LINUX SYSTEM ADMINISTRATION

LINUX SYSTEM ADMINISTRATION

A USER'S GUIDE

Marcel Gagné

ADDISON–WESLEY

Boston • San Francisco • New York • Toronto • Montreal
London • Munich • Paris • Madrid
Capetown • Sydney • Tokyo • Singapore • Mexico City

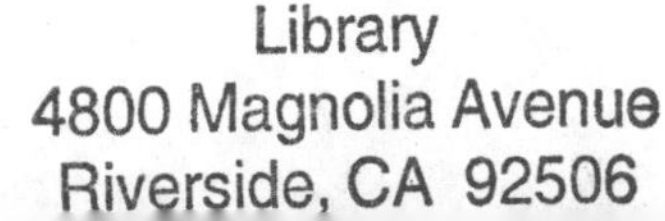

...turers and sellers to distinguish their ... e those designations appear in this book, and Addison-Wesley, Inc. was aware of a trademark claim, the designations have been printed with initial capital letters or in all capitals.

Netscape Communicator browser window ©1999 Netscape Communications Corporation. Used with permission.

The author and publisher have taken care in the preparation of this book, but make no expressed or implied warranty of any kind and assume no responsibility for errors or omissions. No liability is assumed for incidental or consequential damages in connection with or arising out of the use of the information or programs contained herein.

The publisher offers discounts on this book when ordered in quantity for special sales. For more information, please contact:

Pearson Education Corporate Sales Division
One Lake Street
Upper Saddle River, NJ 07458
(800) 382-3419
corpsales@pearsontechgroup.com

Visit AW on the Web: www.awl.com/cseng/

Library of Congress Cataloging-in-Publication Data

Gagné, Marcel.
Linux system administration : the user's guide / Marcel Gagné.
p. cm.
Includes bibliographical references and index.
ISBN 0-201-71934-7
1. Linux. 2. Operating systems (Computers) I. Title.

QA76.76.O63 G34 2001
005.4'469—dc21 2001041245

ISBN: 0-201-71934-7
Text printed on recycled paper
1 2 3 4 5 6 7 8 9 10—CRS—0504030201
First printing, September 2001

I would like to dedicate this book to my parents,
Hector and Marie-Anne,
and
to the love of my life,
my wife and my best friend, Sally Tomasevic.

Contents

Acknowledgments

The book you now hold in your hands is very exciting for me, both to write, and now, to have written.

Sometime during the writing process I came to a rather strange conclusion. Doing a project like this is *insane.* The time, energy, dedication, focus, and so on that is required makes you wonder why anybody, and I do mean *anybody,* embarks on such a project. In some ways, I think it must be something (very remotely) like a mother giving birth. Once it's over, mothers have been heard to say, "Oh, it wasn't that bad." And yet, the sounds from the delivery room would have you think otherwise.

You can't complete a project like this without family, friends, and colleagues helping you out somewhere along the way. I'd like to take a moment to thank a few of them. First and foremost, I have to thank Sally Tomasevic, my wife, partner, best friend, and confidante. Without her, I frankly question where I would be today.

Special thanks must go to Richard Curtis, my agent in New York. I would also like to thank my publisher, Addison-Wesley, and Michael Slaughter, my editor. Thanks also to my friends James Alan Gardner and Robert J. Sawyer, who helped me out with advice and direction in the early days of this whole book thing.

Sincere thanks to those people who reviewed my book along the way. They are (in alphabetical order by last name) Maggie Biggs, Travis Casey, Amy Fong, Scott Lewendowski, Rich Morin, Michael O'Brien, Lew Pitcher, Paul Reavis, Peter Salus, Jan Schaumann, Joe Sharp, Joseph Sloan, and Mark Willey. I am well aware that the process of reviewing is hard work and I truly appreciate their efforts, sharp eyes, and suggestions.

Finally, I'd like to recognize and thank the Linux community: the developers and software designers, the members of Linux user groups, the many who share their experience on Usenet, and all those unnamed folks who give free advice under pseudonyms in IRC groups.

Thank you all.

Chapter 1

Introduction

What Is Linux?

My guess is that if you are reading this book, you already know the answer to that question. You already know that Linux is a fully multitasking operating system based on UNIX.

You may even be aware of this now famous (perhaps legendary) Usenet message from Linus Torvalds to the Usenet group `comp.os.minix`:

```
From: torvalds@klaava.Helsinki.FI (Linus Benedict Torvalds)
       Newsgroups: comp.os.minix
       Subject: What would you like to see most in minix?
       Summary: small poll for my new operating system
       Message-ID: <1991Aug25.205708.9541@klaava.Helsinki.FI>
       Date: 25 Aug 91 20:57:08 GMT
       Organization: University of Helsinki

       Hello everybody out there using minix -
       I'm doing a (free) operating system (just a hobby, won't be
       big and professional like gnu) for 386(486) AT clones. This
       has been brewing since april, and is starting to get ready.
       I'd like any feedback on things people like/dislike in minix,
       as my OS resembles it somewhat (same physical layout of the
       file-system (due to practical reasons) among other things).
       I've currently ported bash(1.08) and gcc(1.40), and things
       seem to work. This implies that I'll get something practical
       within a few months, and I'd like to know what features most
       people would want. Any suggestions are welcome, but I won't
       promise I'll implement them :-)
              Linus (torvalds@kruuna.helsinki.fi)
       PS. Yes - it's free of any minix code, and it has a multi-
       threaded fs. It is NOT protable (uses 386 task switching etc),
       and it probably never will support anything other than AT-hard
       disks, as that's all I have :-(.
```

We've come a long way from Linus's original vision of what his little project would and would not accomplish. What he managed to do was capture the imagination of scores of talented programmers around the world. Joined together through the magic of the Internet, they collaborated, coded, tweaked, and gave birth to the operating system that is now revolutionizing the world of computing.

Notice I mentioned "scores of talented programmers." Linux is not the work of one man alone. Linus Torvalds is the original architect of Linux, its father if you will, but he is not the *only* effort behind it. Perhaps Linus Torvalds' greatest genius lay in knowing when to share the load. For no other pay but satisfaction, he employed people around the world, delegated to them, worked with them, and asked for and accepted feedback in a next generation of the model that began with the GNU project.

GNU, by the way, is a recursive acronym that stands for "GNU's Not Unix," a project of the Free Software Foundation. This project was started in 1984 with the intention of creating a free, UNIX-like operating system. Over the years, many GNU tools were written and widely used by many commercial UNIX vendors and, of course, system administrators trying to get a job done. The appearance of Linus Torvalds' Linux kernel had made the GNU dream of a completely free, UNIX-like operating system a reality at last.

Why Linux?

Because this book is not so much about getting and installing Linux as it is *working* with Linux, I won't spend a long time answering the question "Why Linux?" Frankly, it would take much less time to answer the question "Why not Linux?" Suffice it to say that Linux is a powerful, reliable (some, including your humble author, might even say it's rock solid), expandable, flexible, configurable, multiuser, multitasking, and *completely free* operating system that runs on numerous hardware offerings. These hardware offerings include X86 chipsets (your basic, run-of-the-mill Intel PC), DEC Alpha, Macintosh, PowerPC, and a growing number of embedded processors. You can find Linux in PDA organizers, digital watches, golf carts, and cell phones. In fact, Linux has a greater support base (in terms of platforms) than just about any other operating system you can think of. IBM's entire line of hardware runs Linux!

Completely free?

Hmm . . . Maybe I should explain "free." Free, in this case, isn't a question of cost, although you *can* get a free/gratis copy of Linux and install it on your system without breaking any laws. Of course, because "there ain't no such thing as a free lunch" (to quote Robert A. Heinlein), even a free download costs you connection time on the Internet, disk space, time, and so on.

Linux is distributed under the GNU General Public License (GPL), which in essence says that anyone may copy, distribute, and even sell the program so long as changes to the source are reintroduced back to the community and the terms of the license remain unaltered. Free means that you are free to take Linux, modify it, and create your own version. Free means that you are not at the mercy of a single vendor who forces you into a kind of corporate servitude by making sure that it is extremely costly to convert to another environment. If you are unhappy with your Linux vendor or the support you are getting, you can move to the next vendor without forfeiting your investment in Linux.

The GNU GPL permits a distributor to "charge a fee for the physical act of transferring a copy, and you may at your option offer warranty protection in exchange for a fee." This is further qualified by the statement that the distributor must release "for a charge no more than your cost of physically performing source distribution, a complete machine-readable copy of the corresponding source code." In other words, the GPL ensures that programs like Linux will at best be free of charge. At worst, you may be asked to pay for the cost of a copy.

Everyone should take some time to read the GNU GPL. You'll find a link to its home in the Resources section at the end of this chapter.

The System Administrator's Job

So, this book is about Linux system administration. Just what the heck is system administration anyway? System (or systems) administration is a strange beast. After many years of administering literally hundreds of computer platforms running different operating systems and varying in complexity, I came to have what some might call a strange idea of this job description.

system administrator *n.* Part magician, part juggler, part technical support analyst, and part bartender/psychoanalyst, the system administrator performs the impossible job of keeping all members of his or her company satisfied by making sure that everything works. This usually includes things that are *completely* outside the system administrator's control, such as telephones, photocopiers, fax machines, heating, air conditioning, and paper shortages in the supply cabinet.

I'm being a little silly, I realize, but system administrators get to their exulted position through the strangest of ways. You will find the career system administrator who actually wanted to do the job and worked his or her way to that goal. Along this path, you will also find secretaries who were unfortunate enough (or foolish enough) to say they knew something about computers and were instantly cast into the role. This latter category of *sysadmin* (a popular shortening of "system administrator") is more common than you can possibly imagine. Finally, you have the home user, a relative newcomer to this wonderful calling, thanks in large part to Linux.

About This Book

When I first started thinking about how I would lay out this book, I considered a number of approaches and settled on the following. I don't want to bore you, the reader, with chapters of references to HOWTOs on the Internet (although I will give you appropriate resource links when necessary). Nor do I want to give you verbatim listings of command options or man pages.

What I do want to do is give you real-life examples and things that you can try yourself to get the most out of your system. You will get the theory as well, but only so much. I want you to walk away with an understanding that only comes from actually *doing* things. The most fun I have ever had in the computer biz came from doing things, trying things out, and basically just *playing*. Computers can be fun, even when you are working instead of playing games. This is cool stuff. Imagine—a machine that does what you tell it to do! When the printer is jammed up and your connection to the Internet is down, you tend to forget how marvelous all this really is. So, saddle up to your keyboard, pour yourself a cup of java (that's coffee, not the programming language), limber up those fingers, and start playing.

An assumption I've decided to make is that you already have a Linux system to work with. What you want to know is how to work with it *better.* This doesn't mean I intend to skimp on anything. I will compare various installation philosophies and distributions so that you can satisfy your curiosity about other Linuxes. Which provides me with the perfect segue into another assumption I've decided to make.

> **Marcel's Assumption #312:** You are not all running Red Hat Linux (or Caldera, or Slackware, and so on).

Linux is an operating system kernel supported and bundled into an operating system distribution, which is then marketed, sold, or given away by many different companies or organizations. What this means is that I will try to cover the quirks related to various distributions that may affect you when you try out the things you read in this book. I can't promise that I'll cover every possible distribution here, but what I will do is give you the tools to discover where your version of a particular configuration file or script fits into your system so that you can at least find it. Suffice it to say that even in cases of "my file was here rather than there," the formats, at least, will tend to be constant.

The Command Line Rules!

As you go through this book, you'll notice that I concentrate a lot on the command-line interface. From a system administration point of view, the command line really does rule. It is always available. It is flexible. It enables you to work comfortably on remote systems thousands of miles away even over a slow modem line. Let's face it, all those graphics are a killer on a slow network connection.

Here's one more reason that demands a quick bit of history. Friendly administrative interfaces have been around a lot longer than pretty, front-end GUIs and graphical desktops. Way back when, in my early days of UNIX system administration, there were plenty of menu-driven interfaces to admin tools. This was all very nice and it gave even a novice administrator the means to get the job done without being an expert. The real power though, comes from a real understanding of what is happening under the surface, below that friendly menu or graphical interface.

Learning to wield the command line is akin to getting a black belt in a martial art or earning a first aid certificate. It's not suddenly having the means to crush any obstacle (or opponent) that comes along, but rather having the confidence and the knowledge that you can protect yourself or handle an emergency when it arises. The command line *is* power and it is always there for you.

GUIs Rule!

Okay, now that I've gone off and gotten you all excited about flexing your text-based administrative muscle, I will admit that sometimes it is nice to work in a friendly, graphical environment. More important, if you have to share the load of administering a system, nothing beats putting that comforting graphical tool in front of a timid user. It also impresses the nontechies who view fancy window dressing as the real test of an operating system. ("What do you mean, I can't play solitaire?") With that understanding, I will also cover the graphical ways of doing things.

But I won't hide anything. That means command line first, GUI second. After all, many GUI interfaces are just pretty front ends or *wrappers* for the command line beneath.

Flexibility

Above all, a successful system administrator is flexible. There are only so many hard and fast rules and even those can be bent when necessary. Knowing the entire contents of the Linux man pages by heart is no substitute for the flexibility that is required on a day-to-day basis.

It's not enough to know how to do a backup one way. You need to be able to run a backup at a moment's notice and generate a custom report to go with it. When called on to do so (and you will be), you need to be able to take all the jobs associated with one printer and redirect them to another. Knowing how to print isn't enough.

Flexibility is just one more thing I want to cover in this book. Everything you need to get the job done is on that CD-ROM you received when you got your copy of Linux. It's just a question of mixing and matching the right tools to the needs of the moment and the ongoing needs of your organization.

Is There Anything You Can't Do with Linux?

The answer to the preceding question is increasingly "No." A question like that was originally a euphemism for "Can I run my Windows software with this Linux thing?" These days, the answer is often a resounding "Yes," whether through commercial packages like VMware and Win4Lin or the freely available Wine libraries, you can run a number of Windows software packages without any problem. The VMware and Win4Lin alternatives actually require a copy of Windows whereas Wine does not. You can find out more about setting these up in Chapter 22.

Linux also provides for a vast array of application software. The old warnings about there not being any real software for Linux (word processors, games, and so on) can safely be relegated to your little trash can icon. Yes, Linux even has one of those.

From this author's perspective, Linux has everything I need to work. I have been working without Windows as my primary workstation for a few years now and I can honestly say that I don't miss it. For those times when I can't avoid Windows, I use one of the solutions I mentioned previously. System administration and support are often one and the same, and supporting your customers means working with the things they use, including Windows.

In Appendix A, I have provided a section titled "The Linux-Only Office." It is filled with tips and suggestions for making the jump to Linux once and for all.

Regrets, I've Had a Few . . .

I'll wrap up this Introduction by telling you that I am excited, delighted, and otherwise beside myself that I was given the opportunity to put this book together. My only regret is that I wasn't able to cover everything that is going on in the Linux world.

The Linux world is evolving at an incredible rate. The sheer wealth of talent, dedication, and support in its development makes it an exciting world indeed.

Resources

GNU and the Free Software Foundation

`http://www.gnu.org/`

The GNU General Public License

`http://www.gnu.org/copyleft/gpl.html`

Linux Online

`http://www.linux.org/`

Chapter 2

Linux versus Linux versus UNIX

The UNIX Question

One of the questions I get asked on a regular basis is, "How is Linux different from UNIX?" That question comes, of course, shortly after the "How is Linux different from Windows and why should I care?" question.

The answer I give when I'm short on time is, "It isn't all that different, other than it's free, runs on inexpensive hardware you can buy anywhere, and has a huge number of applications you just won't find on many commercial UNIXes." To address the Linux/UNIX question, the truth is that Linux and UNIX share the same background. A Linux system administrator who finds herself or himself in a UNIX environment will see that things are very familiar and that the learning curve is very slight. The same is true for the UNIX system administrator coming to a Linux shop.

Let's look at a little history.

In the beginning, operating systems (such as they were) were created for specific machines. Each time someone moved from one machine to the other, they had to be prepared to learn a new OS. UNIX was an attempt at standardization. The original attempt concentrated around a new operating system called MULTICS. This first effort was spearheaded by Bell Labs in the late 1960s. Eventually, Bell Labs walked away from the MULTICS effort, leaving a number of people without a computing environment.

In an effort to resolve this quandary, Ken Thompson and Dennis Ritchie (among others) began work on the first UNIX system (originally called UNICS). This first UNIX ran on a DEC PDP-7 computer and was written in assembler. Later, UNIX was rewritten in the C programming language, a change that echoes into the present. Using C, UNIX could easily be transported from machine to machine with a minimum of fuss. In its new form, UNIX began to gain in popularity.

The experiment was not entirely 100 percent successful, but it was far from a failure. There has been fragmentation in the UNIX code with vendors introducing proprietary extensions and code that made the dream of portability seem distant at times—distant, but not impossible. Some of the flavors you may encounter include (in no particular order) the following:

- AIX, from IBM
- HPUX, from Hewlett-Packard
- Solaris, from Sun Microsystems
- DGUX, from Digital Equipment Corporation
- IRIX, from Silicon Graphics

Today, even though many different flavors of UNIX exist, each retains similarities that make moving from one UNIX platform to another relatively painless. UNIX is about as standard as any cross-platform OS gets.

It's interesting to note that UNIX (or UNICS) was never designed to be a commercial product. Today, UNIX is everywhere and its influence touches a number of other (seemingly dissimilar) operating systems. For the purposes of this book, I'll focus on an immensely popular UNIX variant: Linux, the little operating system that *could, can,* and *will.*

The Windows Question

As for the Windows part of the question, the answer (as I mentioned in the Introduction) is becoming more a question of "What can't you do with Linux that you can do only in Windows?"

Let me make a bold statement: *In the OS world, Linux is the future.*

If a Linux company disappears tomorrow—even a big Linux company—Linux lives on. That's because *we all own it.* The source, which is free to all, continues to exist and talented programmers all over the world continue to contribute to it. When it comes to long-term viability, Linux may be the greatest operating system ever developed.

Just when I think I've got this Windows question licked, along comes this question: "How is this Linux different from that Linux?" In this chapter, I'm going to try to answer that question.

A Question of Distribution

When you talk about Linux distributions, you are actually talking about a package of programs or tools put together by a vendor. That vendor's distribution will provide you with a standard configuration, a desktop, admin tools, or anything else the vendor feels might help to differentiate their distribution from the next vendor's. Buying into a specific distribution also buys you a certain installation type—a way of doing things.

If this sounds problematic, consider the following.

> Linux is only the kernel. Therefore, every Linux distribution contains Linux.

That little piece of information is something you can take with you when you are trying to sell Linux as an alternative desktop platform in your office. (I am, of course, assuming that you will want to do this at some point.) Consider this as well: The machine that I use for most of my desktop work was originally a stock Red Hat Linux system. It has been upgraded several times and I have loaded plenty of non–Red Hat or RPM software on it. Its kernel, the *real* Linux if you will, has been replaced with one from the Linux kernel archives as opposed to an RPM from Red Hat. Is it still a Red Hat system? Does it even matter?

The question of distribution, then, becomes one of what makes sense in the long run and that is something that will change from person to person and company to company.

So Which Linux Distribution Should You Choose?

The preceding question is one of the toughest to answer and one that always threatens to spark something akin to a religious war depending on whom you ask. As I mentioned previously, Linux is really the kernel and at any given time, one or more distributions may even use the same version of the kernel. If you were to push me up against the wall, I would probably have to admit that I've installed more Red Hat systems than any other. On the other hand, I have installed and worked with dozens of distributions over the years. In fact, while working on this book, I bounced from release to release so that I could make this guide as non-release-centric as possible.

That's nice, but the question remains: Which one to choose?

Let me try to answer that by taking you on a tour of the various distributions. Armed with that knowledge, you should be able to make a decision that you can feel comfortable with. Now, before I get to the comparisons, you'll notice that I have added a little information box with some quick and dirty notes of each distribution after its description. In those notes, pay special attention to the *package manager,* the means by which software is installed on each respective system. Package managers often have a great deal to do with what people end up choosing in terms of a distribution. I personally like RPM a great deal, but I have also developed a great respect for the power and simplicity of Debian's `apt-get` program.

Also keep an eye on the method of update. In particular, whether or not the distribution allows for Internet updates. Finally, here's the great disclaimer of the decade: Linux is a moving target and, consequently, the details of a specific distribution will change over time. As a result, I am forced to do some amount of generalization and I will not delve into too much detail. At best, I hope that this overview offers just enough information to give you a feel for the differences and to whet your appetite for more.

One final note: There are many, many different Linux distributions out there and I can't possibly hope to touch on all of them. What you have here is a small selection of what is popular at this time. Consider visiting the Linux Weekly News site (`http://www.lwn.net/`) for an impressive list of distributions and links to even more distribution lists.

Enough said. On with the comparisons.

Red Hat Linux

Arguably the most popular Linux distribution, Red Hat has been around since it opened its doors in 1994. It is considered one of the best-supported, most mature distributions. Red Hat offers many boxed sets, specialized configurations, and a variety of support options. You'll also find that third-party support, both in hardware and software, is quite high for Red Hat. A number of computer vendors, including industry leaders like IBM, Dell, and others, have entered into partnerships with the company, further increasing its profile in the marketplace.

On the downside, Red Hat has occasionally taken some flack from the Linux community for releasing a product before it was ready in order to gain a competitive market advantage. That said, patches are released quickly when problems are discovered, just as you would expect in the open source Linux world.

Package manager: RPM
Update: You can update through the Internet with `up2date`.
Installation: Fairly easy install, with multiple, predefined setups based on function.
URL: `http://www.redhat.com/`

SuSE

SuSE (pronounced soo'-sah) was originally born in Germany in 1992, making it the oldest major commercial Linux distribution. At the time of this writing, SuSE was the most popular Linux distribution in Europe. SuSE is a leading-edge, business-oriented distribution that offers a variety of services and support options to its customers. SuSE also offers solutions to the personal Linux market.

To date, what sets SuSE apart from other distributions is the sheer bulk of applications distributed in its boxed set. With over 1,500 applications on six CDs, you may not be looking elsewhere for software for quite some time.

> Package manager: RPM
> Installation: Relatively easy to install and use. A huge amount of software is included in the professional edition.
> URL: `http://www.suse.com/`

Caldera

Caldera made news when it announced that it was buying SCO UNIX, making it, in effect, the company that owned UNIX. Considering that Caldera started out as a Linux company and that Linux has been considered not only a threat to Microsoft, but also to other UNIX releases, there is some delicious irony in this.

Caldera is another major player with a mature, easy to use and administer distribution. Caldera has a reputation as being a Linux distribution for business and has worked hard to position itself in this way. The company has a variety of commercial offerings and support options.

> Package manager: RPM
> Installation: Simple and friendly with the Lizard (Linux wizard).
> URL: `http://www.caldera.com/`

Mandrake

What started out as a Red Hat distribution with a cool desktop (KDE) has grown into a major distribution and a player in its own right. Mandrake has come a long way since its early days and now produces one of the slickest and friendliest Linux distributions out there.

Despite all this, Mandrake is still trying to get business to take it seriously. Unfortunately, in terms of business offerings (support, training, and enterprise options), Mandrake is still behind some of the other major players.

> Package manager: RPM
> Update: Remote Internet update (Mandrake Update) is included.
> Installation: Incredibly friendly install. It's even nice to look at.
> URL: `http://www.linux-mandrake.com/`

Slackware

Before companies like Red Hat and Caldera started selling Linux to the business world, Slackware was *the* distribution. It was certainly my first Linux distribution. As I write this, there is still no graphical install, but you should find it relatively easy, though certainly not the easiest.

This is one of those distributions that longtime UNIX administrators love, and it can't be all nostalgia. I should point out that this is part of the philosophy behind Slackware. It says so right on the Slackware Web page: Its aim is to produce the most "UNIX-like" Linux out there. It's a good, stable product with plenty of documentation, and it is well supported in the community.

> Package manager: installpkg
> Installation: Not very pretty, but it is clean and simple.
> URL: `http://www.slackware.com/`

Debian

Ah, Debian. Loved by true geeks everywhere.

If you are new to Linux, you might find that Debian demands a bit more of you. In a world where most of the major installation procedures are virtually automatic, Debian still requires a fairly in-depth knowledge of what you are doing, how Linux works, your hardware, and so on.

Furthermore, Debian offers no commercial support. Debian is a noncommercial Linux distribution and support is provided through the Linux community through newsgroups, mailing lists, or IRC channels. Keep in mind that you can hire one of the many fine Linux consultants out there (a link to the Linux Consultants HOWTO is provided in the Resources section at the end of this chapter). This may, however, be a showstopper in some companies.

That's the bad. The good is that Debian has been a completely noncommercial product from the beginning. Debian users tout their systems as being reliable, rock solid performers. They benefit from one of the easiest upgrade systems out there (`apt-get dist-upgrade`). They also love their systems.

> Package manager: dpkg
> Update: You can update it through the Internet with the famous `apt-get`.
> Installation: Difficult. Assumes in-depth knowledge. Once installed, updates are a breeze.
> URL: `http://www.debian.org/`

Turbolinux

While this company has been around for some time, it is only recently that the name has started to become well known. That's in North America. Turbolinux is immensely popular in the Asian marketplace (the leader, in fact), and its popularity (and corporate adoption) is growing worldwide.

One technical claim to fame for Turbolinux is that it was the first Linux vendor to offer support for Intel's IA-64 architecture out of the box (though incomplete).

> Package manager: RPM
> Installation: Not the prettiest or flashiest installation, but it's clean and relatively easy.
> URL: `http://www.turbolinux.com/`

Getting Linux

When you are working with other operating systems, getting and trying new releases involve some kind of cash outlay. In the case of Linux, the *most* you need is a spare machine on which to play. If you have a high-speed Internet connection, you can visit any of the vendors covered in this chapter and download their latest and greatest. Remember, though, that while you may download their latest Linux free of charge, technical support is an extra cost.

Don't like the idea of visiting each and every one of those sites? A visit to Linuxiso.org (`http://www.linuxiso.org/`) provides you with a kind of one-stop shop for the more popular Linux distributions.

Getting Others to Try Linux

Okay, here's the sales pitch. The best way for Linux to do everything you've ever dreamed of is for as many people to use it as is possible. One of the arguments against developing for Linux or supporting Linux in an office environment is that nobody uses it. That's not true anymore and it is becoming less and less true as time goes on. The bottom line remains: The more people use the OS, the more people will use it and, perhaps more important, *develop* for it.

While you are the type who obviously has no fear when it comes to trying new things, this may not be the case with your friends. The idea of reformatting their disks and abandoning that other OS may be just too frightening to even consider. If you tell them about dual booting, they may give you a strange look. They don't want to commit. You need to get Linux into their hands with as little fuss as possible. The following section offers some alternatives to consider when you're looking to introduce more "timid" users to the Linux operating system. You'll find links to all of these in the Resources section at the end of the chapter.

Note: The list that follows represents only a small sampling of what is out there.

Sharing Space with Windows

Yes, you can have Linux living on your Windows system. You obviously need disk space for it, and depending on the software you want to run, it could take up a few hundred megabytes, so keep that in mind. Nevertheless, it is a great way to get your flippers wet and the performance is quite good.

Two of my favorites in this arena are DragonLinux and Phat Linux. Both of these distributions come with full graphical desktops (although DragonLinux does offer a "Lite" version) and a bevy of tools, games, and Web browsers. You install them on your hard drive and boot into them using MS-DOS mode. Many video games require that you boot into this mode to run them, so the idea won't seem all that foreign to people.

For those of you who already run and love using Linux, this is a way to get Linux on your PC when you don't have the option of reformatting or repartitioning the hard drive. Linux just becomes another application on your Windows system.

How about No Disk Space at All?

It is possible to run Linux without using your disk at all by running it entirely off a CD-ROM drive. One such distribution is DemoLinux. Based on the Debian distribution, DemoLinux comes with a complete graphical environment, including Web browsers, popular tools, games, and even a full office suite.

The catch here is that it can be slow. That performance wall can be lowered somewhat by using a little workspace on the disk (referred to as an *anchor*), which is a small price to pay because the space required is minimal.

A Changing Landscape

The very idea that anyone could put a final stamp on any specific distribution of Linux is crazy to say the least. Part of Linux's strength comes from the open source network that continues to build on past successes. Consequently, if one company is doing something exciting, it's not unusual to see that organization's ideas adopted by others. After all, they do have access to the source.

What you should do is keep up-to-date on some of the Linux publications out there. Regular "spot checks," or reviews, of where distributions are and what they offer is precisely the sort of thing that magazines do very well. Publications such as *Linux Journal, Linux Magazine,* and the United Kingdom's *Linux Format* are well worth your monthly investment.

Resources

Caldera

`http://www.caldera.com/`

Debian

`http://www.debian.org/`

DemoLinux

`http://www.demolinux.org/`

DragonLinux

`http://www.dragonlinux.net/`

Linux Consultants HOWTO

`http://www.linuxdoc.org/HOWTO/Consultants-HOWTO/index.html`

Linux Weekly News (Linux distribution roundup)

`http://www.lwn.net/`

Phat Linux

`http://www.phatlinux.com/`

Red Hat Software

`http://www.redhat.com/`

Slackware Linux

`http://www.slackware.org/`

SuSE Linux

`http://www.suse.com/`

Turbolinux

`http://www.turbolinux.com/`

Chapter 3

Help (and the Truth) Is Out There

Sooner or later, you are going to need something that is not covered in this book. Hopefully, you won't think this a sign of laziness on my part, but more a sign of the amazing number of things that Linux (that powerful little beast you've unleashed) is capable of. For instance, a comprehensive list of commands and what they do is another book on its own, although you'll find a collection of commonly used commands in Chapter 5 of this book. The point is simply that writing a book with everything you ever wanted to know about Linux (including the things you didn't) is just not possible.

But as it turns out, you don't have to look far for help. Your Linux system is rich with information if you know where to look for it. In this chapter, you are going to find out just where those riches are hidden.

Documentation and Man Pages

One of the great traditions of the Linux (and UNIX) operating system has been to provide full documentation on the system in the form of an online, electronic collection of manual pages, or *man pages* for short. If you installed the documentation package with your Linux system, you have a copy of the man pages on your system. Accessing the man pages is easy.

```
man command_name
```

For instance, if you want to know what the `ls` command does, you type `man ls`. The system then returns a rather wordy explanation of the command (it is amazing what something as simple as `ls` can be trained to do).

Following is a sample man command output. I should point out that this is not the entire man page for the ls command, but rather a small excerpt to give you an idea of the format.

```
Listing 1.1

LS(1)                          FSF                           LS(1)

NAME

       ls - list directory contents

SYNOPSIS

       ls [OPTION]... [FILE]...

DESCRIPTION

       List information about the FILEs (the current directory by
       default).  Sort entries alphabetically if none of -cftuSUX
       nor --sort.

       -a, --all
              do not hide entries starting with .

       -A, --almost-all
              do not list implied . and ..

       -b, --escape
```

If you want to know what a command does and a simple, one-line description is enough, you can use the whatis command. For instance, in wandering through your /usr/bin directory, you may find an interesting command like this one: zipcloak. Now, what (you may ask) is zipcloak? Why not ask your system instead?

```
$ whatis zipcloak
zipcloak [zip]        (1)  - package and compress (archive) files
```

The whatis database may or may not exist on your default system, but have no fear. If you receive a message telling you that the whatis database is missing, you can create it with the makewhatis command.

```
/usr/sbin/makewhatis
```

Depending on the kind of horsepower in your machine, this might take a little while, so be patient.

What If You Don't Know the Command Name?

Luckily, there are ways of finding the command you need even if you don't know what it is. To make this magic happen, Linux has a great little command called `apropos`. What you are doing when you search with `apropos` is using keywords. These keywords are listed in the `whatis` database.

For instance, say you want to know how to create a user, but you don't know what the command is for that. Is it `makeuser` or `inventuser`? Who knows. Well, it's likely that your system does. Try this:

```
apropos user | less
```

The vertical bar (|) is referred to as the *pipe* symbol. It is traditionally located just under or just over the Enter key on your keyboard and is shown as a broken vertical bar. The `less` command is a paging command. It enables you to break up screens and screens of information into manageable chunks. You will visit this sort of thing in more detail in Chapter 5.

I won't bore you with the streams of information that this particular command will output ("user" is a pretty broad term, after all). Let's just take a small snapshot of the output and see what it tells us.

useradd	(8) - create a new user or update default new user information
useradd [adduser]	(8) - create a new user or update default new user information
userdel	(8) - delete a user account and related files
userhelper	(8) - a helper interface to `pam`
userinfo	(1) - a graphical equivalent to `chfn`
usermod	(8) - modify a user account

That first one sounds about right. If you really want to make sure, you can now go back and read the actual man page with the command `man useradd`. Notice the number 8 in brackets just before the definition. If you were to do a `man` on the command `useradd`, you would get this at the top:

```
USERADD(8)                                                USERADD(8)


NAME
       useradd  -  Create  a  new user or update default new user
       information
```

This tells you that the information for the `useradd` command is in section 8 of the man pages. I want to take a moment and tell you about these sections, but before I do, I'll let you in on a secret. All these commands are very closely related. In fact, the `apropos` command is the same as using the man command with a `-k` option. For instance, if you want to find the commands that allow you to log into a system, you might try either of the following:

```
$ apropos login
$ man -k login
```

Either will generate the same result by searching through the `whatis` database for matches to your query. Years ago, I would have argued for `man -k` because it was one less keystroke, but now I've decided to use what I think is more, ahem, apropos. Over time, as you continue to work with Linux and learn its intricacies, you'll find several examples of synonym commands. For instance, the `whatis` command I discussed previously is actually the same as `man -f`. Curious? Why not check out the man page on the command `man`?

Now I'll use the previous example to illustrate the meaning of those man page sections. Use the `apropos` command to call up information on `login`. A partial listing looks like the following.

```
faillog    (5) - login failure logging file
faillog    (8) - examine faillog and set login failure limits
getlogin   (3) - get user name
issue      (5) - prelogin message and identification file
```

Notice the entry for `faillog`. It shows up twice: once with a section 5, and once with a section 8. Table 3.1 displays the meaning of these sections.

If you type `man faillog`, you will see the entry under section 8 and not section 5. The reason for this is that `man` checks command sections first (1, 6, and 8). You might think that a user looking for information strictly through the man pages might never miss out on the other information, but if you scroll

TABLE 3.1: Section Numbers and Meanings

Section Number	What You'll Find There
1	Basic, day-to-day commands
2	System calls
3	Library routines, function calls, and so on
4	Device and special files
5	File formats and configuration files
6	Games and other fun stuff
7	Miscellaneous
8	System administration commands

down to the bottom of the man page, you'll find a SEE ALSO section that provides related commands and corresponding sections. If you want to see the faillog that falls under section 5, you should use this version of the command:

```
man 5 faillog
```

Show Me the PATH, man!

Actually, that's "show me the MANPATH." Not every set of man pages lives in the default MANPATH (usually /usr/man). Different applications install in different places. This is the reason for the -M flag to man. Say, for instance, that you have a package installed in /opt and that the accompanying man pages are there as well. It's likely that on your system there is a file called /etc/man.config that contains your global MANPATHs. Debian users will find they have a /etc/manpath.config file instead. The man pages for cdrecord (a package I will discuss in Chapter 16) are simply not listed there. If you know which directory these pages are in, you can easily read them.

```
man -M /opt/schily/man cdrecord
```

You can now read the man page for cdrecord without any problem.

Graphical Man Pages

If you are already running from a graphical (X) interface, you can call up the X manual page browser by simply typing xman from the command line. Clicking the Manual Page button will bring up a help page with a Sections menu. These are the 1 through 8 sections listed in Table 3.1. As an example, choose section 1, User commands, from the menu and browse away.

info (the Command, That Is)

Before I tell you about info, I should probably start with texinfo. texinfo is a system of creating documentation that makes it possible for a software developer to create a single set of documentation that can be used in many ways. Because developers can use the same source file to generate different types of documents, they can save themselves a lot of time using this format. A file created with texinfo can be used to generate both printed output in a book and electronic documentation that is viewable online. These online documents are info documents and they are read using the info program.

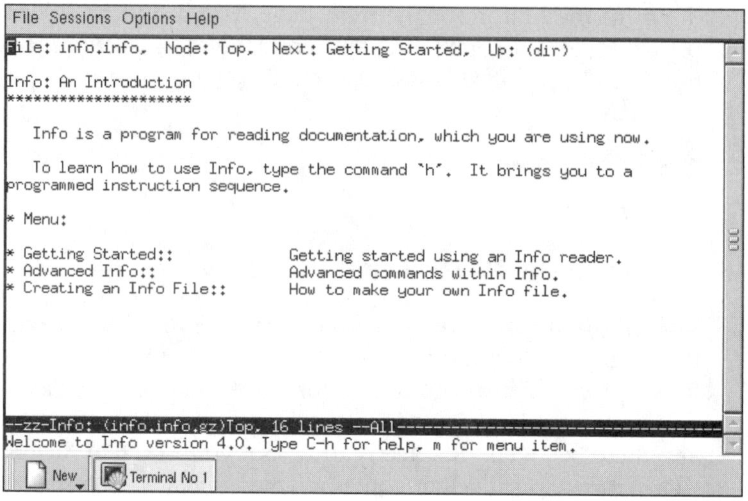

```
File Sessions Options Help
File: info.info,  Node: Top,  Next: Getting Started,  Up: (dir)

Info: An Introduction
*********************

   Info is a program for reading documentation, which you are using now.

   To learn how to use Info, type the command `h'.  It brings you to a
programmed instruction sequence.

* Menu:

* Getting Started::             Getting started using an Info reader.
* Advanced Info::               Advanced commands within Info.
* Creating an Info File::       How to make your own Info file.

--zz-Info: (info.info.gz)Top, 16 lines --All-----------------------------
Welcome to Info version 4.0. Type C-h for help, m for menu item.
New  Terminal No 1
```

FIGURE 3.1 `info` on `info`

Figure 3.1 is a screen capture of the `info` program in action. In this case, it is displaying `info` on the program `info` itself. `info` behaves in much the same way as a Web browser, with hyperlinks between pages that are referred to as *nodes*. Links within the same page are called *menus*. Navigating these pages is not difficult, but it does take a few minutes to get used to. Try this. Start the `info` program with this command:

```
info info
```

Pressing the Tab key takes you to the first menu item. Pressing Enter takes you to that linked node or submenu. While reading a node, you can return to the previous node by pressing n for "next." Going back is just as easy: Press p for "previous." Want to become an info navigation expert? Press Ctrl-h for a full list of navigation commands.

HOWTOs and Distributed DOCs

Man pages and `info` files are only the beginning when it comes to what is already on your system. By default, installed packages put their files into a directory on your system called `/usr/doc`. Note that this path is not quite hard and fast. On some distributions, this is actually the `/usr/share/doc` directory. In fact, with newer releases, you are likely to start finding most of this documentation in `/usr/share/doc`. A quick listing there shows you directories galore, each representing a package and the version number of that package as it exists on your system. For instance, a short listing of the directory shows the following subdirectories:

```
gawk-3.0.4
gd-1.3
gdm-2.0beta2
gedit-0.6.1
getty_ps-2.0.7j
gftp-2.0.6a
ghostscript-5.50
gimp-1.0.4
```

Every one of the preceding subdirectories is a directory with additional files (or directories) containing information pertinent to the specific package. For instance, if you change directories to `gimp-1.0.4`, you'll find a handful of files relating to this release, installation instructions, and a copy of the GNU public license in a file called COPYING. Other packages may even provide HTML manuals that can be read with a Web browser.

Under that `/usr/doc` hierarchy (or `/usr/share/doc`), you may also find a HOWTO directory. Slackware users should look for a Linux-HOWTOs directory here. This directory is another one of those things that can vary slightly from distribution to distribution. Nevertheless, if you start looking here, you won't be far off the mark.

HOWTOs are user- or developer-contributed documents describing in detail (sometimes extensive detail) how to install or work with a specific piece of software. HOWTOs are the heart of the Linux community's attempt to define and describe the various components of Linux packages. They are not command references such as those you find in man pages. Rather, HOWTO documents tend to concern themselves with packages or broader topics such as printing. A word of warning to the new users out there: Your average HOWTO can be a little overwhelming.

The HOWTO also has a smaller sibling called a *mini-HOWTO*. These documents are designed to help a less technical user—certainly a user who wants to get things up and going in short order. While you will find regular HOWTO documents in `/usr/doc/HOWTO`, mini-HOWTOs are located one level deeper in `/usr/doc/HOWTO/mini`.

The Linux Documentation Project

On your Linux distribution CD, you probably have a collection of documents known in the Linux world as HOWTOs. As mentioned previously, these are user- or developer-contributed documents that are maintained and updated by one or more individuals. You can find the latest version of these documents at the Linux Documentation Project (LDP) Web site (`http://www.linuxdoc.org/`).

The mandate of the LDP is essentially to provide a comprehensive base of documentation for all things Linux. If you've been looking high and low for information on installing that FTL radio card on your PC and still haven't found what you are looking for, try the LDP.

The LDP also makes a point of offering the latest versions of the man pages as well as user guides that tend to cover more ground than standard HOWTOs.

Linux User Groups

Let's put technology aside for a moment and explore something else you may have heard about: the Linux community. Yes, there really is a Linux community. All around the world, you will find groups of enthusiastic Linux users gathering for regular meetings, chatting over beer and pizza, and sharing information. This sharing of information is part of what makes Linux so friendly.

Linux user groups, or LUGs, tend to run electronic mailing lists where informal exchanges of information take place. New users are welcomed and their questions are happily answered. These users range from newbies getting their feet wet to seasoned kernel developers. Should you find yourself stuck with nowhere to turn, seek out your local LUG and sign on to the mailing list. Today, someone helps you. As you grow more knowledgeable in administering your Linux system, maybe you will return the favor.

Locating a LUG in your area is as simple as surfing over to the Linux Online Web site (`http://www.linux.org/`). Click the User Groups button and you are on your way. The list is organized by country, then by state or province, and so on.

Go ahead—join a local LUG. They're a fun bunch.

Usenet News

Don't let anybody tell you that Usenet is dead. It is still one of the most vibrant sources of information on the Net today, with literally thousands of newsgroups and thousands of users. Usenet, in case you haven't already heard, is a worldwide system of distributed newsgroups supported freely by Internet service providers (ISPs), colleges and universities, and individual users and companies. Most ISPs offer access to a list of newsgroups that can be accessed through a newsreader, such as Netscape's Collabra, or standard command-line tools, such as `tin` or `trn`. Newsgroups are great sources of information.

That said, Usenet can be a little strange at times. Newsgroups can be pretty busy places and not all that gets posted on a given newsgroup has to do with the subject matter defined by the newsgroup's mandate. Like your personal e-mail package, Usenet is subject to an awful lot of *spam*, or junk postings.

If you are accessing Usenet through one of the methods mentioned previously, try looking first in the `comp.os.linux` hierarchy of groups. For instance, the following listing represents a small snapshot from my own system running `tin`, a small, text-only newsreader. You can see a handful of the more popular Linux newsgroups. The number you see in the first column is the position of that newsgroup in my list of subscribed groups. The second column represents the number of new or unread messages.

```
70   638   comp.os.linux.advocacy
71    47   comp.os.linux.announce
72         comp.os.linux.answers
73   152   comp.os.linux.development.apps
74   211   comp.os.linux.development.system
75   263   comp.os.linux.hardware
76   555   comp.os.linux.misc
77   431   comp.os.linux.networking
78   122   comp.os.linux.security
79   518   comp.os.linux.setup
80   116   comp.os.linux.x
```

I'll let you in on a secret. That listing doesn't even come close to the size of the whole list. The last time I checked, my ISP had nearly 300 Linux-related newsgroups available.

If you are looking for answers to a particularly difficult Linux (or other) problem, there's a good chance that somebody somewhere has already asked that question. They may even have asked it on Usenet. Luckily, there is an archive of Usenet posts (think about that next time you post something to a newsgroup) called Google Groups, formerly Deja.com. (Deja.com was recently acquired by Google, a powerful Internet search engine.) Point your browser to `http://groups.google.com/`. This site features a search engine that enables you to browse through all past Usenet postings.

When you visit Google Groups, you can search postings by keyword, newsgroup, date, and language. I've used this service on numerous occasions. I particularly like using the Advanced Groups Search option to narrow down my searches. Remember, this is an archive of posts going back further than you care to think about. The only catch is that you may have to wade through an incredible amount of information and quasi-information to get what you need.

Sometimes, of course, too much information is just that: too much.

Resources

Google Groups (Deja.com Usenet archives)

`http://groups.google.com/`

Linux Documentation Project

`http://www.linuxdoc.org/`

Linux User Groups Worldwide

`http://lugww.counter.li.org/lugww.php3`

Chapter 4

Linux System Installation

Getting Ready for Your Installation

Okay, I'll admit it right here. It is likely that you already have another operating system (OS) running on your PC as you sit there thinking about installing Linux.

It's not that Linux is that much harder to install than the other OS, but most of the time the other OS (Windows 9*x*/2000) has already been installed for you. In other words, somebody has already done the hard work of figuring out what works with what, what drivers need to be loaded, and so on. A wise move would be to take advantage of all that hard work and make notes on all the hardware in your machine—the type of network and video cards and anything else you can think of. You do that by clicking the Start button; selecting Settings, Control Panel; and then double-clicking the System icon. Now walk through the hardware profiles and take some notes.

If you happen to have a *bare* system—no installed OS of any kind—have no fear. This isn't your grandfather's Linux. Most modern installations have a better than 95 percent hardware detection and configuration success rate, and that's probably conservative.

The average Linux installation takes about 30 to 60 minutes, although I have seen it take as little as 5 minutes on a really fast system. That's a fully network-ready, configured, all-set-to-work machine.

Hardware Considerations

Not every device will work with Linux. You should not think of this as being strange, or that it somehow represents a weakness in Linux. After all, Linux is not unique in this. In fact, Linux may be fairly unique when it comes to the sheer number of devices that it supports. At the time of this writing, only Microsoft Windows 98 has support for a greater number of devices than Linux and that's *only* if you count the Intel (x86) world of computers (arguably what most people are familiar with). Linux will run on numerous platforms, from Intel-based systems to Alpha to RISC to Macintosh. As I mentioned in the Introduction, IBM's entire line of computers, from small, desktop PCs to large mainframe systems like the S/390, runs Linux.

Then there are MIPS, SPARC, and StrongARM. You can also find Linux embedded in microchips, running on portable MP3 players, running on Palm Pilots, and even running on digital watches. That's incredible hardware support!

Still, if you are looking to find whether or not your computer and its associated devices will work with your Linux installation, the first place to look is your Linux vendor's Web site. While Linux is Linux, different releases of different vendors' products may be at different levels of development. Consequently, at one time or another, Red Hat may have slightly more extensive support for hardware than the others, and a month later SuSE may have the widest range of support.

Another great hardware resource is the Hardware HOWTO. You can always find the latest version by surfing on over to the Linux Documentation Project's Linux Hardware Compatibility HOWTO page (`http://www.linuxdoc.org/HOWTO/Hardware-HOWTO/`).

As Linux gains in popularity, you'll find that hardware vendors are increasingly interested in tapping into this ever-growing market. I've had the experience of being on site, adding hardware to a customer's system (Ethernet cards come immediately to mind), and finding that the system did not have the drivers. I quickly visited the Ethernet card manufacturer's Web site and found precompiled drivers ready and waiting for me.

Kernel developers themselves are the determining factor in which devices are supported. If you find yourself in a position where you desperately need to have the super-amazing FJX-2020-XJK FTL card running on your server and you must have it now, a trip to the Linux Kernel Archives (`http://www.kernel.org/`) may be in order. In that case, you may want to look to Chapter 12 for assistance in building your kernel.

Passing Boot Options

Modern Linux distributions have extensive hardware support. While you may still run into problems (some hardware, such as the cheap, built-in "Winmodems" found in some budget PCs, will only work with Windows), they tend to be few and far between. That said, Linux tends to support better than 95 percent of popular PC hardware, and the installation process identifies and loads drivers for most things automatically. The catch is that at installation time, the boot disk only contains so many drivers and you may find that your installation doesn't really get off the ground. It's a kind of catch-22 situation. The driver you need is on the CD, but the CD can't be accessed because you don't have the driver loaded yet. If you could get the system installed, you could load the driver at the command line. But. . . .

A classic example of this problem comes from the fact that Linux is often used to convert some very old hardware into functional Internet and e-mail gateways (I cover just such a process in Chapter 20). Pretend for a moment that your organization's management has given you a 486 SX-25 with an old Mitsumi CD-ROM drive. After all, you told them that with Linux, you can build that useful and inexpensive firewall with just about anything they had lying around. And they took you up on it. The trouble is that the installation diskette doesn't have the Mitsumi driver built into the kernel. Here's what you do: At the SYSLINUX or LILO prompt, rather than simply pressing Enter and letting the build start on its own, you quickly type the following:

```
SYSLINUX : mcdx=0x300,10
```

The `mcdx=` line tells the kernel to load the Mitsumi driver (or module) as it boots. Furthermore, you are telling the system that the CD drive is at address 0x300 and IRQ 10. Yes, it does help to know what kind of hardware you have.

I used the example of a non-IDE or ATAPI CD-ROM drive because that tends to be the real showstopper at this point. The CD is where everything is. If you can't read the CD-ROM, the installation (unless you are doing a network installation) might be cut rather short. Here's another example involving an old Sony CDU-535 drive:

```
sonycd535=0x340,10
```

The parameters tell the installation disk to look for the CD-ROM drive at address 0x340 and IRQ 10. Because an oddball CD-ROM is most likely the problem you will encounter at this point, you might want to visit The Linux CD-ROM HOWTO page (`http://www.linuxdoc.org/HOWTO/CDROM-HOWTO/`) and refer to it if the installation process just can't locate that strange device.

There are many such boot-time parameters. If you find yourself in a real bind, check the installation manual or refer to the Resources section at the end of this chapter.

Dual Booting

Let's pretend for a moment that you are trying to convince a friend to try Linux on for size. Your friend still wants to be able to run Windows from time to time, but he or she genuinely wants to have Linux as well. Usually, this involves something called *dual booting*.

One scenario involves a completely separate disk that you can dedicate to a Linux installation. What you'll normally have, however, is a single disk with Windows already loaded and likely taking up the entire partition table. Even in this environment, you can still set up a dual boot system if the disk has sufficient space. The trick is to shrink the existing partition, thereby creating some space on which to install Linux. You can do this with a little program called FIPS, which you can find on your Linux distribution CD. On Debian, check the `tools` directory. On Red Hat or Turbolinux, check the `dosutils` directory.

> **Note:** You must defragment your disk in Windows 95/98 before you use FIPS. You do this by clicking the Start button and then selecting Programs, Accessories, System Tools, Disk Defragmenter.

If you are going to be dual booting (rather than running a Linux-only system), you might also want to look at PartitionMagic (`http://www.partitionmagic.com/`) as an alternative to using FIPS. It's a nice, friendly, commercial package that enables you to modify partitions on the fly.

> **Warning:** When doing anything this drastic with your drives, *always* make a backup. In fact, no matter what you do with your system, always make regular backups.

Before I move on, don't forget that you also have the option of using a UMSDOS (Linux file system on DOS) type of Linux installation, such as those provided by DragonLinux and Phat Linux, both of which I mentioned in Chapter 2. If you use this kind of installation, you don't need to repartition or format anything. Linux becomes an icon on the Windows desktop that runs in MS-DOS mode. No commitment. No muss. No fuss. The only catch is that you cannot take advantage of Linux's advanced file system and performance because you are still using the Windows/DOS file structure.

The 12 (13, 14, 15 . . .) Steps to Any Installation

Most modern installations offer a nice, graphical process. For the most part, installing Linux today is a point and click experience with help every step of the way. That said, a graphical installation makes a lot of assumptions that might cause you some grief. Should all else fail, try the text-based installation. Most distributions still provide one, and I can't see that changing anytime soon. Let's go through a basic, and very generic, installation. I'll cover some of the problems you might encounter and what to do about them.

Keep in mind that Linux allows you to change your mind about many of the decisions you make during the installation process. Just click the Back button (or use the Tab key to move to it) and reenter the information the way you intended.

> **Note:** One last thing. Keep in mind that what follows is meant to be a generic, "here's what happens" look at installation. The actual order of the steps may vary slightly depending on the distribution.

Step 1: Booting

The installation instructions tell you to pop in the Linux CD-ROM and reboot. The installation should start automatically at this point with the various installation options offered. Somehow, though, the system just booted back into your old OS. What went wrong?

The problem here is that not every computer allows you to boot from the CD-ROM drive. Even those that do allow this may not do so by default. Check your PC's BIOS configuration at start-up. You will see something there that decides the boot order (A drive followed by C drive followed by CD-ROM and so on). You may have to change the order so that it looks at the CD-ROM first.

If that doesn't work, all Linux distributions provide a boot diskette. If you bought a boxed set, look for a boot diskette in the box. Otherwise, look on the CD itself for a `boot.img` file. There should also be a `DOSUTILS` directory there with a program called `RAWRITE.EXE` that enables you to create the boot disk at a DOS prompt.

Step 2: Selecting the Installation Type

This is where you decide on just how much help you want in the installation process. Read the options carefully. Some installations will overwrite your entire disk and this is unlikely to be what you want. This is also where you have the option of deciding between the friendly, graphical installation and the slightly less friendly (though mostly in looks) text-based installation.

My suggestion is that you start graphically. If you run into problems (usually when it comes to setting the display), then try the text installation.

Step 3: Selecting a Language (Parlez-vous Françai?)

You aren't likely to run into anything odd or strange here. Depending on your choice of distribution, you may have a dozen or more languages to choose from. Linux is well represented in the world community and internationalization programs are always under way.

Step 4: Choosing a Keyboard Type

Once again, you aren't likely to have too many problems here, but there are some things to note. In the English-speaking world, the generic 101-key PC-style keyboard will usually work whether it has an extra key or more (like the Windows Start key). Still, to take full advantage of your keyboard's functionality, pick the one that most closely matches what you have.

Pay attention to the enable or eliminate "dead keys" option. This refers to the technique of using key combinations to create accented characters (such as è, ç, ã, or Ÿ). Respond according to your needs.

Step 5: Selecting Your Mouse

Nothing too strange here—usually, your mouse gets detected without any trouble. Pay special attention to the Emulate 3-button mouse option. In the X window environment, you often use features that are based on three buttons. By choosing this option, you make it possible to look as though you are clicking the middle button of your two-button mouse whenever you click both buttons simultaneously. Unless you are actually using a three-button mouse, make sure you set this.

Step 6: Selecting a Time Zone

You are likely to be asked for your location and time zone. I'm not entirely sure who decided on what cities would be represented for time zone locations, but there are a couple of fairly major centers strangely absent from the list. In my case, the closest location was some small northern town far away from any largely populated areas. Ah, well.

Oh, yes. You'll also have to specify whether your location observes daylight saving time.

Step 7: Creating a Partition

There may be some extra steps here that ask for additional information or give you the option of deciding on the complexity of your installation. The latter means that you now want to decide whether you will make the crucial decisions yourself, sometimes referred to as a *custom* or *expert* installation, or whether you will let the system take care of everything. Basically, the custom installation comes down to this: You get to define your own disk partitions and you get to decide exactly what gets installed.

The first and probably most difficult of the custom installation steps deals with disk partitioning. The tools to help you do this, however, have become increasingly friendly and powerful over the last few years. Almost every distribution has some kind of a menu-driven partition manager if not a full-blown graphical tool.

Here is the bare minimum you need on your system:

- A swap partition
- A root (or /) partition

The *swap partition* is a special area designed to allow for virtual memory storage. If you find yourself running hungry programs that use up all your physical memory, your Linux system will start using swap. If you run out of swap, it will swap to disk, but this is not as fast or as efficient as using a swap partition. Unlike other disk partitions, swap is not something you can look at directly with a command like `ls`.

Deciding on the amount of swap is not an exact science. You are supposed to be able to determine the average memory requirements for your day-to-day operations, subtract that from your available real memory, and add a bit for swap. The rule used to be to double what you had for real memory and make that your swap (for instance, if you had 16MB, your swap would be 32MB). On my test system (the one I am writing this on), I have 256MB of RAM and 120MB of swap space configured.

The only other necessary partition is your *root* (or /) *partition*. This can be one large partition for everything (programs and data) on your Linux system.

Alternatively, you might define a separate `/boot` partition, and you can define a `/tmp`, `/usr`, or `/home` partition as well. The reasons for choosing a single partition over individual slices vary depending on individual needs. For instance, while everything will work just fine with the simplistic swap and root configuration, you may discover that you want to have your user directories (the `/home` partition) mounted as a separate disk. Depending on how many people are using the server, it may be wise to limit the amount of `/tmp` space rather than allowing it access to the entire disk. Again, this is not an exact science. You will discover the approach that works best for your environment as you gain experience.

Take care, though: If you do decide to create individual partitions, remember to leave enough room for everything, especially `/usr`. This is where *most* of your programs will live and you don't want to have to reinstall too soon.

Step 8: Formatting the Partitions

This step is pretty self-explanatory. Everything on the partitions you format will be destroyed. That's the big warning.

Note that little check box, however—the one about checking for bad blocks. The upside of checking this box is that the formatting process takes time to check each and every block on the disk. The downside is that this process can take quite a long time.

Step 9: To LILO or Not to LILO

Once the disks are formatted, you'll be asked if you want to use LILO to boot. There should be very little reason to decide on using anything but LILO here—in fact, it is the default. *LILO* is the Linux loader, a boot manager that is flexible enough to offer you the choice of different operating systems at boot time. This is what happens when you dual boot between Linux and another OS. In fact, most installations will recognize the fact that you already have another OS there and will offer a default label for booting it. I'll go into more detail about LILO options when I cover starting Linux later in this chapter.

The next option here has to do with where LILO gets installed. The default is the *master boot record,* or MBR. This is a small portion of your disk and the very first thing that gets read after all the self-tests happen on your PC, and it is the means by which your OS starts loading. Notice that there is another option for installing LILO on the first sector of the boot partition. The reason for this is that you may already have another boot loader. If that is the case, choose this option and then go back and configure your boot loader (whatever it may be) to recognize the presence of Linux.

The only other thing here is an option to use linear mode. Some hard drives use LBA addressing and that is what linear mode refers to.

Step 10: Choosing and Installing Software Packages

If you have enormous amounts of disk space, you might just consider installing everything. Most installations do offer this as an option. Before you choose to do this, though, you should heed this warning: The downside of choosing to install everything is that depending on the release, this can be an incredible amount of software. My SuSE 6.4 boxed set contains five full CD-ROMs. With the average single-CD distribution, this can amount to a full gigabyte of disk space. Odds are pretty good that you don't need all that.

Decide what it is that you want this system to do and concentrate on those things. Always remember that you can go back and reinstall something you missed at a later time.

To help you out, most vendors provide a handful of fixed configurations. These may include descriptions like "minimal," "standard," "workstation," or "network" installation. For instance, Red Hat even differentiates between workstation installations running different desktops.

This is usually a good time to make yourself a cup of tea.

Step 11: Configuring the Network

The only thing you should be aware of here is that this step involves LANs and network cards. This is not dial-up networking or anything having to do with modems. Many network cards will be automatically detected at this point in the installation procedure. If you can't get your network card recognized at this point, don't worry. It may be that you need an updated driver from your vendor. You can always add it at a later time, after the installation is complete. I cover networking later on in the book in fairly extensive detail. Chapter 18 contains a light-speed introduction to TCP/IP networks.

Step 12: Identifying Yourself

It is time to choose a unique password for the root user. If you have questions about what constitutes a good password, you'll find plenty of suggestions in Chapter 6, which covers user and group administration. This step also provides an opportunity to add more users. At this point, I would add *one* non-root account and leave it at that. This is another job you can do later.

You'll also be asked to decide if you want to use shadow passwords, something I highly recommend that you do.

Step 13: The Dreaded X Window Configuration

The X window system is another area that you should not fret too much about if it doesn't work immediately. After all, a Linux system will work just fine without any kind of graphical environment. This isn't to say that I am downplaying the importance of a running desktop configuration—only that it can be taken care of later.

> **Note:** The standard Linux graphical environment is called X, XFree86, or the X window system. The term "X-Windows," while often used, is incorrect.

Most modern installations do a pretty good job of isolating your video card. The monitor is another thing. From the list presented to you, find your monitor's make and model and enter it. There is still a danger of damaging your monitor if you specify incorrect frequencies. If you don't see your monitor listed there, check the manual that came with it.

The X window configuration utility then attempts to start a server with your choices. If everything works out and you like the way things look, you only have one question to answer here: Do you want your system to boot up into the graphical desktop by default? For most people, the answer is "Yes." If you are deploying desktop systems for an office, the answer is an overwhelming "Yes." For strange users like myself (and you, perhaps), it might be more preferable to boot to a text-only screen, leaving the user to start X manually. I discuss some of the reasons for this in Chapter 9, which digs deep into the heart of X.

Step 14: The Boot Disk Question

This is the last question (usually) that you need to answer before you reboot. The answer here is "Yes," you want to create a boot disk. That's the short answer. The following section provides a longer answer.

The (Emergency) Boot Disk

When the installation process asks if you want to create an emergency boot disk, the correct answer is "Yes." If, for some strange reason, you passed this step when you did your installation, it is not too late to go back and create one. Before you do that, however, I'd like to just explain the reasons for this diskette. The first reason is pretty obvious, given the disk's name. In case of an emergency, it is very handy to have a means of booting your system with the current configuration. You'll find this especially important if you are booting from SCSI drives. Should something horrible befall your kernel (for instance, if you rebuilt your kernel and didn't keep the old kernel around for an emergency), you have a quick way back.

The second reason for the disk may not be all that apparent. When you installed your system, you were given the option of using LILO to boot your system. Under normal circumstances, this is the way to go. LILO enables you to boot multiple kernels and allows for easy dual booting, thus making it simple to switch from Windows to Linux and back again. If, for some reason, you decided to opt out of using LILO, the boot disk is the likely means by which you will be booting your Linux system. Either way, you should have a boot disk for emergencies and the following is how you create it after the fact.

Make sure you have a blank, formatted, non-write-protected diskette ready to go. Because the process will actually overwrite whatever is on the diskette, my reason for suggesting a blank diskette is so that you are sure you aren't erasing something important. With the diskette inserted in your drive, type the following command:

```
mkbootdisk kernel-version
```

The `kernel-version` part should be substituted with whatever kernel you are booting from. You can find that out by typing `uname -r` at the command prompt. When I do that on my test systems, I get something that looks like this:

```
2.2.14-test
```

The `-r` flag tells `uname` to return the operating system release. With that information in hand, I create my boot disk by issuing this command:

```
mkbootdisk 2.2.14-test
```

> **Note:** The `mkbootdisk` command looks for a kernel with the name `vmlinuz-release_num` and a module directory under `/lib/modules` with the name `release_num`. In the previous example, I would have a kernel called `/boot/vmlinuz-2.2.14-test` and a modules directory called `/lib/modules/2.2.14-test`. I mention this because you can save your kernel with any number of names, but the `/lib/modules` entry may be different. It is probably a good idea to use the `vmlinuz-release_num` convention when saving your new kernels under `/boot`.

You should be aware that the `mkbootdisk` command does not exist on every system. For instance, on my Debian test system, I used the `mkboot` command to create a boot disk (although I did get an opportunity to create such a disk during the installation).

```
# mkboot
```

The problem I ran into, which is relatively minor, is that the `mkboot` command looks to find `vmlinuz` (the Linux kernel) in the `/boot` directory. Unfortunately, the `vmlinuz` file was under the root directory, and the `mkboot` command failed. To get around this problem, I created a symbolic link to the kernel.

```
ln -s /vmlinuz /boot/vmlinuz
```

If you reexecute the `mkboot` command, all should work fine.

Starting Linux

This sounds far too obvious to spend any time on. After all, you turn on the power switch, sit back, and watch Linux come to life. The truth, however, can be a bit more interesting than that. For instance, you may have opted to use a boot disk, but that's not where I am going with this.

> **Geek Trivia:** The term "booting" comes from "bootstrapping," as in "pulling yourself up by your bootstraps." Your humble author remembers a time when he used a *four-corner boot,* literally booting by entering code into a numeric keypad. The four corners were four essential keys at the corners of that keypad.

When you start your system and you see that marvelous `lilo:` boot prompt waiting for you, there are options other than pressing Enter or typing `win` (or `dos`) if you are set up to dual boot. In fact, it is possible to pass information to the kernel at boot time, right here at the LILO prompt. You may have installed a new piece of hardware that isn't being recognized properly. Just as you did during the installation process, it is possible to pass LILO-specific driver information here as well.

Here's something else you can do. For those times when you're fiddling with the kernel or modifying some system start-up file, it is possible to find yourself with a system that does not want to boot. When you type the following command at the `lilo:` prompt, the system will boot into single-user mode, bypassing a number of steps such as network start-up.

```
linux single
```

For the down and dirty of LILO, go to Chapter 12, which covers kernel building.

Shutting Down Linux

All right. Here is rule number one when it comes to shutting down your system.

> *Never, ever simply power off the system.* You must do a proper shutdown. Oh, and get an uninterruptible power supply (UPS) so that your system doesn't shut down accidentally. I should perhaps make it clear that you *do not need* a UPS to run Linux. However, if you don't want a random power fluctuation or a three-second power outage to take down your system, the added protection of a UPS just makes sense.

Linux is a multiuser, multiprocessing operating system. Even when it appears that nothing is happening, there can be a great deal going on. Your system is maintaining disk space, memory, and files. All this time, it is busy making notes on what is happening in terms of security, e-mail, errors, and so on. There may be open files or jobs running. A sudden stop as a result of pulling the plug can damage your file systems. A proper shutdown is essential.

From the root prompt, type the following:

```
shutdown -h now
```

When shutdown is called with a `-h` option, it is another way of saying, "Shut the system down and keep it down." On some systems (and with proper hardware), this option will power off the system after it is down:

```
shutdown -r now
```

The `-r` option tells Linux to immediately reboot after a shutdown. A reboot option is often used after a kernel rebuild.

```
shutdown -t 60
```

This tells shutdown to wait 60 seconds before shutting the system down. If you have several users still logged onto the system, this gives them a little bit of time to log out.

Resources

Linux CD-ROM HOWTO

`http://www.linuxdoc.org/HOWTO/CDROM-HOWTO/`

Linux Hardware Capability HOWTO

`http://www.linuxdoc.org/HOWTO/Hardware-HOWTO/`

Linux Hardware Database

`http://lhd.zdnet.com/`

Linux.com's Hardware Page

`http://www.linux.com/enhance/hardware/`

PartitionMagic (from PowerQuest)

`http://www.partitionmagic.com/`

Red Hat Linux Hardware Compatibility List

`http://www.redhat.com/support/hardware/`

(Note: Starting with Red Hat 7.0, visit `http://hardware.redhat.com/` instead.)

Chapter 5

Taking Command of Linux

Before I start this chapter, I would like to take everyone and separate you into two groups. Those of you who feel that you are already Linux-savvy enough not to talk about commands that you will use day in and day out, move to the back of the chapter and turn the page. The rest of you will stay here with me and cover some of the basics. Of course, you Linux-savvy folks might still want to stick around. After all, what if you miss something? I plan to continue with a nasty habit I have: I'll start with the basics and build from there. How far will I go? Ah, the pressure.

The things I want to talk about here are basic commands you will need throughout the course of this book and your time with Linux. One of the things I hope to show you is how flexible some of these commands are. With most, you can modify the basic function with command-line switches, flags, or options, and thereby have them yield far more information than a simple execution of the command itself. A little thirst for exploration (which I hope you developed in Chapter 3) will open you up to the real potential of everyday commands.

Before I wrap up this chapter, I will also cover editors. Editors aren't a luxury or an option but an eternal necessity in the life of the system administrator. Every time you turn around, you will have to edit some configuration file or other in order to get your work done. I'll give you some pointers for making this as simple and painless as possible.

Linux Commands: Love at First Sight

When you talk about commands, it invariably means working at the shell level: the command prompt. That's the dollar sign prompt ($) and it is common to many command shells. When logged in as the root user, you will usually have a different prompt. That symbol (#) goes by many names. In North America, we call it the "pound sign" or the "hash mark." My English lit friends tell me it's an "octothorp." Others call it the tic-tac-toe board. I'm going to call it the *root prompt*.

Anyway, you want to be at just such a command prompt to begin your experimentation. If you are running from a graphical environment, click the terminal window icon to start a terminal (or shell) session. KDE users will be starting a Konsole, while GNOME users will likely start up a color `xterm`. To say that there are a great number of terminal emulators might be understating things. You have the venerable `xterm`, and the Konsole, `rxvt`, and Eterm, to name just a few.

As you work your way through this chapter, you'll notice that I toss in little boxes like the one that follows. If these commands are not already in your arsenal, then spend a few minutes playing with them and finding out what they do.

Commands to Know and Love, Part 1

`date`	Date and time.
`who`	Who is logged on to the system?
`w`	Similar to who but with different information.
`whoami`	Who am I, really?
`tty`	Identify your workstation.
`echo`	Hello, ello, llo, lo, o, o, o . . . .
`finger`	Identify a user. Find out more about them.
`last`	Who last logged in and are they still logged in?

Working with Files

Let me tell you the secret of computers, of operating systems, and of the whole industry that surrounds these things: Everything is data. Information is the be all and end all of everything we do with computers. Files are the storehouses for that information and learning how to manipulate them, use and abuse them, and otherwise play with them will still be the point of computers 20 years from now.

The next thing I want to do is talk about the three most overlooked files on your system: standard in, standard out, and standard error. A facility in manipulating these "files" will provide you with amazing flexibility when it comes to doing your work.

Commands to Know and Love, Part 2

`ls`	LiSt files
`cat`	conCATenate files
`sort`	SORT the contents of a file (or any output for that matter)
`uniq`	Return only the UNIQue lines—you do this after sorting
`wc`	Word Count (returns a count of words, characters, and lines)
`cp`	CoPy files
`mv`	MoVe, or rename, a file
`rm`	ReMove, or delete, a file
`more`	Allows easy paging of large text files
`less`	Like the `more` command, but with serious attitude

File Naming Conventions

Valid filenames may contain *almost* any character. You do have to pay some attention to the names you come up with. Once upon a time on some older UNIX systems, a limit of 14 characters existed. However, your Linux systems will allow filenames up to 255 characters in length. How you define filenames can save you a lot of hassle, as I will soon demonstrate.

Some valid filename examples include the following:

```
fish
duck
program_2.01
a.out
letter.to.mom.who.I.dont.write.often.enough.as.it.is
.bash_profile
```

Notice the last name in particular. It starts with a period. Normally, this type of file is invisible with a default listing. This is important because you are going to see this again later on in the book when I discuss crackers and security breaches on your system. For the moment, suffice it to say that if you want a file to be ignored in a normal listing, give it a filename that starts with a period.

Listing Files with Emotion!

The `ls` command seems so simple, and yet it has a number of options that can give you tons of information. Change to something like the `/etc` directory and try these options if you never have:

```
cd /etc
ls --color
ls -b
ls -lS
ls -lt
```

The first listing will show different types of files and directories in color. The second (`-b`) will show octal representations for files that might have been created with control characters. Depending on the terminal you are using, the default is to show question marks or simply blanks. If you need to access (or delete) the file, it helps to know what it is really called. The third and fourth options control sorting. The `-ls` option gives you a long listing (lots of information) sorted by file size. The last option (`-lt`) sorts by time with the newest files at the top of the list and the oldest at the bottom.

A Peek at Metacharacters

I'm going to mention the most basic of metacharacters right now because you will use them a lot. These are special characters that have particular meaning to your shell—that dollar sign or hash mark prompt where you do your work. At this time, I will mention only two metacharacters, but I will visit this topic again in detail when I cover shells later in the book. The two I want to look at are the asterisk and the question mark. The following is what they mean to the shell.

*	Match any number of characters
?	Match a single character

Extending our talk of listing files, you could list all files containing "ackle" by using this command:

```
$ ls *ackle*
hackle hackles                          tackles
```

Similarly, you could find all the words that start with an "h" like this:

```
$ ls h*
hackle hackles
```

Now, if you want to see all the seven-letter words in your directory, use this command:

```
$ ls ???????
hackles                 tackles
```

Each question mark represents a single letter position.

File Permissions: A First Look

When you use the `ls -l` command, you get your first look at Linux security, this time at the file (or directory) level. Here is an example of a long `ls` listing:

```
$ ls -l
```

```
total 3
drwxr-x---   5 root     system    512  Dec 25 12:01   presents
-r-xr--r--   1 zonthar  users     123  Dec 24 09:30   wishlist
-rw-rw----   1 zonthar  users     637  Nov 15 09:30   griflong
```

The first entry under the total column shows a directory (I'll talk about the next nine characters in a moment). The first character is a "d," which indicates a directory. Right at the end of each line, you'll find the directory or filename—in my example, they are "presents," "wishlist," and "griflong." Because the first character in the permissions field is "d," "presents" is a directory.

On to those other nine characters (characters 2 through 10). These indicate permissions for the user or owner of the file (first three), the group (second group of three), and others or everyone else (last three). In the first line, user root has read, write, and execute permissions, while the system group has only read and execute. The three dashes at the end imply that no one else has any permissions. The next two files are owned by the user called "zonthar."

> **Quick Tip:** Remember user, group, and other (ugo). You will find them useful later when I cover changing file and directory permissions.

Not-So-Hidden Files

When you take your first look at valid filenames, remember that I mentioned that files starting with a period are hidden. As a result, creating directories or files in this way is a favorite trick of system crackers. Get used to the idea of listing your directories and files with a `-a` option so that you see everything that's there. Look for anything unusual.

Keep in mind, however, that a number of applications create dotted directory names in your home directory so that you are generally not burdened with seeing all these configuration areas. That's great, except that you should know what you've got on your disk. Always balance your need for convenience with a healthy curiosity. A quick `ls -a` in your home directory will show you some files (and directories) you will become very familiar with as time goes on. Here is an example of what you will see:

```
.Xclients  .bash_history  .bash_profile  .gnupg  .kde
```

Strange Filenames That Just Won't Go Away

Every once in a while, you will do a listing of your directory and some strange file will appear that you just know isn't supposed to be there. Don't panic. It's not necessarily a cracker at work. You may have mistyped something and you just need to get rid of it. The problem is that you can't. Case in point: I *accidentally* created a couple of files with hard-to-deal-with names. I don't want them there, but trying to delete them does not work. Here are the files:

```
-another_file
 onemorefile
```

Here's what happens when I try to delete them:

```
[mgagne@scigate tmp]$ rm -another_file
rm: invalid option -- a
Try `rm --help' for more information.
```

What about that other file?

```
[mgagne@scigate tmp]$ rm onemorefile
rm: cannot remove `onemorefile': No such file or directory
```

The problem with the first file is that the hyphen makes it look like I am passing an option to the `rm` command. To get around this problem, I'll use the double-dash option on the `rm` command. Using two dashes tells the command that what follows is not an option to that command. Here I go again:

```
[mgagne@scigate tmp]$ rm -- -another_file
[mgagne@scigate tmp]$
```

Bravo! By the way, this double-dash syntax applies to many other commands that need to recognize potentially weird filenames. Now, what about the second file? It looked fine, didn't it? If you look very closely, you'll see that there is a space in front of the leading `o`, so simply telling `rm` to remove the file doesn't work either, because "`onemorefile`" is not the filename. It is actually "` onemorefile`". So, I need to pass that space as well, and to do that I give the full name (space included) by enclosing the filename in double quotes.

```
[mgagne@scigate tmp]$ rm " otherfile"
[mgagne@scigate tmp]$
```

More on rm (or "Oops! I didn't really mean that.")

When you delete a file with Linux, it is gone. If you didn't really mean to delete (or `rm`) a file, it is time to find out if you have been keeping good backups. The other option is to check with the rm command before you delete a file. Rather than simply typing `rm` followed by the filename, try this instead:

```
rm -i file_name1 file_name2 file_name3
```

The `-i` option tells `rm` to work in interactive mode. For each of the three files in the example, rm will pause and ask if you really mean it.

```
rm : remove 'file_name1'?
```

If you like to be a bit more wordy than that, you can also try `rm --interactive file_name`, but that goes against the system administrator's first principle.

> **System Administrator's First Principle:** System administrators believe in simplifying things. If your solution makes things more complicated, something has gone terribly wrong.

Of course, in following that principle, you could remove all the files starting with the word "file" by using the asterisk.

```
rm -i file*
```

Making Your Life Easier with alias

You might find that you want to use the `-i` option every time you delete anything, just in case. It's a lot easier to type Y in confirmation than it is to go looking through your backups. The problem is that you are adding keystrokes and everyone knows that system administrators are notoriously lazy people. Then there's that whole issue of the first principle. That's why we shortened "list" to simply "ls," after all. Don't despair, though—Linux has a way. It is the `alias` command.

```
alias rm='rm -i'
```

Now every time you execute the rm command, it will check with you beforehand. This behavior will only be in effect until you log out. If you want this to be the default behavior for `rm`, you should add the `alias` command to your local `.bashrc` file. If you want this to be the behavior for every user on your system, you should add your `alias` definitions to the system-wide version of this file, `/etc/bashrc`, and save yourself even more time. Depending on your distribution, there may already be `alias` definitions set up for you. The first way to find out what has been set up for you is to type the `alias` command on a blank line.

```
[root@website /root]# alias
alias cp='cp -i'
alias ls='ls --color'
alias mv='mv -i'
alias rm='rm -i'
```

Using the `cat` command, you can look in your local `.bashrc file` and discover the same information.

```
[root@website /root]# cat .bashrc
# .bashrc
```

```
# User specific aliases and functions

alias rm='rm -i'
alias cp='cp -i'
alias mv='mv -i'

# Source global definitions
if [ -f /etc/bashrc ]; then
        . /etc/bashrc

fi
```

Well, isn't this interesting? Notice the two other commands here, the `cp` (copy files) and `mv` (rename files) commands, and both have the `-i` flag as well. They too can be set to work interactively, verifying with you before you overwrite something important. Let's say that I want to make a backup copy of a file called `important_info` using the `cp` command.

```
cp important_info important_info.backup
```

Perhaps what I am actually trying to do is rename the file (rather than copy it). For this, I would use the `mv` command.

```
mv important_info not_so_important_info
```

The only time you would be bothered by an "Are you sure?" type of message is if the file already existed. In that case, you would get a message like the following:

```
mv: overwrite 'not_so_important_info'?
```

Forcing the Issue

The answer to the inevitable next question of "What do you do if you are copying, moving, or removing multiple files and you don't want to be bothered with being asked each time when you've aliased everything to be interactive?" is this: Use the `-f` flag, which, as you might have surmised, stands for "force." Once again, this is a flag that is quite common with many Linux commands—either a `-f` or a `--force`.

Imagine a hypothetical scenario in which you move a group of log files daily so that you always have the previous day's files as backup (but just for one day). If your mv command is aliased interactively, you can get around it like this:

```
mv -f *.logs /path_to/backup_directory/
```

> **Musing:** Yes, I know that `mv` looks more like "move" than "rename." In fact, you do move directories and files using the `mv` command. Think of the file as a vessel for your data. When you rename a file with `mv`, you are moving the data into a new container for the same data, so it isn't strictly a rename—you really are moving files. Looking at it that way, it doesn't seem so strange. Sort of.

The reverse of the `alias` command is `unalias`. If you want your `mv` command to return to its original functionality, use this command:

```
unalias mv
```

Standard Input and Standard Output

You are going to use standard in and standard out throughout your Linux administration career, so I'll cover them now. *Standard in* (STDIN) is where the system expects to find its input. This is usually the keyboard, although it can be a program or shell script. When you change that default, you call it redirecting from STDIN.

Standard out (STDOUT) is where the system expects to direct its output, usually the terminal screen. Again, redirection of STDOUT is at the discretion of whatever command or script is executing at the time. The chain of events from STDIN to STDOUT looks something like this:

```
standard in  -> Linux command  ->  standard out
```

STDIN is often referred to as *fd0,* or file descriptor 0, while STDOUT is usually thought of as *fd1.* There is also *standard error* (STDERR), where the system reports any errors in program execution. By default, this is also the terminal. To redirect STDOUT, use the greater-than sign (>). As you might have guessed, to redirect from STDIN, you use the less-than sign (<). But what exactly does that mean? Let's try an experiment. Randomly search your brain and pick a handful of names. Got them? Good. Now type the `cat` command and redirect its STDOUT to a file called "random_names."

```
cat > random_names
```

Your cursor will just sit there and wait for you to do something, so type those names, pressing Enter after each one. What's happening here is that `cat` is taking its input from STDIN and writing it out to your new file. You can also write the command like this:

```
cat - 1> random_names
```

The hyphen literally means `standard in` to the command. The `1` stands for file descriptor 1. This is good information, and you will use it later. Finished with your random names list? When you are done, press Ctrl-D to finish. Ctrl-D, by the way, stands for *EOF,* or *end of file.*

```
Marie Curie
Albert Einstein
Mark Twain
Wolfgang Amadeus Mozart
Stephen Hawking
Hedy Lamarr
^D
```

If you `cat` this file, the names will be written to `STDOUT`—in this case, your terminal window. You can also give `cat` several files at the same time. For instance, you could do something like this:

```
cat file1 file2 file3
```

Each file would be listed one right after the other. That output could then be redirected into another file. You could also have it print out the same file over and over (`cat random_names random_names random_names`). `cat` isn't fussy about these things and will deal with binary files (programs) just as quickly. Beware of using `cat` to print out the contents of a program to your terminal screen. At worst, your terminal session will lock up or reward you with a lot of beeping and weird characters.

> **Quick Tip:** If you get caught in such a situation and all the characters on your screen appear as junk, try typing `echo` and then pressing Ctrl-v and Ctrl-o. If you can still type, you can also try typing `stty sane` and then pressing Ctrl-j.

Redirecting `STDIN` works pretty much the same way, except that you use the less-than sign instead. Using the `sort` command, let's take that file of random names and work with it. Many commands that work with files can take their input directly from that file. Unless told otherwise, `cat` and `sort` will think that the word following the command is a filename. That's why you did the `STDIN` redirection thing. Yes, that's right: `STDIN` is just another file. Sort of.

```
sort random_names
```

The result, of course, is that you get all your names printed out in alphabetical order. You could have also specified that `sort` take its input from a redirected `STDIN`. It looks a bit strange, but this is perfectly valid.

```
[mgagne@scigate tmp]$ sort < random_names
Albert Einstein
Hedy Lamarr
Marie Curie
Mark Twain
Stephen Hawking
Wolfgang Amadeus Mozart
```

One more variation involves defining your `STDIN` (as you did previously) and specifying a different `STDOUT` all on the same line. In the following example, I am redirecting *from* my file and redirecting that output *to* a new file:

```
sort < random_names > sorted_names
```

Piping

Sometimes the thing that makes the most sense is to feed the output from one command directly into another command without having to resort to files in between at every step of the way. This is called *piping*. The symbolism is not that subtle: Imagine pieces of pipe connecting one command with another. Not until you run out of pipe does the command's output emerge. The pipe symbol is the broken vertical bar on your keyboard usually located just below or (depending on the keyboard) just above the Enter key and sharing space with the backslash key. Here's how it works:

```
cat random_names | sort | wc -w > num_names
```

In the preceding example, the output from the `cat` command is piped into `sort`, whose output is then piped into the `wc` command (that's "word count"). The `-w` flag tells `wc` to count the number of words in `random_names`. So far, so good.

That `cat` at the beginning is actually redundant, but I wanted to stack up a few commands for you to give you an idea of the power of piping. Ordinarily, I would write that command as follows:

```
sort random_names | wc -w > num_names
```

The `cat` is extraneous because `sort` incorporates its function. Using pipes is a great timesaver because you don't always need to have output at every step of the way.

tee: A Very Special Pipe

Suppose that you want to send the output of a command to another command, but you also want to see the results at some point. Using the previous word count example, if you want a sorted list of names, but you also want the word count, you might have to use two different commands: one to generate the sorted list and another to count the number of words. Wouldn't it be nice if you could direct part of the output one way and have the rest continue in another direction? For this, use the `tee` command.

```
sort random_names | tee sorted_list | wc -w > num_names
```

The output from `sort` is now sitting in a file called `sorted_list`, while the rest of the output continues on to `wc` for a word count.

STDERR

What about STDERR? Some commands (many, in fact) treat the error output differently than the STDOUT. If you are running the command at your terminal and that's all you want, there is no problem. Sometimes, though, the output is quite wordy and you need to capture it and look at it later. Unfortunately, using the STDOUT redirect (the greater-than sign) is only going to be so useful. Error messages that might be generated (such as warning messages from a compilation) will go to the terminal as before. One way to deal with this is to start by redirecting STDERR to STDOUT, and then redirect that to a file. Here's the line I use for this:

```
command_name 2>&1 > logfile.out
```

Remember that file descriptor 2 is STDERR and that file descriptor 1 is STDOUT. That's what that 2>&1 construct is all about. You are redirecting fd2 to fd1 and then redirecting that output to the file of your choice. Using that program compilation example, you might wind up with something like this:

```
make -f Makefile.linux 2>&1 > compilation.output
```

> **Quick Tip:** The final greater-than sign in the preceding example could be eliminated completely. When using the 2>&1 construct, it is assumed that what follows is a filename.

The Road to Nowhere

If the command happens to be verbose by nature and doesn't have a quiet switch, you can redirect that STDOUT and STDERR noise to what long-time UNIX and Linux users like to call the *bit bucket*, a special file called /dev/null—literally, a road to nowhere. Anything fed to the bit bucket takes up no space and is never seen or heard from again. When I was in school, we would tell people to shut up by saying, "Dev null it, will you?" As you can see, we were easily amused.

To redirect output to the bit bucket, use the STDOUT redirection.

```
command -option > /dev/null
```

If, for some strange reason, you want to sort the output of the random_names files and you do not want to see the output, you can redirect the whole thing to /dev/null in this way:

```
sort random_names > /dev/null
```

Using the program compilation example where you had separate STDOUT and STDERR streams, you can combine the output to the bit bucket.

```
make -F makefile.linux 2>&1 /dev/null
```

That's actually a crazy example because you do want to see what goes on, but redirecting both STDOUT and STDERR to /dev/null is quite common when dealing with automated processes running in the background. You'll see this dealt with in much more detail when you explore system automation in Chapter 15.

Linux Commands: Working with Directories

There is another batch of commands suited to working with directory files (directories being just another type of file—more on this in Chapter 8).

pwd	Print Working Directory
cd	Change to a new Directory
mkdir	MaKe or create a new DIRectory
mv	MoVe directories, or like files, rename them
rmdir	ReMove or delete DIRectories

One way to create a complicated directory structure is to use the mkdir command to create each and every directory.

```
mkdir /dir1
mkdir /dir1/sub_dir
mkdir /dir1/sub_dir/yetanotherdir
```

What you could do instead is save yourself a few keystrokes and use the -p flag. This tells mkdir to create any parent directories that might not already exist. If you happen to like a lot of verbiage from your system, you could also add the --verbose flag for good measure.

```
mkdir -p /dir/sub_dir/yetanotherdir
```

To rename or move a directory, the format is the same as you used with a file or group of files. Use the mv command.

```
mv path_to_dir new_path_to_dir
```

Removing a directory can be just a bit more challenging. The command rmdir seems simple enough. In fact, removing this directory was no problem:

```
$ rmdir trivia_dir
```

Removing this one, however, gave me this error:

```
$ rmdir junk_dir
rmdir: junk_dir: Directory not empty
```

You can only use `rmdir` to remove an empty directory. There is a `-p` option (as in "parents") that enables you to remove a directory structure. For instance, you could remove a couple of levels like this:

```
$ rmdir -p junk_dir/level1/level2/level3
```

All the directories from `junk_dir` on down will be removed, but *only* if they are empty of files. A better approach is to use the `rm` command with the `-r`, or *recursive*, option. Unless you are deleting only a couple of files or directories, you will want to use the `-f` option as well.

```
$ rm -rf junk_dir
```

> **Warning:** Beware the `rm -rf *` command. Better yet, *never use it.* If you must delete an entire directory structure, change directory to the one above it and explicitly remove the directory. This is also the first and best reason to do as much of your work as possible as a normal user and not root. Because root is all powerful, it is quite capable of completely destroying your system. Imagine that you are in the top-level directory (`/`) instead of `/home/myname/junkdir` when you initiate that recursive delete. It is far too easy to make this kind of mistake. *Beware.*

There's No Place Like $HOME

Yeah, I know. It's a pretty cheesy pun, but I like it.

Because you've just had a chance to play with a few directory commands, I'd like to take a moment and talk about a very special directory. Every user on your system has a home directory. That directory can be referenced with the `$HOME` environment variable. To get back to your home directory at any time, simply type `cd $HOME` and no matter where you were, there you are. Actually, you only need type `cd`, press Enter, and you are home. The `$HOME` is implied.

The `$HOME` shortcut is great for shell scripts or anytime you want to save yourself some keystrokes. For instance, say you want to copy the file `remote.file` to your home directory and you are sitting in `/usr/some_remote/dir`. You could use either of the next two commands:

```
cp remote.file /home/my_username
cp remote.file $HOME
```

The second command saves you keystrokes, and the more time you spend doing system administration, the more you will love shortcuts like this.

More on File Permissions

What you can and can't do with a file, as defined by your user or group name, is pretty much wrapped up in four little letters. Each of these letters in turn can be referenced by a number. They are `r`, `w`, `x`, and `s`. Their numerical representations are 4, 2, 1, and "it depends." To understand all that, you need to do a little binary math.

Reading from right to left, think of the `x` as being in position 0. The `w`, then, is in position 1 and the `r` is in position 2. Here's the way it works:

2 to the power of 0 equals 1 (`x` is 1)
2 to the power of 1 equals 2 (`w` is 2)
2 to the power of 2 equals 4 (`r` is 4)

In order to specify multiple permissions, you can just add the numbers together. If you want to specify both read and execute permissions, simply add 4 and 1 and you get 5. For all permissions (`rwx`), use 7.

File permissions are referenced in groups of three `rwx` sections. The `r` stands for "read," the `w` means "write," and the `x` denotes that the file is executable.

While these permissions are arranged in three groups of three `rwx` combinations, their meaning is the same in all cases. The difference has to do with who they represent rather than the permissions themselves. The first of these three represents the user, the second trio stands for the group permissions, and the third represents everybody that doesn't fit into either of the first two categories.

The commands you will use for changing these basic permissions are `chmod`, `chown`, and `chgrp`.

`chmod`	CHange the MODe of a file (aka its permissions)
`chown`	CHange the OWNer of the file or directory
`chgrp`	CHange the GRouP of the file or directory

User and Group Ownership

To change the ownership of file `mail_test` from root to natika, you first have to log in as root because only root can change root's ownership of a file. This is very simple.

```
chown natika mail_test
```

You can also use the `-R` option to change ownership recursively. Let's use a directory called `test_directory` as an example. Once again, it belongs to root and you want to make every file in that directory (and below) owned by natika.

```
chown -R natika test_directory
```

The format for changing group ownership is just as easy. Let's change the group ownership of `test_directory` (previously owned by root) so that it and all its files and subdirectories belong to group accounts:

```
chgrp -R accounts test_directory
```

You can even combine the two formats. In the following example, the ownership of the entire `finance_data` directory changes to natika as the owner and accounts as the group. To do so, you use this form of the `chown` command:

```
chown -R natika.accounts finance_data
```

> **Quick Tip:** You can use the `-R` flag to recursively change everything in a subdirectory with `chgrp` and `chmod` as well.

So now files (and directories) are owned by some user and some group. This brings us to the next question.

Who Can Do What?

From time to time, you will need to modify file permissions. One reason has to do with security. The most common reason, however, is to make a shell script file executable. This is done with the `chmod` command.

```
chmod mode filename
```

For instance, if you have a script file called `list_users`, you make it executable with the following command:

```
chmod +x list_users
```

That command will allow execute permissions for all users. If you want to make the file executable for the owner and group only, you specify it on the command line like this:

```
chmod u+x,g+x list_users
```

The `u` means user (the owner of the file, really), and `g` stands for group. The reason you use `u` for the owner instead of `o` is that the `o` is being used for "other," meaning everyone else. The `chmod +x list_users` command can then be expressed as `chmod u+x,g+x,o+x list_users`. Unfortunately, this starts to get a bit cumbersome. Now let's look at a much more complicated set of permissions. Imagine that you want your `list_users` script to have read, write, and execute permissions for the owner, read and execute for the group, and read-only for anybody else. The long way is to do this is as follows:

```
chmod u=rwx,g=rx,o=r list_users
```

Notice the equal sign (=) construct rather than the plus sign (+). That's because the plus sign adds permissions, and in this case you want them to be absolute. If the original permissions of the file allowed write access for "other," the plus sign construct would not have removed the execute permission. Using the minus sign (–) removes permissions. If you want to take away execute permission entirely from a file, you can do something like this:

```
chmod -x list_users
```

One way to simplify the `chmod` command is to remember that `r` is 4, `w` is 2, and `x` is 1, and add up the numbers in each of the three positions. `rwx` is then 4 + 2 + 1, or 7. `r-x` translates to 4 + 1, and `x` is simply 1. That monster from the second to last example can then be rewritten like this:

```
chmod 751 list_users
```

Who Was That Masked User?

Every time you create a file, you are submitted to a default set of permissions. Go ahead. Create a blank file using the `touch` command. I am going to call my blank file "fish."

```
[mgagne@testsys tmp]$ touch fish
```

Now have a look at its permissions by doing an `ls -l`.

```
[mgagne@testsys tmp]$ ls -l
total 0
-rw-rw-r--    1 mgagne   mgagne          0 Nov  5 11:57 fish
```

Without doing anything whatsoever, your file has read and write permissions for both the user and group, and read permission for everybody else. This happens because you have a default file-creation mask of 002. You can discover this using the `umask` command.

```
[mgagne@testsys tmp]$ umask
002
```

The 2 is subtracted from the possible set of permissions, `rwx` (or 7). 7 – 0 remains 7, while 7 – 2 is 5. But wait—5 stands for `r-x`, or read and execute. How is it that the file only shows a read bit set? That's because newly created files are not set executable. At best, they provide read and write permissions for everyone. Another way to display this information is by using the `-S` flag. Instead of the numeric output, you'll get a symbolic mask displayed.

```
[mgagne@testsys tmp]$ umask -S
u=rwx,g=rwx,o=rx
```

If you have an application that requires you to provide a default set of permissions for all the files you create, change umask to reflect that inside your scripts. As an example, let's pretend that your program or script created text files that you wanted everyone to be able to read (444). Because the execute bit won't be a factor anyway, if you mask out the write bit using a 2 all around, then everybody will have read permission. Set your umask to 222, create another file (called "duck" this time), and then do an `ls -l` to check things out.

```
[mgagne@testsys tmp]$ umask 222
[mgagne@testsys tmp]$ touch duck
[mgagne@testsys tmp]$ ls -l
total 0
-r--r--r--    1 mgagne   mgagne           0 Nov  5 12:58 duck
```

The setuid Bit

Aside from those three permission bits (read, write, and execute), there is one other very important one: the s bit, sometimes referred to as the setuid or setgid bit depending on its position.

The reasoning behind this particular bit is as follows. Sometimes you want a program to act as though you are logged in as a different user. For example, you may want a certain program to run as the root user. This would be a program that you want a nonadministrative user to run, but (for whatever reason) this program needs to read or write files that are exclusively root's. The sendmail program is a perfect example of that. The program needs to access *privileged* functions in order to do its work, but you want regular (nonroot) users to be able to send mail as well.

The setuid bit is a variation on the "execute" bit. In order to make the hypothetical program, ftl_travel, executable by anyone but with root's privileges, you change its permissions as follows:

```
chmod u+s ftl_travel
```

The next step, as you might guess, is to combine full permissions and the setuid bit. Start by thinking of the setuid and setgid bits as another triplet of permissions. Just as you could reference r, w, and x as 4, 2, and 1, so can you reference setuid as 4, setgid as 2, and other (which you don't worry about).

So, using a nice, complicated example, let's make that command so that it has read, write, and execute permissions for the owner, read and execute permissions for the group, and no permissions for anyone else. To those with execute permission, though, you want to have it setuid. You could also represent that command either symbolically or in a numerical way.

```
chmod u=rwxs,g=rx,o= ftl_travel
chmod 4750 ftl_travel
```

The 4 in the front position represents the `setuid` bit. If you want to make the program `setgid` instead, you can change that to 2. And, yes, if you want the executable to maintain both the owner's permissions and that of the group, you can simply add 4 and 2 to get 6. The resulting set of permissions is as follows:

```
chmod 6750 ftl_travel
```

Changing the `setuid` bit (or `setgid`) is not strictly a case of providing administrative access to nonroot users. This can be anything. You might have a database package that operates under only one user ID, or you may want all users to access a program as though they were part of a specific group. You will have to decide.

> **Important Note:** You cannot use the `setuid` or `setgid` bit for shell scripts (although there are Perl hooks to do this). This won't work for security reasons. If you need to have a script execute with a set of permissions other than its own, you will have to write a little C program that wraps around your script, and then allow the program rather than the script to have `setuid` (or `setgid`) permissions.

File Attributes

Unfortunately, the first time most people run across file attributes is usually after their system has been cracked. (I discuss crackers and their techniques in Chapter 25.) What happens is that you try to update a package that you know has been modified and the system will not let you. So you try to delete the file and that still doesn't work. You check your user ID and you are logged in as root and still you cannot get rid of the file or update it with a clean version. What is going on? Isn't root supposed to be all powerful?

You have probably just run across a file with the *immutable* attribute set, which means that under no circumstances can you move, rename, delete, or write to the file.

For the most part, users never wander into this territory and it tends to be a largely ignored aspect of the Linux `ext2fs` file system. The first command to look at here is `lsattr`, which (you guessed it) lists the attributes of any given file. Normally, your stock system will have none of these permission-like bits set, so using the `lsattr` command will show something like this:

```
[mgagne@testsys mgagne]$ lsattr LSAdocs
-------- LSAdocs/LSA01- Introduction
```

The dashes all represent position markers for a number of attributes that can be set (or changed) using the `chattr` command.

```
chattr +attribute file_name
```

You can also use a minus sign (–) to remove attributes or the equal sign (=) to set a number of attributes at the same time. Some of the attributes must be set by the superuser alone. These are `a`, and `i`. The `i` attribute is the one that makes a file immutable—it's the most interesting one to me. Now, why would you want to bother yourself with any of this? Think back to how I introduced this section and my immutable file. You can do the same thing to protect yourself. Take those system files that you absolutely do not want anybody modifying in a remote session and add this attribute.

The other root-only attribute is `a`. Setting this bit means that files are append-only. In other words, you cannot simply overwrite the files. This might be good for log files that you don't want someone suddenly clearing out. Here's an example of this append attribute in action:

```
[mgagne@testsys mgagne]$ chattr +a test.txt
chattr: Operation not permitted while setting flags on test.txt
[mgagne@testsys mgagne]$ su - root
Password:
[root@testsys /root]# touch test.txt
[root@testsys /root]# chattr +a test.txt
[root@testsys /root]# /usr/games/fortune -l > test.txt
bash: test.txt: Operation not permitted
[root@testsys /root]# /usr/games/fortune -l >> test.txt
```

When I first tried to set the attribute, I was working as a regular user and you can see where that got me. I tried again, but this time switched to the root user first. I used the `touch` command to create a blank file, and then set the append attribute. The first time through, I simply redirected the output of the fortune program (using the greater-than sign) but was refused *even though I was running as root.* Only when I started appending my output to the file was I allowed to do so.

The other permissions you can set in this way are as follows.

- Attribute `A`: Don't update the access time information on files. For frequently accessed files that don't change a great deal, this attribute can provide performance improvements. The catch, of course, is that you can't track access time on the files. This can also be set for an entire file system, something that Chapter 6 addresses.
- Attribute `c`: When this file is not being accessed, the system automatically compresses it. Anytime the file is accessed, it is uncompressed. This may or may not be valid on your system because it was not yet fully implemented as of this writing.
- Attribute `d`: Files marked in this way will not be backed up by the `dump` command. (For more on the `dump` command, see Chapter 16.)

- Attribute `s`: Think of this as the paranoia bit. If you set this on a file, it will be completely zeroed out when you delete it. In other words, someone scanning your disk at the bit level will see no trace that it ever existed.
- Attribute `S`: All files tagged with this bit are automatically synchronized to the disk whenever any changes are made.
- Attribute `u`: This is another bit that was not yet implemented at the time of this writing. The idea is that you can undelete a file flagged in this way, even after you have deleted it.

Finding Anything

One of the most useful commands in your arsenal is the `find` command. This powerhouse doesn't get anywhere near the credit it deserves. Generally speaking, `find` is used to list files and redirect (or pipe) that output to do some simple reporting or backups. There it ends. If anything, this should only be the beginning. As versatile as `find` is, you should take some time to get to know it. Let me give you a whirlwind tour of this awesome command. Let's start with the basics:

```
find starting_dir [options]
```

One of those options is `-print`, which only makes sense if you want to see any kind of output from this command. You could easily get a listing of every file on the system by starting at the top and recursively listing the disk.

```
find / -print
```

While that might be interesting and you might want to redirect that to a file for future reference, it is only so useful. It makes more sense to search for something. For instance, look for all the JPEG-type image files sitting on your disk. Because you know that these images end in a .jpg extension, you can use that to search.

```
find / -name "*.jpg" -print
```

Depending on the power of your system, this can take a while and you are likely to get a lot of Permission denied messages (particularly as you traverse a directory called `/proc`). If you are running this as a user other than root, you will likely get a substantial number of Permission denied messages. At this point, the usefulness of `find` should start to become apparent because a lot of images stashed away in various parts of the disk can certainly add up as far as disk space is concerned. Try it with an .avi or .mpg extension to look for video clips (which can be very large).

If what you are trying to do is locate old files or particularly large files, then try the following example. Look for anything that has not been modified (this is the `-mtime` parameter) or accessed (the `-atime` parameter) in the last 12 months. The `-o` flag is the "or" in this equation.

```
# find /data1/Marcel -size +1024 \
\( -mtime +365 -o -atime +365 \) -ls
```

A few techniques introduced here are worth noting. The backslashes in front of the round brackets are *escape characters,* there to make sure the shell does not interpret them in ways you do not want it to—in this case, the open and close parentheses on the second line. The first line also has a backslash at the end. This is to indicate a line break, as the whole command will not fit neatly on one line of this page. Were you to type it exactly as shown without any backslashes, it would not work; however, the backslashes in the second line are essential. The preceding command also searches for files that are greater than 500KB in size. That is what the `-size +1024` means because `1024` refers to 512-byte blocks. The `-ls` at the end of the command tells the system to do a long listing of any files it finds that fit my search criteria.

Earlier in this chapter, you learned about `setuid` and `setgid` files. Keeping an eye on where these files are and determining if they belong there are important aspects of maintaining security on your system. Here's a command that will examine the permissions on your files (the `-perm` option) and report back on what it finds.

```
find / -type f \( -perm -4000 -o -perm -2000 \) -ls
```

You may want to redirect this output to a file that you can later peruse and decide on what course of action to take. Now let's look at another `find` example to help you uncover what types of files you are looking at. Your Linux system has another command called `file` that can deliver useful information on files and what they are, whether they are executables, text files, or movie clips. Here's a sample of some of the files in my home directory as reported by `file`.

```
$  file $HOME/*

code.layout:     ASCII text
cron.txt:        data
dainbox:         International language text
dainbox.gz:      gzip compressed data, deflated, original filename,
last modified: Sat Oct 7 13:21:14 2000, os: Unix
definition.htm:  HTML document text
gatekeeper.1:    troff or preprocessor input text
gatekeeper.man:  English text
gatekeeper.pl:   perl commands text
hilarious.mpg:   MPEG video stream data
```

The next step is to modify the `find` command by adding a `-exec` clause so that I can get the `file` command's output on what `find` locates.

```
# find /data1/Marcel -size +1024  \
\( -mtime +365 -o -atime +365 \) -ls -exec file {} \;
```

The open and close braces that follow `-exec` file mean that the list of files generated should be passed to whatever command follows the `-exec` option (in other words, the command you will be *exec*uting). The backslash followed by a semicolon at the end is required for the command to be valid. As you can see, `find` is extremely powerful. Learning to harness that power can make your administrative life much easier. You'll encounter `find` again at various times in this book.

grep'ping for Dollars (or Anything Else for That Matter) and Piping

`grep`: Global regular expression parser.

That definition of the acronym is one of many. Don't be surprised if you hear it called the "gobble research exercise program" instead of what I called it. Basically, `grep`'s purpose in life is to make it easy for you to find strings in text files. This is its basic format:

```
grep pattern file(s)
```

As an example, let's say you want to find out if you have a user named "natika" in your `/etc/passwd` file. The trouble is that you have 500 lines in the file.

```
[root@testsys /root]# grep natika /etc/passwd
natika:x:504:504:Natika the Cat:/home/natika:/bin/bash
```

Sometimes you just want to know if a particular chunk of text exists in a file, but you don't know which file specifically. Using the `-l` option with `grep` enables you to list filenames only, rather than lines (`grep`'s default behavior). In the next example, I am going to look for Natika's name in my e-mail folders. Because I don't know whether Natika is capitalized in the mail folders, I'll introduce another useful flag to `grep`: the `-i` flag. It tells the command to ignore case.

```
[root@testsys Mail]# grep -i -l natika *
Baroque music
Linux Stuff
Personal stuff
Silliness
sent-mail
```

As you can see, the lines with the word (or name) "Natika" are not displayed—only the files. Here's another great use for `grep`. Every once in a while, you will want to scan for a process. The reason might be to locate a misbehaving terminal or to find out what a specific login is doing. Because grep can filter out patterns in your files or your output, it is a useful tool. Rather than trying to scan through 400 lines on your screen for one command, let grep narrow down the search for you. When grep finds the target text, it displays that line on your screen.

```
[root@testsys /root]# ps ax | grep httpd
 1029 ?        S      0:00 httpd
 1037 ?        S      0:00 httpd
 1038 ?        S      0:00 httpd
 1039 ?        S      0:00 httpd
 1040 ?        S      0:00 httpd
 1041 ?        S      0:00 httpd
 1042 ?        S      0:00 httpd
 1043 ?        S      0:00 httpd
 1044 ?        S      0:00 httpd
30978 ?        S      0:00 httpd
 1385 pts/2    S      0:00 grep httpd
```

Notice the last line that shows the grep command itself in the process list. You'll use that line as the launch point to one last example with grep. If you want to scan for strings other than the one specified, use the -v option. Using this option, it's a breeze to list all processes currently running on the system but ignore any that have a reference to root.

```
ps aux | grep -v root
```

And speaking of processes. . . .

Processes

You are going to hear a lot about processes, process status, monitoring processes, or killing processes. Reducing the whole discussion to its simplest form, all you have to remember is that any command you run is a process. Processes are also sometimes referred to as *jobs.*

So what constitutes a process? Everything.

The session program that executes your typed commands (the shell) is a process. The tools I am using to write this chapter are creating several processes. Every terminal session you have open, every link to the Internet, every game you have running—all these programs generate one or more processes on your system. In fact, there can be hundreds, even thousands, of processes running on your system at any given time. To see your own processes, try the following command:

```
[root@testsys /root]# ps
  PID TTY          TIME CMD
```

```
12293 pts/5     00:00:00 login
12316 pts/5     00:00:00 su
12317 pts/5     00:00:00 bash
12340 pts/5     00:00:00 ps
```

For a bit more detail, try using the u option. This will show all processes owned by you that currently have a controlling terminal. Even if you are running as root, you will not see system processes in this view. If you add the a option to that you'll see all the processes running on that terminal—in this case, revealing the subshell that did the su to root.

```
[root@testsys /root]# ps au
USER       PID %CPU %MEM   VSZ  RSS TTY      STAT START   TIME COMMAND
root     12293  0.0  0.4  2312 1196 pts/5    S    21:23   0:00 login -- mgagne
mgagne   12294  0.0  0.3  1732  976 pts/5    S    21:23   0:00 -bash
root     12316  0.0  0.3  2156  952 pts/5    S    21:23   0:00 su - root
root     12317  0.0  0.3  1736  980 pts/5    S    21:23   0:00 -bash
root     12342  0.0  0.2  2400  768 pts/5    R    21:24   0:00 ps au
```

The most common thing someone will do is add an x option as well. This will show you all processes, controlled by your terminal or not, as well as those of other users. The administrator will also want to know about the l option, which stands for "long." It is particularly useful because it shows the parent process of every process, because every process has another process that launched (or spawned) it. This is the parent process of the process ID. In sysadmin short form, this is the PPID of the PID. When your system starts up, the first process is called init. It is the master process and the superparent of every process that will come until such a time as the system is rebooted. Try this incarnation of the ps command for an interesting view of your system:

```
[root@testsys /root]# ps alxww | more

  F   UID   PID  PPID PRI  NI   VSZ  RSS  WCHAN STAT TTY         TIME COMMAND
100     0     1     0   0   0  1120  120 134005 S    ?           0:07 init [3]
040     0     2     1   0   0     0    0 12d42b SW   ?           0:00 [kflushd]
040     0     3     1   0   0     0    0 12d4a0 SW   ?           0:03 [kupdate]
040     0     4     1   0   0     0    0 123282 SW   ?           0:00 [kpiod]
040     0     5     1   0   0     0    0 126896 SW   ?           0:03 [kswapd]
140     1   336     1   0   0  1212    0 134005 SW   ?           0:00 [portmap]
040     0   350     1   0   0     0    0 1ad198 SW   ?           0:00 [lockd]
040     0   351   350   0   0     0    0 1aa906 SW   ?           0:00 [rpciod]
```

Again, this is a partial listing. You noticed, of course, that I threw a couple of new flags in there. The double w, or ww, displays each process' command-line options. A single w truncates the options at a half a line.

The columns you see there tell you a little bit more about each process. The F field indicates the process flag. A 040 in that position indicates a process that forked, but didn't `exec`, whereas a `140` means the same, but that superuser privileges were used to start the process. The `UID` field represents the user ID while `PID` and `PPID` are the process and parent process ID that I covered earlier. `PRI` and `NI` (priority and nice number) will feature later when I discuss performance issues. In fact, there are quite a number of information flags for the `ps` command. Every system administrator should take some time to read the man page. More important, play with the command and the various flags. You will be enlightened.

Forests and Trees

With all the information displayed through `ps`, you can be forgiven if your head is starting to hurt a bit. It is a little like trying to see the forest but being overwhelmed by the sheer number of trees. And yet, all these processes are linked in some way. Luckily, your stock Linux distribution contains tools to make this easier. One of them is called `pstree`. Here's a sample of what you get by simply typing the command and pressing Enter:

```
init-+-atd
     |-automount
     |-crond---crond---sh---setiathome
     |-gpm
     |-httpd---9*[httpd]
     |-identd---identd---3*[identd]
     |-inetd-+-in.telnetd---login---bash---su---bash---sh
     |       `-in.telnetd---login---bash---pstree
     |-4*[kdeinit]
     |-kdeinit---kdeinit
     |-kflushd
     |-klogd
     |-kmail
     |-kpiod
     |-kswapd
     |-kupdate
     |-lockd---rpciod
     |-login---bash---startx---xinit-+-X
     |                               `-wmaker-+-ascd
     |                                        |-dosexec-+-auserver
     |                                        |         |-dosexec
     |                                        |         |-winsock
     |                                        |         `-xcrt
     |                                        |-gkrellm---gkrellm
     |                                        |-gnumeric
```

This is only a partial listing, but notice that everything on the system stems from one super, ancestral process called `init`. Somewhere under there, I have a login that spawns a shell. From that shell, I start an X window session from which spawns a WindowMaker application. Even so, there are GNOME and KDE applications in there as well.

If you want a similar output, but in somewhat more detail, you can go back to your old friend, the ps command. Try the `f` flag, which in this case stands for "forest," as in forest view. Once again, this is a partial listing, but unlike the `pstree` listing, you also get process IDs, running states, and so on.

```
[root@testsys /root]# ps axf

1143 ?        S      0:00 smbd -D
11640 ?        S      0:00  \_ smbd -D
11641 ?        S      0:00  \_ smbd -D
11642 ?        S      0:00  \_ smbd -D
 1152 ?        S      0:00 nmbd -D
 1195 tty1     S      0:00 login -- mgagne
 1203 tty1     S      0:00  \_ -bash
32118 tty1     S      0:00      \_ sh /usr/X11R6/bin/startx
32125 tty1     S      0:00          \_ xinit /home/mgagne/.xinitrc -- -auth /hom
32126 ?        S    304:12              \_ X :0 -auth /home/mgagne/.Xauthority
32129 tty1     S      0:20              \_ wmaker
32132 tty1     S      7:09                  \_ gkrellm
32141 tty1     S      0:00                  |   \_ gkrellm
32133 tty1     S      0:00                  \_ wmCalClock
32143 tty1     S      0:15                  \_ /opt/win4lin/publicbin/dosexec -W
32156 tty1     SL     5:07                  |   \_ /opt/win4lin/publicbin/dosexe
32157 tty1     S      0:00                  |   \_ auserver 0x0 0x8 0x3000000
32158 tty1     S      0:30                  |   \_ /opt/win4lin/xcrt 0 11 12 vga
32201 tty1     S      0:00                  |   \_ /usr/lib/merge/winsock 0 12 1
32159 tty1     S      0:00                  \_ ascd
11106 tty1     S      1:52                  \_ /usr/lib/netscape/netscape-commun
11122 tty1     S      0:00                  |   \_ (dns helper)
11127 tty1     S      0:00                  \_ rxvt -bg black -fg white -fn fixe
11128 pts/0    S      0:00                  |   \_ bash
11139 pts/0    S      0:00                  |       \_ ssh -l www website
11275 tty1     S      0:01                  \_ gnumeric /home/mgagne/lsatotals.g
11681 tty1     S      0:00                  \_ rxvt -bg black -fg white -fn fixe
11682 pts/3    S      0:00                  |   \_ bash
11694 pts/3    S      0:00                  |       \_ telnet testsys2.salmar.co
11704 tty1     S      0:00                  \_ rxvt -bg black -fg white -fn fixe
11705 pts/4    S      0:00                      \_ bash
11716 pts/4    S      0:00                          \_ ssh -l salmar natika
 1196 tty2     SW     0:00 [mingetty]
 1197 tty3     SW     0:00 [mingetty]
 1198 tty4     SW     0:00 [mingetty]
 1199 tty5     SW     0:00 [mingetty]
 5617 tty1     R    3446:47 wmaker
32395 ?        S      0:06 xscreensaver
 1870 ?        S      0:00 /sbin/mgetty /dev/ttyS0
11081 tty1     S      2:13 kmail
11085 ?        S      0:00 kdeinit: dcopserver --nosid
11087 ?        S      0:00 kdeinit: klauncher
11089 ?        S      0:00 kdeinit: kded
```

```
11091 ?        S      0:00 kdeinit: Running...
11092 ?        S      0:03  \_ kdeinit: kio_pop3 pop3 /tmp/ksocket-mgagne/klaunc
11672 ?        S      0:00 kdeinit: knotify
```

In the Linux world, you can find a number of programs devoted to deciphering those numbers, thereby making it possible to find out what processes are doing and how much time and resources they are using to do it, making it possible to manage the resultant information.

Performance is an administrative topic I sometimes refer to as the "Holy Grail" because as system administrators, it is invariably what we are forever searching for. How do we extract just a little bit more from our machines? How do we make them faster? Stronger? These are such important questions that I am devoting an entire section (appropriately titled "The Search for the Holy Grail") in Chapter 26 to the subject.

Interrupting, Suspending, and Restarting Processes

Once a day or so, I start a process that I think is going to take a few seconds. It will be something like parsing a large log file, scanning for some text, extracting something else, sorting the output, and finally sending the whole thing to a file. All very ad hoc in terms of reporting. The trouble is this: Two and a half minutes go by and I start to get a little impatient. Had I thought that the process would take a while, I might have started it in the background.

When you start a process (by typing a command name and pressing Enter), you normally start that process in the foreground. In other words, your terminal is still controlling the process and the cursor sits there at the end of the line until the process completes. At that point, it returns to the command or shell prompt. For most (not all) processes, you can run things in the background, thus immediately freeing up your command line for the next task. You do this by adding an ampersand (&) to the end of the command before you press Enter.

```
[root@testsys /root]# sh long_process &
```

Unfortunately, I've already confessed to you that I wasn't thinking that far ahead and now I am sitting here looking at a flashing cursor wondering if I did something wrong and just how long this thing will take. Now, I don't want to end the process, but I wouldn't mind being able to temporarily pause it so I can have a look at its output and decide whether or not I want to continue. As it turns out, I can do precisely that with a running process by using Ctrl-Z.

```
[root@testsys /root]# sh long_process
Ctrl-Z
[1]+  Stopped                 sh long_process
```

The process is now suspended. In fact, if you do a `ps ax` and you look for `long_process`, you'll see this:

```
5328 ?        RN   2267:04 ./setiathome -nice 19
 5617 tty1     R     3294:01 wmaker
32118 tty1     S       0:00 sh /usr/X11R6/bin/startx
11091 ?        S       0:00 kdeinit: Running...
11127 tty1     S       0:00 rxvt -bg black -fg white -fn fixed
11128 pts/0    S       0:00 bash
11139 pts/0    S       0:00 ssh -l www website
11177 ?        S       0:00 smbd -D
11178 ?        S       0:00 smbd -D
11219 pts/2    T       0:01 sh long_process
```

> **Quick Tip:** Want to see what jobs you have suspended? Try the `jobs` command.

It is true that I added a few additional processes in this snapshot. That's because I wanted to show you the state of the processes. That `S` you see in the third column of most of these processes means they are sleeping. At any given moment or snapshot of your system, almost every single process will be sleeping and a small handful will show up with an `R` to indicate that they are currently running or runnable, sometimes referred to as being in the *run queue*. The `T` you see beside the suspended process means that it is *traced*, or suspended.

Two other states you might see processes in are `D` and `Z`. The `D` means that your process is in an uninterruptible sleep and it is likely to stay that way (usually not a good sign). The `Z` refers to a process that has gone *zombie*. It may as well be dead and will be just as soon as someone gets that message across.

Getting back to the suspended process, you have a few choices. You can just restart it from where it left off by typing `fg` at the shell prompt; in other words, you can continue the process in the foreground. The second option is to type `bg`, which tells the system (you guessed it) to run the suspended process in the background. If you do that, the process restarts with an ampersand at the end of the command just as it did earlier.

```
[root@testsys /root]# bg
[1]+ sh long_process &
```

Your other option is to terminate the process, or *kill* it.

Killing Processes

You can usually interrupt a foreground process with Ctrl-C, but that does not work with background processes. The command used to terminate a process is called `kill`, which as it turns out is an unfortunate name for a command that does more than just terminate processes. By design, `kill` sends a signal to a job (or jobs). That signal is sent as an option (after a hyphen) to a process ID.

```
kill -signal_no PID
```

For instance, you can send the `SIGHUP` signal to process 7612 like this:

```
kill -1 7612
```

Signals are messages. They are usually referenced numerically, as with the ever popular `kill -9` signal, but there are a number of others. The ones you are most likely to use are 1, 9, and 15. These signals can also be referenced symbolically with these names.

Signal 1 is `SIGHUP`. This is normally used with system processes such as `inetd` and other daemons. With these types of processes, a `SIGHUP` tells the process to hang up, reread its configuration files, and restart. Most applications will just ignore this signal.

Signal 9 is `SIGKILL`, an unconditional termination of the process. Some admins I know call this "killing with extreme prejudice." The process is not asked to stop, close its files, and terminate gracefully. It is simply killed. This should be your *last resort* approach to killing a process and it works 99 percent of the time. Only a small handful of conditions will ever ignore the `-9` signal.

Signal 15, the default, is `SIGTERM`, a call for normal program termination. The system is asking the program to wrap it up and stop doing whatever it was doing.

Remember when you suspended a process earlier? That was another signal. Try this to get a feel for how this works. If you are running in an X display, start a digital `xclock` with a seconds display updated every second.

```
xclock -digital -update 1 &
```

You should see the second digits counting away. Now, find its process ID with `ps ax | grep xclock`. Pretend the process ID is 12136. Let's kill that process with a `SIGSTOP`.

```
kill -SIGSTOP 12136
```

The digits have stopped incrementing, right? Restart the clock.

```
kill -SIGCONT 12136
```

As you can see, `kill` is probably a bad name for a command that can suspend a process and then bring it back to life. For a complete list of signals and what they do, look in the man pages with this command:

```
man 7 signal
```

If you want to kill a process by specifying the symbolic signal, you use the signal name minus the `SIG` prefix. For instance, to send the `-1` signal to `inetd`, you could do this instead:

```
kill -HUP `cat /var/run/inetd.pid`
```

Note that those are backward quotes around the previous command string. Now on to the wonderful world of editors.

"I Am vi, the Great and Powerful"

You can almost hear a fearsome voice echoing eerily around the walls of your office or home. If there is one editor that strikes fear in the hearts of newbies everywhere, it is certainly `vi` (or `vim`), the visual editor. `vim`, by the way, stands for "vi improved" and is the version of `vi` that you will find in your Linux system. Anyhow, pay no attention to that fearsome voice behind the program. `vi` is not so frightening once you get to know it.

Moving around with `vi` is easy. Depending on the terminal emulator you are using, you can usually simply use your cursor keys. In the absence of cursor key control, the up, down, and sideways motions are all implemented with single keystrokes. To move left, press the letter h. To move right, press l. The letter k is up, and j is down.

To recap, on page 74 is a chart to help you remember.

When you work with `vi`, the Esc key is your friend. If you don't know where you are or what mode you are in (insert, replace, append), press the Esc key. You'll go back to normal `vi` command mode. Your second best friend is `u` or `U`, which stands for "undo." The uppercase undo will undo every change to the current line and the lowercase undo will undo the last change only.

:q, :w, :wq, and ZZ

All done editing? When it comes time to save your work, press Esc (to get out of whatever mode you are in) and type `ZZ`. Another way to exit is to type `:wq` (write and quit). At any time during an editing session, you can type `:w` to save your current work. Finally, if you really don't want to save anything you have done, type `:q!`. The exclamation point essentially says that you won't take no for an answer. Had you modified the file and simply typed `:q`, `vi`

Function	Keystroke
These commands let you move around:	
Line (or cursor) up	`k`
Line (or cursor) down	`j`
Single character (or cursor) right	`l`
Single character (or cursor) left	`h`
Move one word right	`w`
Move one word left	`b`
Move cursor to the first character in a line	`^`
Move cursor to the very beginning of a line	`0`
Move cursor to end of line	`$`
Jump to the end of a file	`G`
Jump to the beginning of a file	`gg`
(You can also type a number followed by `gg` and jump to that line.)	
These commands let you start inserting text in various ways:	
Start inserting text before the current character	`i`
Start inserting text at the beginning of the line	`I`
Start inserting text after the current character	`a`
Start inserting text after the last character in the line	`A`
Open a blank line below the current position	`o`
Open a blank line above the current position	`O`
These commands let you delete or change characters, lines, and so on:	
Delete a single character	`x`
Delete three characters	`3x`
Delete a whole line	`dd`
Delete 20 lines	`20dd`
Delete a word	`dw`
Change an entire word (press Esc to finish)	`cw`
Change five words (press Esc to finish)	`5cw`
Replace a single character	`r`
Start replacing text (until you press Esc)	`R`

would warn you that you were trying to exit from a modified file without having saved your changes.

> **Quick Tip:** Need help while in `vi`? Make sure you aren't in insert or replace mode, and then type `:help`.

I urge you to not let `vi` frighten you. Get to know it. The likelihood that you will ever log on to a modern Linux (or UNIX) system that doesn't have some form of `vi` installed is virtually nonexistent. That said, if you need more information than I've given you here, consider the `vi` tutor. This little tool is distributed as part of the vim documentation. It is essentially a text file that tells you what to do and how to do it as you read it. In fact, the tutorial is the file that you actually do your work on. Because you are going to be editing and changing this file as part of the tutorial, you probably don't want to work on the original copy. Copy the tutor file to your home directory and work on it instead. I should probably tell you that on some systems, you can just type vimtutor to start the tutorial, in which case you can skip to the next section. The vimtutor command will make a copy of the file for you and save you a few steps, but it doesn't work on every system. If it doesn't work on your system, then read on.

To get to the tutor, change directory to the vim documentation. The path to that directory is /usr/doc/vim-common-release_num/tutor. To find out the release number of your copy of vi, type vi --version. This will give you far more information than you need, so just pay attention to the first line. You'll get something like this:

```
VIM - Vi Improved 5.6 (2000 Jan 16, compiled Mar  7 2000 12:18:07)
```

What you are interested in is the version number, which is 5.6 in this case. Yours may be 5.7 or 5.5 or whatever the current release is. Use that number to change to the proper directory.

```
cd /usr/doc/vim-common-5.6/tutor
```

If you do an ls in this directory, you should see a README file and another file called tutor. Copy the file, cd to your home directory, and execute the vi tutor like this:

```
cp tutor $HOME/tutor
cd $HOME
vi tutor
```

When the tutorial starts, you should see a picture like the one in Figure 5.1. The entire tutorial takes between 20 and 60 minutes for most people to complete.

Recovering a vim Session

From time to time you may find yourself trying to edit a file but someone else, maybe you, is already editing it. That session may be open or something may have happened to terminate it accidentally. As a result, you get a nice, long-winded message along the lines of "swap file found" and a whole lot of information on what you can do about it. Here's a shortened version of that message:

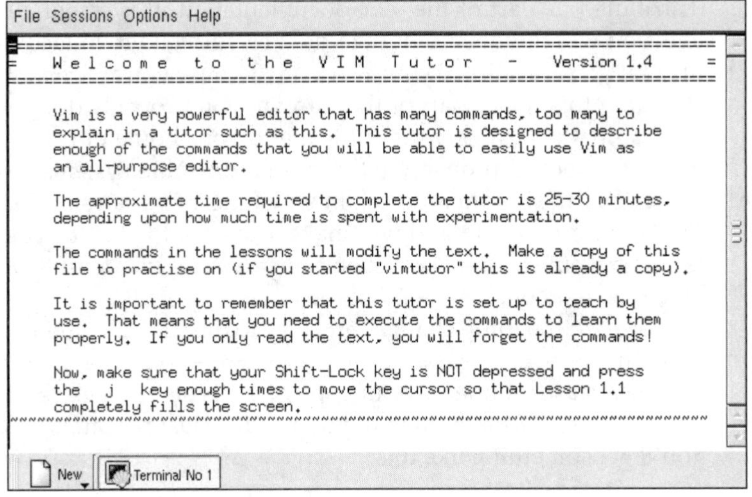

FIGURE 5.1 Learning `vi` with the `vim` tutor

```
ATTENTION

Found a swap file by the name ".testing123.swp"
             dated: Fri Jan 12 16:35:14 2001
          owned by: mgagne
         file name: ~mgagne/testing123
```

To locate these files, you can use the famous `find` command and look for anything with a .swp extension. Another and better way is to have `vi` report on these for you. You can check for the existence of swap files by using the `-r` option, which will provide you with a little more information than the simple `find`.

```
[mgagne@scigate mgagne]$ vi -r
Swap files found:
   In current directory:
1.    .bookstores.swp
             dated: Tue Nov 21 18:31:23 2000
          owned by: mgagne
         file name: ~mgagne/bookstores
          modified: YES
         host name: testsys.mycompany.com
         user name: mgagne
        process ID: 13440
   In directory ~/tmp:
      -- none --
   In directory /var/tmp:
      -- none --
   In directory /tmp:
      -- none --
```

Power vi: Start-up Options

Next time you need a reason to use `vi` over one of the other editors, consider some of these quick tricks for getting to what you want as quickly as possible.

```
vi +100 ftl_program.c
```

This will take you right to line 100 in the file called (in this case) `ftl_program.c`. This can be a great little timesaver when you are compiling programs and something goes wrong, as in the following example:

```
gcc  -O2 -Wall  -c -o ftl_program.o ftp_program.c
ftp_program.c:100: parse error before `<'
make: *** [ftp_program.o] Error 1
```

Another useful start flag is the same one you use to search for text inside a file: the forward slash (/). In the next example, I want to get back to the same place I was working on in my file. To mark my place, I had written my name on a blank line. This `vi` starter gets me right to where I was working:

```
vi +/Marcel ftl_program.c
```

Note the plus sign before the slash.

Here's a last little teaser before you run off to the man pages or a bookstore for the latest and greatest 500-page `vi` reference guide. By design, `vi` is a text editor and basic text is our medium. As demonstrated earlier, you can use Ctrl-V to insert control characters into your text, but you can also edit binary files. Here's a crazy example. There's a great little game that you probably installed when you set up your system. It's called `xbill`, a wonderful piece of strangeness where you must stop a renegade program known only as "Bill" from spreading a most insidious computer virus, which is cleverly disguised as an operating system.

Okay, I know that I can get the source and modify the program without going into the scenario I am about to describe, but trust me, there may be times when you have a binary file (of some kind) with no source and all you need is a simple modification. You don't want to entertain this lightly. Changing things in this mode could leave you with a nonfunctional program or worse, but you are still going to do it. Just remember to make a backup. In my case, I made a copy of the `xbill` program in my home directory. If you pause in the middle of a game, you get the message in Figure 5.2.

For reasons I won't go into at this time, I didn't like the fact that it said "Continue." I would rather it said "Ah go on." Because I only have the source, I start `vi` with the `-b` option which lets me edit a binary file. To make life just a bit easier, I am going to combine that with another helpful little command line option:

```
vi -b +/"Press Continue" xbill
```

FIGURE 5.2 The Pause message in `xbill`

This will put me right on the line I want. There I will change "Continue" to "Ah go on." Figure 5.3 displays the message I receive when I press Pause during a game now.

FIGURE 5.3 The new Pause message

> **Important:** Notice that I used exactly the same number of letters for my change. Because this is a binary, the amount of space I had to work with to make my change was defined at compile time. Breaking this rule may get you the dreaded Segmentation fault (core dumped) message. Using less space is *probably* okay if you fill with spaces.

Pico: A kinder, gentler editor

On many occasions, I have been asked (forced?) to offer an alternative editor to `vi`, something that is still visually oriented ("We'll have none of that line editor stuff here, mister!"), but also somewhat more friendly and intuitive. One of my personal favorites is called Pico, which stands for "PIne COmposer." Pico is the full-screen editor distributed with PINE, a great text-based e-mail client distributed by the University of Washington.

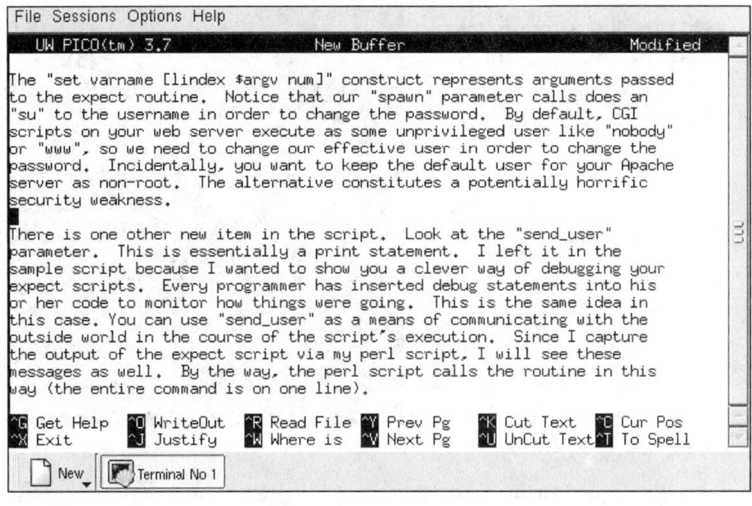

FIGURE 5.4 Pico, a friendly alternative to `vi`

Pico provides you with context-sensitive help and easy access to the commands you need displayed at the bottom of the screen. These commands are accessed in key combinations such as Ctrl-G for "Get help" or Crtl-R for "Read file." For an example of Pico at work, have a look at Figure 5.4.

You can start Pico simply by typing the command name, or you can specify a filename as well.

```
pico chapter5.txt
```

If you choose to start with just the editor, you can then use Ctrl-R to specify a filename if you know the path to it. If you are not 100 percent sure, you can then press Ctrl-T, which will take you to a file manager with which you can navigate to find the file you need.

Emacs

When talking about Emacs, it becomes almost difficult to classify it as strictly an editor. The brainchild of Richard M. Stallman (founder of the Free Software Foundation), GNU Emacs is more than just a nice, powerful, if somewhat complex, editor. It's a mail reader, newsreader, Web browser, program development environment, LISP interpreter, and psychotherapist. (No, really. Check out Figure 5.5.)

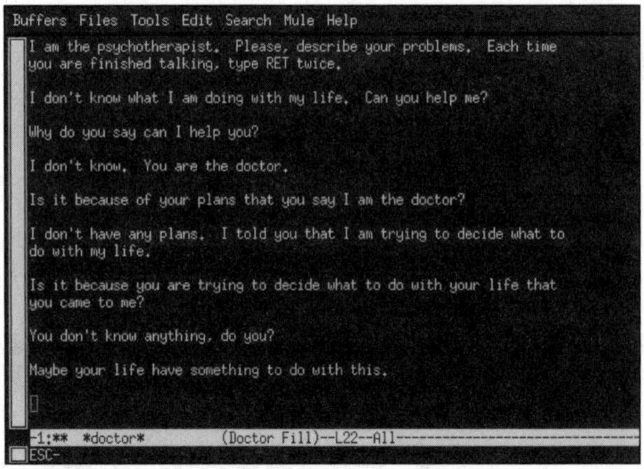

FIGURE 5.5 Getting help from the Emacs doctor

```
Buffers Files Tools Edit Search Mule Help
I am the psychotherapist.  Please, describe your problems.  Each time
you are finished talking, type RET twice.

I don't know what I am doing with my life.  Can you help me?

Why do you say can I help you?

I don't know.  You are the doctor.

Is it because of your plans that you say I am the doctor?

I don't have any plans.  I told you that I am trying to decide what to
do with my life.

Is it because you are trying to decide what to do with your life that
you came to me?

You don't know anything, do you?

Maybe your life have something to do with this.

-1:**  *doctor*          (Doctor Fill)--L22--All-----------------------------
ESC-
```

Because you will want to know how to do this before you do anything else useful, start Emacs by typing emacs. You do not have to specify a filename for this. Now press Esc-x, type doctor, and press Enter. The doctor is in.

And now for something a little more serious. Like Pico, Emacs comes with its own help. At any time, you can press Ctrl-h to get into help mode. You can also go straight to the tutorial by pressing Esc-x and then typing help-with-tutorial. You might want to start your exploration of Emacs with the built-in tutorial by pressing t after you enter help mode.

If you are working in an X interface, you will have likely started the X version of Emacs. The doctor you see in Figure 5.5 is running in X Emacs mode. Even in a nongraphical environment, you can still use Emacs. To do Emacs justice, you would have to write an entire book. For some, this is too much editor. Professional programmers tend to think differently and consider Emacs indispensable. Either way, you owe it to yourself to try this incredibly powerful and customizable tool.

Resources

GNU Emacs

`http://www.gnu.org/software/emacs/`

PINE Information Center (the home of Pico)

`http://www.washington.edu/pine/`

`vim` **Homepage**

`http://www.vim.org/`

Chapter 6

Daemons and Runlevels

When you start your system, a number of messages go scrolling by on the screen. Some have to do with hardware detection, but you will also see a number of things starting (starting `named`, starting `sendmail`, and so on). Unless you have already made changes to your system, these are all the result of either default configurations or requests for services you made when you installed your system.

Now that you are fresh from your exploration of processes, it is time to take it to the next level. As you progress through this book, I suggest that you add various programs or settings to your start-up files. This chapter covers how this is done for the various Linux distributions.

Daemons and Other Not-So-Scary Things

When your system boots up, it starts a number of services. Among these can be a Web server (like Apache), an X window font server, `sendmail` (an e-mail transport system), and any number of other programs, such as the `inetd` daemon, your network *listener.*

> **Definition:** Because I casually tossed out the term "`inetd`" and called it a "daemon," it is only fair that I explain what I mean by that. By definition, a *daemon* is a program that after being spawned (either at boot or by a command from a shell) disconnects itself from the terminal that started it and runs in the background. If you then disconnect from the terminal session that started the program or log out entirely, the program continues to run in the background.

What daemons do there, all by themselves with no one to control them, is a function of what the daemon is for. The `inetd` daemon listens for network connections, while `syslogd`—another process I will discuss in detail when I cover logs—watches, monitors, and logs information.

The inittab File

Of all the processes on your system, one of them is the master process and the parent (grandparent, great-grandparent, and so on) of every other process. Its process ID is always `1` and will always be `1`. That process is called `init` and its main job is to read its configuration file and start processes as defined there.

Which services (or programs) get started are decided by the runlevel at which your system boots. Take a look at the file called `/etc/inittab` for the runlevel in Figure 6.1. The line you are looking for is near the bottom of the following listing (`initdefault`), but on your system, it is most likely near the top of the file itself because Figure 6.1 displays only a partial listing. I included the comment lines so you could see what the levels mean on my test Linux system.

So, my system starts at runlevel 5. To find out what gets started, I do a long listing (`ls -l`) of `/etc/rc.d/rc5.d`.

```
# ls -l /etc/rc.d/rc5.d
```

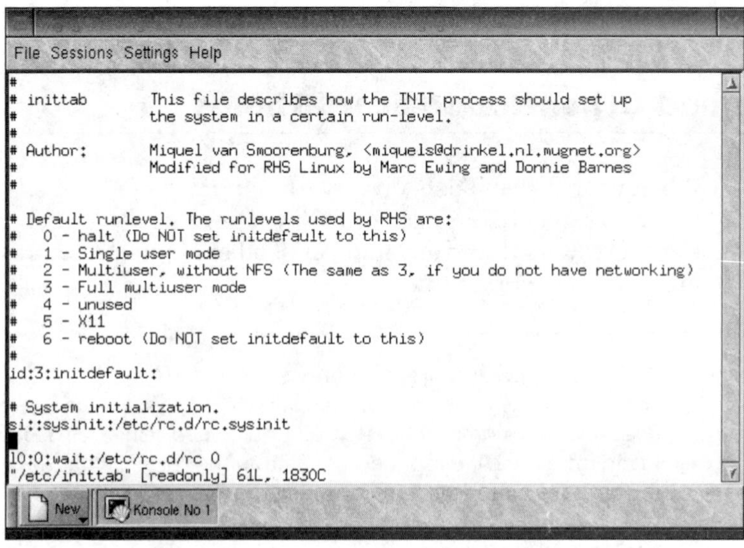

FIGURE 6.1 The `/etc/inittab` file

Here is a partial listing of what I see there:

```
lrwxrwxrwx   1 root   root  17 Jul 18 13:48 S10network -> ../init.d/network
lrwxrwxrwx   1 root   root  17 Jul 18 13:48 S11portmap -> ../init.d/portmap
lrwxrwxrwx   1 root   root  15 Jul 18 13:48 S15netfs -> ../init.d/netfs
lrwxrwxrwx   1 root   root  16 Jul 18 13:48 S20random -> ../init.d/random
lrwxrwxrwx   1 root   root  16 Jul 18 13:48 S30syslog -> ../init.d/syslog
```

Notice the arrows pointing to other files in the `/etc/rc.d/init.d` directory. These are simply symbolic links to the actual files that start and stop the various services. If a link to the file exists, that service is started.

At some point in this book, I might tell you to add a command to your start-up script. This usually refers to the `rc.local` boot script. Depending on your system and the initial configuration, you might not be able to find an `rc.local` file. A Debian system is a good example of that. If the file doesn't exist, then how do you create it and where do you put it? Another question: How do you get the system to recognize it at boot time?

Good questions.

The rc.local File and Runlevels

To get the scoop on `rc.local`, I need to give you the scoop on runlevels and a handful of scripts that run each time your system comes up. What gets executed at boot time is partly defined by symbolic links located in an `rc#.d` file. # represents a number corresponding to the runlevel.

What is this runlevel? In your `/etc/inittab` file, you will find an entry that says something like this:

```
id:3:initdefault:
```

Note the `3` at the beginning of the line. This tells you that when the system comes up, it will, by default, switch to runlevel 3 (which is full multiuser mode with a command-line login). If your system says 5, this tells me you are booting directly to the graphical desktop. What starts at each of these runlevels will be found in an accompanying `/etc/rc#.d` directory; in my case, `rc3.d`. Yeah, it's true. I'm still a command-line guy who starts his X desktop with the `startx` command (I'll talk about that later).

On a Red Hat (or Mandrake) system, you'll find this `rc.local` file hiding under `/etc/init.d`. Didn't I just say that it would be in the `rc3.d` directory? It is. More or less.

If you change directory to `/etc/rc3.d`, you'll see a number of script files either starting with an `S` or a `K`. Do an `ls -l` and you will notice they are all symbolic links pointing back to a directory somewhere else. On a SuSE system, the `rc#.d` directories are under `/sbin/init.d`, but you will still find those `S` or `K` files and they point to `/sbin/init.d`. In the case of my Red Hat system, they point back to the `/etc/rc.d/init.d` directory.

```
lrwxrwxrwx   1 root  root  11 Jul 12 16:09 /etc/rc.d/rc5.d/S99local
-> ../rc.local
```

On a Debian system, these scripts point back to `/etc/init.d`, which is where I would create my `rc.local` file. On my own system, it turns out that `rc.local` is executed by a call to `S99local`. On a Debian system, for instance, look for (or create) an `S99local` file under the appropriate runlevel directory.

My use (or Red Hat's) of `S99local` is (to some degree) convention, but you can (if you want) be somewhat more arbitrary. The first part of that name, `S`, means "start" (`K` means "kill") and 99 is simply a high enough number that it is likely the last thing your system executes on boot. The `local` part is just a name that means something to me. You might call it `rclocal` or `systemlocal` or `iceberg`. So, if I want this file started with my runlevel 3 on a Debian system, I would create a symbolic link like this:

```
ln -s /etc/init.d/rc.local /etc/rc3.d/S99local
```

Switching between Runlevels

It is possible to change runlevels on your system without rebooting. One way is to start and stop a specific initialization script.

```
# /etc/rc.d/init.d/named stop
```

This would stop the name server (covered in Chapter 18) assuming, of course, that the named script was in `/etc/rc.d/init.d`. However, if you want to switch to all processes that are supposed to be running at runlevel 5 and you are at runlevel 3, you can have `init` do this for you:

```
#  init 5
```

Beware of changing runlevels. You may impact other users that are running other processes. If others are using the system, make sure you warn them.

If you aren't sure what runlevel your system is currently at, try typing the `runlevel` command.

```
/sbin/runlevel
```

The system may respond in one of two ways. You may get a letter N followed by a number like this:

```
N 3
```

This indicates that the system is at level 3 and that this is the previous level as well. The other possible answer might be something like `3 5`, indicating that the system was previously at runlevel 3 but that it was recently changed to runlevel 5.

The chkconfig Command

On some systems (Red Hat, for one), you will find another way to add or delete services at boot time. Look for the command `chkconfig`. What this command does is provide a simple interface for updating or reporting on system start-up scripts in the `/etc/rc.d` directory. With `chkconfig`, the process of creating and maintaining the symbolic links that define what services get started is easily taken care of.

```
chkconfig version 1.1.2 - Copyright (C) 1997 Red Hat Software

This may be freely redistributed under the terms of the GNU Public
License.

usage:   chkconfig --list [name]
         chkconfig --add <name>
         chkconfig --del <name>
         chkconfig [--level <levels>] <name> <on|off|reset>)
```

To find out what services get started at boot time, you can use the `--list` option. Adding a service name at the end of it will return information only for that service. For instance, let's see when and where the `inet` service gets started:

```
[root@testsys /root]# chkconfig --list inet
inet        0:off   1:off   2:off   3:on    4:on    5:on    6:off
```

If you want to completely stop a service from starting automatically, you can use the `--del` option and specify the service. In this example, I am removing the advanced power management daemon (`apmd`) from the automatic start-up:

```
[root@testsys /root]# chkconfig --del apmd
```

Adding is the same process, but with the `--add` option. That said, you may also want to specify what services start based on specific runlevels. If I do a list of my `apmd` service after the delete, all runlevels will show as being off.

```
[root@testsys /root]# chkconfig --list apmd
apmd        0:off   1:off   2:off   3:off   4:off   5:off   6:off
```

If, for some strange reason, I did want the `apmd` running but *only* when booting in runlevel 3, I would use this command:

```
[root@testsys /root]# chkconfig --level 3 apmd on
```

To configure multiple runlevels, tack them together as one number. Using the previous example, use this variation on the command to start apmd with runlevels 3, 4, and 5:

```
[root@testsys /root]# chkconfig --level 345 apmd on
```

Runlevels the Graphical Way

Manipulating runlevels is not something you will be doing every day. Still, you may find that a nice, friendly graphical interface makes the job just that much more fun when it does come up. Several tools are available to do this job. The first you might want to look for (if you are running Red Hat) is called `ntsysv` (see Figure 6.2). It is very simple and you may remember its interface from your system installation.

To start (or stop) a service, use your cursor keys to navigate down the list of services, and then toggle them on or off with the spacebar. You can then tab

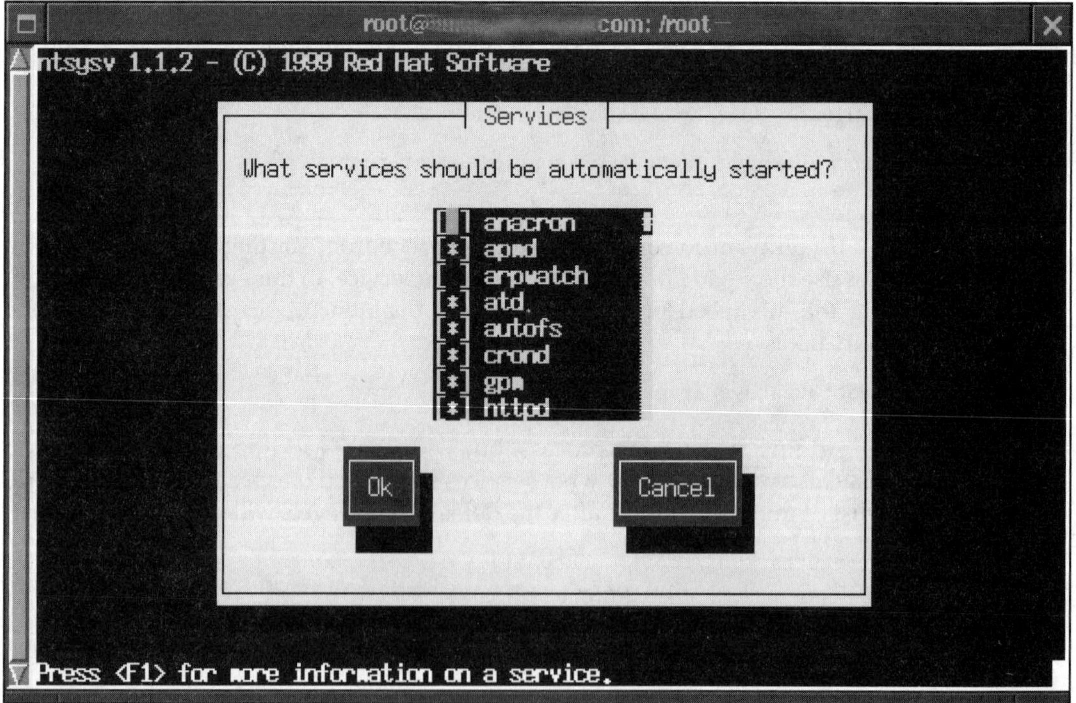

FIGURE 6.2 Red Hat's `ntsysv` runlevel editor

over to the OK button and press Enter. One note of caution here: The program only turns on a service for the active runlevel (the `initdefault` parameter in your `/etc/inittab`). If you want to use the tool to administer multiple levels, this is done in a manner similar to the `chkconfig` command. Let's use the example of wanting to have services turned on for runlevels 3, 4, and 5. Start `ntsysv` like this:

```
ntsysv --level 345
```

This program probably isn't quite what comes to mind when you think about graphical tools, so have a look at `ntsysv`'s graphical X window counterpart, `tksysv`. Actually, `tksysv` is more than just a prettier face to `ntsysv`. It is also more configurable and you may find it easier to work with. If you are running Red Hat, the odds are pretty good that you'll have both of these tools already installed.

Look at Figure 6.3 for a screen shot of `tksysv` in action.

Because I've decided to use `apmd` as my guinea pig daemon, I'll stick with it. Notice in the image that it is in the list for runlevel 3. The interface is a simple point and click. To remove `apmd`, click it in the start column, and then click the Remove button. It is gone. If you want to do multiple changes on a process, click a service and then click the Edit button.

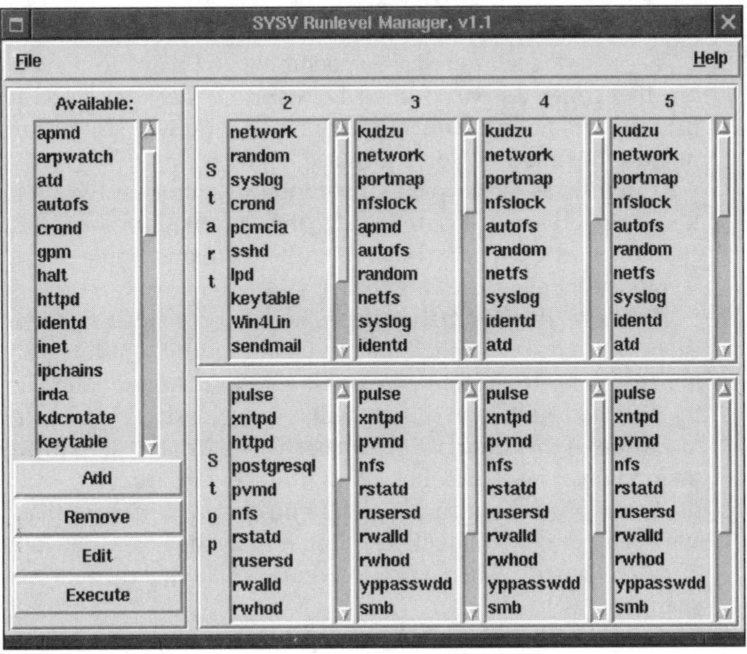

FIGURE 6.3 The `tksysv` graphical runlevel editor

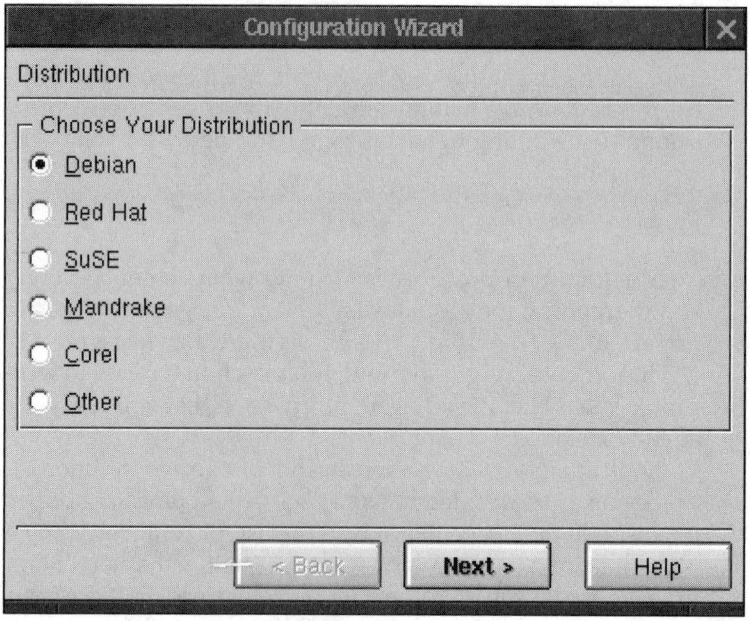

FIGURE 6.4 `ksysv`'s configuration wizard

Because these are release-specific tools, I want to leave you with another one that comes as part of the KDE window manager suite. It is called `ksysv`. Because it is not a platform-specific tool, you will see a configuration wizard pop up the first time you use it (see Figure 6.4).

You'll be asked to pick your Linux distribution type: Mandrake, Debian, Red Hat, and so on. The reason for this is something I mentioned earlier in the chapter. Start-up files haven't yet adhered to one single format or file structure layout (but they are getting there).

That's all there is to that step. The next screen is a confirmation with a Finish button. Once you click that, the main `ksysv` window pops up. It is similar in many ways to the one you saw in `tksysv`. A point and click interface using the polished KDE look (Figure 6.5) is one plus, but it goes further.

Through this interface, you can easily start and stop processes (and restart them in one pass), edit their configuration files directly, or remove them from the list of processes completely. If you choose a process that does not already start in a desired runlevel, just drag it from the list on the left into the runlevel of your choice. When you are done, click the diskette icon to save your changes.

Clicking directly on a service (in an active runlevel) brings up a box that enables you to work with the running process (see Figure 6.6).

From there, you can start, stop, or restart (as I mentioned earlier) but, perhaps more interesting for the new administrators out there, you can also get

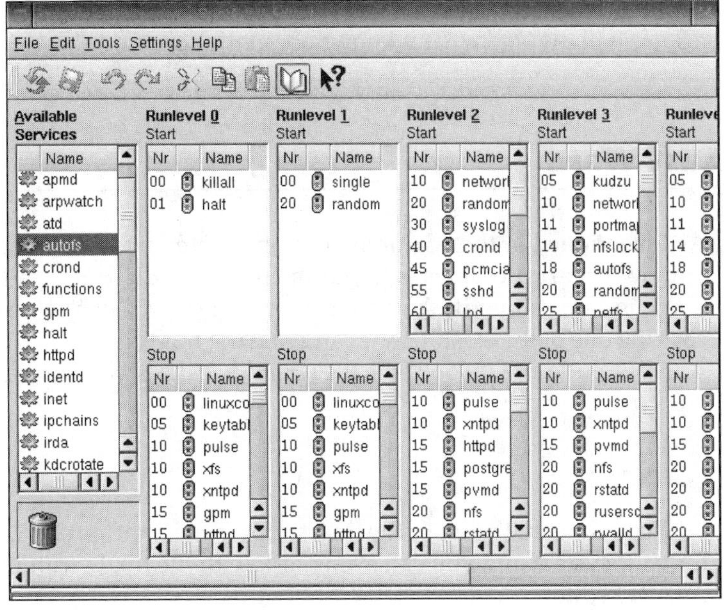

FIGURE 6.5 The KDE `ksysv` runlevel editor

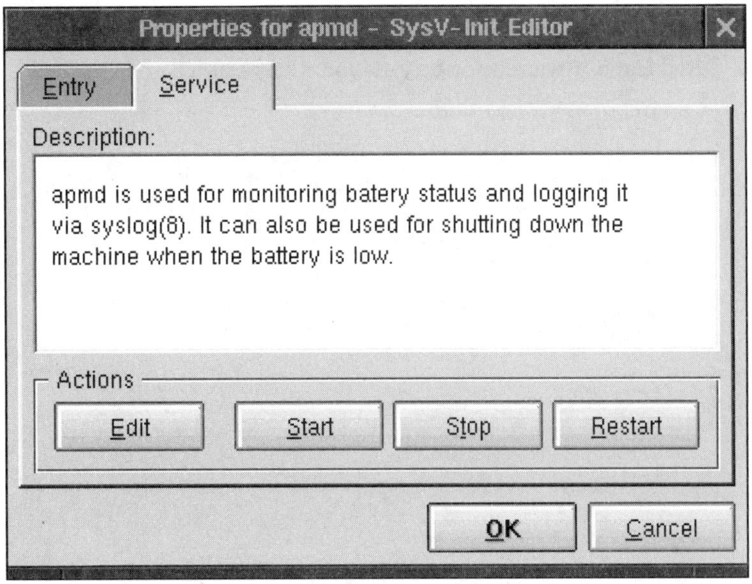

FIGURE 6.6 Getting the skinny on a service

some information on just what this process does. Click the Service tab and ksysv will divulge what it knows about the specified service.

The (Not) Last Word

As I mentioned at the beginning of this chapter, the classic method of adding your own start processes is to put them in the rc.local script (or whatever you wind up calling it). You could just as easily create your own rc script by copying one of the existing ones and making modifications to the new version. A nice, simple one to look at is the script that starts your printer daemon, lpd.

```
cd /path_to/init.d
cp lpd my_service
vi my_service
```

Make sure that you put the final script in the appropriate init.d directory for your system and you can even work with the final script in your graphical runlevel editor.

Resources

The K Desktop Environment (KDE)

http://www.kde.org/

Red Hat Software (for ntsysv and tksysv)

http://www.redhat.com/

Chapter 7

Users and Groups

Living in a Multiuser World

Linux is a multiuser operating system, meaning that one or more users can work on it at the same time. Each user is referenced by a user name. Each user name has a user ID (UID) associated with it and one or more groups. Like user names, group names are also represented by a numeric identifier, this time called a group ID (GID). A user's UID is unique as is a group's GID.

When it comes to your files and directories, security on a Linux system is defined by means of permissions, which directly relate to the user ID. Users are either administrative users or regular users. The chief administrative user is called "root." A user's ID is used to decide what commands can be executed and what files can be read from or written to.

Each user ID also has a password associated with it. That password can and *should* be changed on a regular basis.

When Not to Use the root User

The short answer here is that you should never use the root user unless you absolutely have to. The danger lies in the fact that the root user is virtually omnipotent on the system. A mistake can have serious implications that can wipe out your entire system. Unless you absolutely have to, it is best to work as a nonadmin user. There are other reasons as well.

The first is security. Because the root user has access to everything, it makes sense that only those that really need to have access are given the root password. The fewer people have access to root, the better. Let me give you a few good reasons for jealously guarding root access:

- It makes it easier to maintain security
- It decreases the risk of dangerous code
- Errors do not (usually) have global implications

Yes, it is still possible for a nonroot user to do great damage to a system, but the risk is much, much smaller.

Managing Users

Never manually edit the password file. I'm not saying you can't—simply that you probably shouldn't. You'll notice I told you that even before telling you about the password file which, by the way, is `/etc/passwd`. On systems running with shadow passwords, there is one other file to worry about: `/etc/shadow`.

My reason for introducing this section with a warning is simple. I have seen far too many instances of people getting locked out of their system because of a botched modification to the password file. Suddenly, there is no user access *and* no root access.

> You should know that there is a `vipw` command for editing the password file (and a `vigr` command for the groups file), but I would still recommend against using these. The reason for those commands isn't to prevent dangerous typos, but to allow for proper locking of the file when updating.

Your Linux system has all the tools you need to add and maintain users without having to resort to manually editing your password file. That said, let's start by looking at this file:

```
root:x:0:0:root:/root:/bin/bash
bin:x:1:1:bin:/bin:
daemon:x:2:2:daemon:/sbin:
adm:x:3:4:adm:/var/adm:
lp:x:4:7:lp:/var/spool/lpd:
sync:x:5:0:sync:/sbin:/bin/sync
shutdown:x:6:0:shutdown:/sbin:/sbin/shutdown
halt:x:7:0:halt:/sbin:/sbin/halt
mail:x:8:12:mail:/var/spool/mail:
news:x:9:13:news:/var/spool/news:
```

The format of this file is actually pretty simple. Each field in the password file is delimited by a colon. First comes the user name, then the password field (more on that shortly), followed by a numeric user ID, a group ID, some kind of a comment, a home directory, and a default shell or login program.

The first thing to remember is that all this information is case sensitive. This does make a difference, particularly when you are trying to log into the system. When you choose a user name, make sure that it is no more than eight characters in length. These characters can be letters or numbers and mixed in any way.

> **Geek Trivia:** The eight-character limit is one of those *truths* in transition. On some releases, you can actually create a user name that is more than eight characters. The question then becomes one of whether an application that references the user name will truncate it to eight characters or use the entire field.

I'll discuss the password field in more detail later on. For now, let's move immediately to the user ID (UID) and group ID (GID) fields. The UID is a unique numerical identification. It is used in setting and modifying security information on files and directories. The same goes for the GID except that this number does not need to be unique. That's because it is useful to be able to set permissions based on an effective group. For instance, say you have an accounting application and you want all users in the accounting department to have access to it. GIDs make it easy to offer those permissions.

Notice the root user. Its UID and GID are both 0. GID 0 is also shared by the users sync, shutdown, and halt because they all share root's group permissions.

Next is the comment field. This is pretty much what it sounds like. You can enter comments relating to the identity or purpose of a user on your system. Normally, this means entering the user's full name so that he or she can be identified with commands such as `finger`. For instance, take a look at the `/etc/passwd` entry for natika, one of the users on my system.

```
natika:x:504:504:Natika the Cat:/home/natika:/bin/bash
```

Her command field says "Natika the Cat," which is appropriate because she just happens to be my cat. If I type `who` to find out who is logged into the system, I get the following:

```
# who
natika   pts/1    Dec  7 14:30
```

That only tells me so much. If I then use the `finger` command, I get a lot more information, including natika's plans.

```
# finger natika
Login: natika                           Name: Natika the Cat
Directory: /home/natika                 Shell: /bin/bash
On since Thu Dec  7 14:30 (EST) on pts/1 from localhost.localdomain
   5 minutes 7 seconds idle
No mail.
Plan:
To get my own Natika-only Web site and rule the cat world.
```

> By the way, the "plan" that you see listed is normally blank. This is a holdover from the early days of UNIX. The idea was literally to identify what your plans were or what you were working on. Nobody really does that anymore. Most people use their `.plan` file (if they use it at all) for silly comments like natika's.

Let's get back to our password file. The next field is the home directory. When a user logs in to the system, they are placed here (in an electronic, *virtual* sort of way). This directory contains personal login and user-specific information. For instance, X window client files would be here as would the personal login script, the `.bash_profile`.

Finally, there is the shell itself. You can change your default login shell if you want, but the only valid shells are listed in another system file called `/etc/shells`. Here are the contents of `/etc/shells` on my system:

```
/bin/bash
/bin/sh
/bin/ash
/bin/bsh
/bin/bash2
/bin/tcsh
/bin/csh
```

It's time for me to let you off the hook and finally talk about the password field itself. You may have noticed that in my example, the only thing in the password field was a single letter, `x`. That's because I am using the shadow password file (`/etc/shadow`) for a higher level of security. Traditionally, the password entry was visible in the `/etc/passwd` file. Sadly, that makes it sound like finding out someone's password was as simple as looking at the entry in the password file, and that is not true.

First, let's take a fresh look at the password file from earlier. For simplicity's sake, I'll stick with the root password.

```
root:x:0:0:root:/root:/bin/bash
```

The password entry is a rather cryptic "x." Here is the root entry from a classic password file:

```
root:2IsjW45pb4L56:0:0:root:/root:/bin/bash
```

As you can see, it is far from easy to guess that "2IsjW45pb4L56" might translate into "calculus." The problem is that the encryption algorithm used for creating passwords is well known and it is possible through brute force methods and lots of CPU cycles to crack passwords in the password file, specifically if I have been foolish enough to use a word out of the dictionary. In fact, there are a variety of popular tools available for cracking passwords with names like "crack" and "Nutcracker," all available for free download. (Check the Resources section at the end of this chapter for one of them.) I'll cover rules for choosing good passwords later in this chapter.

Going back to this notion of the shadow password file, the real reason for it is that it makes it hard on users to actually get to the point where they are using something like a password-cracking utility. The reason for this is that the `/etc/passwd` file is readable by all users. The shadow password file, on the other hand, is only readable by root. The format of the file is a little different as well and includes somewhat more flexibility in how users can be configured. Let's have a look at the shadow password file's layout.

```
root:$1$J.tGxREA$nHqbRUyid9.hf4I6UtRBs0:11242:0:99999:7:-1:-1:134540356
```

As in the regular password file, the fields are delimited by colons. There are nine fields in total. Starting with the user name, the shadow password file stores the password itself and then gets into a series of numbers that deal with password expiration.

The first of these (field 3) is the number of days (starting from January 1, 1970) since the last password change, the minimum number of days before a user is allowed to change their password, and the number of days before the password *must* be changed. Then come the warnings. Field 6 is the number of days before a user starts getting warned about changing his or her password. Field 7 represents the grace period. Here's another way of looking at this: How many days are you willing to allow a user to use the system after the user's password has expired before you disable that user's account? This brings us to field 8, which is a representation (in days since January 1, 1970) that the account has been disabled. Finally, there is field 9, which is reserved. Just don't worry about it.

If an entry contains `-1` (as in fields 7 and 8 in my example), it essentially means "never," as in the user never gets warnings and his or her account is never disabled.

Before I get into how to add, modify, or remove users (*delete* just sounds so final), I should talk about the `/etc/group` file. Every user will belong to at least one group. If you use the quick and dirty method of adding a user that I'll cover next, you wind up with a GID that is equivalent to the UID.

The importance of groups is simple. There are times when you want a specific group of people to share access and rights to one or more files or applications. Rather than having to create access rights for each and every user, you can say that the accounting application is available to all the accounting folk. (*Imagine that!*)

I should tell you that I am not quite as worried about someone editing the group file manually. The potential for damage is not as great as with the `/etc/passwd` file. That said, take a look at the format of a sample group file:

```
root:x:0:root
bin:x:1:root,bin,daemon
daemon:x:2:root,bin,daemon
```

```
sys:x:3:root,bin,adm
adm:x:4:root,adm,daemon
users:x:100:marcel,natika,sally
```

Colons separate the fields, as they did with the `passwd` and `shadow` files. The first field is the group name. This is followed by a password field and then the unique group ID. Finally, you see a comma-delimited list of user names that are members of this group. For instance, if you have a group called "finance" and you want users albert, isaac, and marie to be part of the group, you would have an entry like this:

```
finance:x:540:albert,isaac,marie
```

Managing Groups

Dealing with group management is somewhat simpler than dealing with users (at least in the OS world), so let's tackle that first. There is another reason. Strange as it might sound, in some ways there is a logic to the idea that groups precede users. While it is true that a group without users isn't much of a group, people usually define a group before adding users to it. So it is in this world of bits and bytes.

Adding Groups

Adding a group is a simple procedure. The command is `groupadd` followed by a group name.

```
[root@testsys /root]# groupadd finance
```

You can also specify a group ID by using the `-g` flag. By default, the system assigns the next nonadmin group ID in line. Allowing this default is probably the best idea unless you are trying to clone group information from another system.

Modifying Groups

Generally speaking, the reason for modifying groups involves a name change. Realistically, changing the group ID will cause you headaches because it means changing the GID on every file that this group originally had access to. It is possible, however, that you might want to change the `finance` group (as an example) to read `accounts` instead. Here's the command:

```
[root@testsys /root]# groupmod -n accounts finance
```

The -n flag, by the way, is used to refer to the *new* group.

Removing Groups

Group removal is something that too often gets forgotten in the world of managing accounts, whether they are group or user accounts. People leave a company and names change. *Be vigilant.* If the account or group is no longer needed, get rid of it.

To remove a group, use the groupdel command.

```
[root@testsys /root]# groupdel xpilots
```

Adding Users

The simplest possible way to add a user is to use the adduser command or useradd. If you do an ls -l, you'll notice that adduser is just a symbolic link to useradd. In its most basic incarnation, the format is as follows:

```
useradd  username
```

The system assigns the next available UID and equivalent GID, creates a basic home directory under /home, and assigns a default shell. What defines those defaults is a file called /etc/default/useradd (you need to be root to look at it or modify it). Here's what it looks like:

```
# useradd defaults file

GROUP=100
HOME=/home
INACTIVE=-1
EXPIRE=
SHELL=/bin/bash
SKEL=/etc/skel
```

As you can see, the default directory prefix for a user's home directory is /home. The default shell is /bin/bash and what shows up in the user's new home directory is a copy of what is found in /etc/skel. That's a skeleton directory. Using it as a model, useradd decides what to create for the new user.

Several other flags enable you to further customize the account creation process. The more complex form of the useradd command is summed up in this way:

```
usage: useradd  [-u uid [-o]] [-g group] [-G group,...]
                [-d home] [-s shell] [-c comment] [-m [-k template]]
                [-f inactive] [-e expire ] [-p passwd] [-n] [-r] name
```

Should you decide that the default user ID is not for you, you can specify it with the -u flag. While I am going to tell you about it, I'd like you to *forget* about the -o flag. It enables you to override the system's requirement that all UIDs be unique. If you decide (and you shouldn't) to use an existing UID when you create a user, make sure you also add the -o flag.

Next is the -g flag, which enables you to define the group. You might have noticed that there is a capital G, or -G, option as well. This is an optional, comma-separated list of other groups that the user belongs to. Continuing with the finance example, a user might belong to the staff group as well as the finance group.

Note that when you create a user with a default group, that becomes the GID field in /etc/passwd. On the other hand, the optional group list specified by -G will add that user name to the /etc/group file. For instance, I added a group called geeks on my system. With three of the users I created, I used a -G geeks option to specify that they were also part of the geeks group. This is what the geeks group entry looks like in /etc/group:

```
geeks:x:511:mgagne,natika,guitux
```

About Home Directories

Every account you create has a home directory by default. In addition, several files are copied into it, namely those found in the SKEL directory (usually /etc/skel). This is a good thing to remember because this is where you add files or configuration information that you want to appear in every new user's directory or profile.

Should you want to use another account as the model (or skeleton) for the creation of a new account, use the -k flag. Note that you also need to add the -m flag in this case. Let's say that you want to create a user called "aeinstein," but you want him to have the same files and configurations that exist in natika's home directory. This is what you should do:

```
[root@testsys /root]# useradd -m -k /home/natika aeinstein
```

If you look in Mr. Einstein's home directory now, his files are the same as in natika's, but the permissions and ownerships are his.

Group Participation

The -g option is your opportunity to define what group a user belongs to. By default, if you specify nothing, a group is created to match the user's UID. For an environment where users access a database application to which they all have permission and must modify the information, allowing for some kind of group identification is crucial. If you need to specify an additional group (or groups), use the -G option.

```
useradd -g staff -G finance,research aeinstein
```

Here, Mr. Einstein's account is created with an initial group of staff. He is also added to the groups finance and (of course) research.

E-mail-Only Accounts

If you are creating an account that only needs to access e-mail and never needs to log into a shell session, the solution is to simply not give the account a shell. You do this by assigning a shell of `/bin/false` when the account is created.

```
useradd -g popusers -s /bin/false aeinstein
```

The command I just suggested as the user's shell, `/bin/false`, is one of those wonderful little commands that is a stroke of brilliance. Rather than using my own words here, allow me to quote the man page on `false`.

```
FALSE(1)                  FSF                  FALSE(1)

NAME
       false - do nothing, unsuccessfully
```

Yet More User-Creation Controls

Users are the *raison d'être* of a multiuser system. Consequently, the world of user-creation defaults offers another interesting file called `/etc/login.defs`, which controls other, more interesting things. Here's a small sample from that file:

```
PASS_MAX_DAYS   99999
PASS_MIN_DAYS   0
PASS_MIN_LEN    5
PASS_WARN_AGE   7

#

# Min/max values for automatic uid selection in useradd
#
UID_MIN                   500
UID_MAX                 60000

#
# Min/max values for automatic gid selection in groupadd

#
GID_MIN                   500
GID_MAX                 60000
```

This is quite interesting. You can set a system-wide default wherein users must change their passwords every 30 days or however often your office security policy demands. The default is 99,999 days, which translates to roughly 274 years. You can pretty much call that never. The file is well documented, so have a look at it.

Modifying a User Account

The first example I gave you for adding a user was the simple `useradd username`, which is fine, except that it gives you very little control over account creation unless you go ahead and pass the appropriate information at that time. Let's pretend that you are feeling lazy (or you are in a hurry—a classic sysadmin trap) and, as a result, you do not set up any additional information, such as the user's full name. How do you make changes?

With the `usermod` command, that's how.

```
usage: usermod  [-u uid [-o]] [-g group] [-G group,...]
                [-d home [-m]] [-s shell] [-c comment] [-l new_name]
                [-f inactive] [-e expire ] [-p passwd] [-L|-U] name
```

In some ways, `usermod` looks quite similar to the `useradd` command. To change a user's default shell from `/bin/bash` to `/bin/ash`, use this command:

```
usermod -s /bin/ash natika
```

If all you want to do is change the name field, the so-called *comment* field, there is another command that you can use: `chfn`, which actually means "change finger information," as in the `finger` command discussed earlier. Here's how it works:

```
[root@testsys /root]# chfn -f "Tux the Penguin" guitux
Changing finger information for guitux.
Finger information changed.
```

Deleting a User Account

Allow me a moment to say something blitheringly obvious (even if it does sound like I am repeating myself). If a user leaves, you *should* remove that user's login account (or user name, if you prefer). You should also, as part of your regular schedule, run a check on dormant accounts, but I'll get to that shortly. For now, let's talk about getting rid of a user account.

Removing a user is easy. That's why you should be careful. The command that does the job is called `userdel` and it has one optional flag, a `-r`.

```
userdel [-r] user_name
```

The `-r` flag, which is optional, tells `userdel` to not only remove the user, but also the user's entire home directory. If you omit the flag, you will have to manually clean up the directory yourself. Making this decision is where you should be exceptionally careful. Have you checked the user's home directory to make sure it doesn't contain information you might need later? Take a moment and have a look around as root. A good practice might be to do a backup of that account (and maybe two) and file it semipermanently, until such a time as you are *absolutely sure* there is nothing useful in that account.

The bottom line, as always, is to use your good judgment.

> **Note:** If the user has received any mail (even from the system), there may be a mailbox with his or her user name in the `/var/spool/mail` directory. You should remember that as well when removing the user.

Checking the Password File

As if you didn't already have enough things to do . . . well, let me give you yet another job. On a regular basis, you should run a report to identify accounts or logins that have gone dormant. This is a nice way of saying, "people who are gone and who are not coming back anytime soon."

As you might recall from our examination of the `finger` command, it will display the information relating to the last time an account was used. A couple of chapters back, I told you about the powerful things you can do by using your system's command line. Why not try typing the following command to list each user ID and to check the last login time. Note that the single quotes (just before the `sort` command and just before the pipe symbol) are actually back quotes (or back ticks). The back quote is usually found with the tilde (~) just under the Esc key on a keyboard.

```
finger `sort /etc/passwd | cut -f1 -d":"` | grep -i log | more
```

The output of this command looks something like this:

```
Login: aeinstein                        Name: A. Einstein
Never logged in.
Login: guitux                           Name: Tux the Penguin
Last login Mon Jan  8 14:54 (EST) on tty2
Login: halt                             Name: halt
```

```
Never logged in.
Login: lp                               Name: lp
Never logged in.
Login: mail                             Name: mail
Never logged in.
Login: mgagne                           Name: Marcel Gagne
Last login Wed Mar  7 17:29 (EST) on 1 from website
Login: named                            Name: Named
Never logged in.
Login: natika                           Name: Natika the Cat
```

Warning: You must use your good judgment (an absolute requirement for system administration) on this one. Some of these accounts—`sync` and `lp`, for instance—are system accounts. It only makes sense that no one will have ever logged in through them. On the other hand, Mr. Einstein (at the top of the list) has never logged in either, and his is certainly not an admin login. It could be that this is a new account (and it is) or that you created an account for a user and it was never used. In the latter case, you should probably get rid of that account.

I used that example to give you a feel for your command-line prowess. However, I should tell you that there is a cleaner way to do this. Your Linux system comes with a handy little command called `lastlog` that does just this sort of thing.

```
[root@scigate /root]# lastlog | more
Username         Port     From             Latest
root             tty1                      Wed Mar  7 17:18:40 -0500 2001
bin                                        **Never logged in**
daemon                                     **Never logged in**
adm                                        **Never logged in**
lp                                         **Never logged in**
sync                                       **Never logged in**
shutdown                                   **Never logged in**
mgagne           1        scigate          Wed Mar  7 17:29:55 -0500 2001
postgres                                   **Never logged in**
www                                        **Never logged in**
natika           8        localhost.locald Thu Dec  7 14:30:15 -0500 2000
guitux           tty2                      Mon Jan  8 14:54:55 -0500 2001
```

Geek Trivia: You can't edit or modify this file, but the `lastlog` command information comes from the file `/var/log/lastlog`.

Here is another thing you should do. Every once in a while, run the command `pwck`. By default, it walks through your `/etc/passwd` and `/etc/shadow` files and does some basic integrity checks, such as making sure that the right number of fields are present and that each name is uniquely identified.

```
# pwck
```

For the group file, there is a companion command called `grpck`.

```
# grpck
```

User and Group Administration the GUI Way

For those who would rather have a nice, graphical way of handling all this administration, there are some tools that can handle the job quite nicely. For those who are running either the GNOME or KDE desktop, you will find some attractive options.

In the GNOME world, there is `userconf`, which is actually part of the `linuxconf` administrative package (which you will revisit in detail in Chapter 17). Suffice it to say at this point that `userconf` can be called directly from the command line. Because you are updating user information, this must be run as root.

From a shell window, simply type `userconf` and you should get a screen similar to that in Figure 7.1. From there you can add, remove, or modify both user and group information.

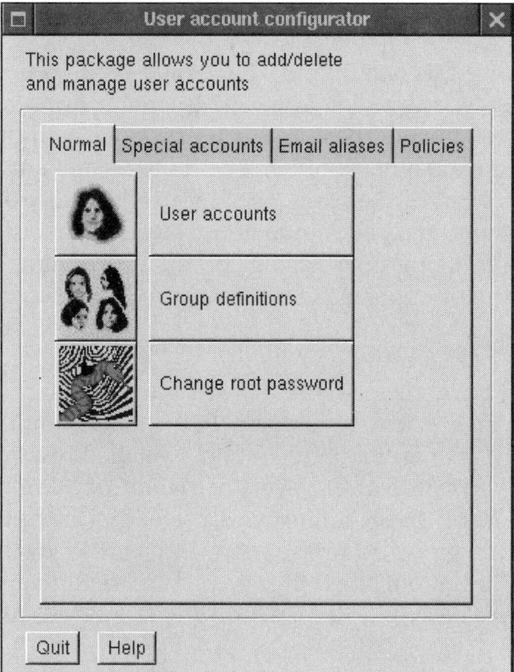

FIGURE 7.1 Managing users with `userconf`

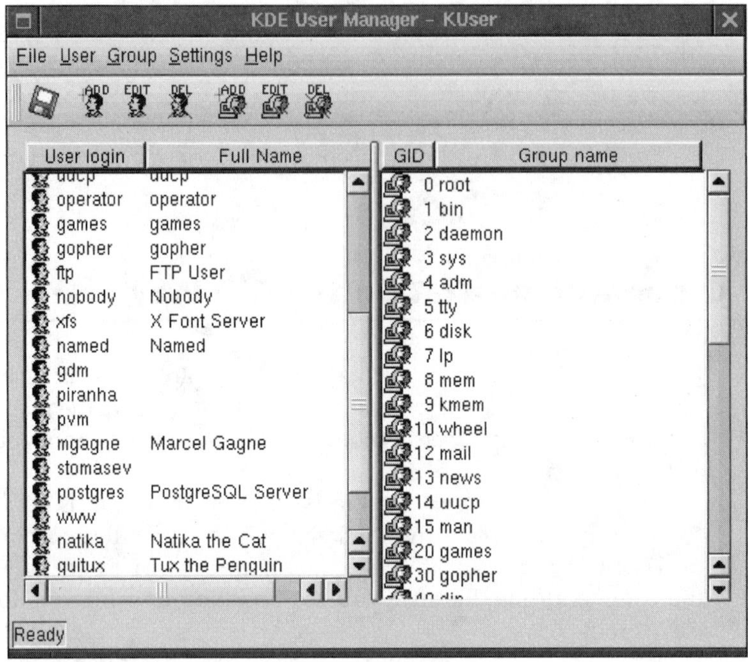

FIGURE 7.2 `kuser`'s interface may look familiar

Another option—this one for the KDE crowd—shows up in the KDE system menu as User Management. You can also call it from the command line with the `kuser` command. Those who have worked with that other OS will note that the interface is quite familiar, as you can see in Figure 7.2.

Have a look at Figure 7.3 as well. You'll see another face of the `kuser` program, but more important, you should notice some of those shadow password date-sensitive fields being put to work. If you are running a small machine with only a handful of users, manually changing these defaults is not a problem (and may even be preferable), but for a large organization, consider using the defaults in `/etc/login.defs` instead.

As you might have guessed, these aren't the only alternative methods of user and group management. In Chapter 19 (the tools roundup), I'll show you other ways to deal with user administration. I've already admitted that I can't possibly cover every system and every variation of administration as provided by those systems. SuSE, for instance, uses YAST as the preferred graphical tool for user and group administration, and another distribution may use something else. The bottom line is this: If you can use the command-line tools, you'll be great.

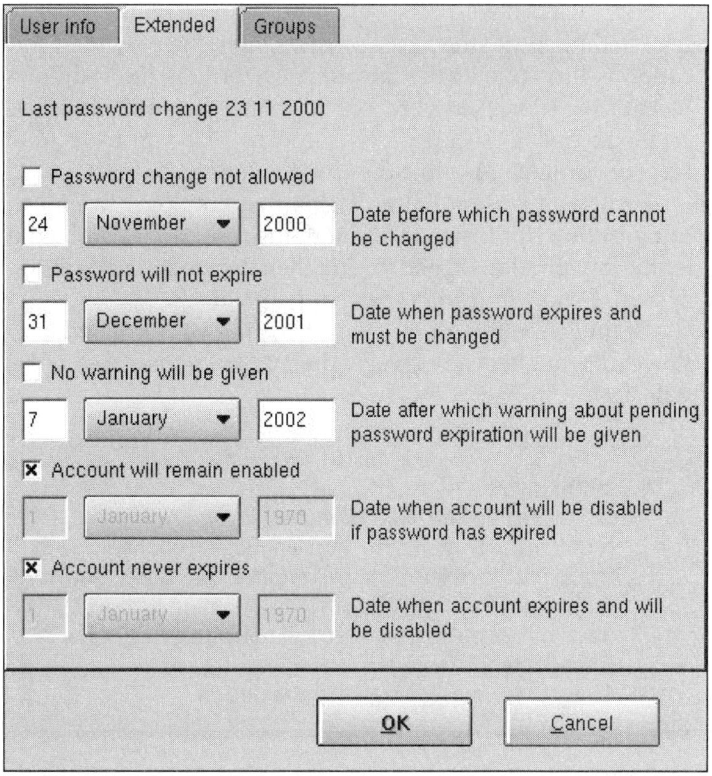

FIGURE 7.3 Using `kuser` to modify expiration dates

Choosing Good Passwords

You'll notice a pattern in this book. Besides being filled with useful information (if I have done my job right), you'll notice that I keep coming back to system security again and again. System security is a big issue and if it isn't, it should be. This is particularly true in the world of the Internet, happily opening our virtual doors to all comers.

Even if your system is not directly connected to the Internet, you should still practice some basic security. Even internally, inside your company's walls, there are security issues to consider. The way to not handle system security is to ignore the following information.

Consider this: There are probably areas in your organization where users will tell you that they all know each other's passwords, just in case. In case of *what* is open to speculation.

Some users have a little yellow sticky note on the corner on their terminals in case they forget their passwords. Often, the password for system authentication is the same as the Novell password, as the Windows password . . . in fact, it's the same password as every other password they use.

Good system security policy means that you have to develop a healthy level of paranoia. Assume the worst and prepare for it.

For example, say that a disgruntled employee wandered back into your organization (for instance, through the front door), walked up to the terminal by the pay phones, logged in, and then decided to have his or her way with the system. I know that will never happen, but. . . .

Granted, there is far more to protecting your system than good passwords; however, your best first level of defense is a good password and that is where I will start.

A good password

- Is between six and eight characters in length
- Is not in any English or foreign language dictionary
- Does not contain personal information (kid's name, driver's license number, birthday, and so on)
- Has a mix of both alphabetic and nonalphabetic characters
- Changes regularly
- Changes whenever a staff member leaves

The level of password security varies from site to site. Some sites have passwords that change weekly—some even go so far as to change passwords daily. On more complicated installations, the daily password requires the entry of an authentication key that also changes daily. The algorithm might take the day of the week as part of the key and multiply it by the user's birthdate divided by the year Steven Spielberg graduated from high school plus the square root of the Hubble Constant divided by. . . . You get the idea.

How Crackers Crack Your Passwords

That previous password formula might be verging on "a bit much" for your organization. Only you know that. The reason for a good password goes right back to my earlier description of the password file, specifically as it relates to the password field in nonshadow files. Here's a quick reminder of the format:

```
root:2IsjW45pb4L56:0:0:root:/root:/bin/bash
```

The password field (field 2) is encoded by virtue of a hashing algorithm. If you are curious as to the gory details, type `man crypt` and you'll find everything you ever wanted to know about encoding passwords. The short form is this: That strange password is actually a coded version of your password based on a two-character, randomly generated *salt*. This salt is then used to seed the hashing routine to generate the final group of characters.

The term "hashing" represents a technique for taking a string of characters (a person's last name, for instance) and generating a unique key (ideally) for easy retrieval of the information from a database. What you are doing is encoding the normal text into a shorter, (usually) numeric representation.

Password crackers figure out passwords by using that salt to generate passwords against every word in the dictionary. While this sounds pretty complex, it's not. A simple program calls the crypt routine, runs the hash on a word, and then compares it to the password entry in the `/etc/passwd` file. If it matches, bingo! They have your password. If it doesn't, they move on to the next word. On a reasonably punchy system, it doesn't take all that long for crackers to work their way through every password in the book.

Don't believe me. Take a look at the output in Figure 7.4 from a little program called Nutcracker, a freeware tool that does the kind of brute force password checking I was talking about.

As you can see in Figure 7.4, picking something you'll remember easily because it is a common word is a bad choice for a password.

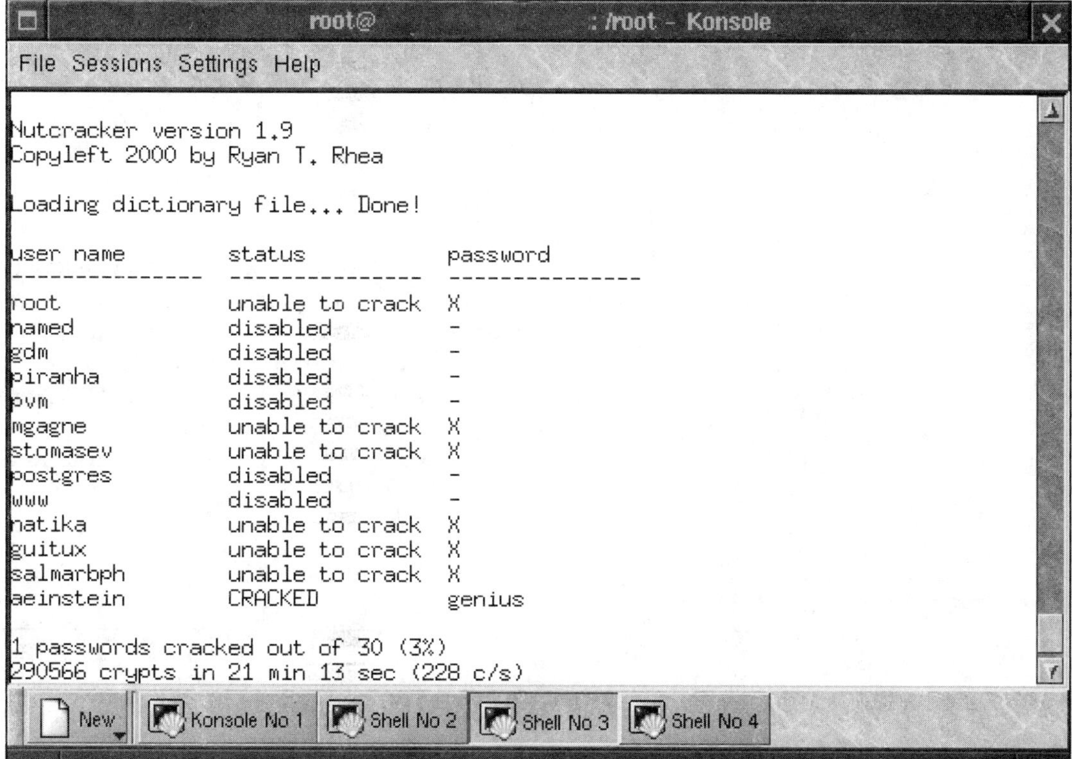

FIGURE 7.4 Why dictionary words make bad passwords

Choosing Better Passwords

Choosing a good password can drive you crazy, it's true (strange combinations of numbers and letters—'7%Bu!=h8'—for some reason, people really seem to hate those), but it can also be fun. Rather than trying for something so completely out of left field that you can't possibly ever remember it, try playing games with familiar phrases or sayings. For instance, you can pick a phrase that means something to you and modify it in some strange way.

For example, let's start with the phrase "Believe in magic!" Now, what can you do with that? Take only the consonants of the first and last word, and you have blvmgc. Then (because you believe in magic) add an "I" at the beginning, except don't use the letter I—use a numeric "1." To finish up, you could put an exclamation point at the end (magic is exciting) but because stars always feature in magic stuff, the final character should be an asterisk. The result is 1blvmgc*, a great password if ever there was one. But don't use that one. Because I've used it in this book, it's too easy a first choice.

Most Linux (and UNIX) systems include some mechanism for password aging as well as password-creation restrictions, all of which were covered earlier in this chapter during the discussion on shadow passwords. What this does is allow an automated system for regular password changes. The rules you establish are enforced whenever a user is told to change his or her password. Rules can be a limit on password length or the number of nonalphabetic characters.

What Next?

For those of you administering your own systems at home or in a small office, I'll leave it there. For others who have to administer their company's system and its however many users, it's time to educate those users. Set a time and date and enforce good passwords as of that date. At first they'll hate you for it, but that's part of your job as IS—to be hated. As we move increasingly (and hopefully) to open and networked systems, we must become increasingly conscious of security on our systems. Passwords are the first level of protection and (properly implemented) still one of the best.

I Logged In from Where?

Have a look at what happens when I log into a machine. Everything looks normal. I have a login name, a request for my password. I enter the password and voila, I am in. But hold on—read that little one-line message that appears after I enter the password:

```
login: mgagne
Password:
Last login: Mon Jan  8 16:00:39 from energize
```

What the heck is "energize"? Energize is the host name of the computer from which I last logged in apparently, except I don't have a system called "energize." Furthermore, let's pretend that I don't know anyone with that system and that I always log in from the same place. The only explanation is that somebody from a system called "energize" logged into the server with my login name and password.

This is just a hypothetical situation, but it does illustrate one other habit that you should consider training your users to adopt. If they are logging in from the same PC day in and day out, that message should never change. If they do not recognize the host name in the last login message, they should make it a policy to alert you.

Security isn't just the domain of the system administrator. After all, you've got plenty on your plate. Any help is appreciated. You need to get the users involved. Let them know that system security is their business as well as yours.

How Not to Be a "Sucker"

Ever heard the saying "There's a sucker born every minute"? That expression is attributed to circus legend P.T. Barnum. In the modern, politically correct world, you might be more likely to run across the term "social engineering." While it may sound a little nicer to the ears, it means the same thing as P.T. Barnum's saying. In the context of system security, it refers to any attempt—no matter how clever or transparent—used to convince people to give up their passwords.

While administrators are all worried sick about people getting through firewalls and breaking into systems, they forget that once in, people still need a password. Sometimes, breaking in is the easy part. Most security violations aren't from some stereotypical hacker in pop-bottle glasses cleverly breaking through all your expensive defenses. It's somebody walking up to someone else and saying, "I forgot my password and I really need that document. Can I use yours?" I've been in a shop where somebody forged an e-mail, sent it to a few people, and told them to change to specific predefined passwords. It's vital that you educate your users.

Tell your users that no one in IS, or anyone on staff for that matter, will ever ask them for their passwords. A Linux system administrator can log in from root to any account without the password. Whether that makes them feel better or worse about the power wielded by their system administrators is another story.

Users should report any attempt to extract password information from them. No one should ever ask for this information for any reason. A classic scenario is someone telling a user that they need to check on system problems and must use a general login to test. The conversation might go something like this:

"Hi, I'm from the phone company and I'm here to check on your phone."

"But there's nothing wrong with my phone."

Remember that personal experience I mentioned? The users showed me a letter they received from "root" or "superuser" telling them to change their passwords to predesignated passwords (supposedly these were passwords selected by the system—for instance, "boot*clock"). The users in question called me because they were unable to change their passwords accordingly. The system password rules that I had in effect forbade that type of password construct (they needed to include two numbers at specific locations in the password and had not). I explained that I would never tell them what password to choose, and if I sent out mail, it would be as myself, not as "root" or "superuser."

As Fox Mulder from "The X-Files" might say: Trust no one!

Resources

Nutcracker (password-cracking tool)

`http://northernlightsgroup.hypermart.net/nutcracker.html`

Chapter 8

Disks and File Systems

My best friend in this world (my wife, Sally) has a saying: "The data comes first." Variations on this little bit of wisdom include "You have to know what the data looks like before you start doing anything at all" and "It's all data." These sayings come from her experiences as a programmer. Before you can possibly write any application, you have to have some idea of what you want the application to do. What kind of input will it have? What will it do with that input? When it finishes doing that whatever, what kind of output are you expecting? While an infinite number of monkeys may hammer out Shakespeare's complete works in an infinite amount of time, I'm not so sure about them doing the same with an accounting or manufacturing application.

Monkey philosophy aside, the bottom line is this: The most important thing on your system is the data. Not the horsepower of your machine, not its monitor, not whether the printer is inkjet or laser, and not even how much RAM it has. It's the data. Ask any accountant. Ask a writer working on his or her book or an artist doing graphic design what is paramount on his or her system and you'll discover that it is the data. Are the files safe and can they access them without encountering problems?

That precious data is stored in Linux's hierarchical file system. By definition, this implies a root directory at the top and all other files and directories branching out below in a kind of upside-down tree. Each branch is a directory and the leaves are files, our precious data.

Everything Is a File

Time to have some fun. Here's what you need to remember in the Linux world.

"Everything is a file." This famous line by Ken Thompson, the developer of UNIX, highlights the simplicity of the Linux (and UNIX) model.

Everything is a file to the Linux operating system. Everything is represented by a file. Your console is a file. So is your disk, your CD writer, and your modem. Linux does not know the difference between a database file, a word-processing file, or a game—nor does it care. That said, there are at least three kinds of files: ordinary files, directory files, and special files.

An *ordinary file* is any file containing data or text in pretty much any format. The source code for a program is in an ordinary file as is its compiled form. Your word-processing document and your client database are also ordinary files.

Directory files enable you to organize your files (all three types) into some kind of logical order. You can think of them as a filing cabinet. The drawers are also directory files as are the hanging folder holders, and the file folders within them are files as well because they continue the logical grouping yet another level. Inside one of these folders, you can have another folder, and inside that folder, an envelope, and inside that possibly a document of some sort. It's directories all the way down until such a time as you get to a document—keeping in mind, of course, that a directory file can contain any kind of file whatsoever.

Finally, you have *special files*. These are usually the files that represent devices, such as your tape drive, your terminal, and your sound card. Everything Linux writes to or reads from is a file. It may seem as though I am over-simplifying things with this definition of a file, but the beauty of this approach quickly becomes evident when you copy files, pipe the output of a command, or play a sound clip.

Understanding Your File Systems

As you work with more and more Linux systems, you'll notice that some people tend to speak about file systems in much the same way that they talk about partitions. This comes from the fact that the past UNIX system architecture enforced a partition division for individual file systems—one for the root file system (`/`), one for `/usr`, `/tmp`, `/home`, `/swap`, `/dump`, and other partitions as required by the version of UNIX, all but the first usually mounted under the root partition.

This was partly due to hardware constraints (and in some cases, operating system design). Your file systems had to be broken up into *slices*, mathematically calculated chunks of space based on the physical disk's mapping. Deciding what area got what slice was the domain of seasoned UNIX sysadmins.

In today's Linux system, we are quite spoiled. While this is another topic capable of sparking heated debate, it is possible to create one swap partition and a single root partition and be done with it. Your system will work just fine and you will have saved yourself a great deal of mental gymnastics.

Despite the possible arrangement of a single data partition, there is some structure out there and these top-level directories (`/usr`, `/etc`, `/home`) are sometimes referred to as file systems, and even (gasp!) partitions. This hierarchical file structure (which has been around as long as UNIX has been around, by the way) is increasingly defined by the filesystem hierarchy standard (FHS). What's interesting here is that FHS was designed to standardize Linux, but it is being adopted by other UNIXes as well.

The File System Tree

Perhaps "tree" is a bit confusing because this is actually more like an *inverted* tree with the root being on top and the directories branching out to leaves (regular files). First, let's take a look at the list of directories that are directly under the root (represented as `/`).

```
# cd /
# find . -type d -maxdepth 1 -print
/
/lost+found
/proc
/var
/tmp
/dev
/usr
/etc
/bin
/boot
/home
/lib
/mnt
/root
/sbin
```

The previous list is typical of what you will find on most Linux distributions out of the box. Some of these directories are often referred to interchangeably as file systems or partitions (remember the earlier partition discussion). What really separates a file system from a simple directory is as follows.

> *File systems* are top-level directories (just below the root) that in and of themselves are responsible for certain functions. As you explore the various file systems, you'll understand what I mean.

You'll notice that there is one missing partition—one you built when you installed your system, but which fails to show up in this list. This is the *swap partition*. That's because swap is not a file system, per se. You can't change directory to the swap file system and do an `ls` to see what files are there. This is a raw chunk of data where programs may be swapped in and out as part of your system's normal operations. It is meant to be a physical extension of your real memory (your RAM). You can't go into swap and delete things or move data around anymore than you can do that with RAM. This does not diminish its usefulness, however. There is a swap argument that goes something like this: If you have enough memory, you don't necessarily need swap. I disagree. Save yourself headaches later and don't take it as a question of choice. Simply stated, you *need* to configure swap.

Incidentally, it is possible to add more swap at a later time as well with the `mkswap` command. I'll talk about that a little later when I cover creating file systems.

The Root File System (aka /, or Slash)

The very name "hierarchical file system" implies an organization from some top level on down. This top level is `/`, commonly referred to as simply *root*. Its purpose is primarily to provide the environment for bringing your system to life. When your system boots, one of the first things it does (after reading the boot record) is mount `/`. What you have here are those files central to a basic boot. This is where `/boot` lives, the directory where your Linux kernel (`vmlinuz`) resides. It is also the home of `/bin`, `/dev`, `/etc`, `/lib`, and `/sbin`.

I'm going to start with what you can think of as the command directories. First, you have the `/bin` directory, which provides all the basic commands necessary to start the system with one criterion—namely, that they are also the nonadministrator commands. Admin-only or system administration commands can be found in the aptly named `/sbin` directory (think "superuser bin"). The other directory in this category is `/lib`, which contains the shared system libraries necessary for start-up. This is also the directory that contains the *system-loadable modules,* small object libraries or drivers that can be pulled into the kernel as needed. For instance, these might include support for your sound card or your Ethernet adapter. When you visit your hardware vendor for an updated driver, this is usually where they wind up.

Next is `/dev`, which contains special files that represent the hardware devices on your Linux system.

Which leaves you with `/etc`. It is here that you will find the things that make your system unique: configuration files, local start-up scripts, passwords, network configurations, and so on. Historically, commands could be found here as well, but this is no longer the case. In a sense, if you were to simply back up the `/etc` directory, you would have all the standard system configurations. Obviously, there is far more that needs to be backed up, but this will represent the system's identity. (For an example of a more comprehensive system identity backup script, see Chapter 16.)

The /usr File System

This is the big one, the largest partition (or file system) on your system. Other than the data areas themselves, this tends to be the busiest and largest directory on your system. It is here that you find the bulk of system tools, applications, and your X window system. The following is a quick overview of what you will find here.

Note that there is a `/usr/local` hierarchy that kind of mirrors some of the directories I'll talk about shortly. These tend to be programs installed after the fact—programs that aren't part of the default distribution. When you download and compile your own programs (as you will in Chapter 11), they will likely wind up here. This isn't to imply that these programs aren't important. The Apache Web server, for example, will by default install its files under `/usr/local/apache` if you build it from scratch.

Some of the logic that goes into this structure has to do with your vendor's distribution. When you upgrade your system, the vendor's programs will likely be overwritten. Those are the ones living in any program directory (`/bin`, `/usr/bin`, `/usr/sbin`) except for the ones under `/usr/local`. Consequently, it's not that unusual for an administrator to have `/usr/local` as a separate mounted partition.

/usr/bin

You can find most user programs that don't fit the `/bin` description and aren't considered strictly admin programs here.

/usr/sbin

This is the administrative counterpart to `/usr/bin`. It is in this directory that you will find admin programs, such as your network daemons, user maintenance programs, and so on.

/usr/include

Most of the system's header files are included here. These are used by the `gcc` compiler for building software. If you do an `ls -l` in this directory, you'll see that a few of the directories actually point to `/usr/src/linux`. These are the kernel header files.

/usr/lib

This is another directory used by the programming environments. A number of programs on your system use *shared libraries*, chunks of code to which they refer but are considered static. These can also be found here.

/usr/man

Several directories exist under here, but they are all related to system documentation. Chapter 3 discussed the man page hierarchy.

/usr/share

One of the busier directories, `/usr/share` is fun to poke around in. A number of application-specific, but non-distribution-related programs create directories here. This is another one of those mirrored (sort of) directories under `/usr/local`. Among the denizens of this directory are background images for your desktop, icons, additional documentation, and other files.

/usr/X11R6

The X window system. The `R6` refers to release 6 of X. It has its own set of `bin`, `lib`, and `share` directories (and a few others). Because I will cover the X window system later on in Chapter 9, I'll leave it at this for now.

/usr/games

Because you can't always be working, there is a directory dedicated to games. In the past, there were a bevy of venerable old games here, like the classic `adventure` (in which you are in a maze of tunnels with identical passages going off in all directions). Depending on the distribution, you'll find very little here these days. My system has `banner` and `fortune` (which I like a great deal). Games usually install under `/usr/local` with the exception of those included with the X window system (such as `xbill`).

The /var File System

The `/var` directory structure contains *variable data,* transient files that are regularly changed or that exist for short periods of time. These include print jobs, mail, lock, locks, system accounting information, and log files. If you decide to go the route of creating separate partitions, consider that this can also be a large partition. The `/var/log` directory is of particular importance from a reporting and security perspective.

If you should happen to find yourself looking at some old distributions, you may notice that some of the structure you find here used to be in `/usr`. For instance, `/var/spool` used to be `/usr/spool`, and `/var/tmp` used to be `/usr/tmp`. In fact, some remnants of this still exist. Check your system for symbolic links in the `/usr` directory. On one of my test systems (a Red Hat 6.2 workstation), `/usr/tmp` is still there, but as a symbolic link to `/var/tmp`.

The /tmp File System

This is yet another file system whose contents can change rapidly. Like the name suggests, this file system is designed for temporary data. Because it is world writable, it is possible for users to use this as a dumping ground for their own temporary data.

This is one of those arguments for making the /tmp file system a separate partition when you install your system. Because users may do precisely what I've suggested, it is possible that they could eat up all the data on your disk. If /tmp is kept separate and they fill it, it is your only problem.

> **Tip:** Consider anything in /tmp as being up for grabs. If it hasn't been claimed in a predefined period, then delete it. Inform your users of this practice. This should keep them honest. It is also used by programs for temporary space, including your X window desktop applications.

The /proc File System

You may not know it, but there is a phantom living on your computer—a file system with lots of directories and files, much like any other file system, except that this one isn't really there at all. In fact, it disappears every time you shut down your computer and is rebuilt every time you reboot. It is /proc (think "process information").

Exploring /proc can be a great deal of fun, not to mention informative. The /proc file system (or pseudo file system, because it doesn't really exist) is a means of looking into your system as it lives and breathes.

So, how can the mysterious /proc file system not really exist? Well, for one thing, if you do an ls -l on the root directory, you'll get a directory of size zero. Try it and see.

```
# ls -l /
(note: only showing partial listing)
drwxr-xr-x    2 root     root         4096 Aug  1 15:07 patch
dr-xr-xr-x   90 root     root            0 Aug 12 19:57 proc
drwxr-x---  113 root     root        12288 Aug 14 14:55 root
drwxr-xr-x    3 root     root         4096 Jul 12 16:40 sbin
drwxrwxrwt    8 root     root         4096 Aug 14 15:21 tmp
drwxr-xr-x   21 root     root         4096 Mar 13 17:07 usr
drwxr-xr-x   18 root     root         4096 Jun 22 18:59 var
```

Notice that /proc does indeed have a zero size. Yet when I change directory to /proc with cd /proc and do an ls there, I see tons of information.

```
# cd /proc
# ls
1 10102 10105 10311 10315 10702 10710 10712 10714 10715
10716 10717 10718 10719 10720 10721 10722 10723 10755 10766
1145 1146 1147 1148 1149 1150 1151 1152 2 3 330 345 346 355
369 4 420 429 443 446 447 449 450 461 475 490 5 508 528 583
6 612 626 675 715 716 717 718 719 720 723 745 752 753 757
771 773 775 776 7922 808 811 8784 8786 8788 8789 8936 9008
9088 911 914 9957 apm bus cmdline cpuinfo devices dma fb
filesystems fs ide interrupts ioports kcore kmsg ksyms loadavg
locks mdstat meminfo misc modules mounts net partitions pci
rtc scsi self slabinfo sound stat swaps sys tty uptime version
```

For an empty directory, there's quite a bit there. Let's begin with some easy stuff. Look at the file called `cpuinfo` for starters. Another zero size file. Now `cat` the file and have a look at the results. This is what mine shows:

```
# cat /proc/cpuinfo
processor         : 0
vendor_id         : GenuineIntel
cpu family        : 5
model             : 2
model name        : Pentium 75 - 200
stepping          : 12
cpu MHz           : 150.342254
fdiv_bug          : no
hlt_bug           : no
sep_bug           : no
f00f_bug          : yes
coma_bug          : no
fpu               : yes
fpu_exception     : yes
cpuid level       : 1
wp                : yes
flags             : fpu vme de pse tsc msr mce cx8
bogomips          : 59.80
```

Actually, in this case it's a Pentium 150, but it is still kind of fascinating to see what my system thinks of itself. Let's see what happens when you look at the file called "interrupts." Guesses, anyone?

```
# cat /proc/interrupts
           CPU0
  0:    6422178          XT-PIC  timer
  1:      43093          XT-PIC  keyboard
  2:          0          XT-PIC  cascade
  5:          3          XT-PIC  soundblaster
  8:          1          XT-PIC  rtc
 10:      34143          XT-PIC  eth0
 12:     541052          XT-PIC  PS/2 Mouse
 13:          1          XT-PIC  fpu
 14:    1622951          XT-PIC  ide0
 15:          6          XT-PIC  ide1
NMI:          0
```

Similarly, doing a `cat` on the `meminfo` file gives you current stats about your memory, both physical and swap. Looking into `/proc/scsi/scsi` reveals your SCSI assignments, while a look at the sound file shows you your sound card configuration. A `cat` of your `/proc/partitions` file displays your disk partition information, and `version` is your running kernel and how it was compiled. Keep looking. There's a lot here and it's tons of fun.

By now, you may have already noticed that I did not tell you the whole truth. When you did an `ls -l` on `/proc`, you actually found two non-zero-size files. One of them is called `kcore` and it can be a fair size for something that takes up no space. This is a "mirror" of sorts for your kernel. Perhaps the lens of a microscope is a better analogy. Notice how the file takes up about as much space as you have physical memory. That is no coincidence. `kcore` is your system's memory—its RAM, if you prefer. In fact, it is everything currently in RAM and as such, it is a dynamic beast. The same can be said for much of what you see in `/proc`. Looking at meminfo from one minute to the next yields a different set of numbers as the demands of real memory versus swap are handled.

The other "big" file (though much smaller than `kcore`) is something called `self`, and if you do an `ls -l` on `/proc`, you'll notice that `self` is actually a pointer to a number. Here's what I get when I do that `ls -l`:

```
lrwxrwxrwx    1 root    root      64 Aug 16 13:28 self -> 2183
```

The reason I asked you to `ls -l` the whole `/proc` directory rather than just `self` is this: I wanted you to see that the number (in my case, 2183) is also a directory under the `/proc` directory. Now, do another `ls -l`. It's gone, isn't it?

What about all those numbers? What are they for? Each one seems to be a directory. What will you find there? Try doing a `ps ax` to get a list of the running processes on your system. Even better, do it this way:

```
ps ax | cut -c1-5
```

That will get you just the process numbers without the long display. Now compare that list to the numbers sitting in `/proc`. Look familiar? Every process currently running on your system has an analog sitting in the `/proc` file system. Now have a look at what you can discover hidden in there. Just for fun, let's take one of the processes on my system. To do my little exploring about, I am using a terminal emulator called Eterm. If you don't have it, get it. You'll thank me later.

The process ID for one of my Eterm sessions is 834 (the result of `ps ax | grep Eterm`). If I change directory to `/proc/834` and do an `ls -l`, this is what I see:

```
total 0
-r--r--r--    1 mgagne   mgagne          0 Aug 16 13:59 cmdline
lrwx------    1 mgagne   mgagne          0 Aug 16 13:59 cwd ->
/usr/share/Eterm/themes/Eterm
-r--------    1 mgagne   mgagne          0 Aug 16 13:59 environ
```

```
lrwx------    1 mgagne   mgagne            0 Aug 16 13:59 exe ->
/usr/bin/Eterm-0.8.10
dr-x------    2 mgagne   mgagne            0 Aug 16 13:59 fd
pr--r--r--    1 mgagne   mgagne            0 Aug 16 13:59 maps
-rw-------    1 mgagne   mgagne            0 Aug 16 13:59 mem
lrwx------    1 mgagne   mgagne            0 Aug 16 13:59 root -> /
-r--r--r--    1 mgagne   mgagne            0 Aug 16 13:59 stat
-r--r--r--    1 mgagne   mgagne            0 Aug 16 13:59 statm
-r--r--r--    1 mgagne   mgagne            0 Aug 16 13:59 status
```

Once again, a number of these can be viewed with `cat` or `more` or `less`. The `cmdline` file shows the command that executed Eterm while `environ` displays the environment variables at work here. Check out `maps` for a list of all the libraries at work with the current executable. Have a look inside that `fd` directory and see if you can figure out what those numbers represent.

Sure, there are system commands that do a fine job of showing what is happening in `/proc`. The command `top`, for instance, is just such a snapshot for your processes. Files like `meminfo` and `pci` can be graphically unwound with the help of KDE's `kcontrol` program. Just check out the Information tab. If you look long and hard enough, you will likely find a tool to display all this stuff in a nice, graphical format. In some ways, that's part of the reasoning behind the `/proc` file system: to give programmers, administrators, and others an easier means of accessing core system information and modifying a running kernel.

Because it is possible to modify your running kernel through `/proc`, changes here can have a profound impact on system performance. Chapter 26 provides more detail on this.

The /lost+found File System

This one will show up as a directory on every partition you create, with the exception of your swap partition. Perhaps before I talk about `lost+found`, I should take a step back and discuss `fsck`.

fsck: The File System Check and Repair Tool

You know that your systems are never supposed to crash, but unfortunately, the worst does indeed happen from time to time. Perhaps someone accidentally pulls the plug or the power goes out and you don't have a UPS. Under those circumstances, it is possible for the file system to suffer damage. If the system was in the middle of writing data out to a file, that operation may have been terminated halfway, leaving behind junk or incomplete data. Anyone who has been using Linux (or UNIX) systems for a long time will tell you that things have improved quite a bit in this area. The `ext2` file system is substantially better at dealing with these types of problems, but they do occur from time to time.

When something like this happens, your system will notice that the disk partition was not properly unmounted as it tries to reboot (think of ScanDisk in your Windows system). The command that does the noticing is the same one that does the repair work afterward. That command is `fsck` (and no, that is not a typo). I made a point of mentioning the `ext2` file system because I wanted to show you something. The `fsck` command isn't really the `fsck` command. It is a front end to various file system repair tools. Using the `whereis` command, you can get an idea of just what I am talking about.

```
[mgagne@testsys marcel]$ whereis fsck
fsck: /sbin/fsck /sbin/fsck.ext2 /sbin/fsck.msdos /sbin/fsck.minix
```

As you can see, the `fsck` front end (or wrapper) tries to determine the file system type and then runs the appropriate version of the program. In the case of `ext2` file systems, the proper program is called `fsck.ext2`, although that program is on your disk by another name, `ext2fs`. Because both are the same, it doesn't matter which one you use.

Because `fsck` normally runs automatically, you might not have considered that it is possible to run it manually. Doing this, however, requires that you unmount the file system you want to check. You can also boot up in single-user mode (`linux single` at the LILO prompt). To check a file system, use this command:

```
fsck /dev/hda5
```

This is the simplest possible scenario for checking disks. If the system was unmounted cleanly, `fsck` will just return to the command prompt. To force a check, use the `-f` option.

```
fsck -f /dev/hda5
```

If there are problems and `fsck` is not sure what to do, it will try to confirm its decisions with you beforehand. You can tell `fsck` to just answer yes to everything by using the `-y` option.

```
fsck -y -f /dev/hda5
```

If `fsck` finds that it is unable to reattach or account for a file fragment, it will put that fragment in the `lost+found` directory for that specific partition. Because `fsck` (and `e2fsck`) is actually very good at what it does, you won't usually find anything here. Still, if your system did not shut down properly and you were forced to run `fsck`, you should probably check `lost+found` for anything that may have been . . . er, well, lost and found.

Bad Superblock?

Let me start by saying that the odds of your getting a message like the following are very, very slim. However, in the event of some serious file system damage, you may find yourself looking at something like this after running `fsck`:

```
The file system superblock is corrupt.
Try running e2fsck again with an alternate superblock using the -b
option.
```

To allow for as robust an architecture as possible, your `ext2` file system has critical information about its layout written at regular intervals in data areas called *superblocks*. These copies can be found at every 8192 blocks, starting with 8193 (because the first is at block 1).

```
fsck -y -b 8193 /dev/hda5
```

If it has gotten to this point, fix the problem and do a backup now. You may actually have hardware problems, so be ready for anything. Keep in mind that the backup you make at this point may have errors as well. If you have a corrupt file on disk, it will wind up on your backup.

How Much Space Have I Got Again?

Disk space is a limited resource and, consequently, you have to keep an eye on it. The `df` command (think "disk free") is what you use to do this. Simply typing `df` will give you information on every mounted file system.

```
[mgagne@testsys marcel]$ df
Filesystem           1k-blocks      Used Available Use% Mounted on
/dev/hda1              1981710    769130   1110144  41% /
/dev/hda5              7903716    520346   6973620   7% /home
/dev/hda6              1981710    714602   1164672  38% /usr/local
scigate:/mnt/data1     6110045   4978257    815310  86% /mnt/scigate
```

A variation of this command involves using the `-h` option, which stands for "human readable format." I don't know that it is any more readable than the other way, but let me show you a sample. Before I do, let's add another interesting flag, the `-T` flag, which identifies the file system type.

```
[root@website /root]# df -T -h
Filesystem        Type     Size  Used Avail Use% Mounted on
/dev/hda1         ext2     1.9G  751M  1.1G  41% /
/dev/hda5         ext2     7.5G  508M  6.7G   7% /home
/dev/hda6         ext2     1.9G  698M  1.1G  38% /usr/local
othersys:/data1    nfs     5.8G  4.7G  796M  86% /mnt/othersys
```

The fourth file system you see in that list is an NFS mount. These file systems do not live directly on your system—they belong to another computer

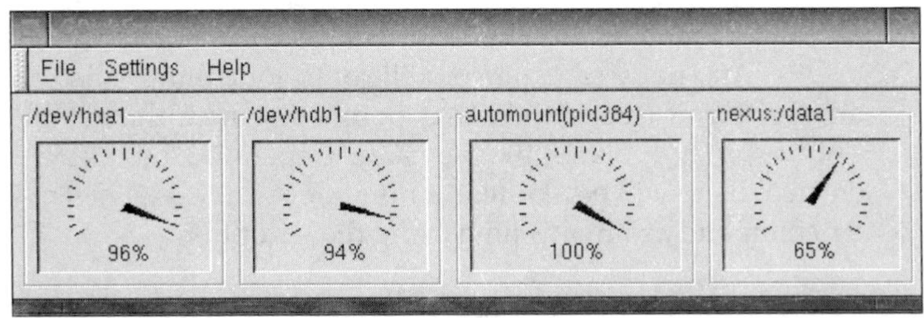

FIGURE 8.1 GNOME's GDiskFree tool

that makes them available across your network. Chapter 18 covers NFS mounts in detail.

You can also specify individual file systems like this:

```
df /usr/local
```

When the situation calls for flash and pizzazz, check out GNOME's GDiskFree program, which is shown in Figure 8.1 (just type `gdiskfree` at the command line). Users of KDE should check out KDiskFree under the System menu (see Figure 8.2).

What's This about Inodes?

Every file and directory (directories being just files) on your disk has a small chunk of data to describe certain attributes such as permissions, creation,

File Options Help

Icon	Device	Type	Size	Mount point	Free	Full %	Usage
	/dev/hda1	ext2	1.78GB	/	66.9MB	96.3%	
	/dev/cdrom	iso9660	N/A	/mnt/cdrom	0.00MB	N/A	
	/dev/fd0	auto	N/A	/mnt/floppy	0.00MB	N/A	
	/dev/hdb1	ext2	5.83GB	/mnt/data1	355MB	94.0%	
	nexus:/data1	nfs	2.40GB	/mnt/nexus	825MB	66.4%	

FIGURE 8.2 KDiskFree: Disk space management, the KDE way

access, and modification times, as well as the location on disk. This is called an inode. An inode can point to a file or to something called an *indirect block*, yet another bit of information that points to where the actual data blocks live. Inodes do not contain the file name. Depending on the size of the file system created, there will be a different number of inodes. Let's have a look with the df command again, this time using the -i option.

```
[root@testsys      /root]#    df -i
Filesystem         Inodes     IUsed     IFree      IUse%     Mounted on
/dev/hda1          514048     59520     454528     12%       /
/dev/hda5          2050048    10923     2039125    1%        /home
/dev/hda6          514048     12126     501922     2%        /usr/local
othersys:/data1    0          0         0          0%        /mnt/othersys
```

Notice that NFS mounted systems do not report inode information.

Inodes are real structures on your disk, and as a result, they take up real space (though not much). They are also a limited quantity (as the previous listing shows under the IFree heading). Their number is fixed at the time the ext2 file system is created and once they are gone, you can no longer write to the disk. Consider that fact if you are running an application that uses large numbers of small files. That said, I should point out that you do have a fair number of inodes by default. The previous /dev/hda1 partition is 2GB in size and has room for over half a million files.

Mounting and Unmounting File Systems

In order for users to be able to use the information in a file system, it must be available to them. This is done through a command called mount. A file system is mounted somewhere in the directory structure. On your system, you have a directory called /mnt and odds are pretty good that you won't see much there if you do an ls. On a stock, out-of-the-box system, you often have a directory called floppy and another called cdrom, although this may vary from distribution to distribution.

A lot of this mounting of file systems is done for you automatically when the system boots. If you watch closely, you'll see messages about this. If you have a dual boot system with a Windows partition, that is, in effect, another file system. If that file system was on /dev/hda6, you could mount that file system like this:

```
mount /dev/hda6 /mnt/windows
```

The /mnt/windows directory would already have to exist for this to happen. The same goes for your CD-ROM drive. You can mount that in this way:

```
mount -o ro /dev/hdc /mnt/cdrom
```

That -o option is a means of passing information specific to the type of file system that you want to mount. In the case of a CD-ROM, ro, meaning "read-only," makes perfect sense. On my system, I can also mount the CD-ROM by simply typing this:

```
mount /mnt/cdrom
```

That's because the mount definition for /mnt/cdrom already exists in a mount configuration file. That file is called /etc/fstab. Here's the file from one of my systems:

```
/dev/hda1       /               ext2     defaults          1 1
/dev/cdrom      /mnt/cdrom      iso9660  noauto,owner,ro   0 0
/dev/fd0        /mnt/floppy     auto     noauto,owner      0 0
none            /proc           proc     defaults          0 0
none            /dev/pts        devpts   gid=5,mode=620    0 0
/dev/hda5       swap            swap     defaults          0 0
/dev/hdb1       /mnt/data1      ext2     defaults          0 0
```

The first column is the device name, which is followed by the mount point, the file system type, and various options. The last two columns are referred to as fs_freq and fs_passno. The first of these is used to determine whether the dump command should be used to back up the system. Finally, fs_default is used to determine the order in which fsck should run.

I want to talk about those options. Notice the /mnt/cdrom entry in that table and that one of the options is ro. That's why I could have just typed mount /mnt/cdrom instead of specifying the device and options. The other thing I would like you to notice ("Mom, he's always asking us to pay attention!") is the defaults keyword.

Defaults are exactly what they sound like: defaults. Unless you want something else to happen (either on the command line or in the fstab file), you don't need to enter the information. Table 8.1 displays the defaults for all file systems.

So, what about the devices /dev/hda1, /dev/hdc, and so on? How can you tell what is even available? One way is to look at that /proc file system I

TABLE 8.1: File System Defaults

Default Option	What It Means
rw	Mount partition as read-write.
exec	Allow binaries to be executable.
suid	Recognize the use of SETUID and GETUID bits.
dev	Interpret device files on this file system.
auto	Can be mounted with the -a option.
nouser	Do not allow nonroot users to mount the file system.
async	All disk I/O should be done asynchronously.

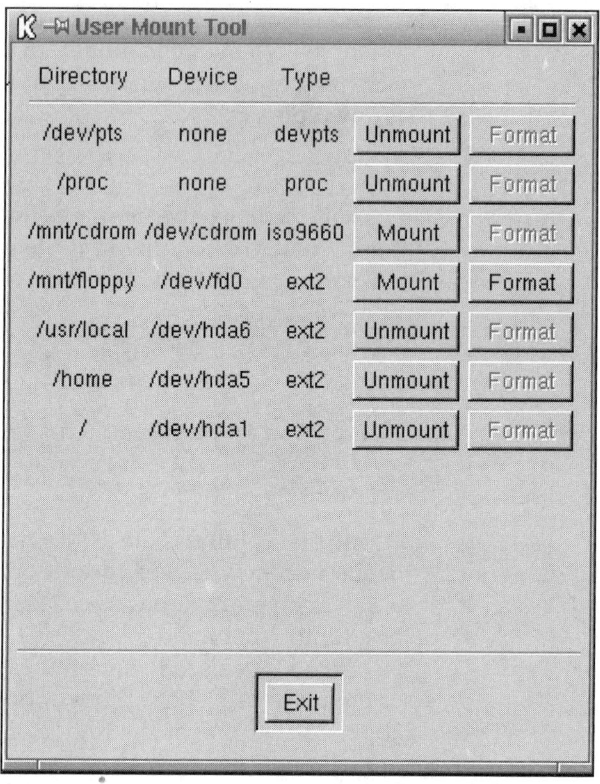

FIGURE 8.3 The usermount tool

talked about. There is a file called partitions that shows you what you have configured and where.

```
[root@othersys /root]# cat /proc/partitions
major minor  #blocks  name

   3     0   12537504 hda
   3     1    2048728 hda1
   3     2          1 hda2
   3     5    8195008 hda5
   3     6    2048728 hda6
   3     7     136048 hda7
  22     0 1073741823 hdc
```

If the file systems are local, you can also gain control of them graphically with the usermount tool (see Figure 8.3). To be able to mount, unmount, and format devices from this interface, you must be root or user must be one of the mount options in /etc/fstab.

Back when we were looking at disk space, I mentioned the KDiskFree tool for KDE. Like usermount, KDiskFree enables you to mount and unmount file systems (with appropriate permissions, of course).

Creating File Systems

So you want to create yourself a file system? Well, in order to create a file system after you have installed the system, you use the `fdisk` command followed by the logical disk. Remember that the first IDE drive is `/dev/hda`, the second is `/dev/hdb`, and so on. To run `fdisk` on the second disk, you use `fdisk /dev/hdb`. Just so that I would have something to demonstrate, I left a tiny bit of space on my first IDE drive.

```
[root@scigate /root]# fdisk /dev/hda
Command (m for help): n
```

This is an interactive session. The `n` you see in the previous code tells the program that I want to add a new partition. I know it says to type m for help and that this isn't particularly intuitive, but try to think "menu" for this program. Continuing with the session, let's add a logical partition.

```
Command action
   l   logical (5 or over)
   p   primary partition (1-4)
l
First cylinder (1002-1023, default 1002):
Using default value 1002
Last cylinder or +size or +sizeM or +sizeK (1002-1023, default 1023):
Using default value 1023
```

As you can see, you don't have a lot of room to play with in terms of partitions, so take everything that is left over. In terms of how big your partition can be, you can specify it in terms of either the last cylinder (which is what I did with 1023), the number of cylinders (I could have typed +6 to specify 6 cylinders), the number of megabytes (+20M means 20MB), or the number of kilobytes by using a K instead of an M. Type p to print the table (just to the screen) and see what you have configured.

```
Command (m for help): p

Disk /dev/hda: 64 heads, 63 sectors, 1023 cylinders
Units = cylinders of 4032 * 512 bytes

   Device Boot    Start       End    Blocks   Id  System
/dev/hda1   *         1       940   1895008+  83  Linux
/dev/hda2           941      1023    167328    5  Extended
/dev/hda5           941      1001    122944+  82  Linux swap
/dev/hda6          1002      1023     44320+  83  Linux

Command (m for help):
```

Now, type w at the command prompt to write the partition table to disk and exit.

> **Warning:** Whenever you do anything that makes drastic changes to your disks, please always do a backup beforehand.

The `fdisk` command enables you to specify a large number of file system types. The default is the Linux `ext2` type, but there are others. To change the system type, use the `t` command and enter a number. You can determine the number you need with the help of the `L` command. Note that this letter is capitalized. Now have a look at Figure 8.4 for an idea of just what is possible.

Using the New File System

Once this information has been written out, you should reboot using the `shutdown` command.

```
# /sbin/shutdown -r now
```

Changes to the partition table are fairly extreme and the OS should have a chance to reread the information without potentially hundreds of programs running. If this is your second disk and you can unmount every partition (this idea automatically excludes the first disk), a reboot should not be necessary. In

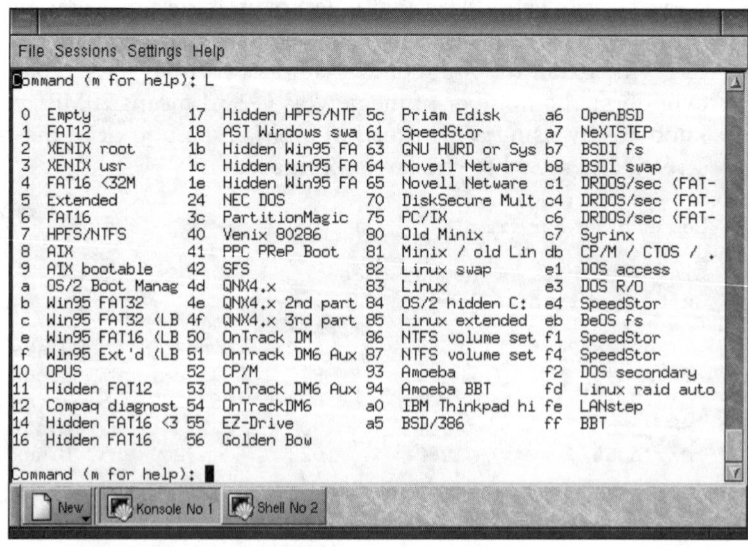

FIGURE 8.4 Choosing a file system type with `fdisk`

the previous example, my free space was on the boot disk, so I have now rebooted (you will just have to trust me) and I am ready to create my new file system.

To do this, I use the `mkfs` command. The `mkfs` command enables me to specify different file system types, but it defaults to the `ext2` file system, which is standard for Linux systems.

```
[root@testsys /root]# mkfs -V /dev/hda6
```

If I wanted to specify the file system type, the command would be similar, but I would use the `-t` flag with a parameter of `ext2`. Here is the output from the command:

```
[root@testsys /root]# mkfs -t ext2 -v /dev/hda6
mke2fs 1.18, 11-Nov-1999 for EXT2 FS 0.5b, 95/08/09
Filesystem label=
OS type: Linux
Block size=1024 (log=0)
Fragment size=1024 (log=0)
11088 inodes, 44320 blocks
2216 blocks (5.00%) reserved for the super user
First data block=1
6 block groups
8192 blocks per group, 8192 fragments per group
1848 inodes per group
Superblock backups stored on blocks:
        8193, 24577, 40961

Writing inode tables: done
Writing superblocks and filesystem accounting information: done
```

Now I have a valid Linux file system. I can create a mount point and start using this partition.

```
[root@testsys /root]# mkdir /mnt/newfs
[root@testsys /root]# mount /dev/hda6 /mnt/newfs
```

Finally, a `df` shows my new file system ready to use.

```
[root@testsys /root]# df /dev/hda6
Filesystem           1k-blocks      Used Available Use% Mounted on
/dev/hda6                42913        13     40684   0% /mnt/newfs
```

Working with Quotas

With quotas, you can use your Linux system to set and enforce limits on disk space usage, and then you simply let the system enforce the policies. If somebody complains, blame the system.

Getting Ready for Quotas

Once upon a time, quota support was something you had to set up in the kernel configuration. Just about any modern Linux distribution will have this support built into the stock kernel, which makes your job that much easier.

To use quotas, you get to revisit the `/etc/fstab` file, specifically those mount options. Rather than show the whole thing, I'll take a couple of lines from that file—two file systems that I will configure for quota support.

```
/dev/hda1       /              ext2    defaults        1 1
/dev/hdb1       /mnt/data1     ext2    defaults        0 0
```

All I have here are the default mount options. To use quotas, I am going to use two new options. One of them enables me to control quotas at the user level, while the other deals with quotas at the group level.

The first is `usrquota` and, as an example, I will set the / (or root) partition so that space is monitored at the user level. The second option, `grpquota`, identifies the partition as being managed at the group level.

```
/dev/hda1       /              ext2    defaults,usrquota        1 1
/dev/hdb1       /mnt/data1     ext2    defaults,grpquota        0 0
```

> Note that the `mount` command doesn't care one way or the other about these options. They are for quota support only.

To actually run things, I will create the quota database files. These files are either called `quota.user` or `quota.group`, depending on whether they maintain information about users or groups. These files live in the root level of the monitored file system. This is not the root directory (/), but rather it is the topmost level of whatever file system you are talking about. In the case of the previous example, this means a `quota.user` file at `/quota.user` and a `quota.group` file at `/mnt/data1/quota.group`. You don't actually have to create these files yourself. If they do not already exist, the system will create them for you in the following command:

```
[root@testsys /root]# quotacheck -uagv
Scanning /dev/hda1 [/] done
Checked 5833 directories and 88825 files
Using quotafile /quota.user
```

```
Scanning /dev/hdb1 [/mnt/data1] done
Checked 5996 directories and 82804 files
Using quotafile /mnt/data1/quota.group
```

The quotacheck command scans the appropriate file systems for quota information and builds the database files. The -a option tells the command to check all file systems. This is the best way to handle this; otherwise, you need to specify the file system on the command line. The -u is actually a default option meaning that you should check for user quotas, but I included it here as a foil to the -g option, which tells the command to scan for group information. The -v, which means "verbose," also does a neat little spinning bar thing while it is scanning.

I haven't actually set any quota limits yet (and I'll get to that), but let's see what kind of information I have just generated. Using the repquota command, I can create a report of just who is using what. In this example, I use the -a flag to specify all file systems, as well as -v, which will report even if there is no usage. Note that the output is truncated because I don't want to bore you with pages of output.

```
[root@testsys /root]# repquota -av
*** Report for user quotas on /dev/hda1 (/)
                        Block limits                File limits
User            used    soft    hard  grace    used  soft  hard  grace
root      -- 1561828       0       0          87038     0     0
bin       --   30476       0       0           1339     0     0
daemon    --    1076       0       0             14     0     0
news      --      80       0       0              2     0     0
uucp      --    4788       0       0             95     0     0
games     --       4       0       0             60     0     0
gdm       --       4       0       0              1     0     0
xfs       --       8       0       0              3     0     0
piranha   --       0       0       0              1     0     0
nobody    --       8       0       0              2     0     0
postgres  --   11516       0       0            594     0     0
mgagne    --   18652       0       0            702     0     0
natika    --     920       0       0            180     0     0
www       --     228       0       0             57     0     0

*** Report for group quotas on /dev/hdb1 (/mnt/data1)
                        Block limits                File limits
User            used    soft    hard  grace    used  soft  hard  grace
root      -- 2566207       0       0          15839     0     0
bin       --   27359       0       0           5686     0     0
daemon    --      12       0       0             13     0     0
disk      --       0       0       0              2     0     0
lp        --       8       0       0              8     0     0
wheel     --   45370       0       0           5020     0     0
mail      --     299       0       0              7     0     0
news      --     412       0       0             10     0     0
uucp      --    4726       0       0            143     0     0
man       --     262       0       0             74     0     0
games     --      32       0       0             73     0     0
```

As you can see, both of the file systems I configured are being reported on. The limits columns are interesting, specifying hard and soft limits as well as a grace period.

The *hard limit* is exactly what it sounds like: an impenetrable wall through which a user may not pass. If a user hits this limit, any further attempts to write to disk are denied.

The *soft limit* is a kind of marshmallow wall. A user can pass through it, but he or she will know because the mark will be upon him or her. The system will warn the user that he or she is past his or her limit and, depending on how the limits have been configured, the user may in time actually be denied access.

This is the *grace period.* Beyond this time, the warnings will ring true as access is finally denied. If you don't want to ever deny access, you can leave the grace period at zero and perhaps, eventually, guilt will overcome your hungry users.

Turning Quotas On and Off

This is one of those weird times when I am going to tell you to reboot your system. Here's why. In order for quotas to really take effect, the file systems being monitored need to be unmounted and remounted in order to set the user limits. If no one is using the file system you want quotas for, you could just unmount and remount it, but this is not possible for the root file system. If you are trying to enforce quotas there, you need to reboot.

Whenever the system reboots, you want to run the `quotacheck` command, so you might as well add this now to your start-up scripts (`rc.local`). Something like this should suffice:

```
/usr/sbin/quotacheck -augv
```

Remember that while the report on usage is cool even at this point, you do want to start enforcing limits, so reboot.

```
# /sbin/shutdown -r now
```

Time passes. . . .

Now that you have rebooted and quotas have been activated, it is possible to turn the whole thing off. No, you don't need to reboot again. You do this with the `quotaoff` command.

```
[root@testsys /root]# quotaoff -auvg
/dev/hda1: user quotas turned off
/dev/hdb1: group quotas turned off
```

To restart the monitoring of quotas, you must reactivate quotas with the `quotaon` command. The `-a` option tells the command to turn on quotas for all file systems appropriately defined in `/etc/fstab`. The `-u` and `-g` flags refer to user and group quotas, and `-v` just gives you a bit of information as it starts.

```
[root@testsys /root]# quotaon -augv
/dev/hda1: user quotas turned on
/dev/hdb1: group quotas turned on
```

Setting Limits

In order to have the system track limits, use the `edquota` command. Using the `-u` flag, specify a user for whom you want to set limits. I'll create a record for the user natika and set some limits. The information for the user will be presented in a temporary file inside a `vi` editor session. If you would rather use a different editor (such as Emacs or Pico), set your EDITOR variable to reflect your preference. In the case of Emacs, the command is this:

```
export EDITOR=emacs
```

Now you can start the `edquota` program with your editor of choice.

```
[root@testsys /root]# edquota -u natika

Quotas for user natika:
/dev/hda1: blocks in use: 280, limits (soft = 0, hard = 0)
        inodes in use: 67, limits (soft = 0, hard = 0)
```

Notice that the soft and hard limits are set at zero. This translates into no limits at all. Let's change it to something reasonable at 5MB of disk space.

```
Quotas for user natika:
/dev/hda1: blocks in use: 280, limits (soft = 5000, hard = 7500)
        inodes in use: 67, limits (soft = 0, hard = 0)
```

Now if natika tries to copy a big file to her account, this is what happens:

```
[natika@testsys natika]$ cp /mnt/data1/packages/apache_1.3.14.tar .
/: write failed, user disk limit reached.
        cp: ./apache_1.3.14.tar: Disk quota exceeded
```

Back to Grace

The `edquota` command enables you to set the grace period as well. You use the `-t` flag for this.

```
[root@testsys /root]# edquota -t
Time units may be: days, hours, minutes, or seconds
Grace period before enforcing soft limits for users:
/dev/hda1: block grace period: 7 days, file grace period: 7 days
```

Finally, it is also possible to define a default user and use that user to clone quotas for others. For instance, if I want to clone natika's limits and assign them to the user guitux, I use the `edquota` command with the `-p` flag.

```
[root@testsys /root]# edquota -p natika guitux
```

Letting the Users Know

The `quota` command itself can be run by any user to let the user know where he or she stands in terms of available disk space. This might be something you decide to put in the `/etc/profile` script so that everybody sees it at login.

```
[natika@testsys natika]$ quota -v
Disk quotas for user natika (uid 504):
    Filesystem  blocks  quota  limit  grace  files  quota  limit  grace
     /dev/hda1     280   1000   5000            67              0      0
```

Resources

Filesystem Hierarchy Standard (FHS)

http://www.pathname.com/fhs/

Filesystems HOWTO (not strictly Linux)

http://www.linuxdoc.org/HOWTO/Filesystems-HOWTO.html

Chapter 9

X and the Graphical Desktop

For the most part, modern Linux systems do all the nasty work of configuring your graphical desktop environment as part of your installation. That is the reason why I have decided to tackle this chapter a little bit differently than the way you'll see X information presented in most books. I am going to start by exposing the world beneath the desktop so that you can quickly delve below the surface and find out what really happens when you run X. Then, I'll cover a few of the desktop environments that are out there and examine how choosing the right one may help the way you do your job, and perhaps more important, help the nonadministrators do theirs. The chapter wraps up with an investigation into fine-tuning X and techniques to deal with some of the problems you may encounter.

It's Just Window Dressing, Right?

I love the command line. It's lean, clean, fast, and powerful.

That said, in all likelihood you will do most of your work in a graphical environment, and if you don't, then others will, including your coworkers. In fact, the prevalence of mature graphical tools and desktops have accelerated the acceptance of Linux in the workforce. Love them or hate them, graphical desktops are here to stay. Furthermore, the proper choice of desktop environment can help make you more productive by enabling you to work the way you want to. Not only that, the configurability and flexibility of the graphical environment can help you solve one of the great challenges of the system administrator: limited resources.

Underneath your fancy desktop is the real graphical engine: the X window system. While there are commercial X window systems, you are more than likely running XFree86, a freeware graphical server. The desktop or window managers, on the other hand, define what your desktop looks like and how it works.

Specifically, window managers control how your windows are resized, what kind of borders programs have, what your background looks like, how icons are set up, how you switch from one application to the next, and so on.

> Here is another way to look at it: Window managers are the graphical user interface *experience.*

Our first stop on this journey is the graphical login manager.

Graphical Login Managers

Linux is a multiuser system by nature. While a number of us instinctively log into the root account when we start up, this is actually a very bad idea (as mentioned in Chapter 7). The root login is there for you to perform administrative functions. While this is the first login you see during an installation, for some users it is also the last. This is not only dangerous, but it also limits the reach of your Linux system.

If you work on the premise that a workstation will be used by a number of different people (either in your company or at home), I recommend that you use a login manager. If your graphical desktop is already up and running and you're not one hundred percent happy with it (maybe it's not enough like another system you may be more comfortable with), you are free to change it. You don't have to work in a desktop environment like everyone else. You can choose what works for you and go with that.

For a multiuser environment in which more than one person will use a workstation, I recommend that you use one of the graphical login programs. For KDE, this is `kdm`, and for GNOME, it is `gdm` (see Figure 9.2). That old favorite, `xdm` (see Figure 9.1), is still available, but those users who are less experienced with Linux may find the default X window environment a little less than friendly.

You can select your default login manager in a couple of different ways. For instance, on a Red Hat system, you set your preference for `kdm` by modifying your `rc.sysinit` script. You'll find that in the `/etc/rc.d` directory. The paragraph you want looks like this:

```
# Set preferred X display manager link
preferred=kdm
if [ -f /etc/sysconfig/desktop ]; then
        if [ -n "`grep GNOME /etc/sysconfig/desktop`" ]; then
                preferred=gdm
```

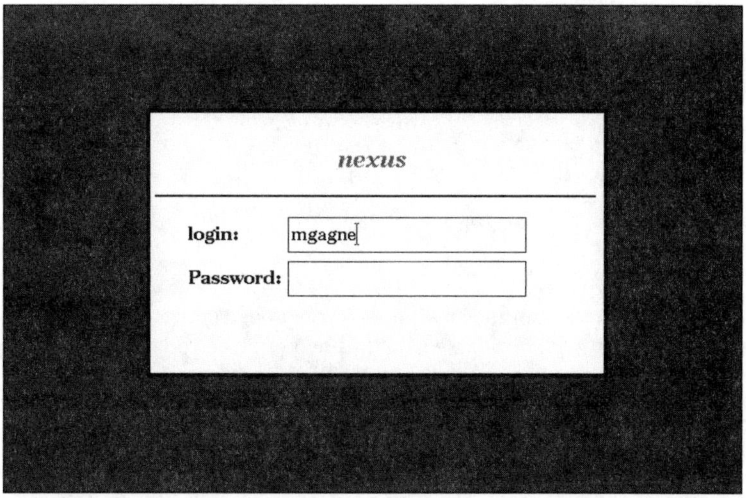

FIGURE 9.1 The simplest of the graphical login managers, `xdm`

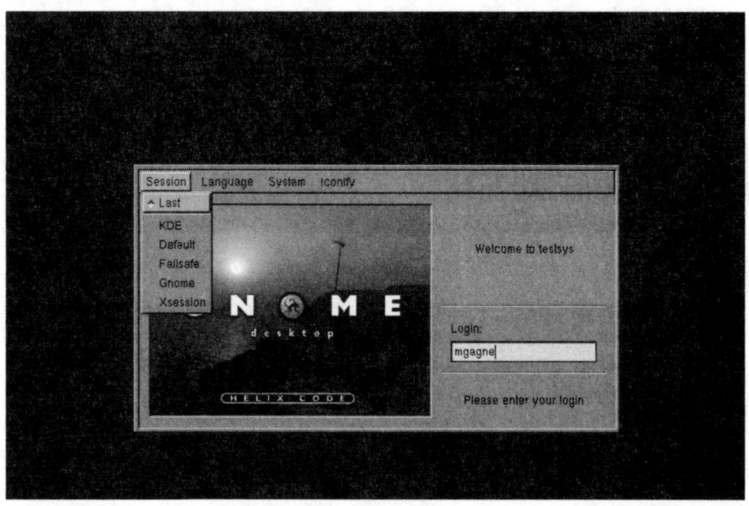

FIGURE 9.2 Advanced login managers like `gdm` offer an alternative to `xdm`.

```
        elif [ -n "`grep KDE /etc/sysconfig/desktop`" ]; then
                preferred=kdm
        elif [ -n "`grep AnotherLevel /etc/sysconfig/desktop`" ];
then
                preferred=xdm
        fi
fi
```

By default, the `preferred=` variable is not set. I changed mine so that it reads `preferred=kdm`. Another way to do the same thing is to edit the `/etc/sysconfig/desktop` file and simply put in the name of your favorite desktop environment. A couple of lines further down (in the next paragraph of the `rc.sysinit`), the system sets the link for `prefdm`, which is then started in your `/etc/inittab` file.

```
ln -snf ../..`which kdm` /etc/X11/prefdm
```

> **Note:** In some incarnations of Red Hat, the decision of where the `preferred` variable is set has been transferred to the `prefdm` script itself.

During your installation, you may have been given the opportunity to let Linux boot into a graphical desktop. If you chose not to do this, you can still change your mind. This is the tail end section of my `/etc/inittab` file:

```
# Run xdm in runlevel 5
# xdm is now a separate service
x:5:respawn:/etc/X11/prefdm -nodaemon
```

Now look at the top, at the line that says `id:5:initdefault:`. As you can see, in this case, the default runlevel (see Chapter 6) is 5. The login manager runs at level 5, which is why it gets started at boot time. If you would rather boot into a text screen and log in at the command line, change your `initdefault` to 3. Then (making sure people are not working on the system) type the following command:

```
# init 3
```

Working without a Graphical Login Manager

This is not really akin to working without a net. Trust me. The various graphical login managers described previously (`kdm`, `gdm`, and `xdm`) are all great ways to provide a means of logging into a multiuser workstation, but for some, the command line login may offer more flexibility, security, or performance despite its plain, unadorned text login screen.

The World beneath the Surface

`xinit` is the master program for starting your graphical desktop. Using various .X files, `xinit` will create, build, and otherwise start up your X window session. But wait—isn't that the idea behind `startx`? Well, in a sense, yes . . .

and no. You see, the problem with using `xinit` to start your X session is that it is so darn complicated (or at the very least, wordy).

`startx` is actually just a Bourne shell front end to `xinit`. In fact, if you take a look through the file `/path_to/startx`, you'll find that after setting a number of variables, paths, and so on, `xinit` is finally called to actually start X. That path, by the way, is pretty much always one of these two:

```
/usr/X11R6/bin
/usr/bin/X11
```

It is actually possible to run X without any desktop or window manager running. The result may look pretty boring, but it's certainly interesting and I invite you to try it. From the command prompt, type the following:

```
xinit /usr/X11R6/bin/xterm
```

You'll notice that you have a completely unadorned X terminal session sitting on a featureless background. The first thing I want you to do is run the `free` command and take note of the change in memory utilization now that this plain and boring X session is running. Now move your mouse pointer. Did you try to grab the terminal window in order to move it? Doesn't work, does it? All right, type a command in that terminal window—`xcalc`, for example. What happens?

The calculator comes up but starts in the same position as the X terminal, which doesn't make for a particularly useful working environment. Press Ctrl-C to interrupt the `xcalc` and type exit at the command prompt. The system returns you to the text-only console.

You can start your desktop system from the command line in the same way. For instance, I could start KDE this way:

```
xinit /usr/bin/startkde
```

The xinitrc File

What happens when you type `startx` is this: The shell script goes out and checks for the existence of a local `.xinitrc` file. In the absence of a local `.xinitrc` file, it looks for the system-wide version. This is called simply `xinitrc` (no dot at the beginning) and is usually found at `/etc/X11/xinit/xinitrc`. Your personal `xinitrc` file, the one that begins with a dot, can be quite simple, as in the case of the one line that read `exec xterm`. That is, in fact, another way to start your unadorned X session. Create (or edit) a `.xinitrc` file in your home directory. If you already have such a file, save it to something like `bak.xinitrc` so that you can restore it afterward. Now create a very simple `.xinitrc` with this one line:

```
exec xterm
```

Notice that you get the same result as you did when you started xterm with xinit. Looking back at the xinitrc files, you will find that the system-wide version is a bit more complex than your personal .xinitrc and it checks for the existence of other .X files to pull into your configuration. For those of you running Red Hat, things are a little tiny bit different. Your system-wide xinitrc file checks for the existence of something called Xclients or its local version, .Xclients.

In a sense, .xinitrc and .Xclients serve pretty much the same purpose. On a Red Hat system, you'll notice that in the absence of a local .Xclients file, it looks to the Xclients file (sitting at /etc/X11/xinit/Xclients). If you don't have a .Xclients file, Red Hat starts GNOME by default. That's a global setting. You can alter this behavior (particularly if you have several users logging into one workstation) by modifying the global Xclients file.

Look for the line near the top of /etc/X11/xinit/Xclients that says PREFERRED=. That variable is set to null right now. Change it to whatever you prefer as the default desktop. If you want KDE, that line should read as follows:

```
PREFERRED=startkde
```

I know that this looks an awful lot like what you did earlier in the chapter to set the default graphical login manager, but these are two different cases.

For the GNOME crowd, replace starkde with gnome-session. There is one other similar file you should be aware of: the .wm_style file. If you follow your global Xclients file, you'll see that it looks to something called .wm_style. This is the local user preference window manager. Just to make things extremely complicated, this is another alternative to .Xclients that allows for some free-form expression. The global Xclients file looks for several variations of the window manager names. For instance, if you want to run Window Maker, you could type WindowMaker, Windowmaker, Wmaker, or wmaker. Scan through the /etc/X11/xinit/Xclients file and you'll find the valid choices.

The .xserverrc File

This is certainly one of the lesser-used files, but you should know about it. .xserverrc defines the X server that you want to run and is almost never used.

The reason for this is that by default, you run one and only one X server, whether it's your SVGA server, your accelerated S3 server, or a straight frame buffer server—namely the one that works for your specific video card. If you don't set anything here, you will run whatever `/etc/X11/X` is linked to. For instance, on the system I am using to write this book on, X is linked to `/usr/X11R6/bin/XF86_Mach64`.

The Xresources File

By now, you may have already started to get the idea that your desktop is an amazingly configurable environment. While the window manager does some things, you can exert further control. For instance, if I start an `xterm` session, I get a nice, flashing blue cursor. Let's say I want that cursor to be red rather than its default blue. I can change that either by creating or modifying my `.Xresources` file.

Before I get into the nitty-gritty of the file structure, you should know that you already have a global file that handles all of this for you. Actually, you have several. Change directory to `/usr/X11R6/lib/X11/app-defaults` and you will find a number of files that predefine some of the standard X applications. In your home directory, you may also find a `.Xdefaults` file that does more or less the same thing. Mine has some defaults set up for several applications, including Emacs, `rxvt`, and `xterm`.

Back to my `xterm`. What changes do I need to make? Well, if I check out the man page for `xterm` with `man xterm` and look for the X resources, I find that cursorColor is the attribute that affects the color of the cursor. If I exit my `.Xdefaults` or `.Xresources` file and add those changes, I get the following. Oh, and I've changed my mind. I would rather change my cursor's color to a hard-to-read wheat.

```
XTerm*cursorColor:       Wheat
```

Notice that I preface the resource with `Xterm*` to tell my X resource file what this resource belongs to (or affects). Because I want these changes to take place without logging out of my X session and logging back in, I need to have the system reread my configuration and incorporate the changes. This is how I do it:

```
xrdb -merge $HOME/.Xdefaults
```

`xrdb`, by the way, is the X resource database utility. This program usually gets run somewhere along the way when you start an X session. On my system, it is called by `/etc/X11/xinit/xinitrc`. If I had created a `.Xresources` file instead, my command would have been as follows:

```
xrdb -merge $HOME/.Xresources
```

I start a new `xterm` and behold, the cursor is a wheat color. Now that you have that down pat, let's try a more interesting example. When I start

Netscape Navigator, I get a menu bar with the word "Help" over on the right. I also get the word "Location" beside my URL address bar. Let's just say for fun that when I need help, it's more like an SOS than a simple request for help. I'd like my browser to display "SOS" for help and "URL" for my location bar. The following is how I tackle this one. At the end of my `.Xdefaults` or `.Xresources` file, I add these lines:

```
Netscape*menuBar.helpMenu.labelString:          S.O.S.
Netscape*urlLocationLabel.uneditedLabelString:          URL:
```

Before I continue, I need to rerun `xrdb` to merge those resources. Now if I close my browser and restart it, things are displayed the way I want them to be. You might be asking by now where I found out how to change these things in Netscape Navigator. I found the X resource for Netscape Navigator in the accompanying documentation distributed with the browser. On my machine (with Netscape Navigator 4.75), this documentation lives at `/usr/doc/netscape-common-4.75/Netscape.ad`.

Specifying Resources on the Command Line

Let's have a look at X resources from a different angle. Start by opening a terminal window and typing `xclock &`. You should get the familiar X window round clock that looks something like Figure 9.3.

Every application that runs during an X session has a number of parameters associated with it. These include geometry, colormap, and others. Using the command `xwininfo` you can find out all sorts of information about the

FIGURE 9.3 The venerable `xclock`

current running application. Simply type `xwininfo -all`, and then click the window you are curious about (`xclock`, for instance).

```
xwininfo: Window id: 0x6400009 "xclock"

  Absolute upper-left X:  690
  Absolute upper-left Y:  20
  Relative upper-left X:  0
  Relative upper-left Y:  0
  Width: 164
  Height: 164
  Depth: 24
  Visual Class: TrueColor
  Border width: 0
  Class: InputOutput
  Colormap: 0x21 (installed)
  Bit Gravity State: NorthWestGravity
  Window Gravity State: NorthWestGravity
  Backing Store State: NotUseful
  Save Under State: no
  Map State: IsViewable
  Override Redirect State: no
  Corners:  +690+20  -170+20  -170-584  +690-584
  -geometry 164x164+686+0
```

Back in the resources discussion, I had you modify things in a `.Xresources` file. Actually, many X applications enable you to modify their resources right on the command line. Let's use that silly `xclock` for an example. When it starts, you see a gray background with black hands. One of the resource flags or modifiers that you can give an X application is `-reverse` (or `-rv` for short). Let's try that.

```
xclock -reverse &
```

Now the hands are white instead of black. Other parameters that you might want to experiment with include `-title`, which lets you change the title text on a window. The `-iconic` parameter starts a window iconified. Don't like the color? In that case, use `-foreground` or `-background` and use a different color. Size matters, so adjust it to your tastes with the `-geometry` flag. I won't show you what the result looks like here, but try these for fun:

```
xclock -iconic &
xclock -title "RoundClock" &
xclock -background "SteelBlue" &
xclock -foreground "Red" &
xclock -geometry 250x250 &
```

Look, Ma! I Can Run Multiple Desktops!

You can, without affecting your current X window session, jump out of that session by pressing Ctrl-Alt-F1. F1 could just as easily be F2, F3, F4, F5, or F6. If you start X from the command line with X, you'll probably see the dialog box for the session when you press Ctrl-Alt-F1. The F2, F3, and other versions should provide you with a text-based login screen. By the way, in case you did not already know this, you can switch from one of these virtual terminals (VTs) to another simply by pressing Alt-F# (where # is the number). To get back to your X window session, press Ctrl-Alt-F7. Go ahead and try it. Flip back and forth. When you are feeling comfortable with this, head on back to your console text screen (Ctrl-Alt-F1).

Now that you have a text screen, let's move on to some fun things. If you are among those running X from the graphical login manager, now is the time to cancel it. Back to those virtual terminals. So, function keys 1 through 6 represent your virtual terminal numbers while function key 7 is your first X session. What about 8, 9, and 10?

A great question that demands a great answer. Well, let's try something fun.

The reason your first X terminal is usually at 7 (*not* 6) is because virtual terminals 1 through 6 are spoken for in your default `/etc/inittab` file. Here's the relevant section from my `/etc/inittab`:

```
# Run gettys in standard runlevels
1:2345:respawn:/sbin/mingetty tty1
2:2345:respawn:/sbin/mingetty tty2
3:2345:respawn:/sbin/mingetty tty3
4:2345:respawn:/sbin/mingetty tty4
5:2345:respawn:/sbin/mingetty tty5
6:2345:respawn:/sbin/mingetty tty6
```

What do you think would be affected if you were to log in as root, take your favorite editor (`vi`, Emacs, Pico, `nano`), and comment out the last line? Give it a try. Remember that like the previous change to the `inittab` (earlier in the chapter), you still need to get `init` to reread the `/etc/inittab` file.

Now, switch to virtual terminal number 6. Suddenly, this is no longer a usable terminal. There is no login prompt. Cool? Well, maybe not, but try this now: Start your X session with the following simple command. You might just remember this from an earlier example.

```
xinit /usr/X11R6/bin/xterm
```

Yes, this is the really boring, plain X screen with a single X terminal up in the top left-hand corner. You have no way to move it and nothing can be done. I'm going to use it to demonstrate something. While you are in that screen, flip back over to your first virtual terminal (Ctrl-Alt-F1). Great. Now, from the text console, go back into your X session by pressing Ctrl-Alt-F7.

Was something wrong? Try Ctrl-Alt-F6 instead. Aha!

What happened here is that `startx` (or `xinit`) in this case started X on the first available free VT, which is now number 6 (because we turned off the `getty` on VT 6). Here comes cool trick number two. Leave your boring X session running and go back to the text console. Now, so that you don't confuse one boring xterm session with another, type this command:

```
xinit /usr/X11R6/bin/xcalc -- :1
```

If you switch back to your text console now, you'll notice some interesting things if you try to revisit your X session. Ctrl-Alt-F6 (assuming you still have VT 6 commented out of the `inittab`) will take you to your `xterm`. To get to your `xcalc` session, press Ctrl-Alt-F7. Because you can't type exit at the command prompt of `xterm`, you need to use the X window escape hatch to close that session.

> **Important Note:** The X window escape hatch or, as some might call it, the "Oh my God, I've tried everything and I can't get out of X" escape clause is Ctrl-Alt-Backspace.

Here's something else that you might find interesting. You can also define which virtual terminal you want X to start on. Say that 10 is your lucky number and you want your X session to start on VT 10:

```
startx -- :1 vt10
```

Backing Up and Restoring the Desktop

The reason for that overview was to get you used to the idea of logging in and creating different profiles for everyone who will use a given PC or workstation. The beauty here is that users are all working in their own *protected* environments. You, as the administrator, can (upon setting up a user just the way you want him or her) back up individual desktops and configurations that can then be stored for quick rebuilds should the user get lost. What's more, you can also create folders or links for all the users on your network from the comfort of your own workstation.

Let's say that a PC is shared by four people and you want each person to have access to a selection of tools. On your own desktop, you have already created this folder (called "Network Tools," for example) and you want all the users to have a folder icon on their desktops. In KDE, this is what you do (note that you are logged in as root, at a shell prompt in your home directory):

```
cd /path_to/home_dir/Desktop
find "Network Tools" -print | cpio -pduvm /home/another_user/Desktop
cd /home/another_user/Desktop
chown -R another_user "Network Tools"
chgrp -R another_user "Network Tools"
```

The next time your users log in, they will find a nice little folder on their desktops with all the appropriate links and icons. Ideally, you would script the previous commands to something that suits you and your environment.

Now, the previous example showed you what to do with a portion of a desktop, but in most cases, you would create a standard desktop layout and provide users with it. The way to do this is to create a skeleton desktop (from a dummy account) and back up the resultant desktop. For this, I might use the `tar` command. My first example is with the KDE desktop.

```
cd /home/skel_user
tar -cvf default_desk.tar Desktop .kde .xinitrc .Xclients
```

Restoring a munched desktop (or preparing for another user) is simply a case of restoring the skeleton desktop in the appropriate directory. For an example, the following uses a user name of "tpeng" and a group name of "staff":

```
cd /home/tpeng
tar -xvf /path_to/default_desk.tar
chown -R tpeng Desktop .kde .xinitrc .Xclients
chgrp -R staff Desktop .kde .xinitrc .Xclients
```

If you use the GNOME desktop, the `.kde` directory is called ".gnome." With the Window Maker desktop, it is called ".wmaker."

Running X Applications Remotely

There's no control like remote control and X provides the tools to run applications from virtually anywhere. While it's true that I think text-based applications make more sense for remote administration, not everything works that way. Sometimes, quite frankly, you would rather run the graphical version of a tool instead.

To administer the runlevels on "marvin" (a host on my network) from my own system, I open up an `xterm` session and run `xhost` to allow client access to my system from marvin.

```
# xhost +marvin
marvin being added to access control list
```

What the `xhost` program does is say that an application from the computer called "marvin" is allowed to run on my machine. From my system, I now `telnet` to marvin. I log in as myself, and switch to the root user in order to do root-level administration.

```
[mgagne@marvin mgagne] su - root
Password: *********
#
```

From here, I set my DISPLAY variable so that X sessions that run on marvin know how to find me.

```
DISPLAY=myhostname:0 ; export DISPLAY
```

That's it. I can now run any of these graphical administration programs (or anything) from the command-line shell prompt.

> **Security Warning:** I don't want to get into this too deeply here, and I will cover it in detail later in the book (Chapters 18, 24, and 25), but this type of environment is only so secure. This type of setup transmits plain-text data and can be picked up by network tools called *sniffers.* Remotely running applications like this may be acceptable for short periods of time, or in a trusted network, but for now be aware that the information transmitted from system to system is in no way encrypted.

Choosing a Window Manager

When I started this chapter, I mentioned that one of the reasons for choosing various window managers was limited resources. The word "resources" can mean an awful lot of things, but what you will often find yourself considering is the memory usage. The modern versions of KDE and GNOME are quite beautiful and powerful, but they do take something out of your system in terms of processor and memory. Processor is a hard resource to manage without buying new hardware. The same goes for memory, of course, but you can manage memory by choosing leaner, less demanding applications.

This is also true for the desktop. Go back to your text-only console screen, type the `free` command, and look at the output. The following is from my own system.

```
              total       used       free     shared    buffers     cached
Mem:         127784      78540      49244      14212      16380      38560
-/+ buffers/cache:       23600     104184
Swap:        122936      70780      52156
```

Notice in particular the second row, under the used column. Not counting memory allocated to buffers and cache, I am using 23600KB of memory (lots of servers running, mail, httpd, postgresql, fonttastic, and so on). I did the same on a Storm Linux system I've been playing with (without quite so many services running) and the numbers were barely 7.5MB. What you are going to do is compare different window managers based on what they offer, how they differ, and most important, the demands they make on your system.

To test the various display managers, you are going to start everything from the command shell. That means using `startx` and working with the simplest possible `.xinitrc` file. That said, let's start with our first candidate for window managers.

The Tab Window Manager (twm)

In your `.xinitrc` file, type the following:

```
exec twm
```

Then start X again. Once again, you have a pretty boring X display, but if you left-click with your mouse, a menu appears (see Figure 9.4).

This is the face of the Tab Window Manager (which is what `twm` stands for). You can move windows around, resize them, and iconize, but not much else. It is possible to modify that menu, by the way. In fact, depending on your version of Linux, you might find that there isn't so much as an `xterm` available in that menu, so modifying it is essential. Your best bet is to just log off

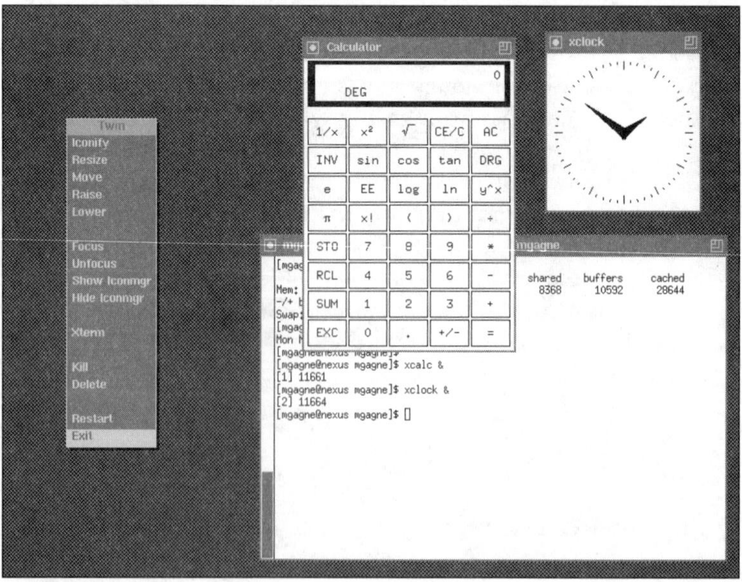

FIGURE 9.4 Plain, but fast, `twm`

(yes, that is on the menu, although you can always use the X window emergency exit: Ctrl-Alt-Backspace).

To add something to that menu, copy the system `twmrc file` from its location in the `/etc/X11/twm` directory into your home directory. The system file is called `system.twmrc` and you want the one in your home directory to be called `.twmrc`. Using your favorite editor, go down near the bottom of the file. The menu section starts with the words "menu defops." After one of the "" `f.nop` lines, add the commands you would like to see on your menu. In my menu, I decided to add the following:

```
""              f.nop
"Rxvt"          !"/usr/bin/rxvt &"
"Xcalc"         !"/usr/x11R6/bin/xcalc &"
```

Run `startx` again and left-click the plain X screen. See your new commands in the menu? Start an X terminal and type `free` again to get a feel for the memory utilization that `twm` demands.

The memory utilization is low, but still that may not seem like much of a reason to run this window manager. Here's a better one: Every release of XFree86 comes with the Tab Window Manager. If you find yourself in an environment where you are looking to use a graphical interface, but nothing other than X exists, you can still work. Then there's that memory thing again. If you do have a need to use an X display but you are running an old, low-memory machine, this may be the only way to achieve your goals with anything resembling decent performance.

Most of us have machines with lots of processor and memory these days, so the lure of the friendly (yes, I'll say it) Windows-like interface is a big deal. Luckily, you don't have to go far to satisfy your needs. The latest Linux distributions usually include several window and desktop managers. One of these is Window Maker.

Window Maker

The GNU Window Maker provides good performance while offering users a rich set of features. It is designed to resemble the proprietary NEXTSTEP desktop. Some of its features include a floating "wharf" for applications and a "dock" for locking in desktop application icons. The dock is the GNUStep icon in the top right-hand corner (in a default installation). You should already see a couple of "dock apps" already docked.

> **Note:** One of the most common problems people run into when trying to run Window Maker for the first time is that the environment is not yet set up. Before you start the program, you need to run a script for the appropriate user. This is the `wmaker.isnt` program.

FIGURE 9.5 A busy Window Maker desktop

Another Window Maker feature is the desktop clip. The clip can be configured to attract icons in the same way as the dock, but its main feature is to provide an easy interface for switching between workspaces and to allow for the creation of additional workspaces.

One of the coolest things about Window Maker is the large of number of dock apps that exist for the window manager. These are icon-sized applications like CD players, performance monitors, calendars, clocks, mini-corkboards, and so on. While I use a number of desktop environments (and I show them off whenever given a chance), Window Maker is one I keep going back to. Figure 9.5 offers a peek at a Window Maker desktop.

Window Maker is quite flashy and enables you to configure your desktop in many different ways. Yes, it even does themes! I will say this, however: Window Maker may not be for the average user and I would think twice about deploying it in an office environment. It is not as intuitive for the Windows-conditioned users out there. If you have relatively fast machines in your office, try either KDE or GNOME (both of which I will talk about shortly). That's the beautiful thing about Linux. You've got lots of choices.

As a Linux user or Linux administrator, you should try all these things out as you get more comfortable with your environment to see what works best for you (and enables you to work efficiently).

Window Maker is probably on your distribution CD. The latest version is always available at the Window Maker Web site (`http://www.windowmaker.org/`).

KDE

Now let's look at one of the two most popular desktop environments out there. Next to GNOME, nothing gets the press and the attention of the KDE desktop environment. Actually, saying "KDE desktop environment" is a bit redundant because KDE stands for K Desktop Environment. What does the K stand for? It stands for "Kool"!

Really.

It's fair to say that KDE deserves all the accolades it has collected. This is a beautiful, polished, and easy-to-use desktop that is rich with applications and tools of every kind. You'll even find a number of games for those times when administrative duties weigh heavily on your mind. Seriously, though, when I set my parents up with their first PC, I loaded Linux and KDE. My parents are people who are very new to PCs and they run Linux.

Once upon a time, the KDE home page used to ask whether UNIX (and Linux) was ready for the desktop. Now, they are talking about the enterprise.

Like the Windows desktops most people are familiar with, KDE includes a nice big button in the bottom left-hand corner that opens up to configuration tools, programs, games, and so on. The desktop switcher is handy in the middle of a familiar looking taskbar that supports dockable applications. (See Figure 9.6.)

In addition to the usual set of tools, KDE features KOffice, a complete productivity suite including a word processor, a spreadsheet program, a

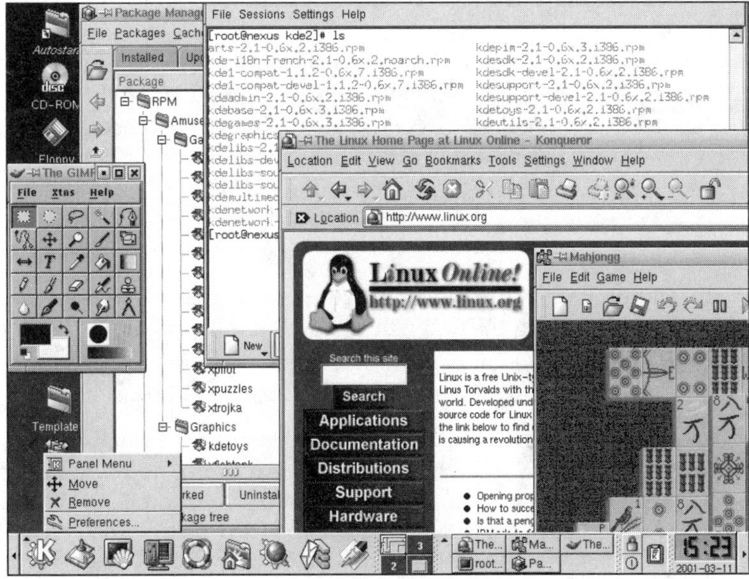

FIGURE 9.6 KDE: An executive-class desktop system

presentation graphics package, and more. To top it off, KDE comes with Konqueror, a multipurpose file viewer and manager that is rapidly becoming one of the best Web browsers on the Net.

The only downside to KDE is that it has become a hungry application and it does require some amount of horsepower, both in processor and memory. A 486 with 16MB of RAM makes a great Linux firewall and Web server, but it won't cut it for KDE.

Like Window Maker, your Linux distribution CD is likely to include KDE, but the latest version is always available at the K Desktop Environment Web site (`http://www.kde.org/`).

Speaking of powerful desktops, allow me to introduce another star in the window manager world: GNOME.

GNOME

GNOME stands for GNU Network Object Model Environment. It is the GNU project's full-featured desktop environment. Under the GNOME panel (a big foot), you'll discover a rich set of applications, system tools, network applications, games, and much more.

The GNOME approach is a bit different from that of the KDE project because it is more of a desktop toolkit than an integrated environment. In some ways, that is part of its strength. Let me give you an example. At the time I was writing this book, GNOME's default window manager was Sawfish. A year earlier, it was Enlightenment.

Because of this plug-it-anywhere approach, a number of window managers (like Window Maker) have integrated GNOME support (sometimes referred to as being "GNOME-aware"). For instance, if you want to run the GNOME environment from Window Maker, you can click Run in the Applications menu and start an `xterm` window. Then type the following:

```
panel
```

If you look at the screen capture in Figure 9.7, you'll see the GNOME desktop running with the Sawfish window manager below.

> **Sneak Peek:** If I've gotten you all excited about trying newer, faster, stronger window managers (maybe even the next very Windows-like candidate) rather than the versions that come with your distribution CD, then have no fear. Getting it means a trip onto the Internet and that is what Chapter 10 covers. Chapter 11 will tell you everything you have ever wanted to know about finding and compiling software but were afraid to ask. Stay tuned.

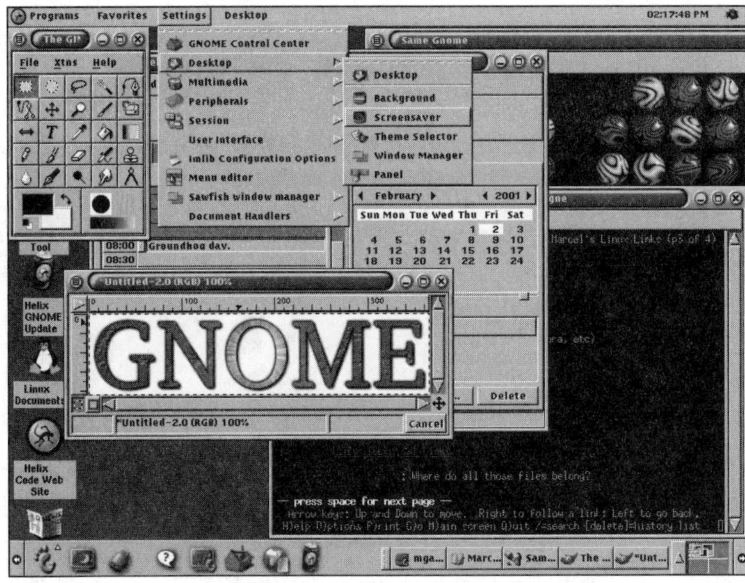

FIGURE 9.7 GNOME offers a slick, polished desktop environment

One of GNOME's strengths at this time comes from its association with HELIX. That strength is an easy-to-use network update and installation facility. In terms of installation, if you have an Internet connection, GNOME is a breeze to install and keep up-to-date. Pay a visit to the Ximian Web site (`http://www.ximian.com/`) and enjoy.

Let's have a look at one more X window manager before we move on.

Qvwm

When I first saw qvwm, I wondered if it was an inside joke on the part of the developer. This particular little window manager is a special treat for those who just can't shake that Redmond habit. If you happen to be administering an office where you have decided to put Linux on some desktops and your people are getting teary-eyed for those days of the Start button and that Windows look and feel, then Kenichi Kourai may have just the thing (see Figure 9.8).

Under the surface, though, it is still Linux. It is not quite as user-friendly as some of the more advanced desktop and window managers, as it requires you to manually edit configuration files rather than the old "right-click, New, and away you go." It does, however, provide you with virtual desktops and a pager, thereby making it quite useful as a Linux desktop.

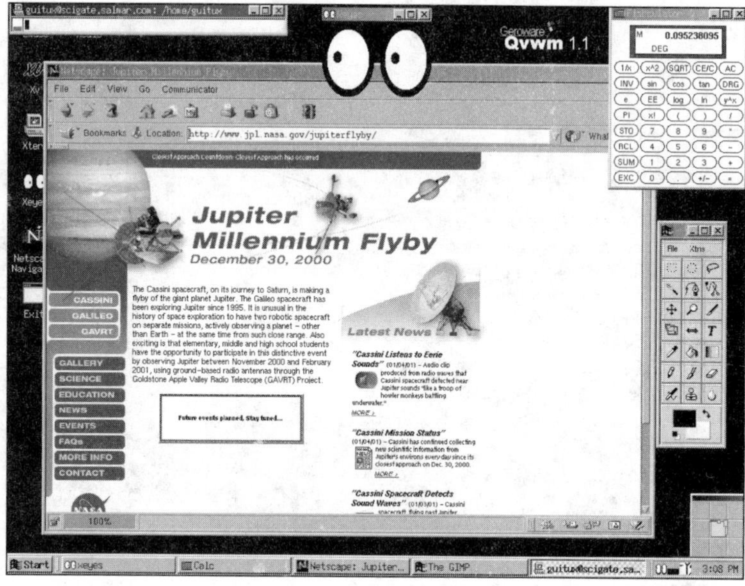

FIGURE 9.8 qvwm's familiar face

Source packages are available free from the qvwm Web site (`http://www.qvwm.org/`) as are precompiled binaries in the form of Red Hat RPMS.

Tweaking X and Dealing with Problems

As I mentioned at the beginning of the chapter, most modern Linux distributions deal very nicely with the whole process of setting up and running X. Most, however, isn't all. From here until the end of the chapter, we are going to look at some of the weirdness you may run into when using X and, best of all, what you can do about it.

Key Mapping

One of the most common and frustrating things that happens when people set up their X window systems has to do with the Backspace key. You open a terminal window (or e-mail or Netscape Navigator), start typing, and nothing works. The easy fix for this is to define a new key with `xmodmap`. This utility is designed specifically to remap keys for use under X. Let's pretend that you have a terminal session open and that your Backspace key does not work (usually the case). Type the following:

```
xmodmap -e 'keycode 22=BackSpace'
```

You can also use the command to modify the behavior of your mouse. Let's say that you have a three-button, right-handed mouse but you are left-handed. It would be really nice if you could reverse the order of the buttons. No problem. Try this:

```
xmodmap -e 'pointer = 3 2 1'
```

If you want to put your mouse back to what it was originally, change the "3 2 1" back to "1 2 3." Of course, this is not what you want to do each and every time you restart X. To make the changes permanent, add the command to your `.xinitrc` file just before your `exec window_manager` command (as discussed earlier).

Tuning Video Modes with xvidtune

When it comes to tweaking your X environment, one fascinating program you should be aware of is `xvidtune`. `xvidtune` gives you an interface through which you can adjust the video modes, making your display wider, taller, narrower, or whatever. There are two sides to the `xvidtune` display. One shows your vertical settings while the other shows your horizontal settings. To make display tweaks with `xvidtune`, simply click any of the adjustment buttons (left, right, wider, taller, and so on), and then click Test to see the results on your screen. If you like what you see, click Show. This will give you an updated ModeLine configuration that you then add to your `XF86Config` file. A quick tour through the file (usually at `/etc/X11/XF86Config`) will show you several defaults. Figure 9.9 shows `xvidtune` in action.

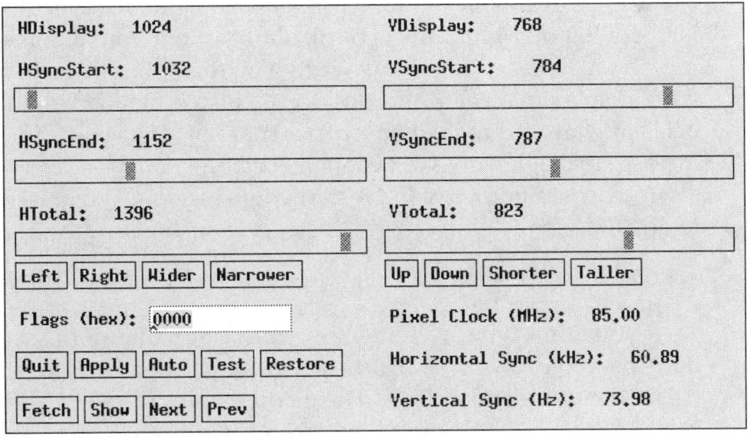

FIGURE 9.9 Modifying video settings with `xvidtune`

If you want to tweak your X display settings, then try this: Immediately after starting `xvidtune` from the command line, click Show and make a note of those settings. Here's what mine look like:

```
Vendor: Unknown, Model: Unknown
Num hsync: 1, Num vsync: 1
hsync range 0:  30.00 -  70.00
vsync range 0:  50.00 - 180.00
"1024x768"      85.00   1024 1032 1152 1360    768  784  787  823
```

The last line is the result of me clicking Show after starting `xvidtune`. The lines before are printed out when `xvidtune` starts. Now, have a look in your `XF86Config` file. Do any of the ModeLine parameters look familiar? One of them should be an *exact* match. After fiddling with the horizontal numbers a bit, then clicking Test followed by Show, I get this modified version of my settings:

```
"1024x768"      85.00   1024 1032 1152 1396    768  784  787  823
```

What this did, by the way (because my screen looked just fine before I started to muck about), was make it narrower. I took the top line and added it to my `/etc/X11/XF86Config` file just below the original line and commented out the original line (always have a backup!). Because my system was working just fine, I didn't want to lose my settings. The point of this is that not every X window configuration looks perfect and not every screen lets you modify its settings through those little buttons. Furthermore, even on a physical screen, tuning the screen through the buttons may mean that your X window display looks great, but your text screens are out of whack.

The "Messed Up" X Session

Every once in a while, your X display is going to do something weird. Things just won't look right. This is particularly true if you, like me, tend to experiment a lot. In the course of my writing on this subject, I have often tried different X display managers and desktops. I also download and test-drive a lot of beta software and more than my fair share of alpha software. Consequently, a messed up display does occasionally occur.

You can shut down X and restart your session, but that isn't the way we like to do things in the Linux world. Instead, try using the `xrefresh` command.

```
xrefresh
```

If you don't type anything else, `xrefresh` blanks the screen (this is very quick) and redraws on a blank background. For a fun effect, try specifying a color from which to redraw. This is done with the `-solid` flag, as in "solid color." In this example, my X session gets redrawn from a flat red background:

```
xrefresh -solid red
```

Screen Captures

Before I wrap up this chapter, I have a special treat for you. I am going to answer one of those questions everybody always seems to ask and that you may be asking yourself as well. Ever wondered how to get great screen captures? I mean, how did I get all the nice screen shots of the KDE, GNOME, and Window Maker desktops presented in this chapter? Is there some complicated magic involved in making this happen?

The truth is that there are several ways of getting screen captures. Desktop packages have their own little utilities. For instance, with KDE, you can click the big K, choose the Graphics menu, and then click Screen capture. Have a look at Figure 9.10 to see how that one works.

Personally, the method I prefer is to use a nice little tool that comes with your system and is probably installed. It is called `import` and here is an example of how it works:

```
import -border -frame -colorspace GRAY image_name.jpg
```

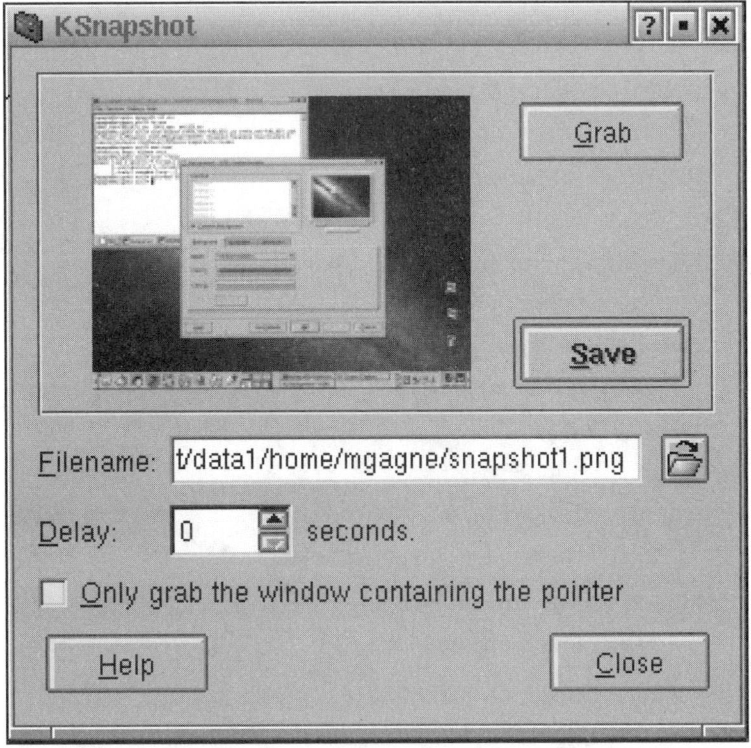

FIGURE 9.10 KDE's screen capture utility

Once you press Enter, the cursor changes to a cross. Click the cursor on the window that you want to capture and it will be saved to whatever filename you decide on. What makes this tool quite flexible and so very nice to use is that you can just define your image type by specifying the appropriate extension. If you prefer a PNG file, change the .jpg extension to .png.

If you want to capture the entire desktop, try this version of the command:

```
import -window root my_screenpic_name.jpg
```

Want something even more fun? You can capture a remote screen on another X display, as long as the proper `xhost` permissions have been granted (as discussed earlier).

```
import -window root -display remotehost:0 screen_cap.tif
```

That will capture the entire desktop of the machine called "remotehost" and save the whole thing to a TIF file called `screen_cap.tif`. Ah, too much fun.

Resources

GNOME Window Manager

http://www.gnome.org/

ICE Window Manager

http://icewm.sourceforge.net

K Desktop Environment (KDE) Home Page

http://www.kde.org/

Qvwm Home Page

http://www.qvwm.org/

Window Maker

http://www.windowmaker.org/

Window Managers for X

http://www.plig.org/xwinman/

XFree86 Project Official Web Site

http://www.xfree86.org/

Chapter 10

Dialing Up to the Internet with PPP

A lot of what I cover in this book requires that you have some means of getting your hands on additional software. You may also want to check out some of the sites I point you to where open source programmers offer you different, sometimes easier, ways of doing things. In fact, the very next chapter talks about finding, getting, and installing software, which makes this chapter seem kind of timely.

There is a common theme to all of this: It requires access to the Internet and I certainly don't want you booting up into some other operating system just so you can get on the Net. In this chapter, I'll show you how it's done.

> **Note:** Whether you have a high-speed connection with a router coming into your home or office, this is still good information to have. Many ISPs offer commercial clients roaming dial-up accounts so that you can easily connect to your network when you are on the road. Knowing the right magic to get your connection up and rolling can be a lifesaver.

The Basics

In the spirit of showing you what goes on underneath first and getting flashy later, let me show you the basics of a Point-to-Point Protocol (PPP) connection. Then I will show you ways to make the whole process even simpler than that. The very first thing you need to do is make sure that you have PPP installed. PPP is the means by which the vast majority of Internet service providers

(ISPs) make it possible for their clients to connect. Chances are you already have the package installed.

PPP can be installed as a package. In Red Hat, Caldera, or any of the Linux distributions that use the Red Hat Package Manager (RPM), you can use this command:

```
rpm -ivh ppp-somereleasenumber.i386.rpm
```

If you are running Debian, Corel Linux, or Storm Linux, the command is similar.

```
dpkg -i ppp_somereleasenumber.deb
```

Actually, for you Debian users, there is a nicer way to do this (called `apt-get`), but I'll talk about that in the next chapter. Besides, it involves already being connected to the Net, which is what you are doing here.

For brevity's sake, I will not try to go into whether your kernel has PPP support compiled in and what to do if it does not. Modifying and compiling your kernel are covered later in the book. Besides, if you have anything resembling a recent Linux distribution, I can pretty much guarantee that PPP support is already there.

What You Need from Your ISP

The next step is to get some information from your ISP: your user name (which will most likely be your e-mail address as well) and password, along with the DNS, or domain name server address. Obviously, you need the ISP's phone number to be able to dial up into their network. If you do have one of those roaming accounts I mentioned earlier, make sure you get a list of local access numbers in areas you might be frequenting. Keep that list on your Palm Pilot, Handspring, or PDA of choice.

You should also have the mail server information for your e-mail package. The sorts of information you need to get are POP and SMTP server addresses.

Some ISPs use a proxy for browsing. Ask about this and, if this is the case with your ISP, keep that information handy. This doesn't have anything to do with connecting, but you will need it when you run Netscape Navigator. Finally, if you plan to make use of services such as network news (and you probably will), make sure you have the NNTP server information handy as well.

Where the Information Goes

When your ISP gives you the DNS address, edit the file `/etc/resolv.conf` with your favorite editor and add that information as follows (the XXXs are of course replaced by the numbers your ISP provides):

```
nameserver XXX.XXX.XXX.XXX
```

Definitions: POP is the Post Office Protocol. Like many Internet protocols, this one has advanced somewhat. Your ISP is probably using (or serving) POP3, or POP version 3. POP is the means by which an e-mail client picks up the mail.

SMTP is the other side of the mail question. It stands for Simple Mail Transport Protocol and it is the program that does the transporting of messages from one location to the other.

NNTP is the Network News Transfer Protocol. This is the communication standard that allows for transfer of Usenet messages between clients and servers. Netscape Communicator has an NNTP-enabled newsreader. As part of your Linux distribution, you will also find `tin` and `trn`. In the graphical world, look for the classic X program, `xrn`, `knode` in KDE, and `pan` in GNOME.

A PPP setup in its simplest form involves a chat script and a properly configured options file. These files are most likely under the `/etc/ppp` directory. There are more elegant ways of setting up PPP, but working with the raw files like this will give you a very good idea of how everything ties in.

The first thing to do is edit the options file. Mine looks like this:

```
/dev/modem
57600
modem
crtscts
lock
defaultroute
noipdefault
connect "/usr/sbin/chat -vf /etc/ppp/chat-script"
```

My modem lives on `/dev/ttyS0`, but I also have a symbolic link to `/dev/modem` for convenience (`ln -s /dev/ttyS0 /dev/modem` is the command to create that link if it does not exist).

What do the other items mean? `57600` is my baud rate, and `crtscts` means that my modem should use hardware flow control. The `lock` statement means that `pppd` should create a lock file to ensure that some other user does not try to use my modem while I am trying to connect to my ISP (remember, Linux is a multiuser system). The next parameter, `defaultroute`, means that a default route to my PPP interface should be established after the connection is up. That means that all nonlocal traffic knows to go out through my point-to-point interface. The last parameter (before `connect`) is `noipdefault`, which means I did not specify a local address for the connection. The `pppd` daemon will try to figure this out on its own by getting the local address from the system.

The connect statement describes how you go about establishing this PPP connection. This is your chat script. `chat` is a command whose purpose in life is to establish a connection with your ISP. This little program talks to your modem and watches for things like the CONNECT string or a login prompt. A sample chat script follows.

```
ABORT 'NO CARRIER'
ABORT 'NO DIALTONE'
ABORT 'ERROR'
ABORT 'NO ANSWER'
ABORT 'BUSY'
"" ATZ
OK ATDT5550000
CONNECT ""
ogin: myISPlogin
ssword: myISPpassword
```

This is the classic `expect/send` script. Expect nothing, and then send `ATZ` to reset the modem. When the modem responds with `OK` (you expected that, right?), send `ATDTyourISPphonenumber`, and so on.

The previous example is extremely simple, but it works. I kill this connection by finding the process ID of `pppd` and terminating it with a `kill` command. For the down and dirty of PPP, check out the latest PPP HOWTO on the Linux Documentation Project Web site (you'll find the URL in the Resources section at the end of this chapter).

The Graphical Alternative

If you are running KDE as your desktop, click the big K, choose the Internet menu and then click Internet Dialer. You can also just start the application with the command `kppp &` from an X window terminal session.

When KDE's Internet connection tool comes up for the first time, there isn't much to see because nothing has been configured. You'll see a blank Connect to list, as well as blank user name and password fields. To get started, click the Setup button. This will take you to the Kppp Configuration screen. This is a nice tool in that you can use it to create and maintain several dial-up accounts. Most people will probably use just one, but you can also use it to set up multiple profiles of the same account. People who travel with a notebook can create profiles for the various cities they visit.

From the Account setup window, click New to create a new account. You'll be asked for a connection name, a phone number for your ISP, and the authentication type (see Figure 10.1). This defaults to PAP authentication (which most ISPs today use). If your ISP still has you go through some kind of authentication script (such as the `expect/send` dialogue I discussed earlier), choose Script-based from the list.

Notice that you have some additional tabs on the menu. The IP tab enables you to manually enter the IP address provided by your ISP. Because most dial-

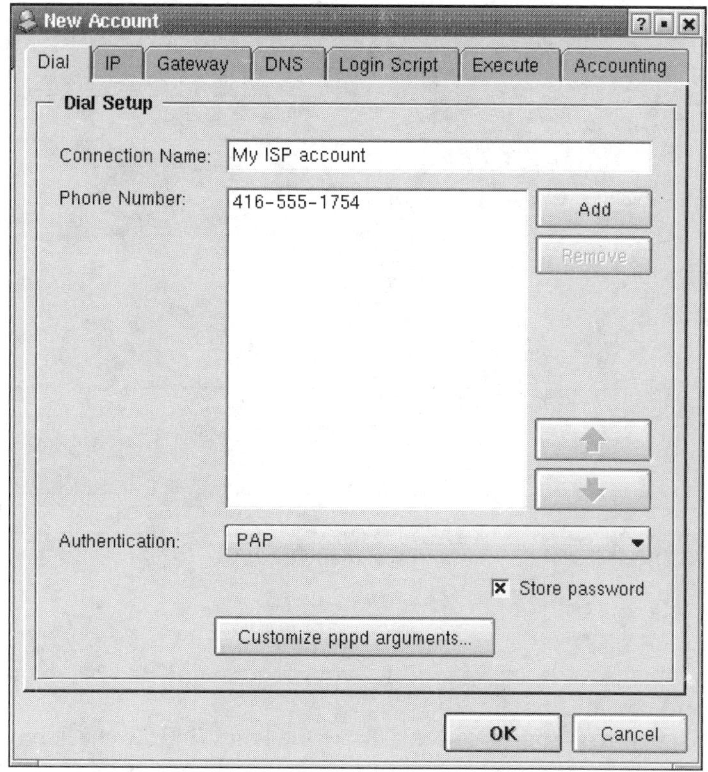

FIGURE 10.1 Setting up an account with Kppp

up accounts use dynamic addresses, that is the default selection and you probably don't have to change anything there. The same goes for the next tab, the Gateway tab. This is usually set for you as you connect. Once again, you can override this setting by providing a static gateway address if your ISP provides it.

In all likelihood, you will want to configure an address here as indicated by your ISP. Click the Manual button. Enter the DNS address you were given into the DNS IP Address field, and then click Add. If you have a second address, enter it in the same way.

Of course, the most work you may have to do comes under the Login Script tab, where you may have to provide your dial-up configuration with the appropriate dialogue for a connection. This is also something your ISP should have supplied you with.

When you click OK, you'll find yourself back at the configuration screen. Click OK one final time and you return to the initial Kppp window, with one difference. In the Connect to connection list, your new connection should be

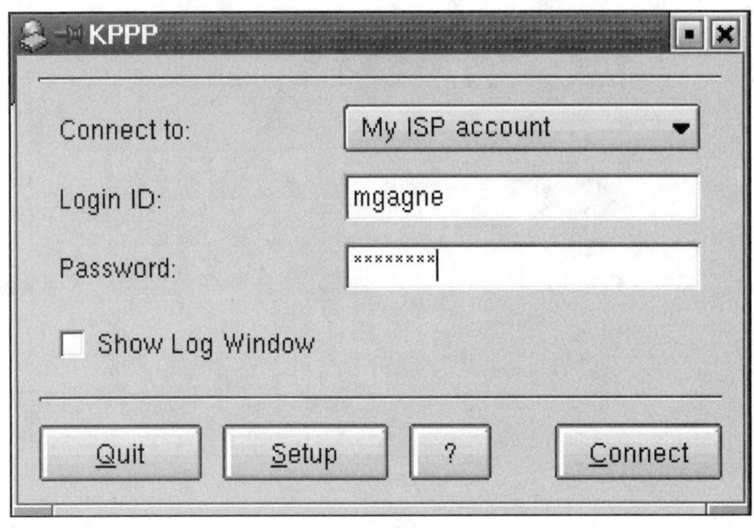

FIGURE 10.2 All configured and ready to surf

visible (see Figure 10.2). Enter your login name and password, click Connect, and you are on your way.

Before I move on, notice the Show Log Window check box. If you find that you are having problems connecting, checking this box will show you a login script window as the connection takes place. This can help you debug any problems you might have with the connection.

Automagic PPP Connections

The whole menu-driven experience is far from complicated. Fill in the blanks and seconds later you are surfing the Net. The truth is that PPP setup is fairly simple; however, little ripples like PAP authentication or CHAP, or even the vagaries of your ISP's login scripting, can make the whole process appear somewhat less than friendly.

To virtually automate the process of whether the connection is PAP, script-based, or whatever, there are a few interesting little programs written for precisely that purpose. I'll cover two programs here: `eznet` and `wvdial`. One of these programs (`eznet`) isn't likely to be on your distribution CD and you may need to get it off the Internet. The catch is that you may not yet be connected, meaning you either use another PC configured for this, or that you have some helpful friend get you the code. Nevertheless, I include it here because of its simplicity.

eznet

Hwaci's eznet software (written by D. Richard Hipp) is a great little piece of software that only needs your login name, your password, and your ISP's phone number, and you are pretty much ready to roll. You don't need to know about the authentication methods, the scripting, or anything else. The program tries to figure all this out on its own. Start by visiting the Hwaci site (http://www.hwaci.com/sw/eznet/) and getting the source code (one single C program file).

The next step is to build the software.

```
gcc -o /usr/bin/eznet -O eznet.c
chown root.root /usr/bin/eznet
chmod 4755 /usr/bin/eznet
```

> **Note:** The eznet binary *must* live in /usr/bin. Notice as well that the binary runs root SUID (as discussed in Chapter 7). For users other than root to initiate the connection, this is necessary. If you are happy dropping to a root prompt to start your PPP connection, you can do a chmod 755 /usr/bin/eznet instead.

That's all there is to it. To use the program, type the following command:

```
eznet add service="MyISP" user=myISPlogin \
    password="myISPpass" phone=555-1754
```

Obviously, you should substitute your own name for the connection, as well as your own login name, password, and ISP phone number. The backslash at the end of the first line is a shell continuation character. It is only there because I couldn't fit the whole command on one line.

To bring this connection up (assuming your service is called "MyISP"), type the following command:

```
eznet up MyISP
```

The program will report on its success (or failure). To bring down the connection, use the same command, but substitute "down" for "up." If you do have problems (bad password?), you can check the log with this command:

```
eznet log
```

There is also an X window front end to the eznet package written by Mark Hall. It is actually a Tcl/Tk (a scripting language) front end to eznet (as opposed to pure X) and it is called xeznet. You get it from the eznet Web site. To run it, you will need to make the script executable.

```
chmod +x xeznet
```

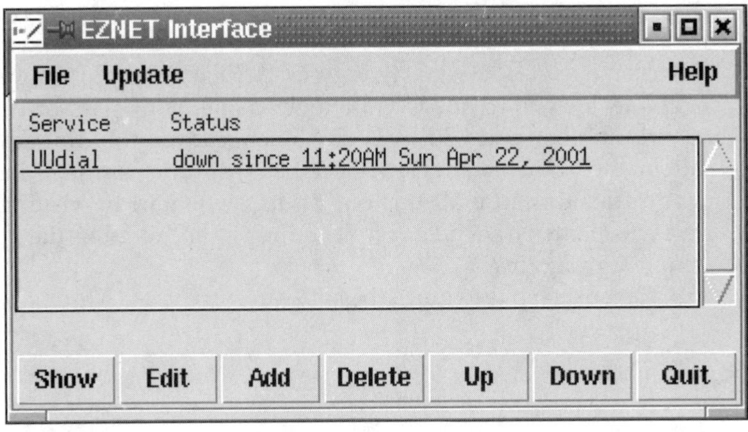

FIGURE 10.3 `xeznet`: An X window interface to `eznet`

Starting the `xeznet` interface is easy. Simply type `./xeznet &` (you can also supply the full path to wherever you have decided to store the script). To see `xeznet` in action, have a look at the screen shot in Figure 10.3.

wvdial

The next program, `wvdial`, comes from Worldvisions Computer Technology, Inc. Like the previous example, this is a wonderfully intelligent tool for connecting to your ISP. Like `eznet`, you can run `wvdial` from the command line or you can use a graphical interface. Here's a treat: Almost every Linux distribution comes with this program and some Linux distributions include their own graphical interface to `wvdial`. In the case of Red Hat, the package is called `rp3` and it includes a wizard-style program called `/usr/sbin/rp3-config` (see Figure 10.4). SuSE has a Tcl script called `wvdial.tcl`. Check your distribution CD before you head for the Net.

Because of its popularity, a number of other graphical front ends to the program have been developed, including Patrick Patterson's KDE-based `kwvdial` and Joergen Scheibengruber's GNOME-based `gppp-wvdial`.

What makes `wvdial` simple is the `wvdialconf` program. Start it like this:

```
wvdialconf /etc/wvdial.conf
```

Those of you who installed it with Debian's `dpkg` have already seen this step. It happens as part of the installation. The first time you run the program, it will go through an autodetection sequence and automatically pick up and configure your modem.

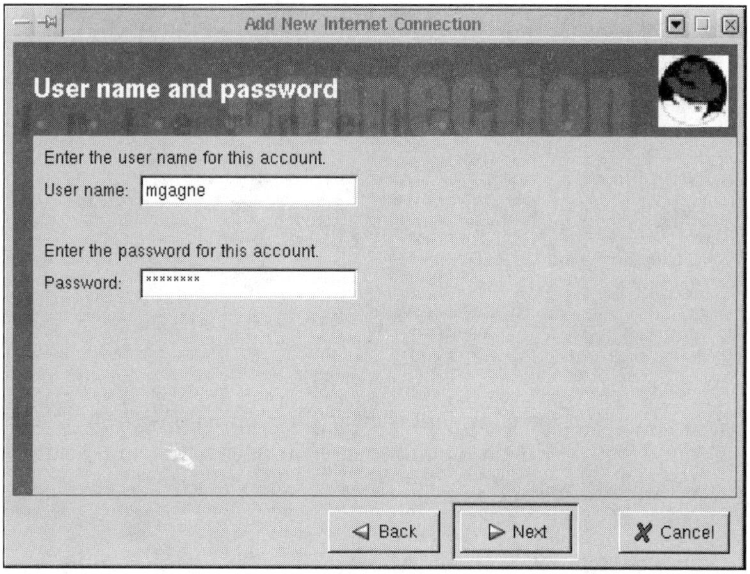

FIGURE 10.4 `rp3-config`: Red Hat's front end to `wvdial`

```
# wvdialconf /etc/wvdial.conf
Scanning your serial ports for a modem.

ttyS0<*1>: ATQ0 V1 E1 -- OK
ttyS0<*1>: ATQ0 V1 E1 Z -- OK
ttyS0<*1>: ATQ0 V1 E1 S0=0 -- OK
ttyS0<*1>: ATQ0 V1 E1 S0=0 &C1 -- OK
ttyS0<*1>: ATQ0 V1 E1 S0=0 &C1 &D2 -- OK
ttyS0<*1>: ATQ0 V1 E1 S0=0 &C1 &D2 S11=55 -- OK
ttyS0<*1>: ATQ0 V1 E1 S0=0 &C1 &D2 S11=55 +FCLASS=0 -- OK
ttyS0<*1>: Modem Identifier: ATI -- 5601
ttyS0<*1>: Speed 2400: AT -- OK
ttyS0<*1>: Speed 4800: AT -- OK
ttyS0<*1>: Speed 9600: AT -- OK
ttyS0<*1>: Speed 19200: AT -- OK
ttyS0<*1>: Speed 38400: AT -- OK
ttyS0<*1>: Speed 57600: AT -- OK
ttyS0<*1>: Speed 115200: AT -- OK
ttyS0<*1>: Max speed is 115200; that should be safe.
ttyS0<*1>: ATQ0 V1 E1 S0=0 &C1 &D2 S11=55 +FCLASS=0 -- OK
ttyS1<*1>: ATQ0 V1 E1 -- ATQ0 V1 E1 -- ATQ0 V1 E1 -- nothing.
Port Scan<*1>: S2   S3

Found a modem on /dev/ttyS0.
ttyS0<Info>: Speed 115200; init "ATQ0 V1 E1 S0=0 &C1 &D2 S11=55
+FCLASS=0"
```

Easy, huh? Now, using your favorite editor, edit the file called `/etc/wvdial.conf`. You'll see something that looks like this:

```
[Dialer Defaults]
Modem = /dev/ttyS0
Baud = 115200
Init1 = ATZ
Init2 = ATQ0 V1 E1 S0=0 &C1 &D2 S11=55 +FCLASS=0
SetVolume = 1
Dial Command = ATDT
Init4 = ATM0
; Phone = <Target Phone Number>
; Username = <Your Login Name>
; Password = <Your Password>
```

Remove the comment marks (the semicolons) from the last three lines and enter your ISP's phone number, your user name, and your password as in the following example.

```
Phone = 905-555-1784
Username = MyISPlogin
Password = MyISPpassword
```

To bring up this connection, type `wvdial`. That's all there is to it. The program will let you know of its progress as the connection is initiated. To terminate the connection, simply press Ctrl-c.

Resources

`gppp-wvdial`

`http://mfcn.ilo.de/gppp/`

Hwaci Home Page (`eznet`)

`http://www.hwaci.com/`

`kwvdial` **Home Page**

`http://www.carillonis.com/~ppatters/kwvdial.html`

Linux PPP-HOWTO

`http://www.linuxdoc.org/HOWTO/PPP-HOWTO/index.html`

`wvdial` **Home Page**

`http://www.worldvisions.ca/wvdial/`

Chapter 11

Finding, Building, and Installing Software

The average Linux distribution CD comes with several gigabytes of software. SuSE, for one, delivers several CDs in a boxed set with enough software to keep you busy for several weeks at least. Sooner or later, though, you will find yourself visiting various Internet sites for new and updated software. Part of your job as a Linux system administrator is to keep on top of security updates for your system. These are usually available from your vendor, but sometimes the quickest way to find an update you need is to go to the software's development site. That means building it yourself.

A perfect example of this is a new security exploit that requires the latest version of BIND (the Domain Name Service suite of programs) or a new `sendmail` to protect you (or even your Windows workstations) from allowing a fast-spreading virus or worm from wreaking havoc. Remember the ILOVEYOU worm from early 2000? An up-to-date version of `sendmail` enabled you to write rules that would filter it out and keep it away from your networked Windows workstations.

In this chapter, you'll find out where to get software and what to do once you have the software. How do you install it? What should you know?

> **Security Note:** When you install software and software packages, you must often do it as the root user. Remember, as root, you are all powerful. Know where your software comes from and take the time to understand what it does. When you compile software (which I cover in this chapter), it might even be a good idea to get into the habit of building as a nonroot user, and then switching to root for the installation portion.

Finding Software and Software Review Sites

It's a techno-jungle out there. Actually, it is probably more like a techno-rainforest in the sense that the landscape is lush with an incredible variety of software offerings. Having identified your software needs represents only the first step in getting the software. Like an early hunter-gatherer, you need to leave the comfort of your local network and venture forth into the world. The hunt is on.

Wait! This is the 21st century, isn't it? We have supermarkets with products from every region of the world nicely stacked, labeled, and sorted on shelves. What we need is a software supermarket and in the following section, I am going to take you on a tour of some of the bigger, more popular software repositories and software review sites. Because much of what you'll find there is *free* software, perhaps you'll be more comfortable thinking of this as a tour of all-you-can-eat buffets.

Hungry? Let's start with your protein.

Freshmeat

When I go looking for something and I don't quite know what it might be, I head to Freshmeat (`http://www.freshmeat.net/`). This site provides a huge database of software projects that are indexed, sorted, and searchable (see Figure 11.1).

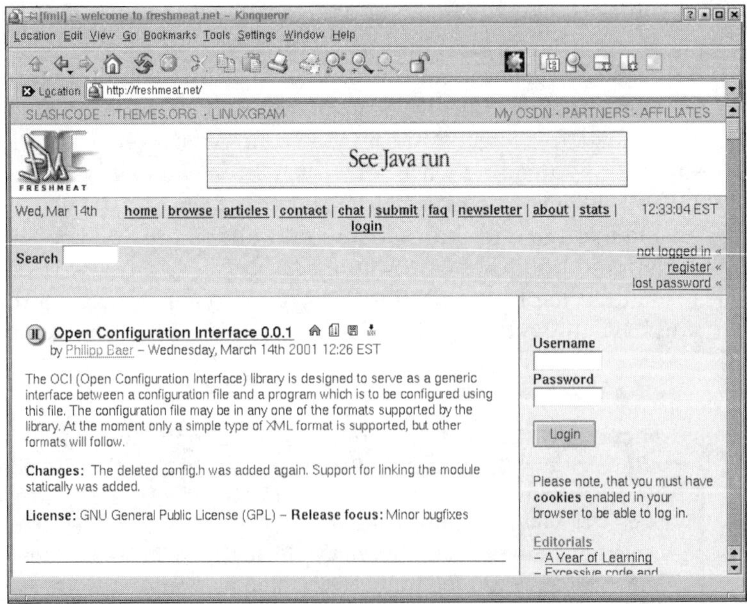

FIGURE 11.1 A visit to Freshmeat

Aside from being a software repository, Freshmeat has daily (sometimes hourly) news clips detailing the latest developments on your favorite software package. The site provides a release history, the number of hits (obviously through the site and not worldwide), links to the project home pages, descriptions, and comments. Freshmeat is a gold mine and a little piece of geek heaven, but it is also a colossal haystack. Luckily, it is a haystack without pins, so jumping in and rooting about may just turn out to be the most fun you've had looking for that elusive bit of code.

TUCOWS Linux

Personally, I liked the name better when it was LinuxBerg, but that's just me. The TUCOWS site (`http://www.tucows.com/`), famous for being a treasure trove of Windows software, has branched out to embrace many other environments. Among these environments, you'll find the various incarnations of that other OS, Palm OS software, Macintosh, BEOS, BSD, and our favorite OS of them all, Linux (see Figure 11.2).

Though not as all-encompassing as Freshmeat, this site does feature a search engine, regular features highlighting hot picks, and so on. You can browse by the type of software you are looking for and narrow it down to your desktop environment of choice (console, X11, KDE, or GNOME). Each of these is arranged by category and most of the packages are rated from one penguin (not so great) to five penguins (really great).

> **Quick Tip:** When you bookmark TUCOWS Linux, make sure you bookmark your local mirror to avoid going through the site selection every time.

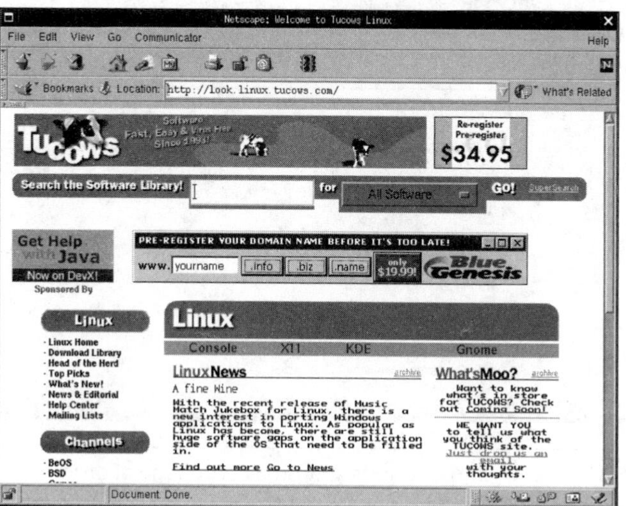

FIGURE 11.2 Touring TUCOWS Linux

SourceForge

If open source development has a meeting place or clubhouse, it may well be SourceForge (`http://www.sourceforge.net/`). SourceForge is a free hosting service for open source development projects. For anyone actively involved in an open source project, this site offers disk space, message boards, bug-tracking systems, archives, backups, and a great deal more. As the price for using this service is certainly right, there is an awful lot here. It is not unusual to find an interesting piece of software reviewed on TUCOWS or Freshmeat only to chase the URL and find yourself at SourceForge.

Like the previously mentioned sites, SourceForge enables you to search by topic, and then narrow down that search to find what you are looking for. For instance, I found an interesting Web-based e-mail client called SquirrelMail by clicking the Communications link (see Figure 11.3) on the Software Map and then clicking the Email link.

If you want to participate in any of these projects or if you want to be able to post your own messages (in case you happen to be tracking a project or looking for support), you can get your own account on SourceForge. It's free. If you are a developer and you want to have SourceForge host your project, it must conform to one of the licenses accepted by the Open Source Initiative (visit `http://www.opensource.org/licenses/` for more information).

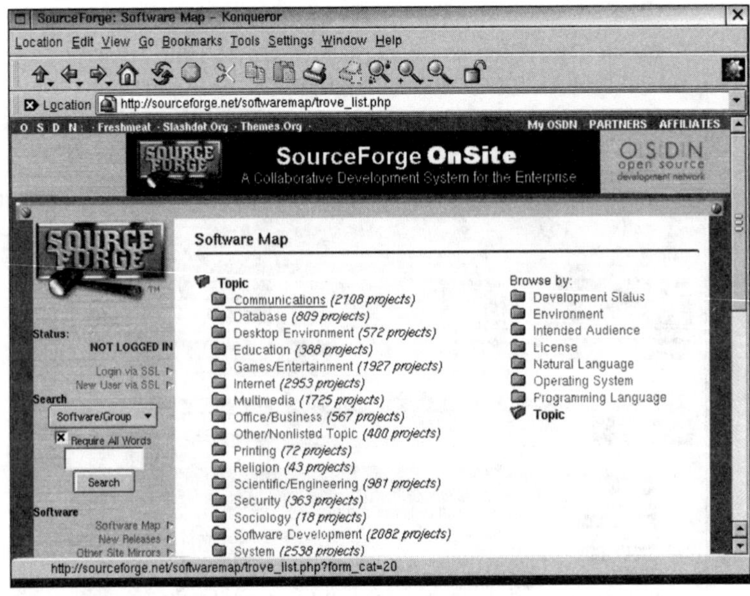

FIGURE 11.3 Browsing development projects at SourceForge

Rpmfind

For those users out there who are running RPM-based Linux distributions, this is a site you *must* know about. The Web site offers a nice search engine where you enter the package name you are looking for and let Rpmfind do its thing. The result is a nice display highlighting various releases, distribution types (Mandrake, Caldera, and so on), and source and binary packages. When the binary (RPM) package you are looking for isn't on your distribution CD and you can't find one on the package Web site either, run, don't walk, to the site at `http://www.rpmfind.net/`.

Another great tool that works with the Rpmfind site is `rpmfind`. Look for it on your distribution CD or download it from the site. Using this tool, you can search the Rpmfind database for RPM packages you may be looking for. The tool is capable of automatically downloading and installing your software for you.

A quick check of Turbolinux and Red Hat Linux distribution CDs shows the `rpmfind` package as being there, so you probably won't have to go looking too far for it. To install it, use the `rpm` command.

```
rpm -ivh rpmfind-release.no.i386.rpm
```

I'll talk more about this, but `-i` tells rpm to install the package. `-v`, meaning "verbose," provides a bit more information, and the `-h` flag prints nice little hash marks on your screen as it does its work. You can get `rpmfind` at its home on the Net. Surf on over to `http://rpmfind.net/linux/rpm2html/rpmfind.html` and get yourself a copy (and yes, they even have it in RPM format).

You can use a simple keyword search to locate software even if you don't know exactly what you are looking for. Use the `--apropos` flag for this. For example, if you were looking for some kind of CD burner, you might use the keyword "burner."

```
rpmfind --apropos burner
```

You might want to redirect this output to a file because a simple keyword search can yield quite a number of hits. Notice the number of candidates found when I did an `apropos` search for "editor."

```
Found 2515 packages related to editor
```

You can also use `rpmfind` to do upgrades of software for you. Now, I would be a little careful about doing this, but in some cases, particularly if you know what you are looking for, it's a nice, quick, and easy way to do the job. For instance, if you're looking for something to upgrade to the latest version of `bluefish` (an HTML editor), use this command:

```
[root@testsys /root]# rpmfind --upgrade bluefish
Installing bluefish will require 1364 KBytes
```

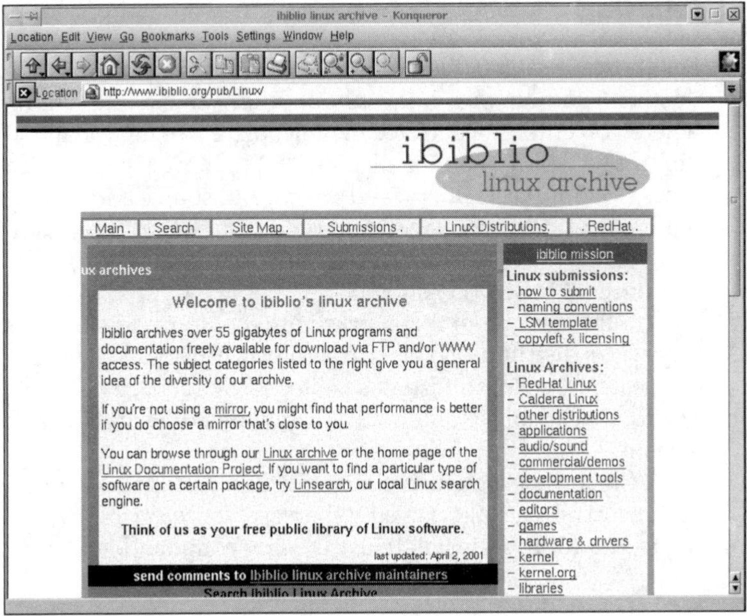

FIGURE 11.4 The monster archive at ibiblio

```
### To Transfer:
ftp://rpmfind.net/linux/contrib/libc6/i386/bluefish-0.6-1.i386.rpm
Do you want to download these files to /tmp [Y/n/a/i] ? : Y
Download bluefish-0.6-1.i386.rpm [Y/n/a/M/?] :Y
transferring ftp://rpmfind.net/linux/contrib/libc6/i386/bluefish-0.6-1.i386.rpm
saving to /tmp/bluefish-0.6-1.i386.rpm
rpm -U /tmp/bluefish-0.6-1.i386.rpm
```

Ibiblio.org

Formerly known as `metalab.unc.edu`, this site should be considered an absolutely essential bookmark for Linux software.

The metalab archive has been around for much longer than Linux has, catering to the UNIX users of the world before Linux arrived on the scene. Point your browser to `http://www.ibiblio.org/` and take a look around.

This is a huge repository that has been categorized and sorted (see Figure 11.4). Ibiblio.org also provides an excellent search engine to locate that hard-to-find package.

It should go without saying that I have only mentioned a few sites here. These are not the only software review sites or repositories on the Internet.

They represent a few that I think every admin should know about. If you need more, check out the Resources section at the end of the chapter. Beyond that, I bid you happy hunting.

Now that you know where and how to get lots of great software, the question becomes one of installation.

Installing and Building Software

Once you've downloaded that new software, you'll no doubt be anxious to take things out for a spin. The catch is that a lot of this software comes in source—not surprising because the GPL license (under which much of the Linux software out there is distributed) requires that you distribute source along with the programs. There are also open source projects that have no relation to the GNU projects that employ the license as a means of copyright. Then, there are other open source projects that use BSD-style licensing, artistic licensing, postcard licensing, and many others, all who distribute their programs in source format.

Another reason for this is apparent when you consider that certain projects go back far beyond the Linux revolution. The software you download may be popularly used by Linux users, but Linux users are by no means the first (or last) to take advantage of that particular package. The authors of the software then provide scripts to allow the product to be compiled on many different systems and still deliver a single package. In comparison, binary distributions (previously compiled packages such as RPMs or DEBs) require a separate bundle for each and every platform.

Compiling from Source

As I mentioned, much of this software is available as source. At first glance, this may appear to be a nuisance, but source makes software portable. The number of platforms on which a single package can be compiled tends to be much higher because the applications can be built using *your* system at *your* operating system level with *your* libraries. It means that if you are running Red Hat 7.1, you don't need to go looking for the Red Hat 7.1 package.

Here's another reason. It takes developers time to provide packages compiled and ready to run on multiple platforms—time they may not have. Consequently, developers sometimes have source code available that is much more recent than the precompiled packages they offer. Why? Because they haven't found the *time* to build the packages for all those platforms. Source often represents the leading edge.

Building from source is not complicated and many of the steps required are common across most source distributions. If you can build one software package, you can build *most* of them.

Step 1: Unpacking the Archive

Most program sources are distributed as *tarballs,* meaning that they have been stored using the `tar` archiving command. For example, a package called "ftl-drive version 1.01" may be found on a site listing looking like this:

```
ftl-drive-1.01.tar
ftl-drive-1.01.tar.Z
ftl-drive-1.01.tar.gz
ftl-drive-1.01.tar.bz2
```

The simple `.tar` extension is pretty basic. You can extract the archive with the command `tar -xvf ftl-drive-1.01.tar`. In the second example (with the `.Z` extension), you are looking at a file that has been compressed using the `compress` command. This is a fairly classic method of compression that you will find on just about every UNIX system out there. To extract the source from this tarball, you first uncompress the file using the `uncompress` command. Then you continue with your `tar` extract:

```
uncompress ftl-drive-1.01.tar.Z
tar -xvf ftp-drive-1.01.tar
```

As you can see, the process of uncompressing strips the `.Z` extension from the file. There is a `-Z` flag to the tar program that theoretically should do the uncompress on the fly (as in `tar -xZvf filename.tar.Z`), but that doesn't always seem to work, which is why I gave you the previous two-step approach. What does work all the time is uncompressing GNU-zipped archives (this `gzip` program should not to be confused with the DOS/Windows PKZIP or WinZip programs). These are the tarballs with the `.gz` extensions. Like the compression example, you can do this in two steps by first gunzipping with the program `gunzip` and then proceeding to untar the source. The second option is to extract in this way:

```
tar -xzvf ftl-drive-1.01.tar.gz
```

One step is all you need. The last of your tarballs represents a relative newcomer to the world of compression. Your Linux system will already have the `compress` and `uncompress` commands as well as the `gzip` and `gunzip`. You may not, however, have the `bzip2` and `bunzip2` programs included with your distribution. Check the Resources section at the end of this chapter for the package's home page if you need to install it.

To extract a `bzip2` archive, you need to perform essentially the same steps you did with `compress`. Use the command `bunzip2 ftl-drive-`

1.01.tar.bz2 to uncompress the file, and then extract using the standard tar command.

Alternatively, you can use a one-line command. The command option for this varies. On most systems I've used, this is the -I option (soon to be replaced with the -j option), but with Slackware, for example, you should try using the -y option. On my test Slackware system, I can use this command to tar and compress with bzip2 in one pass:

```
tar -xyvf ftl-drive-1.01.tar.bz2
```

> **A Note on Compression:** Different forms of compression will deliver different results. Here's an example you might find interesting. Let's start with a tar archive of /etc, which we'll call etc.tar. With my system, the archive file takes up 3502080 bytes. While some 3.5MB of disk space is not a lot, I'll ask you to consider the advantages of the various compression types. Starting with the compress program, I generate a 1170555-byte file called etc.tar.Z. On the other hand, gzip creates a 755073-byte file called etc.tar.gz. Finally, bzip2 creates an astoundingly small 666817-byte file called etc.tar.bz2. My archive now takes up only about 19 percent of the original space.

Step 2: Building Your Programs

Once you have extracted the program source from the tar archive, change directory to the software's distribution directory. Using my current ftl-drive example, type cd ftl-drive-1.01 where an ls listing would likely show a number of files something like this:

```
CHANGES     README          Makefile        Makefile.in     configure
INSTALL     ftl-drive.h     ftl-drive.c     engine.c        config.h
```

The first thing you want to do is read any README and INSTALL files. Those will tell you precisely what you need to do in order to make things work. Many programs provide a configure file, particularly if the software was built to run on different flavors of UNIX and Linux. This file is an executable script designed to identify your system type, release level, whether you have certain code libraries installed, what version of a particular system call your system might use, and so on. You run the configure script from the command line like this:

```
./configure
```

Ninety-five percent of the time, the configure script will make all the changes you need to generate your Makefile. The Makefile is used by the command make, which takes the information and determines what needs to be compiled or recompiled in order to build your software. This brings us to the next step, which is to type `make`. You'll see a lot of information going by on your screen as programs are compiled and linked. Usually (after a successful compile), you follow the make command with a `make install`. This will copy the software into the directories defined in the `Makefile`. A number of programmers also provide a `make uninstall` option should you decide that you do not want to keep the program around.

> **Note:** If you are an open source programmer and you want to make people happy, always provide an uninstall option.

Sometimes, you will be instructed to make changes to the `Makefile` yourself before typing make. In cases where the program was written on and for a Linux system only (and the program is fairly simple) you need only type `make` without any configuration changes.

Unfortunately, there are conceivably as many ways to provide source and build it as there are programmers, so read those `README` files carefully. Luckily, the majority of programmers do follow some standard method of distribution and this introduction will have you running that new game in no time. Did I say "game"? I meant "utility," of course.

Downloading and Installing Perl Modules

Perl is a popular programming language and it is quite likely that you will find yourself installing software that is sometimes based entirely on Perl. This is especially likely if the tools or programs you are looking for are Web-based—CGI scripts tend to be largely written in Perl. Even code that accesses databases in other languages (C, C++, PICK, and so on) often uses Perl as the go-between from Web to data.

Perl's large programmer base has created an archive of modules at the Comprehensive Perl Archive Network (CPAN) that you can download and use in your own Perl scripts and applications. If you find that you have downloaded a package that says something like "You will need the Perl modules `CGI.pm` and `Digest::MD5` to use this application," don't despair. This is what you do.

Start by visiting CPAN and downloading the module you need. The easiest way to do this is to point your browser to the CPAN Web site (`http://cpan.perl.org/`).

For this example, I'll use a real life module called `DBI`. It is used to simplify database development under Perl.

```
cd /usr/local/temp_dir
tar -xzvf DBI-1.13.tar.gz
cd DBI-1.13
perl Makefile.PL
make
make test
make install
```

Package Managers

Downloading, untarring and unzipping source, compiling, installing, and then keeping track of all that doesn't have to be daunting. All right, maybe it can be. In fact, if you lose track of where you've done the installation (remember my call for uninstall scripts in `Makefiles`), upgrading that software can be another trial. This is what a package manager seeks to simplify.

The easiest way to install software is through the package tools provided in your distribution. Here's how packages are identified. Assume that I am talking about a hypothetical package called `ftl_transport`. If I were looking for this package to run my Debian or Debian-like system, I would find it in this type of format:

```
ftl-transport_2.1-1.deb
```

The first part is the package name itself. The numbers just after the underscore (and just before the hyphen) indicate the software version number. The number following the hyphen is the package release number. The final prefix, `.deb`, is a dead giveaway that this is a Debian package, sometimes referred to as a *deb*.

Those of you running Red Hat, Mandrake, Caldera, or one of the other RPM-based distributions will find a similar format.

```
ftl_transport-2.1-1.i386.rpm
```

As you can see, the format is similar to that of the deb package, but with a couple of fairly important differences. For instance, hyphens denote both versions and release numbers. As you might have guessed, `.rpm` denotes an RPM package and while that is an important distinction, the following is somewhat more interesting. The `i386` portion of the package name tells us that it was compiled for a generic x86 processor family. You might also see an "i586" or "i686" in here to denote that the package requires a Pentium class processor or better in order to run. Here are some other things you might see:

```
ftl_transport-2.1-1.ialpha.rpm   # Denotes a DEC alpha-type processor
ftl_transport-2.1-1.sparc.rpm    # Denotes a Sun SPARC processor
ftl_transport-2.1-1.ippc.rpm     # Denotes a Power PC chip
```

If you are wandering around Rpmfind and you locate that great administration game, er, I mean *tool*, make sure that you take your processor type into consideration.

Updating or Installing Packages on a Debian System

This doesn't have to be Debian specifically. Other Debian-based distributions like Storm Linux or Corel will work the same way. The most basic method of installing a package (off your distribution CD or a downloaded file) is with this format of the `dpkg` command:

```
dpkg --install ftl-transport_2.1-1.deb
```

`dpkg` is the basic package installation tool for Debian systems. The previous command installs the package. This one removes it:

```
dpkg --remove ftl-transport
```

> **Note:** If it looks like I am saving keystrokes here, there is a reason. I only indicated the package release number and subsequent extensions at installation time. To remove a package, you only need the package name itself.

You should be aware that there is another step to consider when removing a package. Although the program is now gone from your system, its configuration files remain (which can be a good idea). To get rid of those as well, you need to purge the package.

```
dpkg --purge ftl-transport
```

Great, but Can You Tell Me What Is Already There?

Sure thing. If you want to get a list of every package on your system, use the `--list` option to `dpkg`. You might want to pipe that output to the `more` command.

```
dpkg --list | more
```

If something in that list should prove interesting and you would like to know more about the package, try the `--print-avail` flag. In this example, I try to discover something about the mysterious `mtools` package.

```
speedy:~# dpkg --print-avail mtools
Package: mtools
```

```
Priority: standard
Section: otherosfs
Installed-Size: 311
Maintainer: Mark W. Eichin <eichin@thok.org>
Architecture: i386
Version: 3.9.6-3.1
Depends: libc6 (>= 2.1.2), xlib6g (>= 3.3.5)
Size: 183456
Description: Tools for manipulating MSDOS files
  Mtools is a public domain collection of programs to allow Unix sys-
tems to read, write, and manipulate files on an MSDOS filesystem (typi-
cally a diskette).  Each program attempts to emulate the MSDOS
equivalent command as closely as practical.
```

Finding Out a Package's Current Release Level

To find out what version of a package is already installed on your system, use the `-l` flag. In the following example, I query the system to find out what version of `bash` (the Bourne Again Shell) I am working with.

```
# dpkg -l bash
Desired=Unknown/Install/Remove/Purge/Hold
| Status=Not/Installed/Config-files/Unpacked/Failed-config/Half-installed
|/ Err?=(none)/Hold/Reinst-required/X=both-problems (Status,Err: uppercase=bad)
||/ Name           Version        Description
+++-==============-==============-====================================
ii  bash           2.03-6         The GNU Bourne Again SHell
```

What Is That Strange File?

Let's say that you are wondering what some file is doing on your system. For instance, there is something called `hinotes` in my `/usr/bin` directory and I don't remember installing it. Furthermore, if I try to look it up in the man pages, I am told that there is no information on this file. Using the `-S` flag, I can have `dpkg` identify what package this file was a part of.

```
# dpkg -S /usr/bin/hinotes
pilot-link: /usr/bin/hinotes
```

Because I remember installing the `pilot-link` software (to help me synchronize my Palm Pilot with my Linux system), I can rest a bit easier.

Using apt-get to Install or Update Software

People who use Debian distributions on a regular basis will sometimes point to this wonderful little program as the reason why Debian is so great. Well, I certainly won't be the one to deny that `apt-get` is wonderful.

If you want to install a package called `xpilot`, this is how to do it:

```
speedy:~# apt-get install xpilot
Reading Package Lists... Done
Building Dependency Tree... Done
The following extra packages will be installed:
  xpilot-server
The following NEW packages will be installed:
  xpilot xpilot-server
0 packages upgraded, 2 newly installed, 0 to remove and 2 not upgraded.
Need to get 317kB of archives. After unpacking 1017kB will be used.
Do you want to continue? [Y/n]
```

The great thing here is that you did not have to go to a variety of sites to hunt down and identify appropriate software. You called `apt-get` with the install parameter and off you went. Notice as well that `apt-get` will *automatically* pick up dependencies for a given package and install them when needed. If you want to update to the latest version of `xpilot`, substitute the `install` parameter with `update`. Perhaps the most famous example of Debian's prowess is symbolized by the following command:

```
apt-get dist-upgrade
```

For a command that will do a complete upgrade of your system to the latest release, this is deceptively simple. It's like magic, but it isn't entirely magic. After all, `apt-get` has to get that information somewhere, right?

Educating apt-get

That somewhere is the `/etc/apt/sources.list` file. Ah! A list of sources for software. This is a simple text file that you can modify with your favorite editor. Each line has this format:

```
deb url_path distribution components
```

The first parameter, `deb`, may also be `deb-src` for source distribution lists.

```
# Use for a local mirror - remove the ftp1 http lines for the bits
# your mirror contains.
# deb file:/your/mirror/here/debian stable main contrib non-free
```

For instance, the following line identifies a Debian mirror accessible by FTP. The stable release is identified as `potato` in this case. Generally, this is something like `stable`, `unstable`, or `frozen` but, as you can see, it is possible to identify the specific distribution. The final section is the components section. It will be identified as `main`, `contrib`, `non-free`, or `non-us`.

The following is from a Debian system here at the office:

```
deb ftp://ftp.ca.debian.org/debian potato main contrib non-free
```

From time to time, you should update your local `sources` database with the latest available package information.

```
apt-get update
```

If you are installing Debian files on a regular basis from a development site (the Wine site, for example), you might want to update your local sources file. Edit the file `/etc/apt/sources.list` and add the site information.

In the case of the Wine development site (a package that makes it possible to run Windows applications on Linux), I added the following lines:

```
deb http://gluck.debian.org/~andreas/debian wine main
deb-src http://gluck.debian.org/~andreas/debian wine main
```

> **Note:** Wine is covered in Chapter 22.

Graphical Alternatives

Debian does provide a character-based, menu-driven interface for adding, removing, or updating packages. This is the `dselect` utility (see Figure 11.5) and it is actually a front end to the `dpkg` tool I covered earlier.

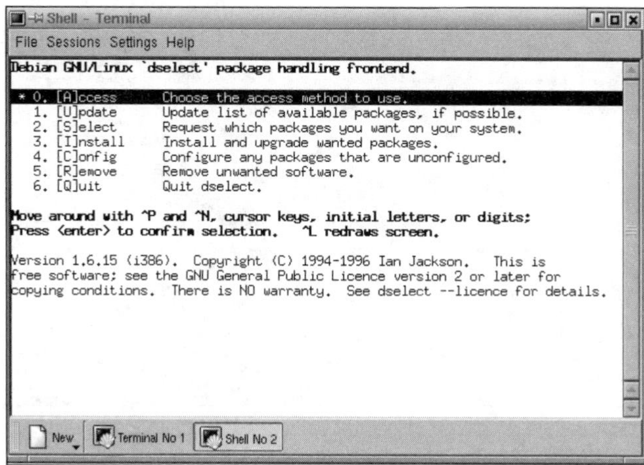

FIGURE 11.5
Upgrading Debian with `dselect`

Start `dselect` from the root prompt like this:

```
dselect
```

It enables you to select an access method that can be an NFS mounted drive, an FTP site, or your CD distribution. If you choose the Select option, you are shown a list of available packages. Using your cursor keys, you then highlight something of interest while keeping an eye on the bottom half of the screen. There, you will see a description of the package in question.

This is not the only package tool available to you. Depending on your desktop environment, you'll find that a number of tools exist. For instance, if you feel the need for something with a bit more flash and you happen to be running KDE, you might try the `kpackage` tool.

To run it, just type `kpackage` from a command line in the desktop. It is very easy to use. First, click the New tab. From the Settings menu, choose Location of uninstalled package.

As soon as you do that, you'll notice that you can select locations for `debs`, `rpms`, and Slackware packages. This is a tool that works nicely with a number of different Linux distributions. Because you are dealing with Debian at this time, click Location DEB (see Figure 11.6).

From there, you merely type in the URL or location of your favorite Debian mirror and click OK. Now, press F5 (or select Reload from the File menu) and wait while your available package list is updated.

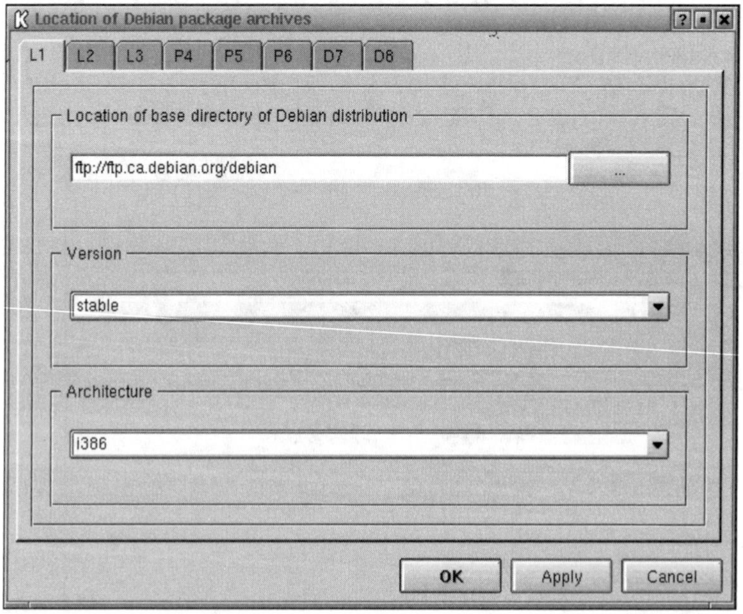

FIGURE 11.6 Selecting a software site with `kpackage`

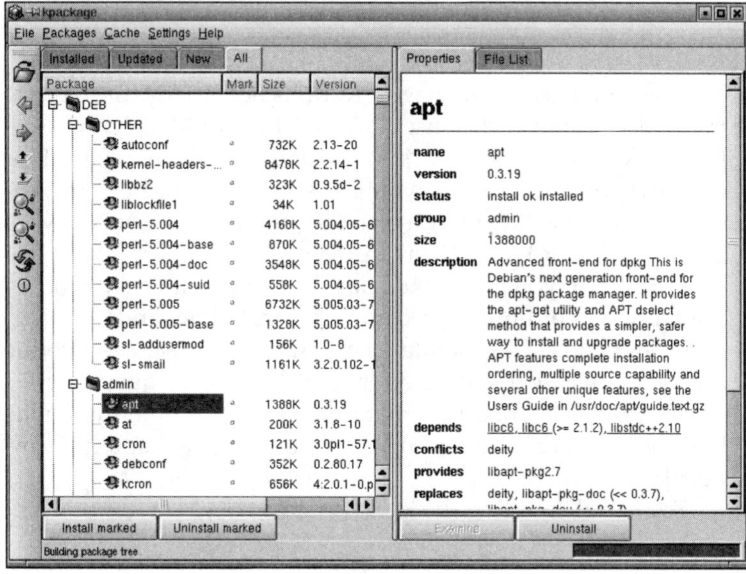

FIGURE 11.7 Debian package updates with style

The Updated tab enables you to choose from a list of packages that are updated from those already on your system. The New tab shows you everything that is available but not already installed.

When you click a package, the right-hand window provides a description of the package (see Figure 11.7). If you then choose to install the package, you will find out that under the surface it all comes back to the basics. This is another front end to the dpkg tool, as Figure 11.8 shows.

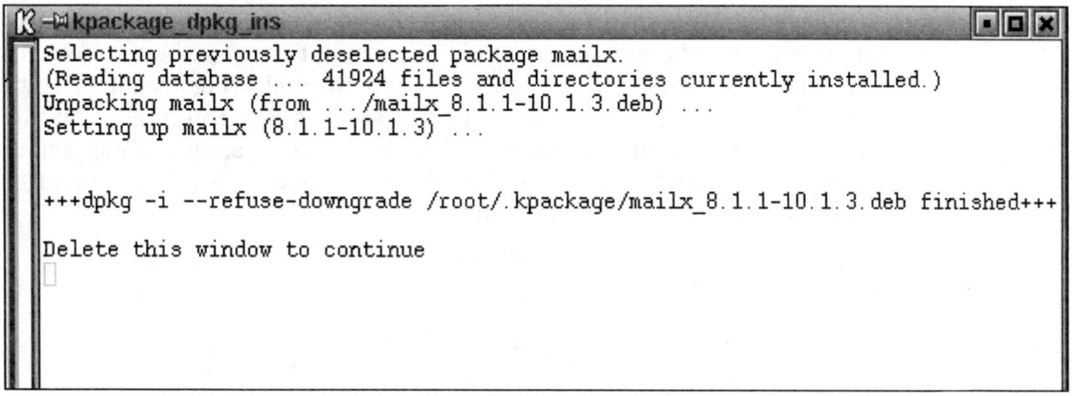

```
kpackage_dpkg_ins
Selecting previously deselected package mailx.
(Reading database ... 41924 files and directories currently installed.)
Unpacking mailx (from .../mailx_8.1.1-10.1.3.deb) ...
Setting up mailx (8.1.1-10.1.3) ...

+++dpkg -i --refuse-downgrade /root/.kpackage/mailx_8.1.1-10.1.3.deb finished+++

Delete this window to continue
```

FIGURE 11.8 Completing a Debian package install with kpackage

Red Hat Package Manager

The Red Hat package manager (RPM) is not strictly for Red Hat. You will find many distributions that use it. You'll find RPM used by Red Hat, Caldera, Mandrake, and Turbolinux, just to name a few. Even if your Linux distribution does not come with RPM, you can still install and use it. What's even more exciting is that RPM will run on a number of other UNIX flavors as well. These include AIX, HP-UX, IRIX, and others.

With RPM, you can make your distribution an easy process by transforming the stages of untarring, compiling, installing, and cleaning up into a one-line command. RPM maintains a database of installed products so that you can verify installed software for completeness or query file locations. This is an exceptionally good tool that you can use to determine whether packages have been modified without your knowledge (Chapter 25 covers security in detail).

You can always find the latest version of RPM at `http://www.rpm.org/`.

Installing an RPM Package

Using my hypothetical package, let's install some great functionality with RPM.

```
rpm -ivh ftl-transport-2.1-1.i386.rpm
```

In reality, you really only need to use the `-i` flag to do this. v gives you some additional feedback and h prints little hash marks across the screen to show you the progress of the installation.

```
# rpm -ivh rpmfind-1.6-1.i386.rpm
rpmfind        ##################################################
```

Some of you are extremely curious, so I am going to let you in on a secret for getting a lot of information out of this process. Drop `h` (although I kind of like this mode) and add two more `v`'s. In the following example, I am installing the `rpmfind` package that I discussed earlier. You might find this quite fascinating. With the double `v` flag, you get to see what is happening during the various stages of the installation. It gives you a fair amount of respect for the simplicity of the RPM tool.

```
# rpm -ivvv rpmfind-1.6-1.i386.rpm
D: counting packages to install
D: found 1 packages
D: looking for packages to download
D: retrieved 0 packages
D: New Header signature
D: Signature size: 149
D: Signature pad : 3
```

```
D: sigsize         : 152
D: Header + Archive: 53825
D: expected size   : 53825
D: opening database mode 0x42 in /var/lib/rpm
D: found 0 source and 1 binary packages
D:   YES    A libxml = 1.8.10-0_helix_1 B libxml >= 1.8.6
D:  requires: libxml >= 1.8.6 satisfied by db packages.
D:  requires: ld-linux.so.2  satisfied by db provides.
D:  requires: libbz2.so.0  satisfied by db provides.
D:  requires: libc.so.6  satisfied by db provides.
D:  requires: libdb.so.2  satisfied by db provides.
D:  requires: libpopt.so.0  satisfied by db provides.
D:  requires: librpm.so.0  satisfied by db provides.
D:  requires: libxml.so.1  satisfied by db provides.
D:  requires: libz.so.1  satisfied by db provides.
D:  requires: libc.so.6(GLIBC_2.0)  satisfied by db provides.
D:  requires: libc.so.6(GLIBC_2.1)  satisfied by db provides.
D: installing binary packages
D: getting list of mounted filesystems
D: New Header signature
D: Signature size: 149
D: Signature pad : 3
D: sigsize         : 152
D: Header + Archive: 53825
D: expected size   : 53825
D: package: rpmfind-1.6-1 files test = 0
D:    file: /usr/bin/rpmfind action: create
D:    file: /usr/doc/rpmfind-1.6 action: create
D:    file: /usr/doc/rpmfind-1.6/BUGS action: create
D:    file: /usr/doc/rpmfind-1.6/CHANGES action: create
D:    file: /usr/doc/rpmfind-1.6/Copyright action: create
D:    file: /usr/doc/rpmfind-1.6/README action: create
D:    file: /usr/doc/rpmfind-1.6/TODO action: create
D:    file: /usr/man/man1/rpmfind.1.gz action: create
D: running preinstall script (if any)
rpmfind-1.6-1
GZDIO:      15 reads,   120508 total bytes in 0.046 secs
D: running postinstall scripts (if any)
```

Sometimes the installation refuses to go ahead for various reasons, but you know better. This usually happens when you are playing with development packages and you want continue anyhow. For instance, RPM may stop if it finds that its version of a font file conflicts with that of another package. In that case, use the `--force` option.

```
rpm -i --force matter_transporter.1.0-3.i386.rpm
```

When the installation scripts occur, a number of sanity checks are performed. Among these are prerequisite or dependency checks. RPM will stop you with a message that you require some package and it will name it in the error message. In this case, the `--force` option will not work. Instead, use the `--nodeps` (do dependency check) option.

```
rpm -i --nodeps matter_transporter-1.0-3.i386.rpm
```

Upgrading an RPM Package

An upgrade is a form of installation. As part of the process, older versions of files will be replaced and the package's default configuration files may be moved or renamed to preserve the originals (you will usually see appropriate messages if this occurs). This works almost exactly like the installation procedure except that you specify a `U` instead of an `i` on the command line.

```
rpm -Uvh matter_transporter-1.2-1.i386.rpm
```

Uninstalling an RPM Package

As part of your tenure as system administrator, you will wind up trying lots of software that you won't necessarily want to keep. RPM makes removing old packages a breeze.

```
rpm -evv matter_transporter
```

Just think "erase" for the `-e` flag. The double `v` flag is there to give you lots of information about what gets deleted and what gets updated during the process of removing this package. All you really need is the `-e` option and things will still be removed.

One other item of note: As you can see, I did not specify a version number with that package. This is only required during the installation.

Everything You Ever Wanted to Know about an RPM Package, but Were Afraid to Ask

RPM can tell you a lot about a package. To find out what version of the `fileutils` packages you have on the system, use the `-q` flag on its own. That is the query flag.

```
# rpm -q fileutils
fileutils-4.0-21
```

To find out what files belong to (or make up) that package, add the `l` flag to list everything in the package.

```
# rpm -ql fileutils
/bin/chgrp
/bin/chmod
/bin/chown
/bin/cp
/bin/dd
/bin/df
/bin/ln
 . . . more follows
```

You can also find out what package a file belongs to by using the `f` flag. In my `/sbin` directory, there is a file called `sysctl`. If I want to know where this file came from and what package it belonged to, I use this command:

```
# rpm -qf /sbin/sysctl
procps-2.0.6-5
```

Now comes a great tool for keeping an eye on changes to files. Using the `-V` flag, you can verify the integrity of an installed package. For instance, if I run the `rpm` command against the previous package, this is the result:

```
# rpm -V procps
#
```

That's right. Nothing happens. The package (in this case) is as it was when it was installed. Let's try another one—a package called "setup."

```
# rpm -V setup
S.5....T c /etc/exports
S.5....T c /etc/hosts.allow
S.5....T c /etc/motd
S.5....T c /etc/printcap
S.5....T c /etc/services
```

In this case, I know that these are all files that I have *personally* modified, so nothing to worry about. This is, however, a great way to keep track of the status of all those packages. This topic is revisited in Chapter 25, which covers security.

RPM: The Graphical Alternatives

I've already discussed the KDE answer to graphical package management (`kpackage`), so now I'd like to tell you about what your GNOME desktop environment has to offer: a slick little package called `gnorpm`. You can either start it from the GNOME menu or type the command at the shell prompt.

```
# gnorpm &
```

From the interface, you can install (you should have your distribution CD-ROM mounted for this), uninstall, query, and verify packages. Yes, just like at the command line.

If you click the Web find button, `gnorpm` will go out, pick up the latest database of available packages, and let you choose what you want to install. There's an interface to Rpmfind (discussed earlier) that enables you to search for a package by keyword. You can then click a package and get additional information. In Figure 11.9, I am looking at information on the `abiword` package.

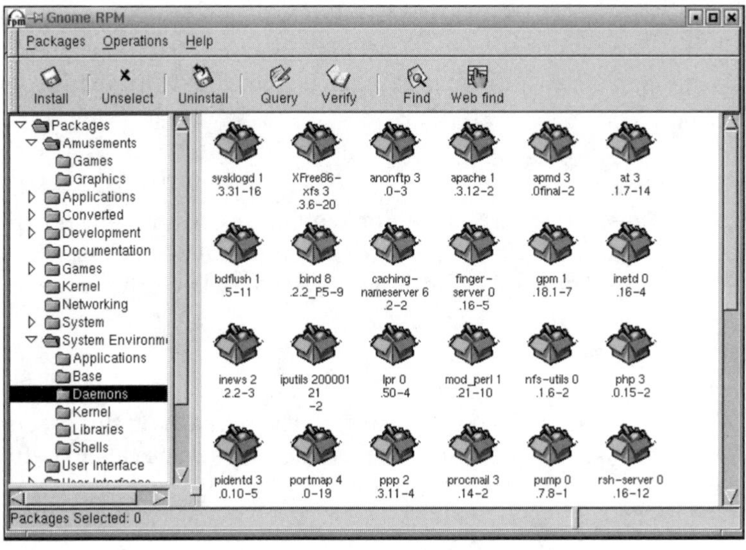

FIGURE 11.9 Managing RPM packages with `gnorpm`

> **Note:** AbiWord, by the way, is a great little open source word processor that offers cross-platform support (it even runs in that *other* OS). You can get it from the AbiSource Web site (`http://www.abisource.com/`).

My next step is to select the version of the package that I want and then click Install (see Figure 11.10). The package is downloaded (you define the temporary directory by clicking Operations and Preferences in the main `gnorpm` window), after which I am given the option of continuing with the installation.

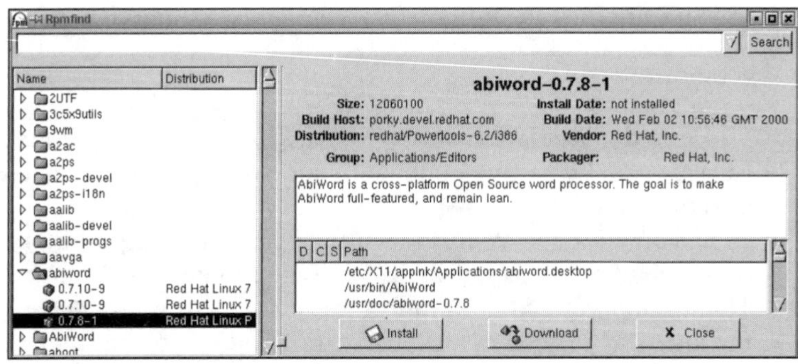

FIGURE 11.10 Using `gnorpm`'s Web find option

installpkg: Slackware's Lonely Child

Perhaps I am being a bit dramatic, but with the prevalence of packages either built as `debs` or `rpms`, it is easy to forget Slackware's package manager, `pkgtool` or `installpkg`. At the time you install your Slackware system and choose which packages to install, you are actually making use of `pkgtool`, the text-based, graphical installation tool.

Packages in the Slackware world are `tarred` and `gzipped` files with a `.tgz` extension. You can actually view the contents of a package by simply using the `tar` command in this way. Here's an example. On my notebook, I forgot to install the PCMCIA package at installation time. I put the CD-ROM in the drive and mounted it as `/mnt/cdrom`. Next, I switched to the directory that contained the PCMCIA installation files and had a look at the `pcmcia.tgz` package.

```
cd /mnt/cdrom/slakware/a11
tar -tzvf pcmcia.tgz
```

Installation of that package can also be done at the command line by using the `installpkg` command.

```
# installpkg pcmcia.tgz
```

Uninstalling packages is done with the `removepkg` command. In this example, I am removing the mini-HOWTOs from my system installation. On my Slackware system, they live in `/usr/doc` under a directory called "Linux-mini-HOWTOs."

```
# removepkg mini
```

The command will then *helpfully* list all the files that are being deleted. (Now, don't you feel terrible?)

Resources

`bzip2` **Compression Utility Home Page**

`http://sources.redhat.com/bzip2/`

CPAN (Comprehensive Perl Archive Network)

`http://www.cpan.org/`

Freshmeat

`http://www.freshmeat.net/`

Ibiblio.org

`http://www.ibiblio.org/`

rpm.org (RPM tool main site)

`http://www.rpm.org/`

Rpmfind

`http://www.rpmfind.net/`

SourceForge

`http://www.sourceforge.net/`

TUCOWS Linux

`http://linux.tucows.com/`

Chapter 12

Kernel Building and Renovation

What Is This Kernel, Anyhow?

The kernel is the heart of your Linux system. In fact, your kernel *is* Linux. All those other things that you think of as your Linux system—the word processors, the editors, the Web browsers, the compilers—are window dressing (not to be confused with window managers, which were covered earlier in this book).

When Should I Rebuild My Kernel?

Ah, great question. Well, the short answer is *never.*

The longer answer probably requires that I explain the short one. In a modern Linux distribution, the odds are *pretty good* that everything you need to run your system is already configured into the kernel. Still, there are times when the distributed kernel will not support your hardware. You may also need specific features that, while uncommon, are required in your environment. You may need to implement a security fix that requires a new kernel. There are and will be other reasons.

This generally implies a requirement for the latest and greatest Linux has to offer. If you want to know what the latest version of the Linux kernel is, whether it is a stable release or a development version, try out the following `finger` command:

```
finger @finger.kernel.org
```

A few seconds later, the system responds with something like this:

```
[zeus.kernel.org]
```

```
The latest stable version of the Linux kernel is:      2.2.17
The latest beta version of the Linux kernel is:  2.4.0-test10
The latest prepatch (alpha) version *appears* to be: 2.4.0-test11/pre5
```

This assumes, of course, that you are currently connected to the Internet. If you are not, check out Chapter 10 for details on how to get there.

Downloading and Building a New Kernel

Armed with the latest kernel information, you can now visit your favorite kernel source mirror and download what you need. Getting to your local mirror is pretty simple. All you have to do is squeeze your country code between the `ftp` or `www` of `kernel.org`. For instance, assume for a moment that I am in Canada (country code ca). The addresses for the `ftp` and `www` sites are as follows:

```
ftp.ca.kernel.org
www.ca.kernel.org
```

If I were in the United States, I would use these mirrors:

```
ftp.us.kernel.org
www.us.kernel.org
```

If you are unsure about any of these codes, visit the main Linux kernel Web site at `http://www.kernel.org/mirrors/` for a complete list. Kernel sources are provided in `tar.gz` and `tar.bz2` formats.

So now you have chosen and downloaded your kernel source distribution. The next step, of course, is to build the kernel.

With source in hand, it is time to uncompress and extract that source. The usual and preferred location tends to be `/usr/src`. Kernels direct from any of the `kernel.org` mirrors tend to extract into a hierarchy called `linux`. This means that your kernel sources would live in `/usr/src/linux`. However, you may find that `/usr/src/linux` is actually a symbolic link to where the actual kernel source lives. For instance, if I do an `ls -l` on one of my servers, I get something that looks like this:

```
# cd /usr/src
# ls -l linux
lrwxrwxrwx   1  1  root  11 Nov 14 1999 linux -> linux-2.2.5
```

Notice that it points to a directory called `linux-2.2.5`. If you want to extract directly from the source, start by renaming the link something else, and then extract the kernel. The tree will be called `linux`. Now, change directory to the `linux` directory and type `make config`. Even before you type that com-

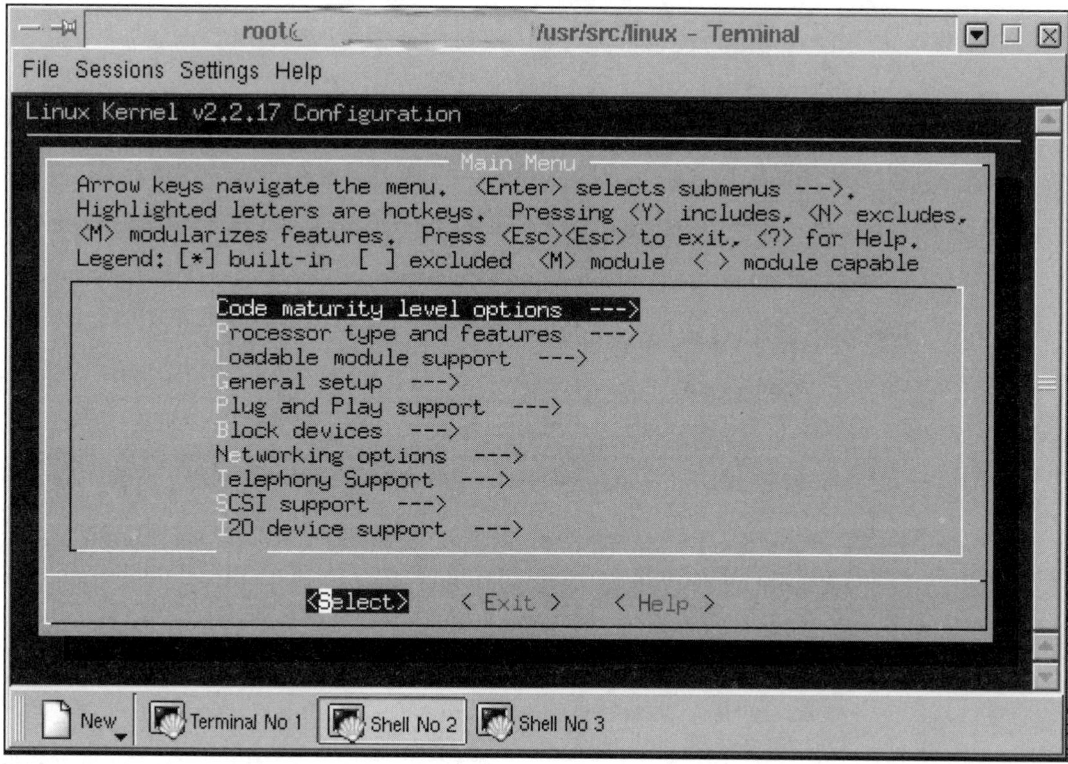

FIGURE 12.1 Configuring a kernel with `make menuconfig`

mand, I should tell you that this is the old way of doing things. You will get a line-by-line question and answer session designed to help you through the configuration process for your new kernel. If you type `make menuconfig`, you will get a ncurses-based screen that is a bit friendlier (see Figure 12.1).

The last option is `make xconfig` (see Figure 12.2), which uses an X window environment for building. This is probably the best way because it makes it easy to switch from one area of system configuration to another. For instance, if you had forgotten to compile in an MS-DOS file system support into your new kernel, it's a snap to click the Filesystems button and just add what you want.

> **Note:** The `make xconfig` command requires that you have the Tcl/Tk package loaded.

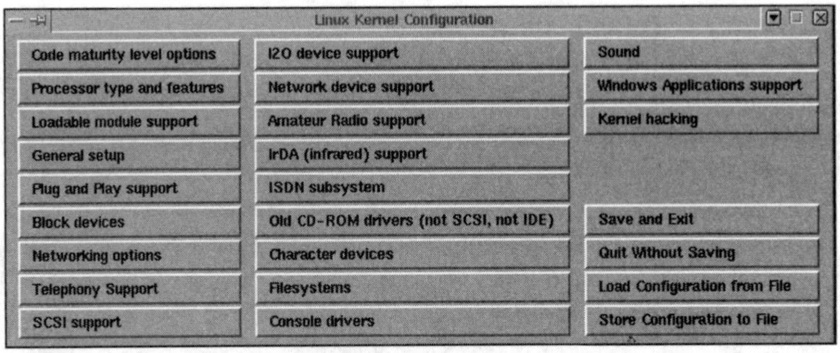

Code maturity level options	I2O device support	Sound
Processor type and features	Network device support	Windows Applications support
Loadable module support	Amateur Radio support	Kernel hacking
General setup	IrDA (infrared) support	
Plug and Play support	ISDN subsystem	
Block devices	Old CD-ROM drivers (not SCSI, not IDE)	Save and Exit
Networking options	Character devices	Quit Without Saving
Telephony Support	Filesystems	Load Configuration from File
SCSI support	Console drivers	Store Configuration to File

FIGURE 12.2 make xconfig

As I mentioned, this is the question and answer session. You decide what you want in your kernel by answering Y for yes, N for no, and M for module. Depending on what you have chosen, you may also be asked to supply device-specific information. Read carefully. At any point in the process, you can ask for help if you don't know what a specific thing does. The kernel `make` process is pretty good at leading you and helping you out through this. If it tells you that you should include something, then do so. Trust the kernel developers.

> **Glossary Note:** When talking about modules, specifically *loadable modules,* I mean kernel support code that is not compiled into the kernel itself. Instead, you load these modules and essentially plug them into the running kernel at will. Usually, "at will" means at boot time, but the fact is that you can install and uninstall kernel support for certain devices on the fly. Not compiling *everything* into the kernel and using modules instead has the advantage of making for a smaller, faster kernel.

Once this is done, you can actually go back and make some modifications if you want to. In the `/usr/src/linux` directory, you will find a file called `.config`. Using Pico, `vi`, or whatever editor makes you happy, you can still make changes. This is especially useful for those using the `make config` method. The menu-driven methods enable you to enter into any portion of the dialog box and edit just what you want. The following is a sample of the `.config` file from a recent build:

```
# CONFIG_M486 is not set
# CONFIG_M586 is not set
# CONFIG_M586TSC is not set
CONFIG_M686=y
CONFIG_X86_WP_WORKS_OK=y
CONFIG_X86_INVLPG=y
CONFIG_X86_BSWAP=y
CONFIG_X86_POPAD_OK=y
```

```
CONFIG_X86_TSC=y
CONFIG_X86_GOOD_APIC=y
CONFIG_1GB=y
# CONFIG_2GB is not set
CONFIG_MATH_EMULATION=y
CONFIG_MTRR=y
# CONFIG_SMP is not set
```

The next step is to do a `make dep` (which handles all the dependencies and creates your `makefiles`) followed by a `make clean`. If this is your first build, you will see messages claiming to be cleaning up and deleting files that aren't really there.

Now, it's time to actually compile your kernel. You do this by executing `make bzImage`.

> **Quick Tip:** Because of old Intel processor limitations, the kernel must be able to load in the first megabyte of memory. This is where this question of kernel image comes into play and why will sometimes get a "kernel too big" message.
>
> You can do a `make zImage`, but in most modern environments, it's best not to try this. Unless you compile everything as a module and trim absolutely everything you don't need, the kernel almost always tends to be too large to fit in this old memory model. This means that you will be required to go back and do a `make bzImage`. The `bzImage` kernel (think "b" for "big") works on the premise that the old limits are not a factor.

This next step may take a while, depending on how fast your computer is, so consider making yourself a fresh pot of coffee or (as an alter ego of mine might say) sitting down with a nice Beaujolais while you wait. When all is done, you'll find your new kernel in the directory `/usr/src/linux/arch/i386/boot`.

Remember that you asked the system to build `bzImage`. Now, copy the new kernel to `/boot`. In the following command, I use `vmlinuz-2.2.17`, but you could call it anything you like. If I am experimenting with various kernel builds, I often name them by date. For instance, the first kernel of November 10 would be `vmlinuz-11101`. You can use whatever naming convention makes sense to you.

```
cp bzImage /boot/vmlinuz-2.2.17
```

Next, you'll want to include your new kernel image in `lilo`'s list of bootable kernels. For this example, I built the 2.2.17 kernel directly from source. Once that was done, I used my `vi` editor to modify my `/etc/lilo.conf` file. Here's what it looked like before I started:

```
boot=/dev/hda
map=/boot/map
```

```
install=/boot/boot.b
prompt
timeout=50
linear
default=linux

image=/boot/vmlinuz-2.2.14-5.0
  label=linux
  read-only
  root=/dev/hda1
```

At the end of the file, I added the following lines:

```
image=/boot/vmlinuz-2.2.17
label=linux-2.2.17
root=/dev/hda1
read-only
```

You'll notice that I did not change anything else in this example. My default boot is still `mlinuz-2.2.14-5.0`, which is the stock kernel that came with my system. The lines that start with `image=/boot/vmlinuz-2.2.17` are the ones I added after the fact. I am now going to have my Linux system reread the configuration file by running this command:

```
/sbin/lilo
```

After `lilo` has worked its way through your `/etc/lilo.conf` file, it should come back with something like this:

```
Added linux *
Added linux-2.2.17
```

> **Quick Tip:** You can never run `/sbin/lilo` too many times, but you can run it too few. If you have made changes to your kernel or your `/etc/lilo.conf` file and you forget to run `/sbin/lilo`, your system will not boot.
>
> This is *extremely important.*
>
> If you are not sure whether you have run `lilo`, run it again.

You have only a couple of things left to do. Because you have no doubt defined several modules to include with your new kernel, you need to make them as well. You do this with the `make modules` command, which you follow up with `make modules_install`.

There you have it. All in all, it's not that the whole process is so complicated, it's just that there are quite a few things to remember and forgetting that all-important `lilo` step can provide you with a great deal of aggravation.

Automatic Build and Install

Now that I have made you do all that work, you might be asking if it could have been easier. The answer is a handful of yeses and maybes. Here's the scoop. You could probably have skipped a few steps by typing this command:

```
make bzlilo
```

This command copies the kernel into place for you and makes things more or less automatic. I don't personally tend to like this because I want to be conscious of each step of the process. If there are errors, I want to know about them. That's a personal decision and one that brings up your level of comfort with doing these things.

What about the 2.4 Kernel?

One of the most awaited developments in the Linux world was the development of the 2.4 kernel. The question of whether or not to run the new 2.4 kernel is already being decided by vendors who are starting to ship their distributions with 2.4 as the default kernel. The advantages are many. The following is a short and incomplete list of some of the benefits.

- Increased RAM capability (from 2GB to 64GB)
- Users and groups go from roughly 65,000 to over 4 million
- Multiprocessor (SMP) support scales easily to 8 processors (I have been told up to 64)
- Journaling file system support
- Logical volume management
- Much larger file sizes (from 2GB to 16TB)
- Raw I/O support (used by large database manufacturers)
- Kernel-level HTTP daemon
- Advanced NFS support
- Better firewalling, network filters, and network address translation (NAT)
- Supports ATM controllers and multiple IDE (10) and Ethernet cards (16)
- And much more!

The 2.4 kernel building process is much the same as the 2.2 series kernel building process. One thing you will notice is that there are more sections in the configuration screen. Compare the image of a `make xconfig` in Figure 12.3 with that of the 2.2 screen in Figure 12.2 and you'll start to get an idea of what I mean.

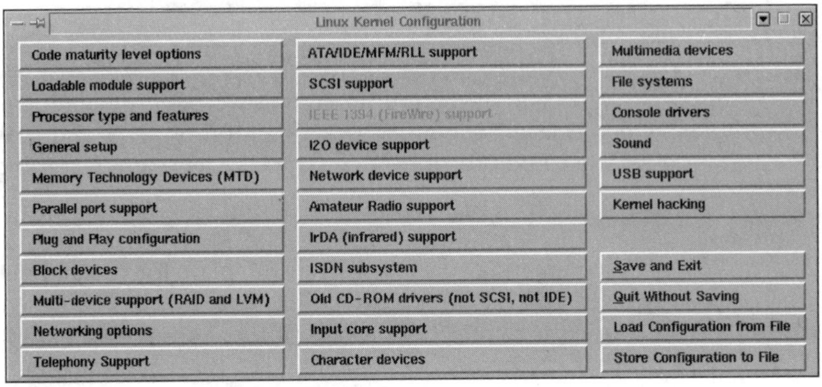

FIGURE 12.3 The new 2.4 kernel provides additional goodies

You should, after unpacking the source, check the Documentation/ Changes file. It is possible that you may need to upgrade your C compiler, libraries, `binutils` package, and possibly other packages on your system. It is best to check here first. If you find that your first attempt at building a 2.4 kernel fails, it may be that your problem is here.

If you are migrating (or merely testing) the new kernel, do not unpack the source into the `/usr/src` hierarchy. Choose a temporary installation directory in much the same way as you do when you install or compile any other software package. The top-level directory will still be called `linux`, but it won't cause you any problems with any currently installed header files. If you have completely abandoned the 2.2 kernel series, putting everything in the old hierarchy should not cause you any problems.

One word of warning, however. The default location for loadable modules has changed. You will want to make sure you have the latest version of the `modutils` package.

Resources

Source Documentation

Check the kernel documentation in the kernel source tree as well. Once you extract the kernel source (say in `/usr/src/linux`), look at the `README` file in that directory, but also check out the `Documentation` directory directly underneath (`/usr/src/linux/Documentation`).

Web Sites

Linux Kernel Archives

`http://www.kernel.org/`

Linux Kernel HOWTO

`http://www.linuxdoc.org/HOWTO/Kernel-HOWTO.html`

Chapter 13

Printers and Printing

Printing seems like one those constants of the computer world that should be so simple as to require next to no thought. Of course, you need to print things. Paper output is a part of doing business. Why, then, does printing continue to confound? Over the years, I have seen and read many different estimates regarding system administrators and printers. In particular, I'm interested in the question of how much time the average administrator devotes to this simple thing. One figure (which had a fairly strong argument backing it up) put printer administration at around 25 percent of a system administrator's time. Granted, this information goes back a few years, but I haven't seen much since then to convince me that this figure has changed.

This chapter examines how printing works and what processes are involved at the system level. I want you to walk away with an understanding, not of graphical printer admin tools, but of printing's dirty underbelly. On the subject of tools, I'll also explore some of the alternative tools that are available to make the whole printing experience just that much easier to deal with. The beauty of working with Linux is that you don't have to do things the way they are defined right out of the box. Many other options exist. Armed with the nuts and bolts of printers and printing, you should be able to print just about *any type of document* to just about *any type of printer.*

Selecting Printers for Linux (and a Note about "WinPrinters")

Beware.

Before you buy any printer to run with your Linux system, make sure you ask your dealer if it will work with Linux. I don't mean to frighten you into thinking that this is an impossible task, by the way. In fact, the "Does it work with Linux?" question is becoming less and less of a problem, but you can still save yourself an awful lot of headaches by asking first. Another way to protect yourself is to check out the hardware compatibility list (see Chapter 4) for Linux systems. This is a great idea for any kind of hardware add-on. For printers, though, you have an additional option that goes one step further.

Even seasoned Linux users like myself occasionally get "stuck" or "caught" with a printer that doesn't work. Some time ago, I bought an HP710C printer, and I just assumed (what do they tell us about assuming) that anything from HP would just work with Linux. After all, they make that great OS, HP-UX. As it turns out, being wrong is extremely easy. This particular printer used something called Printing Performance Architecture (PPA), a closed protocol whose secrets were only available to the Windows platform.

Looking around the Net, I found that an early driver had been put together by a guy named Tim Norman and a group of devoted developers. Unfortunately, at the time, you could only print in black and white, but Tim and his team were working on a color driver. So, I printed in black and white until a color driver finally became available. Had I known about Grant Taylor's printer compatibility list at LinuxPrinting.org (`http://www.linuxprinting.org/`), I wouldn't have had to wait because I wouldn't have bought the printer in the first place.

One of the most useful things at LinuxPrinting.org is a search engine that lets you select a particular manufacturer and get a report of all printers made by them, what level of support they offer, and what kind of tweaking you might need to do in order to make them work. This is especially good if you already have a particular printer and you want to know what filter or drivers are out there for your Linux system. (I'll delve into filters momentarily.)

If you are feeling less than adventurous (or you haven't already spent money on a printer), you can use the safer reporting option. Simply ask to see which color inkjet printers (or laser printers, or whatever type you are looking for) work perfectly. The resulting report lists printers by manufacturer with appropriate links to detailed descriptions of individual models.

The safest approach of all is to get a PostScript printer. These, unfortunately, don't tend to be inexpensive. I'll talk more about PostScript later.

How Printing Works

Linux offers a number of printing options. You can do text, PostScript, and local printers, as well as `lpd` remotes. If you want to, you can even create queues that direct printing to your coworkers' Windows 9*x* printers or provide Windows 9*x* users with Linux print services (using Samba). One printer is mostly okay, but add a handful and it gets a little bit more interesting. What Linux does is provide you with a wide range of options for dealing with this diversity.

Let's go back to the beginning and see how this whole thing actually works, starting with your old friend, the parallel printer.

Basic PC architectures usually have a single parallel port. A printer on that port would actually be connected to `/dev/lp0`. If your PC has more than one parallel connector (or if you added a printer card), the second and third ports would be `/dev/lp1` and `/dev/lp2`, respectively. Now let's pretend that you have a basic, run-of-the-mill text printer attached to the first parallel port. Printing can be as simple as this:

```
# echo "This is a test." > /dev/lp0
# echo "Ignore this print job." > /dev/lp0
# echo "This is nonsense." > /dev/lp0
# echo "^L" > /dev/lp0
```

> **Note:** The last line means "Send a form feed to the printer to eject the page." The `"^L"` is actually a Ctrl-L. I inserted that into the text by pressing Ctrl-V (which allows me to then insert control characters) followed by Ctrl-L.

You may notice that something odd has happened. There is a distinct possibility that the output of this simple job looks something like this:

```
This is a test.
                              Ignore this print job.
                                                                            This is nonsense.
```

This is what my printer configuration tool refers to as "stair stepping of text." You may also have heard it referred to as the "staircase effect." What happens is that my printer, a LaserJet 5L in this case, expects either PCL- (its native printer-command language) or DOS-style text. That means carriage returns and line feeds at the end of each line, unlike Linux files, which default to simply line feeds. This classic problem handily brings us to the topic of filters.

Filters

Let's take exactly the same lines of (non)information (minus the `echo "^L"` line) and create a file called "testfile." I used the Pico editor for this, but you can use whatever editor makes you happy. If you simply `cat` the file to the printer as before (with `cat testfile > /dev/lp0`), the results are the same. Building (or coding) a filter can be quite simple. Here's what mine looks like:

```
#!/bin/bash
echo -ne \\033\&k2G
cat
echo -ne \\f
```

The first echo line sends the command that tells my LaserJet to convert Linux line feeds to a carriage return followed by a line feed, an escape character followed by the printer control sequence &k2G. This is an HP-specific code, so you may have to check your printer manual for your printer's correct code sequence. The next line simply takes the input it got and passes it through unaltered. The final line sends a form feed to eject the page. I called the file dosfilter, moved it to /usr/local/bin, and made it executable.

```
# cp dosfilter /usr/local/bin
# chmod 755 /usr/local/bin/dosfilter
```

I'll resend the job and use my newly created filter.

```
# cat testfile | /usr/local/bin/dosfilter > /dev/lp0
```

Now my text comes out looking normal: one line after the other and properly aligned. Pretty neat, but in real life, you don't usually send jobs to printers in this way. You create printers on the system and send jobs by spooling them. Let's create a spooler definition called lptest. Do this by editing /etc/printcap and adding the following information. Keep in mind that the printcap file is pretty picky about how it is laid out. That's why the guide you received with your Linux system (assuming you bought a boxed set) tells you to use printtool or something like it. Learning to do it the hard way is more fun in the long run and you wind up really understanding how the whole thing works. Later in the chapter, I'll show you how to use nice tools.

The /etc/printcap file looks like this:

```
lptest:\
      :sd=/var/spool/lpd/lptest:\
      :mx#0:\
      :sh:\
      :lp=/dev/lp0:\
      :if=/usr/local/bin/dosfilter:
```

Here's what all this means. The first line is simply a printer name. If you send a job to a printer with the lpr command, you would specify this queue name. The next line refers to the spool directory. In other words, where all the information related to the current job goes. This is a directory under the /var/spool/lpd directory (by default), but it could conceivably go anywhere you like. /var/spool/lpd is convention. I like to use a directory name that is the same as the queue name. mx refers to the maximum file size that you will allow sent to the printer. A zero means "unlimited," which is generally what you want unless you have decided that specific printers will not take jobs beyond a certain size (too slow, perhaps). The next line (:sh:\) means "suppress header page." Because this is a physically connected device, you have the lp option, which defines the parallel device itself (/dev/lp0 because I only have one parallel port). The last line refers to the "input filter," the dosfilter created earlier.

To make all this work, all you really need to do is create the spool directory (/var/spool/lpd/lptest) and send your job to the printer.

```
# mkdir /var/spool/lpd/lptest
# lpr -Plptest testfile
```

Did you get an extra, unwanted form feed with your job? If so, modify your dosfilter and remove (or comment out) the form feed line. Another way to deal with this, if you do not want to modify your dosfilter, is to simply add another parameter to the /etc/printcap definition that tells the printing subsystem to "suppress form feed." The line should look like this:

```
:sf:\
```

The option sh and sf are Booleans. Their presence in the /etc/printcap file means "true." It's up to you to decide what options you will need. For a complete list of printcap options, you can use man and check out the page.

```
# man printcap
```

By default, when you send a job to the printer with the lpr command, it uses a queue definition called lp (as opposed to lptest, or whatever name you gave your queue). If the queue is simply named lp, the only command you need to print is this:

```
# lpr printfile_name
```

That's why you used the long form of the command.

```
# lpr -Pprint_queue_name printfile_name
```

Here's a nice tip that will save you a few keystrokes. If you are always printing to one specific printer, you can add the PRINTER environment variable to your .bash_profile.

```
PRINTER=lptest ; export PRINTER
```

Now, after you log in, all you have to do (assuming you want to print to lptest) is type the first, simpler version of the print command (lpr printfile_name).

Let's look at printing to a remote Linux (or UNIX) printer. In this example, I'll create a printer called "faraway" on the current machine, "nearlinux." The printer (the lptest created earlier) is on another machine called "farlinux." Here's the /etc/printcap entry for nearlinux:

```
faraway:\
  :sd=/var/spool/lpd/faraway:\
  :mx#0:\
  :sh:\
  :rm=farlinux:\
  :rp=lptest:
```

If this is the first time you are trying this, I should tell you it won't work right away. You see, the printing subsystem does have some security associated with it. You must be *allowed* to print to farlinux. This is done by editing the file `/etc/hosts.lpd` and adding the host names or the host IP addresses of the machines that are allowed to print. My `hosts.lpd` file has these entries:

```
192.168.22.2
192.168.22.3
nearlinux
```

It is probably a good idea to restart your `lpd` daemon after making this kind of change. One way to do this is to simply do a `ps ax | grep lpd` and kill the current `lpd` process. The second (this may vary slightly from system to system) is to use these commands:

```
# /etc/rc.d/init.d/lpd stop
# /etc/rc.d/init.d/lpd start
```

On some releases, you can wrap this up in one command by using "restart" instead of "stop" followed by "start." Now from my machine, I can send a really important file to my remote Linux machine for printing.

```
# /usr/games/fortune -l | lpr -Pfaraway
```

HP JetDirect Adapters

A fairly common remote printing situation you may find yourself working with is the HP JetDirect adapter. These are increasingly common in IT shops these days. You'll find both a stand-alone version (to which you can attach any printer) and a built-in version common with network-ready HP LaserJets. You will need to have the JetDirect adapter or printer set up with an IP address. You should refer to the accompanying documentation to do this. Most of the HP network-ready printers enable you to do this setup through the printer's control panel. HP also distributes software packages called JetAdmin and WebAdmin to do this over the network. Once you've got your printer configured, using a JetDirect-connected printer with your Linux system is very easy. As far as Linux is concerned, these are just remote print servers.

In an earlier example, you set up a printer locally referred to as "faraway" to access a remote queue called "lptest." Here's what it looked like:

```
faraway:\
    :sd=/var/spool/lpd/faraway:\
    :mx#0:\
    :sh:\
    :rm=farlinux:\
    :rp=lptest:
```

Keeping that example in mind, let's say that your adapter has an IP address of 192.168.1.225 and a host name of `hpjd1`. To create a queue on your Linux system, use this `printcap` entry:

```
jdqueue1:\
   :sd=/var/spool/lpd/jdqueue1:\
   :mx#0:\
   :sh:\
   :rm=hpjd1:\
   :rp=text:
```

For text-only printing, this is all there is to it. Notice that the remote printer's name is "text." JetDirect cards and adapters have two recognized printer names. The other is "raw." If your output is always PCL or PostScript, you should use "raw" as the remote printer name.

HP also sells three-port HP JetDirect adapters that enable you to connect three printers at one IP address (or one physical network jack). Using one of these is not much more complicated. These cards recognize six different printer names: for simple text output, they are `text1`, `text2`, and `text3`. For raw, or PostScript output, try `raw1`, `raw2`, and (you guessed it) `raw3`.

Printer Job Control

The master control program for printers is `lpc`, a small, interactive command-line program. In its simplest form, you type this:

```
# lpc
```

The system replies with a quiet little prompt.

```
lpc>
```

If you type `status` here, you will get the status of all printers configured on that machine. Here's what the output looks like on my system:

```
lpc> status
   lp:
        queuing is disabled
        printing is disabled
        no entries
        no daemon present
color:
        queuing is enabled
        printing is enabled
        no entries
        no daemon present
lptest:
        queuing is enabled
```

```
printing is enabled
no entries
no daemon present
```

Let's take an example in which my main printer, `lp`, is having problems and I don't want the system to continue trying to print to it while I am trying to fix it. At the `lpc>` prompt, I type the following:

```
down lp "You should not have bothered with this printer."
```

What this will do is take down the printer and stop jobs from getting to it. Notice the message that follows `down lp`. This will print a message to anyone who queries the status of the print queue from his or her computer (I am assuming a remote user here, but the user could be local as well). So, not knowing what my system administrator has done, I still send a job to the printer. I then decide to see where in the queue my job sits, so I use `lpq` to find out. As you might have guessed, `lpq` reports on the status of queued jobs. You invoke it like this:

```
# lpq -Pprinter_name
```

Remember also that if you specify a `PRINTER` environment variable, you don't have to specify the printer. In other words, typing this command means that I can just enter the command `lpq` and leave it at that.

```
PRINTER=lptest ; export PRINTER
```

Here's what happens when I check the status of my job after my system administrator (okay, it's really me) downs the printer:

```
mycomputer.salmar.com: waiting for queue to be enabled on scigate
Rank    Owner      Job  Files                                    Total Size
1st     root       16   /etc/profile                              546 bytes

Warning: lp is down: "You should not have bothered with this printer"
Warning: lp queue is turned off
no entries
```

This tells me that I should consider using a different printer. The other alternative is to remove the job from the queue. This is done with the `lprm` command. To remove my orphaned job (number 16), I type the following:

```
# lprm -Plptest 16
```

Printing Anything to Any Printer

I'd like to talk a little bit more about filters. In my office, I have a small HP LaserJet 5L. It's the one I've been using for all the examples in this chapter. If you've spent any time whatsoever with Linux (or other UNICes/UNIXes), you know that most applications print using the PostScript format. Unfortunately, my printer doesn't print PostScript. Luckily, Linux is distributed with a little package called `ghostscript`.

I won't spend much time on `ghostscript` except to tell you that it is a powerful tool that also makes a great print filter. If I try to print a PostScript file to my printer, it comes out as strange text, which just happens to be a kind of code—code written in the PostScript language. Looking at the first ten lines of a PostScript file on my system, I see this:

```
# head contact.ps

%!PS-Adobe-PS
%%BoundingBox: 54 72 558 720
%%Creator: Mozilla (NetScape) HTML->PS
%%DocumentData: Clean7Bit
%%Orientation: Portrait
%%Pages: 1
%%PageOrder: Ascend
%%Title: Registrant Name Change Agreement
%%EndComments
%%BeginProlog
```

This is also what it looks like if I just send it to my printer without a filter of some kind that can interpret PostScript. Different Linux distributions offer different alternative filters, but all should have `ghostscript` in common.

Here's an example. I'll send my `contact.ps` file to the printer but pass it through a `ghostscript` filter beforehand. (Note that the following line wraps. It is just one line.)

```
    # cat contactm.ps | gs -q -dNOPAUSE -sDEVICE=ljet4 -r300
-sPAPERSIZE=letter -sOutputFile=- - | lpr
```

I know it looks like a lot to take in, but it's really pretty simple. The `-q` means that `ghostscript` should perform its work quietly. Normally, `ghostscript` would put out a lot of "this is what I am currently doing" information, not what I want for a print job. The `-dNOPAUSE` tells `ghostscript` to process all pages without pausing to ask for directions. The first `-s` flag that you see specifies the printer type. The `ljet4` definition covers a whole range of LaserJet printers that can do 600 dpi resolution.

This brings me to the `-r` flag, where I define a 300 dpi resolution. This Netscape Navigator generated page (remember that you can print to a file when using Netscape Navigator) doesn't need a 600 dpi resolution. `ghostscript` also enables me to specify `papersize`, important for those of us in North

America who hold firmly (if not wisely) to the 8½x11-inch letter-size format. Finally, I specify standard out as my output file. Notice the last hyphen in that line. It means that `ghostscript` is taking the input through its standard in. The last thing I do is fire it to the printer.

The great thing about `ghostscript` is its extensive printer support. Visit the `ghostscript` printer support page (`http://www.cs.wisc.edu/~ghost/`) if you want to see the latest and greatest list of support. When you visit the site, scroll down the list and click the "printer compatibility" link.

Armed with this, I could use essentially the same line to create an output filter for printing. Remember the dosfilter example earlier? There was only one real active line in the filter script (other than the staircase effect change) and that was a simple `cat`. That line would now be the `ghostscript` line from the previous code minus the `| lpr` at the end of it.

```
gs -q -dNOPAUSE -sDEVICE=ljet4 -r300 -sPAPERSIZE=letter -sOutputFile=- -
```

You can even use `ghostscript` as a desktop X viewer for PostScript files and documents by simply typing `gv` followed by the name of the file you want to see. `gv`, as you might have guessed, stands for "`ghostscript` viewer" (see Figure 13.1).

```
gv netscape_out.ps
```

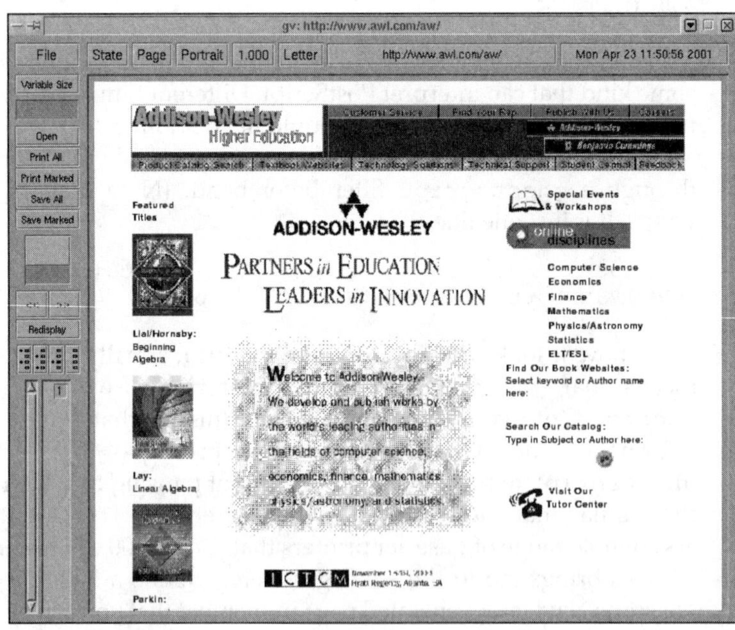

FIGURE 13.1 The `ghostscript` viewer, `gv`

Tying It Up: Advanced Filters with Ghostscript

All right, let's put some of the ideas presented in this chapter together. As I mentioned, a number of programs generate PostScript only rather than trying to create output for different printer types and languages. In the Linux world, that accounts for a lot of programs. Netscape Navigator is one such program, as is StarOffice from Sun Microsystems. So how do you deal with this?

Let's start with a quick reminder of the `ghostscript` output filter to convert PostScript to my LaserJet 5L printer. I've saved this file as `/usr/local/bin/psfilter` and made it executable with `chmod 755 /usr/local/bin/psfilter`.

```
#!/bin/bash
#
# Ghostscript filter so that my HP LJ5 will print PostScript files
#
echo -ne \\033\&k2G
gs -q -dNOPAUSE -sDEVICE=ljet4 -r300 -sPAPERSIZE=letter  -sOutputFile=- -
```

Now I also have a definition for the printer that uses that output filter.

```
pshpljet:\
:sd=/var/spool/lpd/pshpljet:\
:mx#0:\
:sh:\
:lp=/dev/lp0:\
:of=/usr/local/bin/psfilter:
```

Why PostScript?

The simple answer is that PostScript is close to a standard for defining objects (whether text or graphics) to printers, plotters, and even video screens. PostScript was designed to be completely device independent. Consequently, it provides a virtually universal print file format. PostScript (a trademark of Adobe Systems) was developed in the mid-80s and is actually a programming language. Because PostScript files are plain text, you can use a text editor to modify the source—even that of an image.

PostScript has been used in the UNIX world for many, many years. Because a number of the programs that come with your Linux system were originally designed in the UNIX world, it's not surprising that they work with PostScript. This is a plus and not a minus. As a result, you'll find many great tools specifically for working with PostScript. Furthermore, because you can print any PostScript file to any printer, everyone can do this.

A Few PostScript Tricks

Say you've got a two-page document (a program listing or a collection of bad, but funny, one-liners) and you really only want the thing to take up one page (they're not that good). That is where the `mpage` command comes into play. You are now going to print this document so that two pages fit onto one. The output will be rotated, so this will actually come out as portrait orientation.

```
mpage -2 funnyjokes.txt | lpr -Ppshpljet
```

The two pages appear on one page with a nice thin line around both pages. Let's make this just a little fancier, shall we? Try out the next command and see what kind of output it generates.

```
mpage -2 -B-5r-5l-3t-3b3 -M50l50r50t50b -H prog_specs.txt | lpr -Plptest
```

What does this all mean? The `-2`, by the way, could be a `-4` to fit four logical pages per physical page. Just so you are clear on my hastily chosen terminology, I am using the terms *logical* and *physical* to differentiate the printer output from the physical, "hold it in your hand" page. You can even do a `-8`, but that might be getting a tad silly. The `-B-5r-5l-3t-3b3` part means that a bold line (3 point) should be drawn around the box. That's actually the last 3 at the end of that line. The `-5r-5l-3t-3b` part means that you want a three-line margin at the top and bottom and a five-character margin at the left and right. The `-M` line uses a similar format and gives you a 50-point margin all around your virtual page. Remember that you have two logical pages on one physical page in this example. Finally, `-H` means that you want a header on each page. The header has the date on the right, the filename in the center, and a page number on the right.

So, where would you use this? One place that comes immediately to mind (after the one-liners, that is) is source code for your programs. This is a great way to generate compact program listings without having to import them into a word processor. I should point out that there is a non-PostScript way to create simple, numbered pages. All you have to do is use the `pr` command. Try this with a text-only printer definition:

```
pr +2 -h "Secret Kernel Enhancements" -o 5 ftl_travel.c | lpr -Ptextonly
```

`pr` is a command designed to format text for printing. The preceding line says to take the file `ftl_travel.c`, start printing at page 2 (`+2`), add a left-hand indent of 5 spaces (`-o 5`), and print the header "Secret Kernel Enhancements" on each page (`-h` followed by a string). If you do not specify a different header name, you'll get the filename itself, in this case `ftl_travel.c`. Oh, yes . . . it will actually start numbering the pages at page 2.

Alternative Print Systems

You'll get very little argument from the Linux community regarding the need for better and easier printing systems. While the `lp /lpd` printing system is good, works well, and has worked well for decades, a little simplification wouldn't hurt. Luckily, you can find some tools in the Linux world that are changing the face of printing from an administrative nightmare to something more fun and less frightening.

Every distribution differentiates itself with its own interface for system administration tasks such as setting up users and printers. Red Hat has `printtool` and SuSE has YAST. While I could explore each distribution's options for handling this, I'd like to spend some time looking at alternatives that are not release specific. In the next few sections, I'll introduce you to two such systems. Be sure to read Chapter 16 for an admin tools roundup and even more alternatives.

PDQ

According to the author Jacob A. Langford, PDQ stands for "print, don't queue" and a variety of other acronyms. His page is at the following address: `http://pdq.sourceforge.net/`.

PDQ is a nice, friendly little package that works on Linux and a variety of other UNIX systems. I'm not sure I agree completely with Jacob's reasoning on printing, accounting, and queuing, but that doesn't detract from PDQ's value. While it seems quite capable of dealing with large deployments of printers, what I particularly like about PDQ is that it presents the kind of friendly face that users of that other OS find so appealing, complete with a slick X window–like interface and wizards to help you set up your printers quickly and easily. You can even use Grant Taylor's compatibility list (at `http://www.linuxprinting.org/`) to find the latest PDQ drivers and filters.

Downloading the PDQ source and installing it is easy. When you get your copy, just make sure you substitute the appropriate release information. All you have to do is `untar` and unzip, and then do a `make` followed by a `make install`, as follows:

```
tar -xzvf pdq-2.2.1.tgz
cd pdq-2.1.2
make
make install
```

Now set up a base `printrc` configuration file, like this:

```
mv /etc/pdq/printrc.example /etc/pdq/printrc
```

To start PDQ and configure your first printer, simply type this command:

```
xpdq &
```

When the interface comes up, click Printer, choose Add, and follow the steps in the printer wizard. When you move your mouse over a field, PDQ provides context-sensitive, "bubble" help to guide you.

When you get to the driver selection screen, you may find the list somewhat limited—only about a dozen printers are listed, although you may be able to use a generic definition. For my HP LaserJet 5L, I went back to Grant Taylor's printer compatibility list and found my printer. To install this new driver, I typed the following:

```
cd /etc/pdq/drivers/hp
```

In the drivers directory, there are subdirectories for the printer classes (or brands, if you prefer). After changing to the hp directory, I used `vi` (you can use Emacs, Pico, or whatever editor you prefer) and simply cut and pasted the information on the screen. Then I restarted `xpdq`, and my printer was in the list (see Figure 13.2).

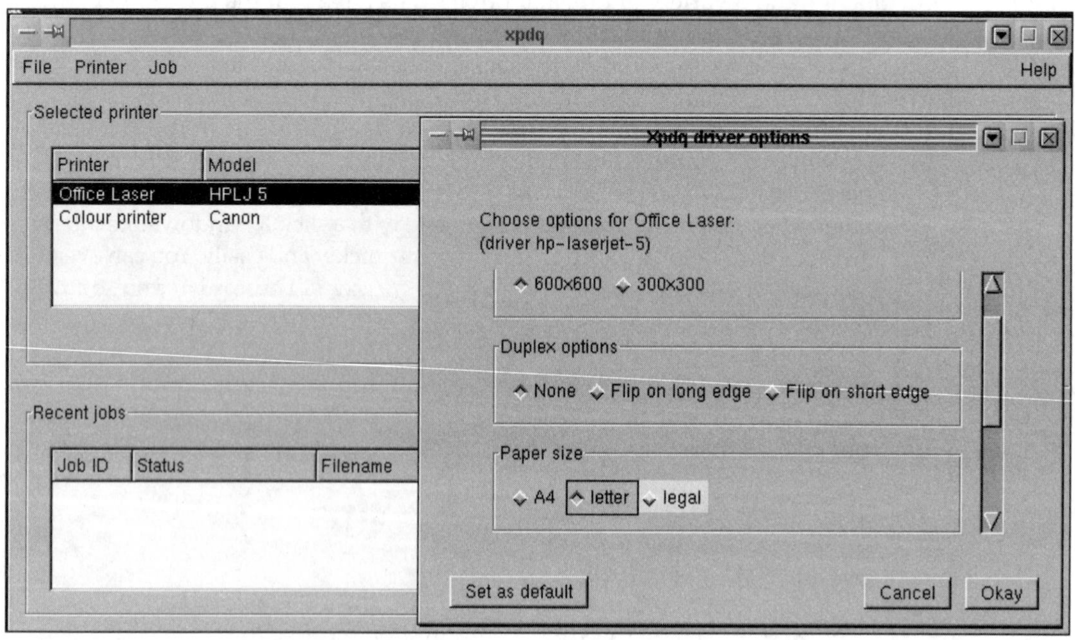

FIGURE 13.2 Printer configuration with `xpdq`

To print a job using PDQ, you send the job through the command line (did I mention there are command-line utilities that let you do what the X interface does?). The format is simple. For my test, I sent a PostScript file. I wanted to see PDQ's drivers and filters in action.

```
pdq -P hp51j /tmp/oneliners.ps
```

The `-P` flag calls the printer name as I defined it in the wizard, while the file called `/tmp/oneliners.ps` is my very important print file. The X interface (`xpdq`) then reports the status of the job and allows me the opportunity to reprint it, get a status on it (if it is deep in the list of jobs), or get information on the type of job.

CUPS

Another alternative to good old-fashioned `lpd` printing is CUPS. CUPS, or the Common UNIX Printing System, is designed to be a platform-independent printing system that works across many different UNIXes (or UNICes, if you prefer). The company that produces CUPS (Easy Software Products) distributes it under the GPL, but you should be aware that the number of print drivers is limited. You'll find the latest software at this address: `http://www.cups.org/`.

For large printer support, you might want to consider their ESP Print Pro, a commercial offering that includes CUPS, lots and lots of printer drivers, and a nice GUI. If you want to explore the commercial side of CUPS, visit `http://www.easysw.com/printpro/`.

CUPS uses the Internet Printing Protocol (IPP), a next-generation printing system aimed at replacing LPD with a "universal" printing environment (although it still supports LPD), where any user anywhere can print to any printer anywhere. It also aims to provide better authentication and security. The proposed standard would even allow for encrypted print jobs. Those who are really curious as to where this is going can visit the Printer Working Group's Web site (`http://www.pwg.org/`).

As I mentioned, CUPS has limited printer support in its free package; however, some popular printers are supported. If you want to go this route but prefer to stick to the freeware version (and you may use the provided drivers), you can still get a nice GUI for your desktop. Actually, you can get *several* nice GUIs, which kind of gives you an idea of the growing popularity of CUPS.

Visit the CUPS-Related Stuff Home Page (`http://cups.sourceforge.net/`) and you will find something to enlighten your CUPS experience. In particular, check out KUPS and QtCups.

Miscellaneous Tips and Tricks

If you are running Red Hat 6.1, you may have found yourself at a loss in trying to figure out why your system does not want to recognize your printer port.

There are two potential problems at work here. The first has to do with a line missing from the /etc/conf.modules file. Try adding this line if you don't see it:

```
alias parport_lowlevel parport_pc
```

Another problem has to do with the version of modutils that was distributed with the system. Visit the Red Hat site and pick up the latest modutils RPM package.

Resources

CUPS

http://www.cups.org/

Ghostscript

http://www.cs.wisc.edu/~ghost/

Linux Printing HOWTO

http://www.linuxdoc.org/HOWTO/Printing-HOWTO/index.html

Linux Printing Usage HOWTO

http://www.linuxdoc.org/HOWTO/Printing-Usage-HOWTO.html

LinuxPrinting.org

http://www.linuxprinting.org/

PDQ

http://pdq.sourceforge.net/

Printer Working Group

http://www.pwg.org/

Chapter 14

Scripting and Scripting Languages

One of my favorite lines is "I am not a programmer," which isn't to say that I don't know how to program or that I haven't wrestled with a number of different programming languages over the years. Names like COBOL, FORTRAN, BASIC, C, C++, Ada, Perl, and the dreaded assembler all come to mind as a reminder. I have been known to write programs and I am likely to do so again. It just doesn't happen to be the sort of thing that excites me. Administration excites me. So does network design, security, systems integration, and the great bugaboo, technical support (I love puzzles).

I'm like the chef who likes to put a number of ingredients together to create a new culinary masterpiece. Like that chef, I rely on others to provide me with the ingredients to do my work. Consequently, I have a deep admiration for professional (and amateur) programmers who can take a complex project and devote weeks or even months to bring out the tools that people like me rely on.

That said, as an administrator, you will need to program on some level. A single tool is rarely the answer to a single problem, but sometimes, assembling the right blend of tools will provide exactly the solution you seek. Putting those tools together requires programming. The average Linux distribution comes with a plethora of programming and program development environments. Luckily, the average administrator can satisfy all his or her programming needs with a couple of very neat languages.

One of those languages is something you are already using.

Shells As Far As the Eye Can See

The shell is the most basic of environments for working with your Linux system. Whatever you may think of working in a text environment, I guarantee that once you have fully experienced the power of simple text, you will be forever convinced. Text is compact. Text is fast. System administration over a network is best experienced at the shell level. Those forced to resort to graphical tools over a slow modem connection are also quickly converted.

What many people do not realize is that the shell is actually a programming language. There are many shells. The most common in the Linux world is called `bash`, the Bourne Again Shell. Other shells you may find on your Linux system include `sh`, the classic Bourne shell (I have yet to find a major Linux or UNIX distribution that did not include it), `pdksh` (the public domain Korn shell), and that old programmer's favorite, `csh` (the C shell).

The list of shells I've given you so far is but a small subset. There's `ash` (stands for "a shell"), `tcsh` (an enhanced C shell), and `zsh` (the Z shell). Like walking along the beach and building a collection of interesting and unique shell specimens, a little tour through your favorite software repository, such as Freshmeat (`http://www.freshmeat.net/`), will show you that people are constantly playing with and designing shells. Far from being an exhaustive list of the shells that exist for Linux, my list is merely a collection of the more popular ones. Certainly, all of these are likely to be on your distribution CD.

Programs written using these shells are collectively called *shell scripts*. Covering all these in detail would constitute another book (or perhaps several books), so I won't even pretend to attempt it. What I want to do in this chapter is get you comfortable with the idea of writing small, useful scripts to do your job as an administrator of your Linux domain, no matter how small or large. To that end, I will concentrate on `bash`. Then, I'll cover some of the other scripting languages out there in order to see how they might best help you do your job.

It's Commands All the Way Down

A shell script can be just a collection of commands saved in a file. Too easy?

Say that throughout the day, I regularly check the time and date, print the disk-free information, and check how long my system has been running with `uptime`. I can open a blank file with my favorite editor and just type each command on its own line.

```
date
df
uptime
```

If I save that as check3 (a completely arbitrary name), I can execute this script by typing the following:

```
bash check3
```

That's it. The shell, bash, executes the three commands in that file and exits. The simplest shell script imaginable is the command itself. For instance, while writing this book, I would occasionally want to capture a snapshot of a particular window. I did that with the import command (which was discussed in Chapter 9). Often, I would capture images from another desktop, a notebook computer that sat beside the main workstation on which I did my writing. The reason for the two was that I could build and rebuild the notebook while leaving my workstation untouched. To capture the images on the notebook, I used this command:

```
import -border -frame -colorspace GRAY -display testsys:0 image_name.tif
```

To simplify my life by saving myself several hundred keystrokes in the course of my work, I created an alias (as discussed in Chapter 5).

```
alias grabwin0='import -border -frame -colorspace GRAY -display\
testsys:0'
```

I also used a grabwin alias for the local system. Now all I had to do was type the command grabwin0 filename.tif and I had my capture, without all the typing. Another way to do this would have been to type the command into a file called grabwin, save it in /usr/local/bin, and make it executable, which would have produced the same effect. Rather than an alias, I would have had a shell script. Here are the steps:

```
vi /usr/local/bin/grabwin
  [Note: Here you type the command in and save your work. ]
chmod +x /usr/local/bin/grabwin
```

But wait—how do I pass the filename that I want to save? If I just run this script by typing /usr/local/bin/grabwin my_file.tif, it doesn't create the filename at all. That's because the script isn't using the information being passed to it. This brings us to the subject of parameters.

Passing Parameters

Here's a really simple way to experience how the shell interprets parameters passed to it. Write this little script and call it paramtest:

```
#!/bin/bash
# This script demonstrates positional parameters
#
echo "This is parameter 0 : $0"
echo "This is parameter 1 : $1"
```

```
echo "This is parameter 2 : $2"
echo "This is parameter 3 : $3"
echo "Here are all the parameters : $*"
```

Make it executable with `chmod +x paramtest`. Now, execute it like this:

```
./paramtest this is a shell script
```

This is the output you will see:

```
This is parameter 0 : ./paramtest
This is parameter 1 : this
This is parameter 2 : is
This is parameter 3 : a
Here are all the parameters : this is a shell script
```

The first thing you should notice is that the script name (or the command, if you prefer) is parameter `$0`. Parameters `$1`, `$2`, and `$3` are the first three words passed to the script. Notice also that the last two words, "shell script," have simply been absorbed by the script. These would have been represented by `$4` and `$5`, which you did not ask to have echoed to the screen. How about the last line? As you can see, the entire list of parameters (not counting the program name) is echoed back.

A First Look at Variables

The `$0`, `$1`, `$2`, and so on, are *variables*. In other words, they can represent different values depending on what parameters are passed to your script. The `$*` variable is a special one in that it represents all the parameters passed to the shell. Like the $number variables, this is one is built into the shell itself. You do not have to define it.

So, going back to the `grabwin` example, I could modify the script by simply adding a `$1` to the end of the command. Then, passing a filename would work. Here's the right script now:

```
import -border -frame -colorspace GRAY -display testsys:0 $1
```

To make the script more intelligent, I could add a check for a parameter using the "if" construct. The following is my updated script. I am also going to specify that I always want to use the `bash` shell for execution.

```
#!/bin/bash
# This script will capture a window on system testsys
if [ $# -eq 0 ]
then
   echo "grabwin : You must specify a filename"
   exit 0
else
   import -border -frame -colorspace GRAY -display testsys:0 $1
fi
```

Lots of stuff here. The script checks to see if there are any parameters at all. If the count of parameters (that's what the variable, `$#` means) is zero, it prints an error message and exits. If I remembered to pass it a filename, I get a much nicer, "job well done" kind of message.

```
$ grabwin eterm.tif
Capture of eterm.tif completed.
```

More on Variables

When you talk about shell programming, you deal with variables on different levels. You have the built-in variables you saw earlier, and you can assign variables. For instance, without writing a script, type this line at your shell (command-line) prompt:

```
hours=24
```

Then type this:

```
echo "There are $hours hours in a typical day"
```

The system responds with this:

```
There are 24 hours in a typical day.
```

You access that variable by putting a dollar sign (`$`) in front of it. If you just enter that line in a shell script (not the `hours=24` line), made that script executable and ran it, you would get this:

```
There are   in a typical day.
```

The shell script did not pick up the `$hours` variable. In order for the shell script to know about the variable "hours," you need to export it. There are two ways to do this. One is to assign the variable as you did and then type the command `export hours`. You can also put the whole thing on one line and save yourself some keystrokes.

```
export hours="24"
```

Running the script now displays a much more intelligent message about how many hours are really in a day.

Aside from user-assigned variables, the script can make use of environment variables. These are variables set for you at login time by the system. Some of these are sometimes overwritten by the `.bash_profile` file in the user's home directory or the global `/etc/profile`. A common one to see modified is the `PATH` variable, which lists the possible search paths for executables. Check your own `$HOME/.bash_profile` file for the references to `PATH`.

```
PATH=$PATH:$HOME/bin:/usr/local/bin
export USERNAME BASH_ENV PATH
```

As you can see, you can modify an environment variable by referencing it in your assignment. The second line exports PATH and a number of other variables so that they are available to you in any shell and any environment in which you might work. To have a look at your environment variables, type this command:

```
env
```

Special Characters

Certain characters mean very specific things to the shell. Following is a sample of what you will encounter.

Characters with special meaning to the shell

Character	Description
$	Highlights the beginning of a variable's name
#	Comment character
?	Matches a character
*	Matches any number of characters
.	Sources or tells the shell to execute the filename that follows
"	Defines a string
'	Defines even special characters as part of a string
`	Executes what is inside the ticks
\	Escapes the character that follows
[]	Lists a range of characters inside the brackets

The dollar sign ($) is one that you have already seen. It indicates the beginning of a variable name. You've also see the comment character (#) and in the next section, I will discuss some of its special properties. And way back in Chapter 5, I talked about the question mark (?) and the asterisk (*). So, let's now look at some of these others (in no specific order).

First and foremost, I want to talk about the backslash (\). When a backslash is put in front of a special character, it stops the shell from interpreting that special character. Here's a simple and, I think, effective demonstration. At your shell prompt, type this command:

```
$ echo *
```

Did you get a listing of every file in your directory separated by spaces? That's what I thought. Try it again, but this time put a backslash in front of the asterisk.

```
$ echo \*
```

Notice that the shell now echoes a single asterisk. Anytime you want to use a special character like those in the shell, but you don't want them treated in any way special, front them with the backslash (which I suppose is a kind of special treatment).

You Can Quote Me on That

Ah, quotes. I have lots of favorites. One of them is "I want to live forever or die trying," which is something Spider Robinson said but I wish I had. Sorry, different kind of quote.

Of course, I should be talking about what quotes mean to the shell. Double quotes ("") tell the shell to interpret what is inside them as a string. This is the way you define variables or echo text back to the terminal.

```
my_variable="This is a double quote \" inside my double quotes."
```

You'll notice that I put a double quote inside my double quotes, but escaped the character with a backslash. If I were to type `echo $my_variable`, this is what I would get:

```
This is a double quote " inside my double quotes.
```

Single quotes (') would seem, on the surface, to do the same thing as double quotes, but they do have another important function. Let's set a couple of variables and build a little shell script.

```
$ os_name="Linux"
$ os_desc="way cool"
$ echo "$os_name is $os_desc."
Linux is way cool.
```

That's more or less what you would expect here. Now, let's put single quotes around that `echo` command and see the difference.

```
$ echo '$os_name is $os_desc.'
$ os_name is $os_desc.
```

Hmm . . . it would seem that single quotes stop the shell from interpreting dollar signs as indicators of variable names. Now, how about those back ticks? Back ticks (`), or back quotes, are special in that they execute what is inside them. For instance, if you had a shell script that echoed `"The current date and time information is . . . "` and you wanted to have that something or other filled in, you would want the output of the `date command`. Here's one way of doing this:

```
the_date=`date`
echo "The current date and time information is $the_date."
```

Another, easier way to do this is to put the back-quoted date command inside the `echo` line itself.

```
echo "The current date and time information is `date`."
```

Really Programming the Shell

One of the things I mentioned was that the shell is a real programming language. This is entirely true. You have access to constructs like "if . . . then . . . else," while and for loops, case statements, and more. Just to give you an idea, here's a little script that runs the fabled Fibonacci sequence (named after famed 13th-century Italian mathematician, Leonardo Pisano, aka Fibonacci).

```
# Run a Fibonacci sequence through 10 iterations
#
last_number=1
previous_number=1
fib_iterations=0
echo "The sequence starts with 1 and 1"
until [ $fib_iterations -ge 10 ]
do
        new_number=`expr $previous_number + $last_number`
        echo "The sum of $previous_number and $last_number is $new_number"
        previous_number=$last_number
        last_number=$new_number
        fib_iterations=`expr $fib_iterations + 1`
done
#
echo "The sequence ends here after $fib_iterations."
```

All right, let's try something with a little more system administration potential. We know that Linux is a multiuser system, but letting people log in time and again when they already have sessions open may not be what you want. You may be running a hungry database application that costs you on resources (or licenses) each time somebody logs in. How can you stop users from logging in multiple times? In the following example, you'll create a file called `user.allow` that you'll put in a hypothetical script directory called `/usr/local/.Admin`. This is one I actually tend to use. The script is simple. If you list a user ID in this plain-text file with a space and a number, that user is allowed to log in however many times the number specifies.

```
marcel 3
tux 2
natika 4
```

In that example, marcel is allowed three logins, tux is allowed two, and natika is allowed a grand total of four. All other users will by default be allowed only one login at a time. To make sure that everyone executes this script on login, add this line to the `/etc/profile` file:

```
. /usr/local/.Admin/logtest
```

Notice the period at the beginning of the line that tells the shell to source (or execute) the filename that follows. Before you get too comfortable with this wonderful idea, you'll also want to make sure that the root user can log in as many times as he or she needs. I think you've got it all, so let's have a look at the `logtest` script.

```
# Test for multiple logins and refuse login if beyond configuration
#
if [ "$LOGNAME" != "root" ]
then
        no_logins=`finger | grep $LOGNAME | wc -l`
        no_allowed=`grep $LOGNAME /usr/local/.Admin/user.allow | cut -f2 -d" "`
        echo "No logins is $no_logins, while allowed is $no_allowed."
        if [ -z $no_allowed ]
        then
                let no_allowed=1
        fi
        echo "There are... $no_logins login processes under your name."
        echo "You are allowed $no_allowed login(s)."
        if [ $no_logins -gt $no_allowed ]
        then
                echo "You have exceeded your allowable limit."
                echo "Please try again later."
                sleep 5
                exit 0
        fi
else
        echo "You are SuperUser and can log in all you want!"
fi
```

Notice the `-z` test in the line that runs `if [ -z $no_allowed ]`. This tests the variable `$no_allowed` to see whether it is zero length or not. If it is zero (in other words, the UID was not listed in the `user.allow` exceptions file), you default that number to one.

> **Note:** Your shell supports a number of tests on variables and file types. You can test to see if a string length is zero sized (as you did in the example with the `-z`), if a file is executable (`-x`), or if a file even exists (`-e`) for that matter. There are a number of such tests built in to be used with files or variables. To see what kind of tests the shell supports, type `man test`.

So, if you try to log in as marcel for the fourth time, you get this message:

```
There are...       4 login processes under your name.
You are allowed 3 login(s).
You have exceeded your allowable limit.
Please try again later.
```

At this point, you get logged out and have to start getting used to the idea of being somewhat less greedy.

Specifying the Shell

If you look through some of your start-up scripts in the /etc/rc.d/init.d directory, or perhaps the /etc/init.d directory, you'll notice that they start with a rather interesting little construct. Here are the first five lines of my inetd start-up script:

```
[root@testsys /root]# head -5 /etc/rc.d/init.d/inet
#! /bin/sh
#
# inet          Start TCP/IP networking services. This script
#               starts the Internet Network Daemon.
#
```

See that #!/bin/sh line at the beginning? This hash-bang, #!/path_to_shell construct is a means of forcing a specific type of shell for execution of a script. Let's say that you created a shell script that used C shell–specific structures to do its work. Letting bash do the execution is certainly not going to yield the results you are looking for. Then, there are system functions, such as the at command (which is covered in the next chapter), that will execute all their commands with /bin/sh. What if you created your script to use some bash commands that the basic sh doesn't understand?

The solution is simple. Just put this line at the top of your shell script:

```
#!/bin/bash
```

Now, even if the shell that runs it is /bin/sh, it will switch to /bin/bash for execution of the script. This is also used to define other scripting environments. Perl scripts will have this line at the beginning:

```
#!/usr/local/bin/perl
```

Keep in mind that the path to the Perl interpreter may vary from system to system.

Perl

Let's just jump right in with a Perl program. Type the following code into a simple text file (call it whatever you like), make the file executable, and run it.

```
#!/usr/bin/perl
#
print "Perl, the Practical Extraction and Report Language, \n";
print "was written by Larry Wall way back in the eighties. \n";
```

Perl has been called the "Swiss Army knife" of programming languages, the "duct tape of the Internet," and other equally interesting things. What Perl is to you, as an administrator, is a means of writing powerful applications without changing vocations and becoming a professional programmer.

The language itself borrows from shell scripting, C, BASIC, and other languages. Perl has several mottos. Perhaps one of the more famous is "There's more than one way to do it." Apparently, this was a motto during the creation of the language.

Part of Perl's strength is its large user base. It is one of the most popular programming languages on the World Wide Web, and it is used in a huge number of CGI (*common gateway interface,* a set of hooks for Web programming) applications. Because of this, it is easy to get fooled into thinking of it in this way and this way alone. Perl is a great little toolkit that you should get to know better.

Remember the CPAN archives I talked about in Chapter 11? There are tons of precreated modules out there to help you with countless tasks.

Perl in Action: A Script for Monitoring Disk Space

There are several books easily as thick as this one covering the topic of Perl, so I won't even pretend to think that I can tell you everything you need to know in a few pages. Instead, I am going to give you a practical example of a Perl script for your day-to-day system maintenance routines. In this case, you'll create a Perl script that can be set to run on a regular basis (see the next chapter on automation) to inform you of critical disk space issues. If the disk space dips below 10 percent of the total, someone is informed. Let's have a look at it, and then I'll discuss what is happening.

```
#!/usr/bin/perl
#
# checkdfusage.pl : checks the usage of the disk space in percentage
#                   and e-mails it to sysadmin if greater than 90 percent

$admin_addr = 'marcel\@my_domain.dom';
&check_dfusage;
exit();
```

```
##### Subroutines #####

sub check_dfusage {
            @diskinfo=`df`;
            $message_text = ' ';
      foreach (@diskinfo) {
                ($dirname, $arg1, $arg2, $arg3, $arg4, $arg5, $arg6) =
                        split (' ', $_, 7);
                ($arg4num,$therest) = split('%',$arg4,2);
                if ($arg4num > "90") {
                     $message_text .= "Directory $dirname is now at
                     $arg4num\n";
                    }
#print $arg4 . "\n";

      }
      if ($message_text ne ' ') {
                &sendmessage;
      }
}
sub sendmessage {
      open(SF,"|mail -s 'Important system info' $admin_addr");
      print SF "$message_text";
      close(SF);
}
```

The first thing you do is set up the mail address of your administrator. That could be you or a comma-delimited list of users who should be informed. Note that the commercial at sign (`@`) in the e-mail address is escaped with the backslash character.

There are two subroutines and each is identified by the reserved word "sub" at the beginning of the line. Depending on the outcome of the first (called `check_dfusage`), you may or may not call the second routine (called `sendmessage`) to do its job.

The variable `@diskinfo` is what is called an *array variable* in Perl. The results of the command inside the back ticks (or back quotes, if you prefer) are used to populate the array. Then you take the array apart into its constituent parts, line by line. This is the `foreach` keyword. Essentially, take each line generated by the `df` command and split it into its various parts. Here's a refresher and a look at one of my disks:

```
/dev/hda1      1865200    1753144      17308   99% /
```

The number I am interested is in the fourth column (after the file system device name), which is represented by `$arg4` in the script. If `$arg4` (minus the percent sign—note the `split` keyword) is greater than 90, you move on to preparing a message and informing your admin people. That 90 is an arbitrary limit that I set here. If you want to be warned at 75 percent, change that limit to 75.

You make this script executable with `chmod +x /path_to/script` and you execute it. With my disk space as shown in my `df` output previously, I get the following message in my e-mail:

```
Directory /dev/hda1 is now at 99
```

Of course, judging by how close you are to the mark here, a more dramatic message might not be such a bad idea.

Other Languages Worthy of Consideration

Space and the desire to cover other topics demand that I stop this chapter somewhere around here. Still, there are many programming languages out there that allow for the rapid development of applications that may help you out on a day-to-day basis. Two that you should certainly consider are Python and Tcl/Tk.

Both Python and Tcl/Tk have large, enthusiastic support and development structures and both have their advantages.

Resources

Books

Programming Perl, by Larry Wall (Cambridge, MA: O'Reilly and Associates, 2000)

Web Sites

BASH Programming HOWTO

`http://www.linuxdoc.org/HOWTO/Bash-Prog-Intro-HOWTO.html`

CPAN (Comprehensive Perl Archive Network)

`http://www.cpan.org/`

Perl's home page (one of them, anyhow)

`http://www.perl.com/`

Python Language Web Site

`http://www.python.org/`

Tcl SourceForge Project

`http://tcl.sourceforge.net/`

Chapter 15

Simplified Administration through Automation

Constructive Laziness

I've joked for years that system administrators are notoriously lazy people. They will work impossibly long hours late into the night with the sole intention of automating a process so they never have to do the work again. That is precisely the kind of system administrator I have always been (which means I pay for my laziness by constantly working to find ways to not work). I am not alone in thinking this way. Larry Wall, the Perl guru, claims that laziness is one of the three great virtues of a programmer. I say "administrator." He says "programmer."

As support for this claim regarding the virtue of laziness, I did a quick search on a popular Internet search engine recently using the words "laziness," "system," and "administrator," and I got over 3,500 hits. Robert A. Heinlein wrote a story about a man too lazy to fail. In fact, one of his characters, Lazarus Long (from *Time Enough for Love*), claims that "Progress is made by lazy men looking for easier ways to do things." Suffice it to say that in the computer world, laziness (combined with a little cleverness) can be exceedingly useful to both the administrator and his or her clients.

In this chapter, I am going to show you how to let your system do some of the repetitious, simple (yet time-consuming) tasks for you. If you are ready to share the load with your Linux system, then here we go.

cron: Punching Linux's Clock

One of the basic processes running on your system is a utility called cron. The actual program is called crond (the cron daemon). cron is a little program that does a great deal. Every UNIX system has some form of cron as part of the system scheduler. On my Red Hat Linux system (and on most distributions), cron is actually "Vixie cron" written by Paul Vixie. Slackware's cron is a little different—it uses Matthew Dillon's dcron package instead.

So, how, you ask, will change your life? What will it do for you? cron enables you to run repetitive tasks at the time and date specified by a user in a file called a crontab. Entries in the crontab run with the user's ID and privileges and are stored as the user name (this is their name from the /etc/passwd file). For instance, root's crontab is called "root." Every minute, cron will wake up and check to see if any jobs need to be run. These jobs can be just about anything you can put into a script file: doing backups, cleaning up log files, removing core files, e-mailing you a daily Linux quote from the fortune program, and so on. This version of cron also checks to see if any of the directories and files it monitors have been changed. If so, it will reread those files and readd them to its to-do list. The plus is that you do not have to restart cron.

The location of the crontab varies slightly from system to system. There are also cron jobs that exist on the system, more or less for the system alone. Have a look in your /var/spool/cron directory. On my Red Hat system, the various user crontabs are all there. On a Debian system, there is a further subdirectory called crontabs under which the user crontabs live.

The times at which the commands in cron.daily, cron.weekly, and others get executed is in the /etc/crontab file. Here's what mine looks like:

```
SHELL=/bin/bash
PATH=/sbin:/bin:/usr/sbin:/usr/bin
MAILTO=root
HOME=/

# run-parts
01 * * * * root run-parts /etc/cron.hourly
02 4 * * * root run-parts /etc/cron.daily
22 4 * * 0 root run-parts /etc/cron.weekly
42 4 1 * * root run-parts /etc/cron.monthly
```

Now that I have that out of the way, here is a crontab entry for the root user:

```
30 2 * * * /usr/local/.Admin/backup.system 1>/dev/null 2>/dev/null
```

Look at the last entry in the previous crontab snippet. The command is /usr/local/.Admin/backup.system and its standard input and output

> There are six fields in a `crontab` entry:
> - The minute, which is usually (always, actually) between 0 and 59
> - The hour, which runs from 0 to 23
> - The day of the month (This where "30 days has September . . ." comes in handy.)
> - The month (Conveniently, Linux uses a 12-month calendar.)
> - The day of the week, numerically speaking, with 0 being Sunday
> - The command string; namely, what you wanted to automate in the first place

is being redirected to `/dev/null`. Using the field definitions as explained previously, you can see that the command runs at 2:30 AM every day of every week of every month. The * (asterisk) means "always."

If you want something to run several times in a day, you don't need a line for each entry. For instance, a process set to run every 15 minutes could be written like this:

```
0,15,30,45 * * * * /path/to/my_15_minute/process
```

You can also indicate sequential periods without multiple lines. Let's take the same process as before, but this time I will make sure it runs Monday through Friday at the same 15-minute intervals. I could enter the day field as "1,2,3,4,5" but you can see that this could get tedious (not to mention ugly) if I tried the same thing for something that ran from the first of the month through to the fifteenth of the month. Try this instead:

```
0,15,30,45 * * 1-15 * /path/to/my_15_minute/process
```

Testing Your Job

A good way to test a `cron` job is to schedule your job for five minutes from now (or whatever) and watch the results. (`cron` will also send messages indicating any output information to the user's mailbox, which is particularly useful when you are redirecting `stdin` and `stdout` to `/dev/null`.)

Editing the crontab

The proper way to edit a `crontab` is to use the command `crontab -e`. This puts you into the `vi` editor where you can make your changes. When you write your changes, `crontab` verifies (to some degree) the sanity of your changes and informs you if you have done something really strange. For those of you who are less than fond of `vi`, you can specify another editor by using the `EDITOR` environment variable.

```
export EDITOR=pico
```

You can also edit another user's `crontab` (assuming you are root) by using the following version of the command. The `-u` flag defines the alternate user.

```
crontab -u user_name -e
```

Could I See an Example?

I know that you are just dying to go out and automate something with `cron`, but what? Here's a thought. Every system builds up a collection of old junk files that no one ever looks at again. Every system accumulates core files, those discards of a program gone bad or interrupted less than gracefully. Let's look at some ways to automate the process of discovery, starting with a look at `find`, which was introduced in Chapter 5.

Here's a little one-line refresher that looks for anything greater than 500K (1,024 512-byte blocks) that hasn't been modified (the `-mtime` parameter) or accessed (the `-atime` parameter) in the last 12 months. The `-ls` parameter simply means that `find` should list what it finds.

```
find /data -size 1024 \( -mtime +365 -o -atime +365 \) -ls
```

> **Note:** Remember not to ignore those backslashes in front of the parentheses; these are shell escape characters that need to be there.

The previous example is fairly simple, but you can use it as the basis of something a bit more complex. How about a job that runs every night, logs what it finds, and e-mails the result to you at another machine?

```
#!/bin/bash
#
# Locate files and report to me.
# Marcel Gagne, 2000
#
search_log=/tmp/foundfiles
rm -f $search_log
touch $search_log
#
echo "-------------------------------- " >> $search_log
echo "Looking for big old files . . . " >> $search_log
echo "-------------------------------- " >> $search_log
#
find /data1 -size +2048 \( -mtime +180 -o -atime +180 \)  \
   -ls -exec file {} \; >> $search_log
#
echo "-------------------------------- " >> $search_log
```

```
echo "Looking SUID / GUID files . . . " >> $search_log
echo "------------------------------ " >> $search_log
#
find / -type f \( -perm -2000 -o -perm -4000 \) -ls >> $search_log
#
echo "------------------------------------------------ " >> $search_log
echo "Looking for core files or old editor files . . . " >> $search_log
echo "------------------------------------------------ " >> $search_log
#
find / \( -name core -o -name "*~" \) -print >> $search_log
#
echo "------------------------------ " >> $search_log
echo "All done!" >> $search_log
mail -s "Big and old file report" myuser@anothersys.com < $search_log
```

I could have modified the search for core files so that it deleted them as it found them, but in this example, I want a complete report so that I can decide what gets deleted after I have had a chance to study the report and be sure. By the way, for those who would like the automatic deletion of core files as a result of this search, try this version of the `find` command:

```
find / -name core -exec rm -f {} \;
```

This will simply "seek out and destroy" any and all core files from your system. Note once again that the backslash with the semicolon is required at the end of the `find` command. The `-exec` option tells `find` that a command string will follow. The double braces (`{}`) at the end of the line tells `find` to substitute all it found and pass it to the command string (which in this case is `rm -f`).

> **Caution:** Normally, I might worry about letting the system simply delete what it finds (even if I am the one who told it to do so), but core files are an exception and I am using `rm -f` rather than `rm -rf`, which does a recursive delete of whatever it finds. Consequently, the only real fear I might have—that the `core` directory under `/proc` might accidentally be deleted—is addressed. It will remain safe, as this script/command will leave it untouched.

Call the script `seekanddestroy` (or whatever else you might like) and save it in your `/usr/local/.Admin` directory. Using `chmod +x`, let's make the script executable and then create a `cron` job to run it. How about every morning at 3:00?

```
0 3 * * * /usr/local/.Admin/seekanddestroy
```

Running Jobs with at

The truly great thing about cron isn't strictly that you can run scripts that automate otherwise tedious processes, but that you can have the system do it when you are not there. Ah, if you could only get your employer to pay you for doing work while you are away from the office.

Another way to run jobs is with the at command. You could, of course, do the same thing by letting cron handle it with a crontab entry. The reason for using at is that it enables you to do some pretty free-form stuff. For instance, say I am going on vacation (leaving Tuesday next week and it is now Thursday) and I want to create a vacation notification for anybody sending me e-mail while I am gone. The trouble is that while I remember to do this now, I might not remember on Monday. I could go through the trouble of creating a cron job or just have at execute the command for me when the time comes.

```
at 6 pm Monday -f /path_to/file_that_updates_vacation_program
```

As you can see, at understands English-like definitions of time and dates, which makes it pretty easy to define when you want something to happen. The -f parameter tells at to read the necessary commands from a script file. At any time, you can find out what jobs you have queued for the at command to execute with the atq command. By the way, atq is synonymous with at -l. The following is a sample of the command and its output. The 12 at the beginning reflects the job number for the at queue.

```
# atq
12   2000-09-26   18:00 a
```

If you don't want to bother with writing a script file, you can do the whole thing from the command line, as follows:

```
at noon today
at> /usr/games/fortune -l linuxcookie | mail -s "Read this" me@here.dom
at> ^D
```

If I type the command as above, specifying only a date and time, the at command will enter a dialogue with an at> prompt where I enter my commands. The command prompt will repeat with each line I enter. To signal completion of my commands, I press Ctrl-D. The following is another way to do it that should give you an idea of the flexibility of Linux shell scripting:

```
at noon today << MY_COMMANDS
/usr/games/fortune -l linuxcookie | mail -s "Linux info" me@here.dom
MY_COMMANDS
```

Finally, if it turns out that you are only kidding and you do not really want to run the job, you can delete it with the atrm command. Using the output from the previous `atq` example, you can remove job 12 from the queue like this:

```
atrm 12
```

A Question of Permissions

I suppose I should have told you about this earlier. Those of you who followed the golden rule of never running from the root account (unless absolutely necessary) probably found yourselves denied from doing any of this. The `at` command simply says, "You do not have permission to use `at`." End of story. Meanwhile, `cron` is a tad more vocal.

```
You (mgagne) are not allowed to use this program (crontab).
See crontab(1) for more information.
```

Access to these commands is controlled by the `/etc/at.allow` and `/etc/at.deny` files in the case of the `at` command and the (you guessed it) `/etc/cron.allow` and `/etc/cron.deny` files in the case of the `cron` command. These are simply text files with a list of users allowed access to either `at` or `cron`. If you want to give everyone access, simply leave an empty `at.deny` or `cron.deny` file in place because these represent a list of who *isn't* allowed access. To limit access to a select few, you can simply create an `at.allow` or `cron.allow` file because this is a text list of the *privileged* users of the `at` or `cron` command. In the latter case, make sure you at least include the root user in that list.

Other Tools for Automation

Your Linux system contains many different tools for simplifying your life as a system administrator. If you are routinely fetching a local copy of a particular file, you can imagine that it would be so much easier if you could simply create a `crontab` for that process. The trouble with that idea has to do with the `ftp` command's interactive nature (you have to log in, provide a password, and so on).

Sometimes the file you are looking for is strictly informational, sitting out on a Web site somewhere. I had a customer who, for internal policy reasons, only allowed external Web access to one workstation through the Linux Internet gateway. That said, this customer still wanted everybody in the office to view the courier service's daily status report (available through the courier's Web site). A local copy of that Web page would have solved the problem, but my customer did not want to start teaching local Web site design to one of the users. It had to be *magic.*

Ladies and gentlemen, it's Linux to the rescue.

Automatic Downloads: ncftp

Let's take a look at that file you need to pick up each and every day (night/hour). Start an `ftp` session and transfer that file to your site (or from your site to the remote site). As I said, this is easy. It is also tedious and repetitious—precisely the sort of drudgery that computers are supposed to eliminate (or so we are told).

Your Linux system comes with a nice little utility called `ncftp` that is designed to make this type of thing nearly painless. With this program, you can create shell scripts that handle these transfers for you automatically. To do this, `ncftp` uses two other programs: `ncftpget` (to get a file from a remote system) and `ncftpput` (to transfer a local file to a remote site). I'll show you how to do this in a moment, but consider having a look at `ncftp` regardless of whether or not you find yourself in the situation of having to automate a transfer. It has some capabilities that the standard command-line `ftp` does not, such as a resume feature for aborted transfers, on-the-fly transfer statistics, and estimated time of completion. It's `ftp` on steroids. For instance, say that I just do regular transfers from my location to one of my remote offices. I can connect to the remote system like this:

```
ncftp -u username ftp://ftp.myremotebranch.net/documents/
```

Furthermore, you can store the current session in a bookmark to completely automate your access next time around. The program will prompt you for details. If I chose to save the session as "branch2," all I have to do next time is connect like this:

```
ncftp branch2
```

Wonderful. But the kind of automation I've been touting here is a bit different. I am usually referring to macros that automatically go through the process of logging into your remote site, pass your user name and password information, get (or put) the appropriate file, and then log out. This is where `ncftpget` and `ncftpput` come into play.

Let's create a transfer of a file called "sales_projections.txt" from a server called "mktg1." To run the whole process on the command line, use this command:

```
ncftpget -u my_user -p my_pass mktg1 /localdir \
/docs/sales_projections.txt
```

The -u and -p parameters can be omitted if this is an anonymous ftp transfer. In the reverse case where you want to transfer a file *to* a remote site, you use the ncftpput command. Let's try it by sending marketing a file called sales_results.txt.

```
ncftpput -u my_user -p my_pass mktg1 \
/localdir/sales_results.txt /docs
```

To fully automate the process, put the command in a script, create an appropriate crontab, and let your system do the work for you.

Automatic Web Fetch: wget

Here's a nice and easy solution to the problem I told you about earlier where my customer decided that no one got to surf the Web from the office but nevertheless wanted everyone to be able to access one page on the courier's Web site.

```
#!/bin/bash
#
# Pick up my courier's delivery updates page for local access
#
cd /home/httpd/html/mycourier
mv deliveryupdates.html olddeliveryupdates.html
wget -l1 http://www.mycouriers_website.com/deliveryupdates.html
chmod 644 /home/httpd/html/mycourier/deliveryupdates.html
#
```

Running from a crontab at regular intervals, this script starts by renaming the current delivery update page. Then, wget picks up the new page from the Web site. Incidentally, the -l1 flag tells wget to stick to one level. There are options that tell wget to spider the remote Web site and create a complete mirror on your system. This is not what I want in this case. The final step in my script is to make the new page readable to all. After the script has run, anyone can now access the deliveryupdates.html page from the internal server by simply pointing his or her browser to the proper page.

```
http://linux_server/mycourier/deliveryupdates.html
```

Now, everyone in the office has access to this vital information without having Internet access.

Scripting for Interactive Sessions: expect

At first glance, it would seem that you are out of luck if what you want to automate requires human intervention. There are things that need someone to pick from menu options, enter passwords, or make decisions based on the information presented. Interactive applications require a user's reaction, don't they? The answer for the cleverly lazy system administrator is "Not always" thanks to a little program called `expect`.

While I had heard of `expect` sometime before, I discovered a few years ago just how useful this language is. My partner and I were developing a Web-based system that required regular updates from the main computer's database, a database that would not allow command-line scripting. The data we needed required the execution of an SQL statement that could only be entered through the vendor's menu interface. That SQL statement would then generate the data file we needed for the Web interface. The whole process hinged on writing something that mimicked a user sitting at a terminal entering information as the various prompts were presented to him or her. Expect, a software suite/language based on Tcl, was the answer to our dilemma. Later, Expect would make it possible to stretch our Web-tool well beyond what we, ahem, expected at the time.

Still wondering if you need it? Remember that laziness discussion at the beginning of the chapter? Well, pretend that you are working late and that the last thing you need to do before leaving is to log onto your remote site, make sure that a specific application has completed (it is always done by 3:00 AM), and then download the file that application generates back to your local site. It is now 10:00 PM and you would much rather go home than wait for the magic moment when the file is ready. You could just launch an `at` job that starts `ncftp` for the download, but you don't know the filename because the output name changes at each run. You find the name by logging into the menu system and checking the completion log. (I am purposely making this complicated to demonstrate that there are instances that are hard to automate with a simple shell script.)

The basic format of an `expect` script is this:

```
#!/usr/local/bin/expect
# Comments on this script (name, what it does, optional)
spawn some_command
set response myanswer
expect "Some prompt . . . . "
send $response\r
close
```

Here's what happens. The `spawn` keyword tells `expect` to begin some program. This could be a shell (`spawn /bin/bash`) or any kind of command through which the session will take place. With the `set` keyword, you set the variable `response` to some predetermined response. The language's namesake, the expect keyword, does exactly what it sounds like it does. It scans the output of whatever command you invoked with spawn, searching for matching text. Then, send responds to the expected text with the first variable, $response. Let's do something real now.

I run an Apache Web server on my system with OpenSSL extensions for secure transactions. Starting Apache with the OpenSSL extensions running requires me to enter a security pass phrase in order for it to start up because the private key files on the server are encrypted. This is all fine if I am there to enter the pass phrase, but what happens if the server goes down when I am not there? It hasn't happened for months, but these things can happen and I do go on vacation sometimes. It could be something as crazy as me adding a SCSI card for my new tape drive. I might have forgotten (it has happened) to restart the Web server with OpenSSL running. What then? To get around this problem, I wrote the following simple expect script:

```
#!/usr/bin/expect
# Routine: startapachessl
# Purpose: Start Web server with OpenSSL active
#
log_file -a /tmp/expectlog
#log_user 0
spawn /bin/bash
sleep .2
send "/usr/local/apache/bin/apachectl startssl\r"
expect "Enter pass phrase*"
sleep .2
send "mysecretphrasegoeshere\r"
sleep .2
close
```

When the system restarts, whether I am there or not, this script will restart my Apache Web server with OpenSSL running. Looking at the script, you'll notice a couple of interesting things. For instance, the log_file parameter is new. What this does, as you might expect, is define a log file for the execution of this script. Whether the file is written to or not is defined by the log_user parameter. If the parameter is set to 1, logging will take place. I tend to use log_user when I am still testing the script, but you may decide you want to capture the output at all times. Notice as well that I am spawning a bash shell to execute the script that starts my server. Then, there are the sleep statements. In all cases, I have the shell wait ⅕ second before continuing on. Finally, the close statement tells the spawned process that there is nothing more to come. At this time, expect terminates and returns to the process that spawned it.

There is no doubt that you could program these functions with other languages, but expect makes it easy. What you will find as you go along is that not every tool is perfect for every job. For quick and dirty automation of interactive applications, nothing beats expect.

Fully exploring expect would require a book on its own (in fact, there is one) and what I am trying to do is give you a taste of what you can do with it rather than explaining every aspect of the language. Before I let you run off to do your own exploring, let me take these examples one step further.

We all know that changing passwords on a regular basis is a good thing, as is choosing good passwords (see Chapter 7), and it is a fairly easy thing to have a user do when he or she logs in but somewhat more difficult if the user does not have a login account. I'm talking about e-mail-only users, the ones who you allow POP3 mail pickup (or Web-based e-mail) but no actual command prompt access. A number of offices have precisely this kind of setup for their Linux systems—it serves as an e-mail or Internet gateway and allows no logins. So, how do you allow users who aren't allowed to login to change their passwords? After all, changing passwords is an interactive activity as the following dialogue will attest.

```
[root@myhost] # passwd
New UNIX password:
```

Even more complicated is that in order for a nonroot user to change his or her password, that user must first enter his or her old password, so the dialogue is even more complex. What now?

You could create a Web-based form whereby a user could enter all that information up front (see Figure 15.1).

A Perl script behind the form would extract the variables and pass them to an `expect` script that does the rest. If you are curious about this little

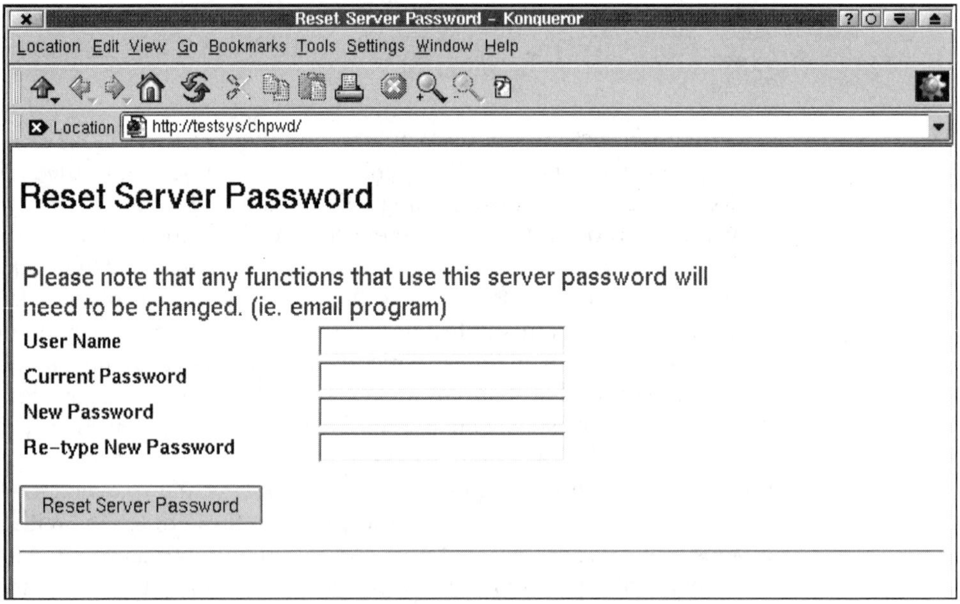

FIGURE 15.1 Modifying passwords through a Web browser

Web application or would like to use it, feel free to download it from my Web site (`http://www.salmar.com/marcel/`). Look in the Downloads section.

In the meantime, have a look at this segment from the application:

```
#!/usr/bin/expect
# Routine: psdcmd
# Purpose: to change a user's password with expect
log_user 1
set uservar [lindex $argv 0]
set currpassword [lindex $argv 1]
set newpassword [lindex $argv 2]
set renewpassword [lindex $argv 3]
#
# log_file -a /tmp/expectlog
# send_user "Spawning passwd command with uservar.\n"
spawn su -l -c "passwd" $uservar
expect "Password:"
sleep .1
send "$currpassword\r"
sleep .1
#
expect {
       "(current) UNIX password:" {send "$currpassword\r"}
"su: incorrect password" {exit 0}
     }
sleep .1
expect {
     "su: incorrect password" {exit 0}
             "New UNIX password:" {send "$newpassword\r"}
}
sleep .1
expect {
"BAD PASSWORD:" {exit 0}
        "Retype new UNIX password:" {send "$renewpassword\r"}
}
sleep .1
expect {
"su: incorrect password" {exit 0}
        "New UNIX password:" {exit 0}
}
#End of password change routine
```

The `set varname [lindex $argv num]` construct represents arguments passed to the `expect` routine. Notice that the `spawn` parameter call does an `su` to the user name in order to change the password. By default, CGI scripts on a Web server execute as some unprivileged user like `nobody` or `www`, so you need to change your effective user in order to change the password. Those names aren't etched in stone, by the way. The latest Red Hat 7.0 uses `apache` as the user name that runs the Web server. You could specify just about anything you want.

> **Warning:** You *want* to keep the default user for your Apache server as non-root. The alternative constitutes a potentially horrific security weakness.

There is one other new item in the script. Look at the `send_user` parameter. This is essentially a print statement. I left it in the sample script because I wanted to show you a clever way of debugging your `expect` scripts. Every programmer has inserted debug statements into his or her code to monitor how things were going. This is the same idea in this case. You can use `send_user` as a means of communicating with the outside world in the course of the script's execution. Because I capture the output of the `expect` script through my Perl script, I will see these messages as well.

By the way, the Perl script calls the routine in this way (the entire command is on one line):

```
$return_code = `./psdcmd "$username" "$currpassword" "$newpassword"
"$renewpassword" `;
```

As you can see, the `expect` script is called with the user name, current password, the new password, and the new password repeated. I could simply have passed the new password twice, but I wanted to keep the verification aspect of the password change routine as close to what the user would experience as possible at the command line. More to the point, it is probably also a good idea to force the user to confirm the password before changing things on him or her.

Automating Interactive Automation

Now that you have had your introduction to scripting with `expect`, I am going to make the process almost impossibly easy. Rather than manually creating an `expect` script, how about letting a program do that for you, too? When you install `expect`, you will also install a little program called `autoexpect`. Simply put, `autoexpect` watches whatever you are doing in an interactive session and creates the `expect` script for you. Here is the format of the command:

```
autoexpect -f script_outputfile command_string
```

For instance, imagine that you want to log into a remote system that is behind a firewall—essentially a two-step login process. After you log into the firewall, you execute a login (`telnet`, `ssh`, and so on) to yet another system on the internal network, and then you execute a standard menu program. What you would like is to have this whole process of logging in twice and starting the menu automated for you. From the command prompt, type this command:

```
autoexpect -f superlogin.script telnet firewall.mycompany.com
```

When you have finished your login, you can exit the menu and log out. Just like magic, `autoexpect` will have captured the entire session for you. Now, you will probably want to do some editing in there, but the basics of the script and all the prompts are captured there for you. Make the script executable and you are almost done. There is still one other thing you will want to add. At the end of your new `expect` script, add this command:

```
interact
```

This tells `expect` to return control to you after it has done its work. Without it, `expect` closes the spawned process and all you've managed to do is log in and log out very quickly.

In no way do I intend this to be the definitive reference on `expect`. I do, however, hope that this little introduction (indeed, this whole chapter) will serve to whet your appetite and inspire you to explore other ways of developing constructive laziness. After all, we all have other work to do.

What's all this on your screen about a magic cloak?

Resources

Books

Exploring Expect, **by Don Libes (Cambridge, MA: O'Reilly and Associates, 1994)**

Web Sites

Expect Home Page

`http://expect.nist.gov/`

GNU Wget

`http://www.cg.tuwien.ac.at/~prikryl/wget.html`

NcFTP Software

`http://www.ncftp.com/`

Salmar Web site (click the Downloads link to find the Password Change Web Form)

`http://www.salmar.com/marcel/`

Tcltk.com

`http://www.tcltk.com/`

Chapter 16

Devices, Devices, and More Devices

At some point, you will likely add a new device to your system—for example, a tape drive to do your backups or that really great new CD writer for making long-term archives of software or data.

This chapter deals with the creation and support of those devices that might not fall into the basic categories of disk drives and printers.

Creating Device Definitions

This little side trip will seem a bit like file systems revisited. It is only natural to view devices as hardware. After all, the console is a large, glowing screen in front of you and your keyboard feels real enough. When you bought a new hard drive for your computer, it sure had some heft to it. Without sounding too metaphysical, devices, from the Linux kernel's perspective, are nothing but special files in the `/dev` directory. The way in which you define those files also defines how the system treats devices in the real (physical) world.

Major Minor

The definitions for these devices are created with a command called `mknod` by passing it a device type, a major number, and a minor number definition. For example, I can create a copy of my null device like this:

```
mknod /dev/null2 c 1 3
```

The second parameter is the device name. You should already be in the /dev directory or you must specify the full path. This is followed by the device type, which in this case is c, for "character" device. Another option is to create a block or "buffered" device using the b option. Each of these options is followed by the major and minor numbers.

> **Note:** There is one exception to the major/minor rule. You can also create a *named pipe,* also known as a *FIFO,* using the p option. This file type is used by applications for interprocess communication. Essentially what happens is that one process writes to the named pipe, and another reads from it. Think of it as a file that lives mostly in system memory rather than disk: one that is emptied as it is read.

The *major* number tells you (or rather, tells the system) what kind of device you are talking about. The *minor* number identifies which device of that type you are talking about. For instance, you'll find that your IDE hard drives have a major number of 3, while your SCSI disks have a major number of 8. Meanwhile, all serial ports are 5 (including the console, by the way), parallel ports are 99, and SCSI tape drives are 9. If you are curious, do an `ls -l` on /dev.

```
ls -l /dev | more
```

On the minor side, you'll notice an interesting pattern as well. My first IDE disk drive is called /dev/hda. Its major number is 3 and its minor number is 0. The first partition on /dev/hda (hda1) is major 3 and minor 1. The second partition is major 3 and minor 2. Same story goes for my second IDE hard drive. Called /dev/hdb, its first partition, hdb1, is major 3 with minor 64. On the second partition, the minor number is incremented to 65 and then to 66 for the third partition.

```
brw-rw----    1 root     disk       3,   0 May  5  1998 /dev/hda
brw-rw----    1 root     disk       3,  64 May  5  1998 /dev/hdb
brw-rw----    1 root     disk       3,   1 May  5  1998 /dev/hda1
brw-rw----    1 root     disk       3,  65 May  5  1998 /dev/hdb1
```

All the commands necessary to regenerate these files are contained in a script called MAKEDEV, which lives in /dev. To do its work, the script uses the same mknod command I talked about earlier.

Incidentally, if you ever find yourself having deleted a device, you can use this script to recreate it. For instance, let's pretend that you accidentally deleted your audio devices (/dev/audio and /dev/audio1). You can recreate them as follows:

```
cd /dev
./MAKEDEV -v audio
```

The `-v` option is not necessary, but it does give you some information as the script executes. For instance, here is a small portion of the output from the previous command:

```
create mixer        c 14 0 root:sys 666
create sequencer    c 14 1 root:sys 666
create midi00       c 14 2 root:sys 666
create dsp          c 14 3 root:sys 666
```

SCSI versus IDE

By definition, a SCSI device is one that is connected to your system through the Small Computer Systems Interface. SCSI, which is pronounced "scuzzy," is an interface design created to allow a standard means of connecting anything from disk drives and CD-ROMs to scanners and printers. Another driving force for the standard was to allow for faster devices than what was available. SCSI devices can be daisy-chained with each device identified by a number. In the original SCSI standard, that meant a number from 0 through 6—the number 7 was reserved for the SCSI card itself, the actual interface through which all these pieces of hardware *talk.*

SCSI has evolved since the early days. There are SCSI-2, SCSI-3, Fast/Wide SCSI interfaces, and even Ultra Fast/Wide SCSI cards. The number of devices on a single chain has grown to 15 now. The allowable length of the SCSI chain has doubled for some cards.

IDE, on the other hand, stands for Integrated (or Intelligent) Drive Electronics and has been the most common form of disk device available on inexpensive PCs. We also have EIDE (Enhanced Integrated Drive Electronics) drives as well. What made IDE drives revolutionary in their time was the inclusion of the controller on the drive itself, which meant that a separate card for each disk was no longer required.

Why Choose One over the Other?

For starters, SCSI is more flexible in terms of the kinds of devices that you can add to your Linux system. Second, SCSI devices tend to be faster than IDE.

Adding another SCSI device is simply a matter of setting an address and plugging it in to the chain. The only catch is something called *termination* (all SCSI chains must be physically "closed" with a device called a *terminator).* Some SCSI cards provide automatic termination. Whether or not you require a physical terminator may depend on the card you purchase. Check your hardware manual to make sure.

Performance issues aside, SCSI also means fewer headaches in configuration. SCSI devices generally report their identities to the SCSI system, which means less work for you when it comes time to use your new devices.

> **Quick Tip:** If you are out there considering SCSI versus IDE CD-rewritable, and you are trying to decide which way to go, stop wondering. Go SCSI. Sure, you'll have to install a SCSI card and sure it tends to cost a bit more, but you'll have an easier configuration and fewer headaches.

Scanners or CD writers usually represent what are called "generic" SCSI devices, meaning that the kernel doesn't specifically know what those devices are. For these generic devices, a `/dev` special file is created that allows communication to the device with this understanding: The application program does the talking and the interfacing, not the kernel. SCSI devices have `/dev` entries starting with `sg`.

You can get information on what SCSI devices your system knows about by looking in the `/proc/scsi/scsi` file. You can see that information simply by doing a `cat` on the file.

```
# cat /proc/scsi/scsi
Attached devices:
Host: scsi0 Channel: 00 Id: 02 Lun: 00
  Vendor: AIWA     Model: GD-8000          Rev: 0119
  Type:    Sequential-Access               ANSI SCSI revision: 02
Host: scsi0 Channel: 00 Id: 03 Lun: 00
  Vendor: YAMAHA   Model: CRW4416S         Rev: 1.0f
  Type:    CD-ROM                          ANSI SCSI revision: 02
Host: scsi0 Channel: 00 Id: 04 Lun: 00
  Vendor: HP       Model: C1130A           Rev: 3540
  Type:    Processor                       ANSI SCSI revision: 02
```

In this scenario, my scanner is `/dev/sgc`. Notice that the device is actually SCSI ID 4 and not 3 as you might expect. That's because SCSI devices are assigned as they are located by the system. Because I only have three devices, they are `/dev/sga`, `/dev/sgb`, and `/dev/sgc`.

CD-ROMs and CD-RWs

An increasingly common addition to new systems is the CD-RW, or CD-rewritable, compact disc. The beauty of CD-ROMs and CD-RWs is that they are now extremely inexpensive, though CD-ROMs cost a bit less than CD-RWs. Your local business-supply store probably sells CD-ROM blanks in stacks of 50 and 100. For long-term archiving or sharing files, CD-ROMs have become the way to go.

Writing CDs is often referred to as *burning*, a term you will see over and over again. In fact, programs that record CDs are usually called *burners*. For Linux, the tool of choice is a program called `cdrecord`, available from Jörg Schilling's Web site (`http://www.fokus.gmd.de/research/cc/glone/employees/joerg.schilling/private/cdrecord.html`).

Pick up the latest source and extract it into a temporary directory. The steps to build the software are reasonably simple. Always keep in mind that the version numbers included in this book represent those that were in effect at the time the book was written. Despite the fact that these things change (as well they should), the format usually remains the same.

```
tar -xzvf cdrecord-1.9.tar.gz
cd cdrecord-1.9
./Gmake.linux
make install
```

By default, `cdrecord` is installed in the `/opt/schilly` directory. The programs are there under `/opt/schilly/bin`. For the sake of this discussion, the two programs you are most interested in are `cdrecord` and `mkisofs`. The first (`cdrecord`) does the actual writing to your recordable compact discs, while `mkisofs` creates the ISO9660 or Joliet-type file system with optional Rock Ridge extensions. It is this image (or file system) that will be copied to the CD. I suggest that you take some time to read up on what the many options do on both of these commands, but for now, I am going to give you just enough to start using the programs.

To see if your CD-RW is being recognized by `cdrecord`, type this command:

```
/opt/schilly/bin/cdrecord -scanbus
```

This is what comes back on my system:

```
Cdrecord 1.9 (i686-pc-linux-gnu) Copyright (C) 1995-2000 Jörg Schilling
Linux sg driver version: 2.1.39
Using libscg version 'schily-0.1'
scsibus0:
      0,0,0     0) *
      0,1,0     1) *
      0,2,0     2) 'AIWA    ' 'GD-8000         ' '0119' Removable Tape
      0,3,0     3) 'YAMAHA  ' 'CRW4416S        ' '1.0f' Removable CD-ROM
      0,4,0     4) 'HP      ' 'C1130A          ' '3540' Processor
      0,5,0     5) *
      0,6,0     6) *
      0,7,0     7) *
```

As you can see, my CD-RW is sitting at address "0,3,0" and it is a Yamaha CRW4416S. `cdrecord` has identified other devices as well, including my old AIWA 4mm tape drive and my HP scanner (I'll talk about scanners next).

Starting with a simple test, I am going to put in a CD-RW disc. Because this is a rewritable disc, it might already have data on it, so I will start by erasing the disc.

```
cdrecord -blank=fast dev=3,0
```

The dev= option tells cdrecord where to find my CD-RW. After all, I could have more than one. The program gives me a few seconds to change my mind (ten seconds, actually) and then continues with erasing the CD-RW disc.

```
Starting to write CD/DVD at speed 4 in write mode for single session.
Last chance to quit, starting real write in 1 seconds.
```

Let's try writing to the CD-RW. On my system, I have raw, ISO-format files similar to the ISO files you might download from your favorite Linux distribution site. This is an image file I created when I backed up the documents that constitute this book (I'll talk about CD backups in the next chapter). Here's how I write this to the CD-RW:

```
cdrecord -v dev=3,0 lsadocs.raw
```

The feedback that I get from this operation is quite interesting, which is why I added the -v flag.

```
Total size:       5 MB (00:35.37) = 2653 sectors
Lout start:       6 MB (00:37/28) = 2653 sectors
Current Secsize: 2048
ATIP info from disk:
  Indicated writing power: 5
  Reference speed: 2
  Is not unrestricted
  Is erasable
  ATIP start of lead in:  -11615 (97:27/10)
  ATIP start of lead out: 335925 (74:41/00)
  speed low: 0 speed high: 4
  power mult factor: 4 5
  recommended erase/write power: 3
  A2 values: 5C C6 26
Disk type:    Phase change
Manuf. index: 18
Manufacturer: Plasmon Data systems Ltd.
Blocks total: 335925 Blocks current: 335925 Blocks remaining: 333272
Starting to write CD/DVD at speed 4 in write mode for single session.
Last chance to quit, starting real write in 1 seconds.
Waiting for reader process to fill input buffer ... input buffer
ready.
Performing OPC...
Starting new track at sector: 0
Track 01:   3 of   5 MB written (fifo 100%).
Track 01: Total bytes read/written: 5429248/5429248 (2651 sectors).
Writing  time:   39.181s
Fixating...
```

As the write operation proceeds, I get information about how much has been written and how long it will likely take before this is all completed. When it has completed, I can mount the resulting CD and navigate it like any other file system.

```
mount /dev/scd0 /mnt/cdrom1
```

The Graphical Way to Burn

There are somewhat more attractive ways to burn CDs. X-CD-Roast (`http://www.xcdroast.org/`) is a graphical package you can build from source. There are some binary distributions as well, but (as you know by now in this world of Linux) while precompiled binaries aren't always available, the source usually is.

```
tar -xzvf xcdroast-0.98alpha8.tar.gz
cd xcdroast-0.98alpha8
make
make install
```

To start `xcdroast`, just type the program name at your shell prompt.

The program is easy to use. The setup page enables you to autodetect your CD-RW, which makes that part painless. You will need a directory for images, so that part is something that you will have to specify on your own. Other than that, click the Master CD button, choose Master from/to, and then highlight the directory structure you want to write to your new CD.

The next step is to click the Master Image button, which then enables you to specify a filename to write your ISO image to. (I have a directory on my system where I keep all CD images.) The next step is to pop in a blank CD, click Write Image and you are off and burning.

Figure 16.1 shows an `xcdroast` session where I burn the same image I used in the `cdrecord` example.

Without a doubt, there are a number of CD burners out there, and a quick browse through Freshmeat or your favorite Linux applications site will show you several. I am going to introduce you to one other because it shows what you can do with a simple script—in this case, written using the Tcl/Tk language.

Check out Ian Kjos' CDR Toaster program at `http://www.jump.net/~brooke/cdrtoast/`.

No compilation is necessary, although you do still need the `cdrecord` and `mkisofs` programs. Just copy the file into a location where you can find it (`/usr/local/bin` perhaps), make the script executable, and run the program by typing this command:

```
cdrtoaster-1.12
```

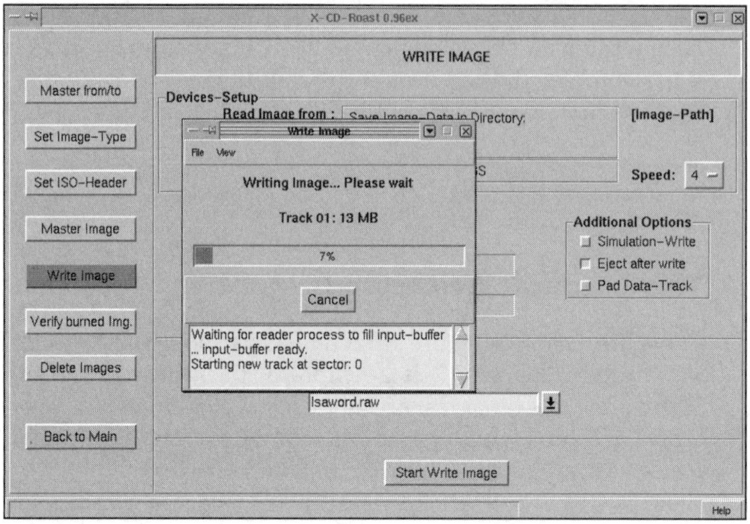

FIGURE 16.1 Burning a CD with X-CD-Roast

Because the program is just a version numbered script, you may want to rename it to something more intuitive, such as `cdrtoaster`. Figure 16.2 shows the program ready to make a CD copy of my e-mail directory.

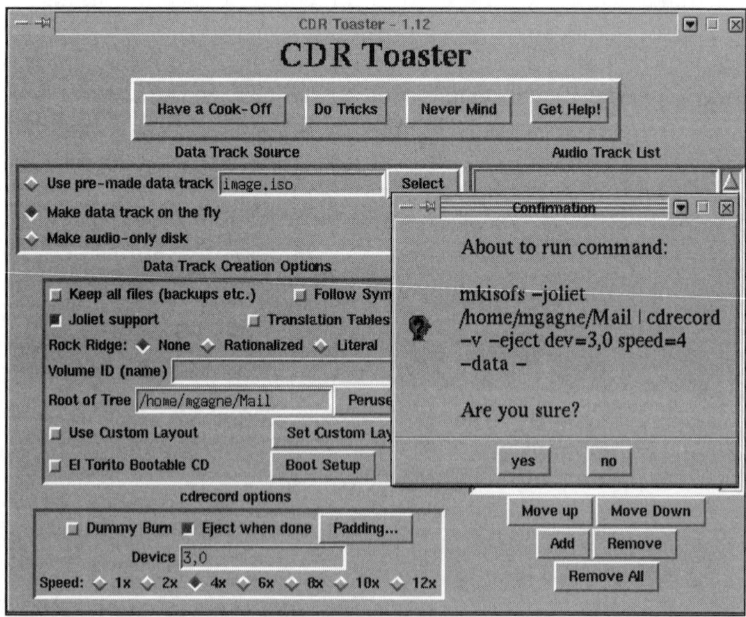

FIGURE 16.2 `cdrtoaster`, a simple Tk front end to `cdrecord`

Scanners

Scanners are incredibly handy devices for the office. I use mine as a photocopier, as a means to get nondigital pictures on my Web site (or to e-mail family), and as a way to send faxes. As I mentioned earlier on, scanners are part of the "generic" device category. For the most part, SCSI devices should work without too much fuss. If you are not running a SCSI scanner, then it gets a little bit weirder.

First you need to get the appropriate driver for your scanner. Then, you will "fake" a SCSI device. You do this by loading the appropriate driver for your scanner. Then, you load the SCSI generic module.

```
modprobe myscannermod
modprobe sg
```

To be able to use a scanner, you should download and install the Scanner Access Now Easy (SANE) libraries. The idea behind SANE was to create a consistent interface for writing software that would access scanner devices. Before that, each application that was written had to take each device type into consideration. While SANE is generally used for scanners, it also enables you to capture frames from video and still cameras as well. For now, let's stick to scanners.

SANE consists of a back end of support libraries and drivers and a front end that provides the programs that interact with the scanner. To run SANE on your system, get download binaries or source from `http://www.mostang.com/sane/`.

Back Ends

You need to install the SANE back end before you do anything else. If you are building from source, start by extracting the software into a temporary directory. The process goes something like this:

```
tar -xzvf sane-backends-1.0.4.tar.gz
cd sane-backends-1.0.4
./configure
make
make install
```

This back-end package does have one basic front-end (or application) package: the program `scanimage`. Using that program, you can look for available scanners currently connected to your system.

Earlier on in this chapter, I mentioned that you could find out about SCSI devices recognized by your system by looking into the `/proc` file system with `cat/proc/scsi/scsi`. Here is the output from mine (strictly the scanner information):

```
Host: scsi0 Channel: 00 Id: 04 Lun: 00
  Vendor: HP       Model: C1130A           Rev: 3540
  Type:    Processor
```

Because I know that my HP scanner is out there, I'll use `scanimage` and make sure that it sees it as well. To do this, I use the `-L` flag.

```
$ scanimage -L
device 'hp:/dev/sgc' is a Hewlett-Packard C1130A flatbed scanner
device 'hp:/dev/scanner' is a Hewlett-Packard C1130A flatbed scanner
```

Excellent, and I apparently already have a symbolic link to `/dev/sgc` (my generic SCSI device) called `/dev/scanner`. If the link like that doesn't exist on your system, then create it because it usually makes more sense to call your scanner `scanner` than `/dev/sg_somenumber`. Using this information, I can even try scanning a picture.

```
scanimage --mode Color --format tiff -d hp:/dev/scanner > myimage.tif
```

The default scan mode is black and white line art, which is why I specified a mode of `Color` on the line. Furthermore, the default image format is pnm and I chose to override that with the `--format` flag. If all goes well when you try this process, you should be able to fire up the GIMP (a free, graphical program similar to Photoshop), or your favorite image viewer, and look at the scanned image.

Front Ends

This is all wonderful, but it is a bit clunky. The ideal approach when dealing with a scanner is to use a somewhat more elegant, graphical front end. The `sane-frontend` package provides a couple of these (and you will want those so go ahead and build them). The format for building this package is almost identical to that of the back-end package.

```
tar -xzvf sane-frontends-1.0.4.tar.gz
cd sane-frontends-1.0.4
./configure
make
make install
```

Now, you can use `xscanimage` to provide a graphical interface to your scanning (see Figure 16.3). In truth, it isn't much more than the command-line version, but if you use the GIMP, you'll find that `xscanimage` is very useful indeed. To be able to use it as a plug-in, however, you will need to have a couple of things. One of them is the GIMP itself as well as its development libraries. If you have any major Linux distribution, you can be quite sure that the GIMP has been included. Of course, the latest version is always available at `http://www.gimp.org/`.

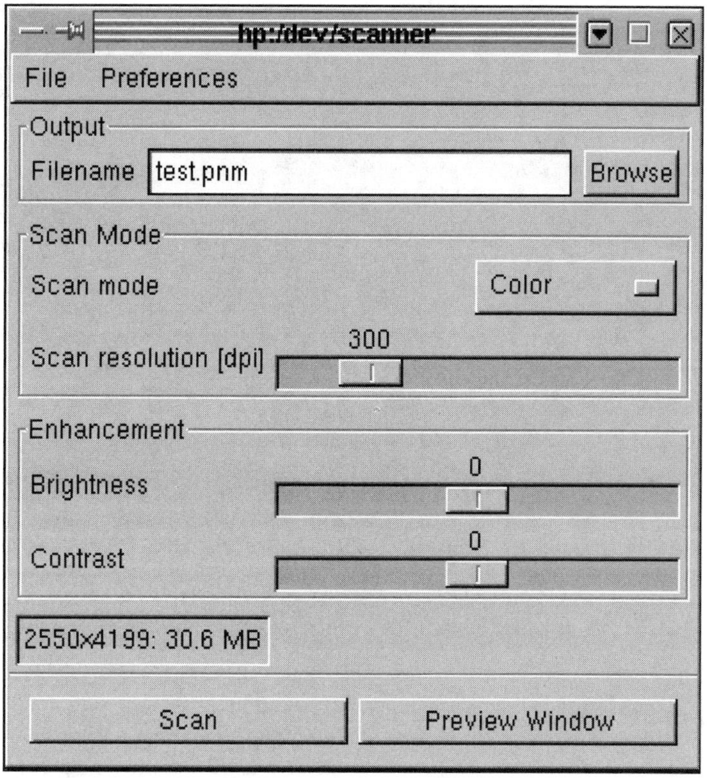

FIGURE 16.3 Scanner access with `xscanimage`

I am going to leave the GIMP as something for you to discover. After playing with it for a while, you'll wonder how you ever lived without it. That said, you do need to do one more thing in order to use the `xscanimage` as a plug-in to the GIMP. Create a symbolic link from the `xscanimage` executable to your GIMP plug-ins directory as follows (note that the release number of the GIMP may vary from system to system):

```
ln -s /usr/local/bin/xscanimage ~/.gimp-1.1/plug-ins/
```

XSane

For any kind of long-term work with a scanner, you are going to want something easy, configurable, and flexible. Something that enables you to preview, photocopy, and fax is good too. That's why you should get XSane.

XSane works in an X window environment. You can actually get the source from the Mostang site where you picked up SANE, or you can go directly to

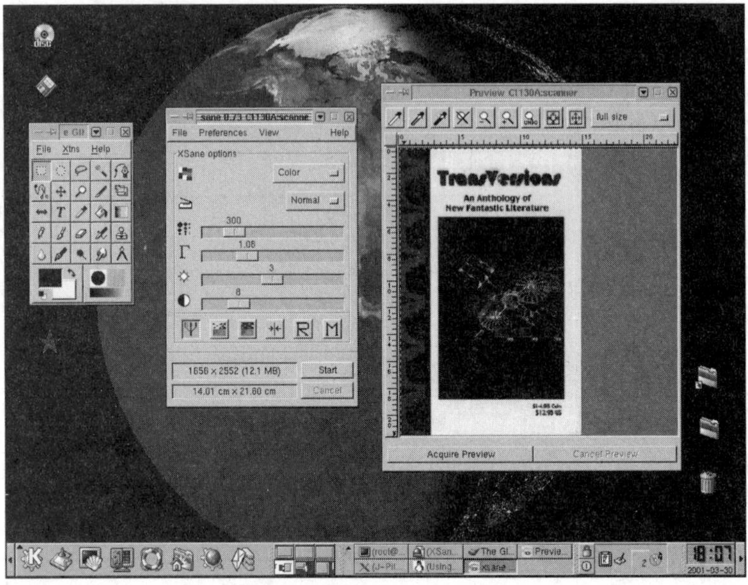

FIGURE 16.4 Using `xsane` as a plug-in to the GIMP

the XSane Web site (`http://www.xsane.org/`). When you build this program, you'll follow the same steps as the other two packages.

```
tar -xzvf xsane-0.73.tar.gz
cd xsane-0.73
./configure
make
make install
```

To start the program, simply type `xsane`. You'll find options for copying, faxing, or image capture in line art, halftone, grayscale, and color.

Here's something else that's great: Like `xscanimage`, you can use `xsane` as a plug-in to the GIMP for graphic manipulation (as shown in Figure 16.4). Just create the symbolic link.

```
ln -s /usr/local/bin/xsane ~/.gimp-1.1/plug-ins/
```

Tape Drives

The next chapter is in some ways a direct follow-up of this section. It deals with backing up and restoring your system, while this section deals with tape drives. Tapes aren't the only way to back up a system, but to date they still make the most sense. Consequently, if your system is more than just a hobby and if you need larger scale backups, you will want a tape drive. There are other options and I will talk about those soon.

When it comes to tape drives, Linux has great support, particularly if you are using a SCSI device. These devices are supported directly by the kernel. The drives should be automatically recognized and configured when the system loads your SCSI driver (which may be compiled in or loaded as a module). If you are compiling your kernel from scratch, make sure you turn on SCSI tape support.

A SCSI tape drive will show up as `/dev/st0` for the first device and `/dev/nst0` for the no-rewind device. Because tape drives are sequential devices, it is possible to write a file to the device and then write another (assuming there is enough space on the tape). Normally, when you finish writing to a tape, the device automatically rewinds the tape. If you try to write anything else here, you simply overwrite the first file (or backup). By specifying the no-rewind device, your tape will stop at the end of the write and wait for the next command.

> **Quick Tip:** Additional SCSI tapes will show up as `/dev/st1`, `/dev/st2`, and so on. Each will have a corresponding no-rewind device.

The standard program for talking to a tape drive is called `mt`. The command format is as follows:

```
usage: mt [-v] [-h] [ -f device ] command [ count ]
```

There are many command options; `rewind` is just one of them. If you want to rewind your first SCSI tape after (or before) your backup, you type this:

```
mt -f /dev/nst0 rewind
```

The `-f` specifies the tape drive that you want to work with. On the next page are a few other options you may find useful.

As you have probably noticed, some of these options aren't exactly intuitive. Get a scratch tape (one without an important backup already on it) and practice. Write a few files to the no-rewind device and then try to read the data back (into a temporary directory). Use the positioning options for the `mt` command and get comfortable with what they do. How do you do that? The next chapter covers what you need to back up and restore your precious data.

`command` options for `mt`

`fsf count`: Advance the tape a certain number of files as defined by `count`. The tape will be positioned at the first block of that file. No `count` assumes one file. Note that this is a file *skip*. To get to the beginning of the third file, you use `fsf 2`.

`bsf count`: Same as `fsf count`, but go backward in the tape.

`asf count`: Position the tape at the beginning of the file indicated by `count`. Note the difference between this and `fsf count`, which skips a certain number of files.

`offline`: Rewind the tape and, if applicable, eject it. Not all tape drives support eject.

`retension`: Every once in a while, you need to do this with tapes. What this does is rewind the tape, run it all the way to the end of the reel, and rewind it again.

`status`: Depending on your tape drive, this will return information about the tape drive, whether or not it is online, the tape block size, and its position.

`tell`: Reports the current block number. Like `status`, this depends on the tape drive.

`erase`: As you might expect, this erases the tape.

Other Tape Formats

IDE/ATAPI tape drives are also supported and have been for some time. The story here is the same: If you are building your own kernel, make sure you turn on IDE tape support if you plan to use these devices. The device files here show up as `/dev/ht0` (and up from there).

If you happen to have an inexpensive tape drive that hooks up into your floppy controller (such as QIC-80, Iomega Ditto, and others), you should look into using the `ftape` module. Luckily, this tends to be part of most modern distributions. Visit the Ftape HOWTO (`http://www.linuxdoc.org/HOWTO/Ftape-HOWTO.html`) to learn how to deal specifically with this type of tape drive.

Miscellaneous Devices

There are as many options for extra devices as there are devices. We've got video cameras (Webcams), accelerator cards, video tuners and capture boards, joysticks, amateur and FM radio cards, touch screens, and much, much more. Consequently, it is impossible to cover everything you could conceivably hook up to your Linux system in this chapter.

Your best bet is to go back to the Hardware Compatibility HOWTO and make sure that what you want is supported. If you are into the idea of experimentation, Linux user groups (LUGs) are a great place to blue sky with others about your gizmo of choice. Somebody may even be able to point you toward someone else who has already managed to make it work.

Resources

CDR Toaster

`http://www.jump.net/~brooke/cdrtoast/`

cdrecord and mkisofs

`http://www.fokus.gmd.de/research/cc/glone/employees/joerg.schilling/private/cdrecord.html`

Ftape-HOWTO

`http://www.linuxdoc.org/HOWTO/Ftape-HOWTO.html`

The GIMP

`http://www.gimp.org/`

SANE (Scanner Access Now Easy)

`http://www.mostang.com/sane/`

X-CD-Roast

`http://www.xcdroast.org/`

XSane Web site

`http://www.xsane.org/`

Chapter 17

Backups and Restores

The Need for Backups

Okay, I won't preach. Well, maybe just a bit. You can get pretty much anyone you ask to agree that backups are a good idea. You can also pretty much guarantee that people don't back up as often as they should. While I won't name names, I've known a number of people over the years who (despite touting the benefits of regular backups) treat their important data as follows:

- Backups are done "occasionally" or "very occasionally."
- Backups are not verified. ("They must be okay, right?")
- Backups are not labeled. ("What did I back up and when?")
- A backup is put on a single diskette that is used over and over.
- A backup is put on a single tape that is used over and over.
- Backups are saved to another directory on the *same* disk.

The single diskette entry in that list is a true story. The user in question had only a single diskette for all his important documents, because he was worried about the hard disk crashing! (Yes, the diskette eventually failed and all data was lost.) Still, in the world of that other operating system, backups often mean nothing more than a few diskettes somewhere with your documents on them. Because there is no point in boring you with a list that goes on and on, I'll stop for now. Suffice it to say that when the system crashes and data has to be recovered, it's always *important* data.

So, what's the best way to protect that important data? In one word: *backups*.

For a lot of people dealing with simple systems, the data that is our accounts, word-processing documents, and e-mails is the only truly important part. The problem with diskettes is that they hold only so much information. Backing up your whole system could take years (hours, anyway) and you may require sedation afterward. Every system should have some kind of large storage capacity backup, such as a tape drive. That's right. Whatever you may have heard, tape is alive and well. In the previous chapter, I talked about setting up other devices, tape drives being an important one. That wasn't just a coincidence.

Network backups are possible (and many large-scale backup systems are built this way), but they add a layer of complexity. I will discuss some of these systems later in the chapter.

Basic Tools in Every Linux System

Your Linux distribution contains an incredible collection of tools for a variety of applications. The same is true for keeping your data safe. Without buying or downloading anything else, you can start getting into a healthy habit of regular backups.

The most popular commands out of the box are `cpio` and `tar`. Other command-line tools such as `dd`, `dump`, and `afio` are also available (although `afio` might not be included in all distributions). For simplicity and universality, `tar` and `cpio` are quite useful and powerful, and they are the ones I use on a regular basis.

Using cpio

The main advantage of `cpio` over `tar` is that it does a somewhat better job of packing data on your backup medium and it handles errors better as well, particularly when dealing with tape. There is one other advantage: When using `tar`, you tend to work in terms of short lists of directories or files. With `cpio`, you can largely customize the files that wind up in an archive. For instance, you can work from a list of files and pipe that list directly to `cpio`:

```
cpio -ov > /dev/st0 < /tmp/list_of_files
```

The `-o` option writes out an archive directed to `/dev/st0` (the SCSI tape drive) and takes the list from a file called `list_of_files`. You can then go back and check the backup by reading the tape and checking the table of contents. This is done with the `-t` option:

```
cpio -ivt < /dev/st0
```

To extract a file from that archive, you need to know how it was stored (the path to the archive). The command is fairly simple. Let's say I want to restore a file called `lost_file`. I can do so as follows:

```
cpio -iv lost_file < /dev/st0
```

Working with tar

The next candidate for included backup tools is my old friend, `tar`. I confess that I probably use tar more than any other command. It's partly out of habit, because I have been `tarr`ing files for a number of years, and it's also partly because single-file archives are always delivered `tarr`ed and in some way compressed (as in `cool_new_software.tar.gz`).

Linux's `tar` isn't your plain old `tar`; it's GNU `tar`. This means it has some advantages over the regular `tar`, which makes it that much more interesting. For instance, with GNU `tar` it's possible to do compression on the fly (with both standard `compress` compression and `gzip` compression). You can also specify multivolume backups. Here's an example:

```
tar -cvf /dev/fd0 /mydata
```

In this example, I am backing up the directory `/mydata` to a floppy. Yes, I know what I said about diskettes, but every once in a while, nothing beats the convenience of using diskettes. Unfortunately, as I mentioned earlier on, there's only so much space on a diskette. What if your floppy is really too small for that amount of data but you still want to use diskettes? No problem (assuming you don't need a *huge* number of floppies). To get around this problem, use the `-M` flag. When `tar` gets to the end of the first diskette, you will be prompted for the next volume in your multivolume backup, as follows:

```
tar -cvMf /dev/fd0 /mydata
```

To compress data (you can't use compression on multivolumes—sorry), you can use the `-z` flag. For instance, if I want to archive `/mydata` and `gzip` it to my SCSI tape drive on the fly, I use this command:

```
tar -czvf /dev/st0 /mydata
```

For a good, old-fashioned `zcat`-type of compression (as with the command `compress`), use a capital `Z` flag instead of the lowercase `z`.

Another compression type I discussed (back in Chapter 11) was `bzip2`. You can also have `tar` do `bzip2` compression on the fly. On most systems, you specify this with the `-I` option. However, if you are running a Slackware system, please note that it is probably using the `-y` option to do the same thing.

> **Quick Tip:** The `-p` option may well be the most important `tar` option of them all. This tells `tar` to *preserve* permissions and ownership information in both backups and restores. If you are using `tar` to back up system files, you definitely want to do this.

Backing Up Windows Workstations

Linux works nicely with a number of other computer systems, including Windows. With a few simple commands, Linux will happily safeguard data in those systems as well.

You probably already have Samba installed. If you don't, never fear. I will cover it in detail in Chapter 22, which covers integration with Windows. For now, here's a quick Samba example. Pretend that you have a Windows PC called "speedy" on your network. The user has shared the C drive with the name "SPEEDY_C." I can mount that share on a Linux system running Samba like this:

```
smbmount //speedy/speedy_c /mnt/linux_mount_point
```

Then, I simply back it up to my tape drive like this:

```
cd /mnt/linux_mount_point
tar -cvf /dev/st0 .
```

I'm jumping ahead a little bit, but I just wanted to show you that it is possible to use Linux tools to do Windows backups. More on this later.

Everything works. So, what's wrong with that? Well, for one thing, straight `tar` isn't the greatest when it comes to error recovery. While errors don't generally occur, this is a concern. I've seen systems backed up with `tar` for years with few problems or none at all, so while I urge caution, it's not all bad. You could use `cpio`, which has better error handling in case of a read error, but both `tar` and `cpio` aren't particularly quick if you want to restore something. In the case of older versions of these commands (they still exist on some platforms), they don't back up all files. Here's another minus. To find a file, you have to travel the *entire length* of the tape searching for it. There is no index at the beginning and just finding out where the file actually is (assuming you don't remember the exact pathname) can take quite some time.

The real plus with `cpio` and `tar` is this: Every Linux/UNIX under the sun (including Sun OS) has `cpio` and `tar`. This assures cross-compatibility, a consideration I will mention again.

Selecting a Backup Medium

On the question of medium, here's how I see things. Floppies are extremely convenient for storing small collections of files, but their capacity is very limited. CD-RW is reliable and access is reasonably quick, but the capacity (while much larger than diskette) is still limited. A 2GB Jaz drive is quite hot, but 2GB is pretty much it at the moment, and spare cartridges can be pricey. It's good for infrequent backups and data that doesn't change much, but there are limits. You could use a spare hard disk, but multiple archives of your data are a bit difficult with that scenario. It's very fast, though. Then there's tape.

Tapes themselves are relatively inexpensive (currently, I can buy a 12GB DDS tape for about $20). The number one advantage to tape, however, is capacity. There is no other medium, short of maybe another disk, that provides the backup capacity of today's tape drives—certainly not at a comparable cost. In terms of capacity, it is now possible to get Linux-compatible tape drives that will back up an astounding 50GB on a single tape.

Large capacity makes for another great advantage: unattended backups. You can pop in a tape before you head out for the night, rather than sitting around watching files list to the screen. With a little ingenuity, you can verify a backup, capture a list of what has been backed up, and have the result mailed to you in the morning. For instance, take a look at the following hastily constructed script that (I am quite sure) could be a lot prettier.

```
#!/bin/bash
#
# 4mm.dataonly      -  This Short Backup Script backs up only my data
# 2000 - Marcel Gagne
#
# Set up some file pointers for short backup
sb_log=/usr/local/.Admin/dataonly.log
sb_errlog=/usr/local/.Admin/dataonly.err
# Do we capture the file list, or send it to dev null?
# file_log=/usr/local/.Admin/backup.log
file_log=/dev/null
admin_dir=/usr/local/.Admin

# Do a little cleanup.
mv $sb_log $sb_log.old
mv $sb_errlog $sb_errlog.old

# Prepare report headers
#
echo "==============================================" > $sb_errlog
echo "What follows is a report of errors encountered" >> $sb_errlog
echo "during the backup or its subsequent verify." >> $sb_errlog
echo "==============================================" >> $sb_errlog

echo "Data Only Nightly Backup. <'date'>" >> $sb_log
echo "===================================================" >> $sb_log

#Get on with actual backup
#
echo "** Moving to data directory..." >> $sb_log
cd /root

echo "***Nightly Backup Starting : `date`..."  >> $sb_log

echo "Backup errors ..." >>$sb_errlog

tar -cvf /dev/st0 . 2>>$sb_errlog
```

```
# Verify Backup
# start by rewinding the tape
mt -f /dev/st0 rewind

echo "****Verifying the Backup : `date` *** " >> $sb_log

echo "Restore and verify errors . . ." >>$sb_errlog
tar -vtf /dev/st0 2>>$sb_errlog

echo "*****Nightly Backup Completed : `date`..." >> $sb_log

# Report on this, will you?
cat $sb_errlog >> $sb_log
mail -s "Dataonly backup status report" root < $sb_log
```

When I come in the next morning, my backup has completed and I have an e-mail message telling me when it started and how long it took. If the tape generated messages to STDERR (standard error), I'll see it in that message.

Another thing I toss in there is an option to list the files on backup and restore. *Warning:* This can chew up a *lot* of disk space, which is why my `file_log` has the option of going to either a file or to `/dev/null`. Because my 4mm DAT can back up 4GB to 8GB, I can have this happen every night with a `cron` job (see Chapter 15) and not worry about it. All I have to do is remember to put the tape in. Here's a `cron` entry for a backup that runs at 11:00 PM every night, Monday to Friday:

```
0 23 * * 1-5 /usr/local/.Admin/4mm.dataonly
```

Backing Up with dump

The `dump` command is half of a duo, the other part being the `restore` command. The idea behind this command is to take a complete backup of a file system as opposed to a single directory or a list of directories. The first backup you do with `dump` is called a "full backup." From there, you can speed up the backup process by doing incremental backups. In other words, you can back up only what has been modified since the last full backup. You do this by instituting *levels.* A level 1 backup only saves those files that have changed since the last level 0 backup. A level 2 backup only saves files that have changed since the last level 1 backup. (Are you seeing a pattern developing?) There are nine possible levels of incremental backups. The following is the essence of a full backup that I have just run on my system. The zero indicates a level 0, or full backup. The `u` flag tells `dump` to update `/etc/dumpdates` after it has successfully completed. Immediately after the `f` flag, I specify the device to which the backup will occur. Finally, just before the pipe symbol, I specify the file system.

```
# dump -0uf - /dev/hdb1 | cat > /dev/st0
  DUMP: Date of this level 0 dump: Wed Apr 18 16:43:54 2001
  DUMP: Date of last level 0 dump: the epoch
  DUMP: Dumping /dev/hdb1 (/mnt/data1) to standard output
```

```
  DUMP: Label: none
  DUMP: mapping (Pass I) [regular files]
  DUMP: mapping (Pass II) [directories]
  DUMP: estimated 1590653 tape blocks.
  DUMP: Volume 1 started at: Wed Apr 18 16:44:03 2001
  DUMP: dumping (Pass III) [directories]
  DUMP: dumping (Pass IV) [regular files]
  DUMP: 6.25% done, finished in 1:15
  DUMP: 13.09% done, finished in 1:06
  DUMP: 19.90% done, finished in 1:00
  DUMP: 26.99% done, finished in 0:54
```

Notice anything strange? Instead of specifying my tape drive directly (after the `f` flag), I used a hyphen to redirect to standard out, and then I piped the whole thing to `cat` and redirected that to the tape drive. If that sounds convoluted, consider this: The `dump` command wants to know the density of the tape in bits per inch (the `d` flag) and the number of feet in the tape (the `s` flag) so that it can figure out how many tapes it will need. As it turns out, the only thing I know for sure is that my tape drive can back up 30GB (uncompressed) and that I only have 15GB of data. Doing it this way overrides the need to supply the tape size information.

Now, here is a `dump` of the same file system one day later, using a level 1 backup:

```
# dump -1uf - /dev/hdb1 | cat > /dev/st0
  DUMP: Date of this level 1 dump: Thu Apr 19 17:16:35 2001
  DUMP: Date of last level 0 dump: Wed Apr 18 16:43:54 2001
  DUMP: Dumping /dev/hdb1 (/mnt/data1) to standard output
  DUMP: Label: none
  DUMP: mapping (Pass I) [regular files]
  DUMP: mapping (Pass II) [directories]
  DUMP: estimated 29280 tape blocks.
  DUMP: Volume 1 started at: Thu Apr 19 17:16:49 2001
  DUMP: dumping (Pass III) [directories]
  DUMP: dumping (Pass IV) [regular files]
  DUMP: 94.33% done, finished in 0:00
  DUMP: Volume 1 completed at: Thu Apr 19 17:22:06 2001
  DUMP: Volume 1 took 0:05:17
  DUMP: Volume 1 transfer rate: 91 KB/s
  DUMP: DUMP: 29072 tape blocks
  DUMP: finished in 317 seconds, throughput 91 KBytes/sec
  DUMP: level 1 dump on Thu Apr 19 17:16:35 2001
  DUMP: DUMP: Date of this level 1 dump: Thu Apr 19 17:16:35 2001
  DUMP: DUMP: Date this dump completed:  Thu Apr 19 17:22:06 2001
  DUMP: DUMP: Average transfer rate: 91 KB/s
  DUMP: DUMP IS DONE
```

As you can see, the whole thing took just over five minutes and only backed up what had changed since the day before. My `/etc/dumpdates` file looks like this now:

```
/dev/hdb1 0 Wed Apr 18 16:43:54 2001
/dev/hdb1 1 Thu Apr 19 17:16:35 2001
```

From this, you can see that Wednesday's backup was a level 0 (second column) while the following day's backup was a level 1.

Restoring with (You Guessed It) restore

When it comes time to `restore` from a `dump` tape, you must recreate the file system with the `mke2fs` command (as in Chapter 8), change directory to that file system (`/mnt/data1` in this case), and then `restore` your data to it.

```
# restore -rf /dev/st0
```

This will overwrite everything and you must start with your level 0 backup. You can also do an interactive restore by specifying the `-i` flag. You will find yourself at a `restore>` prompt where you can enter an interactive session and specify individual directories or files.

I'll admit that the `dump` and `restore` system is not the prettiest of systems, but it works well and comes with every major Linux distribution.

Identity Backups

Despite my wish that every Linux system administrator have his or her own tape drives for backups, I admit that there are instances when you don't have a proper backup device and you need solutions.

For instance, a number of people have taken advantage of Linux's powerful network tools and masquerading (not to mention price) to create simple mail servers and Internet gateways for their companies (I describe such a technique in Chapter 21). The company gave you this machine because nobody else was using it and you told them Linux works for *sardines*. (It's that penguin thing again.) Say this machine is an old 486 with a two-speed CD-ROM and no tape drive. You asked for one, but your insistence that Linux would cost them nothing and give them the world made you break one of the cardinal rules and cut corners on backups.

On this server of yours, you may be running `diald`, `fetchmail`, IP masquerading, and e-mail. Not particularly complex, and the data (the e-mail) gets transferred to the user PCs anyway. Not much to worry about there, right? Well, keep in mind that it took you several hours to properly tweak this machine and to get just the right settings for dialing out and connecting to your ISP. Sure, Linux is stable as can be, but disks crash. You can reinstall Linux from the CD-ROM in minutes, but getting everything just right might take a little longer than that and users want their e-mail and Internet access yesterday.

It's a good idea to have everything, but everything is not always a requirement. Because this type of system is essentially the sum total of its configuration files, you can do what I call an *identity backup*. This script will collect all the files that make your put-together server unique among all other put-together servers. Here's what it looks like:

```
#!/bin/bash
#
# Identity backup for Linux systems
# This script does a backup of important files
# Marcel Gagne, 2000
#
clear
echo "Identity backup for Linux systems"
echo "2000: Salmar Consulting Inc."
echo " "
#
echo "Please enter a directory name for temporary image storage."
echo "ie: /data1/PROTECT"
#
read PROTECT_dir
#
#####################################################
# Start by copying config files in etc

mkdir -p $PROTECT_dir/etc/rc.d
mkdir $PROTECT_dir/root
mkdir -p $PROTECT_dir/usr/local/.Admin

cd /etc
for file_names in passwd group shadow profile bashrc sendmail.cw \
sendmail.cf hosts hosts.allow hosts.deny named.conf named.boot \
hosts.lpd diald.conf aliases
do
    cp $file_names $PROTECT_dir/etc
done

find nsdata -print | cpio -pduvm $PROTECT_dir/etc
find ppp -print | cpio -pduvm $PROTECT_dir/etc
find sysconfig -print | cpio -pduvm $PROTECT_dir/etc
cp rc.d/rc.local $PROTECT_dir/etc/rc.d

#
cd /
cp /root/.fetchmailrc $PROTECT_dir/root
find usr/local/.Admin -print | cpio -pduvm $PROTECT_dir/usr
```

The basics are as follows. After obtaining a temporary backup directory, I make the structure by creating the directory hierarchy that I want to recreate. (Using the `-p` flag on `mkdir`, I can save myself a few keystrokes and create the entire subdirectory I need in one pass.)

I often save little admin scripts to a directory called /usr/local/.Admin, as is the case with this one. Consequently, in the script I make sure to back up that directory as part of my identity backup. If you want to use a different directory, make sure you take this into consideration. After writing the script, I make it script-executable and run it.

```
# chmod 700 /usr/local/.Admin/identity_backup
# /usr/local/.Admin/identity_backup
```

When the script runs, I give it a directory name on my server. Something I use pretty regularly is data1/PROTECT or /something/PROTECT, but you can use anything that makes sense, making sure, of course, that the file system you copy to has enough disk space. What you wind up with here is a kind of configuration "mirror" of your system. Without too much fuss, you can quickly pull back the files you need from a copy of the structure that originally existed.

This list of backed-up items is *by no means complete.* Not only that, this list is something I have found useful. You may have important configuration files in user directories or over in the /usr/local directory. What you are doing here is taking the bare minimum files and configurations to recreate a functional system as quickly as possible should disaster strike. Now that you have this quick identity snapshot, what should you do with it? If you created your PROTECT_dir in /data1, you would do the following:

```
# cd /data1
# tar -czvf hostname.identity.tar PROTECT_dir
```

This creates a tarred and gzipped file of your system configuration. The next step is to get it off the system and put it somewhere safe. If the file is small enough (as is sometimes the case), you can save it to a floppy. In fact, you could tar the whole thing to a floppy and save yourself a step. Alternatively, you can ftp the file to another server, a Windows PC, or (if you are a sysadmin working remotely) to your own server.

> **Trivia Time:** I paused briefly while writing this paragraph and tested the script as you see it on a remote Linux system that acts as a corporate e-mail/Internet gateway. The resulting file was about 35K. You can store an awful lot of those on your own system.

If you wanted to extract this "identity" to your local system, you might do something like this:

```
# mkdir -p /home/remote_servers/hostname
# cd /home/remote_servers/hostname
# tar -xzvf hostname.identity.tar.gz
```

There you have it! A copy of what makes that system unique that is saved someplace other than the server itself.

> **Warning:** I know I have already said this, but I want to make it clear. This is *not* an all-encompassing answer to backups. For that, you need to consider other ways of looking at your system, your data, and how you store it. In the meantime, let's look at another popular alternative, the CD-RW.

Backing Up to a CD-RW

The question of whether a CD-RW is a good backup choice is sometimes settled in this way: You can afford either a tape drive (sometimes more expensive than the CD-RW) or the tape. When our machines get used for both business and pleasure, as is often the case with home offices, we tend to lean in the direction of "I want both."

Making collections of favorite songs and burning extra Slackware or Debian CDs is usually done with something called `cdrecord`, which is discussed in Chapter 16.

For now, I'm going to work on the premise that the reason we are having this discussion is you already have a working CD writer setup. (If not, go back and read the previous chapter.) You went to your local office-supply store (the modern hardware store) and got a great deal on a SCSI CD-RW, the writer makes great song collections, and now you think using that same device for backups is a great idea.

So, here is the bad news: The problem with doing backups using CD writers and rewriters is that they were *never* intended for that. A raw image, based on a mirror of the data you intend to capture, is written to disk. You then write that image back to your CD or CD-RW. Translation: You are going to need *twice* the amount of free space you are trying to back up. In the case of a full CD at something like 650MB, you must have 1.3GB of space. Using a CD-RW is not necessarily the friendliest way to do backups and it is certainly far from being the space-friendliest. Luckily, there is a way to cut the necessary space in half and still get your backups done. With a sufficiently fast system, you can simply pass the ISO9660 image data that is being created directly to the `cdrecord` command. That means you do not need to have double the space available, the backup tree, and an ISO image to then burn onto the CD.

One way to do this is to beef up the identity backup script I talked about earlier. If you remember, I created a temporary directory with a hierarchical "mirror" of my important data, and then I backed up that smaller mirror to a diskette. With that script, I gave you a very small list of files and suggested that your choice of what's *important* may be different from mine. After all, you can fit roughly 1.4MB on a single diskette, and my example identity backup used only 37K.

With the CD-RW, you can increase that size to roughly 650MB, which may be all you need for the things that change day to day. Remember the catch (or half-catch, now): You still need that spare 650MB into which you can recreate the structure you want to back up. You don't get away that easy. If you plan on backing up only 300MB of data, you'll need 300MB of space.

You start by creating your mirror. In this case, it is a directory called `/mnt/data1/data_backup`. On my system, `/mnt/data1` is a separate drive with a fair amount of free space. On your system, the mirror will most likely be in a different location. Just make sure the space is available. Here is the modified identity backup script:

```
#!/bin/bash
# script name : backup_to_cd
# This script does a backup of important files onto the CD-RW
#
# NOTE: my "data mirror" is /mnt/data1/data_backup
#
echo "Starting by Blanking the data_backup area"
rm -rf /mnt/data1/data_backup
echo "Recreating the data_backup mirror ..."
mkdir /mnt/data1/data_backup
mkdir /mnt/data1/data_backup/usr
mkdir /mnt/data1/data_backup/etc
#
echo "Backing up to data1 disk mirror area ..."
cd /
find home -print | cpio -pduvm /mnt/data1/data_backup
find root -print | cpio -pduvm /mnt/data1/data_backup
find usr/local -print | cpio -pduvm /mnt/data1/data_backup/usr
#
echo "Backing up system identity."
cd /etc
for ident_names in passwd group shadow profile bashrc sendmail.cw
sendmail.cf hosts hosts.allow hosts.deny named.conf named.boot aliases
do
cp -v $ident_names /mnt/data1/data_backup/etc
done
find nsdata -print | cpio -pduvm /mnt/data1/data_backup/etc
find sysconfig -print | cpio -pduvm /mnt/data1/data_backup/etc
find mgetty+sendfax -print | cpio -pduvm /mnt/data1/data_backup/etc
#
echo "All files saved. Ready to begin CD copy."
echo "Shall I blank the CD first?"
read the_answer
#
cdrecord -blank=fast dev=3,0
#
echo "Shall I start the CD burn now?"
read the_answer
#
mkisofs -R /mnt/data1/data_backup | cdrecord -v dev=3,0 -
```

Notice that in my /mnt/data1/data-backup mirror, I am capturing /home, /usr/local, and /root, none of which I was paying much attention to with my original identity_backup script (when I was talking about diskettes). After creating your mirror, you immediately burn the data to your disk.

You may have noticed that I'm not really doing anything at those prompts for blanking and copying the CD (where it says "read the_answer") other than pausing. Because the amount of data in my mirror can be pretty dynamic, not to mention downright huge, I want an opportunity to verify that I'm staying within that 650MB limit. I do that with the du command.

```
du -sk /mnt/data1/data_backup
```

Because I am using a rewritable CD, I blank my CDs before starting. This is done with the line

```
cdrecord -blank=fast dev=3,0
```

I use the -blank=fast option to quickly erase the table of contents from the disk. You have the option of blanking the entire disk, but that can take a long time.

The real magic happens at the end of the script with mkisofs and cdrecord. The -R option on mkisofs means I want the Rock Ridge extensions to be used. In other words, I want a Linux file system with user and group information, long filename support, and so on. (If you want to be able to load this compact disc onto a Windows PC to have a look at, remember to specify the -joliet flag as well.) That's about it. Like the previous example, this script is meant to be a jumping-off point for your own CD backup. What I consider important in my backup may differ wildly from yours.

For the curious, here is the normal chain of events in creating a CD. You have mkisofs write out an ISO9660 image, which then gets recorded on the CD. The final backup onto the CD happens in two passes. For instance, the commands are

```
# First we create the image based on a previously done "mirror" backup
mkisofs -o /another_dir/image.iso -R /mnt/data1/data_backup
# Now, we record the image to CD
cdrecord -v dev=3,0 /another_dir/image.iso
```

Quick Tip: If you have a few ISO images hanging around on your hard disk, you can mount those images and navigate them as you would any CD file system. Here's how: Pretend your debian.iso image is sitting out there on your disk, and you want to look at it. First, you create a mount point (mkdir /mnt/debdist). Next, using this command, you can mount the image:

```
mount debian.iso -r -t iso9660 -o loop /mnt/debdist
```

The -r option means "read-only." As you can see, it is very much like a CD file system.

Backups the Graphical Way

The friendliness of the desktop is attractive to many and there is no lack of backup tools for this environment. You'll find that most of these tools are designed to work with tape in one way, shape, or form. Another reason you may want to consider a tape drive for doing backups (just in case I have not yet convinced you) is that for better or worse, tapes are the medium that the data-protection world has grown up with, and the vast majority of backup tools are designed to work with tape. These tools range from free to very expensive. I'll cover a few of them here, starting with free tools.

Taper: A Text-Based Backup Utility

One of the tools I've taken a liking to (despite the fact that it is limited to 4GB per archive) is something called taper. While taper will work with things like a floppy drive or a disk file, it is really a tape tool. Taper also has a nice `ncurses` (text-based) screen.

Taper, written by Yusuf Nagree, shows up on a number of distribution CDs, so you probably already have it, but you can also find it at the taper Web site (`http://www.e-survey.net.au/taper/`).

The installation is pretty simple. All I did was download the latest version (`taper-6.9b.tar.gz`) and follow a few steps. The page also contains a warning about making sure you have `ncurses` version 4.1 or better.

```
tar -xzvf taper-6.9b.tar.gz
cd taper-6.9b
make
make install
```

You then start taper with a command switch to define what medium you want to back up to. Yes, despite my ramblings about tape, I am mentioning a tool that is quite at home with a file on disk, a floppy drive, a Zip drive, or (you guessed it) a number of different tape drives.

You have options other than tape with this little program. Using command switches, you can define your destination. Here's a little sampling:

```
taper -T s      # starts taper with a SCSI tape drive
taper -T r      # starts taper with a floppy
```

The `-r` option can be further modified to use things like Zip drives, although I personally have not tried it.

The interface is simple and menu-driven. To back up your data, choose the Backup Module (see Figure 17.1). The software will identify your tape at the beginning and ask you for an archive and volume title. For instance, I used "Web server archive" and "Volume 1" as my storage information.

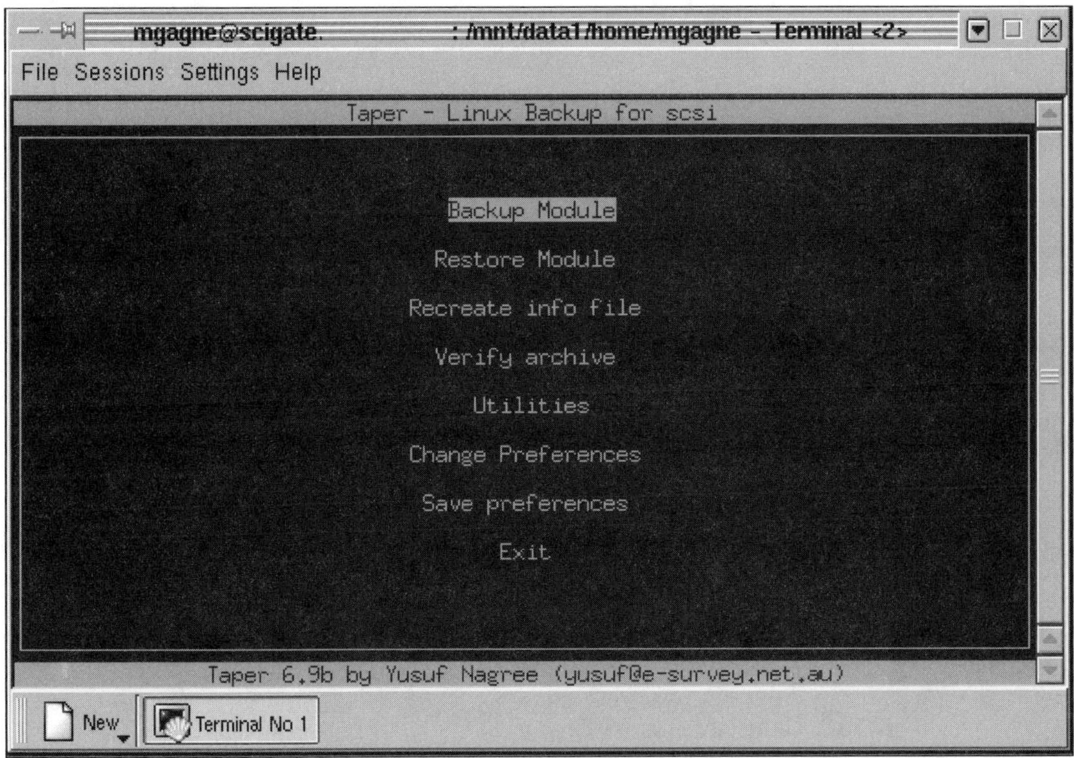

FIGURE 17.1 Taper, a text-based backup tool

You are then presented with a list of directories, relative to where you started taper. You select files for inclusion in your backup with single keystrokes. Pressing i tells the program to "include" the file (or directory), while pressing u means to "uninclude" should you change your mind. When you are done selecting, simply press f for "finish" and taper goes to work with a running report of where it is, how long it expects the whole process to take, and how far it has gone.

In order to restore, choose the Restore Module. You will be presented with a list of your backups and archives. Choose from the list and press Enter. You'll be prompted for the directory where you wish to restore the archive (you might not want your files in precisely the same directory as you started). Choose the files you want to restore (in the same way you did previously), and press f when you're done.

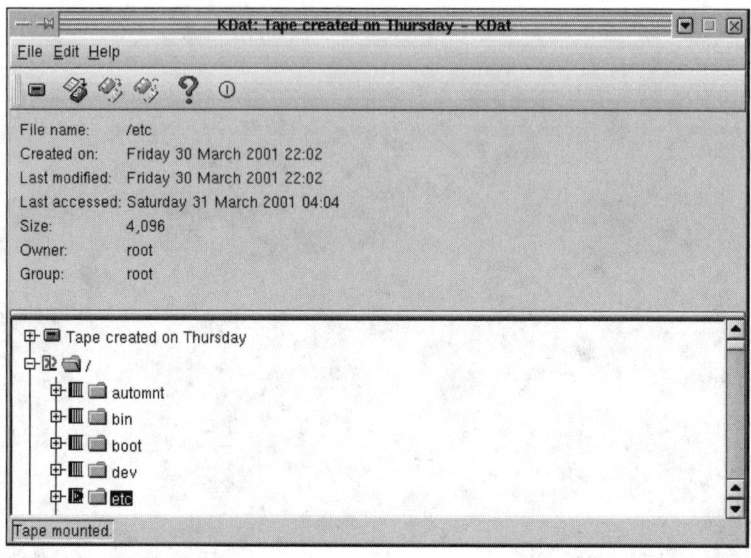

FIGURE 17.2 Backing up with `kdat`

KDat: Graphical and Free

For those of you who are running KDE as your graphical desktop, you already have a nice backup tool sitting there waiting for you: `kdat`. You start `kdat` by clicking the Tape Backup Tool under the Utilities menu under the big K. If you feel so inclined, you can also start it from an `xterm` simply by typing `kdat` at the command line (which is the way I did it).

When the `kdat` window comes up, you may have to click Edit and choose Preferences to select the type of tape you are using. I have a 4GB SCSI DAT at device `/dev/st0` and I had to enter that information. The default was `/dev/tape`. The other thing I did was click Eject tape on unmount, just because I think it is fun to have the system toss out the tape when I am done with it.

The next thing you do is `mount` the tape (under the File menu). `kdat` will tell you it is reading the tape's "magic string," which is its way of identifying whether it is a previously prepared `kdat` tape. If it cannot identify the tape as one of its own, it will ask you to format the tape. Click OK to continue. You'll get one last warning that all data will be lost if you format the tape. Click Yes (assuming, of course, that you want to use this tape for a backup). The next prompt asks you for a label. The default format is "Tape created on today's date." Change that label to something that makes sense. Perhaps it is Thursday (see Figure 17.2).

Next, confirm the tape size that you determined earlier (you can still override the defaults at this point) and click OK. After a few seconds, you should see the tape icon in the top left change, with your label on its right.

To start a backup, you must first decide what you want to back up. Directly under the tape icon is a folder with / (slash) beside it. On its left is a check box. If you check this box, you are selecting everything under the root directory. You can also click the plus sign (+), which opens up your directory tree and enables you to choose individual files and directories. In my example, I clicked the plus sign, moved to the home folder and clicked its check box. A backup icon is highlighted (just under Edit), which you can then click to start the backup. One more "Are you sure?" type of confirmation, and you are on your way to a quick and friendly backup.

Commercial Solutions

In your search for the perfect backup solution, you need to carefully weigh your requirements. Casual backups that don't require you to have a great deal of information backed up may be ideally suited to a simple `tar` or `cpio` script. And while the graphical tools mentioned previously may also be just fine for noncritical, casual backups, enterprise computing or large IS shops generally require something with a little more bite and reliability.

Case in point: `kdat` is still based on `tar`, which, while generally quite reliable, does not recover well from media errors. In fact, when it does fail, it pretty much crashes and burns. I don't mean to be overly frightening here; for the most part, you won't have any problems. Having a large pool of tapes in rotation pretty much insures that you can find a good tape somewhere and if your setup doesn't change all that much, you are probably fine with any of these.

Unfortunately, fine for some applications is not fine everywhere, and for many, good backups can mean the very *life* of their business.

BRU

My first suggestion is BRU from Enhanced Software Technologies. In the world of commercial backup solutions, BRU, or Backup and Restore Utility, is one of the all-time favorites for Linux users. You can get a demo copy of the program from the Enhanced Software Technologies Web site (`http://www.bru.com/`).

The installation for BRU is extremely simple. After answering a few questions about your tape drive, you are pretty much ready to roll. You can start BRU with the command `xbru`. You'll be presented with a wonderfully simple, uncluttered interface for your backup needs. Large, clean buttons enable

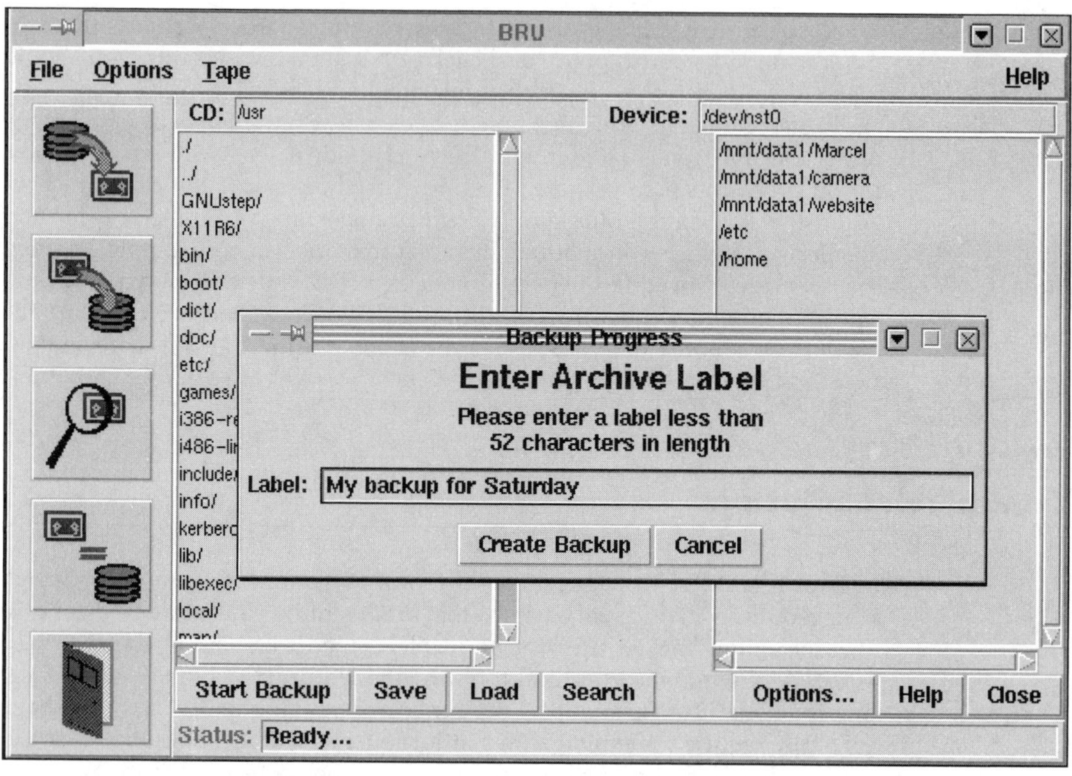

FIGURE 17.3 The BRU backup and recovery utility

single-click access to full, level 1, and level 2 backups. You'll be asked for a tape label and away you go (see Figure 17.3). The key to BRU seems to be simplicity. Even the scheduling options (daily, weekly, any day of the month) are easy to set up and use. Restoring a file or group of files is no more difficult.

While its graphical interface is simple and pleasant to work with, BRU will run from the command line as well. On that note, you can visit the BRU Web site and pick up contributed scripts for unattended or customized backup needs. You'll find those in the Tech Tips section of the site.

BRU comes in a variety of offerings. For truly large-scale networks where multistreaming backups and automated tape libraries are the order of the day, you should have a look at BRU's enterprise class package called BRU-PRO. Besides Linux backups, you can also take care of your various Windows platforms, AIX, Solaris, and more. Check the site for more details and currently supported platforms.

BRU is a commercial product, but the company also offers a noncommercial version that does a nice job of backing up your system and giving you peace of mind without the dollar pinch. The Personal Edition BRU is for non-commercial personal use only.

Arkeia

If you are trying to impress non-Linux users with a little pizzazz, look no further than Arkeia. For out-and-out looks, I have to give Arkeia from Knox Software the "coolness" award. Like BRU, you can run Arkeia from the command line, but the GUI is so cool to look at and use that even if you could use the command line and speed things up, why would you? A flashy speedometer records your backup speed in megabytes per minute, while the odometer keeps track of the total data already backed up, as shown in Figure 17.4. You can judge whether or not this is just silly, but it sure is fun.

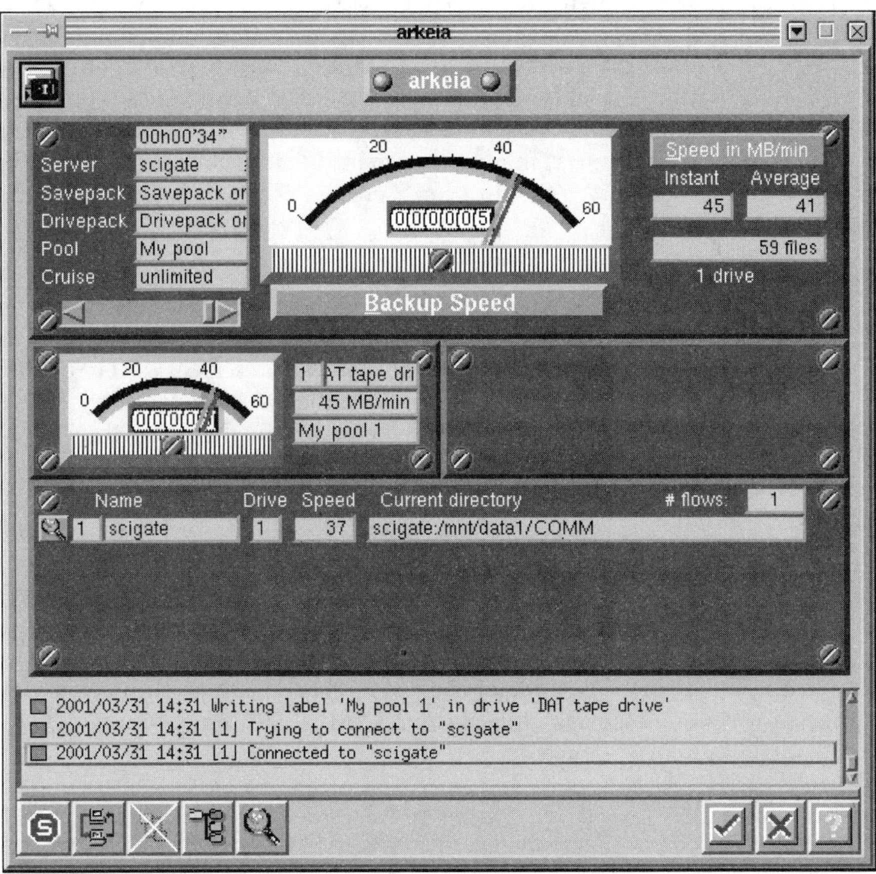

FIGURE 17.4 Backups appear to "race" along with Arkeia

All kidding aside, Arkeia is a powerful tool with clients that run on a number of platforms. For example, you can run a network backup onto your Linux system's DLT that comprises an IBM RS/6000, an HPUX machine, a couple of NT servers, and some Windows 9*x* boxes. Arkeia handles full, incremental, and on-demand backups. You can even back up multiple systems (and architectures) simultaneously while maintaining permissions, symbolic links, and so on.

The whole notion of pools management, tape management, and so on takes some getting used to. Consequently, it's not as intuitive (or as simple) as running BRU, where you push the Full backup button and are then on your way. You don't just load Arkeia and start using it. Before you can run that first tape, you have to do a fair amount of setup, which on reflection is warranted.

You see, Arkeia enforces good backup practices and strict tape rotation (a good thing, really). You cannot just choose a specific tape from the list. Of course there are ways to override anything if you are stubborn enough, but it kind of defeats the purpose. Tapes must follow rotation.

Arkeia is a commercial package; however, like our friend BRU, Arkeia is also available in a freeware version. The difference is one of scale. The free version supports only one server, one tape drive, and two clients (either Linux or Windows 9*x*) in a noncommercial, personal environment. Surf on over to the Arkeia Web site (`http://www.arkeia.com/`) and check it out.

Other Considerations

Products such as Arkeia and BRU lend a great deal of credibility to the maturity of Linux. They also provide the graphical tools that (like it or not) are often seen as the determining factor of whether something is "modern" or not. "Modern" is then usually equated to "good."

Still, those looking for a sophisticated and powerful backup solution should also check out AMANDA, the Advanced Maryland Automatic Network Disk Archiver, from the University of Maryland at College Park (`http://www.amanda.org/`). AMANDA is a non-GUI tool, but it provides the means to back up a large number of clients to a single location on a high-capacity tape drive. Windows clients can also be backed up using Samba (which I cover later in the book), and standard Linux backup tools are used to store the data. Furthermore, AMANDA is free software.

Final Words

Do your backups.

Label your backups.

Do backups regularly.

Remember that no piece of data is ever as important as the day you need to recover it.

Resources

AMANDA

`http://www.amanda.org/`

Arkeia

`http://www.arkeia.com/`

BRU

`http://www.bru.com/`

KDat

`http://www.kde.org/`

Taper

`http://www.e-survey.net.au/taper/`

Chapter 18

Network Administration

Linux is almost synonymous with the server world. When asked, I tend to champion the use of Linux on the desktop as quickly as I champion it in the server world. Nevertheless, Linux's strength and flexibility comes through in the server world. You might argue that the whole point of running Linux is to have access to the unparalleled networking capabilities inherent in the OS. That and rock-solid reliability. And excellent performance. And flexibility. And open source code that you can modify as needed. And . . . .

Before I discuss Linux's networking capabilities, I need to cover the basics of TCP/IP networking.

> **Security Warning:** As you start to work your way through this chapter, you'll notice that a number of networking protocols, environments, tools, and so on will be presented. I could warn you every step of the way about the dangers of these tools, but I want to cover the concepts here. Once you have finished this chapter, please make sure that you read Chapter 24 (which covers secure computing) and Chapter 25 (which covers security) and take what you find there to heart.

Because I am going to cover a lot of ground, I'll give you some good markers to let you know when it makes sense to take a breather. How much information am I talking about? Well, think of this chapter as a Wagner opera.

The Light-Speed Introduction to TCP/IP (Act 18, Scene 1)

Let's talk about basic TCP/IP configuration for a moment, shall we? Once again, I'll start with the non-GUI approach and discuss the bits and bytes of networking as it relates to TCP/IP, which we all know stands for Talk Clearly Please, Internet Politeness. Actually, that's a lie. It really stands for Transmission Control Protocol/Internet Protocol and it is the basic, underlying means by which communications is possible across the Internet.

Protocols and Suites

In discussions of TCP/IP, you will often hear the word "protocols." In fact, TCP/IP is often referred to as the "TCP/IP protocol suite." In other words, it is a collection of protocols that speak the same language. Any information transmitted using the TCP/IP protocol suite is done with *IP packets,* the fundamental bundles of information for IP-based protocols. Eventually, everything either becomes a packet or comes from a packet.

Packets are transported across your network to the various application protocols in this suite. These transport protocols tend to be either Transmission Control Protocol (TCP) or User Datagram Protocol (UDP).

TCP is referred to as a *connection-oriented protocol,* which means that you connect to a specific application and this connection stays up until such a time as you disconnect. When you telnet into another computer, you are using TCP as your transport protocol. TCP also breaks up large chunks of information into numbered IP packets and routes them to their final destination. The packets are numbered because they can theoretically take different paths to get to their destination, where they are reassembled according to their numbers.

On the other hand, UDP is referred to as a *connectionless protocol.* No connection has to be created (other than running the specific application daemon). UDP sends information through *datagrams,* which are small, packet-like chunks of data. Unlike with TCP packets, there is no numbering information and no checking to make sure that the datagrams arrive in the right order. There is *no guarantee* of delivery either. Any consistency checking must be done by the application. So why would anyone in his or her *right mind* want to use UDP as his or her transport protocol?

> **Trivia Time:** Most application protocols that use UDP can also use TCP. The reverse is also true, but somewhat fewer TCP protocols use UDP.

The answer is performance. Because UDP doesn't have to worry about numbering, disassembling, and reassembling packets, it tends to be more efficient (if you don't need to worry about getting all the data all the time). For fast, private networks, UDP is probably not a bad transport mechanism for certain less-critical applications. The Simple Network Management Protocol (SNMP) is an example of a UDP application protocol.

In this TCP/IP protocol suite, you also have a number of application protocols (some UDP, some TCP, and some both). These include the Simple Mail Transport Protocol (SMTP), Post Office Protocol (POP), and File Transfer Protocol (FTP) to name just a few. These are called *services*, and services are addressed by their respective port numbers.

Services and Ports

Your system's master process, the one that got the system going (after you pushed the On switch, that is) is called `init`. `init`'s process ID is 1. It is always 1. If you want to explore it further, you can find `init` in your process table using `ps`.

```
# ps ax | grep init
     1    ?      S          6:03  init
```

One of the services that `init` starts when your system boots is `inetd`. Its job is to listen for network requests, which it references by way of Internet socket numbers or ports. For instance, when you telnet to your system by typing `telnet mysystem`, you are actually requesting that `inetd` on `mysystem` starts an `in.telnetd` process that handles communication over port 23. So far, so good. Then, `in.telnetd` starts a process that eventually asks you for your login name and password and, miraculously, you are then logged in.

Basically, `inetd` listens to find out what other daemons should wake up to answer the port request. If you want to see what those service numbers translate to, do a `more` (or `less`) on `/etc/services`, a text file that lists the known TCP service ports. Here's a small sample from that file:

```
tcpmux          1/tcp                       # TCP port service multiplexer
echo            7/tcp
echo            7/udp
discard         9/tcp            sink null
discard         9/udp            sink null
systat          11/tcp           users
daytime         13/tcp
daytime         13/udp
netstat         15/tcp
qotd            17/tcp           quote
msp             18/tcp                  # message send protocol
msp             18/udp                  # message send protocol
chargen         19/tcp           ttytst source
chargen         19/udp           ttytst source
ftp-data        20/tcp
```

```
ftp             21/tcp
fsp             21/udp          fspd
ssh             22/tcp                          # SSH Remote Login
Protocol
ssh             22/udp                          # SSH Remote Login
Protocol
telnet          23/tcp
```

Notice that I have services that use both TCP and UDP as their transport protocols. Your own /etc/services file will contain a list of the more common port numbers. The services file has a very simple format. First, the service is listed, followed by some white space, a port number, a slash, and then the transport protocol for that service. You can also leave some white space again and add descriptive comments. Your version of this file will have a couple of hundred (or more) services listed. Even so, this is by no means an exhaustive list. The Resources section at the end of this chapter provides a link to a much more complete list.

From a resources perspective, it makes sense to have a single process listening rather than one for each and every service. For those of you who can remember and visualize such things, picture Lily Tomlin as the telephone operator who (eventually) patches people through to the party to whom they wished to speak. She is inetd and the people to whom you wish to speak are the service deamons. You request extension 23 and eventually she puts you through.

When inetd starts, it reads a file called inetd.conf. You'll find this one in your /etc directory, just like the services file. Here are a couple of sample lines from inetd.conf:

```
#
# These are standard services.
#
ftp  stream    tcp  nowait    root /usr/sbin/tcpd in.ftpd -l -a
telnet    stream  tcp    nowait  root    /usr/sbin/tcpd    in.telnetd
#
# Shell, login, exec, comsat and talk are BSD protocols.
#
shell     stream    tcp  nowait    root /usr/sbin/tcpd in.rshd
login     stream    tcp  nowait    root /usr/sbin/tcpd in.rlogind
#exec     stream    tcp  nowait    root /usr/sbin/tcpd in.rexecd
```

IP Addresses, Networks, and Subnets, Oh My!

Pay no attention to that man trying to scare you away. While the following terms may appear like arcane words from a strange alternate universe, they are in fact the stuff that networks are made of. All those packets have to go somewhere and getting them there is what I am going to talk about next.

When you address a snail-mail envelope, you are triggering a chain of events that has its equal in the network world: moving something from one address to another.

What Are Domains?

Anybody who has ever surfed the Net from a browser knows about domain names—the dot-coms, the dot-orgs, and the dot-whatevers. Domain names always appear in the following format:

```
somecomputer.somedomain.top_level_domain
```

The idea behind all these names is to provide an easy-to-remember address to a specific computer in much the same way that your house or apartment has an address. The reason I say "easy-to-remember" is because the real address is something entirely different. This is the `number.number.number.number` format of addressing and the only one that actually really matters to computers on the Internet. In fact, the whole point of a *domain name server (DNS)* is to translate those friendly names back into something the computers and routers of the Internet can deal with.

The `somecomputer` part of the domain is pretty much arbitrary. If I have a machine called "natika," that becomes my host name. What you usually call the domain is actually the domain name itself combined with the top-level domain (TLD). The TLDs most North Americans are familiar with are .com, .org, .edu, .net, .gov, and .mil, but there are substantially more than just these. If you live outside the United States, your top-level domain is your country's two-letter code. For instance, .ca represents Canada and .jp represents Japan. Canadians, with their proximity to the United States, can use either the .ca TLD or three of the classic United States TLDs, .com, .org, and .net, as shown in Table 18.1.

The rules have relaxed quite a bit since these original domains were put in place. Anybody can get a .com, .org, or .net TLD without necessarily being a

TABLE 18.1: Traditional U.S. Top-Level Domains

Domain	Description
.org	Organizations, nonprofits, and so on
.com	Businesses
.edu	Universities and educational institutions
.mil	Military
.gov	Government
.net	Networks and service providers

TABLE 18.2: New Top-Level Domains

Domain	Description
.aero	Aerospace and air transport industry
.biz	Businesses
.coop	Nonprofit cooperatives
.info	Pretty generic (no restrictions)
.museum	Museums
.name	Personal and family names
.pro	Accountants, lawyers, and physicians

business, an organization (non-profit or otherwise), or a network services provider. Furthermore, several new TLDs were introduced just recently (in addition to the two-letter country TLDs). These new domains are presented in Table 18.2.

Believe it or not, there isn't a lot more that can be done in terms of coming up with new .com names. Pretty much anything you might want has already been registered. That is the reason that for the first time new TLDs were considered. While the new TLDs listed in Table 18.2 were just recently approved by ICANN, the story is far from over. Many companies and organizations were vying for new TLDs and a legal battle was launched to challenge ICANN's choices.

> The job of administering all those two-letter country codes or TLDs goes to the Internet Assigned Numbers Authority (IANA). When you see an e-mail coming in from `somebody@mydomain.gr`, you can use IANA's listing (`http://www.iana.org/cctld/cctld-whois.htm`) to find out just what the .gr stands for. (It is Greece, by the way.)

IP Addresses and Networks

Getting back to those IP address numbers—how are they defined?

Finding the answer to this question requires looking at public and private addressing schemes. Because both use the same format for defining IP addresses, let's start there. An IP address, say 192.168.22.56, is often referred to as consisting of four octets. In other words, four dotted 8-bit sections. All told, this gives you a 32-bit addressing scheme that can generate nearly 4.3 million separate IP addresses. While that's an awful lot of computers, it just isn't enough. This is why the IPv6 standard is replacing the old IPv4 standard. The new standard ensures that the addresses don't run out any time soon.

Geek Trivia: My local IP address of 192.168.22.2 can also be read as 3232241154. "How is this possible?" you might ask. Well, follow me through these little calculations and you'll see. Take the first octet (in this case, the left-most) and multiply it by 256 cubed. Add to that the second octet times 256 squared plus the third octet times 256 plus the fourth octet. Confused? Here it is as I fed the calculation into the command-line calculator, `bc`:

```
((192*256^3)+(168*256^2)+(22*256)+2) = 3232241154
```

If I `ping` 3232241154, the system responds as though I had typed `ping 192.168.22.2`. Try it yourself. It's more work than you ever want to do, but it is fun.

This whole "running out of network addresses" issue does have a positive effect. As it turns out, the odds of your ISP being willing to provide you with IP addresses for every machine on your network are pretty slim, but as I said, that's a good thing. The standard nonprivate network addressing scheme is (by necessity) routable throughout the Internet. Your local network should not be. Making every machine visible to the world just increases the amount of work you are going to have to do in order to keep crackers out. Crackers might be able to see and work at breaking through your Web server, but the internal network is problematic because they have to get through your gateway or firewall before they can direct their attention to the rest of your network.

Warning: You *must not* assign IP addresses willy-nilly. Even if your network is not connected to the Internet in some way, do not use a routable address. As system administrator, it is your job to make sure that the IP addresses you assign to PCs and other devices in your office environment are unique, sane, and legitimate.

The three common network classes are Class A, Class B, and Class C. Class A networks cover a range of addresses starting at 1.0.0.0 and going all the way to 127.0.0.0. Class B networks run from 128.0.0.0 all the way through to 191.255.0.0, while Class C networks occupy the space from 192.0.0.0 to 223.255.255.0. There are also two other classes of networks (which I won't spend a lot of time talking about): the multicast addresses, which run from 224.0.0.0 to 239.255.255.255.0, and the "don't touch because this is reserved" space, which runs from 240.0.0.0 through to 255.255.255.255.

If you are creating a local network in your home or company, you should use a subnet of addresses as defined by RFC1918. While the other addresses require that they be assigned to you, the private network addresses can be used any way you see fit. This private space is defined as shown in Table 18-3.

TABLE 18.3: Private Network Addresses

Class	Address Range	Number of Hosts
Class A	10.0.0.0 to 10.255.255.255	254 possible hosts
Class B	172.16.0.0 to 172.31.255.255	Around 65,000 hosts
Class C	192.168.0.0 to 192.168.255.255	Over 1.5 million hosts

Definition: RFC stands for Request For Comments. These documents (started in 1969) were and continue to be efforts to define the Internet (originally the ARPANET), computer communications, networks in general, protocols, and so on. Some of these documents eventually became the standards for the Internet under the Internet Engineering Task Force (IETF). RFCs are a kind of *blueprint* for the Internet.

You'll notice that when addresses are used in this book, they follow the pattern in Table 18-3. In fact, I tend to gear my examples to the Class C network scheme because it represents a small network of just a few computers, which is what my own office is using.

Subnets, Netmasks, and Broadcast Addresses

Even when you have a large network assigned to you, you may want to break up the network into small subnets. This is, in fact, what is happening when your ISP gives you an address within a Class A, B, or C network. Normally, you won't subnet a Class C network because it's already quite small (254 possible hosts), requires minimal maintenance, and is well within the capacities of most office backbones. ISPs will routinely subnet a Class C network because they rarely assign complete Class C networks anymore (the running out of addresses thing again). Class B and Class A networks almost demand subnetting (which I will talk about shortly). Imagine some 65,000 hosts hanging off a batch of routers in your office (Class B), or even worse, over 1.5 million hosts (Class A).

The netmask is designed to isolate your network from every other network. Talking to other computers inside that network then requires a router, which is how your computer winds up talking to other computers on the Internet. Here's what constitutes being part of a subnet: Any computer you can talk to without the aid of a router is on your subnet. Specifically, if your computer's network is the same as another's and your netmask matches the netmask of that other computer, you are on the same subnet.

The following line shows the IP address 192.168.22.2 as a binary representation:

```
11000000 . 10101000 . 00010110 . 00000010
```

Each octet is represented by 8 bits and, as it turns out, 8 bits is just enough to represent the numbers 0 through 255.

Netmasks

What about the netmask? If you are dealing with an internal private network, you almost don't have to worry about it. When you give a host an IP address, there is what is called a *default netmask.* The standard netmask for a Class A network is 255.0.0.0. For a Class B network, it is 255.255.0.0. Finally, for a Class C network, it is 255.255.255.0. To understand why these are the defaults, it helps to understand what a netmask does. The answer is pretty much what the name implies: A netmask masks (or covers up) those parts of the IP address that aren't part of your subnet. The default subnet mask for my 192.168.22.2 address is 255.255.255.0. Let's line them up as in my earlier example:

```
11000000 . 10101000 . 00010110 . 00000010
11111111 . 11111111 . 11111111 . 00000000
```

The first line is the address. The second line is the netmask. Because the 255 translates to 11111111, the 192 in my address is *masked.* In other words, my computer in that part of the network effectively becomes invisible. The same goes for the 168 and the 22. You can't touch those. Those numbers represent my network and the only thing I can see are other computers in that same network. That's what the netmask does. It defines what part of your IP address is your network. So, what's left over for you to play with are those last 256 numbers (0 through 255), right? Not quite.

If you accept this standard netmask, your networks have not been divided into subnets themselves. The Class C network, for instance, will only have 254 usable addresses. That's because the .0 address is reserved to represent the network itself (192.168.22.0) and the .255 becomes the broadcast address (192.168.22.255). Everything else is up for grabs.

Broadcast Addresses

"So, what's a broadcast address?" you ask. Well, I'll tell you. Sending information (a packet) to the broadcast address is akin to sending it to every host on the network. You are, in effect, *broadcasting.* For instance, I could broadcast `ping` over my network with this command:

```
ping -b 192.168.22.255
```

Some versions of the `ping` command require that you use the `-b` flag when you do a broadcast `ping`.

Participation in a network is defined by the network side of your IP address, your netmask, and your broadcast address. Any host within the same network can, by definition, talk to any other host within that network without the need for a router. A *router,* quite simply, is a device that enables a computer to talk to another computer not on the same network by taking care of moving information between those networks.

Subnets

If I break up a network into small networks, that's called *subnetting*. If I create subnets from my larger network, I then need a router for those subnets to talk to each other. Routers cost money. Separating your network from somebody else's just makes sense when you think of the Internet and several million other hosts, but how about in your own company? Why would you want to do such a thing?

A Class A network can consist of over 1.5 million hosts. From an office administration point of view, that's insane. A Class B network can consist of some 65,000 hosts. Not quite insane, but still crazy. On the other hand, a Class C network of 254 hosts, while more than okay for a small office, isn't much for a medium-sized office of a hundred employees or so. Toss in a few network printers, a handful of servers, and a PC on every desk, and it's amazing how quickly you can use up 254 addresses. But 65,000 hosts? That's a bit much and there's no in-between network definition.

Pretend that you have 2,000 hosts and a couple hundred network printers that you want to configure into your corporate network. That still qualifies as an administrative nightmare. Still, let's say you could do it. Standard Ethernet rules say you can have no more than 1,024 hosts on a single network segment. That leaves you a bit short if you just try to string them all together. Even if you could, *long* before you get to that number, you'd discover that collisions, errors, and just plain traffic on your network would make the network unusable. Breaking up the network into something manageable and efficient is what subnetting is all about.

Before I continue with how this happens, I should talk about Classless InterDomain Routing (CIDR). That means taking all that stuff I told you about default netmasks and putting it away for a few minutes. Pretend I never told you about all of that—but only for a few minutes.

Intermezzo

To help me explain CIDR, let's continue with the 2,000-host network. You'll use the private Class B network so every host will have an address somewhere between 172.16.0.1 and 172.31.255.254. The default netmask under normal conditions would be 255.255.0.0, which in binary format looks like this:

```
11111111 . 11111111 . 00000000 . 00000000
[ network portion ] . [   host portion  ]
```

Those first two octets define your network as being 172.16.0.0. A computer at 172.16.10.1 can then *see* another computer at 172.16.12.17 if both computers are on the same backbone. The 172.16.10.1 computer cannot, however, talk to a computer at 172.21.10.1 because the subnet mask won't allow it. Now, if you apply a subnet of 255.255.255.0 to that large Class B network, you have essentially created a whole bunch of 254-host networks (or subnetworks) with which to work. The host portion is as a result much smaller.

```
11111111 . 11111111 . 11111111 . 00000000
[      network portion        ] . 00000000
```

Because these are now separate networks, they will need routers to transport packets from one segment to another. The problem is that you still have a minimum of 254 hosts per network (or subnetwork). On the Internet itself, this waste of addresses was a formula for disaster as IP address space quickly ran out. Is there a way to divide even a Class C network into smaller networks?

Let's go back to my 255.255.255.0 subnet mask. The network portion is identified by the number of bits—in this case, it's 24 bits. In the example before that, it is 16 bits. (Just count the 1s.) Finally, in a Class A network, the netmask is 8 bits. You can write the network and netmask definition like this:

Class A	10.0.0.0/8
Class B	172.16.0.0/16
Class C	192.168.22.0/24

That's eight 1s for the Class A network's netmask, 16 for the Class B, and 24 for the Class C. This is the important part here. The netmask defines the network. So what would happen if you mucked about with this nice, clean netmask? That was the whole point of CIDR.

What CIDR did was permit the use of a netmask of anything from 13 to 27 bits to define the network, thus giving up. Using the CIDR scheme, you could take a Class C network and split it into two or more networks by adding bits to the netmask. For instance, if I want to break my Class C network of 254 possible hosts into two separate networks of 128 hosts, I should use a netmask of 255.255.255.128, which (using the CIDR format) I can write as 192.168.22.0/25 instead. How does this work? Have a look at the following:

```
11111111 . 11111111 . 11111111 . 10000000
```

Notice the extra 1 in the preceding binary representation. Those 1s are my netmask. They define my network. That means I only have 7 bits left in which to specify IP addresses. That's because I can only create the numbers 0 through

127 with seven binary digits. Get it? I also wind up with two networks. Like any network definition, I need to reserve space for one network address and one broadcast address, leaving me with 126 hosts. My first network would be 192.168.22.0 with a broadcast address of 192.168.22.127. That extra 1 in the last octet is the break, the wall through which neither network is allowed to pass without a router. The second network would be 192.168.22.128 with a broadcast address of 192.168.22.255.

Using CIDR notation, you can create more interesting subnets yet. Sticking with the Class C example, 192.168.22.0/26 would create four class C networks of 64 hosts each. Why? Because 6 bits is only enough to define the numbers 0 through 63. And 192.168.22.0/27? That becomes eight Class C networks of 32 hosts each because 5 bits is only good enough to define the numbers 0 through 31.

What happens if you go in the other direction? What happens when you use a /23 mask? The host part of the network now has 9 bits. That's good enough to generate numbers running anywhere from 0 to 511, meaning you could create two Class C networks of 512 hosts each. A /22 mask leaves 10 bits, which allows four networks of 1024 addresses each because 10 bits enables you to define numbers from 0 to 1023. This process is called *supernetting,* and other than getting you all excited about the prospect, I'm going to slide back to the discussion on local network configuration and leave you with those thoughts. Check the Resources section for the RFC editor link and put CIDR into the Search field if you want the deep-down, nasty details.

Setting Up Your PC Network (Act 18, Scene 2)

Back in Chapter 10, I talked about setting up a dial-up connection to the Internet using PPP and a modem. This is not the way you set up an office network. You could try, but it would get complicated, ugly, and run very slowly. Instead, install Ethernet cards into your computers and link them through RJ45 Ethernet cabling through hardware such as hubs and routers.

Drivers

An Ethernet card is configured by loading the appropriate driver into the running system. While it is possible to compile these drivers into the kernel, the favored approach is through loadable modules. These are defined in `/etc/conf.modules`. The Linux system I am writing this book on has two cards installed. Here's the relevant information from my `conf.modules` file:

```
alias eth0 rtl8139
alias eth1 tulip
```

In this case, I have a couple of no-name (low-name) PCI cards, one running the RealTek 8139 driver and the other running the Tulip driver.

On the Debian system running across from me, things are a little bit different. There is a modules file at `/etc/modules` that performs more or less the same function, but it is a bit less wordy. This is the only line in that one:

```
3c59x
```

Other modules are listed in `/initrd/etc/conf.modules`, and that file is managed by a program called `update-modules`. This is further represented in `/etc/modules.conf`. That, too, should not be edited by hand. Rather, the information that you see there comes from several files under the `/etc/modutils` directory.

Setting the IP Address

Again, setting the IP address depends on the system. More on that in a moment.

Before I get into the system specifics, there is actually a universal way of setting an address. In fact, this is what actually happens under the surface by the scripts that bring up interfaces at boot time. The command is called `/sbin/ifconfig`. To see all the interfaces on your system, type this command:

```
/sbin/ifconfig -a
```

You should see something like this come back to you:

```
eth0      Link encap:Ethernet  HWaddr 00:20:18:89:29:A6
          inet addr:192.168.22.100  Bcast:192.168.22.255  Mask:255.255.255.0
          UP BROADCAST RUNNING MULTICAST  MTU:1500  Metric:1
          RX packets:1318777 errors:0 dropped:0 overruns:0 frame:0
          TX packets:1238307 errors:0 dropped:0 overruns:0 carrier:0
          collisions:26510 txqueuelen:100
          Interrupt:9 Base address:0x1000

lo        Link encap:Local Loopback
          inet addr:127.0.0.1  Mask:255.0.0.0
          UP LOOPBACK RUNNING  MTU:3924  Metric:1
          RX packets:108877 errors:0 dropped:0 overruns:0 frame:0
          TX packets:108877 errors:0 dropped:0 overruns:0 carrier:0
          collisions:0 txqueuelen:0
```

You may actually see more information, depending on the number of cards you already have configured. What's interesting here is that you can do everything having to do with starting, stopping, and reconfiguring the interface from the command line. Let's have another look at the first three lines for `eth0`:

```
eth0      Link encap:Ethernet  HWaddr 00:20:18:89:29:A6
          inet addr:192.168.22.100  Bcast:192.168.22.255  Mask:255.255.255.0
          UP BROADCAST RUNNING MULTICAST  MTU:1500  Metric:1
```

The interesting piece of information in the first line is the hardware address (`HWaddr`). This is also referred to as the Media Access Control (MAC) address. This is your card's hardware address and like the Little Prince's rose, it is unique in all the world. The second line is what you think of as the normal network address (IP, netmask, and so on). Finally, in the third line, you see that the card is up and running (UP). Taking that card down can be done with your friend, `ifconfig`:

```
/sbin/ifconfig eth0 down
```

To change the address to something else (like the answer to life, the universe, and everything), you can use the same command:

```
/sbin/ifconfig eth0 192.168.22.42 netmask 255.255.255.255 up
```

Notice that I changed the card address and brought it up with one command.

Of course, in real life, these things happen automatically when you boot your system. There is no need to manually bring up interfaces (other than for testing). On a Red Hat (or similar) system, you'll find most of the configuration files exist in a directory called `/etc/sysconfig`. Your default network address is defined in the `network` file.

```
NETWORKING=yes
HOSTNAME=mailhost.mydomain.dom
GATEWAY=192.168.22.10
```

The details of various interfaces are sitting in the `/etc/sysconfig/network-scripts` directory. On my test machine, I have four interfaces: one for `lo` (the loopback address), another for `eth0` (my first Ethernet card), `eth1`, and finally, a `ppp0` interface for my dial-up connection. For each interface, there is an `ifcfg-interface` file with the details of that interface. When the system boots and the `/etc/rc.d/init.d/network` script is executed, it is this information that the scripts read to bring up the interfaces. The following is from the `ifcfg-eth0` file in the network-scripts directory:

```
DEVICE=eth0
IPADDR=192.168.22.10
NETMASK=255.255.255.0
NETWORK=192.168.22.0
BROADCAST=192.168.22.255
ONBOOT=yes
BOOTPROTO=none
```

While working on this book, I had two Debian versions to play with. On the older system, the information is sitting right in the network script at `/etc/init.d/network`. This is what it looks like:

```
#!/bin/sh

cat /proc/net/dev |grep : | cut -d : -f 1 | grep lo >/dev/null 2>&1
```

```
if [ $? -eq 0 ] ; then
   ifconfig lo 127.0.0.1
   route add -net 127.0.0.0 netmask 255.0.0.0 dev lo
fi

IPADDR=192.168.22.2
NETMASK=255.255.255.0
NETWORK=192.168.22.0
GATEWAY=192.168.22.10

cat /proc/net/dev |grep : | cut -d : -f 1 | grep eth0 >/dev/null 2>&1

if [ $? -eq 0 ] ; then
   ifconfig eth0 ${IPADDR} netmask ${NETMASK}
   route add -net ${NETWORK} netmask ${NETMASK} dev eth0
   [ "${GATEWAY}" ] && route add default gw ${GATEWAY} metric 1
fi
```

On the newer system (Potato release), things have changed somewhat. All the information has moved to the `/etc/network/interfaces` file. Here is a sample configuration on my network, including a single `loopback` interface (127.0.0.1) and one card for the internal network interface at `eth0`:

```
# This is the loopback interface
iface lo inet loopback

# Our single ethernet card
iface eth1 inet static
address 192.168.22.3
network 192.168.22.0
netmask 255.255.255.0
broadcast 192.168.22.255
gateway 192.168.22.10
```

My `eth0` interface can then be brought up with the `ifup` command and taken down with the `ifdown` command.

Routing

The reason I showed you the whole Debian script is twofold. First, it is short, and second, it brings up the subject of routing. Simply having a configured network interface isn't enough. Your system needs to know what to do with packets once they leave your Ethernet card (or dial-up modem). You do this with the `route` command. Let's look at the previous line from the Debian `network` script:

```
route add -net ${NETWORK} netmask ${NETMASK} dev eth0
```

By plugging in the appropriate numbers, you wind up with this line:

```
route add -net 192.168.22.0 netmask 255.255.255.0 dev eth0
```

By executing this command after configuring your card with `ifconfig`, you are telling the system what to do when it sees packet addresses within that 192.168.22.0 network—redirect them to the `eth0` interface. When the packets generated belong to something outside that network, you rely on a different kind of `route`: the `default route`. This address usually refers to a router that is connected to other routers and hosts. Eventually, one of these will hopefully know where this packet belongs. That, in a rather crude nutshell, is how the Internet works. In the following example, I configure my system to look to another host on my network as the default route for all nonlocal network traffic:

```
route add default gw 192.168.22.10
```

The simplest form of this command is `/sbin/route`.

```
$ /sbin/route
Kernel IP routing table
Destination     Gateway         Genmask         Flags Metric Ref    Use Iface
testsys.mydomai *               255.255.255.255 UH    0      0        0 eth0
192.168.22.0    *               255.255.255.0   U     0      0        0 eth0
127.0.0.0       *               255.0.0.0       U     0      0        0 lo
default         netgate         0.0.0.0         UG    0      0        0 eth0
```

The previous command goes ahead and tries to resolve the numerical addresses into symbolic ones. You can speed up this process by passing the `-n` flag and using only a numerical display.

Using netstat

You can also use the `netstat` program to display essentially the same information (as displayed by the `/sbin/route` command above) by using the `-r` flag. The `netstat` program is important for other reasons as well. By using the program with the `-a` and `-p` flags, you can find out about every connection (or port) open on your system and what programs are using those ports.

> **Security Note:** Learn to use and appreciate the `netstat` program; it can be extremely useful in determining if there are people using your system who should not be there. Does every one of those connections make sense to you? Are there live connections from a host you don't recognize? These are things to think about when you explore network security later on in this book.

In the following example, I also use the `-n flag`. This tells `netstat` not to worry about resolving IP addresses into symbolic addresses. It also makes the program run a bit faster because no name resolution is performed. Finally, this can be quite a long listing, so I pipe the whole thing to `more`.

```
# netstat -apn | more
Active Internet connections (servers and established)
Proto Recv-Q Send-Q Local Address           Foreign Address         State
PID/Program name
tcp        0     20 192.168.22.10:22        192.168.22.100:1014     ESTABLISHED
4003/sshd
tcp        0      0 192.168.22.10:22        192.168.22.100:1015     ESTABLISHED
6122/named
tcp        0      0 192.168.22.10:53        0.0.0.0:*               LISTEN
6122/named
tcp        0      0 127.0.0.1:53            0.0.0.0:*               LISTEN
6122/named
tcp        0      0 0.0.0.0:80              0.0.0.0:*               LISTEN
1231/httpd
tcp        0      0 0.0.0.0:443             0.0.0.0:*               LISTEN
```

The PID is the process ID of the running program that is using the connection.

Domain Name Services (Act 18, Scene 3)

This whole discussion of IP addresses brings up one of the more frightening topics in the world of Linux administration: the ever-unpopular domain name server (DNS). The job of the DNS, quite simply, is to provide a mechanism whereby you can turn those IP numbers into a symbolic name, such as `arbitrary.domain_name.com`, and vice versa.

You don't necessarily need a DNS. In fact, running your own DNS (if you don't have to) is often more trouble than it is worth. Even on a home system where you've decided to share that one Internet connection with the other PCs in your house, you may find a DNS is completely unnecessary. Simple entries in your hosts file can define your local network.

> **Security Warning:** All right, this isn't meant to scare you away from running a DNS. You may, in fact, need to run a DNS. That said, one of the most common holes in networks, not to mention one of the most common means by which networks are compromised, continues to be DNS. If you must run a DNS, stay on top of your `bind` package releases. Keep an eye on security bulletins and upgrade your DNS software whenever necessary.

The /etc/hosts File

Once upon a time, a long time ago, there was no DNS. There was a simple file on every network-connected host: the `/etc/hosts` file. You still have a hosts file on your computers, but it isn't used to define every network-connected system, just yours and perhaps a handful of others that you need quick access to. The format is quite simple: an IP address followed by some white space (I like to use tabs) followed by the fully qualified domain name of the computer and then any aliases by which that host is known. Here's an example:

```
# /etc/hosts file
# IP Address          Fully qualified domain name    Aliases
127.0.0.1             localhost.localdomain          localhost
192.168.22.100        scigate.mycompany.com          scigate      devsys
192.168.22.2          nexus.mycompany.com            nexus
192.168.22.3          speedy.mycompany.com           speedy
```

The first two lines are comments. The first "real" line is the 127.0.0.1 line, which defines my `localhost` interface. The next three lines define different systems on my network. Notice that the machine called "scigate.mycompany. dom" has aliases of "scigate" and "devsys." That means I can get to that machine by using either of those names.

The `/etc/hosts` file is only visible to users on the machine on which that file resides. That means you need to have a `/etc/hosts` file on every system in your network and those files have to be up-to-date. I'm sure you can see where this is going. If you only have two or three hosts on your network, managing the appropriate files is not time-consuming. Once that list starts to grow, it is time to start thinking about running some kind of local name service.

> **Hold That Thought:** Incidentally, DNS is not the only solution to consider. Another is network information service (NIS). Where DNS is strictly a name resolution system, NIS performs a number of other lookup functions that I'll explore later in this chapter.

Your own computer's host name, by the way, is contained in a file called `/etc/HOSTNAME`. That's how the system remembers to set that information between reboots. On a Debian system, that file has the same name in lowercase letters: `/etc/hostname`.

Will the Real DNS Please Stand Up

BIND is the de facto package that runs DNS. If you see something called `named` running on your system, you have BIND. BIND stands for Berkeley Internet Name Domain, and despite the "Berkeley" in the name (that's where it all began), the home of BIND is actually the Internet Software Consortium (ISC) (`http://www.isc.org/`), where you can always find the latest and greatest BIND. Your Linux distribution vendor will also have precompiled binaries of this DNS software, but it usually follows behind what you can find at the ISC site.

Setting up your own DNS can be a fairly complicated affair (and I will cover that), but as I have already mentioned, you may not need to do so. If you are already tied in to an existing network that is connected to the Internet, the simple solution is to point to existing name servers by adding them to your /etc/resolv.conf file. I talked about this in Chapter 10 when I discussed a dial-up connection to the Internet. A single line (or two) pointing to your ISP's name server will serve under the circumstances. For example:

```
domain mydomain.dom
nameserver XXX.XXX.XXX.XXX          (first DNS)
nameserver YYY.YYY.YYY.YYY          (second DNS)
```

What this does is set up as a DNS client, rather than a server. The first line is your default search domain (usually your own). If you try to do a lookup (using the host or nslookup programs), you do not need to specify your domain name. For instance, if I were trying to find the address of a host called "speedy" on my network, I would type this command:

```
$ host speedy
speedy.mydomain.dom has address 192.168.22.3
```

As part of doing the lookup, the default domain is appended to the host name I specified.

Before I get into the nitty-gritty, you should also be aware of the /etc/nsswitch.conf file. This text file is one that I will visit in more detail later in this chapter when I discuss NIS. For now, simply be aware that the order in which certain information (like host names) is looked up is defined in this file. The line that refers to the hosts file looks something like this:

```
hosts:       files nisplus nis dns
```

With this configuration, the local host file is searched first (files), followed by the NIS (nisplus and nis), and finally the DNS (dns). This is designed to speed up the lookup process. If you want to telnet to a host called host1.natika.dom, and that information is in your /etc/hosts file, the system looks no further. Consequently, it is possible to modify this file to force a different order.

Setting Up Your Own Name Server

Generally speaking, if you are running a single site with a simple dial-up connection to the Internet and you're not running server services, you do not need to set up a DNS. As previously mentioned, you should save yourself some trouble and let your ISP do it for you. If, however, you're running a public Web server, if multiple servers and clients are sharing a connection, or if you're distributing mail through a local domain, then read on, brave hearts. It's time to set up a real DNS. But first, consider the following weasel words about BIND and DNS.

> **Security Note:** Unfortunately, the prevalence of BIND and a permanently available service on most servers makes it a tempting target for crackers and script kiddies. In fact, the SANS Institute (`http://www.sans.org/`) routinely places DNS and BIND at the top of its list of means by which security is compromised.
>
> Please make sure that you are running the latest version of BIND.

> **Quick Tip:** Before you dive into this whole DNS configuration thing, I'll make it easy on you. If you visit my Web site (`http://www.salmar.com/marcel/`) and check the Downloads section, you'll notice some *generic* DNS configuration files. If you want to save yourself a lot of typing and all you need is a DNS for your small PC network, look for the quick and easy package there.

Defining Your Domain

The point of this exercise is not to turn you into an ISP. If this is what you are trying to do, you are going to be doing quite a bit more reading on DNS services and you'll certainly need more information than I will give you here. Nevertheless, the following is the premise for this DNS.

You have a Linux server that provides printing, telnet (or SSH) access, maybe Web services for your Intranet (see Chapter 20), a little mail perhaps, and it also shares your outside connection with an internal network. The internal network in this example is going to be based on a private address Class C network at 192.168.22.0.

The /etc/named.conf File

Starting with BIND 8, the `/etc/named.conf` file represents the top of your DNS pyramid. On a Debian system, you may find the file in the `/etc/bind` directory, although the latest BIND I have running on my Debian box installed in `/etc`, just like Red Hat. The first thing to note is that anything starting with double forward slashes (`//`) or slash-star star-slash constructs (`/* stuff goes here */`) represents comments. The first version is C++-type comments, while the second is good, old-fashioned, C-style comments.

Let's start by having a look at a pretty basic `named.conf` file. This one is actually from a Red Hat system, from a base package called `caching-nameserver`. While you are at it, install the `bind` and the `bind-util` packages. The Debian people will want to pick up the `bind` and the `dnsutils` packages.

Listing of /etc/named.conf

Let's start with something simple. The following information is a listing of the default configuration file for a caching-only name server. This is what `named` reads when it starts up:

```
// generated by named-bootconf.pl

options {
        directory "/var/named";
        /*
         * If there is a firewall between you and nameservers you want
         * to talk to, you might need to uncomment the query-source
         * directive below.  Previous versions of BIND always asked
         * questions using port 53, but BIND 8.1 uses an unprivileged
         * port by default.
         */
        // query-source address * port 53;
};
//
// a caching only nameserver config
//
zone "." {
        type hint;
        file "named.ca";
};

zone "0.0.127.in-addr.arpa" {
        type master;
        file "named.local";
};
```

The very first line is interesting because even though I said I wasn't going to cover the old BIND 4 name server files, you are looking at the name of the utility that will enable you to convert an old-style `named.boot` file to a new `named.conf` for BIND 8. The program listed is a Perl script called `named-bootconf.pl`, which you will find in `/usr/sbin`. Should you have that old BIND 4 `named.boot` file lying around from a previous name server, here is what you do:

```
cd /etc
named-bootconf < named.boot > named.conf
```

Going back to your `named.conf` file, notice also the comments in both C and C++ formats. The format of the file is pretty much the same throughout: some statement definition with various options inside curly brackets.

```
zone "0.0.127.in-addr.arpa" {
        type master;
        file "named.local";
};
```

The statement in this case is "zone" with options called "type" and "file." Let's have a look at these, starting with the ones you see in the default `named.conf` file.

- `options`: The very first statement you run across is `options`. This statement refers to things that affect the name server configuration globally. The best example in this case is the `directory` option, which defines where all name server configuration files will live. While you can specify another place for your files, this is the accepted standard.
- `zone`: This is the heart of your DNS. These sections define parts of your domain, specifically as they relate to networks and subnetworks inside your organization. The most basic zone references the entire domain because the domain and the network are essentially one and the same. Large organizations may have hundreds of zones in their domains.
- Other options include `acl` (which enables you to define IP address lists for access control of some definition), `logging` (what to log and where), and `include` (which enables you to include other files in your configuration, rather than putting everything in this one file). And yes, you guessed it, there are even more.

Zones

Ack! Don't zone out yet. You're almost there.

The first zone you'll encounter is the `named.ca` zone, which is listed as type `hint`. Essentially, this is exactly what it sounds like: If your DNS can't find the answer, it would at least like some kind of hint. That hint is a list of the top-level domain name servers in the world and their addresses. This is your cache file. Because this is a list of top-level servers and the list does change from time to time, it is in your best interest to keep this copy up-to-date. To get the latest and greatest copy, use this command:

```
dig @e-root-servers.net > newcache_file
```

You will want to be connected to the Net (of course) and you will want to use the same name as your current cache file (`named.ca`) when you have what you need. `dig`, by the way, is a command-line tool used to query name servers.

> **Geek Trivia:** Your DNS is not alone. In fact, the whole point of DNS is that each server is actually part of some greater entity—a distributed database of address information that spans the world.

The next zone is your `localhost` zone. The file name is `named.local` in the example (and in the caching name server defaults). The file type is `master`, meaning that it is the primary source of information for anything having to do with this zone. For this zone, it doesn't make sense, but in another zone, you might find the type set to `slave` with a list of `masters` followed by an IP address list to get the appropriate zone information, as follows:

```
zone mydomain.dom {
type slave;
masters { ip_addr; };
}
```

> **Quick Tip:** Notice the semicolons at the end of each option.

Let's have a look at that `named.local` file.

```
@       IN      SOA     localhost. root.localhost.  (
                                    1997022700 ; Serial
                                    28800      ; Refresh
                                    14400      ; Retry
                                    3600000    ; Expire
                                    86400 )    ; Minimum
              IN      NS      localhost.

1       IN      PTR     localhost.
```

The first line has a very important keyword: `SOA`, which means "start of authority" (as in "This is where it all begins"). `IN` tells the system that this is an Internet record. (They pretty much always are in DNS files.) `localhost.` followed by `root.localhost.` represent (first) the fully qualified domain name (or FQDN) for this domain and (second) the place to e-mail the domain administrator (you). The period instead of an at sign (`@`) is not an error in this file, so leave it as is.

> **Important:** Notice as well the trailing period at the end of the domain name. This is important. A period indicates that this is the whole domain name and not relative to the domain in the zone record. The at sign (`@`) indicates the called domain. If you set up a zone for `mydomain.dom`, `@` might be replaced with `mydomain.dom`. Once again, note the trailing period. This is also true for IP addresses inside zone files.

The next thing to look at is the serial number, which you can see is a date. The last two zeroes in that example represent 100 possible changes to the file within that day. Why the changes? Every time you modify a name server record, you must increment that serial number for the zone to be reloaded. If you make changes (add a host) and you find that your updated information is not showing up in a query, you probably haven't updated the serial number. At that point, you need to restart the named daemon.

The second number (Refresh) tells secondary name servers how long they should wait before refreshing their information by contacting the primary name server. If contact fails or the primary is offline, the next number (Retry) becomes important. How long, in seconds, do you wait before trying to contact the primary again? If the primary server cannot be contacted after repeated trials, you might have to start thinking that it is gone for good and that any cached information relating to its domain is quite possibly useless. For that, you have an Expire number.

Your Own Zone File

To get information to and from that 192.168.22.0 domain I told you about, you need to create your own zone records. You will need two files: the primary zone file and a corresponding reverse lookup file. The primary zone file is called in the named.conf file as follows:

```
zone "mydomain.dom" {
        type master;
        file "named.hosts";
```

It looks quite similar to the zone definition for localhost, but instead of that reverse number address (0.0.127.in-addr.arpa), you list a domain name. This is what a simple file for this zone might look like:

```
@               IN      SOA     mydomain.dom. root.mydomain.dom. (
                        200103131       ; serial, todays date + todays serial #
                        28800           ; refresh, seconds
                        14400            ; retry, seconds
                        604800          ; expire, seconds
                        86400 )         ; minimum, seconds
                0       IN      NS      ns.mydomain.dom.

                0       IN      MX      10 mail.mydomain.dom.
                                        ; Primary Mail Exchanger

ns              0       IN      A       192.168.22.10
mail            0       IN      A       192.168.1.11
gateway         0       IN      A       192.168.22.99
www             0       IN      CNAME   gateway.mydomain.dom.
@               TXT     "My Company Name, maybe."

;       Other hosts
natika     0    IN    A       192.168.22.1
mgagne     0    IN    A       192.168.22.2
speedy     0    IN    A       192.168.22.3
```

Some interesting new records here include the MX record, which indicates where mail to this domain should be sent—in other words, where the machine that handles delivery of mail sent to that domain is. The 10 that you see is called the *weight*. A lower number implies a server whose weight is more important in the hierarchy of finding a valid mail exchange host. If one server is down, the second (or third) will be tried.

```
IN      MX      10 mail.mydomain.dom.  ; Primary Mail Exchanger
IN      MX      20 mail2.mydomain.dom. ; Secondary Mail Server
```

The NS record specifies the location of the DNS. You can have multiple NS records. In fact, if you are connected to the Internet through your ISP, you may use them as a secondary DNS and put the address here.

The A type records simply indicate maps from the host name to relevant IP address, while the CNAME (or canonical name) is just an alias for a previously defined A record.

> **Note:** Do not use an alias (CNAME) for your MX record.

Finally, you'll see the TXT record. This is pretty much what it looks like: a free-form text field where you can put company information (who this DNS belongs to) or contact information. You can also choose to have nothing there at all.

And Now the Reverse DNS Zone

The last file you are going to look at is your local reverse IP mapping. Internet hosts must be able to resolve your address not only by name, but also by doing a lookup on the IP number. The first thing you need to do is look at how this is configured in the named.conf file. Notice that the zone name is your network address (192.168.22.0) minus the trailing zero and mapped in reverse format. The in-addr.arpa is always suffixed in this way:

```
zone "22.168.192.in-addr.arpa" {
        type master;
        file "named.rev";
};
```

Now, here is the named.rev file:

```
@               0       IN      SOA     mydomain.dom.
ns.mydomain.dom. (
                                200101311       ; Serial
                                28800   ; Refresh
                                14400    ; Retry
```

```
                                    604800   ; Expire
                                    86400)   ; Minimum TTL
                    0        IN      NS       ns.mydomain.dom.

11                  0        IN      PTR      mail.mydomain.dom.
99                  0        IN      PTR      gateway.mydomain.dom.
1                   0        IN      PTR      natika.mydomain.dom.
2                   0        IN      PTR      mgagne.mydomain.dom.
3                   0        IN      PTR      speedy.mydomain.dom.
```

> **Geek Trivia:** This whole `in-addr.arpa` thing is meant to specify that the file and its addresses conform to the Arpanet addressing methodology. The truth is that *all* DNS files conform to the Arpanet addressing methodology. In the early days of the Internet, however, several methods of addressing were either being used or worked on. This method of naming the reverse lookup file is there for historical reasons (and perhaps a little nostalgia).

Other than the fact that you use this file for reverse address mapping, the records you find here are pretty much the same as in the previous file (`named.hosts`). The new records are `PTR` records. These serve more or less the same purpose as the `A` records in the previous file, but the information is reversed. First, you have the number (of which only the last octet is required), which is followed by the host name.

Does It Work?

Now that you have everything, it is time to shut down your `named` process (if it is running) and start or restart it. Next, use the `dig` command to see how well you did. In the previous files, you have a host on the network called "speedy" at 192.168.22.3. Let's try doing a lookup on the address to see if it finds speedy.

```
# dig -x 192.168.22.3
;; Got answer:
;; ->>HEADER<<- opcode: QUERY, status: NOERROR, id: 25921
;; flags: qr aa rd ra; QUERY: 1, ANSWER: 1, AUTHORITY: 1, ADDITIONAL: 1

;; QUESTION SECTION:
;3.22.168.192.in-addr.arpa.      IN      PTR

;; ANSWER SECTION:
3.22.168.192.in-addr.arpa. 0     IN      PTR      speedy.mydomain.dom.

;; AUTHORITY SECTION:
22.168.192.in-addr.arpa. 0       IN      NS       ns.mydomain.dom.
```

```
;; ADDITIONAL SECTION:

ns.mydomain.dom.         0       IN      A       192.168.22.10

;; Query time: 2 msec
;; SERVER: 127.0.0.1#53(127.0.0.1)
;; WHEN: Sun Apr  1 03:50:37 2001
;; MSG SIZE  rcvd: 112
```

What's All This about "Lame Servers"?

If you watch your logs closely, there is a distinct possibility that you will see messages about "lame servers" being reported. Simply stated, a *lame server* is one that has been designated as being authoritative for the domain but that doesn't agree. Unfortunately, if you are regularly communicating with such a server and it is not yours or under your control, these errors are of little use. In fact, they can be downright annoying precisely because you can't do anything about them. To get rid of these annoying little messages, edit your `/etc/named.conf` file and add these lines:

```
logging  {
category lame-servers{ null; };
};
```

Who Gets to See the Information?

When you run a name server, you are usually offering services for your network, but you may also be providing information about your mail exchange server or your Web site to the rest of the world. Obviously, the world needs to know how to get vital information to you. What they don't need to know is what is inside your network. Queries about your private network should not be for public consumption. Furthermore, restricting access reduces malicious use of your DNS.

You can disable queries for any zones you don't want public by adding the `allow-query` option to the global options paragraph at the top of your `/etc/named.conf` file.

```
// generated by named-bootconf.pl

options {
        directory "/etc/nsdata";
        /*
         * If there is a firewall between you and nameservers you want
         * to talk to, you might need to uncomment the query-source
         * directive below.  Previous versions of BIND always asked
         * questions using port 53, but BIND 8.1 uses an unprivileged
         * port by default.
```

```
         */
        // query-source address * port 53;
        allow-query { 192.168.22.0/24; localhost; };
};
```

From here on in, only the internal 192.168.22.0/24 network and the localhost address are allowed free reign of the DNS. To allow remote sites to query valid zones in the DNS, add an `allow-query` option that specifies "any" host access, as follows:

```
zone "mydomain.dom" {
        type master;
        file "mydomain.hosts";
        allow-query { any; };
};
```

If you try to do an `nslookup` on an address on your internal 192.168.22.0 network from a remote machine on the Internet, you'll get a message similar to this:

```
*** www.mydomain.dom can't find 192.168.22.3: Query refused
>
```

DNS Wrap-up

The previously presented information should be enough to get you going with a simple DNS setup. While it is fairly easy to set up your own domain name services, it can also be quite complex. If you need additional information, check the various man pages or the Resources section at this end of this chapter.

File Sharing Under Linux (Act 18, Scene 4)

When it comes to file sharing, you've got a number of options. For instance, you can choose from NFS, Samba, CODA, AFS, and others. When all that fails, there's always sneakernet. That last one doesn't require an awful lot of explanation—if you've got sneakers (and even if you don't), you're connected. Throw that file onto a diskette or tape and *walk* it over to the remote system.

Understanding what the various systems do and how they do it is the first step in deciding what makes sense for your environment. You might have noticed Samba in that previous list. I'm going to leave this one until Chapter 22. In this chapter, I'll concentrate on Network File System (NFS).

Network File System

From a historical perspective, NFS is the granddaddy (or grandmamma—I can't be sure) of network file-sharing technologies. It was developed by Sun Microsystems and has been around since the '80s. Its great strength is that it is on just about every Linux and UNIX distribution.

Network shared directories are used for more than just extra space (although that is a good reason to use them). They also provide the means to have large programs or applications inhabit one linked system, thus saving the hassle of installing the same thing over and over again on every workstation. Shared directories are routinely used for e-mail. Rather than having each user's mail distributed to each and every workstation, the mail lives in a central location, a one-stop place for backups. Speaking of backups, why not have each user's home directory remotely mounted so that his or her personal information is backed up when the server is backed up? This saves you the aggravation of worrying about each person's "important" data going missing.

Like just about everything in the world of Linux, NFS is still evolving and different incarnations exist on different releases. Nevertheless, NFS has been around a long time, and while it has problems (which I will discuss later), it is a good, stable file-sharing mechanism that is worth looking at. On most Linux machines out there, the Linux implementation of NFS is sitting around version 2. NFS version 3, which includes improved performance, better file locking, and other goodies, is still in development and requires that your kernel level be at 2.2.18 or higher, although there are patches for other kernel levels. This discussion will concentrate on version 2. For those of you who want to explore the latest and greatest in the world of Linux NFS, you can visit the NFS project at SourceForge (`http://nfs.sourceforge.net/`).

How Does NFS Work?

NFS is a client/server system that enables a local directory (on the server) to be made available to other client computers. These can be other Linux machines, UNIX workstations, or any other machine that can mount NFS directories. To do this, the server runs a number of processes that handle things such as permissions, authentication, maintenance of established connections, and so on. NFS uses remote procedure calls (RPC) as its mechanism for communicating information.

Starting the NFS server is usually done at boot time if you have those services set to come up at boot time. On a Debian server, most of these daemons are brought up by the `nfs-server` script.

```
/etc/init.d/nfs-server start
```

On a Red Hat or Mandrake system, you may find that you need to start both the `nfs` and the `nfslock` scripts.

```
/etc/rc.d/init.d/nfs start
/etc/rc.d/init.d/nfslock start
```

There is actually one other program that needs to be up and running. When a directory is "exported" by the server, another program, the portmapper, tells the client what directories are available on the server.

Using the `rpcinfo` program, you can determine what RPC services are running on a server machine. The format of the command is simple. In the next example, I query a system called "testsys." Here's what I get:

```
# rpcinfo -p testsys
   program vers proto   port
    100000    2   tcp    111  portmapper
    100000    2   udp    111  portmapper
    100011    1   udp    764  rquotad
    100011    2   udp    764  rquotad
    100005    1   udp    772  mountd
    100005    1   tcp    774  mountd
    100005    2   udp    777  mountd
    100005    2   tcp    779  mountd
    100003    2   udp   2049  nfs
```

The `-p` flag tells the `rpcinfo` program to ask the portmapper on a remote system to report on what services it offers. This means, of course, that I need to be running the `portmap` daemon. If I shut down the `portmap` daemon, the results are less than stellar. Before I show you the results, let's shut down the portmapper. On a Red Hat or Mandrake system, you use this command:

```
/etc/rc.d/init.d/portmap stop
```

On a Debian or Storm Linux system, try this instead:

```
/etc/init.d/portmap stop
```

Now, here's the result of an `rpcinfo` probe of the same system (testsys):

```
rpcinfo: can't contact portmapper: RPC: Remote system error -
Connection refused
```

Now that you know how to check on what is available and whether or not NFS services are running, let's examine each of the daemons and see what they do.

- rpc.statd: This daemon is started by the nfslock script along with rpc.lockd. Together they handle file locking and lock recovery (in the event of an NFS server crash) upon reboot. Depending on the system, you may not see rpc.lockd in your process status. Instead, you might simply see lockd.
- rpc.quotad: On a machine where quota support has been set up, rpc.quotad will handle this, making sure that any limits that were set up are imposed on the exported directory.
- rpc.nfsd: What you have here is the real workhorse of the whole NFS group of programs. This is the program that actually handles all the NFS user requests.
- rpc.mountd: When the client initiates a request to mount an exported directory, this is the program that looks to see whether the request meets with the permissions defined in the /etc/exports file.

Making a Remote File System Available

In order for a server to make a directory (or file system) available to one or more clients, you must add an entry to the /etc/exports file. Entries in this file (which you can manually edit with your favorite editor) have this format:

```
/name_of_dir      client_name(permissions)
```

The name part is pretty simple. That's the full path to the directory you want to share on your network. The client name is the host name of the client machine. This can just as easily be an IP address. Furthermore, you can use a wildcard to make every host within a domain available. For instance, say your domain is myowndomain.dom and you want all machines in that domain to be able to access /mnt/data on the machine acting as your NFS server. You create an entry that looks like this:

```
/mnt/data1        *.myowndomain.dom(permissions)
```

You can also use an asterisk to make every single host on every network privy to your NFS services, but this would be a very bad idea. Still, sharing that drive is pretty simple so far. Which leads us to the permissions aspect of things.

Permissions are a bit more complex and should be discussed in some detail. Options for the permissions (or security) section are secure, ro, rw, sync, no_wdelay, nohide, and no_subtree_check. Other groups of permissions exist that are related to the way individual users get treated. I like to think of these as the "squashing permissions." They are root_squash, no_root_squash, all_squash, anonuid, and anongid.

- `secure`: This option specifies that an NFS mount request must be from an Internet port number below 1024. This option is on by default. If you don't want this behavior, then specify `insecure`.
- `ro/rw`: The `ro` permission option allows for read-only access. This is the default. It allows the client to see the files, but doesn't let the client change anything. To allow read and write access, specify `rw` instead.
- `sync`: This option is what you might call a mixed blessing. What it does is make sure that a commit of data follows every write operation. This is great in the event of a server crash, but the cost is a slight performance hit. The default is `async`, which means that the system just writes and doesn't worry about whether the operation completed before it moves on.
- `no_wdelay`: This is a cousin to the `sync` option. If you decide that your data is relatively safe (but you still want the commit option), you can elect to set this option, which lets the system do multiple commits simultaneously. The default, `wdelay`, delays the next write until the first is committed.
- `no_hide`: Say you have two directories exported in the same tree. If one of those directories is below the first, you would normally mount both on the client. If you only mounted the parent directory, you would see the second directory but it would have no data beneath it. It is hidden. If you want to have the entire subtree visible as well, use this option. *Use it with care,* however, because clients have been known to have problems with this, specifically as it relates to assigning duplicate inodes. The default option is `hide`.
- `no_subtree_check`: If the directory you are exporting is actually a subdirectory of a file system, the directories above it may have something to say about permissions. Because you only have access to the files and directories that are exported, you must check to ensure security throughout the chain. The default is to allow "`subtree_check`," which may have minor security implications. If this is a concern, remember to specify `no_subtree_check`.

I call the next few permissions "squashing permissions" because there seems to be so much talk about squashing in the list. Generally, they have to do with how the server deals with the problem of user IDs (UIDs) and group IDs (GIDs) while assigning permissions.

The thing to remember here is that NFS in a default installation deals with permissions by assuming that UIDs and GIDs are the same on both the server and the client. This isn't such a big deal if you are the one setting up all the machines and you define the rules and you can make sure that all machines have identical `/etc/passwd` files, but unfortunately this isn't always the case. The real problem starts when the user "natika" on the server has UID 505, but "natika" on the client has UID 501.

One way to deal with this is to run NIS. (I'll explain how to set up an NIS server later in this chapter.) Another way is to use some of the following "squashing permissions" options to change the default behavior of NFS when a mount request is honored.

- `no_root_squash`: When a user tries to gain access to a remote NFS directory, the UID and GID are treated as though they are the same on the client and server. This is not true of the root UID by default. NFS maps root's UID (0) to the anonymous user, or "nobody," for security reasons. If you are the administrator of NFS domain and you are root on all machines, this might not be a problem and you may want root to have equal rights to the exported directories. To make sure this happens, use `no_root_squash`. You can also specify the default, `root_squash`, if you like to see all these things spelled out.
- `all_squash`: As you might expect, this option means that all UIDs should be treated like root, mapping them to the anonymous user. `no_all_squash` is the default.
- `anonuid/anongid`: This option enables you to specify the UID and GID of the anonymous user to which a `root_squash` or an `all_squash` will map permissions.

Have a look at the following example:

```
# /etc/exports file
# These are just comments
#
/mnt/data1          natika(rw,no_root_squash)
/usr/local          speedy(rw)
/mnt/acctng         *.mycompany.dom(rw)
```

Obviously, the first three lines (starting with the # symbol) are just comments. The `/mnt/data1` line makes that directory available to the client called "natika." It also allows root to be treated as root on this directory. The second line gives the client called "speedy" read-write access, but it maps root's UID to the anonymous user. Finally, the third line enables any computer in the `mycompany.dom` domain to mount the `/mnt/acctng` directory with read-write access.

Once you have all your directories ready to export, you can restart NFS or reboot to reread the `/etc/exports` file, but this is Linux. You don't reboot or restart if you don't need to. This is why you use the command `exportfs`. The following are some examples showing the more common formats for the command. In all cases, you can add the `-v` flag to up the command's level of verbosity.

```
exportfs -a
```

The preceding command exports all the entries in `/etc/exports`. *Be careful with this one* because it is a Boolean command. If you execute it again, it unexports all the entries in `/etc/exports`.

```
exportfs -r
```

The preceding command is probably the safest option and usually what you want to do. It reexports all the entries in /etc/exports. If it finds that something has been deleted from the /etc/exports file, it unexports it. Now, using a command called showmount, I can look to see what my server has exported.

```
[root@testsys /root]# showmount -exports

Export list for testsys.mycompany.dom:
/mnt/data1 192.168.22.10
```

As you can see, I have one directory exported for use by a client at 192.168.22.10. You can also export directories on the fly by using a -o option to the exportfs command. This enables you to manually export a directory without updating the /etc/exports file without re-editing it. For instance, if I want to export a directory called /etc for use by a client called "speedy," I can use this version of exportfs:

```
[root@scigate /root]# exportfs -o rw,no_root_squash speedy:/etc
[root@scigate /root]# showmount --exports
Export list for testsys.mycompany.dom:
/etc        speedy.mycompany.dom
/mnt/data1 192.168.22.10
```

Mounting an NFS Partition

When you mount a directory through NFS, you can use a fairly simple version of the mount command similar to what you would use for a local file system (as in Chapter 6). Using the previous /mnt/data1 example, you might do this:

```
mount -t nfs testsys:/mnt/data1 /mnt/local_data1
```

For starters, the -t flag (which specifies the type of file system) is sort of optional in that the mount command is usually able to deal with many different mount types without being explicitly told what it is mounting. Next, /mnt/local_data1 is a previously created directory on my client system. The name is entirely up to you. As you can see, the format is not at all complicated for most common requirements. There are, however, other options on the mount command that you may want to consider. The most compelling reason for other than default options is the issue of hard versus soft mounting.

By default, NFS mounts are *hard* mounts. What that means is that if the server goes down, your client just keeps right on trying to contact the server. If the server was to go down, you would know this is happening when you issued a df command on the client with an NFS mounted directory. The command lists your other file systems, but it just hangs as it waits for the server to respond. You can solve this with a *soft* mount, which lets the kernel stop waiting after a while. For instance, let's use the previous command, but as a soft mount:

```
mount -f nfs -o soft,timeo=120 testsys:/mnt/data1 /mnt/local_data1
```

Yes, it's true. I added something extra there, the `timeo=` option. For starters, you can see that mount options are added to the command line with the `-o` flag. The reason for the `timeo` option is to specify the number of seconds I want the system to wait before it times out on the mount. You can also specify a `retrans=n` where `n` is the number of retries you want the mount to attempt before giving up.

Now that I've told you all about soft mounts, I'm going to let you know that *for the most part, you don't want to do this.* When people are in the middle of editing a file or updating information, you don't want the client system to just drop them without them having had a chance to finish their writes. The connection may come back 122 seconds later. Who knows?

That said, let me tell you about two other mount options. You can also issue the `mount` command with a `bg` option, which puts the `mount` command in the background. That way, if the system you need mounted is unavailable, `mount` will keep trying without hanging at the command line. The last option is `intr`, which enables you to interrupt the `mount` command (should it be taking too long). Because the process of mounting a file system is a kernel function, you don't normally have the option of interrupting it, but on systems where the server's presence may be unreliable on the network, the hard and soft mount options I've talked about may be worthy of consideration.

> **Performance Tip:** Other NFS mount flags you'll want to know about are `rsize` and `wsize`. Try adding these to your `mount` command, as they can definitely improve read and write performance. The default `rsize` and `wsize` is 1024. You might want to use `rsize=8192` and `wsize=8192` instead.

Specifying Mounts with /etc/fstab

When your system boots, several file systems are automatically mounted. The most obvious is the root directory (`/`), but there are others. These others may be `/boot`, `/usr/local`, or `/home`, depending on your system configuration. Furthermore, you may, like me, have a separate data drive that always needs to be available. Mounting it each and every single time isn't practical.

Think back, way back, to the chapter on file systems (Chapter 6). The following listing from a `/etc/fstab` file is essentially the same as the one you saw in that chapter. The very last line is one I added after the fact. In this case, it mounts a remote file system on an NFS host called "testsys."

```
/dev/hda1         /              ext2              defaults          1 1
/dev/cdrom        /mnt/cdrom     iso9660           noauto,owner,ro   0 0
/dev/fd0          /mnt/floppy    auto              noauto,owner      0 0
none              /proc          proc              defaults          0 0
none              /dev/pts                  devpts gid=5,mode=620    0 0
/dev/hda5         swap                      swap          defaults   0 0
/dev/hdb1         /mnt/data1                ext2          defaults   0 0
testsys:/home     /mnt/tshome    nfs               rw,bg        0 0
```

If you look back to the last section, you'll notice that the mount happens in the background (bg) and that the default permissions are read and write (rw). The local directory is called /mnt/tshome.

By the way, the fstab isn't just for booting. It can simplify mounting and unmounting because all the defaults and requirements that you have for a specific mount are already there. Rather than typing the name of the device, the file system type, the various options, and the mount point, once you have an entry in fstab you can just type mount/whatever. (The "whatever" is, of course, replaced with whatever.)

Simplifying Network Mounts with Linux autofs

If you start using NFS in a big way, you may find that this whole business of mounting and unmounting file systems gets to be a bit tedious. You could just put the various mounts in your /etc/fstab (as described previously) and have them come up automatically, but that has its problems as well. What if that system is not always available? It may also be that you only need this file system from time to time. If that is the case, you don't want to have it permanently mounted. Then, when somebody does need it, do you really want him or her to disturb you?

The Linux autofs can make your life a lot easier. The idea is that you define file systems for mounting in a *map* file. This map describes the file system types, where they are, and what permissions may be required to mount them. The beauty is that you don't have to manually mount these file systems or even have them mounted. As soon as a user requests something in the map path, that file system is automatically mounted.

To use this tool, you need to have the autofs package loaded on your system. It is probably already on your distribution CD. Alternatively, you can go to the ftp.kernel.org Web site and look in the /pub/linux/daemons/autofs directory for the latest and greatest.

Setup is easy. Start by setting up your /etc/auto.master file. The format is as follows. You define a top-level directory where your automatic mounts occur. This points back to another file (your map), which takes care of individually defining these mounts and their file system types. Here's my `auto.master` file:

```
/automnt        /etc/auto.automnt
```

You can have many such definitions. For instance, you might have mount points defined under `/misc`, `/home`, or the perennial `/mnt`. The convention is to use a `/etc/auto.map` file where `map` is the same name as the mount point. You can use pretty much any name you like, however, and it will still work. Now, let's have a look at the map I have defined:

```
# automount locations

# This is an automounter map and it has the following format
# key [ -mount-options-separated-by-comma ] location

# nfs servers
testsysdata       -fstype=nfs,rsize=8192,wsize=8192              testsys:/data1
testsysroot       -fstype=nfs,rsize=8192,wsize=8192              testsys:/

# samba servers
testsysdos        -fstype=smb,username=mgagne,password=secret    ://testsys/dosdir
winsoft           -fstype=smb                                    ://nexus/win95

# Windows PCs
natika_c          -fstype=smb,username=natika,password=secret
://speedy/natika_c
```

Notice that I have listed Samba file systems and a Windows PC as well. The Linux `autofs` can handle many different systems—it's not just for NFS. Before you can start using things, you need to start (or restart) the `autofs` process. On my test system running Red Hat, I start it from a script like this:

```
/etc/rc.d/init.d/autofs start
```

On a Debian system, the script will likely be in `/etc/init.d` instead but it will use the same keyword to start the automounter.

> **Geek Trivia:** The program that actually does the work is called `automount`, so if you look for the program in a `ps ax`, you'll see that program name instead of `autofs`.

To access information on any of these systems, I only need to change directory or reference a file there. The `autofs` system will do the rest for me.

Network Information Service (Act 18, Scene 5)

Like NFS, NIS is a child of Sun Microsystems, and also like NFS, it goes back to the '80s. At that time, it was called Yellow Pages, but because "Yellow Pages" happens to be a registered trademark, the name was changed to avoid legal troubles. Nevertheless, an echo of those Yellow Pages days is still with you when you deal with NIS. As you will soon discover in this section, the letters "yp" show up in configuration files and commands alike.

When I talked about NFS, I mentioned that NFS assumes that user and group information on the server are equivalent to user and group information on the client. The problem with this scenario is that is it requires an administrator to create and maintain identical `/etc/passwd` and `/etc/group` files on each and every computer. That's not always practical, or for that matter, desirable. One way to get around this problem is NIS.

NIS (and more recently, NIS+) does far more than allow these files to be consistent across a network. Other files can be maintained as well. You can use the `ypcat -x` command to get a list of the databases already known or managed by your system. You need to have the portmapper running, so make sure it is running and then try it on your system.

```
[root@scigate /root]# ypcat -x
Use "ethers"    for map "ethers.byname"
Use "aliases"   for map "mail.aliases"
Use "services"  for map "services.byname"
Use "protocols" for map "protocols.bynumber"
Use "hosts"     for map "hosts.byname"
Use "networks"  for map "networks.byaddr"
Use "group"     for map "group.byname"
Use "passwd"    for map "passwd.byname"
```

Now you have an idea of just what kind of information you can use NIS to distribute. Of particular interest to the topic of permissions on NFS are the group and password databases. Remember that NFS expects that a user on one machine has the same UID on another. Short of always updating each and every server to reflect user and group name changes, NIS is the answer.

The first thing you need to get NIS rolling is an NIS domain name that bears no resemblance whatsoever to your Internet domain name (although it could be the same if you so choose). Let's create an NIS domain name called `mydomain.nis`. On my Red Hat system, this is done by setting the `NIS_DOMAIN` variable in `/etc/sysconfig/network`.

```
NIS_DOMAIN=mydomain.nis
```

On a Debian system, the `domainname` is pulled from `/etc/defaultdomain`. In that case, add a single line with the domain name and nothing else.

There's more to do, but before you can get there, you need to start the `ypserver` process (it is actually called `ypbind`). If you are running Red Hat, try the first of the following commands. Debian users should try the second version of the command.

```
/etc/rc.d/init.d/ypserv start
/etc/init.d/nis start
```

Configuring the NIS Master Server

With NIS, you can set up backup servers as well—hence the master specification in that title. For now, you'll concentrate on the primary master. You've defined the domain name, so now you'll move on to defining what databases will be shared. You do this by modifying a file called `/var/yp/Makefile` (it's starting to look an awful lot like you are compiling a program, isn't it?). Open the file into your favorite editor and you'll see something like this:

```
GROUP       = $(YPPWDDIR)/group
PASSWD      = $(YPPWDDIR)/passwd
SHADOW      = $(YPPWDDIR)/shadow
GSHADOW     = $(YPPWDDIR)/gshadow
ADJUNCT     = $(YPPWDDIR)/passwd.adjunct
#ALIASES    = $(YPSRCDIR)/aliases  # aliases could be in /etc or /etc/mail
ALIASES     = /etc/aliases
ETHERS      = $(YPSRCDIR)/ethers     # ethernet addresses (for rarpd)
BOOTPARAMS  = $(YPSRCDIR)/bootparams # for booting Sun boxes (bootparamd)
HOSTS       = $(YPSRCDIR)/hosts
NETWORKS    = $(YPSRCDIR)/networks
PRINTCAP    = $(YPSRCDIR)/printcap
PROTOCOLS   = $(YPSRCDIR)/protocols
PUBLICKEYS  = $(YPSRCDIR)/publickey
```

The list is fairly long and it is possible to add others. Comment out what you don't need or want. What actually gets built is decided a little later in the file. Notice the `YPPWDDIR` variable. It is set earlier in the file and by default is `/etc`, where most of these files live. Pay attention because this isn't always true. For instance, later incarnations of `sendmail` put the aliases file in `/etc/mail` instead of `/etc`. Once you have the databases you want defined, look for this:

```
NOPUSH=true
```

Because you are setting up a single master NIS server in this example, set this to true. If you had secondary or "slave" servers, you would set this to false. Notice as well these two settings:

```
MINUID=500
MINGID=500
```

This is the *default* UID and GID information being served. As you might guess, there are security reasons for this. You don't want to advertise administrative IDs across your network. If you want to change this, do it here. If you are setting this up on a Debian system, you may find that these are already set to 100 instead of the Red Hat default of 500.

All right. Two more very important settings before you get ready to wrap up your server configuration. Look for these two in the file:

```
MERGE_PASSWD=true
MERGE_GROUP=true
```

In all likelihood, you are using a shadow password file (see Chapter 7), and if you are not, go back and implement shadow passwords now. NIS will merge the information from your `/etc/shadow` file into its shared copy of `/etc/passwd`. This is normally set to true, but you can override it. The `MERGE_GROUP` setting defaults to false on some systems (my Debian test system is one), so you might wind up changing the setting of this one. Look for a `/etc/gshadow` file. If your system is using it, set this one to true as well.

Now you are almost ready to build the new databases. The last thing you do is confirm what you want (or don't want) built. This is where you *really* decide what gets out the NIS door. Look for this text in the `Makefile`:

```
# If you don't want some of these maps built, feel free to comment
# them out from this list.

all:  passwd group hosts rpc services netid protocols netgrp mail \
        # shadow publickey # networks ethers bootparams printcap \
        # amd.home auto.master auto.home passwd.adjunct
```

Once again, the settings as they exist are probably what you want, but you can set things like automount files (`auto.master` and so on) that you'll remember from the previous sections.

Ready? No, you don't type `make`.

The command that initializes all these databases is called `ypinit`.

```
[root@testsys /root]# /usr/lib/yp/ypinit -m
The local host's domain name hasn't been set.  Please set it.
```

If you get this message, it is because the domain name is in your boot time scripts. Next time the system comes up, you won't have to worry about this because it will already be set. Because you don't want to reboot right now, manually set the domain name with this command:

```
domainname mydomain.nis
```

Run the `ypinit` command again.

```
[root@scigate /root]# /usr/lib/yp/ypinit -m
At this point, we have to construct a list of the hosts which will
run NIS
```

```
servers.  testsys.mydomain.nis is in the list of NIS server hosts.
Please continue to add the names for the other hosts, one per line.
When you are done with the list, type a <control D>.

        next host to add:  testsys.domain.nis
        next host to add:
```

Unless you want to set up secondary servers at this point, just press Ctrl-D and you are done. If you want to add servers, it's easy to do so after the fact. These get added into a file called `/var/yp/ypservers`. If you change to this directory, you'll see that this is a simple text file. When you are finished here, the `ypinit` process will do a `make` for you and create the databases. You should see output like the following:

```
The current list of NIS servers looks like this:

testsys.mydomain.nis

Is this correct?  [y/n: y]
We need some  minutes to build the databases...
Building /var/yp/mydomain.nis/ypservers...
Running /var/yp/Makefile...
gmake[1]: Entering directory '/var/yp/mydomain.nis'
Updating passwd.byname...
Updating passwd.byuid...
Updating group.byname...
Updating group.bygid...
Updating hosts.byname...
Updating hosts.byaddr...
Updating rpc.byname...
Updating rpc.bynumber...
Updating services.byname...
Updating netid.byname...
Updating protocols.bynumber...
Updating protocols.byname...
Updating mail.aliases...
gmake[1]: Leaving directory '/var/yp/mydomain.nis'
```

It is possible that when you run this the first time, it won't work quite so cleanly. The most likely scenario for a failure here is that you have told the `Makefile` to create databases that don't exist on your system. Pay attention to the messages and edit the `Makefile` accordingly. Then simply rerun `ypinit`. At this point, you can also just type `make` (if you really, really want to).

Configuring the NIS Client

Although it is wonderful that you've done such a great job of setting up the NIS server, it isn't much good without clients. Well, clients are fairly simple, so feel free to set up lots of them.

Start by opening the file /etc/yp.conf in your favorite editor. There are three possible ways of setting up the client to look for NIS servers.

```
domain NISDOMAIN server HOSTNAME
#       Use server HOSTNAME for the domain NISDOMAIN.
```

If you choose this method, specify the NISDOMAIN and the HOSTNAME to which you would like the client to connect. You can have more than one entry of this type. Using my example of domain.nis, my yp.conf entry would look like this:

```
domain domain.nis server testsys.mydomain.dom
```

You can also set up your client to listen for NIS servers through a broadcast. The only catch here is that the servers must be on the same subnet. You cannot listen for NIS servers outside your network.

```
domain NISDOMAIN broadcast
#       Use  broadcast  on  the local net for domain NISDOMAIN
```

Once again, you replace NISDOMAIN with the NIS domain name. The advantage of this method is that you only need configure one entry and you are done. The final option is perhaps the easiest of the bunch in terms of flexibility.

```
ypserver HOSTNAME
#       Use server HOSTNAME for the  local  domain.
```

Type the host name of the NIS server and that is all. Make sure, however, that the HOSTNAME is listed in /etc/hosts. For my test, I used the final example with this entry:

```
ypserver testsys
```

The /etc/nsswitch.conf File

There is one last file to edit before you are finished. This one is called /etc/nsswitch.conf and while there is more here than in yp.conf, the format is equally simple. Basically, it is a list of file names and service options associated with it. Here's a sample from my file:

```
passwd:     files nisplus nis
shadow:     files nisplus nis
group:      files nisplus nis

#hosts:     db files nisplus nis dns
hosts:      files nisplus nis dns
```

The service options are files, nis (or yp—both are the same), nisplus, dns, and [NOTFOUND=return], as shown in Table 18.4.

TABLE 18.4: Service Options

Option	Option Meaning
`files`	Use the local files to look up information.
`nis` (or `yp`)	Use NIS for this information.
`nisplus`	Use NIS+.
`dns`	Use DNS to find the information (only applies to hosts).
`[NOTFOUND=return]`	If you haven't found the information, stop searching.

Of course, each file has several options listed that can only mean that the order is somehow important. This is the search order for information retrieval. You almost always want to search your local host first, so `files` is usually the first option. It is only when you don't find the information locally that you want to look elsewhere, but even that can be changed.

Let's test things, shall we? As with the server, you need to have the NIS domain name set. You still want the information hard-coded in the appropriate configuration files, but a quick way to set it (if you haven't already) is with the `domainname` command.

```
domainname domain.nis
```

Great! Now, you need to start `yppasswdd` (to allow for password changes on the NIS server) and the NIS listener, `ypbind`. With Debian, this is the `/etc/init.d/nis` start script. With Red Hat, you'll need to start `/etc/rc.d/init.d/yppasswdd` and `/etc/rc.d/init.d/ypbind` as well.

To see the contents of the NIS server's password file, try this command:

```
ypcat passwd
```

To get the host information, use this:

```
ypcat hosts
```

Notice that you are simply specifying the name of the file served by NIS services.

Miscellaneous Network Tricks: Time Synchronization

In the world of PC hardware, the whole notion of trying to keep time can be quite a frustrating experience. Cheap PC clocks have been known to drift wildly, leaving you asking that age-old question: "What time is it really?"

rdate

If you take a look at your /etc/inetd.conf file, you'll notice an entry like this one:

```
time    stream  tcp     nowait  root    internal
time    dgram   udp     wait    root    internal
```

Using the rdate command is one way of synchronizing with a trusted machine. For this to work, however, you must check that the services are active on the server machine by making sure that their entries in the /etc/inetd.conf file are not commented out. Then, a client can synchronize with this trusted time server by using the following command:

```
rdate -s server_name
```

The -s flag means "set." If you are logged in as root, you can use this to reset your own computer's clock with another on your network. If you are just curious, use the -p flag ("print"). This only reports the date and time, making no changes to your system.

While this is often referred to as a "brute force" approach to synchronizing the time and date, it does work. If your operation doesn't require a huge amount of accuracy (down to the split second) and you just want to make sure that your systems more or less agree with each other, putting this command in a nightly cron job is probably sufficient.

If you'd like more information, read on.

NTP

What if you have a network of inexpensive PCs that all have wandering clocks? What if you don't have a host on this network that you can trust?

This is where NTP comes in to play. Originally maintained by professor David L. Mills with the assistance of numerous volunteers over the years, the idea of NTP is to make it possible to synchronize the time of one Internet-connected computer with another.

You will probably find that NTP is on your Linux system distribution CD. The odds are, however, that it did not get installed by default, so you may have to do that. A word of caution: When you look for it, you may find it as `xntpd` rather than `ntpd`.

NTP is configured using the `/etc/ntp.conf` file.

There are also a handful of programs you should be aware of. The first is the NTP program itself, called `xntpd`, a daemon that runs on both the server and client sides, enabling the synchronization to take place.

When you first set things up, you may want (or be tempted) to quickly synchronize with a time server out there on the network. A common method of doing this is through the use of the `ntpdate` command. Say that my `/etc/ntp.conf` file is all set up and things are ready to roll. Now I want to quickly set up my machine to some reasonably accurate standard. I type the date command and get something like this: Thu Dec 7 15:41:14 EST 2000. This is, as it turns out, at least an hour off. I then run `ntpdate` as follows:

```
ntpdate server_ip_address
```

When I run the date command again, it returns Thu Dec 7 14:46:40 EST 2000, so I guess my clock was off. Ideally, I don't want to do this again because the `ntpdate` command is considered a brute force approach to setting system time, as mentioned previously. It's time to start `xntpd`.

```
xntpd
```

The NTP client/server will now start to run in the background and update itself according to the defaults set up earlier.

Wait! What about the GUIs?

"You said there would be GUIs."

Yes, I did promise that I would show you graphical ways of doing things whenever possible. This chapter is not an exception, although server and network configurations are largely done in the somewhat less glamorous world of text editors. For ongoing administration; maintaining NIS, DNS, interfaces, printers, and other assorted network functions; and just about anything else you can think of, join me in the next chapter for some real heavy hitters in the world of graphical administration.

Resources

Common IP Port Numbers (IANA Web site)

http://www.iana.org/assignments/port-numbers

DNS HOWTO

http://www.linuxdoc.org/HOWTO/DNS-HOWTO.html

ISC (BIND and DNS)

http://www.isc.org/

Linux Router Project

http://www.linuxrouter.org/

RFC Editor

http://www.rfc-editor.org/

Time Server Web site

http://www.eecis.udel.edu/~ntp/

Chapter 19

Tools, Tools, and More Tools

If you are timid about administering a Linux system or, worse yet, turning portions of the administrative duties over to your more timid coworkers, this chapter is designed to put your fears (and theirs) to rest. The chapter examines a collection of tools designed to make the job of administration easier across multiple systems and, in some cases, even different architectures. The chapter also covers tools, graphical and not, that no administrator should ever be without.

> **Security Warning:** Just as in Chapter 18, I want to remind you that because I am talking about tools that work across networks, all the weaknesses (and strengths) of TCP/IP networking are also in effect here. For in-depth coverage of security and encryption, refer to Chapters 24 and 25.

The Web Browser Angle

The Web browser is ubiquitous. Pretty much anybody who works with a computer on a regular basis knows the power of the Web browser. Whatever your choice of browser (and by the way, Linux only increases that choice), the modern user knows how to work with one, how to connect to his or her favorite Web sites, pick up news and information, bank online, and fill in forms. What could be better than doing your administration through a friendly browser interface, an interface that no one has to learn?

Linuxconf

The first administration tool I would like to look at crosses three distinct interfaces. You can use it from a text-only terminal, an X window session, or that comfy browser of yours. If you use a Red Hat system, or if you are running GNOME as your desktop, you probably already have the `linuxconf` program loaded. If not, you can get it from the source by visiting Jacques Gelinas' Web site (`http://www.solucorp.qc.ca/linuxconf/`), the official home of `linuxconf`.

The program is available in a source tarball as well as prebuilt distributions for Caldera, Red Hat, Slackware, and SuSE.

As I mentioned, `linuxconf` is particularly interesting in that it is designed to work in a number of different environments. Nevertheless, the interface is similar whether you are using the text-based interface, the X interface (on my Red Hat system, it is based on GNOME), or the Web interface. Another thing that distinguishes this program is that it views itself in two different ways. One is as a configuration utility and the second is as a control system where you can do things like shut down and reboot the system, create `cron` entries, or install software. For a peek at `linuxconf` in action, check out Figure 19.1 (text-based) and Figure 19.2 (X/Tcl-based).

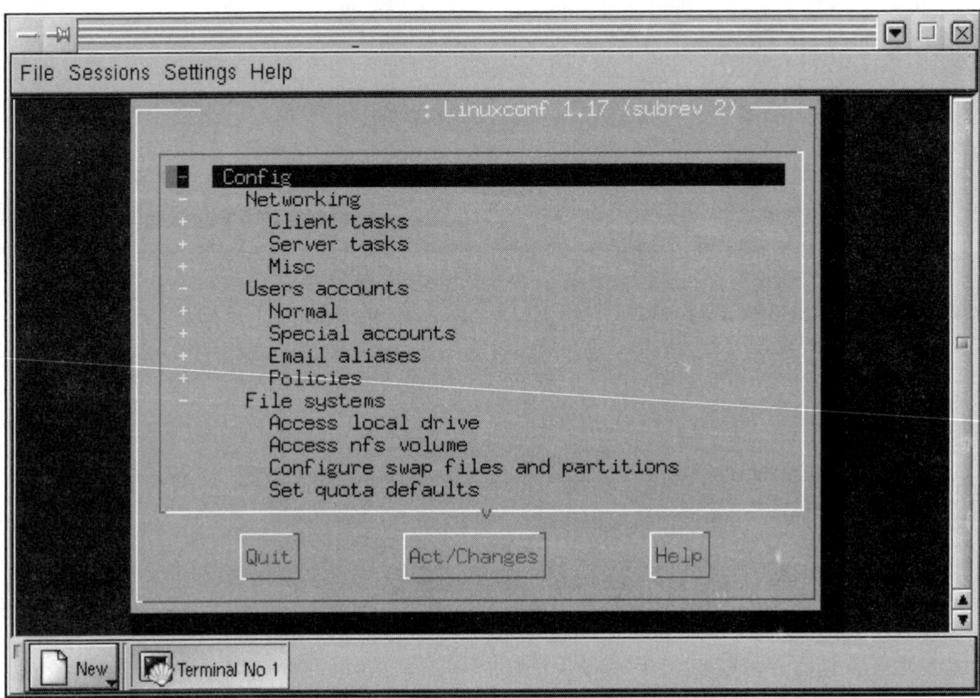

FIGURE 19.1 The text-based `linuxconf` screen

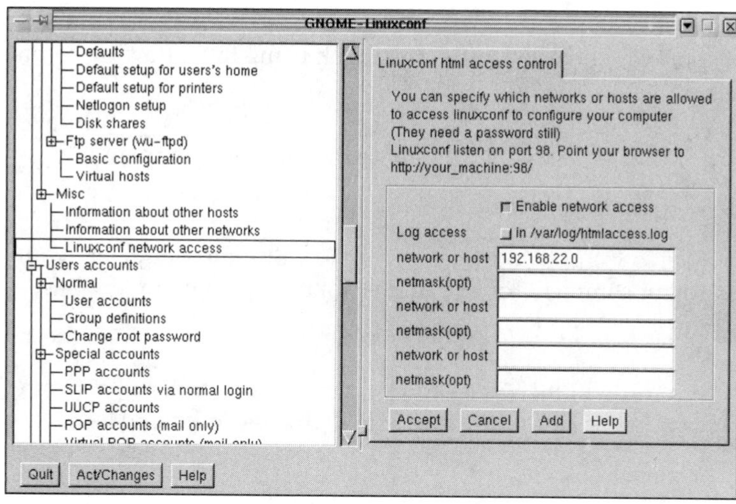

FIGURE 19.2 `linuxconf`'s Tcl/Tk X window face

Because I am touting browser-based administration, I'll concentrate on that. In order to activate the Web interface, you will need to do a few things first. The tool you'll use is the text (or X) version of `linuxconf`, thus giving you a perfect excuse to tour these alternative interfaces. Start `linuxconf` from the command line, as follows:

```
# linuxconf &
```

You will notice `linuxconf` starts with a simple menu that is essentially a hierarchical view of its functions. The layout is much the same as you would find in graphical file managers. There are two major sections: Config and Control. Each section can be expanded or collapsed by clicking the plus (+) or minus (-) sign in front of each section (or subsection). If you are using the simple text version, navigating from one section to another is simply a matter of tabbing from one area to another and moving up and down with your cursor keys.

To activate the Web interface, click Networking followed by Network and then Misc. Under the Misc branch (or menu), choose the option linuxconf network access. This is your HTML access control. Now click the radio button labeled Enable network access. If you want to log access through the Web interface, click the Log Access radio button. The default output for the log file is `/var/log/htmlaccess.log`.

The last step you really need to perform is add either a host or a domain entry. On my system, I added my whole internal network, 192.168.22.0. Finally, click Accept and then click Quit. `linuxconf` will then inform you that changes have been made to various configurations. You can accept and activate these changes or just plain quit. Activate the changes and `linuxconf` will terminate.

To use `linuxconf` through a Web browser, you should know it runs on port 98. Check this out for yourself using the following command:

```
# grep linuxconf /etc/services
```

You should get this reply to the previous command:

```
linuxconf   98/tcp
```

Now check your `/etc/inetd.conf` file, and using your favorite text editor, uncomment (or add, if it is not there) the following line:

```
linuxconf stream tcp wait root /bin/linuxconf linuxconf --http
```

You will then need to restart `inetd` in order to activate this change. You can do this by finding the `inetd` process and doing a `kill -SIGHUP`.

```
# ps ax | grep inetd
  395 ?        S   0:00 inetd
 7332 pts/0    S   0:00 grep inetd
# kill -SIGHUP 395
```

If you are feeling particularly brave, you can do a `kill -1 pid`. Just keep in mind one of my favorite warnings.

> **Important Note:** I've said it before and I'll say it again.
> A `kill -1` looks an awful lot like `kill 1` (which will crash your entire system).

To start the Web interface, enter a URL with the following format:

```
http://your_site_address:98/
```

When `linuxconf` starts up in your browser (see Figure 19.3) it will inform you of the modules currently installed and provide you with a Start button. Clicking the Start button causes an authentication window to pop up, where you will enter your user name and password.

Try experimenting with the various interfaces to decide what you like best. I should point out that the X window GUI provides some interesting direct access commands that are somewhat slicker than their `linuxconf` menu alternates. For instance, you can access network functions simply by typing `netconf`. User administration is also a single command away with `userconf`.

You can also access linuxconf modules directly from the command line. To find out what these options are (and there are many), type the following command:

```
linuxconf --help
```

There is one last file you might want to take a look at: the configuration file, located at `/etc/conf.linuxconf`. Here's what mine looks like right now:

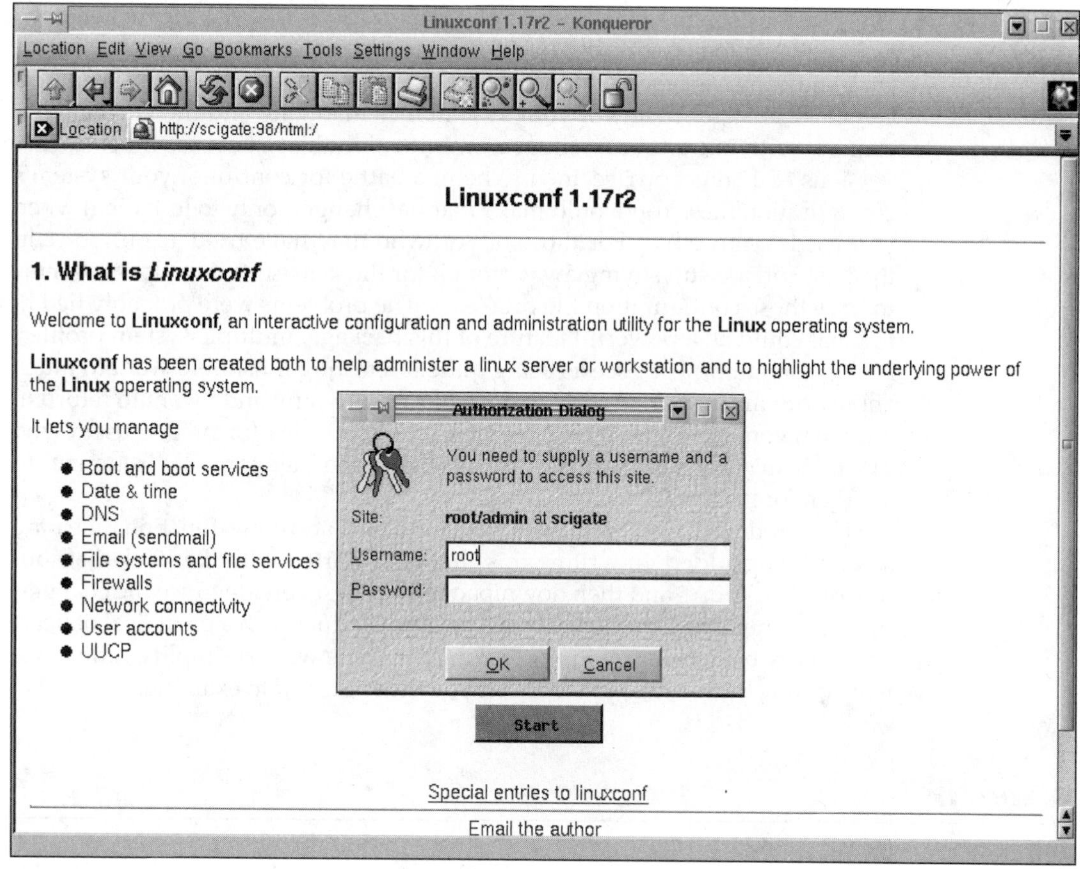

FIGURE 19.3 Browser-based administration with `linuxconf`

```
[base]
LINUXCONF.distribution redhat
module.list 1 redhatppp
module.list 1 treemenu
module.list 1 inittab
module.list 1 motd
module.list 1 dnsconf
module.list 1 apache
module.list 1 samba
module.list 1 mailconf
module.list 1 wuftpd
kmaildbtype./etc/mail/virtusertable hash
notice.10-welcome.help 924195811
[netaccess]
htmlaccess.from 192.168.22.0
htmlaccess.dolog 1
   htmlaccess.enable 1
```

Note the change to the `netaccess` paragraph at the end, where I enabled `htmlaccess` to network 192.168.22.0.

`linuxconf` is flexible in that it works with your regular system files. You can make changes in any of your system files manually and then make other changes with `linuxconf`. The reason I mention this is because much earlier versions of `linuxconf` seemed to be in a battle for control of your system's configuration files. You would make manual changes, only to lose them when you used `linuxconf`. For those of you who may have tried `linuxconf` in the past and are still shying away from it for those reasons, it no longer seems to have those configuration file problems. The problems were probably tied in to what could be a powerful feature of this package: multiple system profiles. This is something I can see as being quite interesting if I should want to muck about with my system (testing various bits of software) and I want to return to a known configuration. It also seems like a good idea for mobile users who move from one configuration to another (one network environment to another, for instance).

The product is in continuous development, and new functionalities are always being added. In writing this chapter, I started with the stock distribution of `linuxconf` and then downloaded the latest version to see the changes. Indeed, `linuxconf` proved to be a dynamic product with a great deal of heart and energy behind it. If you are looking for some way to simplify Linux system administration, this is a tool that you owe yourself to examine.

Webmin

Webmin is exactly what the name implies: a Web-based system administration tool. In many ways, Webmin is more advanced than `linuxconf`, but it is strictly a browser-based utility. Its strength comes from its multiplatform support. One other reason you should consider Webmin is that it is flexible enough to let you offload some of that administrative work on others. You'll see what I mean when you start working with the program. I have turned Webmin over to other users who aren't very Linux-savvy but who can deal with those system functions that I've provided them on a custom-tailored menu.

This package requires only that you have Perl loaded on your system (in all likelihood you do). Webmin comes with its own Web server so Apache isn't even necessary. You can get Webmin from the official Web site (`http://www.webmin.com/`). The latest version as I write this is 0.85, so I will use those numbers in this example. Don't let the pre-1.0 version numbers scare you. Webmin is ready now.

```
# tar -xzvf webmin-0.85.tar.gz
# cd webmin-0.85
# ./setup.sh
```

The Webmin installation will now prompt me for a number of things. For the `config` file directory, I accept the default of `/etc/webmin`. For the log directory, I once again take the default of `/var/webmin`. The next prompt is interesting because it tells me about what I've already told you, namely that all it really takes to run Webmin is Perl. The whole thing is written in Perl, which is why the installation now wants to know where your Perl binary is located. Odds are that the default it offers is the right place.

Next, you'll get a prompt that will tell you one of the coolest things about Webmin. Notice your choices:

```
 1) Sun Solaris                          2) Caldera OpenLinux
 3) Redhat Linux                         4) Slackware Linux
 5) Debian Linux                         6) SuSE Linux
 7) Mandrake Linux                       8) Delix DLD Linux
 9) MkLinux                             10) FreeBSD
11) BSDI                                12) HP/UX
13) SGI Irix                            14) DEC/Compaq OSF/1
15) IBM AIX                             16) SCO UnixWare
17) SCO OpenServer                      18) MacOS Server X
```

As you can see, Webmin runs on a whack of different platforms with the same basic interface. If you learn to administer your Linux system with Webmin, you can pretty much do it with HPUX, AIX, and so on. In no time at all, you'll be a master of all UNICes (not that you need anything more than Linux, though). By the way, I have personally run Webmin on both AIX and HPUX.

On my system, I choose number 3 for Red Hat. The next prompt wants to know what release of Red Hat. I tell it 6.2.

Because Webmin runs its own little Web server, it then asks for the port on which I intend to run it. The default is 10000. Following are the next couple of prompts. No, I won't tell you what user name and password I chose.

```
Web server port (default 10000):
Login name (default admin):
Login password:
Web server hostname (default testsys.mycompany.com):
Use SSL (y/n):
```

Isn't that last question interesting? Should you use SSL? For those of you who built or are running OpenSSL on your systems, this is an opportunity to use it. (If you are looking to run a secure server and need some help, be sure to read Chapter 24.) While the Webmin server is protected (good CGI scripts and so on), you might still worry that somebody with a sniffer running on your network might just pick up the user name and password of the person you are adding through the user interface. If you want to add SSL to your Webmin, you'll need a little Perl module besides your already installed OpenSSL. This is where you get it: `ftp://ftp.cpan.org/pub/CPAN/modules/by-module/Net`.

When I picked mine up, I got version 1.05, which meant grabbing the file `Net_SSLeay.pm-1.05.tar.gz`. If you've never added Perl modules (from CPAN) to your system, here is an easy lesson in adding them. On my system, I keep a directory called `/data1/packages/perl` where all my Perl module distributions are kept (in the event of some major catastrophe). To install any of these modules, follow these guidelines:

```
# tar -xzvf modules_name.rev.tar.gz
# cd module_name.rev
# perl Makefile.PL
# make
```

The last step is usually to do a `make install`, although you'll find that some of these distributions come with a few test programs to make sure everything went fine. In that case, you'll do a `make test`, convince yourself that all is well, and then do your `make install`.

Finish your Webmin installation. You probably want to answer Yes to the idea of having the server running automagically at boot time. You can start it manually as well with the command `/etc/webmin/start`. I'll let you guess the command that stops the server. Now, start your browsers and let's see what you get. For the plain, ordinary, non-SSL server, the URL is

```
http://your_server:10000/
```

For the SSL-enabled version, try this instead:

```
https://your_server:10000/
```

The default admin options include modules for a wide range of administration functions. From the included modules, you can add users, create and administer printers and queues, modify your apache server configuration, maintain disks and partitions, tweak your DNS, configure `sendmail`, shut down or restart your system, and more (see Figure 19.4). There's even a great Java file manager that enables you to copy, rename, and even transfer files to the remote system.

Way back when at the beginning of this chapter, I mentioned that you could unload some of your administration work to another user. Suppose you want someone to take care of the printers. From the master Webmin menu, you can create another Webmin user. You simply create the user and click the modules you want that user to have. When you are happy, click Save and you can start forgetting about those printers.

If you feel really ambitious (and there's something missing from the master menu that you really want to have), visit the Webmin Web site (`http://www.webmin.com/`) for information on creating your own modules. There's a wish list there just waiting for someone like you.

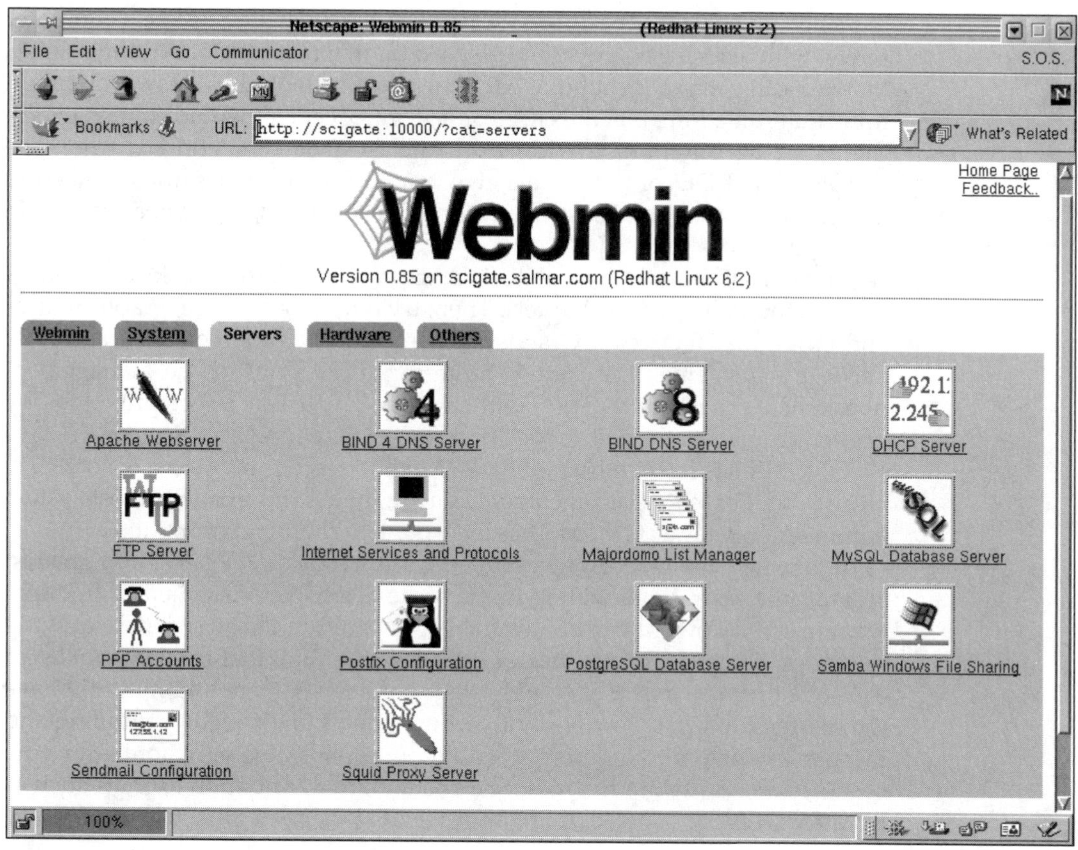

FIGURE 19.4 The face of Webmin

Graphical Administration Tools

Let's take a tour of what your desktop offers, and then I'll talk about remote administration with KDE or GNOME. You can access these tools from their respective Start buttons. On your GNOME desktop, that's the big foot on the left. KDE has a large K. Both GNOME and KDE offer a variety of great tools, but at this time, I am still more impressed with the collection of tools the standard KDE installation offers. In the world of open-source development, things change quickly. In three months, I may feel differently. The beauty, of course, is that I can run my GNOME tools from KDE or my KDE tools from GNOME.

To control the basics of your environment, use GNOME's sessions manager, `gnomecc`. You can find it under the Utilities menu as system info. On the GNOME panel, it is likely under that toolbox icon. KDE, on the other hand, has its control center (kcontrol). On the KDE panel, it looks like a computer screen with a circuit board superimposed on it. One of the nice things here is that you can get a snapshot of what your machine looks like. Now, you might think that something that bills itself as a "control center" would contain everything having anything to do with your system—not entirely true. The GNOME and KDE control centers give you some control (desktop themes and looks, colors, styles, and so on), but for other functions, you'll need to pull in other tools.

In the KDE bundle, you will find kdat, a tar-based backup system (I talked about it in the last chapter). Then, try out kuser, a nice, graphical user and group manager. ksysv is a system run-level editor. For RPM and DEB package management, try out kpackage. In the print queue management department, check out klpq. With this tool, you can select print jobs by printer, reorganize the print order, or remove jobs entirely.

GNOME has its own crop of tools. Need to reset your system's clock? Try timetool. For RPM package management, there's gnorpm. For most system administration tasks, GNOME has incorporated the linuxconf tool.

If, like me, you just can't wait to get your hands on the latest and greatest system administration tool for your favorite desktop environment, you might want to scroll down the list of available packages on the appropriate desktop Web sites. Before I give you those URLs, keep in mind that the software listed can sometimes be in the very early stages of development and may still have the odd bug to swat. For those of you who don't really enjoy compiling and installing your programs from distribution tarballs, this may not be for you, because some software might not be in standard distribution formats such as RPMs or DEBs.

Tiny but Powerful Tools

As a system administrator, you are all set. You've got the knowledge and you've got your notebook or desktop system loaded with Linux. You are ready for anything and any eventuality. But what about when you aren't within easy reach of that desktop? What if your notebook is in another building (or maybe you don't have a notebook)? Once you have been working with Linux for some time, you'll discover that you can find yourself almost lost without it. There are just too many situations where you will find yourself saying, "You know, if I was running Linux on this puppy, I'd have this problem cleared up in no time."

The solution? Carry your own Linux distribution around with you. The best possible scenario would be something that fits in your pocket—an entire Linux OS on a single diskette would be great.

Go-Anywhere Linux

Luckily, Linux developers have answered that call on many occasions. A number of portable, single-diskette Linux systems exist, making it possible to rescue downed systems (Linux and Windows), back up and restore data, diagnose network problems, or gain access to a computer when its password has been forgotten. In the next few pages, I'm going to cover a few of these micro-Linuxes, starting with the aptly named Linux On A Floppy (LOAF) (`http://www.ecks.org/projects/loaf/`).

When you visit the LOAF Web site, you'll notice there are several versions (or images) available. Each image contains a specific network driver, so you'll want to get the one (or ones) that best suit the environment in your office. I picked up `loaf3.img`, which contained the 3Com 3x59x driver. Then I popped in a blank diskette and created my diskette using this command:

```
dd if=loaf3.img of=/dev/fd0
```

Throw a label on it, and that's all you need. To test this out, take the diskette to another PC (I am assuming that you don't want to shut yours down), put it in the driver, and reboot the PC.

When the login prompt comes up, just type `root` and away you go. To get LOAF to recognize your network and work on it, you need to execute the following commands:

```
ifconfig eth0 local_ip_address
netmask your_network_mask
broadcast broadcast_address
route add -net network_address
echo "nameserver gateway_address" > /etc/resolv.conf
route add default gw gateway_address
```

In my case, I was using a local private Class C network at 192.168.1.0 and the client address was at 192.168.1.2. My gateway and name server were at 192.168.1.10 (a Linux server doing IP masquerading). Here's what it actually looks like:

```
ifconfig eth0 192.168.1.2 netmask 255.255.255.0 broadcast
192.168.1.255
route add -net 192.168.1.0
echo "nameserver 192.168.1.10" > /etc/resolv.conf
route add default gw 192.168.1.10
```

I typed `lynx http://www.linuxjournal.com`, and suddenly I was surfing the Web.

LOAF includes a nice set of useful tools. You get things like `ifconfig`, `traceroute` and, of course, `lynx`, which enables you to happily surf either the Web or your local network. Incidentally, if you just type `lynx`, you get the local LOAF documentation. (Don't worry—it's a quick read.) You also get an ssh (secure shell) client for secure access to your network, good old telnet, and ftp. LOAF is a great lightweight networking client. Heck, if all you want to do is run dumb terminal applications with an old 386, LOAF may be for you. The only catch is that LOAF doesn't know anything about hard drives. For a micro-Linux that enables you to have local hard disk access, read on.

tomsrtbt

Another cool, super-tiny Linux is tomsrtbt, which stands for "Tom's floppy, which has a root file system and is also bootable." Hey, I couldn't make this stuff up. What Tom has achieved here is practically a miracle of miniaturization. He uses a great little trick to stretch what he can put on a floppy by using 1.7MB of diskette space rather than the normal 1.4MB. You can get tomsrtbt at http://www.toms.net/rb/.

As I write this, the latest distribution in a tarred and gzipped file is tomsrtbt-1.7.185.tar.gz. After you download it, you simply extract it and create the diskette from the installation script. In its simplest form, the installation goes as follows. Start by putting a blank diskette in your drive and follow these steps:

```
tar -xzvf tomsrtbt-1.7.185.tar.gz
cd tomsrtbt-1.7.185
./install.s
```

That is all you really need in order to create the tomsrtbt diskette. Earlier with LOAF, you had to configure the network settings with each boot, but not so with tomsrtbt. Consequently, you will find that the default installation boots to a preconfigured set of network addresses, including DNS entries. To customize tomsrtbt for your own network, edit the settings.s file in the distribution directory. After my changes, the file looks something like this:

```
DOMAIN=yourcompany.com
IF_PORT=10baseT
DNS_1=192.168.22.10
IPADDR=192.168.22.3
NETWORK=192.168.22.0
NETMASK=255.255.255.0
PASSWD=xxxx
FD=/dev/fd0u1722
FN="b 2 60"
```

The original network numbers were in the network 192.168.1.0 and the domain was rb.com.

When you first boot the diskette, you will be delighted to learn that the date is something rather odd, such as "Boomtime, the 14th day of Discord in the YOLD 3166." Never fear. This is the ddate, a small program courtesy of the Church of the SubGenius that translates Gregorian dates into those of the Discordian calendar. Push on and explore.

The sheer bulk of tools available is impressive, to say the least. `tomsrtbt` has SCSI support and PCMCIA support. It contains a handful of useful shell tools (in no particular order), such as `find`, `grep`, `vi`, `e2fsck`, `tar`, `cpio`, and a host of other command-line tools. This tiny Linux *does* know about hard drives, and it enables you to mount them. For instance, if you create a directory called `/mnt/cdrive`, you might mount your Windows partition like this:

```
mount /dev/hda1 /mnt/cdrive
```

With access to your client PC's hard drive, you can now do such things as creating `tar` archives on the disk that you can then `ftp` to another server on your network. Because there are a number of Linux file system tools available, this makes an ideal generic rescue diskette for when all else has failed. The possibilities are, as they say, virtually endless. You can also mount network drives with NFS. What LOAF gets you that `tomsrtbt` does not is a Web browser (`lynx`) and a secure shell client (`ssh`).

While this doesn't really have anything to do with what `tomsrtbt` does, I like Tom's logo and decided to include it here.

Trinux

The last pocket Linux I want to look at is something that bills itself as the "Linux Security Toolkit." It is Trinux, a two-floppy (or more) Linux distribution whose claim to fame is the concentration of network tools that are included with the system. You get programs for network mapping, packet sniffing, network performance monitoring, and a whole lot more. The implication of these programs requires that I spend a fair amount of time on them. I'll cover some of those topics in the final chapters of the book that explore network security.

You can get Trinux from the Trinux Web site (`http://trinux.sourceforge.net/`). Click the Images link over on the left-hand side. You'll be transported to the Trinux FTP site, where you'll find the basic distribution. The images to get are `boot` and `classic`.

The installation is simply a matter of copying the images onto a couple of blank diskettes.

```
dd if=boot of=/dev/fd0
```

For the second diskette, it's the same thing.

```
dd if=classic of=/dev/fd0
```

To use Trinux, simply boot from the first diskette. You will be prompted for the second diskette, after which you'll be asked if you have any more diskettes. For now, answer N. (You can read more about other add-on software on the site itself.)

Your Trinux system is now up, with a nice welcome message and the shell prompt (`Trinux 0.version->`). There is no need to log in here—you are automatically root. You might wonder if this qualifies as a security problem. The answer is a kind of qualified "No." Under normal circumstances, Trinux runs entirely stand-alone. Its whole being is in RAM. If you take those diskettes out after boot and put them back in your pocket, no one will make changes to them. That said, if you mount the hard disk drive partition, you do have access to that computer and all its information. No login means no restrictions if you walk away in the process of your testing. Please be careful.

Your next step will be to configure your Trinux network IP address and start using the system. Network activation is done through the `netcfg` command. What you do is change directory to `/etc/conf`, edit the `/etc/conf/eth0` file, edit the `/etc/conf/network` file, and run `netcfg` to bring up `eth0`. I will show you how this is done in a moment; but first, consider the following.

Working in different offices and on different networks means you will have to go through the set-up dialog each and every time. However, if you are always working in the same office, you can probably safely assign all network information to your Trinux distribution diskette beforehand by modifying the diskette you've already created. Here's an example of what I mean.

Log back into the Linux system on which you created the Trinux disks. If you do not already have one defined, create a mount point for the floppy. I created mine with the command `mkdir /mnt/floppy`. Now, mount the diskette as an `msdos` file system and change directory to `/mnt/floppy/conf`.

```
mount -t msdos /dev/fd0 /mnt/floppy
cd /mnt/floppy/conf
```

If you do an `ls` here, you'll find that the architecture is somewhat different than the final booted product. For instance, the `conf` directory is under `/etc` when the Trinux system is running, but not at this time. With your favorite editor, edit the `eth0` file to reflect the address you want for this highly portable workstation (it doesn't get much more portable than a diskette or two). On my network (I use a class C at 192.168.2.0 in this case), I gave the Trinux machine an address of 192.168.2.4. Here's what my `eth0` file wound up looking like:

```
export IPADDRESS NETWORK BROADCAST NETMASK
IPADDRESS=192.168.2.4
```

```
NETMASK=255.255.255.0
NETWORK=192.168.2.0
BROADCAST=192.168.2.255
```

You will also want to set the network information as it relates to your default gateway and name server. This is the `network` file. On a booted Trinux system, it is at `/etc/conf/network`. On the distribution diskette, it is simply under the `conf` directory. After a quick edit, my `network` file looked like this:

```
GATEWAY=192.168.2.10
DNS=192.168.2.10
GWDEV=eth0
```

As I mentioned earlier, Trinux comes with a small treasure trove of tools for the security-conscious network administrator. For instance, you get `nmap`, one of the best port scanners I know of. If you are not sure what services the hosts on your systems have open, you will want to run `nmap`. You may be surprised at what turns up. Because there is always more than one way to do it, you can also use `exscan` for network mapping.

Trinux also features `ntop`, a really cool tool that displays network usage interactively. You can sort the information in various ways, concentrate on specific protocols, and zoom in on your network bandwidth hogs. One feature I really like is a display that enables me to toggle between the IP address of the card and its MAC address. One more keystroke and those MAC addresses are identified by the manufacturer of the card. Another included network monitor is `iptraf`.

If you are looking for sniffers, there's `tcpdump` or `ipgrab`. Your Trinux station can be configured as a firewall with `ipchains` or run a `proxy`.

If you are looking for the latest and greatest package to add to your toolkit (check the Web site), you can take a blank DOS diskette, mount it as described previously, and copy the packages you need to it with a simple `cp` command.

```
cp newpackage.tgz /mnt/floppy
```

Then, if you want to load such a package after the fact (while your Trinux workstation is actually running), you mount the diskette in exactly the same way and use the `pkgadd` command to load the new software.

```
cd /mnt/trinux_mount_point
pkgadd newpackage.tgz
```

Now, just type the command name and start using it.

Here is something to think about. With a little package like this at your disposal, you are carrying around the kind of network tools that would have cost *thousands of dollars* just a few years ago. I remember when a packet sniffer was a *big* deal that came in its own black-box hardware with a little hard-to-read screen and cost a small fortune! (I also remember walking ten miles to school, uphill in both directions, with 14-foot-high snow banks on either side of the road—but that's another story.)

> Here is something else to think about. *<Soapbox mode on>* My reason for showing you these tools is twofold. For network and system administrators, these tools are invaluable for determining problems, bottlenecks, and a host of other day-to-day headaches. Because these same tools are used by the enemy, the system cracker, they are also great tools for determining the weaknesses the cracker will try to exploit. Knowing your own weaknesses is the first step toward making sure no one else can take advantage of you or your network. The bottom line is this: *Be ethical.* Scan only your own systems and networks. Protect yourself, your company, and your customers, but leave other people alone. *<Soapbox mode off>*

The Tiny Conclusion

Whether you choose LOAF, `tomsrtbt`, or Trinux will depend on precisely what you need to do. Heck, considering how little pocket space these guys take up, why not carry a few different flavors? That way, you can be ready for anything. Here's a parting thought that might encourage you to carry one of these diskettes around: If you are working on a network where you question the security of the various machines (maybe someone is watching or listening), you have the guarantee of an OS that is completely untainted by whatever compromise may exist on the network. After all, when your OS resides entirely in RAM, not much will be able to touch it.

> **Security Warning:** Just as you can use your micro, floppy-based Linux to repair/rescue another system or scan a network for trouble, so can unscrupulous users. Unfortunately, they aren't scanning for trouble. Their scanning *is* trouble. There is a way to protect against this. Many modern PCs enable you to set a hardware boot password in the BIOS. If you are concerned about this type of threat, consider password-protecting your computers and not just your computers' operating systems.

There's No Control Like Remote Control

A system administrator in a large company with a number of Windows workstations knows the headaches of all the simple "operator" error calls that nonetheless require a great deal of work and time as he or she walks users through the right steps to solve their problems. Wouldn't it be great if you could take control of users' desktops and do it for them while they watch and learn?

I am talking about a remote administration tool that works not only with Windows, Solaris, and DEC Alphas running OSF1, but also with that old favorite of the desktop publishing world, the Macintosh.

This great tool is Virtual Network Computing (VNC) from AT&T Laboratories in Cambridge, England. VNC is a package that enables you to view other computer desktops from your own desktop. For instance, I could be running an X server on a Linux machine from a Windows 95 or NT box, or doing the reverse. I can do it from my internal network or across the Internet.

Now, I know there are commercial packages that can do this, but not necessarily from your Linux desktop. They also cost more than VNC. That's right—VNC is distributed free of charge.

To get your free copy of VNC, surf on over to `http://www.uk.research.att.com/vnc/`.

From the download page, select the version that works for your system. I picked up both the Linux and the Windows versions. Installation is a breeze. For Linux, simply extract the `tar` archive and follow the installation procedures described in the accompanying `README` file. For the impatient, here it is in a nutshell:

```
# tar -xzvf vnc-3.3.3_x86_linux_2.0.tgz
# cd vnc_x86_linux_2.0
# cp vncviewer vncserver vncpasswd Xvnc /usr/local/bin
# mkdir -p /usr/local/vnc/classes
# cp classes/* /usr/local/vnc/classes
```

The last two lines copy the Java classes to use with the Java VNC viewer. You do not have to do this, but considering what I tell you later on about the browser side of VNC, you'll be glad you did. For the installation part, there's not much else to do. Let's start with the heart of VNC: the server.

```
vncserver
```

This is actually a Perl script that runs the Xvnc server. Use it to run Xvnc. You may have to change the first line of the script to reflect the location of your Perl binary.

You start a `vncserver` by logging on to the Linux (or UNIX) system you want to administer remotely. To start the command, type the following:

```
vncserver hostname:session_number
```

With VNC, you can run multiple sessions and connect to different servers. By default, the session numbers start at 1 and go up from there, but you can specify session 3 (for instance) right from the start by typing `vncserver hostname:3`. This highlights another benefit of VNC. Until you kill a VNC session, it retains its current state. That means you can disconnect from a session, reconnect later, and return right where you left off. In fact, you can even share a session so multiple users can access it. More on that later.

When you start the `vncserver` for the first time, you will be prompted for a password to access the server. You can always change it later using the `vncpasswd` command. Once the server is activated, you can connect to it using the `vncviewer` command. The format is as follows:

```
vncviewer host:session_number
```

To exit the viewer (or send specific key sequences), press the F8 key, and then click Quit Viewer to close the session. You can also start a shared session so that others may use the same X window session with this version of the command:

```
vncviewer -shared host:session_number
```

When you start the `vncserver`, it creates a `.vnc` directory under your home directory (`/root/.vnc`). Several files are kept here. You'll find a log file associated with each server you run and a `.pid` file to allow for removal of the server. By the way, you kill a `vncserver` process like this:

```
vncserver -kill :1
```

Remember that the `:1` could be a `:2` or `:3`, depending on the session you are trying to kill. That said, the other file I want you to look at is `xstartup`. If you do a `cat` on the file, you get something that looks like this:

```
#!/bin/sh

xrdb $HOME/.Xresources
xsetroot -solid grey
xterm -geometry 80x24+10+10 -ls -title "$VNCDESKTOP Desktop" &
# twm &
startkde &
```

Notice the second-to-last line is commented out and a `startkde` line is added below. This is because VNC uses `twm` (the Tab Window Manager) as its default desktop. I chose to run KDE instead, and added the line that follows. If you prefer another window manager, change it in the start-up here.

Just when you thought it couldn't get any better, the VNC viewer can also be run from your favorite Web browser through a small Java applet. From your Netscape browser, use this URL (substituting `host` and `session_number` with yours) to access the Java client:

```
http://server_name:580session_number/
```

Let me clarify that a bit. I have a machine with a hostname of `gateway` (as in a gateway to my intranet) on my network. If I want to connect to `vncserver` session number 1 on that machine, my URL looks like this:

```
http://gateway:5801/
```

Java starts on your browser and you are presented with a password prompt, the one you gave when you first started the server. Unlike the command-line viewer, you don't use function keys to cut and paste or disconnect from the session. Four small buttons remain at the top of the screen for you to use.

This is a small, fast client that responds very quickly. With the browser client, you can access your Linux (or UNIX) server from any PC (with a Java-capable browser, of course).

How about Windows? Earlier on, I mentioned that VNC offers a server for Windows as well. Using this product, you no longer have to spend hours on the phone walking a user through a problem with a Windows application—you simply take control. To do this, you will need to install the Windows product that comes as a `.zip` file. The current version of the file is `vnc-3.3.3r2_x86_win32.zip`. This works with all Windows 9*x*, Windows NT, and Windows 2000 products. Have a peek at Figure 19.5. This is a Windows 95 session running Mozilla that is being accessed from my Linux system running a KDE session.

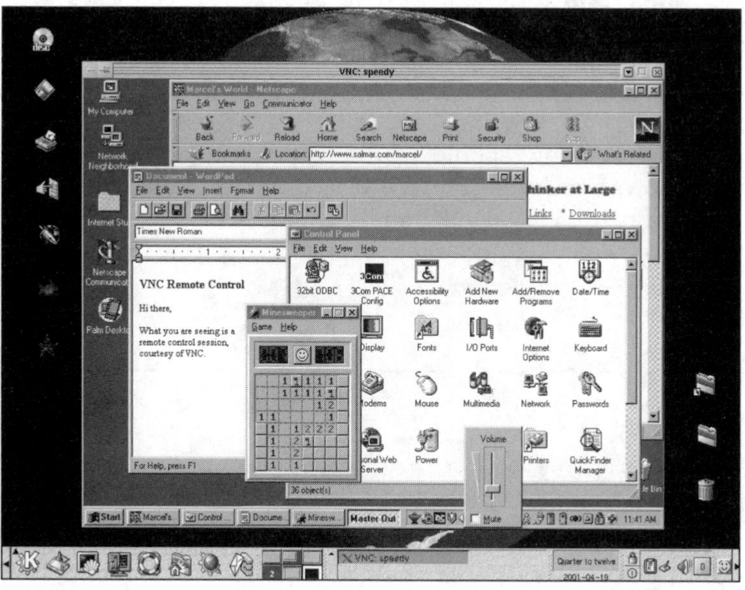

FIGURE 19.5 Controlling a Windows 95 machine using VNC

To get in on the action, extract the file into the directory of your choice (using your favorite Windows archive client, such as `pkzip` or WinZip). Two folders will be created. One is `vncviewer`, which contains a single executable, `vncviewer.exe`, that can be run to access your Linux server (or any VNC server) without any special installation. You can put this file on a diskette and carry it around with you if you do not want to install it on every PC. The other directory is `winvnc`, which contains the full distribution, including the VNC server for Windows. To install VNC for Windows, simply run the `setup.exe` file in the folder.

Next, click the Start button and then select Program Files, VNC, Administrative Tools. Click the Install Registry Key link, and then click Install WinVNC Service. To run the server, either reboot or click Start WinVNC Service. You should see a little VNC icon appear in the tray of your Windows task bar (over by the clock on the right-hand side). Now, go back to your Linux machine and run your `vncviewer` (either from the command line or the browser) by connecting to the host at service number 0. In other words, for me to connect to my PC called "natika," I run either of the following two commands (the second actually being a URL and not a command):

```
# vncviewer natika:0

http://natika:5800/
```

> **Important Note:** Unlike on the Linux server, you *cannot* run multiple sessions of VNC from Windows. You are not magically given a multiuser Windows system. This is strictly remote control.

The last thing I should mention is that you can also run a VNC viewer from Windows by selecting it in the VNC program group (click the Start button and select Program Files, VNC, and so on).

Resources

Linuxconf

`http://www.solucorp.qc.ca/linuxconf/`

LOAF

`http://www.ecks.org/projects/loaf/`

tomsrtbt (Tom's root and boot disk) Home Page

`http://www.toms.net/rb/`

Trinux Security Toolkit

`http://www.trinux.org/`

Webmin Software

`http://www.webmin.com/`

Chapter 20

Proof of Concept, Part 1

Of Web Servers and Intranets

This is the first of two "proof of concept" chapters. The reason I use that term is that both chapters will explore a *complete* office solution created with the aid of a Linux system and readily available tools. In the process, I'll cover some new techniques and administrative ground as well.

Communication and sharing information are important in an organization. Whether interoffice communication comes in the form of a company-wide memo, a list of useful Web sites, or the announcement of Jackie and Paul's new baby girl, it makes an office a place for people rather than just machines.

The corporate intranet, or internal network, is an ideal marriage of human needs and machine capabilities—capabilities that came bundled with your Linux system distribution.

You can think of an intranet as your own private Internet, a networked environment where users can share information, participate in discussions, and use networking technologies to make getting to information as easy as possible. It can be many things, really—a database providing access to corporate documents, an information center for job postings, a discussion board, or a place to find the results of the hockey pool. It can take many forms, but the essence of an intranet is a high-tech bulletin board that lets you post simple notices as well as entire multipage documents. Unlike that corkboard in most company lunch rooms, a good Web-based intranet has virtually unlimited room.

I like to think of this chapter as a proof of concept because it proves that you can provide a complete solution working with your Linux server. The solution, in this case, is a fully functional intranet, complete with discussion boards, file and Internet link management, an online telephone directory, and an employee in-out board. The package is called Grand Salmar Station and it was written by Sally Tomasevic (who just happens to be my wife and partner). It is freely distributed under the GPL.

As part of its functionality, Grand Salmar Station automatically creates and maintains all links for you and even expires old postings or dated information without you having to lift a finger. Any newly added item magically appears on the intranet's What's New page to highlight it. Normally, such adding and deleting requires user intervention and links must be verified and re-created. No such problem with this intranet—it does it all for you.

In order to use this software, you'll build and configure an Apache Web server, build and configure an SQL database system (PostgreSQL), and deliver that intranet solution I talked about.

Building Your Own Corporate Portal

The heart of your intranet is your Web server. Luckily, you don't have to go far for it. Linux distributions come with the world's most popular and most flexible Web server: the Apache server. Like other open source projects, the Apache server can be built from scratch and customized at will. It also provides extensive module support, allowing you to "plug in" additional functionality, such as database support modules or SSL encryption.

The name "Apache" is actually a homonym for the original description of the server in its early development. Originally, it was based on the NCSA httpd Web server. Developers kept patching and enhancing the code. When asked what their project was, legend has it that the developers called it a "patchy" Web server. I suppose they could have said a "patchwork" server, but "Apache" caught on and the rest, as they say, is history.

You can always pick up the latest code for the Apache server from the Apache Web site, but it is almost guaranteed to already be in your Linux distribution, providing you with a precompiled, easy-to-install version. If you want to build your Apache server from scratch, I'll show you how in the next section. You may also want to check out the chapter on encryption and secure computing (Chapter 24). Not only do you build the Apache server, but you build it with SSL encryption as well.

Building Apache from Source

The first thing to do is get the latest source from the Apache Software Foundation Web site (`http://www.apache.org/`).

From there, download the source and save it to a temporary directory. For this example, I'll work with release 1.3.14. The first thing I did was extract the source into my directory, as follows:

```
#  tar -xzvf apache_1.3.14.tar.gz
#  cd apache_1.3.14
#  ./configure
```

This configures Apache for installation into the default directory structure of `/usr/local/apache`. In the case of a Red Hat installation (along with some others), the default directory is `/home/httpd`. If you want a different installation directory, use the `--prefix` option, as follows:

```
#  ./configure --prefix=/home/httpd
```

The configure script has a number of additional flags or options that you can set. You might want to have a look at the `README.configure` file before you start your installation. For now, I'll keep it simple and use the defaults as in my first example. When the configure script has finished creating its `Makefiles`, type `make` followed by `make install` to complete the installation.

```
#  make
#  make install
```

A number of defaults are assumed if you choose the standard configuration. For instance, your document root is assumed to be `/usr/local/apache/htdocs`, while your `cgi-bin` directory is assumed to be `/usr/local/apache/cgi-bin` which, for the most part, should be just fine.

Once your server is installed, you need to start it with the `apachectl` command.

```
/usr/local/apache/bin/apachectl start
```

You stop the server by using the `stop` option instead of `start` (but you already knew that, didn't you?). Now, in order to test your installation, fire up your favorite browser (Netscape, Lynx, or Konqueror), and point it to your new server. Assuming that the server on which you just did your installation is called "natika," you use this URL:

```
http://natika/
```

You should get a page that looks very much like that in Figure 20.1.

If you look at your running processes, the server itself will generally show up as `httpd`. If your Web server was installed as part of a Debian `apt-get` or basic installation, there is a good possibility that the executable is actually called `apache` rather than `httpd`. You can verify this by listing the `apache` package files with this command:

```
dpkg -L apache | more
```

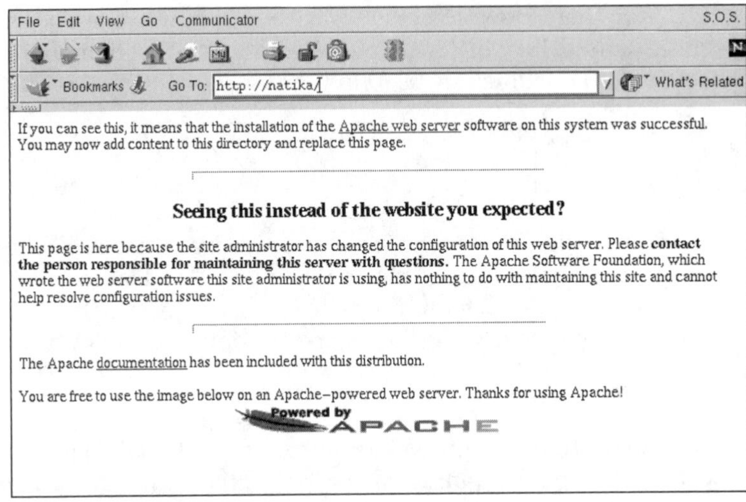

FIGURE 20.1 Your new Apache server

Basic Apache Configuration

As of release 1.3.4, all configuration information is in one file: the `httpd.conf` file. If you built from scratch, you'll find the configuration file(s) in `/usr/local/apache/conf`. On my preinstalled Debian Apache server, the `httpd.conf` file lives in the `/etc/apache` directory. One way to find out exactly where this thing is on your system (other than running the `find` command) is to ask the Apache executable itself by calling it with the `-V` flag. This will show you the compile time settings of a number of parameters, including paths to configuration files. For the sake of this example, I am going to assume that the Apache executable is in your `PATH`.

```
httpd -V
```

On my Debian system, I type `apache -V` instead. Look for a line that says `SERVER_CONFIG_FILE`. It indicates the full path to the configuration file.

Any change to the Web server requires a restart of the server. With any current Apache installation, this is done using the `apachectl` program (as demonstrated previously).

Common Changes

The first thing I want to look at is the server name. Your host may be known by different names on the same network. A common example is the classic `www.domain.dom` format. Your server may respond initially as `myserver.domain.dom`, but you want to force the latter. Note that this has to be a valid host name for your server. Change the `ServerName` setting.

```
ServerName www.domain.dom
```

Other parameters you may want to change are the user ID and group ID your server runs as. These are the `User` and `Group` configuration parameters. The root user still starts the server, but the Apache binary switches to this user for its operation. Some sites have a user called "www" to run Web services. Others use "nobody." You may use whatever your server is configured for. This is defined in the `httpd.conf` file where you find these lines:

```
User www
Group www
```

Every once in a while, something will go wrong with a document and the server will generate an error message with a note to contact the administrator of the site. The server maintains this information in the `ServerAdmin` parameter. The administrator may well be at some address other than that of the server. Find and modify the line that looks like this:

```
ServerAdmin webmaster@somedomain.dom
```

There are other changes you may want to make and there is certainly a lot that you can do with those changes. As luck would have it, Apache comes with its own HTML documentation. After the default installation has completed, you should see a link to the documentation on the test page.

The Basics of Web-Connected Databases

Databases are some of the most useful and crucial items in the modern computing environment, so much so that we take their existence largely for granted. To most users, databases are invisible and yet they consult them on a regular basis throughout the workday.

The World Wide Web has provided the next generation of database application in that the information you need to access may be located in another office, another city, or another country thousands of miles away.

As system administrator, making information available is an excellent way to make your job easier. Web-connected databases answer that need by giving you a means to share information without having to load complicated database software on each PC, play with shared drives, and constantly worry about revisions to that software. Pretty much every PC has a browser loaded, whether it is Netscape Navigator, Internet Explorer, or Lynx. It's time to take advantage of that fact.

An Introduction to PostgreSQL

PostgreSQL is an advanced multiuser relational database management system (RDBMS) distributed freely along with its source code. Originally written in 1985 and worked on by many developers worldwide, PostgreSQL is fast, powerful, supports most (if not all) SQL standards, and best of all, it is free. You probably don't even have to go looking for PostgreSQL because it is packaged as part of most major Linux distributions. In fact, on some systems, PostgreSQL is part of the default installation.

Still, if you want to work with the latest and greatest version of the software, it makes sense to download the source and build it yourself. Even if you do have PostgreSQL preinstalled, there are some basics that you will need to configure, so let's go through the process together.

The latest version is available by visiting the PostgreSQL Web site (`http://www.postgresql.org/`) or by visiting one of the mirrors (the main site can get busy, so it provides a list of alternate sites).

After downloading the latest bundle, extract it to a temporary location, change directory to the source directory, and build PostgreSQL using these steps:

```
tar -xzvf postgresql-7.0.3.tar.gz
cd postgresql-7.0.3/src
./configure
make
make install
```

The distribution directory (`postgresql-7.0.3`, in this case) has a nice `INSTALL` file that you'll want to take a moment to read because there are some options related to the configure script that you may find useful. For instance, by default, PostgreSQL installs in the `/usr/local/pgsql` directory, and you may want to use another location.

When the compile is done, PostgreSQL has to know how to find its libraries. You can always modify your environment variable to include `/usr/local/pgsql/lib` in the `LD_LIBRARY_PATH`, but it's probably easier to add the path to the `/etc/ld.so.conf` file. This is a text file that tells the system where to search for libraries. Because it is straight text, just add the path to your libraries and run this command as root:

```
ldconfig
```

If you decided to install a PostgreSQL binary from your CD, a `postgres` user will likely already have been created as part of the installation. Otherwise, create a `postgres` user with its home directory being the PostgreSQL install directory. Then, assign a password to the user and log in as `postgres`. If you built your database along with me, you will be in the `/usr/local/pgsql` directory. The next step is to create a data directory.

```
mkdir data
```

To initialize the database for the first time, use the following command:

```
$ bin/initdb -D /usr/local/pgsql/data
```

That is, of course, the data directory that you just finished creating. You will see a number of messages going by as PostgreSQL reports on what it is doing. Some default permissions will be set. In addition, a default database will be created along with PostgreSQL's own database (`pg_database`) for user and other database information. Several views are then created after which you should get a message like this:

```
Success. You can now start the database server using:

/usr/bin/postmaster -D /var/lib/pgsql
    or
/usr/bin/pg_ctl -D /var/lib/pgsql start
```

Either option will work, but the second is a better choice because it launches the process in the background for you. You will also want to add this to your start-up files (`rc.local`) for system boot.

Next, you will need to create some default PostgreSQL users. root will have to be added. So will the user "nobody." Start by logging in as your `postgres` user and execute the following commands to add users "root" and "nobody" to your PostgreSQL system:

```
$ bin/createuser root
```

You'll be prompted for root's UID (accept the default) and you'll be asked whether or not user root is allowed to create databases. Answer y. When asked whether root is allowed to create users, I answered n. Now, do the same thing for user nobody. The only difference is that I answer n to the question of whether user nobody is allowed to create databases as well. Depending on the version of PostgreSQL you are using, the question of whether or not a user is allowed to create other users may be worded this way:

```
Is user "whoever" a superuser?
```

The answer is still n. Finally, with the creation of user nobody, you will then be asked whether `createuser` should create a database for nobody. Answer y and you are finished creating users.

Perl DBI and DBD for Database Access

In order to make programming database access easier with Perl, DataBase Interface (DBI) modules were developed. DBI modules consist of a collection of routines that offer standard hooks into an SQL database. DBI is an application program interface (API) for `perl5` to interface with database systems. The idea is to provide a consistent set of modules and calls so that database access code is portable without too much fuss.

Now, because there are a number of database formats out there (PostgreSQL, MySQL, Sybase, Oracle, and so on), there is some variance in accessing and talking to those various databases. This is where DataBase Dependent (DBD) modules come into play. DBD modules are identified by the database they support by a simple suffix. For instance, DBD-Pg is the DBD module for PostgreSQL. Meanwhile, DBD-Informix is the DBD module for the Informix database.

Essentially, the DBI module is common to all the various databases, but the DBD module must be (and is) database specific.

Downloading and Installing the Modules

Both the DBD and DBI module can be found at the CPAN FTP site, a huge Perl resource on the Web. You can find the DBI module at `ftp://ftp.cpan.org/CPAN/modules/by-module/DBI/`. You can find the DBD module at `ftp://ftp.cpan.org/CPAN/modules/by-module/DBD/`.

At the time of this writing, the latest and greatest DBI version was `DBI-1.14.tar.gz`, whereas the DBD release number was `DBD-Pg-0.95.tar.gz`. It probably makes sense to get the latest and greatest when it comes to these modules. The reason for this is that the modules grow and develop with the databases they reference. The most recent PostgreSQL database is best served by the most recent DBD-Pg.

Install the DBI module first by unpacking the distributions into a temporary directory and following these steps:

```
cd /usr/local/temp_dir
tar -xzvf DBI-1.14.tar.gz
cd DBI-1.14
perl Makefile.PL
make
make test
make install
```

The DBD module installation process is similar. Please note that more recent versions of the DBD module now require you to set a couple of environment variables, `POSTGRES_LIB` and `POSTGRES_INCLUDE`, before the installation can occur.

```
POSTGRES_LIB=/usr/lib/pgsql ; export POSTGRES_LIB
POSTGRES_INCLUDE=/usr/include/pgsql ; export POSTGRES_INCLUDE
```

On a Debian system, you might find that these environment settings work better:

```
POSTGRES_LIB=/usr/lib/pgsql ; export POSTGRES_LIB
POSTGRES_INCLUDE=/usr/include/pgsql ; export POSTGRES_INCLUDE
```

Now, you can run the installation.

```
cd /usr/local/temp_dir
tar -xzvf DBD-Pg-0.95.tar.gz
cd DBD-Pg-0.95
perl Makefile.PL
make
make test
make install
```

The CGI Back End

The final item you will need is the `cgi-lib.pl` library for Perl. This has become a virtual de facto standard for CGI design using forms. For the latest and greatest version, surf over to `http://cgi-lib.berkeley.edu/` and save the file into your `/usr/lib/perl5` directory.

If your Perl libraries live in a different directory (for instance `/usr/local/lib/perl5`), you will need to modify the required `/usr/lib/perl5/cgi-lib.pl` line near the top of each `cgi-bin perl` script to reflect your own directory structure.

The Face of the Intranet

Start by downloading the latest release of Grand Salmar Station from the Salmar Web site (`http://www.salmar.com/gss/`), and then extract it into a temporary directory. The package comes with a little `README` file that you may want to read. For the impatient, this is all you do:

```
tar -xzvf sciintra.tar.gz
cd installintra
```

Before you begin the actual install, you must pause and modify one little configuration script. This is a small text file called `sciintra_conf.pl`, and you can edit it with your favorite text editor. Here is what you will find in the file:

```
#!/usr/bin/perl
#
# Local configuration parameters for intranet
# installation script
#
# Set the path to whatever your Apache server root is.
# On Red Hat, this may be /home/httpd
# The standard source build from Apache uses
# /usr/local/apache
#
# You will also need to know the document root:
# this is usually document_root/htdocs or
# document_root/html
#
#
$apache_path="/usr/local/apache";
$apache_doc_root="/usr/local/apache/htdocs";
$apache_cgi_bin="/usr/local/apache/cgi-bin";
#
```

The first thing to do is make sure that the path to your Perl executable is correct. It will either be `/usr/bin/perl` or `/usr/local/bin/perl`. Now, go down to the last three lines and fill in the path to your Apache server's document root and `cgi-bin` directory. What you see in the previous code is the file's default configuration. If this fits your own system configuration, you don't have to change anything.

Now that you have these paths taken care of, it is time to finish your installation.

```
./install
```

When you press Enter, the script does a couple of sanity checks to make sure that you have PostgreSQL running and Perl installed. Once it is satisfied, it will ask you the following question:

```
Do you also wish to install the phonebook (Y/N)?
```

The correct answer is probably Y (for "yes"). In the installation script, we have separated the online telephone directory from the intranet itself. If you choose to have it installed, it will then be available from the Grand Salmar Station Intranet menu. Next, you will be asked whether you want to install the intranet. Again, the answer is probably Y. A Perl script is then called to do the rest of the installation.

If you decide to post a date-sensitive item, the software can automatically remove this item from the intranet after a specific date. To activate this feature, add the following command to run with `cron`:

```
/usr/local/apache/cgi-bin/scimaint/dailyclean.pl
```

You can, if you want, copy it to some other location. I will discuss the security aspects of the administrator shortly.

There are two different faces to the intranet: what everyone else sees and has access to and a few little items strictly for the administrator's eyes. The Administrator's menu is available through your favorite browser at `http://yourmachine_name/scimaint/admin/`.

From here, you can set various configuration parameters. The first option enables you to create, modify, or remove posting categories. You'll see that as Update Categories on the menu. The Posting Category heading is what your users will see when they look at the public face of the intranet. The default category is News, but you can set it to Documents. News items will show up in the user menu under All the News while documents will show up under All the Documents. Both will appear briefly in the What's New menu, but you can decide to override that default at this point.

You can also define who is allowed to post here. Your choice is between allowing only administrators or making it a public category and letting everyone have a go at it (see Figure 20.2).

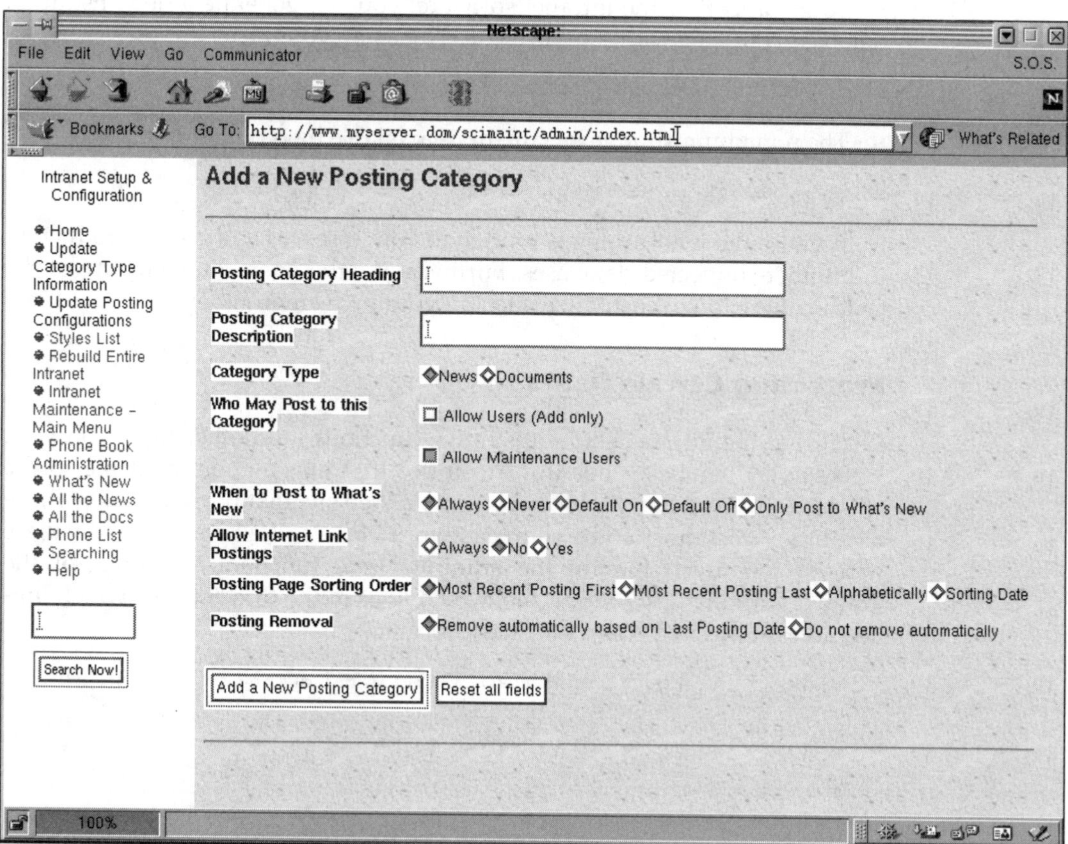

FIGURE 20.2 Adding a posting category in a Grand Salmar Station intranet

Another choice you have at this point is whether or not to allow Internet links. Links can refer to sites anywhere on the Internet or internally—or for that matter, they can refer to company documents somewhere on your local network. You can then decide on posting order: alphabetically or by date, ascending or descending. Finally, you specify if the system will take care of expiring and removing these links automatically.

Have a look around. Explore. Grand Salmar Station offers many other options. For instance, you can change the style of the intranet—in essence, the look and feel of it. You will find six styles included with the distribution with such exotic names as Beach Time, Copper Kettle, and Blue Skies. You can even create your own. Any style you choose can then be propagated across your entire intranet.

The phone book can also be administered from here (if you chose to install it), as can other intranet defaults, such as expiration dates. Be sure to read the accompanying documentation, which is also available from the Administrator's menu.

To get a feel for the intranet software, you can generate a demonstration database complete with sample records by using your browser.

```
http://yourmachine_name/scimaint/admin/demoreset.html
```

The nonadministrative user menu is available by typing this address:

```
http://yourmachine_name/sciintranet/
```

Because the whole thing is written in Perl, it serves as a great introduction to Internet-connected databases. Furthermore, the open source nature of the code enables you to customize it to suit your own environment.

Protecting Certain Pages

Regarding the intranet's administrative functions (and other things on your Web server), you may not want to make that information available to the whole world. You have no doubt been to a Web site that pops up one of those nice little "You must enter your password" boxes. Well, you can add these without too much fuss in the administrative function directories of the intranet with the `.htaccess` file, which lives in the directory for which limited access is desired. Here's the basic format:

```
AuthName        "Intranet Admin:  Restricted access"
AuthType        Basic
AuthUserFile    /usr/local/apache/.intranetadmin

<Limit GET POST>
require valid-user
</Limit>
```

The `AuthUserFile` parameter points to the location of the actual password file. Notice that I have mine sitting outside of my Web server's document root. In that way, the file cannot be downloaded with a simple HTTP request. Passwords are added to this file with the `htpasswd` command, as follows:

```
htpasswd -c passwordfile username
```

Incidentally, if you built your Apache server from source, the program will likely be in the `/usr/local/apache/bin` directory. A note of caution here: The `-c` flag creates a new password file if none existed before. You shouldn't use this unless you want to flush the whole file and start over. Another flag you may want to use (and probably should) is the `-m` flag, which forces MD5 encryption on the passwords.

```
htpasswd -m /usr/local/apache/.intranetadmin natika
```

As soon as I add natika to the list, I am prompted for a password and then asked to confirm that password.

You are *almost* done.

Now that I have told you how to add password protection to your Web directories, I am going to take a step back and tell you what you need to change in your Web server's configuration in order to make all this possible. By default, the Apache server does not honor `.htaccess` files. You need to turn this feature on. To do that, bring up the `httpd.conf` file in your favorite editor and look for this line:

```
AllowOverride None
```

You'll find at least four different areas where this line appears. One covers the server root, one the document root (`htdocs` or `html`), one is for `cgi-bin`, and another is for the `icon` directory. You need to change the `None` to `All`.

```
AllowOverride All
```

I tend to set all but the `icon` directory because I don't have a lot there that I feel needs protecting (just the default icons from the Apache installation). That's it. Restart Apache, relaunch your browser, and you should be rewarded with a nice password authentication prompt (see Figure 20.3).

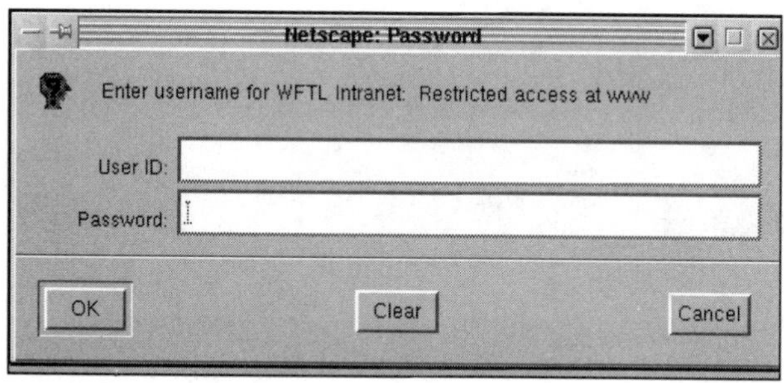

FIGURE 20.3 Authentication à la `.htaccess`

Resources

The Apache Web Server

`http://www.apache.org/`

DBI Mailing Lists

`http://www.isc.org/services/public/lists/dbi-lists.html`

Grand Salmar Station Intranet

`http://www.salmar.com/gss/`

Grand Salmar Station Mailing List

`http://www.salmar.com/mailman/listinfo/gss-users`

PostgreSQL

`http://www.postgresql.org/`

Chapter 21

Proof of Concept, Part 2

The Connected Office, Linux Style

Welcome to the second "proof of concept" chapter (the first being Chapter 20).

In this chapter, you are going to put Linux through quite a set of paces. With the information covered here, you will be able to set up a complete Linux-based Internet and e-mail gateway. With the information that follows, you can use a single, inexpensive machine (do you have an old 486 sitting around?) to provide connectivity to every member of your office. I'll show you how to do it for a small cost—one company sharing a single phone line, a single modem, and a single dial-up account to an Internet service provider. This is the magic of IP forwarding and masquerading, a technique that makes all hosts in a network appear as though they are coming from the single, Internet-connected Linux server.

"Online" means many things to many people. Arguably, e-mail is still the most powerful reason to provide company-wide access to the Internet. Consequently, the requirements will no doubt include providing e-mail as well as the ability to browse the Web. Furthermore, you can define who gets access and to what.

The solution I will present here actually consists of two major components. One is the technical side, the nuts and bolts of using Linux to create this simple, powerful server. The second is business and marketing related and involves the services upon which all our nuts and bolts will attach. This is where we will start. The search for a friendly Internet service provider (ISP) begins.

What to Look for in an ISP

One of the great things about this solution is that you can keep the costs of Internet access for a small company down to a minimum. Depending on your Internet service provider (ISP), service costs can range from a few dollars a month for a casual dial-up connection to a few hundred dollars a month for dedicated, 24/7 service.

I recommend that you contact the smaller ISPs in your area. Strange as it may seem, smaller ISPs often provide more service options than their larger competitors. Over time, I have also found that smaller providers are often extremely knowledgeable. Their small staffs mean that their people truly understand the nature of the service they provide and technical support is second nature to them.

While Internet accounts at both large and small providers generally make it easy to share a single phone line and dial-up connection, you may find your choices a bit more limited if you want to provide mail as well as Web services. This is particularly true if you want to have your mail delivered to your domain address. For example, you want all people in your office to get mail addressed to `user_name@mycompany.dom`. Don't despair. There are still a couple of ways to do this.

Some ISPs will allow a domain or multidrop mailbox. This means that any and all mail directed to `mycompany.dom` gets delivered to the individual who has the dial-up account. You then use a program like `fetchmail` (more on that later) to disassemble the messages and deliver them to the individuals to whom they are addressed. Some ISPs will also set up individual accounts for the various people in your office. The first of these options, the multidrop mailbox, is the most flexible because you can create new users or mail aliases locally on the fly.

The single most flexible option involves a 24-hour connection to your ISP through a dedicated access service. This is also, unfortunately, the most expensive option.

Setting Up Your ISP Dial-up Connection with diald

For automatic, friendly dialing, you are going to use a program called `diald`. It is also possible to use the `pppd` program's own dial-on-demand capabilities, but it is not as flexible, especially when considering limited time connections.

Let's work with the idea that you have purchased a dial-up PPP connection from a mythical company called "we-are-an-isp.com." This connection provides us with a multidrop domain mailbox and is limited to 200 hours per month. While that may seem like a fair amount, you don't want to stretch that too far. That is why you will use `diald` for your dialer.

You should have everything you need already installed on your machine. The one exception is the `diald` program. It was not included in my Red Hat distribution, but it was present on my Caldera 2.3 CD, so you should check before deciding if you need to hunt it down. `diald`, by the way, is an intelligent dial-on-demand program originally written by Eric Schenk. Eric has since handed over the reins to a new maintainer, Mike Jagdis. Look for links to Mike's site in the Resources section at the end of this chapter.

You are going to set up `diald` with a minimum of fuss. On this system, I am using an ordinary 56K modem on my COM1 port. You can either install `diald` directly from the `tarred` and `gzipped` distribution from the `diald` Web site, or you can pick up one of the binary distributions that are available. The main control file for `diald` is `/etc/diald.conf`. The one from my system looks like this:

```
#
# Diald configuration script for Internet gateway
#
mode ppp
connect "/etc/ppp/ppp-on-diald"
device /dev/ttyS0
speed 115200
modem
crtscts
local 192.168.1.150
remote 192.168.1.151
dynamic
defaultroute
include /usr/lib/diald/standard.filter
```

I'll show you the connect script in a moment, but for now, I'd like to point out what some of these things mean. In particular, look at the `local`, `remote`, and `dynamic` entries. For `diald` to work, it sets up a temporary SLIP connection that "waits" for requests from the network.

> **Note:** SLIP is the Serial Line Interface Protocol, another means of connecting through an ISP or setting up a dial-up network connection. It has, for the most part, been replaced by PPP, the Point-to-Point Protocol. It's extremely unusual these days to find an ISP that supports SLIP but not PPP.

For instance, a user clicking a link in a Web browser is just such a request. When the PPP connection is established, the `dynamic` entry tells `diald` to assign this new address to the PPP connection. Then, `defaultroute` tells `diald` to assign the new address as the default route to the Internet.

And now, the connect script:

```
#!/bin/sh
```

```
#
# This is the diald connect script.
#
exec /usr/sbin/chat -v                                    \
      TIMEOUT              3                                    \
      ABORT             '\nBUSY\r'                              \
      ABORT             '\nNO ANSWER\r'                         \
      ABORT             '\nRINGING\r\n\r\nRINGING\r'            \
      ''          \rATZ                                   \
      'OK-+++\c-OK'     ATH0                                    \
      TIMEOUT           30                                      \
      OK          ATDTmy_isp_phone_number                 \
      CONNECT           ''                                      \
      ogin:--ogin:             Pmy_isp_login              \
      ssword:           my_isp_passwd
```

Incidentally, the `ogin` (or `ssword`) is not a typo. You don't need to scan for the entire string for this to work. Furthermore, some sites may use "Login" while others use "login." Shortening the prompt to something more or less common to all simplifies things.

This script must be executable. All you need to do is substitute your ISP's phone number as well as the login name and password.

To start `diald`, use the following command:

```
# /usr/sbin/diald
```

The `diald` program runs as a daemon and, under normal circumstances, requires no further user intervention. You may want to include `diald` in the start-up scripts so that it runs on boot up.

Automatic Remote Mail Pickup with fetchmail

`fetchmail` is a remote mail collection agent written by Eric S. Raymond. This package is so popular that it is included in virtually every Linux distribution and is available in source form to run on many different flavors of UNIX. This great package pretty much handles any and every mail-collection protocol out there. You'll only concern yourself with POP3 at this time. POP3 is still the most popular and common mail-collection protocol offered by ISPs. You can set `fetchmail` to log in with your ISP login and password and collect mail for a single account or many accounts. One of the really great things about `fetchmail` is that it can take apart the header information of incoming e-mail messages and decipher their intended location.

At this time, I would like to point out that the author of `fetchmail` does not wholeheartedly recommend this method. The reason for this is that not all messages are so easily decoded, and some header information may be lost or misinterpreted. Messages delivered through large mailing lists where the To:

information is buried or rewritten represent the most common problem area for `fetchmail`. For the most part, and for most day-to-day messaging, you should find `fetchmail` more than capable. Any mail messages that cannot be delivered wind up in the root mailbox where the system administrator can reroute them at a later time.

`fetchmail` can be run as a daemon at system start-up, from the command line, or from a shell script run through a `cron` job. The first option is by far the simplest but the third option enables you to add other options when `fetchmail` runs, such as a date and time stamp to confirm mail pickup. It also enables you to define exactly when `fetchmail` runs. For instance, in a number of environments where I have configured `fetchmail`, I am limited by a certain number of hours allotted by the dial-up account. Running `fetchmail` from `cron` enables me run it every 15 minutes during business hours and not at all otherwise.

Most of what you need to configure is done in a file called `.fetchmailrc`, which lives in the root directory. A sample script is provided with the distribution and is well documented. Using `vi` (or your favorite editor), edit the file `/root/.fetchmailrc`.

> **Note:** Information in this file is stored in plain text. Make sure that you set the permissions to 600 (read and write for root only).

Near the bottom of the file, there are several sample entries. You should see a paragraph that looks something like this:

```
# Use this for production
poll mail.myisp.dom with protocol pop3:
no dns, aka mycompany.dom mailserv.mycompany.dom
user myaccount with password mypassword to root bob carol
     ted alice natika marcel office info here;
```

The poll line defines the mail server connection. As you can see, I am connecting to `myisp.dom`'s mail server (as defined by the ISP) with the POP3 protocol. Then, in the next line, I tell my `fetchmail` program to not do DNS lookups for every address and list my mail server aliases. In other words, accept mail for those domains and host names listed.

Finally, have a look at the line that begins with "user." Substitute "myaccount" and "mypassword" with the login name and password your ISP has provided for you. Then, before the word "here," add your new users' names. Save the file and exit. You might want to put in other names than those listed here if these people don't work for you. Keep in mind that these have to be real names on your system or aliases in your `/etc/aliases` file. This is the case for the `office` and the `info` addresses.

If you want to run `fetchmail` as a daemon, look for or add the line that defines the interval in the `.fetchmailrc`. This is what it looks like:

```
set daemon 300
```

Then, start `fetchmail` in this manner:

```
fetchmail -d
```

You can also add the time interval directly to the `daemon` command if you don't want to include it in the `.fetchmailrc` file. That variant looks like this:

```
fetchmail -d 300
```

This means that `fetchmail` should run every five minutes. The *catch* here is that `diald` will bring your connection up every five minutes 24 hours a day. Even if you change the line to every 30 or 60 minutes, it still polls around the clock. I prefer to use a simple script like the one that follows along with a `crontab` entry to control when `fetchmail` runs. I call the script (strangely enough) `pickup.mail`. It also leaves a time and date stamp so that if something were to go wrong with mail pickup, I could verify the last time that `fetchmail` ran successfully.

```
#
# Pick up mail using fetchmail
#
/usr/bin/fetchmail -a -s
echo "Fetchmail ran at `date`" > /usr/local/.Admin/fmranlast
```

The `-s` flag means that `fetchmail` should run silently, while the `-a` flag tells `fetchmail` to pick up all mail regardless of its status on the server (it may have been read on the mail host itself with a reader such as `pine`). As I mentioned, I run `fetchmail` from a `cron` job. The following `crontab` entry ensures that mail pickup (which does a call to `diald` and brings up my connection) happens Monday through Friday, 7:00 AM to 7:00 PM, at 30-minute intervals—essentially during business hours, thus preserving my limited hours.

```
0,30 7-19 * * 1-5 /usr/local/.Admin/pickup.mail 1> /dev/null 2> /dev/null
```

IP Forwarding and Masquerading

Modern stock distributions of Linux have made things much simpler for setting up a networked office. For instance, it used to be that IP forwarding and masquerading needed to be compiled into the kernel after the fact. This wonderful means of sharing access has long since left the experimental stage and now comes built in. This doesn't mean that you will find IP forwarding pre-enabled.

Let's look at a Red Hat system for an example of this. In the directory `/etc/sysconfig`, you will find a file called `network` that quite simply defines the basic network rules. The one for my Internet server looks something like this:

```
NETWORKING=yes
FORWARD_IPV4=yes
HOSTNAME=mailserv.mycompany.dom
DOMAINNAME=mycompany.dom
GATEWAY=
GATEWAYDEV=
```

The important line here is the second one. FORWARD_IPV4 is by default set to "no." To enable an office of PCs to access your single dial-up connection, you need to set this to "yes" and restart networking. Notice also that GATEWAY and GATEWAYDEV are not set. As mentioned earlier, these are set when `diald` brings up the PPP connection.

On the PC side, you should make sure that your Internet gateway is set up as the default gateway for the server. On your Windows 9*x* system, click the Start button and then select Settings, Control Panel. Double-click the Network icon and then double-click the TCP/IP configuration line. If you have one for your network card and a dial-up networking TCP/IP line, make sure you pick the one for your network card. Finally, click the Gateway tab and add the address for your Internet server. In this example, the address is 192.168.1.100.

Finally, turn IP forwarding on for the PCs on your network. Please note that this example shows the simplest possible form of the `ipchains` commands for external routing of an internal network. I will talk about this in more detail in Chapter 25.

```
# Set up IP forwarding and IP masquerading using ipchains
#
/sbin/ipchains -A forward -j MASQ -s 192.168.22.0/24 -d 0.0.0.0/0
```

DNS Revisited

I covered DNS in Chapter 18, but I'll give you a very simple example for this discussion. For those who do not run full-fledged, round-the-clock domains on their sites, I'll explore a scaled-down DNS. The simple answer is to run the caching-only name server with a simple entry in your `/etc/resolv.conf`. A single line (or two) pointing to your ISP's name server will serve under the circumstances.

```
nameserver XXX.XXX.XXX.XXX          (ISP's first DNS)
nameserver YYY.YYY.YYY.YYY          (ISP's second DNS)
```

You can also set your Windows 9*x* PCs to point to your ISP's name server by adding DNS entries through your control panel. In this example, you point to the Internet server as your primary name server.

If you want to put together a simple (but completely functional) DNS for your site, visit my own Web site (check the Resources section at the end of this chapter for the URL). The tarball is called `easydns.tar.gz`. Change the references to reflect your domain and ISP name server entries, and you are all set.

Putting It All Together

After making all these changes, it's probably time to reset your network. On my Red Hat system, I simply stop and restart both networking and `inetd`.

```
# /etc/rc.d/init.d/network stop
# /etc/rc.d/init.d/inet stop
# /etc/rc.d/init.d/inet start
# /etc/rc.d/init.d/network start
```

This assumes that I am logged in directly to my server. If I am logged in through the network, the first line will pretty much bring an end to the rest of my commands.

Because you will no doubt want all these services activated at boot time, it would be wise to add them to one of the boot-up scripts. I recommend the `rc.local` file (see Chapter 6). If you are following this example, the things you need to start are `diald` and your IP forwarding and masquerading. If you want around-the-clock mail checking, add your `fetchmail` process to the start-up script as well.

Basic Firewall Services

Once you expose yourself and your company to the Internet, you will want to institute some basic security at the very least. *Nearly* bulletproof security is not impossible with your freeware Internet gateway.

> **Security Warning:** At no point should you become complacent about network security. Basic measures can be *very* effective. You may look at your logs (see Chapter 23) and decide that your security is doing a great job of refusing and controlling access to your system. But stay on top of things. The following information is designed to provide you with a quick and dirty start to security and the chapters that follow (Chapters 24 and 25 in particular) explore security in much greater detail. Don't pass them up.

That said, it is fairly easy to say "Stay out!" with a few simple configurations. TCP wrappers are a means by which you can control access to network services provided by your machine. Those services that can be controlled by the wrapper are listed in your /etc/inetd.conf file. The giveaway is this: Programs controlled by the TCP wrapper have a listing with tcpd in the line. For example, here's the line dealing with the rlogin service:

```
#login    stream  tcp     nowait  root    /usr/sbin/tcpd    in.rlogind
```

As you can see, the line is commented out, which means that this service is not available to the outside world. The problem is that it is not available to my inside network either. If I want to turn on that service (by uncommenting the line and restarting the inetd process), I can use the TCP wrapper to regulate access.

Access through the TCP wrapper is handled by two main files: /etc/hosts.allow and /etc/hosts.deny. If you want to maintain services in your inetd.conf file open to you but cut off from the outside world, you start by adding this line to /etc/hosts.deny:

```
ALL:ALL
```

Simply put, it means stop *all* people everywhere from accessing your system. Because that means your internal site as well, the next step is to add an entry for your local network in the /etc/hosts.allow file. This network, as you may recall, was an internal Class C network using the format 192.168.1.xxx. To be safe, you should also add the localhost address for the Linux server itself.

```
ALL: 127.0.0.1
ALL: 192.168.1.
```

In other words, allow all localhost access and all local network traffic as well. To activate these changes, you should now reset the inetd process.

Setting Up the Mail Server with Linux

At this point, your server is connecting happily to the Internet, and if you so choose, you can even surf the Net from a browser on the server. If you are running from the console outside of the graphical environment, you can even use a little program called lynx to surf. The world is yours. Unfortunately, it is yours alone and you are trying to connect an entire office through one machine. In the following section, I'll show you how to get your users' PCs set up to share your new Internet connection and to allow them to send and receive e-mail.

Defining the Network

To get the e-mail part of this running, you'll continue with your hypothetical network consisting of your hot new Linux system and six PCs. The Linux server is at address 192.168.1.100 while the PCs are at addresses 192.168.1.31 through 192.168.1.36. You are using the private internal network addressing scheme as defined in RFC1918 (see Resources section). You'll call the Linux server "gateway." The fully qualified domain name is `gateway.mycompany.dom`.

Each PC will have its own mail client. All mail traffic will go through your Linux server. There should be little here that you cannot directly relate to your specific distribution. Any RPM-based distribution (Caldera, Turbolinux, Mandrake) will behave in much the same way as I describe.

The Components

On the server end, the basic components are a mail transport agent (MTA) (usually `sendmail`), and a local delivery agent (LDA) (usually a program called `deliver`). The client side consists primarily of a mail user agent (MUA), which usually lives on the user's PC. This will be your favorite e-mail package. I often recommend Pegasus Mail, a great Windows e-mail package that just happens to be freely distributed (though not GPL'ed). Your MUA can also be something like Netscape Communicator, Eudora, or Microsoft Outlook.

I should mention that you do have one other alternative that would make things amazingly simple, though not as exciting from the user perspective. Your users could connect to the server (with `ssh`, for instance), log into a shell prompt, and use a text-only mailer, such as `pine` or `elm`. No fancy Windows packages and no GUIs. Going that route requires no MUA setup.

The packages you need (if not already installed) are as follows:

```
sendmail (your MTA)
imap (for POP mail services)
```

I've opted for `sendmail` rather than `qmail` (or some other alternative) because `sendmail` is pretty much universal. My second reason is that `sendmail` will likely already be installed. `imap`, on the other hand, was not part of my default Red Hat installation. Because the `imap` package contains the POP3 server, I will spend a moment to deal with it.

Setting Up the POP3 Server

The POP3 server listens for mail pickup requests from users. To check if you have `imap` installed, use this version of the `rpm` command:

```
# rpm -q imap
```

If the system responds with something like `imap-4.5-3`, the package is already loaded. If not, mount your distribution CD-ROM and install `imap`.

```
# mount /mnt/cdrom
# cd /mnt/cdrom/RedHat/RPMS
# rpm -ivh imap-somereleasenumber.i386.rpm
```

One last thing before I leave POP3 and move on: You will probably also need to activate those services in `inetd.conf`. Here's the line pertaining to POP3 before I change it in `/etc/inetd.conf`:

```
#pop-3    stream   tcp     nowait   root     /usr/sbin/tcpd    ipop3d
```

Uncomment the line by removing the hash mark (#) at the beginning. You will now need to refresh the `inetd` process in order for this change to take effect. Find `inetd`'s process ID and send a `SIGHUP` to it. Careful with that `-1`! Remember that forgetting the hyphen in this case could down the whole system because `init`, the master process, has a PID of 1.

```
kill -1 `cat /var/run/inetd.pid`
```

The next step is to configure `sendmail`.

Setting Up sendmail

Depending on how your account is set up with your ISP, the domain name of your server may be something like `dhch3-ip1.theirdomain.dom`, which is probably not what you want in setting up your e-mail gateway. For a return address, user "fred" would wind up as `fred@dhcp3-ip.theirdomain.dom` when sending mail from the local system. You can have your `sendmail` program put in your domain name by making the one modification that I will recommend in your `sendmail` configuration file.

Using your favorite editor, open `/etc/sendmail.cf` and look for the following lines:

```
##################
#   local info   #
##################
```

```
Cwlocalhost
# file containing names of hosts for which we receive e-mail
Fw/etc/sendmail.cw

# my official domain name
# ... define this only if sendmail cannot automatically determine
your domain
#Dj$w.Foo.COM
Djmycompany.dom

CP.

# "Smart" relay host (may be null)
DSlocalhost
```

Notice the part that contains "my official domain name." The line that reads `Dj$w.Fo.COM` has been copied and rewritten with your domain name to define the `Dj` macro. A macro in `sendmail` parlance is very much like an environment variable in your Bourne, Korn, or C shell. The `Dj` macro references your canonical host name. For this example, call your domain `mycompany.dom`.

That is the only change you want to make to your `/etc/sendmail.cf` file. The next file you need to modify is `/etc/sendmail.cw`. This file contains a list of all the domains and systems that your server will accept mail for. For instance, if you edit the file with your favorite editor (`vi`?) and add your domain name (`mycompany.dom`) and the localhost name (`localhost`), you wind up with this simple file:

```
# sendmail.cw - include all aliases for your machine here.
gateway
gateway.mycompany.dom
mycompany.dom
localhost
```

This tells your `sendmail` daemon to accept mail messages addressed to either `user@localhost` or `user@mycompany.dom`, or any of the aliases you have set up.

Next, you will need to edit `/etc/mail/relay-domains`. One of the great annoyances of modern e-mail is *spam,* those unwanted bits of advertising that seem to flood your e-mail box. My personal favorites are the ones that promise to help me make money fast. Particularly galling are the spammers who use other people's e-mail servers to route their mail traffic. The modern incarnations of `sendmail` make it difficult for spammers to use your machine as a relay. In fact, unless otherwise specified, `sendmail` will refuse to deliver messages from machines or domains it has not been told about. That is where the `relay-domains` file comes into play.

Edit the file and add the following:

```
localhost
127.
```

```
mycompany.dom
192.168.1.
```

This should cover all hosts in your small, networked office, including any need you may have for using `sendmail` to relay messages on the server itself. Make sure you include the dot at the end of your localhost domain address (127.) and at the end of your private network and domain (192.168.1.).

Stopping and Restarting sendmail

After making these configuration changes, you need to restart `sendmail`. The different distributions will vary slightly. If you are using Red Hat or Turbolinux, simply do the following:

```
/etc/rc.d/init.d/sendmail restart
```

If your distribution of choice is Caldera, you can use the following command:

```
/etc/rc.d/init.d/mta restart
```

Caldera defines the MTA in "options" under `/etc/mta`.

If all else fails, you can kill the `sendmail` process and restart it the old-fashioned way by issuing this command:

```
/usr/sbin/sendmail -bd -q5m
```

Guess what? That's all you really need to do with `sendmail` and `imap` in order to send and receive mail on your small network. If it weren't for the fact that there are other pieces to the mail server puzzle, I could stop here.

Your DNS Setup

For `sendmail` to route mail properly, it must be able to locate other machines throughout the world. To do this, it uses a DNS. Usually, the standard Linux installation fires up with a DNS already present. This is a very simple version called a "caching name server," which I discussed in Chapter 18.

Setting Up Users and Aliases

You can add users to your Linux system with the `adduser` command I discussed in Chapter 7. See how it is all coming together? If you are running a desktop environment such as KDE, you have access to `kuser`, a nice user and group maintenance program, while GNOME provides `linuxconf`. I confess that for user maintenance (as well as many system administration functions) I still prefer doing it the old-fashioned way—at the command line.

So use adduser and add your users' names. Remember that you must be logged in as the root user to do this.

```
adduser user_name
```

You then assign a password with the passwd command.

```
passwd user_name
```

One of the things you will likely want to do is create an alias for your office (or perhaps several aliases). This is a fairly simple process. Aliases are also useful if you want to add something like sales@mycompany.dom that you want redirected to two salespeople. Another useful alias, office@mycompany.dom, sends mail to everybody. Here's how it's done.

The file you need to edit is called /etc/aliases. Using your favorite editor, open the file. The format of the aliases file is simple.

```
alias_name:    real_name1,real_name2,real_name3, . . .
```

The alias_name part is the name you are creating the alias for. In the preceding example, this is "sales" or "office." After the colon, press Tab (or just insert spaces) and type your list of user names separated by commas. White space at the beginning of a line implies the continuation of an alias. Here's an example using "office":

```
office: john,myrtle,bonnie,gilbert,elvis,tux
```

The six e-mail addresses listed after "office:" will receive a copy of any mail addressed to office@mycompany.dom. Now, save your work and run the following command:

```
/usr/sbin/sendmail -bi
```

The -bi part stands for "build index." You can also just run the newaliases command, which is just a synonym for -bi. Running either version of this command should return a message something like this:

```
/etc/aliases: 14 aliases, longest 10 bytes, 152 bytes total
```

Your new aliases are ready to roll.

Now you have your server with sendmail and a super-simple DNS set up, your users have been created (in a virtual sense, that is), and you have aliases for the office and sales team. The only thing left is your clients.

Setting Up Your Client MUAs

After spending all this time on the server side, it is finally time to tie it all in together by bringing your clients online.

The number of ways that a user can collect his or her mail has changed and continues to do so. A popular newcomer to the field is the browser-based e-mail package. Still, most people in an office environment will have some kind of preferred e-mail package. Earlier, I mentioned Pegasus Mail and Netscape Communicator, among others. Because your e-mail server will both send and receive mail, your MUA configuration is simple.

If you are using Netscape Communicator for e-mail, click Edit, Preferences. When the Preferences window pops up, click Mail and Newsgroups in the Category menu. There are two sets of settings you will want to change. The first is Identity (see Figure 21.1) and the second is Mail Servers (see Figure 21.2).

In the Identity dialog box, enter your full name (Tux M. Penguin) and e-mail address (`tux@mycompany.dom`). At a minimum, this is all you need. In the Mail Servers dialog box, click the Add button to specify an incoming (POP3) mail server. You will get another dialog box asking you to specify the

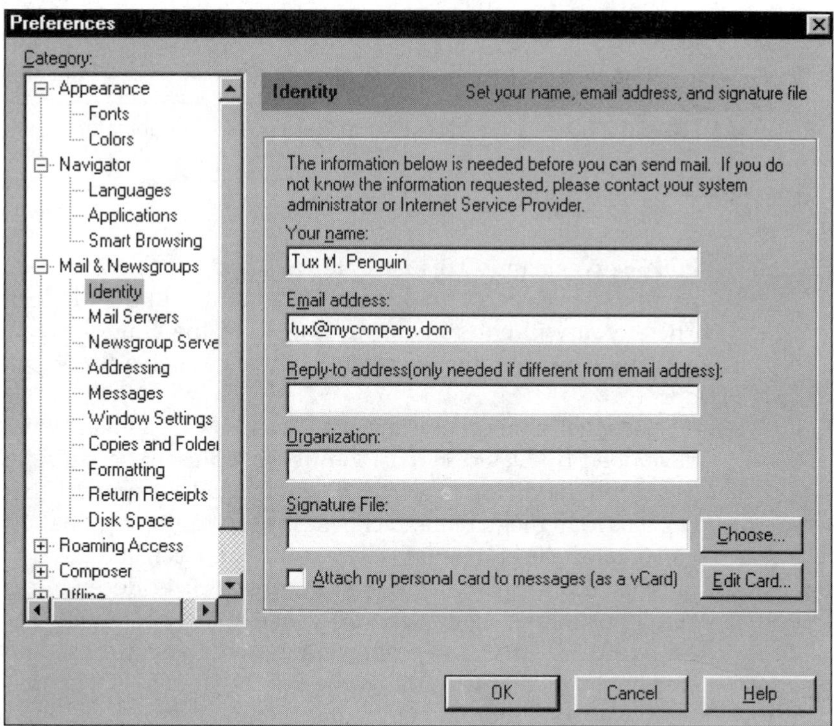

FIGURE 21.1 E-mail Identity setup in Netscape Communicator

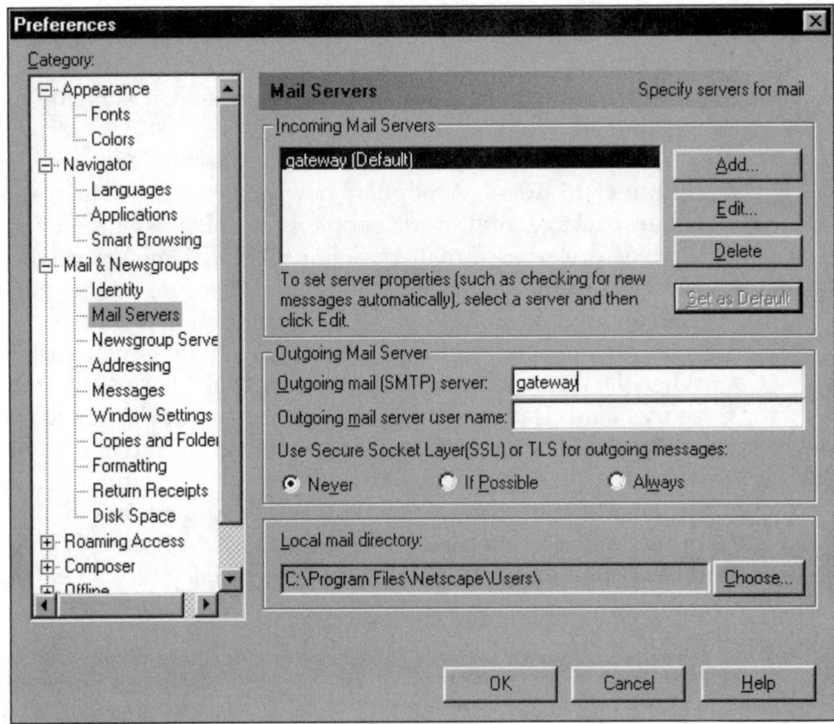

FIGURE 21.2 Mail Servers setup in Netscape Communicator

POP3 server name. This is "gateway" and the Server Type is POP. The user name in this case is "tux." Click OK to return to the Mail Servers dialog box. There, you will enter "gateway" again in the Outgoing mail (SMTP) server text box. The outgoing user name is Tux's e-mail address, `tux@mycompany.dom`.

Let's look at another example: Pegasus Mail, a great Windows e-mail client developed by David Harris. Figure 21.3 presents a snapshot of the Internet Mail Options dialog box from Pegasus Mail version 3.1 (click Tools on your Pegasus Mail menu bar and choose Internet options). On the first tab (General) you enter the user's e-mail address—in this case, `tux@mycompany.dom`.

The second tab (pictured in Figure 21.3) is Receiving (POP3). For your POP3 host, enter "gateway," your machine's hostname. The user name and password are "tux" and whatever password you assigned him when you created him earlier. Finally, under the Sending (SMTP) tab, you only need to enter "gateway" one more time, because your server is handling both the sending and receiving of mail.

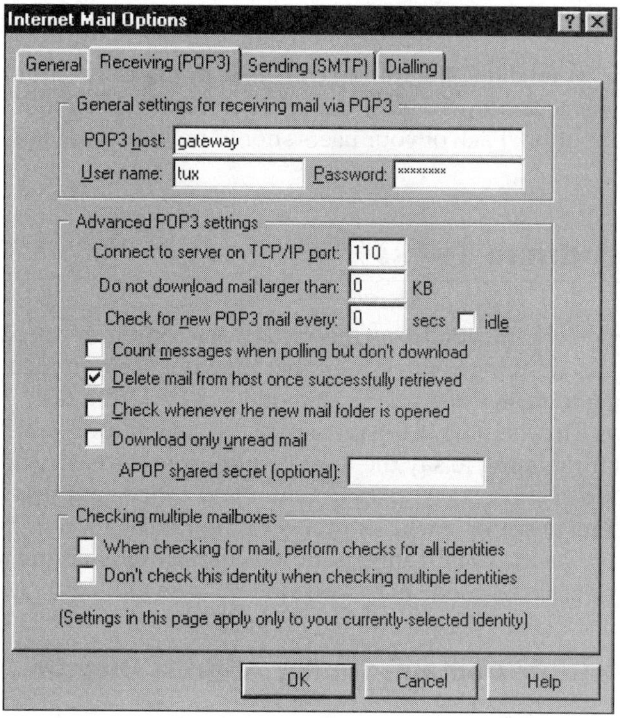

FIGURE 21.3 POP3 mail configuration in Pegasus Mail

I've included two examples to show you that most Windows e-mail clients follow a similar setup. You need the SMTP and POP3 host defined, a user name and password to pick up mail and, of course, an e-mail address.

One last little bit.

Because you are not setting up a DNS at this time, the PCs need to have the address for your gateway in the `HOSTS` file. This file is located in the `C:\WINDOWS` directory. Edit the file by clicking the Start button, selecting Run, and typing this command:

```
EDIT C:\WINDOWS\HOSTS
```

Then add this single line:

```
192.168.1.100  gateway.mycompany.dom gateway
```

Click File in the editor and choose Save, Quit.

Let's Send Some Mail

Bring up your mail client and send mail to the office. In the To field, enter `office@mycompany.dom`. Enter some clever subject and text, and then click the Send button. Each of your users should now receive mail.

Not-So-Stupid sendmail Tricks

Once your organization becomes relatively complex, you will find yourself wanting to do things with e-mail that may not seem immediately important. Becoming a master of `sendmail` alone is a daunting task. This is a massive program. The classic, 1,000-page `sendmail` reference from O'Reilly & Associates is intimidating to say the least. In my experience, you don't need to have every one of those 1,000 pages memorized to create a useful, simple e-mail server. I just wanted a few shortcuts to the information in the following sections, but I had to dig through hundreds of pages to find them.

Let's get to the good stuff, shall we?

The Multiple Domain, Similar Address Dilemma

Imagine for a moment that you have decided to register several domains, all of which reside on the same machine. After all, your Linux system is more than capable of handling the load and you don't want to bother starting from scratch for what might be low-traffic domains anyway. What you do want, though, is a standard method of getting information-only mail to your virtual companies. You might even want that mail to go to different places. Here's what you want in a nutshell:

```
info@mycompany.dom
info@myseconddomain.dom
info@myinfosite.dom
```

Now, you can only have one "info" login on your system. If "info" is not a user on your system, you could add an info alias to direct info mail to a real user (rather than creating the pseudo-user). For instance, if "mary" was to get info's mail, you would have a `/etc/aliases` entry like this:

```
info:      mary@somedomain.dom
```

The problem comes when you want all these different info addresses to go to different people. You can't have two alias entries for info. The way to get around this is to use `sendmail`'s `virtusertable` feature. Look for this line in your `/etc/sendmail.cf` configuration file:

```
Kvirtuser hash -o /etc/mail/virtusertable
```

This will give you the path to the virtual user table and the means to set up these different domains with equivalent users. The format of the file is simple.

```
username@somedomain.dom        realuser@someotherdomain.dom
```

In the case of my info example, my `virtusertable` would look like this:

```
info@mycompany.dom             mary@localdomain.dom
info@myseconddomain.dom        tom@remotedomain.dcom
info@myinfosite.dom            natika@bigschool.edu
```

Stop and restart `sendmail` and everything should now work as advertised.

The Multidrop Domain

Here's another scenario. Pretend that mail bound for `myinfosite.org` was to all go to one user because there is only one user at `myinfosite.org`. You don't want to lose important mail if people send to that address but use "Webmaster" when you only have "info" set up as an alias. Generally, mail that is improperly addressed is probably not mail you want, but if you want to play it safe, how do you make sure that all mail gets through no matter who it is addressed to within that domain?

Strangely enough, the answer is the same as in the previous section—namely, your old friend `virtusertable`. Here's an entry that directs all mail for `myinfosite.dom` to `andy@mycompany.dom`:

```
@myinfosite.dom                andy@mycompany.dom
```

Once again, stop and restart `sendmail` and you are on your way.

Stop the Spam!

Here's a great tip for getting rid of some of the spam that keeps pounding your mail server. In case you've been away for a while, *spam* is a euphemism for unwanted e-mail. The sheer bulk of spam directed at your server can slow things down to a crawl. A new technique used by spammers involves sending out e-mail to thousands of people on your server and just hoping that some of the e-mail addresses are valid. Because they are already relaying through a site other than their own anyway, they don't care if some of it bounces. It doesn't affect them. The problem is that it affects you.

```
# privacy flags
O PrivacyOptions=authwarnings
```

Add a comma and the word "goaway" to the PrivacyOptions flag.

```
O PrivacyOptions=authwarnings,goaway
```

This flag switches on a number of options that require a valid connection to identify itself properly. It also refuses VRFY queries, which a potential cracker might use to locate valid user names on your system. The only downside is that someone who tries to send e-mail to a nonvalid address on your system will find that his or her message just falls into the ether.

Another trick is to block access to e-mail from particularly annoying domains. Here's an example. Some time ago, I dealt with an incident of bulk e-mails being sent through a relay. The format of the spam was this: hundreds of e-mail addresses to the same domain, mostly to users that did not exist on that system anyhow. Presumably, the spammers were looking to hit at least some legitimate e-mail addresses.

Once again, the solution is a sendmail-specific trick. Start by editing your /etc/mail/access file, the same one you used to allow local relay of mail.

```
spammer.dom                    REJECT
```

The REJECT flag is just one of a few that can be used.

```
makemap hash /etc/mail/access.db < /etc/mail/access
```

Resources

Books

sendmail, by Bryan Costales with Eric Allman (Cambridge, MA: O'Reilly & Associates, 1997)

Web Sites

diald Web Site

http://diald.sourceforge.net/

Marcel's Website (for easydns files)

http://www.salmar.com/marcel/downloads.html

Netscape Communicator

http://home.netscape.com/computing/download/

Pegasus Mail (Windows)

http://www.pmail.com

RFC Editor

http://www.rfc-editor.org/

sendmail **Home Page**

http://www.sendmail.org/

Chapter 22

Integrating Windows with Linux

People will tell you that I spend a fair bit of time championing Linux as an alternative to Windows—perhaps to the level of evangelism. While I might argue about the ferocity with which I push Linux, I will admit that (for the time being, anyhow) it is a Windows world. One of the wonderful things about Linux is that it plays so well with Windows and Macintosh and Novell and . . . .

In this chapter, you are going to investigate the many ways in which Linux and Windows can play together. Using Samba, you'll see how easy it is to share files with Windows users using Windows networking. Heck, you'll even look at ways to replace that NT server with a Samba server and get on the road to a Windows-free existence.

"On the desktop as well?" you may ask. Indeed. With the tools available to today's Linux user, it is possible to boot into Linux and stay there and still run Windows. But first, you will learn to work with Windows, not against it.

An Introduction to Samba

Samba was originally developed by Andrew Trigdell in the land down under. Using the server message block (SMB) protocol, Samba makes it possible to share resources between a surprisingly wide variety of operating systems. SMB, like many networking protocols, continues to evolve as developers do what developers do. Consequently, the current version (or incarnation, if you prefer) of the SMB protocol is actually called CIFS, for common Internet file system.

In case you are wondering where NetBIOS fits into this picture, that's what SMB evolved from, although NetBIOS isn't a protocol so much as an application programming interface (API) designed to provide the building blocks for creating LAN software.

Samba can provide file-sharing services between Windows 95/98/NT, OS/2, VMS, AIX, HPUX, Linux (of course), and many others. While most people tend to think of Samba as the means by which you replace NT servers with Linux machines, Samba is much more flexible than that. For instance, the lone Windows PC in my office has Client for Microsoft Networks loaded so that it can share files in the Network Neighborhood.

Let's say that this PC (called "speedy") has a share called "natika_c," which is actually the entire C drive. From my Linux workstation, I can mount that drive like this (note: command is all on one line):

```
# mount -t smbfs -o username=natika,password=secret //speedy/natika_c
/mnt/natika
```

If I had a Samba share defined on my Linux server, I could mount it from another Linux server as though I was mounting a Windows share. I've got a small notebook (called "wiltravl") running Linux. On a somewhat larger server (called "testsys"), I've got Samba running. It has a share defined called "winstuff." You might recall that with NFS, I specified the file system type with the `-t` flag, passed the appropriate options, and told it about the directory I was mounting to (note: command is all on one line).

```
# mount -t smbfs -o username=marcel,password=itsasecret //testsys/
winstuff
```

If I use the `df` command, I will see the file system mounted as one of my local drives.

```
[root@wiltravl /root]# df
Filesystem           1k-blocks      Used Available Use% Mounted on
/dev/hda1              1517920   1405640     35172  98% /
/dev/hda5              2514172   1737840    648620  73% /data1
//testsys/winstuff      6109952   4611072   1498880  75% /mnt/winstuff
```

Pretty cool stuff. (Note: The ability to mount Windows shares on a Linux system is actually supported and configurable in the Linux kernel.) With Samba, you can also make printers available to the Windows machines on the network. By the way, nothing stops you from being able to use Samba-exported printers from Linux either. If you want to, you can even use Samba as your file-sharing system across your network, thereby replacing NFS.

Now that I have told you about some of the great things you can do with Samba, I suppose I should tell you how you go about doing them.

Getting and Building Samba

Just about every Linux distribution CD-ROM comes with a version of Samba, which you can install using `rpm` or `dpkg`, depending on your distribution. Debian users can, of course, use `apt-get` to pull in the latest distribution from the Debian site. But if you really want the latest and greatest, you need to get yourself to the Samba Web site (`http://www.samba.org/`).

Go to the Download section. The latest source is always called `samba-latest.tar.gz`. If you prefer, you can also find recent binaries for a variety of platforms, but they won't necessarily be as up-to-date as the source files. To build and install Samba from source, unpack the tarball into a temporary directory and follow these steps:

```
tar -xzvf samba-latest.tar.gz
```

This will create a directory suffixed with the current release number of the Samba source. When I wrote this chapter, the Samba code was sitting at version 2.0.7.

```
cd samba-2.0.7
more README
cd source
./configure
make
make install
```

By default, Samba will install in the `/usr/local/samba` directory. If you prefer to have it install in another directory, you can use the `--prefix=/path/to_dir` flag when you do the `./configure` step. After the installation has completed (assuming that you accepted the defaults), you need to create a Samba configuration file, which will live in `/usr/local/samba/lib`. The easiest way to do this is to copy the sample file provided along with the source into the appropriate directory.

```
cd /tmp_install_dir/samba-2.0.7/examples
cp smb.conf.default /usr/local/samba/lib/smb.conf
```

If you are working from a preinstalled Samba, particularly if you are running on an RPM-based system, you should look for a default `smb.conf` file in the `/etc` directory.

Using your favorite editor, open the `smb.conf` file and change these two parameters: `workgroup =` and `server string =`. For the `workgroup` parameter, I called mine "MYGROUP" with a server name of "Testsys Samba Server." Now, let's start the Samba daemons.

```
# /usr/local/samba/bin/smbd -D
# /usr/local/samba/bin/nmbd -D
```

You'll want to add this to your start-up scripts in `rc.local`. Say that your server is called "myserver." To test Samba and see if you have done everything right, type the following command:

```
/usr/local/samba/bin/smbclient -L myserver
```

If everything worked smoothly, you should see something like this appear on your screen:

```
added interface ip=192.168.1.100 bcast=192.168.1.255 nmask=255.255.255.0
Password:
Anonymous login successful
Domain=[MYGROUP] OS=[Unix] Server=[Samba 2.0.7]
Sharename      Type      Comment
          ---------      ----      -------
          IPC$           IPC       IPC Service (Testsys Samba Server
          lp             Printer
          hp710c         Printer
          colour         Printer
          win            Printer

          Server               Comment
          ---------            -------

          Workgroup            Master
          ---------            -------
```

Notice anything interesting when you did that? Without doing anything other than starting Samba with a valid configuration file, your printers are available as resources on the network. It is not necessary to define each printer individually—Samba takes for granted that they are shared resources (you are running a server, after all).

You can also use your Windows workstations to test all this. Keep in mind that you need to have Client for Microsoft Networks installed on the PC in question. If you are doing this on an existing network of Windows PCs, this is very likely the case. Double-click the Network Neighborhood icon and then double-click Entire Network. You should see the workgroup you just specified in your list. If you don't see it right away, don't despair. Windows can take a while to notice that a new workgroup or server has been added to the Network Neighborhood. If you are in a hurry, reboot the Windows PC.

A Note on Passwords

Before you continue to configure Samba to make it really useful, you need to look at the subject of SMB password encryption. It's okay. It won't hurt much.

Later versions of Windows 95 through Windows 98 (as well as later versions of NT) started using encrypted passwords, thus not allowing connections to or from servers that did not support SMB encryption. When a Windows workstation wanted to authenticate with a server (whether NT or Samba), it used to pass plain-text passwords. This made life very simple when setting up Samba servers. Unfortunately, that is no longer the case. What this means to you is that you have a decision to make on how you will deal with passwords, because Linux passwords use a different encryption method than Windows passwords.

The first way to address this is to go back to nonencrypted passwords. If you are running a small network with only one or two PCs, this isn't a bad option. You can go back to nonencrypted passwords with a modification to the Windows 9*x* registry, as follows:

1. Start the Registry Editor by clicking the Start button, choosing Run, and typing `regedit`.
2. Double-click `HKEY_LOCAL_MACHINE`.
3. Now, walk down the registry structure and locate the following: `System/CurrentControlSet/Services/VxD/VNETSUP`
4. From the menu bar, choose Edit, New, DWORD Value.
5. Rename the new entry from `New Value #1` to `EnablePlainTextPassword`. Make sure you type it exactly—case is important.
6. Press Enter and then double-click your new entry. A dialog box appears that enables you to change the value of this new key. Set the value to `1`.
7. Close the registry editor and reboot.

The other method is to have Samba use encrypted passwords. In a larger network, it doesn't make sense to wander around to every PC in order to remove SMB encrypted authentication. To start using encrypted passwords, look for this section in the `smb.conf` file:

```
;   encrypt passwords = yes
```

The semicolon in front denotes a comment in the `smb.conf` file. To uncomment this parameter, simply remove the semicolon. The default file for these new passwords is called `/usr/local/samba/private/smbpasswd` if you built Samba from source (and used the defaults) or, as is often the case with distributions, it is `/etc/smbpasswd`. It is possible to override this with another parameter in the `smb.conf` file.

```
; smb passswd file = /etc/smbpasswd
```

If you want to use a different file, uncomment (or add) the following line with the appropriate path to your Samba password file. To add a Samba encrypted password for a user named "guitux" on my system, I use this command:

```
/usr/local/samba/bin/smbpasswd -a guitux
```

The system asks for a password and then asks for confirmation of that password. This part should seem quite familiar.

Configuring the Server

The order in which I've taken you through this process may seem a bit strange, but there is some method to my apparent madness. Samba is a complex beast with more parameters and configuration tweaks than I can possibly cover here. In fact, entire books have been devoted to Samba. Still, I can present you with the information you need to set up a server and start doing useful things. Because configuring a server exactly the way you want it will probably be a work in progress, you'll find that taking this process in stages reduces the chance of things simply not working. You have a working server and you've decided on a means of password authentication. Now, let's get to the meat.

The notion of using a server like this is to provide what Samba calls *shares:* exported directories that can be mounted by Windows (or Linux) systems as drives. In Windows, these drives are associated with a drive letter such as `M:`. There are also a number of configuration sections. Both shares and configuration sections are identified by a header in square brackets. Some of the ones you'll see as you look at your `smb.conf` file are as follows.

- `[global]`: These are parameters that affect the whole server and, as a result, everything that comes after it. You already encountered this when you set up encrypted passwords, a server name, and a workgroup. Because you are going to go ahead with the encrypted passwords, define your security as being at the user level.

  ```
  security = user
  ```

- `[homes]`: This section defines home directories for users connecting to the system. By using a specific configuration macro in this section (and there are many), the Samba server automatically attaches the client to a share based on the user name. To set up a home section in this way, use the following example.

  ```
  [homes]
     comment = Home Directories
     browseable = no
     path = /home/%u
     writable = yes
  ```

  The `%u` macro substitutes the user's name as they authenticate with the Samba server. This assumes that you use `/home` as your top-level directory for people's home directories (as discussed in Chapter 7). In a system where home directories start from `/disk2/users`, the path changes accordingly.
- `[printers]`: The printers section is magic. With Samba, you can define individual printers as shares, or you can have it automatically make any printers you have defined in your `/etc/printcap` file available without any additional work. I'll cover more on this when I talk about printing.

Go ahead and start using Samba's file sharing. Rather than testing this from a Windows PC at this time, try it from the command line. You do not have to be on a different machine to do this. Assume that you are still working with the user guitux.

```
smbclient //myserver/guitux -U guitux
```

The `-U` option specifies your Samba user login. Next, the system will prompt for that user's password. This is the Samba password you created earlier.

```
Password: ********
Domain=[MYGROUP] OS=[Unix] Server=[Samba 2.0.7]
smb: \>
```

At the prompt, you should be able to type `dir` and see the files in guitux's home directory. While you are there, type `help` at the `smb` prompt and have a look around.

The PC Side

The simplest setup involves setting up your Windows workstations to be part of the workgroup you have defined. Click the Start button, and then select Settings, Control Panel. Double-click the Network icon. When the dialog box comes up, the Configuration tab is visible.

Look for the list as defined by "The following network components are installed." Before you can do any kind of Samba networking, you need to have Client for Microsoft Networks installed. The same is true for File and Printer Sharing for Microsoft Networks. If these are missing, get your Windows CD (the files may actually be on your disk if the system was preinstalled) and perform the following steps.

For Client for Microsoft Networks, click Add, choose Client, and then click the Add button again. You'll get a list of clients on the right and their manufacturers on the left. Click Microsoft in the left-hand window. You should now see Client for Microsoft Networks at the top of that list. Click OK and you should find yourself back at the network components list.

To install File and Printer Sharing for Microsoft Networks, you do the same sort of thing you did to install Client for Microsoft Networks, except you specify Service instead of Client. When you get to the list of manufacturers, you should see it there. Click OK.

Now, click the Identification tab, and enter your PC's name and the workgroup name in the fields provided (see Figure 22.1). The Computer Description text box is just a comment field that would appear if you were to query the client in Network Neighborhood (choose View, Details) or with `smbclient -L`.

Printing with Samba

As I mentioned earlier, the basics of printer definition and sharing are in a paragraph called, strangely enough, `[printers]`. This is what mine looks like:

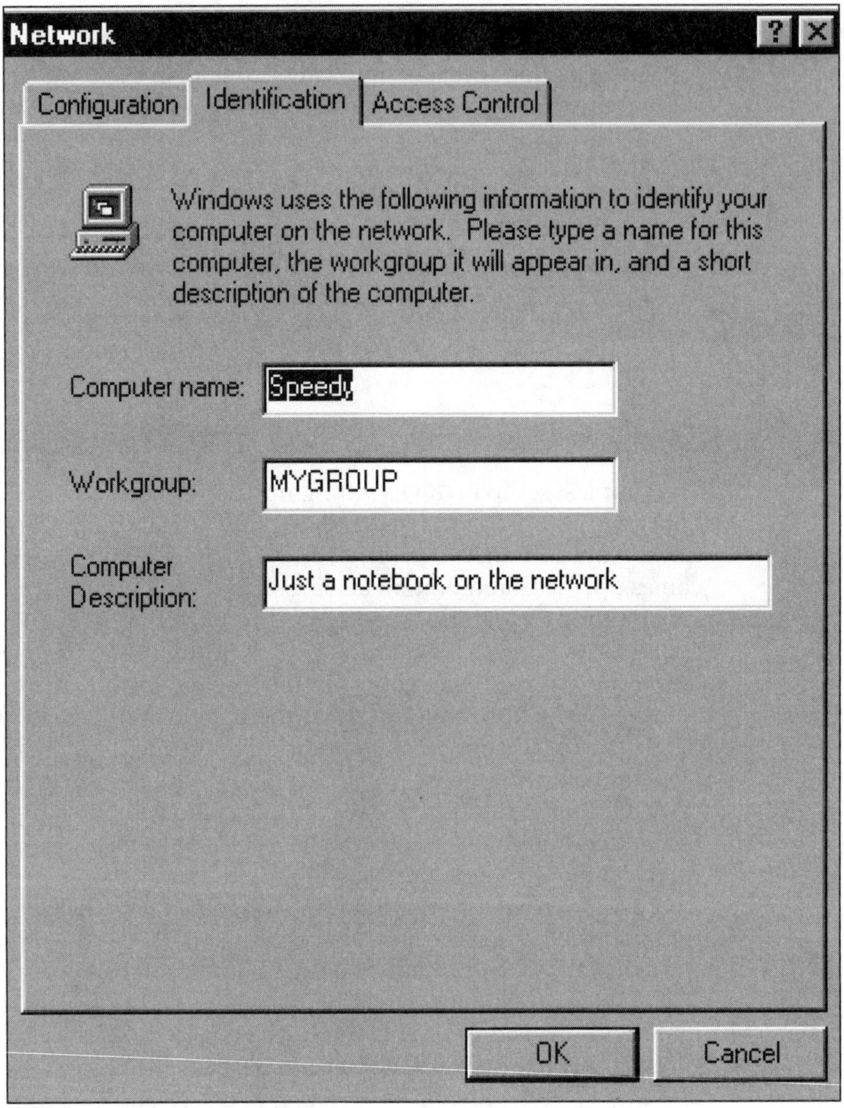

FIGURE 22.1 Specifying a workgroup in Windows networking

```
[printers]
        comment = My System Printers
        path = /var/spool/samba
        print ok = Yes
        guest ok = Yes
        browseable = No
```

The permissions here are pretty wide open. Anybody can browse these printers on the network and anybody can print to them. The `path =` variable is the temporary spool directory where print files are kept while they are printed. In the case of printers, `browseable` is set to No here because this isn't a share. All `/etc/printcap` printers will automagically appear in the browse list.

You might recall that when I checked on the newly created server by executing `smbclient -L new_server`, it automatically listed all the printers that were available. The normal method of creating a new printer in Windows is to click the Start button and then select Settings, Printers. Next, double-click the Add Printer icon and select a network-connected printer. When you click Browse, you get the Network Neighborhood list of servers that you can navigate to find the printer you want.

From the Linux side, you can also create print queues that print to remote Samba printers and I'll talk about that, but if you are in a hurry, you can do something even simpler and quicker. If all you want to do is momentarily use a printer on the network and it is managed by a Samba server, try the following trick. Pretend that you are on a notebook called "wltravl" (with no printers configured) and that you want to be able to do a quick text print to a printer on a server called "testsys." The printer is called "hplj5." From the command line, type this command:

```
smbclient //testsys/hplj5
```

Assuming that you still have your printer settings so that guest printing (or public access) is allowed, press Enter at the password prompt and you should see this:

```
Password:
Domain=[MYGROUP] OS=[Unix] Server=[Samba 2.0.7]
smb: \>
```

At the prompt, type `print` followed by the name of the file you want to print.

```
print /etc/profile
```

When you are done, all you have to do is type `quit` at the `smb: \>` prompt. The really cool thing about this is that you can do that with Windows printers on the network as well: If a PC has a printer that you need and that printer is shared on the network, you can do the very same thing. Do you want to see what a PC has available to share? Use `smbclient` with the `-L` option to list the information.

Printing from the Windows Client

To set up a printer in Windows, click the Start button and select Settings, Printers. Double-click the Add Printer icon. You should now see the Add Printer Wizard. Click Next, choose Network Printer by clicking the radio button, and then click Browse. You should see a window similar to the one in Figure 22.2 pop up.

You may need to click the plus sign (+) beside the appropriate host. Figure 22.2 shows a list of Samba printers serviced by a host called "Netgate." Click the appropriate printer and then click OK. The wizard then asks you for the printer type and manufacturer. At this point (because I don't know what printers you own), the rest is up to you.

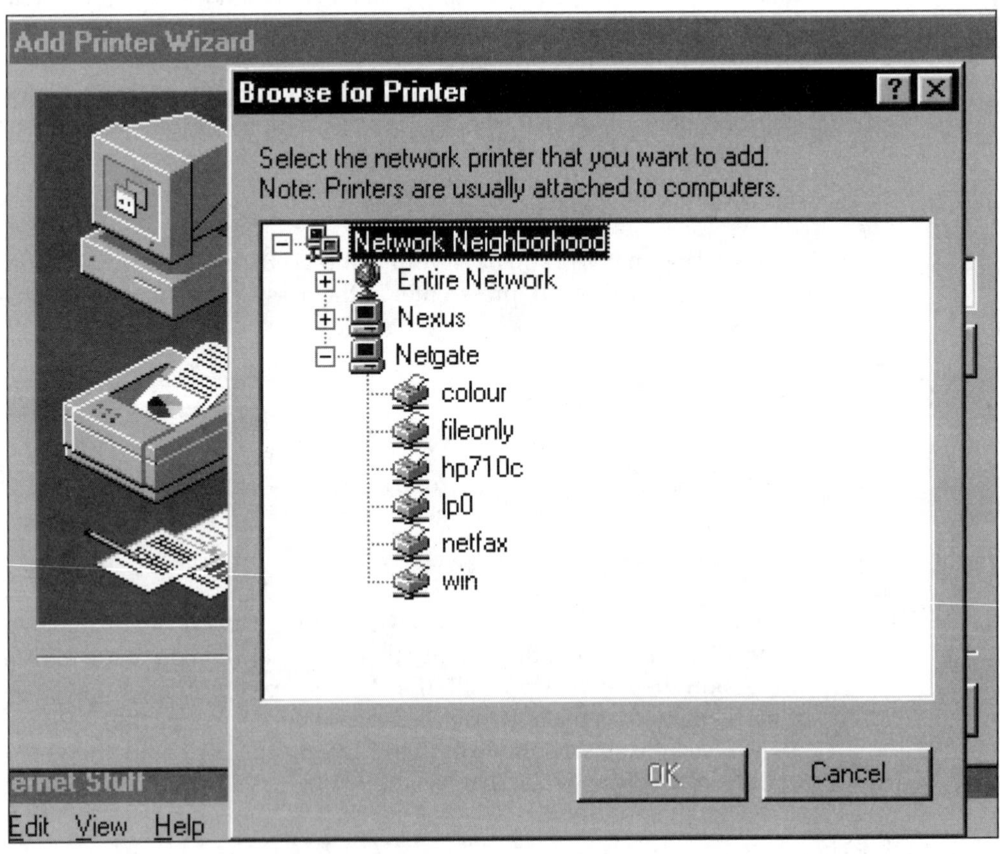

FIGURE 22.2 Adding a Samba network printer in Windows

The GUI Way to Administer Samba

Now that I have gone ahead and made you do all this the command line way, let me show you the GUI way as provided by the Samba team. When you installed Samba, you also installed a Web client called SWAT. Aside from providing an easy-to-use, point-and-click means of setting up shares, printers, and configuring various functions of the server, SWAT also offers complete online help for any of the configuration parameters you might run into. Figure 22.3 shows SWAT in action.

To use SWAT, you may need to set up the service in your `inetd.conf` file. The following entry comes from an RPM-based installation of Samba:

```
swat      stream  tcp     nowait.400      root /usr/sbin/swat swat
```

The path to the SWAT executable depends on how you installed Samba. If you did a default source build (as I did earlier), you'll find it in `/usr/local/samba/bin` and that is the path that you specify in the `inetd.conf` file. When you've made that change, remember to reset the `inetd` master process.

```
kill -HUP `cat /var/run/inetd.pid`
```

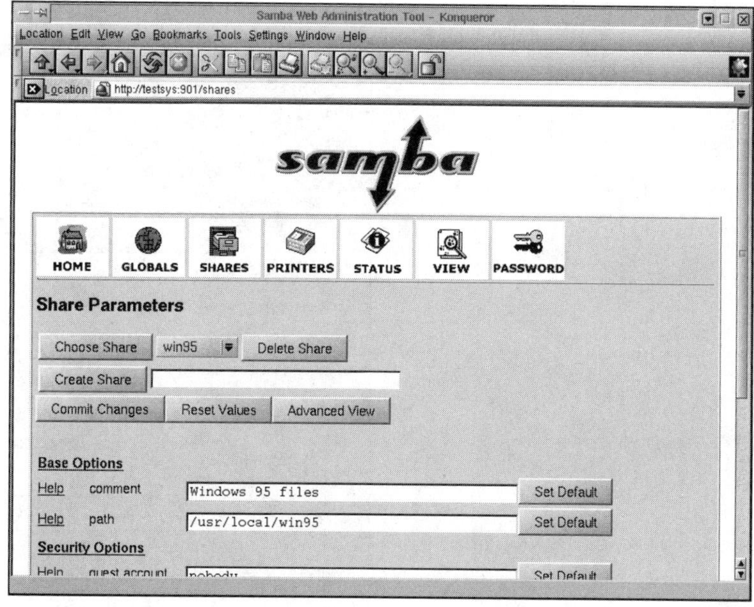

FIGURE 22.3 SWAT, the Samba browser administration tool

Note that those are back quotes in the last line. The URL to get to SWAT is as follows, where `my_server` is your server's IP address:

```
http://my_server:901/
```

Backing Up Windows Workstations

I touched briefly on backing up Windows workstations in Chapter 16. To back up a PC client using a Linux system running Samba, the easiest solution is to use `smbtar`.

To use `smbtar`, you must first set up shares on your Windows 95/98 PCs. To do this, bring up Windows Explorer (right-click the Start button and choose Explore).

Locate the directory you want to set up a share for and right-click that folder. You can click the drive icon itself and share the entire disk. I suggest backing up only your data files. When your Windows 95 system needs a restore, it usually needs a clean Windows and registry installation as well.

Anyhow, right-click the folder and choose Sharing, which brings up the SCSI Properties dialog box shown in Figure 22.4. In this example, I used a folder called SCSI under my C drive.

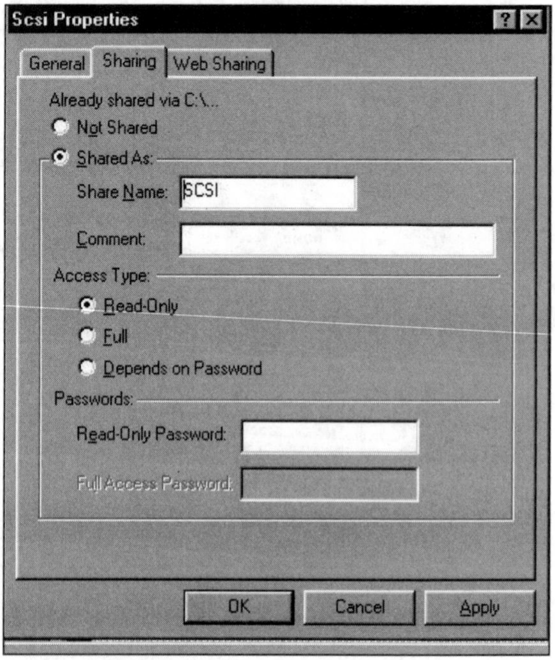

FIGURE 22.4 Sharing a drive in Windows

Click the Shared As radio button and give it a share name. The default is the directory name itself but you may want to give it a more intuitive name—it's up to you. Click OK.

Back on your Linux machine, you can now use `smbtar` to back up this directory. The format is as follows:

```
smbtar -v -s server_name -x share_name -t tarfile
```

For `server_name`, enter the PC's network name. For `share_name`, enter the name used in the previous example. In my scenario, I would enter SCSI. `tar_file` is the output device, which could be a file name. (*Danger!* Don't use up all your disk space!) In the case of a SCSI tape drive, it might be `/dev/st0`.

```
smbtar -v -s MARYPC -x SCSI -t /dev/st0
```

You will now see a list of files scrolling to the console screen.

Other options to `smbtar` include the following:

```
Usage: smbtar [<options>] [<include/exclude files>]
Function: backup/restore a Windows PC directories to a local tape file
Options: (Description) (Default)
-r Restore from tape file to PC Save from PC to tapefile
-i Incremental mode Full backup mode
-v Verbose mode: echo command Don't echo anything
-s <server> Specify PC Server
-p <password> Specify PC Password
-x <share> Specify PC Share backup
-X Exclude mode Include
-N <newer> File for date comparison
-b <blocksize> Specify tape's blocksize
-d <dir> Specify a directory in share \
-l <log> Specify a Samba Log Level 2
-u <user> Specify User Name root
-t <tape> Specify Tape device tar.out
```

If you specified an access type dependent on a password (in your Windows 95 sharing options), you need to specify the user name (`-u` option) and password (`-p` option) to access the PC.

Running Windows on Linux

When I speak to the Linux curious, one of the questions I get on a fairly regular basis goes like this: "But does it run Windows applications?" Because I don't want to scare people with talk of dual booting (after all, that's one of the pluses we keep offering them—the end to constant reboots), I then follow up with this great, cryptic response: "Under the right circumstances."

Those "circumstances" come in several different packages. I am going to cover a few of them here. What each of these solutions can offer you depends, to some degree, on what you need to be able to do.

Wine

It is possible to run some Windows applications on your Linux system without running Windows at all with a great little package called Wine. To paraphrase from the Wine Web site, Wine is not an emulator. Rather it is a compatibility layer, a set of APIs that enable Windows applications to operate on a Linux system running the X window system.

Wine will not run every Windows application, but the number of applications it is capable of running is increasing all the time. Some commercial vendors (Corel and IBM among them) have ported certain Windows applications to Linux by making some of the code run in Wine. This has sped up the normal production cycle and made it possible for them to get their programs to Linux users faster.

For Linux users, getting Wine is as simple as visiting the Wine Web site (`http://www.winehq.com/`). You will find both source and binary downloads available for a number of platforms. Also worth checking out is the CodeWeavers site (`http://www.codeweavers.com/`) for their version of Wine. What they have done is provide an installation wizard to guide you through the installation and configuration process for Wine. It makes the whole process extremely simple.

Have a look at Figure 22.5. This is a nice little Windows terminal emulation client called Tera Term Pro that is running under Wine. Everything works and the client is quite capable of using the Linux network layer (as you can see).

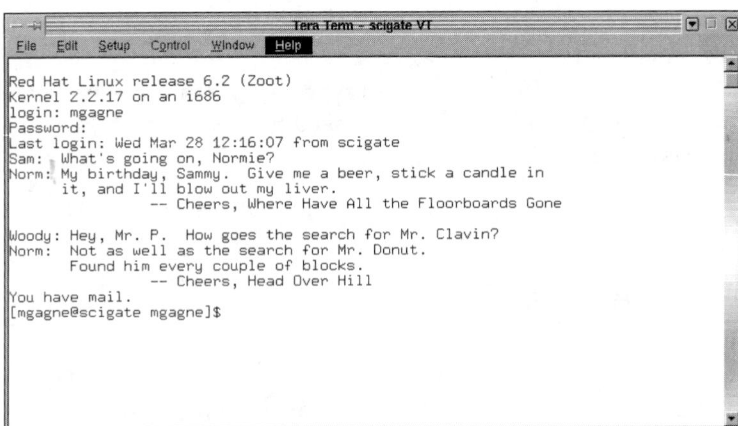

FIGURE 22.5 Tera Term Pro, a Windows terminal emulator running under Wine

VMware

Sometimes you need to run the whole shebang, and that means a full copy of Windows. Because you don't want to boot back and forth between Windows and Linux, it would be nice if you could run Windows entirely on your Linux machine. This is the philosophy behind VMware—and it doesn't stop there.

VMware enables you to create virtual machines on your computer. Complete with boot-up BIOS and memory checks, VMware virtualizes your entire hardware configuration, making the PC inside the PC as real as the one you are running. Furthermore, VMware enables you to run (not emulate) Windows 95, 98, 2000, NT, FreeBSD, or other Linuxes. For the developer or support person who needs to work (or write code) on different platforms, this is an incredible package. Yes, you can even run another Linux on your Linux, making it possible to test different releases without reinstalling on a new machine. VMware knows enough to share your printers, network cards, and so on. You can even network between the "real" machine and the virtual machine as though they were two separate systems.

All this capability comes at a price, however. Aside from the dollars that you spend on this package (and it can be well worth it), there is a considerable price in performance. VMware is a hungry beast. The more processor and memory you have, the better. A Pentium III with 96 or more megabytes should be your starting point. Unlike Wine, you need a copy of Windows (or whatever OS you are installing) to run.

VMware comes in a variety of packages and price points. Visit the VMware Web site (`http://www.vmware.com/`) for details.

Win4Lin

If all you want to do is run Windows and you don't have a particularly powerful machine, consider Win4Lin. It is much more lightweight than VMware, but then it doesn't perform all the magic that VMware does either. This is a package designed to let you run Windows on your system. Only Windows. Not FreeBSD and no other Linux distributions. If all you need Windows for is to run Microsoft Office, look no further. If you want to run the latest multimedia, intergalactic, shoot-'em-up extravaganza, you might have to stick with dual booting.

Where VMware comes with a performance gotcha, Win4Lin's is with the kernel. Its magic is performed at the kernel level and consequently requires that you download a patched kernel equivalent to what you are currently running or that you patch and rebuild your own. If you have compiled custom drivers into your kernel, you are going to have to go through the process again to get Win4Lin going. The other catch is that the Win4Lin patches (understandably) lag somewhat behind kernel development. If you are running the bleeding edge for whatever reason, Win4Lin may hold you back.

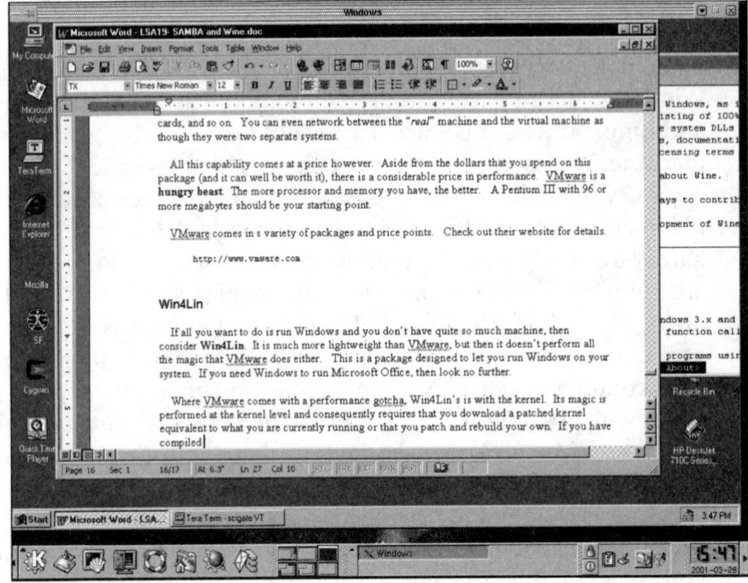

FIGURE 22.6 Using Win4Lin, Windows runs inside KDE on a Linux system

Like VMware, Win4Lin *requires* you to have a full Windows CD in order for the installation to take place. Interestingly enough, Windows installs and loads much faster under Linux than in native mode. Have a look at Figure 22.6, then come back to this chapter, look back a couple of paragraphs, and tell me if it doesn't look familiar.

On the upside, Win4Lin works very well indeed and requires surprisingly little in terms of resources. I have run it on a Pentium 233 notebook with 64MB of RAM and found that it was reasonably peppy. You do take a performance hit, but it feels minor and should not distract you under most circumstances.

For most basic Windows applications, Win4Lin is a great solution to the running Windows on Linux question.

Resources

Usenet Groups

```
comp.emulators.ms-windows.wine
linux.samba
```

Web Sites

CodeWeavers

`http://www.codeweavers.com/`

Samba Web site

`http://www.samba.org/`

VMware

`http://www.vmware.com/`

Win4Lin

`http://www.netraverse.com/`

Wine

`http://www.winehq.com/`

Chapter 23

System Logs and Accounting

Your System Logs

Many people keep a diary. Even if you don't, it is likely that you know someone who does. Over the years, I've known many people who were so inclined. They busily jot down details about those events in their day-to-day lives that, in some way, stand out. At some later time, they (or some future biographer or historian) can go back over their notes and try to make some sense of what was happening to them at that point in their lives.

In a similar way, your Linux system is keeping its own diary in the form of logs. These logs are generated and gathered at many levels from the kernel to application programs running on the system. Constantly updated, you'll find logs that relate to security, file transfers, electronic mail, login dates and times, boot-up and shutdown information, error messages, and much more. In fact, a server running in a small office will generate hundreds (if not thousands) of messages on any given day.

As system or network administrator, it is your job to check these logs and through them make the decisions that your job requires. If this is starting to sound like some kind of impossible task, have no fear. In the pages that follow, I will spend some time shedding light into the dark corners of your system logs.

Looking at Your Log Files

Luckily, from a system perspective, most things (with a few exceptions) tend to be kept in the same place: the `/var/log` directory. On your own system, change to that directory and have a look around with `ls`.

```
# cd /var/log
# ls
```

Here's a sample of what you should see there:

```
boot.log        cron            cron.1        cron.2        dmesg
lastlog         lastlog.1       maillog       maillog.1
maillog.2       messages        messages.1    netconf.log
netconf.log.1   netconf.log.2   secure        secure.1      secure.2
secure.3        secure.4        spooler       spooler.1     spooler.2
uucp            wtmp            wtmp.1        xferlog       xferlog.1
xferlog.2
```

Notice how the various log files have a .1, .2, .3, or .4 extension. This numbering sequence is the result of your system's automatic log rotation. The files that do this are in the `/etc` directory. To be a bit more exact, `cron.daily` is a directory under `/etc` that contains a number of administration scripts your system runs automatically. Without you having to do anything extra, Linux uses these scripts to keep things tidy—for example, it rotates your log files so they don't grow to enormous proportions. In the old days of UNIX, we had to do our own log file trimming. Tell that to kids today!

All kidding aside, have a look at those `cron` jobs. Take some time and familiarize yourself with what they do. In some cases, you'll find that each script is part of a simple package to do one job or another. For instance, the files `tmpwatch` and `logrotate` are two such packages. If you type `file *` in this directory, you will notice that these are text files. To discover their secrets, simply `more` or `less` them. Notice as well that the system also has `cron.hourly`, `cron.weekly`, and `cron.monthly` directories. A couple of those directories may be empty. The actual dates and times for these hourly (or weekly, and so on) `cron` jobs are in the `/etc/crontab` file.

What the Names Mean

As you can see from the previous sample list, the `/var/log` directory has a fair bit of information. Let's see what we can make of that information.

The `messages` log file is the busiest of the log files. You'll find boot time and shutdown messages here, DNS errors, kernel-level errors, `pppd` connection messages, daemons starting and stopping, `su` authentication, and more. User-written programs and even simple scripts will often use the `messages` file. Writing to it is easy with a great little utility called `logger` (more on that later).

From a cracker-detection point of view, your `secure(.1,.2,.3, and .4)` file will be of particular interest. If you turned off all access (other than your local network), you can check for possible attempts like this:

```
grep refused /var/log/secure*
```

The listing below is a sample of a connect attempt from an unauthorized host.

```
Sep 12 07:52:42 netgate in.rlogind[7138]: refused  connect from 2??.?.5?.?42
Sep 12 07:52:52 netgate in.rshd[7139]: refused  connect from 2??.?.5?.?42
Sep 12 07:52:55 netgate in.rexecd[7144]: refused  connect from 2??.?.5?.?42
Sep 12 07:52:59 netgate imapd[7146]: refused connect  from 2??.?.5?.42
Sep 12 07:52:59 netgate in.fingerd[7142]: refused  connect from 2??.?.5?.?42
Sep 12 07:53:00 netgate ipop3d[7143]: refused  connect from 2??.?.5?.?42
Sep 12 07:53:07 netgate in.ftpd[7147]: refused  connect from 2??.?.5?.?42
Sep 12 07:53:10 netgate gn[7145]: refused connect  from 2??.?.5?.?42
Sep 12 07:53:22 netgate in.telnetd[7149]: refused  connect from 2??.?.5?.?42
Sep 12 07:56:34 netgate imapd[7150]: refused connect  from 2??.?.5?.?42
```

From the log information, you can see the cracker tried several ports, or services, on my netgate server. For more information on what is happening here, refer to Chapter 25. In the meantime, let's continue exploring your logging subsystem.

You can also use the `more` command to scan some of the other files for additional information. The `maillog` files will give you a picture of what e-mail messages are routing through your machine. If you'd like to see `ftp` transfers to and from your machine, have a look at the `xferlog` files.

To find out who logged into your system and when, you will want to pay special attention to the `wtmp` file. Unlike most of your log files, `wtmp` cannot be viewed by simply using normal text commands like `cat`, `more`, or `less`. To view the contents of `wtmp`, use the `last` command. You might want to pipe the output of `last` to `more`.

```
# last | more
 fishduck ttyp6        nexus            Tue Sep 28  16:03   still logged in
 birdrat  ttyp5        speedy           Tue Sep 28  15:57   still logged in
 root     tty1                          Tue Sep 28  12:54   still logged in
```

This will give you the contents of the `wtmp` file, which details who logged in when, for how long, and whether or not they are still logged in. Make sure these are all people who you want to have access.

If you haven't checked your logs in a while and you would like to see what is in `wtmp.1`, use this version of the `last` command:

```
# last -f /var/log/wtmp.1 | more
```

Cleaning Up and What the Numbers Mean

Log files can get pretty large. An active server is a talkative one, and talk from your Linux system means log entries—lots of log entries. Over the years, I've seen log files grow unchecked until the system crashes for lack of disk space.

Sure, now that we all have 40GB drives on our PCs, it's not as bad, but a mess is a mess and it needs cleaning from time to time.

It is possible that you do not have `logrotate` on your system (although many distributions do include it). In case you don't know, `logrotate` is a utility written by Erik Troan that takes care of all this ugly business of archiving logs and recreating them. If you are running Red Hat, you almost certainly have `logrotate` running. In fact, you should see an entry for it in your `/etc/cron.daily` directory. This is a simple script that calls `logrotate` with the default configuration at `/etc/logrotate.conf`. Another giveaway is the presence of files in your `/var/log` directory with .1, .2, .3, and .4 extensions.

Before I get into the gory details of log rotation, I should probably remind you that you can find the times for execution of your `cron.daily`, `cron.weekly`, and `cron.some_time` files in `/etc/crontab`. This is just a text file, and you can view it with `cat /etc/crontab`.

Now back to `logrotate`. If you do not have the program on your system, the source for `logrotate` is available from `ftp://ftp.redhat.com/pub/redhat/code/logrotate/`.

Extract and build `logrotate` as follows:

```
tar -xzvf logrotate-3.3.tar.gz
cd logrotate-3.3
make
make install
```

The next step is to edit `/etc/logrotate.conf`, which defines what `logrotate` does and how. Configuration parameters exist in a global configuration file and in a configuration file for each subsystem. The global file is (by default) `/etc/logrotate.conf`, while the subsystem-specific definitions are in the directory `/etc/logrotate.d`. For instance, in my default global file, I have the following parameters:

```
rotate 4
create
errors marcel
include /etc/logrotate.d
```

The `rotate` parameter tells the system to keep four copies of archived logs. The fifth rotation will dump the .4 file specified. The `create` keyword tells `logrotate` to create a new, empty file after archiving. `errors marcel`, meanwhile, tells `logrotate` to e-mail me with any errors. Normally, this is set to root.

The next line is a Red Hat line that defines each package to log individually. The directory listed is where these files are kept. You can, if you want, write your own definitions into your `/etc/logrotate.conf` file. The format is as follows:

```
"/var/log/some_log_file" {
     rotate 5
```

```
    weekly
    mail user@mydomain.dom
    postrotate
        /sbin/killall -HUP syslogd
    endscript
}
```

Each definition, or paragraph, starts with the full pathname for the log file, followed by a number of options inside squiggly brackets. Let's take apart the previous example. `rotate 5` will override the default of 4 that I set up in my global configuration. `weekly` tells `logrotate` to rotate the file every seven days rather than the default daily (remember, I have `logrotate` running in `/etc/cron.daily`). The program then mails me the latest file, after which it restarts the `syslogd` daemon. This restart is a kind of a "script within a script," with a `postrotate` parameter to start followed by one or more commands to execute afterward. Finally, `endscript` ends this miniscript. Another angle bracket closes off the whole thing.

Even if you have `logrotate` already installed and set up on your system, things change and you may decide it makes more sense to change the times at which the process runs and how often. Very recently, I had reason to change it myself. On my Red Hat system, `logrotate` did a nice job of taking care of my Apache server files until I downloaded a new Apache, recompiled it with `mod_ssl`, `mod_php`, and did a few other things. Red Hat stores the Apache log files in `/var/log/httpd` while the new Apache installation stores its logs in `/usr/local/apache/logs`.

I realize I could have changed all this when I first built Apache, but I didn't and decided to leave it, as Apache seemed to like it. The trouble was that my logs were growing and growing with nothing but disk space standing in their way.

syslogd: The Master Logger

A good deal of the logs your system generates come to you courtesy of the `syslogd` daemon. The `syslogd` daemon is a program that runs in the background. It is independent of whatever else you may do on your system, but it does pay attention. That's its job: to collect information on what is going on and report it. You may recall from earlier in the book that by definition a *daemon* is a program that after being spawned (either at boot or by a command from a shell) disconnects itself from the terminal that started it and runs in the background. If you then disconnect from the terminal session that started the program or log out entirely, the program continues to run in the background. What it does there is a function of what the daemon is for. The `inetd` daemon listens for network connections, while `syslogd` watches, monitors, and logs.

What syslogd logs is defined in a file called /etc/syslog.conf. The format of the file consists of two sections: a selector and an action field. The *selector* (which is broken up into facility and priority) defines what you log by identifying where the information came from and the level of its importance or severity. The *action field* tells syslogd where the information goes or what to do with it. Not counting comment lines, the file looks something like this:

```
facility/priority                                  /var/log/filename
```

That's the basic format. Now let's have a look at a few lines from my file.

```
# Log anything (except mail) of level info or higher.
# Don't log private authentication messages!
*.info;mail.none;authpriv.none                     /var/log/messages

# The authpriv file has restricted access.
authpriv.*                                         /var/log/secure

# Log all the mail messages in one place.
mail.*                                             /var/log/maillog
```

Consider the filenames you saw in the earlier example and see where these fit in to your current configuration.

The filenames you see there may already be familiar ones (messages, maillog, and secure), but as you can see they can also be changed. A listing of your /var/log directory will show you the various log files your system keeps. Some of the files you'll see there (the Samba logs, for instance) are written by other processes.

Actually, the previous filename can be an additional process or even another host where its syslogd process will do whatever its own log file tells it to. More on that shortly—but first, the selector field. This section is auth (security info), authpriv (more or less the same as auth), cron (your cron scheduling system), daemon (various daemons), kern (messages generated by the kernel), lpr (spooler), mail, mark, news, security, syslog, user (user programs), uucp, or local0-local7. Not all of these are useful or even used. For instance, mark is basically no more (it just gets ignored) and security has been superseded by auth.

Each of these facilities has a priority to define the severity of the report. These priorities are debug (debug statements), info (whatever doesn't fit elsewhere), notice (getting important), warning (very important and potentially a bad thing), err (error conditions), and finally the biggies: crit (critical), alert, and emerg (it doesn't get any worse). Notice as well that you can specify a wild card (*) to indicate that you want reports on every priority level associated with a given facility.

```
kern.*                                /dev/console
```

The bottom line here is that any given Linux system is generating an awful lot of information. Pretend for a minute that you are the system administrator on a small/medium/large network. You have your own Linux machine running as your desktop, but somewhere on your network is your main machine. It runs mail, firewall services, and so on. Should something dreadful happen to that machine in the form of a disk crash, a cracker breaching security, or you name it, it is entirely possible that by the time you have a chance to look at the logs to determine what happened, it is already too late. They may be gone for good. Pretend again that you have several of these critical systems to keep an eye on. How can you possibly keep an eye on every one of them?

Here's what you do: Modify the `syslog.conf` file (in `/etc`) and add a new line with a very different action to the file. In the example that follows, I have added another line that defines what to do with `authpriv` messages. In other words, if I get a message telling me that someone is trying to log into my machine, I want to know about it. But just in case the evidence is removed before I have another chance to look at the logs, it would be nice if a copy of that log entry were passed on to my other machine, a machine I call "shadow."

```
# The authpriv file. has restricted access.
authpriv.*                                             /var/log/secure
authpriv.*                                             @shadow
```

When messages that normally show up in the `/var/log/secure` file are generated, I will get them in shadow's `/var/log/secure file`. Those messages will be prefaced by the host name on which they were generated. For example:

```
Jun 21 12:22:06 shadow in.telnetd[17002]: connect from 192.168.22.2
Jun 21 12:22:10 shadow login: LOGIN ON 5 BY natika FROM shadow
Jun 22 12:57:31 website in.telnetd[1245]: connect from 192.168.22.2
```

Notice that the first two lines from shadow's `/var/log/secure` line are fronted by shadow's host name. The last is reporting from my Internet gateway, a machine called "website." In order for shadow to accept and record these messages, I need to stop my system logger and restart it with a different set of options. If I do a `ps ax` to look at how my `syslogd` is running on shadow, I get something like this:

```
[root@shadow /root]# ps ax | grep syslog
17171 ?        S      0:00 syslogd -m 0 -r
17220 pts/6    S      0:00 grep syslog
```

If you do it on your machine, you will notice that the `-r` option is probably missing. You need to stop `syslogd` and restart it with the `-r` option, which tells `syslogd` to listen for remote `syslogd` messages. To stop `syslogd` on my Red Hat system, I can use this command:

```
/etc/rc.d/init.d/syslogd stop
```

You can also stop the process with this command:

```
kill pid_of_syslogd
```

To restart, I could just reissue that command with start instead of stop, but I would get the same version of `syslogd` running. If you want to try this for yourself, you can (as root) simply type `syslogd -m 0 -r` and your machine should start accepting logs from your other machine. For this to happen each time you boot, you need to change the boot script itself. On my Red Hat system, that is `/etc/rc.d/init.d/syslog`. Here are a few lines from that script:

```
# See how we were called.
case "$1" in
  start)
        echo -n "Starting system logger: "
        # we don't want the MARK ticks
        daemon syslogd -m 0
```

That last line is the one you want to change. Now when you reboot, `syslogd` will start with your new options. Incidentally, any changes you make to `/etc/syslog.conf` also require a restart (of the process, not the whole system). On my Debian system, the script (this time in `/etc/init.d`) is called `sysklogd` instead.

If you are particularly concerned about what is going on with your various systems, you could check your new, enriched log files with occasional `tail -10 /var/log/log_file_name` commands in a terminal window. You could also try a variation on the `tail` command, as follows:

```
tail -f /var/log/secure
```

The `-f` flag means "follow" the file. You can now keep a terminal window open and any changes to the file will appear on your screen. To stop this, press Ctrl-c (or whatever your interrupt key has been set to).

Back to the logger Program

With every passing second, your system is busy writing this wordy diary, but there may be situations in which you want to be able to write to the system log yourself. To do this, you use a little program called `logger`. What `logger` does is provide you (or your scripts) with a command-line interface to the `syslog` system. So why, you ask, is this a good thing? I'll start by saying that I genuinely admire real programmers. I, for one, am not given to spending hours hacking C code when I can get away with writing a quick and dirty script. A real C programmer uses the syslog libraries and writes him- or herself a classy little daemon. I, being a lazy system administrator type, write a script that uses a clever tool written by a C programmer—a tool such as logger. With logger, I can log information into a standardized system location (`/var/log/messages`) where my `syslogd` daemon is busy taking care of other business. You may also remember `syslogd` can even be writing to another system's logs as well.

Imagine a script called "natika" that watches some critical system resources on my server. If those resources drop below a certain level, the system writes a message to the system log file—in this case, `/var/log/messages`. The command I put in my script to accomplish this is as follows. The `-f` flag enables me to identify the log file I want to write to. The `-i` flag includes logger's process ID.

```
logger -f /var/log/messages -i "Low on coffee.  This is very important."
```

If I `tail` my `/var/log/messages` file, I get this result:

```
# tail -1 /var/log/messages
Jul  5 14:32:06 natika logger[1355]: Low on coffee.  This is very important.
```

Because my system is listening for natika's syslog messages, I will know right away if something important is happening on the other system.

Along with your own user-generated log entries, you may have noticed it is starting to get rather busy in your system's personal diaries. So how do you know what to look for? Even though running a `tail -f` of your messages log to your screen is great if you are connected and you happen to be watching at the time, what about other times? Your logs also demand attention for those times you are not there, and (believe it or not) even system administrators have to sleep. It's time to automate the process.

Automating the Log-Checking Process

Where to start? This is the real question when trying to decide what to automate. In time, you'll find that there are things important to your specific environment, and you'll write scripts to deal with those things. For instance, I could write a Perl script that monitors the status of disk space on my system. If the space drops below a specific level, the script alerts the appropriate system administration or support individuals.

The following script is written in Perl. It will check for and send an alert when disk utilization rises past a predetermined "safe" level. It can be set to run automatically with an appropriate `crontab` entry.

```
#!/usr/bin/perl
# 1999: Sally Tomasevic & Marcel Gagné
# Salmar Consulting Inc. www.salmar.com
# checkdfusage.pl : checks disk usage in
# percentage and alerts sys admin if greater
# than 90%
&check_dfusage;
exit();
# Subroutines #
sub check_dfusage {
```

```
  @message=`df`;
  $message_text = '';
  foreach (@message) {
    ($dirname, $arg1, $arg2, $arg3, $arg4, $arg5,
        $arg6) = split (' ', $_, 7);
    ($arg4num,$therest) = split('%',$arg4,2);
    if ($arg4num > "90") {
      $message_text .= "Directory $dirname is now " .
      " at $arg4num\n";
      }
#print $arg4 . "\n";
  }
  if ($message_text ne '') {
    $smbclient = "/usr/bin/smbclient -U root";
    $smbhost = 'speedy';
    &sendmessage;
  }
}
sub sendmessage {
  open(SF,"|$smbclient -M $smbhost");
  print SF "$message_text";
  close(SF);
}
```

Logcheck

There are things that are pretty constant across systems that you'll want to check for and a program that tirelessly watches various files for items of interest or concern can be a great help. This is where Logcheck (`http://www.psionic.com/abacus/logcheck/`) from Psionic Software comes into play. Logcheck is an automated log file analyzer that works while you sleep, and it is available free of charge and GPL'ed.

To install the software, extract the files into a temporary directory and build the software. You may want to read the whole `INSTALL` file, because it contains some good information about securing your log files. Odds are that if you are running a standard Linux distribution, the permissions on your log files are probably fine (`rw-------`).

Logcheck consists (more or less) of two programs: `logcheck.sh` and `logtail`. The first, `logcheck.sh`, is a script that walks through your log files, notes any weirdness, and reports back. The second, `logtail`, remembers where in your log files it last checked so that it doesn't repeat itself in feeding information to `logcheck.sh`. There are also a few additional configuration files, which I will cover a little later. Here's what you do to install the package:

```
tar -xzvf logcheck-1.1.1.tar.gz
cd logcheck-1.1.1
make linux
```

The installation runs pretty quickly—in a matter of seconds, you are ready to roll. The first thing you need to do is a little local configuration. Using your favorite editor, modify the `/usr/local/etc/logcheck.sh` script in the following way. A little ways down, you will notice an entry that looks like this:

```
# Person to send log activity to
SYSADMIN=root
```

The reports generated will then be e-mailed to that user. On my system, I use `SYSADMIN=security`. `security` is a mail alias that e-mails a handful of people in different locations (just in case). If something terrible were to happen (for example, if an evil cracker were to strike), I still have the evidence because it has been mailed off system.

You will also find another section titled LOG FILE CONFIGURATION SECTION, where the log files monitored by Logcheck are located. You can add or delete files as needed. Here are the ones from my own script file:

```
$LOGTAIL /var/log/messages > $TMPDIR/check.$$
$LOGTAIL /var/log/secure >> $TMPDIR/check.$$
$LOGTAIL /var/log/maillog >> $TMPDIR/check.$$
```

Now that everything is configured, you need to set up `cron` to run the `logcheck.sh` script on a regular basis. The following is a sample entry for a root `crontab` (remember, you can add a `cron` entry with the command `crontab -e`). In this example, `logcheck.sh` will run four times every hour (at 15-minute intervals).

```
0,15,30,45 * * * * /usr/local/etc/logcheck.sh
```

When Logcheck runs, it divides the report into three main sections: Active system attacks, Security violations, and Unusual system events. Note that some of these items may be reported in all three areas, such as anything that qualifies as an ACTIVE SYSTEM ATTACK. The keywords that will trip such a message are in one of those other files you may remember me mentioning earlier—in this case, `logcheck.hacking`. Three other files are called `logcheck.violations`, `logcheck.violations.ignore`, and plain old `logcheck.ignore`. You will find them all in `/usr/local/etc`.

`logcheck.hacking` has nasty little keywords like ATTACK, LOGIN FAILURE, and so on. Messages matching anything in this file are sent to your e-mail address with a subject line reading ACTIVE SYSTEM ATTACK. Apparently, this is designed to get your attention, and it does. Messages matching the keywords in `logcheck.violations` will show up under the Security violations heading. The last file, `logcheck.violations.ignore`, is exactly what it sounds like: a list of keywords for Logcheck to ignore. For instance, in the case of my own internal network, I tell Logcheck to ignore anything that has 192.168.1. by adding that to the file. By default, the only thing in that file is `stat=Deferred`.

The last file, `logcheck.ignore`, applies to any and all types of messages. If you scan through that file, you'll see a fair bit there: `named lame` messages, `cron` start-ups, `sendmail` stats, and others. Type `more /usr/local/etc/logcheck.ignore` to look these over. As with the other files, you can customize them to your needs.

> **Warning:** You'll be tempted to add a lot of things to these ignore files as a result of the volume of information Logcheck generates (it's not that bad), but be careful. You don't want to start filtering out important data for the sake of a cleaner report. More information is almost always better than less.

Here's a (very) small sample of Logcheck's output:

```
Security Violations


=-=-=-=-=-=-=-=-=-=
Jul  5 16:05:03 netgate PAM_pwdb[3908]: authentication failure; (uid=0) ->
+edgarc for pop service
Jul  5 16:05:04 netgate ipop3d[3908]: Login failure user=edgarc
+host=[192.168.1.6]
Jul  5 16:06:36 netgate PAM_pwdb[3912]: authentication failure; (uid=0) ->
+edgarc for pop service
```

It seems that user edgarc may have forgotten his password.

As you can see, with a package like this, the job of filtering and looking through logs can be greatly simplified. As you get more comfortable with what you expect to see in those logs, you can customize the keyword files to deliver the information you want. Even with the default files, Logcheck is a great little package.

You're not finished with Logcheck quite yet. In Chapter 25, you will revisit the program with its big brother, an intrusion detection program called PortSentry.

Web Site Log Analysis

What about Web server logs? A quick peek at the log files for any Web site (even a fairly quiet one) displays an amazing amount of chitchat. Every HTML document or graphic image is captured, along with information about times, dates, browser types, and much more. You see, every time someone requests a page, you get at least one entry in your Web server's log files. Why "at least" one, rather than only one? In all likelihood, your pages aren't simple text documents. You may have a half-dozen graphics and a Web counter in addition to text. Each and every one of those will generate a log entry. If your Web page uses frames, that means even more log entries.

Before you can examine this wealth of information, you need to know where to look. For a Red Hat RPM installation, take a look in `/etc/httpd/logs`. If, like me, you built your own Apache server from source, you should probably look in your `/usr/local/apache/logs` directory. Either way, the file to look at is `access_log`. Another way to get the information you need no matter what system you are running is to use the following command:

```
httpd -V
```

This will print out the configuration settings of your Web server binary. The piece of information you want looks like this:

```
-D DEFAULT_XFERLOG="/path_to/your/access_log"
```

As I mentioned earlier, every link, image, or piece of text is in that file, along with the address of the site that clicked it. That's a lot of information, but how can you tell which page is most popular? What do visitors look for on your site? Here's an interesting thought: If you could count the types of browsers that visit your site, you could make some changes in your page layout to accommodate the majority of visitors.

Analog

The first log analyzer I want to look at is called Analog, which was written by Stephen Turner at the University of Cambridge Statistical Laboratory. The Web page for Analog (`http://www.analog.cx/`) proudly proclaims it to be "the most popular log file analyzer in the world." (For those of you who want to check those numbers out for yourselves, Stephen has provided links on his site to the research.)

Analog can sift through literally thousands of Web site log entries and generate an easy-to-read report in very little time. I took an old `access_log` file from my Web site and let Analog do its thing. On my old 150MHz Pentium notebook, Analog processed 800,000 lines of log in 1 minute and 39 seconds. That's reasonably impressive. At the time I downloaded my copy of Analog, the latest version was 4.11. For those of you who run other platforms besides Linux (maybe a Solaris or BSD Web server), this program will compile on many different UNIX platforms.

You should extract Analog into the directory structure where you will eventually want it to live. Normally, you do your `make` and `make install`, and then delete the installation directory. Not so here. If I want Analog to live in /usr/local/analog-4.11, I can change to the /usr/local directory and perform the following steps:

```
cd /usr/local
tar -xzvf analog-4.11.tar.gz
cd analog-4.11
```

Before you go ahead and type make, you will want to edit the anlghead.h file. The most obvious changes are the following lines:

```
#define HOSTNAME "[my organization]"
#define HOSTURL "none"
#define ANALOGDIR "/usr/local/analog-4.11/"
#define LOGFILE "/usr/local/apache/logs/access_log"
```

The HOSTNAME variable refers to a banner that will be displayed at the top of your HTML report. This can be pretty much anything—if you have only one Web server, your company or organization name is an obvious choice. If you have several Web servers, you might want to identify a specific host. Next you have HOSTURL, which simply puts a link back to your home page (or whatever page you like) on the report head. ANALOGDIR is the path to the Analog program and support files. You decided on this when you extracted the program. Finally, LOGFILE is the full path to your Web server log file—in my case, the path is /usr/local/apache/logs/access_log.
Now you are ready to make the program.

```
make
```

Before running the program for the first time, you are going to edit one more thing. This one is in the installation directory for the program and is called analog.cfg. The directory examples contain variations of .cfg files with ideas on how you might set yours up. Quite a number of parameters can be set in analog.cfg that will enable you to customize the report generated to better suit your site. The following is a (very small) sample of those parameters and their meanings:

```
LANGUAGE ENGLISH  (My choice, although I did try FRENCH)
HOST ON           (The host name of the system)
DOMAIN ON         (Country codes get listed)
REFERRER ON       (What page did they come from to find you)
SEARCHQUERY ON    (Search terms used to find you)
BROWSER ON        (What kind of browsers were they using)
OSREP ON          (What were they running: Linux, Windows, and so on)
```

You'll find tons more if you check out the big.cfg file in the examples directory, because it contains pretty much anything you could possibly want to consider. I should point out that in order for Analog to report certain things, you have to make sure your Web server is actually collecting that information. For instance, my server collects IP addresses of visitors and does not do a DNS lookup for each connect. This is the default Apache configuration these days, and it is done in the interest of speed. Consequently, I would not get HOSTNAME or DOMAIN reports on my system. In case you are curious, that parameter is `HostnameLookups` in your Apache configuration file. Beware of the cost, though—the default is off for good reason.

Anyhow, I digress. To run the Analog program, type either the full path to the command or execute it from the installation directory.

```
cd /usr/local/analog-4.11
./analog
```

Wait a short time, and you will have your report. You can then view it in your favorite Web browser. If you are running it locally on your system, you can simply type in the pathname to the report in your browser's location bar. If you would like to see an example of an Analog report (before installing it), click the See a Sample Report link from the Analog home page.

Analog is cool. It's fast. It's free (although it is not GPL—read the included license for details).

The Webalizer

We've all gotten used to those colorful charts in our daily papers and magazines. The same is true for the Web. That's one reason why you might find The Webalizer more interesting than Analog. For a peek at the kind of output you can expect from The Webalizer, have a look at the sample in Figure 23.1.

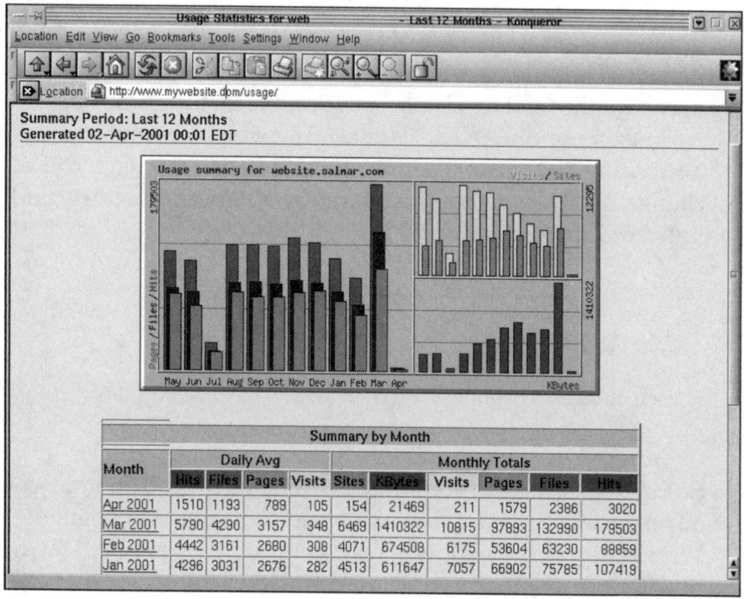

Summary by Month										
Month	Daily Avg				Monthly Totals					
	Hits	Files	Pages	Visits	Sites	KBytes	Visits	Pages	Files	Hits
Apr 2001	1510	1193	789	105	154	21469	211	1579	2386	3020
Mar 2001	5790	4290	3157	348	6469	1410322	10815	97893	132990	179503
Feb 2001	4442	3161	2680	308	4071	674508	6175	53604	63230	88859
Jan 2001	4296	3031	2676	282	4513	611647	7057	66902	75785	107419

FIGURE 23.1 Web stats generated with The Webalizer

In an instant, you can see how the access to your site has changed over recent months with charts displaying weekly (and even hourly) averages based on pages, files, and the number of hits. Even if you personally are not moved by The Webalizer's output, your company's management will be. (They love that sort of thing. Trust me.) Best of all, The Webalizer is free and distributed under the GNU Public License.

The official Webalizer Web site (`http://www.mrunix.net/webalizer/`) is fine for information, but I have found it tends to get bogged down with download requests. If you get refused because of too many `ftp` transfers, try the European mirror (in Austria) at `http://webalizer.dexa.org/`.

You'll find a 2.*x* development version of The Webalizer code out there as well, but I'm going to deal with the current (stable) 1.3*x* release in this example. Those of you who are dealing with multiple platforms will be happy to learn that The Webalizer works on a variety of systems, including Solaris, BSD, MacOS, and others. Binaries are available for some platforms, but if you don't see yourself listed there, fear not—building from source is easy.

Okay. Side trip. There is just one possible catch: The Webalizer uses the GD graphics library to build those "oh-so-cool" pseudo-GIF inline graphics, and the compression algorithm for the GIF file format is subject to patent restrictions that lately have generated much controversy. Part of what this means is that the GD library may or may not be included in your Linux distribution. The Webalizer's download page provides a link should you need it. I built my The Webalizer binaries on a Red Hat 6.2 system that still provided the libraries—odds are that for now, your system will likely have them as well. For that reason, The Webalizer development is shifting toward PNG format graphics even as I write this. In fact, version 2.*x* uses the PNG format by default. Those who would like more details on this whole GIF patent issue may visit the GNU Web site (but don't forget to come back).

Let us continue. The latest 1.3*x* version turned out to be `webalizer-1.30-04-src.tgz`. The installation steps are easy: You extract the source, change directory to the resultant distribution directory, and compile. Here's how I did it on my system:

```
tar -xzvf webalizer-1.30-04-src.tgz
cd webalizer-1.20-04
./configure
make
make install
```

You can perform all these steps with whatever user ID you want, but the `make install` portion must be done as root. Now that you have The Webalizer installed, you will make some configuration changes. (Surprised?) The Webalizer needs to know where your log files are kept, as well as where and how reports should be generated and stored.

You might have noticed that the build process created a `/etc/webalizer.conf.sample` file. The default location for the configuration file is `/etc/webalizer.conf` and I recommend you leave it at that. First, make a copy of the sample file and edit that file. Let's pretend I am going to use Pico as my editor in this case.

```
cp /etc/webalizer.conf.sample /etc/webalizer.conf
pico /etc/webalizer.conf
```

All I did was change four lines in this file, which were as follows:

```
LogFile          /etc/httpd/logs/access_log
OutputDir        /home/httpd/html/usage/
Incremental      yes
HostName         myhost.mydomain.dom
```

The `LogFile` parameter identifies the location of my `access_log` file. The previous path is typical of a Red Hat installation.

The next parameter, `OutputDir`, defines the location for the The Webalizer reports. I created a directory called `usage` on my Web server under my document root. Again, the previous path implies a Red Hat system. Next in line is `Incremental yes`. This is a useful little parameter (and I do recommend it) if your log files rotate more than once a month. It lets The Webalizer continue from where it left off, even if that means starting on a brand-new log (remember those .1, .2, and so on files created by `logrotate`?).

The last parameter, `HostName`, may not be necessary. It depends on whether your system returns the proper host name (which is put at the top of the report). If you are running a number of virtual domains (as I do on my Web server), you should pick one for the report headers. Read the configuration file and decide whether you want to change anything else. In my case, those were the only changes.

The last thing left to do is run The Webalizer. You do that simply by typing this command:

```
/usr/local/bin/webalizer
```

While I did not find The Webalizer as quick as Analog—it processed my 800,000-line `access_log` file in 2 minutes and 55 seconds compared to Analog's 1 minute and 39 seconds—it is still pretty darn fast. The data generated from The Webalizer is cumulative. That means you can run The Webalizer whenever it suits you and it will just build on what it already has. If you want to do daily updates, you will certainly want to put the following command in a `crontab` entry (the `-e` flag, of course, means "edit"):

```
crontab -e
```

Once in the editor, I add the following line, which will run The Webalizer every day at 6:00 AM:

```
0 6 * * * /usr/local/bin/webalizer 1> /dev/null 2> /dev/null
```

Whether you decide to use Analog or The Webalizer is a matter of personal taste. In terms of sheer "flash" and bright, shiny colors, The Webalizer is definitely ahead.

Resources

Analog Web site

`http://www.analog.cx/`

`logrotate` **Program**

`ftp://ftp.redhat.com/pub/redhat/code/logrotate/`

Logcheck

`http://www.psionic.com/abacus/logcheck/`

The Webalizer

`http://www.mrunix.net/webalizer/`

Chapter 24

Secure Computing

A Brief History of Encryption

You've probably heard the terms "public key encryption" and "DSA" bandied about. You've probably received messages with a "PGP signature" attached to the message. What does that mean?

When you were a kid, you may have played with secret codes. Heck, you may even have invented your own. One of the earliest secret codes I remember being shown involved reversing the alphabet and using that as an encryption key, like this:

```
a b c d e f g h i j k l m n o p q r s t u v w x y z
z y x w v u t s r q p o n m l k j i h g f e d c b a
```

If I want to write the words "secret message" using this encryption method, I wind up with `hvxivg nvhhvtv`. That's not particularly difficult to crack, I realize. Consequently, over the years, people have created increasingly complex forms of encryption, particularly during wartime. Historically, encryption methods worked on the premise of a shared key file. You would give the person with whom you wanted to communicate the same key by which the message was encoded. That meant getting the key to your coconspirator (or whatever) through a channel separate from the message.

The catch was that anyone intercepting the key could then decipher all your messages.

Personal Encryption

Personal encryption technologies generally center around *public key encryption.* Essentially, the concept works this way: My messages are encrypted with two keys. One is my private key, which I guard jealously and never hand out to anyone. I take a copy of this key, print it out, save it to a diskette, and store both the original and the copy in a safe-deposit box. Anyone knowing the whereabouts of the key would have to be . . . well, that's a bit dramatic, but you get the idea.

When I encode a message, I do so by combining my key with a public key. This is not my public key, but one supplied to me by the person I want to communicate with. Both keys are required for the encryption/decryption process, but anyone having just one half of the key pair has nothing, and you should never hand out your private key to anyone.

The reason for this whole encryption thing has to do with our old friend, TCP/IP. You see, while TCP/IP is truly wonderful and has given us this bright, beautiful Internet, it is inherently insecure. In the early days when the protocol was first created, people were a little less worried about others looking over their electronic shoulders and watching them work. After all, computers were big, magical, scary things that only a handful of people really understood. There were also very few connected computers. It is highly doubtful that anybody back then imagined the interconnected world in which we now live.

An Introduction to the Secure Shell

Imagine you are the system administrator at Big Company, Inc., and you've read all the security articles and books you can lay your hands on, you've tied down your Linux server, you've done more reading, you've tied the server down even further, and a few days later you discover a break-in. What happened?

One possibility is that Joe Cracker plugged into your 200-port network with his Linux notebook (it's easy to hide in a 200-station office if you look official and wear a nice suit), started a sniffer, and waited while people logged in and left their plain-text user names and passwords. The grand prize was the root password, which you let slip by as you started a telnet session to your Samba server. Suddenly, Joe Cracker has full access to your system all over again.

One way to avoid this is to never log in as root (or `su` to root) across anything but a direct serial connection or the console itself.

That's the idea behind the `/etc/securetty` file, which is simply a list of terminals at which root is allowed to log in.

```
# cat /etc/securetty
tty1
tty2
tty3
tty4
tty5
tty6
tty7
tty8
```

This doesn't stop you from logging in as yourself and doing a su - root in order to gain root privileges, thus exposing yourself to Joe Cracker.

What Are Your Options?

One way to beat this problem is with ssh, or the Secure Shell. For the purpose of this chapter, I started at the source (literally) by downloading a copy of the software and building it on my system. You can get the software at http://www.ssh.com/. After downloading the gzipped and tarred bundle, I extracted the software and compiled it as follows:

```
# tar -xzvf ssh-2.0.13.tar.gz
# cd ssh-2.0.13
# ./configure
# make install
```

There are several components to ssh: a client and server component, utilities for generating public and private encrypted keys for strong authentication, and a secure ftp server. For brevity's sake (whoever he or she is), I will concentrate on the telnet or shell client.

Before you can run a secure shell, you need to start a secure server. By default, the sshd daemon (or server) runs on TCP port 22 (check it out by doing a more or less on your /etc/services file), but you can specify a different port with the -p option. I started my new sshd on my server from the command line with the default port.

```
# sshd
```

Before I try out my spiffy new secure shell, I'll just telnet to my server and type pwd. This is your regular, run-of-the-mill telnet to port 23. Just for fun, I will also switch to the root user after I've logged in. In my sniffer window, I get this result:

```
pwd../mnt/data1/packages/ssh-2.0.13
[root@server_name ssh-2.0.13#
```

> *Ouch!* That should be more than a little bit frightening. What I did not show you came before this little tidbit. My user name and password, including the su to root and its password, were displayed for anyone to see. Basic TCP protocols, such as telnet, do all their work in plain text. Everything you type and everything the system writes back is there, *in plain text,* for anyone on your network to see. This is just the sort of thing that can make someone afraid to turn on his or her computer.

Let's try that again, this time with emotion—er, encryption. From my notebook (where I have also built and installed `ssh`), I initiate a connection to my server.

```
# ssh server_name
```

After responding to the password prompt, I go back to my sniffer session, click the new port 22 session, and start capturing the output. Here's what I see this time:

```
..>.V.eC?q.\./...F.D.vR.._rl.j..k.U..;J...X....g*.
KW..D.VSq.A.[Qy.E[.e...p'..s...1.n.....|.M..B..?..
...HE....,xB
```

Quite a difference, eh?

If you want to get your hands on a copy of `ssh`, you can visit the official `ssh` Web site (`http://www.ssh.com/`).

You can also obtain Red Hat RPMs at `http://www.replay.com/redhat/ssh.html` if you do not want to build from the source distribution.

Keep in mind that `ssh` (the official SSH) is a commercial product that can be ordered online from the F-Secure Web site (`http://www.datafellows.com/`)—you'll find a link on the `ssh` Web site as well. While the product is not free, this doesn't stop you from downloading and evaluating it or experimenting with it (the evaluation period is 60 days). If you happen to qualify for the noncommercial or educational use category, you may use `ssh` without cost. Check the license agreement for details.

OpenSSH

Although `ssh` is almost certainly the de facto standard, a freeware implementation exists as well and you may want to use it instead. While it is not a 100 percent drop-in replacement for SSH, it comes pretty darn close and supports both SSH1 and SSH2 protocols. OpenSSH (`http://www.openssh.org/`) is primarily developed and distributed by the OpenBSD project. It is, however, an international effort. OpenSSH is distributed under the BSD license and is freely distributed.

This version of the secure shell environment is an easy build, but it does require two additional support packages: zlib (ftp://ftp.freesofware.com/pub/infozip/zlib/zlib.html), a patent-free compression and decompression library, and OpenSSL, the Open-sourced Secure Sockets Layer package (SSL).

I want to spend a little time working with and talking about OpenSSH, but *first* I need to talk about that second piece I just mentioned, OpenSSL—a very *important* piece indeed.

Secure Sockets Layer

Before we examine OpenSSL, let's get a little historical background.

Secure Sockets Layer (SSL) is a secure network protocol originally created by Netscape Communications. It is one of several Transport Layer Security protocols (SSH is another). The chief application and drive for SSL was and remains electronic commerce. For users to willingly send their credit card information over the Web, they needed to be convinced that no one could intercept and decode their information.

For e-commerce to flourish, something like SSL was needed, and Netscape answered that call. The current version of the SSL protocol is version 3.0. If you're really curious, you can visit the Netscape Web site (http://www.netscape.com/eng/ssl3) for the current SSL 3.0 specifications.

Some time after SSL was created, the model was distributed to the World Wide Web Consortium (W3C). I mention W3C because it is an international organization dedicated to taking protocols like SSL and directing them toward some kind of global interoperability. The World Wide Web Consortium's Web site (http://www.w3c.org/) is the place to go if you want to explore Web-related standards. But, I digress.

You can find the OpenSSL package by surfing over to http://www.openssl.org/ and downloading the latest version. At the time of this writing, it was version 0.9.6.

After downloading the package, extract the files and build the distribution.

```
# tar -xzvf openssl-0.9.6.tar.gz
# cd openssl-0.9.6
# ./config
```

You can, if you want, change the configuration option to load OpenSSL into a different directory structure. The default is /usr/local/ssl. Check the INSTALL file if you want to go outside the defaults. You may want to omit a particular cipher or change the default install directory. For example, the following will create a Makefile that will install OpenSSL in /usr/myspecialdir/ssl instead of /usr/local. It will also build the software without the rc5 cryptographic algorithm.

```
# ./config --prefix=/usr/myspecialdir -no-rc5
```

Note: With the recent expiration of the RSA patent, the door seems wide open for encrypted communications and software built on these technologies. That said, there are still parts of the world where encryption technologies may not be entirely legal and where the transport or exchange of such technologies may have legal ramifications. Unfortunately, it is still up to the individual to be aware of what laws may be in effect in his or her country regarding such technologies.

Next, you need to do a `make` followed a few minutes later by a `make test`. The `make test` will do all sorts of neat things, such as run through encryption and decryption tests on all the ciphers you have built. Some of them will take a while.

Now do a `make install`. When this build happens, two interesting libraries are created: `libcrypto.a` and `libssl.a`. Because you use these again when you create your Apache Web server with SSL, you need to know where they are. For the Apache build to find them, you need to set your `LD_LIBRARY_PATH` variable to find them later.

```
# LD_LIBRARY_PATH=$LD_LIBRARY_PATH:/usr/local/ssl/lib
# export LD_LIBRARY_PATH
```

You might want to throw those two lines into your `$HOME/.bash_profile`. If you are lazier than that, why not simply create a symbolic link to the files from `/usr/lib` where all package builds will look?

```
# ln -s /usr/local/ssl/lib/libcrypto.a /usr/lib/libcrypto.a
# ln -s /usr/local/ssl/lib/libssl.a /usr/lib/libssl.a
```

Or, if you are lazier still (much like I am), you can do it nice and clean by adding a line to `/etc/ld.so.conf` that reads `/usr/local/ssl/lib` and then runs `ldconfig`. Then you never need worry about it again. Note that this must be done as root.

Because I've already told you that you are eventually going to use this Secure Sockets Layer package for the OpenSSH package, you might want to know what else you can do with this monster now that you've built it. Well, you can build an SSL-enabled Apache server, but I'll talk about that later.

SSL is not so much a final product as the foundation for many others, such as OpenSSH and the Apache server I mentioned. A good place to look for SSL applications is the OpenSSL Web site (`http://www.openssl.org/related/apps.html`).

While I was hunting around for applications for SSL, I found a cool little text-only browser called w3m. Personally, what I like about w3m is that it renders tables and frames very well (with the `-F` option). It also does color and you can even use your mouse (with gpm) to click your way from URL to URL. Finally, as it relates to this chapter, you can build it using your SSL libraries. All this for the low, low price of . . . nothing. The programmer has a sense of humor, evident from his README file. Here it is in its entirety:

```
If you can read English, see doc/*.
If you can read Japanese, see doc-jp/*.
If you can read both, read both and correct English. :-)
```

w3m is well worth checking out. The w3m address is as follows: http://ei5nazha.yz.yamagata-u.ac.jp/~aito/w3m/eng/.

Another application for OpenSSL that you may not have immediately thought of is Samba, your Windows-style file and printer server. If secure communications between your PC clients and your Samba server are desirable, you can compile Samba from the source with SSL enabled. Why would you want to run SSL-enabled Samba? If you flip back a few pages to that section on port sniffers, you'll remember that every keystroke you type on your network can be picked up by a port sniffer. The same holds true for a document you may have open on an SMB-shared drive. Think about this as you edit that spreadsheet detailing executive salaries.

Your stock Samba server does not have these services built into the code. If you want this feature, you can now add it with the help of your brand-new SSL toolkit and libraries. When you run your ./configure script for the Samba build, just add --with-ssl to the command (./configure --with-ssl). Visit the Samba Web site (http://www.samba.org/) for the latest Samba source.

So there you have it. As mentioned, there are other applications that use OpenSSL as the basis for secure communication. Check out the OpenSSL Web site and see for yourself. All right, now that you have an SSL library and you know what to do with it, let's go back and finish what you started.

OpenSSH (Right Back Where You Started)

In order to have some fun with OpenSSH (and work, too), you need to get the program and get it running. If you haven't already done so, visit http://www.openssh.org/ and download the latest copy. Then extract the source and build it like this:

```
tar -xzvf openssh-2.5.2p2.tar.gz
cd openssh-2.5.2p2
make
make install
```

The last thing you are going to see as part of this installation is a handful of messages telling you that SSH is generating some public/private key pairs. If you installed from source using the defaults, these will be under /usr/local/etc. It might be a good idea to back these up now.

In order to use the OpenSSH server, you need to start it with the following command. Note that you probably want this in your rc.local boot time script as well.

```
# /usr/local/sbin/sshd
```

From another machine, I can now connect to the server like this:

```
ssh -l marcel testsys
```

When I initiated this connection to my server testsys, I used the -l option. That's because I was working with a different account name on my current machine than the one I wanted to log into on testsys. For instance, if I had been logged in as marcel on my notebook and wanted to ssh over to testsys, all I had to do was this:

```
ssh testsys
```

Just like that—simple, secure communication.

Secure File Transfers

OpenSSH lets you do some other things besides just logging in and working away on your system (incognito, as it were). Another application is secure file transfer. This is much like using rcp (remote copy), but with an encrypted data stream. For this, you use the scp command, part of the OpenSSH package and one of the tools you built previously.

To copy a file called ap_file from a remote system called "faraway_sys" to my local system, I would do this (this assumes that I have a user login called "marcel" on the remote system):

```
scp marcel@faraway_sys:/directory/path/ap_file ap_file
```

Remember that the software was installed in /usr/local/bin, so if you don't have that in your PATH, you will need to use the full pathname. As in the secure shell connection, the remote system will ask me for a password to go with my user name. In the second example, I have a file called ap_file that I want sent to the remote system called "faraway_sys."

```
scp ap_file marcel@faraway_sys:/directory/path/ap_file
```

You see? It's the same (more or less) as saving copy from location 1 to location 2. In the first case, location 1 is remote because I am copying *from* the remote. In the second case, the file is here, and I want to send it *to* the remote system.

Here are some other options that you may want to consider:

```
scp -p FROM TO
scp -r FROM TO
scp -v FROM TO
```

The `-p` means that you preserve modification times, creation dates, and so on from the original file. If what you are copying is a directory, you can use the `-r` flag, which means a recursive copy. Be careful with that one. You want to be darn sure that this is *really* what you had in mind. You could be transferring an awful lot of data. Finally, the `-v` gives you some nice, verbose feedback on what the copy process is doing.

Does the transfer seem kind of slow compared to something like a regular FTP? Chances are that if you tried a small file, you would not have noticed, but larger files may seem sluggish in their travels from one system to the other. Well, that's not surprising considering `scp` encrypts every file it transmits (which takes time) making them larger (which takes more time) as they move from location to location. You can try the `-C` flag, which turns on compression. You might find that helps a great deal.

You do have another option for secure file transfers: the `sftp` program, a secure replacement for the stock `ftp` program. This isn't quite a drop-in replacement, however, so don't expect it to behave exactly like the `ftp` program you are used to. To connect to testsys as user natika, you would use this format:

```
sftp natika@testsys
```

At this point, you'll be prompted for a password, and then you'll find yourself at an `ftp`-like prompt.

```
sftp>
```

Type help and have fun.

PGP and GnuPG

For public key encryption of electronic mail, Pretty Good Privacy (PGP) is the de facto standard. The official release of PGP is available from the PGP Security Web site (`http://www.pgp.com/`). Depending on your needs, PGP provides a number of packages of varying price. There are also freeware clients available. Visit the site for more information.

I would like to spend some time talking about the open source alternative to PGP: GnuPG. To get the latest GnuPG, surf on over to the GNU Privacy Guard site (`http://www.gnupg.org/`). You'll need the `gmp` or GNU MP libraries in order to compile. You can get this from the GNU Web site or one of its mirrors.

Surf to `http://www.gnu.org/order/ftp.html` and look for one of the many mirrors. For the impatient, the GnuPG site also provides a link for an RPM version.

Obviously, the first thing you need to do is make the package.

```
# tar -xzvf gnupg-1.0.4.tar.gz
# cd gnupg-1.0.4
# ./configure
# make
# make install
```

Once you've got GnuPG built and installed, you will need to generate your personal key. Before I explain the various commands, I should tell you that this will create a *key pair,* meaning both your private (and jealously guarded) key and your public key (the one you hand out to all your friends).

Here is the command (note the double hyphens):

```
# gpg --gen-key
```

You will now be prompted to answer a number of questions. The first has to do with the encryption algorithm, or cipher. The default is DSA and ElGamal. I recommend choosing the default.

The next question concerns key length. You have a choice of 768, 1024, or 2048 bytes. Because the DSA standard is 1024, I recommend choosing that. Granted, 2048 bytes is more secure, but it takes much longer to generate. The question-and-answer session continues with the expiration date of your key. The default here is to not expire the key, but you can define days, weeks, months, and even years. Choose the default and confirm your choice. You will then be asked to supply the name of the key user, e-mail address, and a comment.

Now comes the fun part. You will be asked to enter a pass phrase. All this information will be used to create the key, and too much information is better than too little. The catch, of course, is that more words means more typing when it comes to deciphering your encrypted messages. For my test, I will use `I f33l v3ry s3cure n0w` as my pass phrase. Now, GPG runs off and generates your secure key pair. This can take awhile, depending on your processing power, and you may have to help the system along by doing some other kind of work in order to create "entropy" for random number generation. The program suggests moving the mouse. I started a `find /-print` and waited.

When you're done, you have a bright, shiny new key pair. You'll also notice a new entry in your `$HOME` directory: `.gnupg`. If I list the contents of the directory, I see this:

```
$ cd /home/marcel/.gnupg
$ ls
options     pubring.gpg    random_seed    secring.gpg     trustdb.gpg
```

The options file contains a list of default flags on the `gpg` command. You can add your command-line options here (without the double dashes) and they will be automatically added. Also notice the `pubring.gpg` and `secring.gpg` files. It is a good idea to make backups of these files immediately and store them somewhere other than your computer. This is particularly true for the `secring.gpg` file, because it contains your personal secret key. The last file is your database of trust. It defines the level of trust that you assign to the public keys you collect. More on this later. Right now, let's take your GnuPG package out for a spin.

Every day, I run the fortune program and have it generate a new message of the day, like this:

```
/usr/games/fortune -l > /etc/motd
```

I'll use that file as my encryption test. Here's the basic command:

```
gpg -ear marcel --output /tmp/fish /etc/motd
```

The dash-e option means "encrypt." The dash-a option means that `gpg` should create "armored" ASCII output. You've seen it in e-mail messages, usually starting with BEGIN PGP MESSAGE and then a bunch of letters, numbers, and various other characters. The next part of the command is the user for whom I am encrypting the message—in this case, myself. The dash-dash-output tells the command where to write this output. You can see I am sending my output to `/tmp/fish`, but it could be anywhere, including standard output (your screen) by using `--output -`. The last part of the command is the file I want to encrypt. Here's the output of that command (the contents of the fish file):

```
-----BEGIN PGP MESSAGE-----
Version: GnuPG v1.0.0 (GNU/Linux)
Comment: For info see http://www.gnupg.org

hQEOAzlo5+tIbkclEAQA5Pj0CRm5eXfHouFEiTGQA5YKKVhLaoo2zGFuWnuugfBq
kDALlUI1a7oNAUff4n2hca6N5ff0erKjOnXGj/GTnEUZpZbWfDJTjZgOg5lS0IQ2
VNlLFKN5WuM2mSNstxs/uezSIdv0s5zmQ+rbW+aKM4NETUil9IOGNUEvEf3clLoD
/AsvIAk+ucMzGxYVXNUVCfqEelViK5YnDoDE1rdX8hgTgZxCelg/YcaNS1dVRaOr
/orTP2eMCO91krhy2RohMNvxWxJ7FRj8LELztEIGqiqYnjwIKaJae2bxRB/KOB7l
aeT+MuUR8qCpdyL5mzv6vaOx/LTWtfTKBAVA3HH6g1b3ycDw3Ys25w6N6EOq1IRn
XflKhEt6Ix4zvmB7v1rMORE+R8luyiVPsbweG+P4TZuqBp2uetx8VhFgRF/2RPMc
el7NM01tHISIVPaX5w/P+SKtxx70DnLW1cQEx8O9YUokLC9qw7oHFOp/ETIE+tXr
bl+ZeUtoBIHZd8EPEKzh919R4z5Rh3+FGJZjFM66KwCFxjRfwX7hgdVG35+N+CpK
t4vHg4izT5yjZyTL9ZJfdapV6XH9yvp8Y1nOToylOFxwb26YZsoq6UeLCW5da1vD
SWW3HwvXx/lew/yVnLQhKdfmMpdgJN4oQAfkn2lmPwJJJQcImQh6sm8B9xIzC+vJ
4R0Fq5RwU3osZ6hIk1KpCMAvF9RUOEYldZSEle3Fu7pDczt7nH0EgAkaKdrg6FmQ
Hmp9wFSqTzBy55x+I+pVFSu8F/J2J/9Z3UjxnpWNMip0Vt+3w2DP1RR9/JKo1uko
+1mIWpisB6WSEajBTZot05CzgmPn3Y2I8n4cJVV9Dx35FRy3Ih7xUKrrB8FC9YBC
ZDHsas9qLplseVZHB9LEbIyEUfCEOVpoQo0dU4qKd9470PFk
=h47B
-----END PGP MESSAGE-----
```

Difficult to read, even on one's most clever of days. It's also one of the hardest things to crack. No wonder the military is upset by the idea of civilians having this kind of technology at their disposal. To decode the message, simply use this command:

```
gpg -d /tmp/fish
```

You will then be able to read your message of the day in plain English (or whatever language it was originally written in). Here it is:

```
My boss has pointy hair just like ...
```

Hmm . . . maybe stuff like that is better left encrypted.

Before you can get anyone to send you encrypted information in any way, shape, or form, you need to provide that person with the public half of your key. This key can then be imported into another GnuPG package or a Windows 9*x* client such as PGP. To start, publicly export the key you created earlier.

```
gpg --export -a --output mykey.asc mgagne
```

The `-a` flag creates an ASCII output to the file `mykey.asc`. This can then be sent as an e-mail attachment. As with all security-related things, there are items to be careful with, which I'll cover in a moment with the concept of importing keys. In the meantime, here are the first few lines of the ASCII output generated:

```
-----BEGIN PGP PUBLIC KEY BLOCK-----
Version: GnuPG v1.0.0 (GNU/Linux)
Comment: For info see http://www.gnupg.org

mQGiBDgM4HkRBAC+Tzf9NOHx0fCOEE8zH2pSGKoz6g5ocqwu/4p3bMfJCWNDYo0Y
Pd2JWFKindbRdrerTpQYBvL+1OdgsrZgDBFxiqd10A1EkpN0NCnmCG2BCwdgygaB
jV6RSBumrABvVgcjc/1AmAkH3SHZR3xd81Pi26jqWsdOmLXZD7r+fTWEJwCg8IOl
```

Now you have your public key, ready for others to import.

Importing keys is a multistep process. The reason for this is that after importing the public keys, you want to "sign" them to verify authenticity. What good is an encrypted message if it comes from a source you can't be sure of? This verification can be a tricky process, especially if you picked up the key from a key server or simply had it e-mailed to you. It's always a good idea to contact the individual providing the public key and arrange another method of verification (fax, voice, and so on) before you verify keys with your digital signature. Checking over that long PGP KEY BLOCK can be quite a job.

A way to shorten this is with the `--fingerprint` option.

```
 $ gpg --fingerprint
 pub  1024D/A8C01167 1999-11-19 Natika (This is our cat's key)
<natika@salmar.com>
```

```
Key fingerprint = E895 FCCE 76A4 1007 D890  FE30 EC9C 57EC A8C0 1167
sub  1024g/9E7F38F7 1999-11-19
```

As you can see, the fingerprint is much shorter and easier to verify with a phone call than the full PGP KEY BLOCK.

Let's say I want to send an encrypted message to a user on my system whose login name is "natika." Natika starts by exporting her key as described previously. She then sends me the ASCII file that contains her key, and I import it like this:

```
$ gpg --import natika.asc
gpg: key A8C01167: public key imported
gpg: Total number processed: 1
gpg:               imported: 1
```

My key ring now contains two keys, the one I generated for myself and the one belonging to Natika. To see what is currently in your key ring, use the following command:

```
$ gpg --list-keys
```

This gives me the following output:

```
/home/mgagne/.gnupg/pubring.gpg
------------------------
pub  1024D/0E0EF396 1999-10-19 Marcel Gagne (Marcel's personal
Key) <mggagne@salmar.com> sub  1024g/486E4725 1999-10-19

pub  1024D/A8C01167 1999-11-19 Natika (This is our cat's key)
<natika@salmar.com> sub  1024g/9E7F38F7 1999-11-19
```

By the way, if you want to see the contents of your secret key ring, use this command instead:

```
$ gpg --list-secret-keys
```

The next step is to sign Natika's key in order to verify the authenticity of the key. You do this with the `--edit-key option.`

```
$ gpg --edit-key natika
```

The result is a command-driven dialogue that offers you a number of different options from a command prompt. To list the available commands, type a question mark and you'll get a short description of what each command does. The one you want to take is sign. The program will ask you to confirm that you really, genuinely want to sign this public key, and then it will ask you to confirm again with your pass phrase. I can now send Natika an encrypted message that only she can decrypt.

```
$ cat my_message | gpg -ear natika | mail natika
```

Because you need both the public and the private key to decrypt the message, even I cannot decrypt the message I just sent her.

Earlier on, I mentioned key servers. Sometimes it makes more sense to distribute your public key through a public key server, rather than e-mailing it to each and every person you want to communicate with. You could post the key on your Web site or `ftp` server if you had one, or you could upload your key to a key server where others could find it. A good place to start for this is Keyserver.net (`http://www.keyserver.net/`). From this site you can upload keys, search for other public keys, and even find other key servers.

At some point, you may want to delete a key from your public key ring (particularly if you start collecting vast quantities from public key servers). You can do that with the command `gpg --delete-key user_id`.

Graphical Front Ends to GnuPG

This may be sacrilege to some. I know that there are those who appreciate a nice, menu-driven interface for GnuPG key management (or PGP, for that matter). Now that you can do all this at the command line, you are allowed to relax behind the friendly face of a GNOME or KDE program. In fact, there are several very nice-looking packages for key maintenance, including the GnuPG project's own GPA (see Figure 24.1).

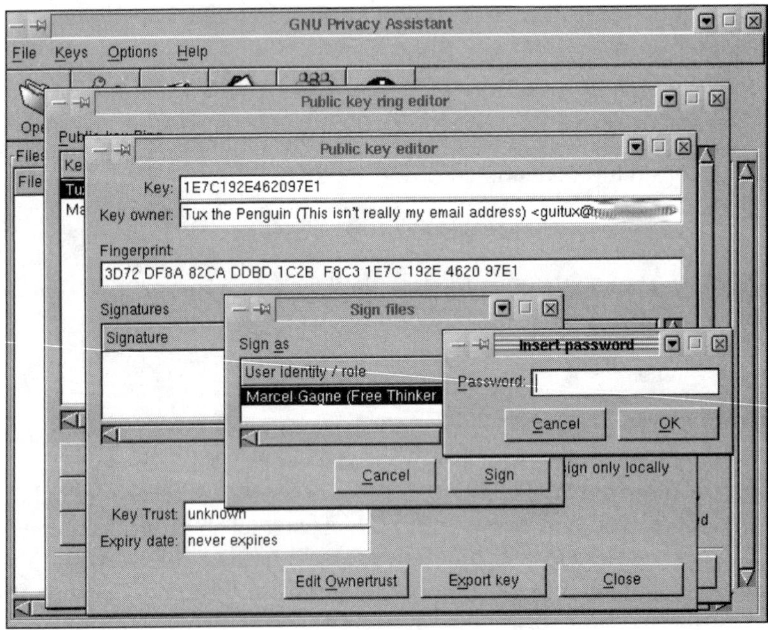

FIGURE 24.1 Key management through GPA

The GnuPG site is pretty equal opportunity and lists many other similar projects including Geheimnis, GnomePGP, and TkPGP. So, pay it a visit. Try others and see what you like.

While you play with these tools, one or more of you may be asking some naive-sounding questions at this point, such as "How can I trust a public key?", "Just because someone picks up my key and encrypts a message to me, does that make it legitimate?", and "How am I supposed to check the validity of possibly hundreds of keys?"

These are all excellent questions that open the door to a discussion of signing authorities and trust relationships.

Building Trust Relationships

Suppose you work for MegaCorp InterUniversal, Inc. (if such a company exists, it is strictly coincidental), and corporate policy says that all company e-mail must now be signed and encrypted for it to be accepted by the system. Lately, your competitor, UltraCorp MultiDimensional (same disclaimer as before), has been trying to finagle information from employees through bogus e-mails. No problem—your public keys are posted on a key server so anyone can send you encrypted e-mail. The problem is that MegaCorp has 23,000 employees and business contacts. Again, how can you possibly verify all those signatures?

In essence, that's the idea behind companies such as VeriSign and GlobalSign. They provide a certificate signing authority that validates public keys. Whenever you visit a Web site that runs a secure Web server (SSL), that server will present your browser with a certificate generated by that site. Normally, you do not see this exchange at all. That's because Netscape (and Microsoft) browsers employ various top-level signatures from trusted certificate authorities to basically say, "Yes, that's a good signature. You don't need to bother the user with this one." The question of trust has already been answered for you.

If you want an example of what I am talking about, just visit your bank's Web site and then enter a secure page (check your bank balance, or do something else that requires secure access). Other than that little padlock icon on your browser changing from the open lock to the glowing, closed lock, nothing really different happens. Now, surf on over to my Web server at `https://www.salmar.com/marcel/securepage.html` and check out the difference. Your browser will let you know it is receiving a certificate from the Salmar Web site. Because this certificate has not been purchased (or signed) by someone, your browser has deemed it untrustworthy, and you are now asked to verify that trust on your own. (Sure. Sure. Of course you can trust me.)

Now, click that padlock icon in your Netscape browser. A window pops up with the title Security Info. On the left-hand side, click Signers under the Certificates menu. A long list of certificate authorities will appear (see

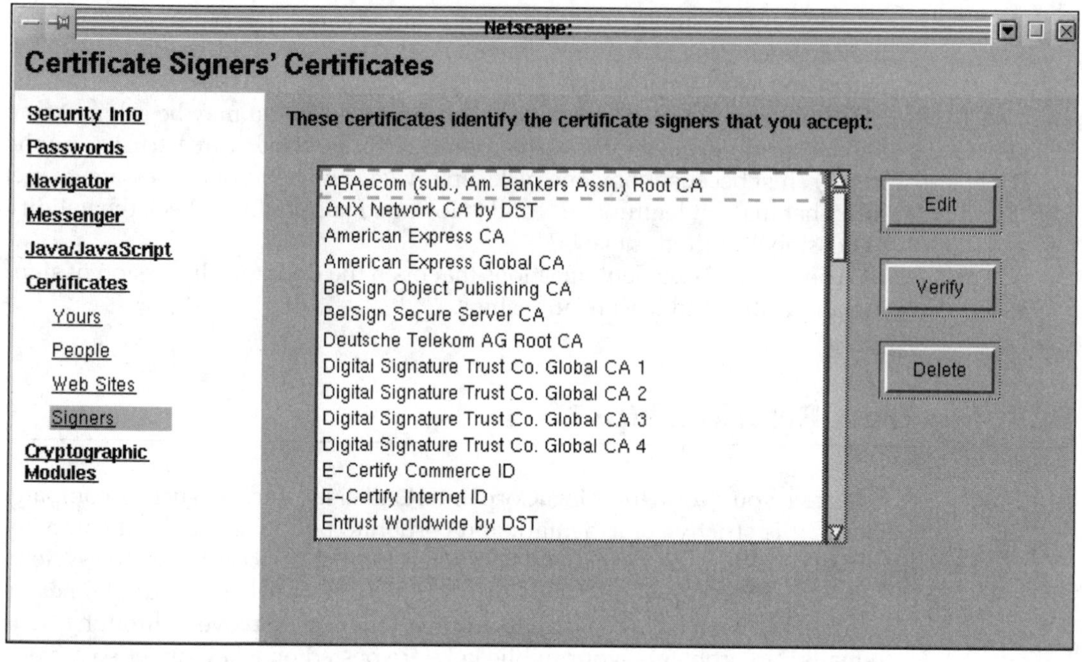

FIGURE 24.2 Using a Netscape browser to view "signers" for SSl certificates

Figure 24.2). Any certificate sent to your browser that has been signed by any of these CAs will simply be accepted.

The concept of a GnuPG or PGP web of trust is essentially the same.

Let's say I've just imported the key for user natika with the command `gpg --importnatika.asc`. Immediately, I decide to encode a message to her like this:

```
# gpg -ear natika message.txt
```

The system promptly responds with this message:

```
Could not find a valid trust path to the key.  Let's see whether
we can assign some missing owner trust values.

No path leading to one of our keys found.

1024g/486E4725 1999-10-19 "Marcel Gagne (Marcel's personal key)
<mggagne@salmar.com>"
          Fingerprint: C337 4781 C7CD E8EE EBF0  0E2B 3968 E7EB 486E 4725

It is NOT certain that the key belongs to its owner.
If you *really* know what you are doing, you may answer
the next question with yes
Use this key anyway?
```

That's a good question. Natika is a user in the jungles of Antarctica, and phone service is spotty. Getting in touch with her is difficult at best. How can I verify that this key is valid? Here's a quick refresher on the `--edit-key` option:

```
# gpg --edit-key natika
```

If you type help at the command prompt, you will notice an option called "trust" and another called "check." A couple of pages back, I had you simply sign the key so that you wouldn't go through this question-and-answer dialogue. Let's type check and see what natika's key says.

```
Command> check
uid Natika Feline <natika@antarctic.dom>
sig!       9486A537 1999-10-20   [self-signature]
sig!       2E5230F8 1999-11-25   Australian Rainbow <rainbow@downunder.dom>
```

The key has two signatures: one from the key owner herself and the other from someone who goes by the handle "rainbow." This is where trust comes into play. It turns out I know rainbow and his signature. What does that mean to my level of trust regarding natika's key? When I first imported rainbow, I entered my `--edit-key` dialogue and chose trust. I was given four options, from 1 (don't know) to 4 (I trust this person with my credit card). Depending on the trust relationship I have assigned to the user rainbow (in this case, complete and total), I can now accept natika's key and will sign it based on his recommendation. That's because rainbow is my third party, the signing authority I can safely use to verify another's signature.

As you sit back and watch the machinations of governments, security agencies, and large conglomerates vying for their piece of the pie in trusted PGP certificates, it's worthwhile to have a look the Global Internet Trust Register site (`http://www.cl.cam.ac.uk/Research/Security/ Trust-Register/index.html`) and read the organization's fourfold statement of purpose (in particular, number 4).

Not everyone needs something like this, of course. If you just want to exchange trusted or encrypted e-mail between a few friends, a worldwide signing authority is not a requirement. Even now, though, companies are selling validated PGP certificates, and business is growing. All those interested in secure e-mail and secure communications would do well to keep an eye on associated developments.

Encrypting Electronic Mail

Because I mentioned signing e-mail messages with my GnuPG (or PGP) key earlier on, let me show you what that looks like. Using my KDE mail client (`kmail`), I can either sign my messages with my public key (so that others may verify it) or pick up messages signed in the same way (see Figure 24.3).

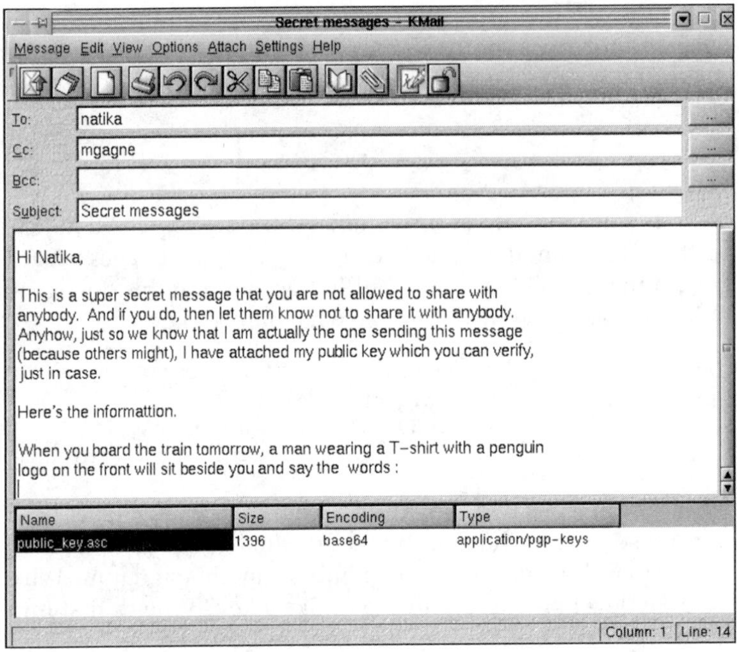

FIGURE 24.3 GnuPG-signed messages in `kmail`

While this is no longer a big deal anymore, there are still mail clients that do not yet support GnuPG or PGP. Don't be discouraged. Once again, check the GnuPG Web site for a list of e-mail clients and links to the appropriate Web sites.

Building a Secure Web Server

The notion of running a secure Web server may seem like an obvious need if you (or your company) is looking at running an e-commerce Web site. Anyone submitting credit card information will want to know that his or her transaction is indeed secure, hidden from the prying eyes of techno-snoops.

For those running corporate intranets, this may still be an excellent idea. Ask yourself whether the information on your Web site is for public consumption. In your home office, this may not be a problem, but how do you know that your communications between your notebook and your Web site aren't being monitored when you are visiting a friend or customer?

My office has a personal little application we call "gatekeeper" that allows us to authenticate with our server before being granted access to private e-mail and other services. When visiting a client, I don't want to risk my password being picked up during this authentication (or at any time, for that matter). I need peace of mind and so do you.

An SSL-enabled Web server will give you that peace of mind.

Building the SSL-Enabled Apache Server

You might find yourself asking why you need to build another Apache Web server if you already have one installed on your server. Remember, your stock Apache distribution from Caldera or Red Hat does not come SSL-enabled. You will need two packages for this one. The first is your Apache Web server source. You can get that one by surfing over to `http://www.apache.org/httpd.html` or going directly to the FTP site at `ftp://ftp.apache.org/dist/`. The current bundle (as of this writing) is version 1.3.19. That means you should download `apache_1.3.19.tar.gz` for this example.

You will also need the `mod_ssl` package from `http://www.modssl.org/source`. The release corresponds (partially) with the Apache release in numbers; in this case, I downloaded `mod_ssl-2.8.2-1.3.19.tar.gz`. In order to build from a fixed point of reference, I will put all my SSL builds in a directory called `/usr/local/src`. From this directory, I will extract the files for the Apache server and the `mod_ssl` source distribution.

```
# mkdir /usr/local/src
# cd /usr/local/src
# tar -xzvf apache_1.3.9.tar.gz
# tar -xzvf mod_ssl-2.4.9-1.3.9.tar.gz
```

Strange as it may seem, I will not go into the Apache directory to set up `mod_ssl`. Instead, I `cd` to the `mod_ssl` directory and configure with these options. Keep in mind that there are several options that can be changed. If you're curious or you want to install in different default locations, try the command `./configure -help` before you start. Here's my final build command:

```
# ./configure --with-apache=../apache_1.3.19 --with-ssl=shared
```

The configure script will run happily for a while. When I am returned to the command prompt, it is time to build my server.

```
# export SSL_BASE=/usr/local/ssl
# cd ../apache_1.3.19
# ./configure --enable-module=ssl
# make
```

If you follow the documentation, the next step is described as simply `make certificate`. This, unfortunately, makes only a test certificate (and it shows up that way when presented to your users). The real command to use is this:

```
# make certificate TYPE=custom
```

I am asked several questions now. The dialogue goes something like this (look for my answers in Step 2).

```
# make certificate TYPE=custom
make[1]: Entering directory
`/usr/local/src/apache_1.3.19/src'
SSL Certificate Generation Utility (mkcert.sh)
Copyright (c) 1998-2000 Ralf S. Engelschall, All Rights Reserved.
Generating custom certificate signed by own CA [CUSTOM]
______________________________________

STEP 0: Decide the signature algorithm used for certificates
The generated X.509 certificates can contain either
RSA or DSA based ingredients. Select the one you want to
use.
Signature Algorithm ((R)SA or (D)SA) [R]:
______________________________________

STEP 1: Generating RSA private key for CA (1024 bit)
[ca.key]
117545 semi-random bytes loaded
Generating RSA private key, 1024 bit long modulus
..........+++++
.............................................+++++
______________________________________

STEP 2: Generating X.509 certificate signing request for CA
[ca.csr]
Using configuration from .mkcert.cfg
You are about to be asked to enter information that will be
incorporated into your certificate request. What you are
about to enter is what is called a Distinguished Name or a
DN.
There are quite a few fields but you can leave some blank.
For some fields there will be a default value.
If you enter '.', the field will be left blank.
-----
1. Country Name             (2 letter code) [XY]: CA
2. State or Province Name   (full name)     [Snake Desert]: Ontario
3. Locality Name            (eg, city)      [SnakeTown]: Toronto
4. Organization Name        (eg, company)   [Snake Oil,Ltd]:
Super MegaUniversal Corp.
5. Organizational Unit Name (eg, section)   [Certificate Authority]:
6. Common Name             (eg, CA name)   [Snake Oil CA]:SuperMega CA
7. Email Address             (eg, name@FQDN)
[ca@snakeoil.dom]:ca@supermegauniversal
```

There's more. Without giving you all the gory details, here are the next steps:

```
STEP 3: Generating X.509 certificate for CA signed by itself
[ca.crt]
STEP 4: Generating RSA private key for SERVER (1024 bit)
[server.key]
```

```
STEP 5: Generating X.509 certificate signing request for
SERVER [server.csr]
STEP 6: Generating X.509 certificate signed by own CA
[server.crt]I
STEP 7: Encrypting RSA private key of CA with a pass phrase
for security [ca.key]
```

The last step is an important one. I will now encrypt my server's private key with a pass phrase. I must remember this pass phrase, because I will need it to start my server.

```
STEP 8: Encrypting RSA private key of SERVER with a pass
phrase for security [server.key]

The contents of the server.key file (the generated private
key) has to be kept secret. So we strongly recommend you to
encrypt the server.key file with a Triple-DES cipher and a
Pass Phrase.
Encrypt the private key now? [Y/n]: y
read RSA private key
writing RSA private key
Enter PEM pass phrase:
```

Now for the big final step:

```
# make install
```

If you followed along with the instructions more or less as I wrote them, your new Apache server will be installed in `/usr/local/apache`. Make sure you shut down your old server first (assuming you were actually running an old server). To start the new server, use this command:

```
/usr/local/apache/bin/apachectl start
```

This starts up your run-of-the-mill Web server with no SSL. To start the SSL version, use this command instead:

```
/usr/local/apache/bin/apachectl startssl
```

To run the secure server, you will be asked to provide the pass phrase you used when you generated the site certificates. Next, start your browser and surf to your new secure server with the following:

```
https://your_server_name
```

Notice the `https` instead of the usual `http`. For the curious, I will also tell you that SSL Web services run on port 443 by default, unlike the port 80 of standard Web services. Check it out by looking in your `/etc/services` file. Notice, also, that your browser has just popped up a warning, telling you it can't verify the authenticity of the certificate it has just received. You must now decide if you can trust yourself (I don't need to include a smiley here, do I?).

Resources

Apache

http://www.apache.org/

GNU Privacy Guard (GnuPG)

http://www.gnupg.org/

ModSSL

http://www.modssl.org/

Netscape SSL 3.0 Specifications

http://www.netscape.com/eng/ssl3

OpenSSH

http://www.openssh.org/

OpenSSL

http://www.openssl.org/

Pretty Good Privacy

http://www.pgp.com/

SSH (Secure Shell)

http://www.ssh.com/

World Wide Web Consortium (W3C)

http://www.w3c.org/

Chapter 25

Security: The Battle for Your System

Your system is a battleground. The day you expose your computer to the Internet, you present a tempting target for others. You might ask why someone would want to break into your system. After all, there may be nothing of value on your system other than some documents you make publicly available. These hardly qualify as industrial secrets or concerns of national security. That machine of yours may be nothing more than the computer that you surf the Net with. What the heck would a cracker want with you?

Answer: A beachhead.

The attack on your system may be nothing but a prank, but your compromised system may also be the beachhead from which the cracker launches attacks on other systems. Recently, there have been a few famous instances of distributed denial of service attacks, where major corporate servers were brought down using the combined force of many, many systems. Under the weight of e-mails or Web requests sent by the thousands every second, the server under attack collapses. Your compromised system might end up as one of those pawns doing another's bidding.

What about your own system? Rarely does a cracked system work as well as it did before the attack. Weird little things that you can't quite put your finger on start happening. Certain e-mails don't get through. Your `su` command doesn't work anymore. Information you are expecting to see in your logs goes missing. Your system performance has taken a turn for the worse.

Not so bad? How about this: *You are being watched!* Your logins to other systems are being monitored. Your credit card information now belongs to an unknown cracker. Your private documents have stopped being private.

It is up to every system administrator and every owner of an Internet-connected system to do his or her best to deter the system cracker. By helping yourself, you help others as well.

What Is a "Script Kiddie"?

Most people would like to think that crackers are super-genius whiz kids with an IQ of 250 sitting up late in their high-tech computer rooms (assembled from old toasters, telephones, and pop-can pull-tops). Well, here's a real shocker: It doesn't take any great brains whatsoever to break into a system, just the right set of tools.

The term "script kiddie" says it all. Using a script downloaded from a warez Web site or a cracker newsgroup, script-kiddies literally follow the script. They run the programs, scan your network, and when they find the right signature (an insecure version of BIND, for instance), they follow the next step on the script. Usually, this means running a program that exploits that network program's particular weakness—for instance, they may cause a buffer overrun in a susceptible program.

A script kiddie is not necessarily a genius. A script kiddie is just persistent and has a lot of time on his or her hands. It's time to shut the script kiddie down.

The Basics: Your TCP Wrappers

Over time, I've answered an increasing number of calls from people whose systems have been cracked. Usually they're not aware of this, and the call starts out something like this: "There seems to be something wrong with my e-mail. Could you have a look at it?"

I log on, do a quick look around, and see his footprints everywhere. The wily cracker has struck again.

When you set up your Linux system, you brought up a powerful, high-level, multitasking network operating system—one that was maybe a little too powerful. Out of the box, some distributions start a large number of services (`rlogind`, `inetd`, `httpd`, `innd`, `fingerd`, `timed`, `rhsd`, and others). Do you know what they all are? You should. As system administrator, you've got enough things to worry about, such as that hung printer, but if your machine is exposed to the Internet, you should pay particular attention.

Crackers will use the latest distributed exploits (programs and/or techniques) to break through a well-known or recently uncovered security hole in your system. The good news is that you, as a security administrator, are just as capable of becoming aware of these exploits. Regular visits to your Linux distribution Web site, such as Red Hat or Caldera Systems, can keep you on top of the latest patches to stop those exploits. While you're at it, find out about the exploits themselves by checking out the BugTraq forum or CERT (check the Resources section at the end of the chapter for URLs). Innovators or not, cracking a system is made so much easier if the door to your server is left wide open.

The simplest means of controlling access (short of turning off your machine) is through a program called a *TCP wrapper*. Chances are good that you loaded it as part of your system installation. Using the wrapper, you can restrict access to some of those services I mentioned earlier. Best of all, the wrapper logs attempts to gain entry to your system, so you can track who is testing the locks on your virtual doors. If you do not need to have people logging in to your system (using `telnet`, `ssh`, or `rlogin`), you should close the door to remote access by adding this line to your `/etc/hosts.deny` file:

```
ALL:ALL
```

The first `ALL` refers to all services. The second `ALL` refers to everybody. Nobody gets in.

Now, you should probably let the people on your internal network have access. Pretend you've set up your LAN with the approved internal network addressing scheme as detailed in RFC 1918 (a document that describes this standard). You'll use a class C network at 192.168.1.0 for the example. You'll also add your localhost (127.0.0.1) network. Here's the `hosts.allow` entry:

```
ALL: 127.0.0.1
ALL: 192.168.1.
```

Yes, that's right. There's a dot after the `1` and nothing else. Now everyone in the 192.168.1.whatever network can get in to your system. For the changes to take effect, you must now restart your `inetd` process. One that should work for everyone is as follows (note that the quotes are back quotes):

```
kill -1 `cat /var/run/inetd.pid`
```

Safe, right?

Not exactly. The `hosts.deny` file controls access only to services listed in `/etc/inetd.conf` and wrapped by `/usr/bin/tcpd`, your TCP wrapper. The wrapper looks at incoming network requests, compares them to what is in your `hosts.allow` and `hosts.deny` files, and makes a decision on what to allow through. You could be running services not covered by the wrapper, or you may not have had the wrapper configured and the cracker has already gotten through. How can you tell? How can you make your system even more secure?

What Your TCP Wrapper Is Telling You

Your Linux system does a great job of tracking access through its system logs, and denying access through the wrapper means you've just added some useful information to those logs. I talked about this in the last chapter; now it is time to take some of this information to heart as it pertains to securing your system against intruders.

If you recall, `/var/log` contains a number of files (`messages`, `secure`, `cron`, and so on) that are written to and updated on an ongoing basis. Not only is it important to be familiar with these from a day-to-day operations standpoint, but they are also invaluable when it comes to monitoring system security.

From a cracker-detection point of view, your `secure.?` file will be of particular interest. If you turned off all access (other than your local network) as described earlier, you can check for possible attempts as follows:

```
grep refused /var/log/secure*
```

Here's the output of an actual attempt. I've blanked out the address for security reasons.

```
Sep 12 07:52:42 netgate in.rlogind[7138]: refused
connect from 2??.?.5?.?42
Sep 12 07:52:52 netgate in.rshd[7139]: refused
connect from 2??.?.5?.?42
Sep 12 07:52:55 netgate in.rexecd[7144]: refused
connect from 2??.?.5?.?42
Sep 12 07:52:59 netgate imapd[7146]: refused connect
from 2??.?.5?.42
Sep 12 07:52:59 netgate in.fingerd[7142]: refused
connect from 2??.?.5?.?42
Sep 12 07:53:00 netgate ipop3d[7143]: refused
connect from 2??.?.5?.?42
Sep 12 07:53:07 netgate in.ftpd[7147]: refused
connect from 2??.?.5?.?42
Sep 12 07:53:10 netgate gn[7145]: refused connect
from 2??.?.5?.?42
Sep 12 07:53:22 netgate in.telnetd[7149]: refused
connect from 2??.?.5?.?42
Sep 12 07:56:34 netgate imapd[7150]: refused connect
from 2??.?.5?.?42
```

As you can see, my cracker tried several ports, or services, on my netgate server, all of which were refused because of my wrapper's configuration and the resulting logs. I took the information from this log and e-mailed it to the security authority of the ISP the cracker was using.

Now, this doesn't mean the cracker will never get in, but you know he or she is trying and that's a great start.

You can also use `more` to look at some of the other files for additional information. The `maillog` files will give you a picture of what e-mail messages are routing through your machine. If you'd like to see `ftp` transfers to and from your machine, have a look at the `xferlog` files. Because attempts at breaching system security can zero in on many different aspects of your networked system, it is important to monitor even these files. For instance, this extract from the `maillog` file shows a cracker trying to write `.forward` information into my mail spool directory:

```
Dec 11 23:45:16 netsite sendmail[2384]: XAA02384: from=<cracker@bigcompany.dom.tld>,
size=1652, class=0, pri=91652, nrcpts=3,
msgid=<00003b4d4011$000033fd$00002ec5@www.somewebsite.tld>, proto=ESMTP,
relay=www.questionablesite.dom [???.2?.?6.39]
Dec 11 23:45:16 netsite sendmail[2385]: XAA02384: forward
/var/spool/mail/.forward.netsite: Group writable directory
Dec 11 23:45:16 netsite sendmail[2385]: XAA02384: forward
/var/spool/mail/.forward: Group writable directory
```

The original address was likely forged (and I did change it to protect the potentially innocent) and you'll notice that my cracker tried to relay his or her message through another unsuspecting host in an attempt to cover his or her tracks. If this attack had been successful, the `.forward` might have contained code that provided a back door into the system.

The other file of interest here is `wtmp`. To view the contents of `wtmp`, use the `last` command—you cannot simply `cat` or `more` this file. However, you might want to pipe the output of `last` to `more`.

```
# last | more

fishduck ttyp6        nexus             Tue Sep 28
16:03    still logged in
birdrat  ttyp5        speedy            Tue Sep 28
15:57    still logged in
root     tty1                           Tue Sep 28
12:54    still logged in
```

Make sure these are all people who you want to have access. Maybe you don't know who "birdrat" is.

If you haven't checked your logs in a while and you would like to see what is in `wtmp.1`, use this version of the `last` command:

```
# last -f /var/log/wtmp.1 | more
```

"Hey, My Logs Have Nothing in Them!"

This is a sure sign of trouble.

Consider the state of your log files. If you find too little activity in your logs, or the logs tend to be sized at 0 bytes or missing altogether, it's time for damage control. In the script kiddie's book of instructions, it clearly says to cover your tracks. The easiest way to do this is to get rid of the log files and that's invariably one of the steps the script kiddie will take (although blowing away all the log information is a bit messy). Which brings me to the next topic, which can be summed up in the following way: "How can I discover whether I've been cracked?"

Detecting the Cracker

In one of his famous monotone stand-up routines, comedian Steven Wright expresses an interesting dilemma. Someone broke into his house, he says, stole everything and replaced all those things with an identical copy. In the world of the system cracker, this isn't such a crazy idea.

Here's what happens. Using some well-known hole or exploit, a cracker finds his or her way onto your system. Yet, when you do a `ps`, there is no evidence. When you do an `ls`, there is no evidence. You think your password file looks normal but you can't be sure. What to do?

One of the first things a cracker will do is replace certain files on your system. You will wind up with a new version of `netstat` so that a `netstat -a` does not show any evidence of the cracker's presence. The cracker will also replace any file that might give him or her away.

Some of those files are as follows. This is just a sample of many possibilities.

```
/bin/ps
/bin/netstat
/usr/bin/top
```

Because the files have been replaced, simply doing an `ls` will only confirm that the files are there. There are a number of ways that you can detect modified files on your system. If you are running Red Hat, Caldera, Turbolinux, or any of the releases that use the Red Hat Package Manager (aka RPM) concept, I'm going to show you a way to do this.

The first thing you need to do is find out what package these files came from. Using the `rpm` command, you can identify the location of a file (say `netstat`) with this version of the command:

```
# rpm -qf /bin/netstat
```

The system comes back with this reply:

```
net-tools-1.51-3
```

I can scan this entire package to find out what has been changed with this version of the `rpm` command:

```
rpm -V net-tools   (You can leave off the version info)
```

Now, on my test system, I've modified my `/bin/netstat` binary (I replaced the 6.0 version with 5.2, in this case). The result of the previous command should be nothing—a return to the shell prompt (the hash mark). Instead, I get this:

```
.......T   /bin/netstat
```

The `/bin/netstat` file shows up as having been modified. If I check using `rpm` (`rpm -qf /bin/ps`) for the location of `ps` and `/usr/bin/top`, I find that they belong to the `procps` package. I then run an `rpm` verify on `procps`. Here's sample output from a cracked system:

```
# rpm -qf /bin/ps
procps.2.0.2-2

# rpm -V procps
SM5..UGT   /bin/ps
SM5..UGT   /usr/bin/top
```

The cracker has gone in and replaced my version of `ps` and `top` so that I cannot see the processes he or she is running—maybe a sniffer or IRC "bot." A *sniffer,* by the way, is a program that essentially watches all your users' comings and goings and traps their passwords so that the cracker can use valid user logins to do his or her work, further hiding his or her tracks.

I'll give you a quick script now to run through your entire `rpm` database and check all your packages for tampering. Before I do that, I want to give you a warning: Not every file flagged by this report represents a compromised file. For instance, the password file on your system is not the same as it was when it was first installed. After all, you added at least one user and changed at least one password. Any file that is different from the original installation will show up as modified. Binaries, or compiled programs such as `netstat`, should never show up in this list. Here's the little script:

```
#!/bin/bash
#
# Run through rpm database and report inconsistencies
#
for rpmlist in `rpm -qa | sort`      # These quotes are back quotes
do
    echo " ====== $rpmlist ======"
    rpm -V $rpmlist
done > /tmp/rpmverify.out
```

When you run this script, the output is redirected to the temporary file /tmp/rpmverify.out. The packages are nicely sorted alphabetically, and each package is separated by a header with the package's name. You can then use more or less to view the contents of the file.

Because I mentioned that configuration and text files (/etc/passwd, /etc/inetd.conf, and so on) will very likely show up as changed when you run this script, how do you know if these are your changes and not those of a cracker? If your system is pristine, or in a state you can be sure of—such as immediately after an installation or an upgrade—you can take "fingerprints" of your files, print out the information, and refer to it if you suspect something has changed.

A way to do this is with md5sum. Those without rpm (Debian and Slackware users, for instance) can use this method to fingerprint their binaries as well. The following is the way to do it. I'll use a few files, including some binaries.

```
# md5sum /etc/passwd
d8439475fac2ea638cbad4fd6ca4bc22  /etc/passwd

# md5sum /bin/ps
6d16efee5baecce7a6db7d1e1a088813  /bin/ps

# md5sum /bin/netsat
b7dda3abd9a1429b23fd8687ad3dd551  /bin/netstat
```

Keep in mind that these are the numbers from my system. You don't want to write these down. The information will vary based on release and what you have in your text and configuration files. Other than the ones mentioned, you might want to check the following. Remember, print the results out and check them from time to time to help you determine if a wily cracker has entered your domain. Here are those files:

```
/usr/bin/passwd
/sbin/portmap
/bin/login
/bin/ls
/usr/bin/top
/etc/inetd.conf
/etc/services
```

This should give you a good starting point. Crackers will not change every file on your system and monitoring a few specific files is enough to give you a good idea as to whether or not something has been changed without your knowledge.

> You may be asking the following question at this point: "What if the cracker changes `rpm` or `md5sum`?"
>
> Questions like this demonstrate just how tricky this whole security business is. One solution to this issue is this: Immediately after installing your system and before you hook up to the Internet, get `md5sums` of `md5sum` and `rpm`, print out the results, and store them for future reference. Furthermore, have a clean copy of the `md5sum` and `rpm` programs on a write-protected diskette (or CD-ROM) stored away somewhere for safekeeping. Even if the versions of those programs on the server have been modified, your diskette version will still be clean.
>
> It's nice to know people are paying attention.

The Cracker's Not-So-Invisible Footsteps

Let's talk about what happens next. You notice that after using the `rpm` trick, files like `netstat` and `ls` have actually been modified. The question that follows is fairly obvious: "What now?"

You have a fair number of options. Depending on the importance of the system, I usually recommend taking a backup of the user directories, password, and other critical system files, and rebuilding the system without these files, using the backup as a reference for the new system. I won't just copy those files back. The cracker may have hidden things in legitimate places and you don't want to let him or her back in quite that easily.

You can also leave the system alone, tie down the host access with TCP wrappers, shut down nonessential services, and replace affected packages. This is yet another reason why you should perform regular backups (see Chapter 17). A clean, reliable backup is your best solution. Starting clean is important, but you don't always have that luxury—not immediately, anyway.

> **Quick Tip:** You may want to make copies of modified files in order to study the attack and to determine precisely how the cracker got in and what he or she was doing there.

If you discover that your `procps` or `net-tools` package has been modified by a cracker, the first thing to do is to reinstall the package. Because that package may have been the hole through which the cracker entered, it is usually a good idea to get the latest build from your vendor (Red Hat, Caldera, Debian, and so on). For the truly paranoid, the fact is that once a cracker has access to your system, he or she can replace anything, including the very files you use to track down the damage. Like the Shaolin priests in the old TV series "Kung-Fu," the cracker succeeds by being invisible.

Now, let's have a look at those invisible things.

Here is a real-life example. After a cracker attack, the machine was tied down, TCP wrappers were installed, and all affected packages were replaced. It was time to scope out the damage while keeping a close eye on the logs for repeated attempts at break in. Looking at the `/etc/passwd` file, I noticed a user, "jon," that did not belong on the system. It looked like a normal `passwd` entry and did not have root privileges. With several users on this machine, the cracker hid nicely in the `passwd` list.

When I went to jon's home directory (`/home/jon`) and did an `ls -a`, all I got was this:

```
.    ..    ..   .bashrc   .bash_history  .screenrc      emech.tar.gz
```

Other than a file called `emech.tar.gz`, things did not look that strange. Could that be all that was wrong? With a closer look though, you'll notice that there are two `..` directories (pointers to the previous directory in your file system hierarchy). That's strange. However, if I change directory to `..` with `cd ..`, I just wind up in the `/home` directory. What's up?

What's up is that there is an extra space after the second dot-dot. I can find this out as follows:

```
  # cd /home/jon
  # echo .* | cat -v

. .. ..  .bashrc .bash_history .screenrc emech.tar.gz
```

Look very closely. Notice how each item is separated by only one space. Now look between the second dot-dot and `.bashrc`. There are actually two spaces, which means the directory is actually dot-dot-space. To get into that directory and have a look around, I do this:

```
# cd ".. "
```

An `ls` shows me all this fun stuff:

```
randfiles mech.set  mech.pid  checkmech cpu.memory
mech.help mech.usage     mech mech.levels    emech.users
psdevtab
```

That is definitely interesting. Let's see if jon has any more files hidden around the disk. Using the `find` command again, I specify a search for files belonging only to this user ID.

```
# find / -user jon -print
```

Aside from what is in the `/home/jon` directory, I get this partial list:

```
/usr/local/bin/.httpd
/tmp/cl
/tmp/.l/bcast
/tmp/.l/.l
/tmp/.l/imapd
/tmp/.l/log
/tmp/.l/pscan
/tmp/.l/pscan.c
/tmp/.l/rpc
/tmp/.l/slice2
/tmp/.l/sniffer
/tmp/.l/sxploit
/tmp/.l/thc
/tmp/.l/ufs.c
```

It is starting to look as though my friend jon has been getting around. And what have we here? Sniffers. Port scanners. My cracker was making quite a home for himself. Furthermore, I discovered two other users coming from different hosts with their own files. My cracker was either operating from different locations with different IDs or he had friends.

In doing this search, I found there were even files belonging to this cracker in legitimate user directories, including one very scary file: something called `tcp.log`. This file was several hundred lines long and contained every `telnet` and `ftp` login that had come to and from the machine. *Every one!*

Aside from telling the person whose machine had been broken into that he should rebuild the whole thing from scratch, I also told him to change each and every password, not only on this system but on every system he had access to.

Here's the scoop: Part of the information the cracker collects is a list of logins and passwords you use on other systems. Why? So he or she has an easier time breaking into someone else's system. Every system you have been accessing while the cracker has had access to your system is at risk. You should contact the system administrators of those other systems and inform them of the risk they face. The flip side is that someone logging into your system on a regular basis whose system had been compromised may have given the cracker a valid login and password on your system.

Spooky, huh?

Here are a few examples to help you search for the hidden and dangerous. For starters, check the user directories for `suid` or `sgid` files. These are programs that have an `s` instead of an `x` when you do an `ls`. For instance, an `ls -l` on `/usr/bin/passwd` returns this information:

```
-r-s--x--x   1 root     root     10704 Apr 14  1999 /usr/bin/passwd
```

Chapter 7 covered this, but let's do a quick refresher. The `s` in the fourth position means that the `passwd` program acts as root when it is being executed (because root has ownership of the file). This is necessary in order to allow users to change their passwords. The second `x` is simply an `x`, but an `s` in this position means that any user in that group acts as that group. Programs that can act as a specific user or group are not a bad thing—usually. That said, for the most part, no regular (nonadministrative) user needs to have root-`suid` files in his or her home directory. Look for them this way (the command assumes that your users are created in the `/home` directory):

```
# find /home -perm -4000 -o -perm -2000 -print
```

What else can you do? Because you want to speed up the process of finding programs and files left behind by the cracker, a quick way to look for hidden directories would be good. The following command will show you those. It will also show you things like `.kde` and so on, but you'll find things like dot-dot-space and dot-dot-dot, perfect hidey-holes for the cracker.

```
# find / -type d -name ".*" -print
```

The `-type d` option means to list directories only. This can be a big list, but it is certainly a smaller one than you would get if you just walked through every file and directory on the system. What's nice here is that your proper dot and dot-dot directories (`.` being the current directory and `..` being the parent directory) do not show up in this list. If you see a dot-dot, it will have some other hidden character following it.

More Thoughts If You Have Been Cracked

What can you conclude from all this? Blowing away everything on your cracked system and starting over clean is a quick and dirty approach that enables you to create a properly secure system right from scratch. Eventually, this is what you should do anyhow. In fact, it is the *only way* to be absolutely sure that you are not still, in some way, open and compromised.

If your system must be up, using a new box and making that your new production system is probably the next best bet, but providing a brand-new system while you investigate the damage to the old one can be costly. PCs are inexpensive, but not everybody is ready to shell out a few thousand dollars to bring another system online.

The catch is this: Your cracker has left a wealth of information behind—information you may need. Getting rid of that information is a bit like getting rid of the evidence. It's tough to do an investigation without evidence.

Weigh the costs of both decisions and then act. *But do act.*

Port Scanners, Sniffers, and the Cracker's Tools

Before I get into this topic, here's a quick little refresher from Chapter 18 on network administration (just in case you skipped the earlier parts of the book because you wanted the security information *now*). On a really, really basic level, here's how this whole thing works.

One of the services started by the initialization process (aka "powering on your computer") is called `inetd`. What `inetd` does is listen for network requests. These requests are referenced by way of Internet socket numbers or ports. When you telnet to your system by typing `telnet mysystem`, you are actually requesting that `inetd` on `mysystem` start an `in.telnetd` process that handles communication over port 23.

Those services are all listed in a file called `/etc/services`. There are hundreds of these services and, unfortunately, hundreds of possible ways into your system (but I'll get to that in a moment).

When `inetd` starts, it reads a file called `inetd.conf`. You'll find this one in your `/etc` directory. Here are a couple of sample lines from `inetd.conf`:

```
#
# These are standard services.
#
ftp  stream    tcp  nowait    root /usr/sbin/tcpd in.ftpd -l -a
telnet    stream  tcp    nowait  root    /usr/sbin/tcpd     in.telnetd
#
# Shell, login, exec, comsat and talk are BSD protocols.
#
shell     stream    tcp  nowait    root /usr/sbin/tcpd in.rshd
login     stream    tcp  nowait    root /usr/sbin/tcpd in.rlogind
#exec     stream    tcp  nowait    root /usr/sbin/tcpd in.rexecd
```

When a cracker first visits your site with the intention of breaking in, he or she will often employ a tool known as a *port scanner* to find out what `inetd` is listening for on your system.

One of my favorite port scanners is Nmap. You can pick up Nmap from `http://www.insecure.org/nmap/index.html`. The latest version even comes with a nice GUI front end called `nmapfe`. Let's run the `nmap` command against my test system and see what happens.

The options are `-sS` for TCP SYN, or half-open scan, and `-O` for OS fingerprinting. *OS fingerprinting* means that `nmap` will try to guess the OS version running on the system. A cracker who knows what release of an OS you are running will use that information to decide on the most likely exploits for a successful entry. Here's the `nmap` command and the output from my test system:

```
# nmap -sS -O localhost

Starting nmap V. 2.3BETA5 by Fyodor (fyodor@dhp.com,
www.insecure.org/nmap/)
Interesting ports on localhost (127.0.0.1):
```

```
Port     State         Protocol  Service
21       open          tcp       ftp
23       open          tcp       telnet
25       open          tcp       smtp
53       open          tcp       domain
79       open          tcp       finger
80       open          tcp       http
98       open          tcp       linuxconf
111      open          tcp       sunrpc
113      open          tcp       auth
139      open          tcp       netbios-ssn
513      open          tcp       login
514      open          tcp       shell
515      open          tcp       printer
TCP Sequence Prediction: Class=random positive increments
                         Difficulty=4360068 (Good luck!)
Remote operating system guess: Linux 2.1.122 - 2.2.12

Nmap run completed -- 1 IP address (1 host up) scanned in 2
seconds
```

Those open ports are the jumping-off point for a cracker. With this information, he or she knows what to bother with and what to forget about. If there is no daemon listening on a network port, why bother trying to get in that way?

Now, go back and look at the `/etc/inetd.conf` file. Notice that `exec` is commented out (there's a hash mark at the beginning of the line) but `login` is not. If you reference that with the output of `nmap`, you'll see that those services not commented out in `inetd.conf` are listed, while those with the hash mark at the beginning are not.

This is how you shut down unnecessary ports monitored by `inetd`. Your TCP wrapper is keeping an eye on those ports, but if no one needs to have access to remote shell, why have `inetd` listen for it at all? The wrapper's job is to provide access to specific services for specific IP addresses. Earlier in this chapter, you did the quick lockdown with the wrapper. Now, go through your list of services, decide what you need and what you don't, and then disable the don'ts by commenting out those lines.

To activate the changes, you need to restart `inetd`.

```
# kill -1 `cat /var/run/inetd.pid`
```

Now, rerun `nmap`.

```
Starting nmap V. 2.3BETA5 by Fyodor (fyodor@dhp.com,
www.insecure.org/nmap/)
Interesting ports on localhost (127.0.0.1):
Port     State         Protocol  Service
21       open          tcp       ftp
23       open          tcp       telnet
25       open          tcp       smtp
53       open          tcp       domain
80       open          tcp       http
```

```
111      open       tcp        sunrpc
113      open       tcp        auth
139      open       tcp        netbios-ssn
515      open       tcp        printer

TCP Sequence Prediction: Class=random positive increments
                         Difficulty=3487082 (Good luck!)
Remote operating system guess: Linux 2.1.122 - 2.2.12

Nmap run completed -- 1 IP address (1 host up) scanned in 3 seconds
```

This last run is the same as the previous from a command standpoint, but `finger`, `linuxconf`, `shell`, and `login` are gone. I could argue that the smart thing to do would have been to leave `rlogin` in place and deactivate `telnet`, but keep in mind that this is an example. Disabling `telnet` may not be appropriate for your location. Ideally, if you needed to access your system remotely, you would close both `telnet` and `login` and run `ssh`, the secure shell, instead.

For those services that are run by `inetd`, disabling them in this manner completely removes them from external access, even beyond your `/etc/hosts.allow` file.

What should you disable? If you are running a single, private machine that does not require anyone from the outside world to access it, then just about everything in the list can go. However, if you have a small network with a couple of PCs, you may still want to run `ftp`, `telnet`, or `rlogin`. Some things must be weighed on a case-by-case basis.

One final note: Use tools such as port scanners wisely. Use them only to test the security of your own systems and never, never use them to scan other people's systems. Remember, just as you are learning to deal with and watch for the cracker, so can others watch you.

Sniffers

I firmly believe that the best way to beat the cracker is to understand how the cracker works, what his or her tools are, how they work, and how your system works. It's vital to understand that the tools I present here are for use on your network. As much as I would like to make every reader an expert, there will always be things I miss. I'd like everyone to walk away from these discussions just a little bit paranoid.

Now, I mentioned in my earlier real-life example that my cracker was using a sniffer to monitor network traffic and collect user names and passwords. Because I did not go into much detail then, I'll try to clarify what I meant by "sniffing." Simply put, a *sniffer* is a tool that enables you to monitor packets as they "fly" across your network interface. You could simply monitor your machine's own traffic, but sniffers use promiscuous mode to scan all packets bound for your network.

Allow me to demonstrate.

If I run the command `ifconfig eth0` on my machine, I get the following output:

```
eth0      Link encap:Ethernet  HWaddr 00:C0:4F:E3:C1:8F
          inet addr:192.168.22.2  Bcast:192.168.22.255  Mask:255.255.255.0
          UP BROADCAST RUNNING MULTICAST  MTU:1500  Metric:1
          RX packets:49448 errors:0 dropped:0 overruns:0 frame:0
          TX packets:33859 errors:0 dropped:0 overruns:0 carrier:0
          collisions:6 txqueuelen:100
          Interrupt:10 Base address:0x300
```

Now I'll open up a couple of terminal or `xterm` windows. In one window, I'll start a sniffer program. The one I'm using is called Sniffit and I will start it in interactive mode.

```
# sniffit -i
```

In the second window, I'll rerun the `ifconfig` command and look for the differences. I'll focus on the important line here:

```
UP BROADCAST RUNNING PROMISC MULTICAST  MTU:1500  Metric:1
```

Notice the addition in this line of the word PROMISC, short for "promiscuous mode." What that means is your network interface is indiscriminate as to what network traffic it is listening for. Normally, your system is capturing only information bound for your IP address. If you put your network interface in promiscuous mode, it will receive all packets on the network.

Sniffit is a light, curses-based program that will work in a regular terminal window. I obtained my copy from my Linux vendor's contrib FTP site. You can also visit the Sniffit Web site (`http://reptile.rug.ac.be/~coder/sniffit/sniffit.html`). One of the cool things about this package is if you press Enter on one of the open sockets in the interactive list, you can watch the plain-text traffic going to and from the user's process. Yes, you can actually see what the user is typing, hence my suggestion that you consider using the secure shell as your method of remote access.

Another similar product is Netwatch (`http://www.slctech.org/~mackay/netwatch.html`). This is also a network monitoring tool that shows you what connections are alive on your network.

Now, if you are busy collecting commands to run as part of your system administration toolkit, you could do worse than to check for interfaces running in promiscuous mode. Simply run the `ifconfig` command and `grep` for PROMISC, as follows:

```
ifconfig | grep PROMISC
```

When you installed your Linux system, you probably also installed a little package called `tcpdump`. While not as flashy as the other two sniffers I mentioned, this little program will do the same thing. If you've ever wondered what goes on across your network, you'll find this enlightening. From the command line, type the following:

```
# tcpdump
```

In a few seconds, you should start seeing packets coming from and going to your system. The following is some output from my system. I told `tcpdump` to watch for traffic coming to and from `http://www.linuxjournal.com/` (a Linux magazine and information site). Notice the `-l` flag. That tells `tcpdump` to show me the output I was busy capturing to a file for later perusal.

```
# tcpdump host www.linuxjournal.com -l | tee /tmp/tcpdump.out
```

This is what the output looked like when I clicked the Web site address:

```
16:41:49.101002 www2.linuxjournal.com.www > marcel.somedomain.dom.1432: F
2303148464:2303148464(0) ack 1998428290 win 16352
16:41:49.101206 marcel.somedomain.dom.1432 > www2.linuxjournal.com.www: . ack
1 win 32120 (DF)
16:41:50.001024 www2.linuxjournal.com.www > marcel.somedomain.dom.1429: F
1805282316:1805282316(0) ack 1988937134 win 16352
16:41:50.001215 marcel.somedomain.dom.1429 > www2.linuxjournal.com.www: . ack
1 win 32120 (DF)
16:41:50.840998 www2.linuxjournal.com.www > marcel.somedomain.com.1431: F
1539885010:1539885010(0) ack 1997163524 win 16352
16:41:50.841198 marcel.somedomain.dom.1431 > www2.linuxjournal.com.www: . ack
1 win 32120 (DF)
16:41:51.494356 marcel.somedomain.dom.1429 > www2.linuxjournal.com.www: P
1:335(334) ack 1 win 32120 (DF)
16:41:51.497003 marcel.somedomain.dom.1433 > www2.linuxjournal.com.www: S
2019129753:2019129753(0) win 32120
(DF)
16:41:51.671023 www2.linuxjournal.com.www > marcel.somedomain.dom.1429:
R
```

There are many sniffer programs available. Some are stripped-down packages that simply keep track of logins and passwords from any `telnet` or `ftp` session (more good reasons to use `ssh`). Your cracker may use a modified `ps` to hide the presence of the sniffer as it logs away the hours. It may also have a perfectly innocent name in the process table, even if your `ps` is fine.

PortSentry: Active Intrusion Detection and Response

One thing you are looking for, of course, is a sign that the dreaded system cracker may be trying to infiltrate your system. The problem with crackers is that they don't just sit there and telnet to your system and try different passwords—not if they want to keep attention away from themselves as they try to break your security. The most likely first attack is a stealth port scan done with a tool like nmap.

"Stealth" means hidden, and normally this information does not show up in your log. The best defense against a potential cracker is to catch him or her and report the cracker to his or her ISP while he or she is still busy scanning your network for weaknesses. So if the scans are stealthed, how are you going to find them? Good question. A good answer comes from those crazy folks at Psionic (the same people who brought you Logcheck, which I covered in Chapter 23): a tool called PortSentry. In conjunction with Logcheck, PortSentry is an ideal way to help you identify potential threats to your system. You can pick up the latest version of PortSentry from the Psionic Web site (http://www.psionic.com/abacus/portsentry/).

The latest version is portsentry-1.0.tar.gz. To install it, extract the files into a temporary directory and build the software.

```
tar -xzvf portsentry-1.0.tar.gz
cd portsentry-1.0
make linux
make install
```

Before you actually type make, you might want to read the README.install file, which will give you far more detail than I can give you in a short description. You may also want to modify the path to certain files by editing portsentry_config.h before you compile. On my system, I simply took all the defaults and went ahead with the compile.

After you have built and installed the program, you will probably want to edit the portsentry.ignore file. You'll find it in the directory /usr/local/psionic/portsentry/. This file contains a list of IP addresses you do not want blocked. By default, you will have 127.0.0.1 and 0.0.0.0 listed. It's a good idea to put in your local host address here.

Next, you should edit the portsentry.conf file, which is located in the same directory as portsentry.ignore. Look for the section that talks about the KILL_ROUTE command. Depending on your OS or your kernel revision, you may be using route, ipfwadm, or ipchains to dynamically block offending traffic. Here's the section I uncommented for my Red Hat 6.1 system (note that you can uncomment only one KILL_ROUTE command):

```
# New ipchain support for Linux kernel version 2.102+
KILL_ROUTE="/sbin/ipchains -I input -s $TARGET$ -j DENY -l"
#
```

The `portsentry.conf` file has a number of other options, and I recommend that you at least take a look at it. For instance, you can configure PortSentry to run specific commands when a scan is detected. The text suggests paging you. Psionic also includes some warnings about how you should react on detecting a scan. Rightfully so. Here's another Marcel soapbox speech, shortened so as not to try your patience.

> **Note:** Whenever an automatic lockout occurs, you should review the report to decide whether or not the action is valid. The scan may have been accidental. *<Marcel steps onto one of his soapboxes>* You have to use your judgment. Just because some people are out to get you doesn't mean everybody is. A single port scan is not necessarily a break-in attempt. For instance, I have on occasion started my Web server without SSL. Someone attempting to connect with `https://` instead of `http://` will set off alarm bells. I don't want to report this person for my forgetfulness. *<Marcel now steps off his soapbox>* Of course, if one address scans all your ports, that address is likely up to no good.

Finally, you want to start PortSentry. I use the most sensitive mode, and I always restart it at boot time by putting it in my `rc.local` script. Here's how you run it in advanced TCP mode:

```
/usr/local/psionic/portsentry/portsentry -atcp
```

When PortSentry detects an attempt at break in or a port scan, it can automatically lock out that address by putting an entry in your `/etc/hosts.deny` file, thereby denying all TCP-wrapped services. As I mentioned previously, it will also issue route commands to block the offender or add rules to your firewall configuration with `ipfwadm` or `ipchains`. The following is a sample of a scan of my system, as reported by PortSentry and Logcheck. The actual report was several hundred lines long, because the would-be cracker scanned *every* port on my system, whether real or imaginary. I know you'll thank me for keeping it as short as possible. I've also mangled the IP address to hide the origin of the scan.

```
Active System Attack Alerts
=-=-=-=-=-=-=-=-=-=-=-=-=-=
Jul  7 21:46:04 website portsentry[462]: attackalert:
SYN/Normal scan from host:
264.63.97.521.some.domain.dom/264.63.97.521 to TCP port: 449
Jul  7 21:46:04 website portsentry[462]: attackalert: Host
264.63.97.521 has been blocked via wrappers with string: "ALL: 264.63.97.521"
Jul 13 17:44:53 website portsentry[31279]: attackalert:
Host 264.63.97.521 has been blocked via dropped route using command:
"/sbin/ipchains -I input -s 264.63.97.521 -j DENY -l"
```

There's a lot more, with hundreds of ports being listed, but you get the idea. The Logcheck program e-mailed this information to me off-site, where I could study it and take appropriate action. This is by no means a surefire cure-all against a break-in. Always keep an eye on your system and make regular backups. Watching for possible intruders is no guarantee that no one will ever break through your security. As I've said before, you have to sleep sometime. Nothing is perfect, but staying on top of and monitoring your logs regularly, as well as using tools like Logcheck and PortSentry to highlight trouble spots, will do wonders for prevention.

ipchains and Firewalls

The `ipchains` program is the successor to the older `ipfwadm` program. Most newer Linux distributions will require `ipchains` for packet filtering. If you have read the `ipchains` documentation, you've probably also felt a twinge of panic as you started to realize how complex this can all be. I'll spend the next few paragraphs providing some simple (I hope) explanations of the process, and then I will show you some nice tools for making the process just a bit easier.

To begin with, `ipchains` is a command-line utility that enables you to create packet filtering rule sets called *chains*. These chains come in a few different flavors: `input` (packets coming in from the outside), `output` (packets bound for the outside world), and `forward` (packets being routed through your system, as in the case of IP forwarding and masquerading). There is actually a fourth chain that can be user-defined and named. The format of the command is similar to the following:

```
/sbin/ipchains -A forward -j MASQ -s 192.168.1.0/24 -d 0.0.0.0/0
```

`-A` means to add a rule to the existing chain. Other options are `-D` to delete; `-R` to replace; `-I` to insert; `-N` to create a new, user-defined chain; and a handful of others. The previous command creates a rule set that will forward packets from any host on my internal network and masquerade them to appear as though all traffic was originating from one machine only. The `0.0.0.0` part means the packet destinations can be anywhere. The `-j` flag defines the action for this rule. Other than the previous options, which will do masquerading for your site, you can also specify ACCEPT (let the packet through), REJECT (reject the packet, but let the other side know it is being rejected), and DENY (don't allow the packet through and don't offer any explanation).

What else can you do with this? For one thing, you can create a pretty safe system by adding this single rule:

```
/sbin/ipchains -A input -j DENY -s 0.0.0.0/0 -d 0.0.0.0/0
```

No one will get into your system, and no one will ever know why. It might be a good idea, then, to insert the following rule into the chain *before* you add the previous rule. Then at least your local network will have access to your server.

```
/sbin/ipchains -I input -j ACCEPT -s 192.168.22.0/24 -d 0.0.0.0/0
```

Let's try something a bit more complex. Starting from scratch, you might set up the following input chain. Note that there should be no broken lines here. Each command in the list begins with `/sbin/ipchains`. You will probably also notice that the Internet address is an imaginary one. (No IP address starts with 259.)

```
#
# Input Rules
  /sbin/ipchains -F input
  /sbin/ipchains -P input ACCEPT
  /sbin/ipchains -A input -j ACCEPT -s 192.168.1.0/24 -d 0.0.0.0/0
  /sbin/ipchains -A input -j ACCEPT -s 0.0.0.0/0 -d 0.0.0.0/0
  /sbin/ipchains -A input -j DENY -p tcp -s 0.0.0.0/0 -d 259.25.132.55 137:139
  /sbin/ipchains -A input -j DENY -p udp -s 0.0.0.0/0 -d 259.25.132.55 137:139
  /sbin/ipchains -A input -j ACCEPT -p tcp -s 0.0.0.0/0 -d 259.25.132.55 80
  /sbin/ipchains -A input -j DENY -s 0.0.0.0/0 -d 0.0.0.0/0
```

You start by "flushing" your input chain. That's the `-F` option at work. You then assign a default policy of ACCEPT with the `-P` option. The next two rules allow all traffic from your local network and the outside world to enter. Next, you DENY all traffic bound for the NetBIOS services (Windows or Samba file sharing) at ports 137 through 139. A range of TCP ports is expressed by a starting number, a colon, and an ending number. Because you do want to allow Web server access on this mythical system, you then open port 80. Finally, you catch anything that is still open and does not fit the previous rules by closing off access as earlier with an all-inclusive DENY.

You might be wondering why the example started out with a policy of ACCEPT instead of DENY. The reason is a calculated risk based on administration choices. When constructing this example, I considered the creation of a rules set, added line by line remotely, whether from your own internal network or from outside. If you DENY everything immediately, you deny yourself as well. Now, when it comes time to script all these commands, you may want to consider setting up a default DENY policy rather than ACCEPT. Even so, when the rules are executed in a script at boot time, with the final result being that you DENY anything that has not been specifically ACCEPTed, the window for a cracker to exploit this policy is very small.

At any point, you can list all the rules by typing `/sbin/ipchains -L`. You can also flush the table of all chains, rule sets, and so on, by typing `/sbin/ipchains -F`. This is by no means a complete firewall setup, nor is it entirely realistic. In a real setup on a real server, there are other ports I would like open (such as e-mail or DNS services). I would also like to explicitly close access to my X window sockets (ports 6000, 6001, and so on).

Quick and Easy Firewall Solutions

While it is certainly preferable to know this stuff inside out, you can still set up a great little `ipchains` firewall with some clever programs available for free.

If the prospect of creating a firewall from scratch seems a bit daunting and you would prefer a quick and dirty approach to a rules-based IP filtering system, look no further than the `ipchains-firewall` script distributed by Ian Hall-Beyer. You can pick up the latest script at this address: `http://firewall.langistix.com/`.

To create a basic firewall, you need only call the script with your outside interface and inside interface as the parameters. Here's how I did it on my system with an external PPP connection:

```
./firewall.sh ppp0 eth0
```

As the script runs, it will set up masquerading and block out remote access to things like NetBIOS (Samba and Windows file sharing) and X sessions. Using `/sbin/ipchains -L`, you can list the rules created by the script. Ian's script is the beginnings of a firewall system taking into consideration the "usual." Customization can be done just by editing the script, which you will no doubt want to do. The defaults are fairly restrictive. For instance, vital services like SMTP are, by default, denied. The following example comes from the script itself showing where I have uncommented port 25 (among other things):

```
# telnet (23)
# $IPCHAINS -A input -p tcp -s 0/0 -d $1 23 -j ACCEPT
# echo -n "."
# smtp (25)
$IPCHAINS -A input -p tcp -s 0/0 -d $1 25 -j ACCEPT
echo -n "."
# DNS (53)
$IPCHAINS -A input -p tcp -s 0/0 -d $1 53 -j ACCEPT
$IPCHAINS -A input -p udp -s 0/0 -d $1 53 -j ACCEPT
echo -n ".."
```

Some nice graphical methods of doing this exist, but I like the idea of using something like this as the means to generate the beginnings of a firewall. Then, using something a bit friendlier perhaps, you can tweak the results.

The brainchild of Daniel Roche, EasyFw (Easy Firewall) is a Tck/Tk (version 8.0) application that provides a nice interface for firewall administration (see Figure 25.1).

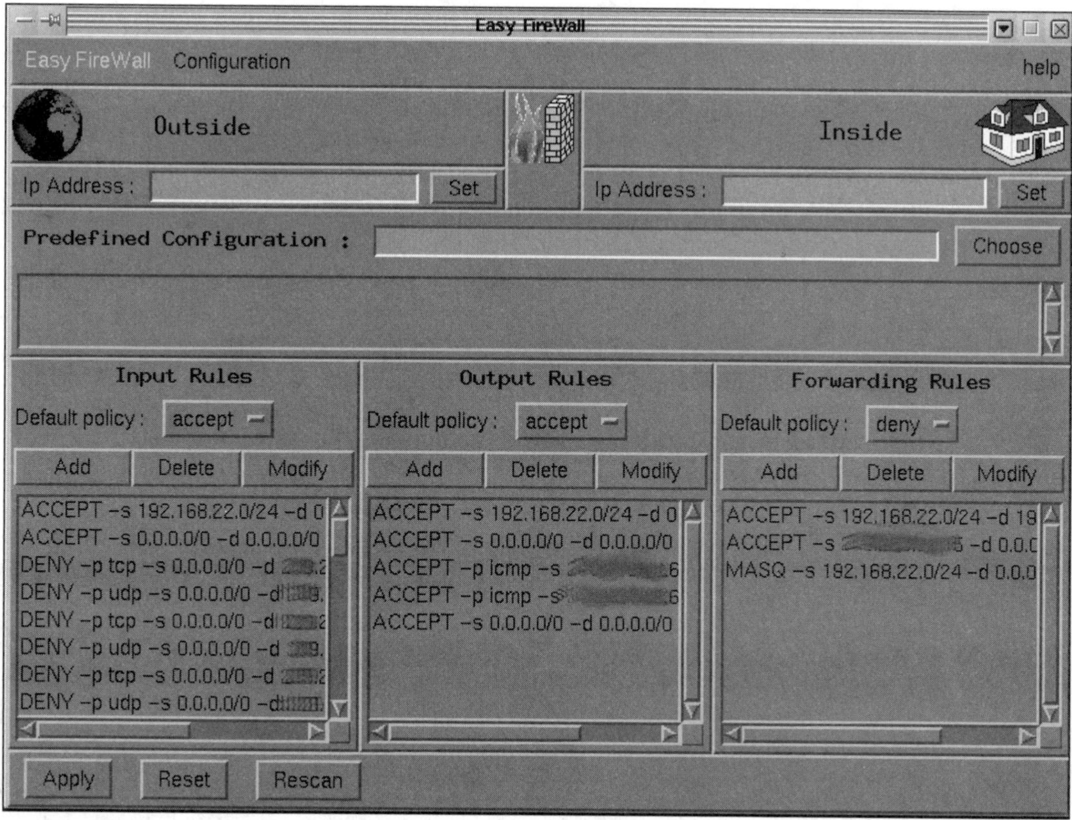

FIGURE 25.1 Using EasyFw to create or maintain a firewall

For those running older Linux versions out there, this application also works with `ipfwadm`. The program is available in a `tarred` and `gzipped` bundle or a Red Hat RPM. Because it is a Tcl/Tk application, it's also very easy to work through the program in case you happen to be curious. Installation is easy in either case because there is no compiling to do with the Tck/Tk script.

EasyFw (`http://www.linux-kheops.com/pub/easyfw/easyfwGB.html`) comes with a few predefined firewall configurations that are easily modified. Start the program with the command `easyfw`. The big friendly screen lets you choose your internal and external interfaces with the click of a button. It will then scan your system for any `ipchains` rules that may already be in effect (remember what I said about starting with the script) and display those in the interface. Modify, add, or delete rules as you see fit. When you have a satisfactory configuration, you can choose to "apply" that configuration to your running network (now or at boot time) as well as saving it to a file. The file option is great for a glimpse into the structure of the firewall rules.

Furthermore, because that file is a shell script, you can call it from your `rc.local` script at boot time.

Another nice tool for manipulating IP firewall rules was written by Koo Kyoseon. The program is called GTK+ Firewall Control Center, or gfcc for short (`http://icarus.autostock.co.kr/`). This is another clean, friendly interface to `ipchains` administration (see Figure 25.2).

This program is available in either RPM or source code format. If you will be building gfcc from source, note that you will also need the `libipfwc` library. Luckily, this is included with the source for gfcc. At the time I was writing this, I picked up version `gfcc-0.7.4.tar.gz`. The build is simple.

```
tar -xzvf gfcc-0.7.4.tar.gz
cd gfcc-0.7.4
```

Once inside this directory, you can build `libipfwc`.

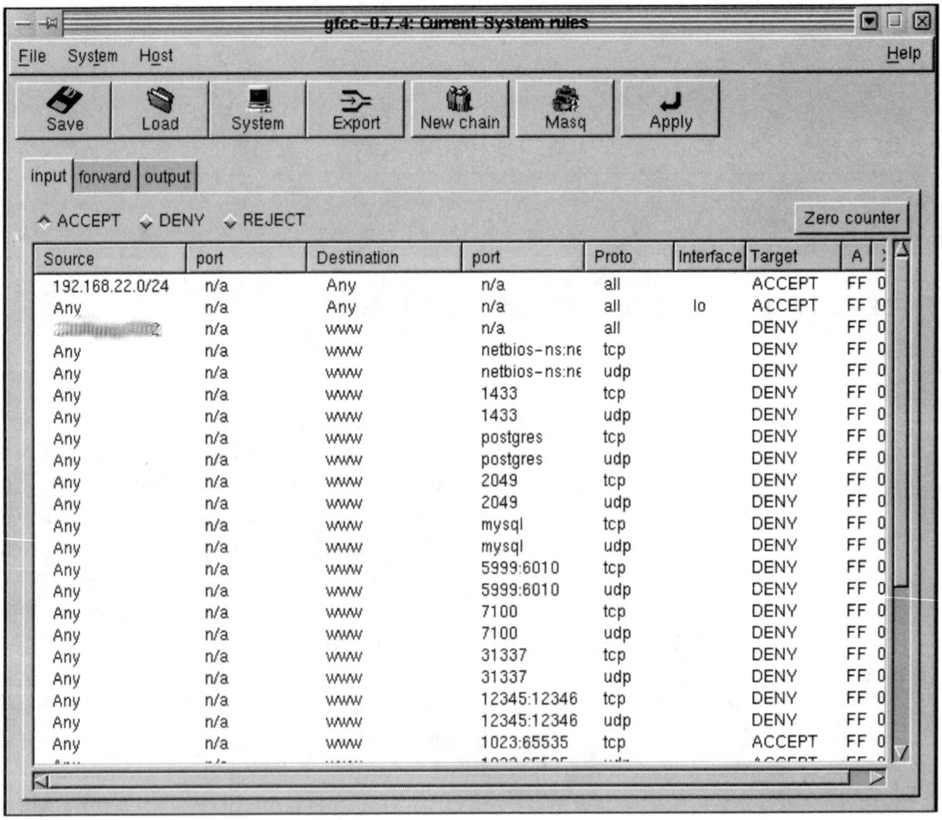

FIGURE 25.2 More easy firewall administration with gfcc

```
tar -xzvf libipfwc.tar.gz
cd libipfwc
make
Now change back to the gfcc directory and build it.
cd ..
./configure  --with-ipfwc=./libipfwc
make
make install
```

Start the program by typing `gfcc`. This program has actually two different ways of saving information. One is a list of rules very much like what you will see if you look at the existing rules in the `/proc` file system. You can do so by typing this command:

```
cat /proc/net/ip_fwchains
```

If you want a nice shell script like the one I mentioned earlier, you can use the Export function to create the script. For instance, if I export my rules to a script called `fwrules.sh`, I can load it the next time I reboot by including that path as a single line command at the end of my `rc.local` boot script.

Locating the Cracker and Reporting Him or Her

The first rule I follow for intrusion detection on any of my systems is this: Follow up on all break-in attempts. Don't let anybody get away with it. If that sounds a little heavy-handed (after all, the cracker did not make it through your security, so why bother?), consider this: Your security held today, but how about tomorrow? The cracker who failed with your system will move on to another system where he or she will continue his or her work. It's karma. Eventually, it's going to come back around to you.

The best approach is to deal with a break-in when you know it's happening. Other system administrators out there will thank you for it. Just as you will thank those system administrators who stop a cracker before he or she can get to your system. That's the policy I follow and that's the policy I recommend to everyone who is responsible for a network, whether it's one machine or 1,000 machines.

When the IP address of a cracker shows up in your logs as `dialup-11.somecompany.dom`, reporting the cracker is usually just a matter of sending mail to `postmaster@somecompany.dom` or `abuse@somecompany.dom`. Another approach is to visit `www.somecompany.dom` and looking on their page for details about reporting network abuse. What do you do if you only have an IP address? How do you know what ISP that address belongs to?

One way to find out just where the cracker is coming from is to do a `traceroute` on the address. The format is simple:

```
/usr/sbin/traceroute xxx.xxx.xxx.xxx -i ppp0
```

The `-i` flag specifies the interface through which the `traceroute` occurs. If you do not have multiple interfaces, meaning you are one PC on a masqueraded network (or something like that), you can skip the `-i` flag. A dial-up connection would follow the previous format. While `traceroute` output can be quite interesting and will sometimes yield the identity of the ISP (somewhere near the end of the chain), in most cases you'll find yourself scratching your head. If the cracker's IP address does not resolve with a simple host XXX.XXX.XXX.XXX command, I then search for who owns the address space of that IP address by visiting the American Registry for Internet Numbers' (ARIN) Whois database (`http://www.arin.net/whois/index.html`).

Entering an IP address into the search form will return the block of IP addresses that correspond to the one you just entered, including the owner of that block. You can then click the owner and find the domain record for that person or organization, along with contact information. Even armed with the technical contact's name, I usually also send mail to `abuse@thedomain.dom` (where `thedomain` is, oddly enough, the domain) as well as `postmaster@thedomain.dom`. The odds are pretty good that you will get the right person.

You won't find everything in the ARIN database. For instance, military IPs aren't listed with ARIN. You will, however, be able to locate just about anything else either there or through one of the links to other Whois databases.

Keeping Up-to-Date

Security is an ongoing battle for system administrators in charge of a network-connected machine, which nowadays is probably most of them. Your best defense is information. The more information, the better. Because new exploits are uncovered on a regular basis, it makes sense to keep an eye on the resources that are available to you.

One of the resources you should probably pay attention to is CERT. Carnegie Mellon University runs the CERT Coordination Center (`http://www.cert.org/`). If your system has been cracked, you should consider reporting the incident to CERT.

The CERT Web site also has extensive security information and "alerts" describing security issues or software weaknesses. One thing you can and should do is subscribe to the CERT advisory mailing list (`http://www.cert.org/contact_cert/certmaillist.html`).

Resources

ARIN Whois Database Search

`http://www.arin.net/whois/index.html`

BugTraq list

(To subscribe, send mail to `subscribe-bugtraq@securityfocus.com`)

`http://www.securityfocus.com/`

The CERT Advisory Mailing List

`http://www.cert.org/contact_cert/certmaillist.html`

EasyFw

`http://www.linux-kheops.com/pub/easyfw/easyfwGB.html`

GTK+ Firewall Control Center (gfcc)

`http://icarus.autostock.co.kr/`

Linux IPCHAINS HOWTO

`http://www.linuxdoc.org/HOWTO/IPCHAINS-HOWTO.html`

Linux Security HOWTO

`http://www.linuxdoc.org/HOWTO/Security-HOWTO.html`

Netwatch

`http://www.slctech.org/~mackay/netwatch.html`

Nmap Web site

`http://www.insecure.org/nmap/index.html`

RFC Editor (archives of RFC documentation)

`http://www.rfc-editor.org/`

Sniffit

`http://reptile.rug.ac.be/~coder/sniffit/sniffit.html`

Chapter 26

Performance Monitoring and Tuning

The Search for the Holy Grail

For some, performance monitoring and tuning might sound like the search for the Holy Grail. Are there any system administrators in this world who would not love to squeeze just a few more performance points out of their system—a few CPU cycles or increased disk access rates? We'll explore some of those possibilities.

Resource management is the other side of performance. Monitoring how much you have and how best to use those resources is equally important. Do you have enough memory? Is your processor up to the job? There are ways to tell. If you are all quite hungry for this Holy Grail of computing, I shall tarry no longer.

Monitoring and Analyzing Performance

As part of the ongoing job of administering one or more systems, you should keep a regular watch on just what those systems are doing. What kind of draw are you experiencing on finite limits and how will you decide when it's time to extend those limits? Luckily, every Linux system comes with the tools necessary to help you get the answers.

The uptime Command

Of all the tools that can report on a snapshot of your system, `uptime` is an old favorite of mine. Longtime Linux users like to use this command to show their Windows-using friends just how long a system can run without needing to be rebooted.

```
# uptime
9:04am  up 219 days,  2:46,  4 users,  load average: 0.31, 0.29, 0.26
```

That doesn't look too bad—219 days, 2 hours, and 46 minutes without a reboot on a Web server that gets an average of *140 thousand hits* each and every month. (Ahem, I'd like to point out that the last reboot was a *planned* one.)

Besides providing you with the opportunity for some friendly ribbing, the `uptime` command offers useful information relating to just how your system is performing. For instance, I have four users logged in. The load average is 0.27 over the last minute, 0.23 over the last 5 minutes, and 0.19 over the last 15 minutes. Load average is just that—an average. It is an indication of the number of processes in the CPU's run queue; that is, the number of processes active or waiting to execute.

Think of the load average as the number of patients in a waiting room queued up to see a doctor. In my previous printout (from my Web server), I had an average of ⅓ of a process waiting to be dealt with. The higher the number for load average, the more likely it is that your system is starting to suffer under an excessive load and the more likely that users will start ringing your extension. As the popular expression goes, "your mileage may vary," but I tend to think of anything under 4 as acceptable. Any higher and it starts feeling slow. It's virtually impossible to tell just what an acceptable load is because the user experience will define that for you. As I mentioned earlier, when the phone starts ringing, you'll know.

The top Command

For a more comprehensive peek into what your system is doing, try the `top` command. The first thing you'll notice is that the load average numbers from the `uptime` command are also part of the `top` display. Running top delivers far more information than the `uptime` command does by itself, including the actual number of processes, distribution of work done between system and user processes, memory utilization, and more.

To run `top`, simply type `top`. Here's a little sample output from one of my systems:

```
 1:39pm  up 127 days,  6:20,  4 users,  load average: 0.01, 0.01, 0.03
43 processes: 42 sleeping, 1 running, 0 zombie, 0 stopped
CPU states:  0.1% user,  0.1% system,  0.0% nice, 99.6% idle
Mem:   61864K av,  57876K used,   3988K free,  33484K shrd,   1836K buff
Swap: 136040K av,   4496K used, 131544K free                 32752K cached
```

```
  PID USER     PRI  NI  SIZE  RSS SHARE STAT  LIB %CPU %MEM   TIME COMMAND
24382 root      19   0  1000 1000   824 R       0  0.3  1.6   0:00 top
    1 root       0   0   104   52    36 S       0  0.0  0.0   0:05 init
    2 root       0   0     0    0     0 SW      0  0.0  0.0   3:39 kflushd
    3 root       0   0     0    0     0 SW      0  0.0  0.0   0:00 kpiod
    4 root       0   0     0    0     0 SW      0  0.0  0.0   1:22 kswapd
```

Notice the load average numbers there as well. From this interactive screen, you can `kill` (send SIGNALs to) processes (press k at any time and enter the PID and signal) and `renice` processes that don't need the system's full attention by pressing r. (I'll cover renicing processes a little later on.) You can also change the sort order of the fields by pressing o. If you are curious as to the various combinations, try pressing h for help while `top` is running. One of the things I like to do is run `top` in its own window, where it reports real-time activity and gives me a feel for just what is eating a system's resources. A note of caution here: If you are going to do this and you have a habit of walking away from your terminal without locking your screen (which is probably a bad idea anyway), you might want to start `top` like this:

```
top -s
```

This starts `top` in secure mode. If you try to press k now, you'll get a nice "Can't kill in secure mode" message. Think of if as leaving the safety on.

Graphical tops

For those of you who are running either KDE or GNOME as your desktops, you have some alternatives to using `top` that do essentially the same thing, but with a bit more flash. These programs are available from the desktop menus, but you can also call them from the command line.

To access KDE's `top` program, select Process Management from the Utilities menu. To run it directly from the command line in KDE, simply type `kpm`. Figure 26.1 is a screenshot of the `kpm` command at work.

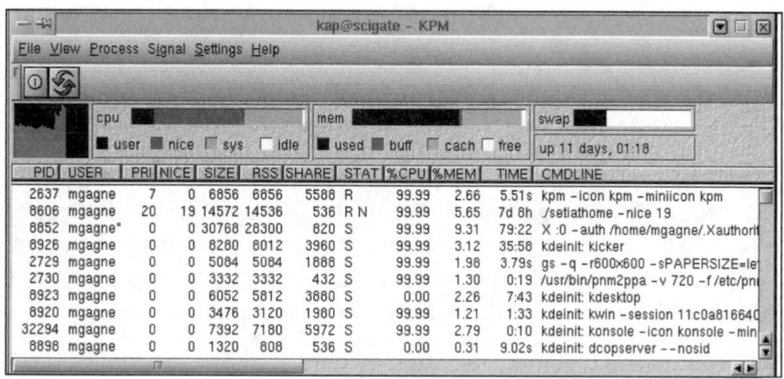

FIGURE 26.1 kpm, KDE's graphical "top"

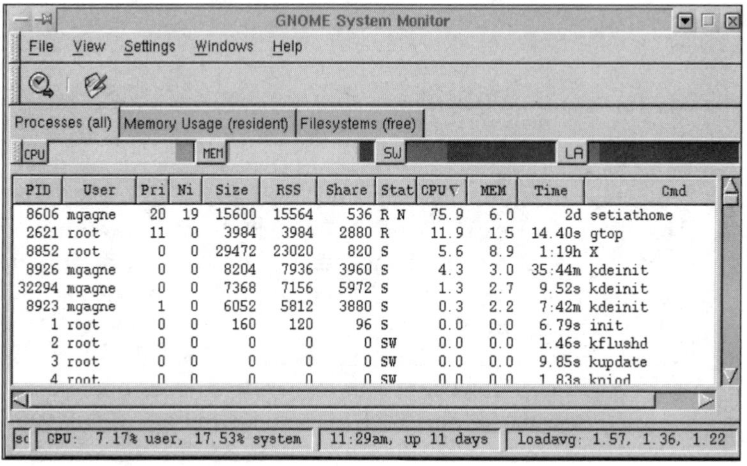

FIGURE 26.2 `gtop`, GNOME's "top"

The GNOME desktop's tool is called System Monitor and you can also find it in the Utilities menu (this time in GNOME, of course). Type `gtop` to start it from the command line.

> Do you really need all those processes?
>
> This is a very important question and answering it should require more than a few seconds of your time. The average Linux installation turns on a lot of processes by default. Do you need to run `NFS`, `portmap`, or an `HTTP` daemon? If you don't need some of these, they are best left off (see Chapter 6 on daemons and runlevels). Furthermore, a lot of these programs, if improperly configured or monitored, represent a security risk to your system. Shutting them down may buy you more than just a few extra cycles.

The free Command

The only real catch with `top`, and even more so with the graphical tools, is that it has a fairly big footprint in memory, CPU, and so on. If you run `top` (or `gtop` or `kps`) on your system, you'll notice that the program itself (`gtop` or `kps`) spends a fair amount of time as the `top` process in terms of its demands on the system. This is why I still find myself using small, lightweight command-line tools such as `free`.

```
# free
             total       used       free     shared    buffers     cached
```

```
Mem:            63004      60768       2236      24448       3720      19956
-/+ buffers/cache:         37092      25912
Swap:          128480      13996     114484
```

free reports on memory, both real and swap. You get a snapshot of the amount of real memory split across programs sharing the same memory space (shared), buffers used by the kernel (buffers), and what has been cached to disk. The -/+ line reflects the total versus used memory as reflected by the combination of the disk buffer cache and memory actually written to disk.

Working with vmstat

vmstat is everywhere. This little command is ubiquitous in some form or another in that you can find it on most UNIX systems (including, of course, Linux). It represents another means of taking a peek into current CPU usage. The format of the command is as follows:

```
vmstat interval_in_seconds  number_of_intervals.
```

In the following example, I am taking a sample every two seconds for five iterations.

```
# vmstat 2 5

 procs                       memory  swap    io      system     cpu
r  b  w  swpd   free  buff  cache si so bi bo    in  cs us sy  id
0  0  0  14004  2288  2960  22992  0  0  1  1    21  23  4  3  16
0  0  0  14004  2168  2968  23104 28  0 15  0   225  18  3  2  94
0  0  0  14004  2168  2968  23104  0  0  0 23   285   9  2  1  97
0  0  0  14004  2168  2968  23104  0  0  0  0   105   9  1  2  97
0  0  0  14004  2168  2968  23104  0  0  0  3   125  10  1  2  97
```

Let's look at vmstat in more detail, including what you can decipher from some of the other columns. Notice the columns us, sy, and id. They represent the percentage of CPU time spent dealing with user programs or requests (us); the percentage of CPU time dealing with system tasks (sy), such as waiting on I/O, updating the system stats, maintaining priorities, and all the other systemy stuff; and the percentage of CPU time spent doing nothing at all (id). If your computer were human, it would be flipping through the television program guides at this point.

One pass using vmstat 1 1 won't tell you anything worthwhile. For the numbers to actually mean something, you should take regular samplings or let vmstat run for several iterations, such as vmstat 1 20. Let's say that you consistently see the us column at a high percentage with sy taking up the rest and next to no idle time. You might guess (remember, there are lots of factors) that the system is overloaded with tasks. Essentially, the system is doing nothing but servicing system or user tasks.

Disk I/O is the great bottleneck of any system and I will talk about it more in the performance tweaks section later in this chapter. Because of this bottleneck, anything that impacts disk access time can make a substantial difference to your system. For instance, demands for memory can cause your system to swap heavily, which can cause your disks to thrash as pages of information start a manic dance from memory to disk and back to memory. Let's have a look at another `vmstat` output:

```
    # vmstat 2 5
  procs                          memory  swap     io      system      cpu
 r  b  w  swpd   free  buff   cache si  so bi bo    in   cs   us sy  id
 1  0  0   3684  1120  1308   25692 0  1   19  2    267 1270   8  3  89
 1  0  0   3684  1376  1308   25052 0  0 2687 0     172 2483 19 15  67
 1  0  0   4172  1412  1308   25408 0 4883230 122 205   346   2  6  92
 1  0  0   4168   724  1308   24768 0  0 1417 0     180  699 24  5  71
 1  0  0   4300   548  1308   25376 0 1322528 33   204 2790 13  3  84
```

This is a system where several interesting things are happening. The `r` column shows how many processes are currently in the run queue. The `w` tells me that no processes are swapped out. This is a good thing. In fact, that number should ideally always be zero. Have a look at the `swap` set of columns (`si` and `so`) and you'll see that I am starting to use more and more swap space. The `free` column is rapidly shrinking as whatever is happening continues to happen. The system, faced with a shortage of real memory, starts to swap a great deal of memory out to disk as well. You can see that activity in the `si` and `so` columns, which can be a great indicator of how your system is doing as far as memory is concerned. The `si` column refers to the amount of memory swapped in from disk, while `so` is memory swapped out to disk. That's memory, not processes, by the way. You should not immediately panic when you see this. This kind of swapping in and out is a pretty common thing to see, particularly when you first start up a huge application such as a graphical word-processing program or even your X desktop. When everything finishes loading, you'll see those numbers settle down again. Some real memory will be freed up and the amount of used virtual memory (`swpd`) will likely be somewhat higher. The real problem becomes evident when you start hitting the ceiling with virtual memory and `si/so` activity never seems to settle down.

What about Good Ol' ps?

In playing with all these high-tech tools, it's easy to forget that some very basic tools can be quite useful. For instance, the `ps` command is a great way to find out who is doing what and how much it is costing you in terms of resources. By using the `-o` flag to define what fields I want displayed, I can create a custom process-status display. Then I can specify a single field on which to sort. In the following example, I am sorting on the percentage of CPU usage.

```
# ps -eo pid,%cpu,user,rss,args --sort -%cpu | more
  PID %CPU USER      RSS COMMAND
 8606 75.8 mgagne   14536 ./setiathome -nice 19
 8852  1.1 root     23312 X :0 -auth /home/mgagne/.Xauthority
22698  1.0 mgagne   17652 kdeinit: konqueror --silent
8926   0.3 mgagne   6568  kdeinit: kicker
20996  0.1 mgagne   15636 kmail -caption KMail -icon kmail -miniicon
kmail
    1  0.0 root      120  init
    2  0.0 root        0  [kflushd]
    3  0.0 root        0  [kupdate]
    4  0.0 root        0  [kpiod]
    5  0.0 root        0  [kswapd]
```

The `-e` flag specifies that I want to see all processes. Notice as well that when I specified what field I wanted to sort on I put a hyphen in front of it (`-%cpu`). Leaving out the hyphen (a minus sign in this case) means that I want a reverse sort, with the highest usage first. Another useful field to sort on is `rss`, or "resident set size," which is the amount of real memory (RAM) in use.

In the following example, I am reverse sorting on `rss` and introducing another interesting element: `vsize`, the virtual memory in use.

```
# ps -eo pid,%cpu,user,vsize,rss,args --sort -rss | more
  PID %CPU USER       VSZ  RSS COMMAND
 8852  1.1 root     30420 22980 X :0 -auth /home/mgagne/.Xauthority
22698  1.0 mgagne   27708 18128 kdeinit: konqueror --silent
20996  0.1 mgagne   24732 15636 kmail -caption KMail -icon kmail -miniicon
kmail
 8606 75.8 mgagne   17640 15564 ./setiathome -nice 19
20038  0.0 mgagne   16752 6916 kdeinit: konsole -icon konsole -miniicon
konsole
 8926  0.3 mgagne   19936 6572 kdeinit: kicker
 8923  0.0 mgagne   18684 5344 kdeinit: kdesktop
```

I could probably spend several pages showing you how useful the `ps` command can be in determining how your system resources are being used (but I won't). I suggest that when you have a few moments, you spend some time and read that stirring work, the `ps` man page. Play with the command. Learn what it can teach you. Not only will it open your eyes to what is going on in that system of yours, but I guarantee you'll have fun too (well, maybe a little bit).

Performance Enhancing Tweaks

Back a million years ago when I first started working with UNIX systems, I always had to compile my own kernels (as in the early days of Linux). I did this because every system was different in terms of hardware, drivers, number of users, and so on, and all these parameters had to be taken into consideration before I ever booted my systems. Otherwise, the twentieth person would log in and the system would go down in flames. Resource and capacity planning as well as performance tuning were low-level issues that had to be considered. This is not so much the case with today's systems. For those who want my answer as to why and when you should rebuild your kernel, take a quick jump to Chapter 12, and then come back here. The next few pages deal with how *not* to rebuild your kernel. I am going to cover ways to improve your system performance without tweaking the kernel and without rebooting.

Caution: Please, be very careful when doing any kind of OS-level tweaking. The same command that sends your system speeding along as if by magic can slow it down to a crawl if used improperly. While I realize that the point is to speed up your production system, please remember that you are experimenting with live data (and tweaks are *always* experiments). *Always have a backup.* Performance tweaking is fun and the results can be nothing short of impressive, but there is an element of risk involved.

/proc Revisited

Way back in Chapter 6, I talked about the `/proc` file system and all the information it reveals about your running system. I also promised that I would revisit it in this chapter on performance tuning. That's because the `/proc` file system contains files that when modified will change the performance of your running system, in effect allowing you to modify your running kernel. This is an exciting part of your system and one that warrants some investigation.

The following example is from a Red Hat system (to make a point). Change to the `/etc/sysconfig` directory and do a `cat` on your network file. It should look something like this:

```
NETWORKING=yes
FORWARD_IPV4=no
HOSTNAME=netgate.mycompany.dom
GATEWAY=192.168.22.10
GATEWAYDEV=
```

In particular, look at the second line (`FORWARD_IPV4`). For those who aren't already familiar with this concept, IP forwarding means routing. *Routing* means a networked computer will forward or direct packets between networks—specifically, packets from other computers on your network. In this manner, a computer with a single dial-up Internet connection can act as a gateway for a whole network of computers. By default, your system does not do IP forwarding. If you want to change it so that at boot time (or network restart) you have forwarding turned on, change the value of `FORWARD_IPV4` to "yes" instead of "no." Now, here's a little problem for all you upgraders.

If you are upgrading to Red Hat 6.2 and are currently running with IP forwarding, you may find that things don't seem to work with your old configuration scripts. If you start with a squeaky-clean 6.2 system, your `/etc/sysconfig/network` file will have an entry that says something like this:

```
# FORWARD_IPV4 removed; see /etc/sysctl.conf
```

The `/etc/sysctl.conf` file looks like this:

```
# Disables packet forwarding
net.ipv4.ip_forward = 0
# Enables source route verification
net.ipv4.conf.all.rp_filter = 1
# Disables automatic defragmentation (needed for masquerading, LVS)
net.ipv4.ip_always_defrag = 0
# Disables the magic-sysrq key
kernel.sysrq = 0
```

In both cases, the same thing is happening. As a result of these parameters being set, changes are made to an entry in the `/proc` file system—in this case, `/proc/sys/net/ipv4/ip_forward`. If you `cat` this file, you'll see a simple 0 sitting there or a 1 if you are running forwarding. To make a short story long, changing your network to go from not forwarding to forwarding is as simple as changing the `/proc` entry.

The way to write your own entry into a `/proc` entry (`ip_forward`, in this case) is as follows:

```
echo "1" > /proc/sys/net/ipv4/ip_forward
```

That has exactly the same effect as mucking about with the other network start-up scripts.

> This procedure works on *any* Linux—it isn't restricted to Red Hat. If you can't figure out where the configuration parameter is or where the system thinks it should go, it doesn't matter.

To make sure this happens at boot time, just add that line (with appropriate comments for yourself) to your `rc.local` script. Remember, depending on your system, this script might be in `/etc/init.d` or `/etc/rc.d`.

Cool. The point (was I making one?) is that you can change things on your running system, essentially modifying your running kernel. In fact, a number of the entries in `/proc` can be modified while your system is running. The reason for doing this varies from changing the behavior of things to extending limits that are otherwise built into your kernel at compile time to improving performance.

The downside is that you can wind up with things being worse than they were before you started touching them, which is why I offer the following warning.

> **Warning:** Be *careful*. Be very careful whenever you change things in `/proc`.

Let's look at something else. By now, you're probably all familiar with denial of service (DoS) attacks. A fairly simple one is the `TCP SYN` flood. The lowdown on this one is that in establishing communication with a remote network, you send a packet that is then acknowledged by that network, whose acknowledgment you then acknowledge. Sort of like this silly conversation:

"Hey there, remote."

"Hey yourself."

"Good, you're home and you're talking. Let's chat."

Usually when you call someone on the phone, you expect that person to say "Hello," at which point you say "Hello" back. If I were to call your house a thousand times in a matter of seconds and hang up immediately, I might be well on my way to making you either nuts or dangerous. In the case of your system, a `TCP SYN` flood is that phone ringing thousands of times in a very short period of time. Meanwhile, your system is still keeping an ear open, looking to hear a reply to its "Hello," a reply that isn't coming. Force a system to keep track of too many such one-sided messages (there's a system/kernel table that does this), and your network may become unavailable (or worse). This is what `syncookies` are for: a mechanism for your system to dump unacknowledged acknowledgments (what a mouthful) if it is taking too long for a reply. If your network happens to be under attack, `syncookies` will also dump any SYN packets that would push your system over the edge.

Now, any recent Linux kernel has support for TCP `syncookies` compiled in but not necessarily turned on. If your system is connected to the Internet as a gateway, you will definitely want to turn this feature on. To do that, go back to `/proc`. A `cat` of `/proc/sys/net/ipv4/tcp_syncookie` will show it to be set to 0 (for "off"). To turn `syncookie` protection on, change the 0 to a 1 just as you did with IP forwarding.

```
echo "1" > /proc/sys/net/ipv4/tcp_syncookies
```

Here's another interesting one before you go. Do a `netstat -a` and have a look at the display. You'll see something like this:

```
Active Internet connections (servers and established)
Proto Recv-Q Send-Q Local Address          Foreign Address       State
tcp        0      0 gate1.mycorp.dom:2354  www.mycorp.dom:pop3   TIME_WAIT
```

```
tcp        0   6 gate1.mycorp.dom:2344   news.whodat.ca:nntp    ESTABLISHED
tcp        1   0 gate1.mycorp.dom:2277   visit.rsite.org:www    CLOSE_WAIT
tcp       57   0 gate1.mycorp.dom:2195   host.somsite.org:ftp   CLOSE_WAIT
```

Notice the numbers attached to the local address (that is, `gate1.mycorp.dom:2195`). These are TCP sockets, and their numbers are assigned as needed by the system. As you might guess, there is an upper limit to these sockets (or ports) through which remote sites can communicate with yours. That number has a lower and an upper limit. The lower limit is 1024 and the upper limit is 4099. Check it out for yourself.

```
# cat /proc/sys/net/ipv4/ip_local_port_range
1024 4999
```

If you are running a busy Web site, you may find yourself hitting that wall. On such a (busy) site, the recommended procedure is to change the limits from 1024 4099 to 32768 61000, as follows:

```
echo "32768   61000" > /proc/sys/net/ipv4/ip_local_port_range
```

Okay, one last little question. How does the system do the things I am having you do manually? Here is the first method. On one of my systems (Red Hat 6.0), there's this bit of code in the `/etc/rc.d/init.d/network` script:

```
if [ "$FORWARD_IPV4" = "no" -o "$FORWARD_IPV4" = "false" ]; then
    value=0
    message="Disabling IPv4 packet forwarding"
else
    value=1
    message="Enabling IPv4 packet forwarding"
fi

if [ $value != `cat /proc/sys/net/ipv4/ip_forward` ]; then
    action "$message" /bin/true
    echo "$value" > /proc/sys/net/ipv4/ip_forward
fi
```

Notice the `echo "$value" >` line near the bottom. Looks pretty much like the same thing you've been doing at the command line. Now here is the second method. Earlier, I mentioned that Red Hat 6.2 does it a bit differently. That was back when you looked at the `sysctl.conf` file earlier to set IP forwarding. How does that figure into what the system does for setting these parameters? The answer is that the file `/etc/sysctl.conf` is used by the command sysctl. Have a peek at your `/etc/rc.d/init.d/network` script (with `vi` or `cat`) and look for the following line:

```
action "Setting network parameters" sysctl -p /etc/sysctl.conf
```

Note: On certain Linux distributions, this file may be in `/etc/init.d`. Later versions of Debian use the `/etc/init.d/networking` file rather than the `/etc/init.d/network` file.

The -p for sysctl tells the command to read its parameters from the named file (in this case, /etc/sysctl.conf) and one of those parameters is ip_forward. Here's my final question to you before I move on to other things. Without looking at the source code, what do you think sysctl does?

File System Tweaks

In past lives (working with other UNIX operating systems), the environments I administered ran complex databases, often with hundreds of users. I'm fond of the following tweaks because they represent parameters that required a kernel rebuild if you found yourself starting to run low. You made your best guess, but invariably it would be kernel rebuild time soon enough. With Linux, these parameters are simple /proc tweaks. If you are running a busy database system with a large number of users, this is one you might run into. The file-max parameter defines the maximum number of open files on your system at any given time. For most, the default of 4096 is plenty. For a busier system, you might want to push that limit up somewhat. As an example, let's just double that number.

```
echo "8192" > /proc/sys/fs/file-max
```

If you are getting errors telling you that you are running out of file handles, it's definitely time to change that number, but don't wait for users to start ringing you up. You can look under the hood and see when this limit is approaching without waiting for errors. (Preventative maintenance—what a concept!) If you do a cat on /proc/sys/fs/file-nr, you will get three numbers. The third number will be your file-max. The first number is allocated file handles and the second number is actual used file handles. Why the two numbers? When the Linux kernel allocates a file handle, it does not release it. If you increase the file-max value, you should also increase inode-max. Considering that each open file requires an inode for stdin and stdout (and possibly a network socket), this needs to be somewhat higher than your file-max. Take your file-max value, triple it, and write it back out to inode-max.

```
echo "24576" > /proc/sys/fs/inode-max
```

Busy Web server? News server? Here's another tweak for your files, and this one has nothing to do with /proc. One of the options for the mount command is noatime. In other words, do not update the access time on visited files. Each time a file is read, the access time is updated, which can yield useful information about file usage (with the find command, for instance). Odds are that you may not need that information. In the case of a Web server getting a few thousand hits a day (an hour?), this little change can make a difference. Historically, this option was a suggestion for directories on news servers. Today, we are usually talking Web servers. This is an environment where small files are accessed over and over again (versus a database environment which traditionally has a few very large files).

To mount a file system `noatime`, use the `-o` flag as follows. In this example, I'll use the pretend drive `hda5`.

```
mount -o noatime /dev/hda5 /data1
```

If you want this to happen automatically, you can also edit your `/etc/fstab` file so that you have an entry similar to this one:

```
/dev/hda5        /data1          ext2    defaults,noatime       1 2
```

Improving Disk Drive Performance

As I've mentioned, the real bottleneck in terms of performance is often (usually?) disk. In modern systems, we run large databases where numerous users have real-time access to data. Any improvement in disk performance is a blessing in that kind of environment. Hidden away on your Linux system is a little command called `hdparm`. This is a command-line utility with a fair amount of flexibility and power. With it, you have the ability to modify certain I/O-related parameters on your actual hard drives, which can lead to substantial changes in disk access performance.

> **Note:** If your system did not come with `hdparm`, you can find it at `http://www.ibiblio.org/pub/Linux/system/hardware/`.

> **Warning:** Remember my constant badgering on this topic. If you don't have a backup, this is a good time to stop and do one. Yes, I know. The book is almost over and the man is still preaching backups. Nevertheless . . . let's continue.

You should probably start by having a look at the hard drive before you go changing anything. Using the `-i` flag, `hdparm` will return a little information about the type of drive you have and some of the basic capabilities. Here's what happens when I run it on one of my Linux machines here in the office (devsys1):

```
[root@devsys1 /root]# hdparm -i /dev/hda

 /dev/hda:

    Model=QUANTUM BIGFOOT TS12.7A, FwRev=A21.0G00, SerialNo=38190552
    Config={ HardSect NotMFM HdSw>15uSec Fixed DTR>10Mbs }
```

```
RawCHS=24876/16/63, TrkSize=32256, SectSize=21298, ECCbytes=4
BuffType=3(DualPortCache), BuffSize=418kB, MaxMultSect=16, MultSect=off
DblWordIO=no, maxPIO=2(fast), DMA=yes, maxDMA=2(fast)
CurCHS=1658/240/63, CurSects=-1656749698, LBA=yes, LBAsects=25075008
tDMA={min:120,rec:120}, DMA modes: sword0 sword1 sword2 mword0 mword1 mword2
IORDY=on/off, tPIO={min:120,w/IORDY:120}, PIO modes: mode3 mode4
```

There's a lot of good stuff here. For instance, take note of that DMA information. This will come in handy as you start playing with the settings. To find out whether anything you do will have any benefit, it is a good idea to get a baseline reading of what kind of access you have beforehand. There are two hdparm flags that deliver this type of information. The first, -t, will provide a kind of benchmark report of a physical read of sequential data on the disk. The second parameter is -T, which reports on cached buffer reads. In essence, this involves no real read of physical data but is more of a performance report of your processor, memory, and so on. For simplicity's sake, you can use the two parameters in conjunction with each other; hdparm will take this into consideration and make some corrections. The hdparm documentation suggests running this test a few times to get a good average reading. In this example, I will only show you the report of one such run (they were all extremely close).

```
[root@devsys1 /root]# /sbin/hdparm -Tt /dev/hda

/dev/hda:
Timing buffer-cache reads:   64 MB in  0.74 seconds =86.49 MB/sec
Timing buffered disk reads:  32 MB in 10.54 seconds = 3.04 MB/sec
```

Keep those numbers in mind because the change will be quite dramatic. By default, data transfer from your disk is happening in 16-bit chunks. On an IDE or EIDE drive, this is what the hardware does, but by the time it hits the controller, it could travel across your system's bus in 32-bit chunks. To find out whether 32-bit I/O support is enabled, use the -c parameter.

```
[root@devsys1 /root]# /sbin/hdparm -c /dev/hda

/dev/hda:
I/O support  =  0 (default 16-bit)
```

As you can see, I am running bare 16-bit. Let's change that with a -c3 switch to hdparm. The 3 tells the program to turn on 32-bit I/O with sync.

```
# /sbin/hdparm -c3 /dev/hda

/dev/hda:
setting 32-bit I/O support flag to 3
I/O support  =  3 (32-bit w/sync)
```

When I run hdparm with the -Tt flags again, I get a set of numbers that is starting to look quite a bit more interesting than the first run-through.

```
# /sbin/hdparm -Tt /dev/hda

/dev/hda:
```

```
 Timing buffer-cache reads:   64 MB in  0.65 seconds =98.46 MB/sec
 Timing buffered disk reads:  32 MB in  6.23 seconds = 5.14 MB/sec
```

Notice that while the buffer cache reads (the reads from memory) have not changed in any major way, my disk reads have changed quite dramatically. Because disk access is generally among the slowest of random access operations on your system (not counting CD-ROM or floppy), this is starting to look very interesting.

So 32MB of disk reads went from 10.54 seconds to 6.23 seconds. I suppose I should be happy with that, but can I do better? There is one other parameter to consider. Whether I can do better or not should be evident in my `-i` (information) `hdparm` operation from earlier on. You'll notice that in my example, I have a `DMA=yes` reading followed by some additional DMA information:

```
DMA modes: sword0 sword1 sword2 mword0 mword1 mword2 .
```

This tells me that my disk supports direct memory access (DMA). Essentially, this means that my drive can send information directly from the drive to system memory. The processor does not have to be involved in the operation. To set DMA access, use the `-d1` parameter (`-d0` means "off").

```
# /sbin/hdparm -d1 /dev/hda

/dev/hda:
setting using_dma to 1 (on)
using_dma     =  1 (on)
```

All right. Now let's check that little benchmarking result again, shall we?

```
/dev/hda:
Timing buffer-cache reads:   64 MB in  0.65 seconds =98.46 MB/sec
Timing buffered disk reads:  32 MB in  2.32 seconds =13.79 MB/sec
```

From an original 10.54 seconds to 6.23 seconds to 2.32 seconds. Some IDE/EIDE drives out there also support UDMA but, sadly (not having a handy UDMA drive), I cannot speak for those.

Do-It-Yourself Benchmarks

The previous examples with `hdparm` actually show you some numbers you can nail down, but how can you be sure that things have actually improved? You've done all this tweaking and it feels like commands are executing faster, but "feels like" is hardly what you would call scientific. Loading and running complex benchmark software and trying to come up with some kind of baseline system on which to test everything is not what happens in a real, working environment. That's why you buy and read those benchmark reports. What, then, can you do?

There's a little command on your system called `time` that you should be aware of. The purpose of this tool is to time command execution. The format is as follows:

```
time -v command_string
```

The `-v` option tells the `time` command to provide more verbose output. For instance, how much time and what kind of resources are used by your system when you run a `ps ax` command? Let's find out. Because I can't do this on your system, I'll do it on mine and you can try it later.

```
#  time -v ps ax
```

When the `ps` command has finished running, `time` does its thing and shows me this:

```
Command being timed: "ps ax"
        User time (seconds): 0.08
        System time (seconds): 0.12
        Percent of CPU this job got: 41%
        Elapsed (wall clock) time (h:mm:ss or m:ss): 0:00.48
        Average shared text size (kbytes): 0
        Average unshared data size (kbytes): 0
        Average stack size (kbytes): 0
        Average total size (kbytes): 0
        Maximum resident set size (kbytes): 0
        Average resident set size (kbytes): 0
        Major (requiring I/O) page faults: 197
        Minor (reclaiming a frame) page faults: 60
        Voluntary context switches: 0
        Involuntary context switches: 0
        Swaps: 0
        File system inputs: 0
        File system outputs: 0
        Socket messages sent: 0
        Socket messages received: 0
        Signals delivered: 0
        Page size (bytes): 4096
        Exit status: 0
```

There is one other flag you might be interested in if you are taking regular performance measurements: the `-o` flag. What it will do is report the statistics of your command to a file. Because each successive run with `-o` overwrites the file, you may also want to use the `-a` switch. This tells `time` to append its output to the end of the specified file rather than overwriting each time—er, I mean *iteration*. This is what my complete command looks like with all the options set:

```
time -a -o psout.txt -v ps ax
```

I can run this at regular times from a `crontab` with another program analyzing or graphing the results. The possibilities are limitless.

Resources

`hdparm`

`http://www.ibiblio.org/pub/Linux/system/hardware/`

KDE Desktop

`http://www.kde.org/`

GNOME Desktop

`http://www.gnome.org/`

Appendix A

The All-Linux Office?

Let's face it. For now and for the foreseeable future, this is still a Windows world. While Linux is rapidly taking command of the server world, the desktop belongs to the boys from Redmond.

Nonsense!

The first paragraph is my twisted way of making a point. Here's the truth and the whole truth. The time for the all Linux office is *already here*. It is possible to make the switch and run an office environment with each and every desktop system running Linux. All the tools you need are there for you—"you" being the administrator *and* the user. This section isn't specifically about system administration; it's more about choices and alternatives—hence its position as an appendix to the rest of the book.

Running Linux desktops throughout the office makes sense for the system administrator as well. Armed with what you find here, you should have enough in your hands to convince the CIO, the CEO, and the CFO too.

The System Administrator's Tale

When it comes to administering the various systems scattered across an office, the less work you have to do with individual PCs, the better. While PC users now accept regular system hangs, blue screens, and general protection faults as part of everyday life in the office, their problems are still yours—even if those problems are things they are used to. This is the first bonus of deploying Linux in the office: reliability.

The second has to do with user profiles and individually catered desktops. In the world of Windows, when a user totally mangles their desktop (or their PC), it is up to the administrator to provide a quick fix (often involving a reboot), or worse, reloading their PCs from scratch. That last option sounds a bit drastic, but with the nearly complete absence of log information, no access to source, and proprietary APIs, sometimes the only answer is reformatting and reloading Windows. With Linux, however, you set up individual user accounts with specific permissions. Then you take backups of individual user desktop configurations. If a desktop gets "mushed," you simply restore the default desktop. If something doesn't work right, you have logs that you can refer to in order to help you isolate the problem. User and group permissions mean that you can keep users away from the parts of the system they should not be modifying.

Speaking of users and groups, now you can completely customize the user environment based on who logs in. Each user's desktop (even if multiple users are on the same PC), can be unique if you so wish.

You can also save yourself a lot of walking. Linux is built for networking. From a remote workstation, you can easily install software on those desktops. I talked about different methods of remote control in chapter 9 and again in chapter 19. Furthermore, the simplicity and power of access to the command line means you can work in the background without affecting your users. Finally, changes to a Linux system rarely require a reboot.

This is great for you as systems administrator, but what about your users?

The User's Tale

If you take a moment to get to the heart of the matter, you will realize that the desktop experience for most users (though, I grant, not *all*) consists of a handful of core applications. Pretty desktop environments aside, these core applications are the word processor, the e-mail agent, and the web browser. Following close behind are the spreadsheet, the scheduler, and the graphical or presentation package. All of these tools are well served by Linux. Better yet, the selection is more impressive than you may have thought.

Of course, users do more than just that—they burn CDs, play music, watch videos, and enjoy a game or two. As important as these tools are, we'll leave them aside for now and start with word processing.

Word Processors

The word processor is the killer app. It's the one application that no desktop user can be without, and its invention, like that of the typewriter before it, revolutionized the office environment. Consequently, I think it is safe to say that the word processor is *the* office application. Sure, we read e-mails, surf the web (but only for business reasons), and work on the odd spreadsheet, but mostly we write. We write letters, memos, and reports. Almost everyone in the office needs to use a word processor at one point or another. In our "paperless society" (just kidding), we generate an amazing amount of written, printed information. Word processors are the engines that let us do the job.

The first question, sadly, that will spring forth from many of your users—not to mention their managers—is "Does it work with Microsoft Word?" While this may not be a problem for the home office or the small one-person business, this is a real concern for larger companies that must exchange documents back and forth between other offices that use Microsoft's very popular word processing package.

On that note, if you are trying to woo people away from their MS applications, then StarOffice from Sun may well be the ticket. Its word processor is called **StarWriter** and it is pretty darn close to 100 percent compatible with the MS Word product in terms of features and document format. In fact, StarWriter reads and writes MS Word files with near perfect accuracy. Furthermore, its interface is very much what your users are familiar with. Speaking from personal experience, I can tell you that I've watched users (who are familiar with Word) sit down in front of Sun's word processor and start working as though they had always used it. StarOffice, the suite that contains StarWriter, is distributed free of charge to businesses and private individuals alike. You can pick it up from Sun at the address below. Sun also sells a boxed set with full documentation.

While trying to decide what you will use in your office, you should also consider taking a look at **KWord**, KDE's word-processing package, part of their KOffice suite. KWord is a little different as word-processing packages go. It uses a frame-based approach to document layout that won't be unfamiliar to those who have used Adobe's FrameMaker. While the idea here is to provide a level of flexibility in document design that exists primarily in desktop publishing packages, KWord is still more than capable of handling your simple letters.

Complexity is not necessary for every environment. If you are looking for a simple, *standalone* word processor, a final candidate might be **AbiWord**. Aside from being able to import a number of document formats, AbiWord is cross-platform so that you can interchange documents between Linux, Windows workstations, BEOS systems, or FreeBSD.

http://www.abisource.com	AbiWord
http://www.koffice.org	KWord
http://www.sun.com/staroffice	StarWriter

SpreadSheets

In this area, you'll see some of the same players start to appear: KOffice with **KSpread** and StarOffice with **StarCalc**. Both are well integrated into their respective environments, but as I mentioned in the last section, sometimes all you need is one solid, standalone application. This is where **Gnumeric** comes into play.

While technically part of the GNOME desktop environment, you don't need to run GNOME (unless you want to) in order to use Gnumeric. For even the most demanding spreadsheet user, this is an excellent package that will import your existing Excel or Lotus 1-2-3 files (and others).

http://www.gnome.org/projects/gnumeric	Gnumeric

Integrated Office Suites

In the last couple of sections, I alluded to the idea that when talking about office applications such as word processors and spreadsheets, we often speak in terms of *suites,* integrated collections of these crucial applications that share the same look and feel across the various components. Linux is no different here and provides several suites. Once again, I am going to start with StarOffice from Sun, but I'm going to extend that option.

In 1999, Sun Microsystems released StarOffice under the GPL, turning the whole thing into an open source project. This gave birth to the **Openoffice.Org** Project, which continues to develop the StarOffice suite of applications. Actually, there are two licenses in effect here. The other is the SISSL, the Sun Industries Standards Source License, which provides some flexibility in the development of commercial applications based on the source. You should check out both the StarOffice site and the OpenOffice.org Project site.

You should also consider **KOffice**, the KDE office suite that contains KWord, KSpread, KPresenter (for presentation graphics), and others. Another suite worth looking into is **Applix Office** from VistaSource. It provides extensive support for document formats in a comfortable interface. Finally, just before you run off, have a look at **SIAG** (which stands for Scheme In A Grid), one of the most lightweight office suites I've run across and still loaded with features.

http://www.vistasource.com	Applix Office
http://www.koffice.org	KOffice
http://www.openoffice.org	OpenOffice.Org Project
http://siag.nu	SIAG
http://www.sun.com/products/staroffice	StarOffice at Sun Microsystems

E-mail agents

E-mail is the modern heart of business communication. We rely on it to keep us in touch with vendors, suppliers, customers, and coworkers. It has become a means of keeping in touch, sending memos, tracking business plans, and so on. We depend on it, and we always expect it to be there.

Numerous text or curses-based e-mail packages exist for Linux. You'll find **elm**, **pine**, and **mutt** to be very popular (and likely already installed as part of your distribution), but in an office environment, we are usually talking graphical desktops. The two *big* desktop environments, KDE and GNOME, both come with their own e-mail packages, **KMail** and **Balsa** respectively. These are full-featured e-mail packages, well-integrated into their respective environments. I use KMail almost exclusively, but these choices are so often a matter of personal, or corporate, preference.

Both KMail and Balsa are straight e-mail packages rather than combination address book, planners, and contact managers (a la Outlook). Collectively, we call these things *PIMs* (Personal Information Managers). If you want an e-mail package that more fully integrates these additional features, consider using your StarOffice package. Its mail package will be very familiar to users of Outlook.

Also worth a look is **Aethera** from the Kompany, and **Evolution**, part of the GNOME office development. The last thing I would like to mention here, though certainly not your last choice, is Netscape or Mozilla. Your web browser (which I will discuss in the next section) often comes with its own integrated e-mail package.

http://www.thekompany.com/projects/aethera	Aethera
http://www.balsa.net/main.html	Balsa
http://www.ximian.com/apps/evolution.php3	Evolution
http://kmail.kde.org	KMail

Web Browsers

Once a tool or curiosity, the web browser is now an essential part of the office environment. Through its ubiquitous interface, we have learned to use the Web's incredible wealth of information as readily as we would once have opened a dictionary or an encyclopedia. Indeed, those resources are available on more than one website. That's not all—with office intranets, we also use web browsers for access to corporate documents and other essential pieces of information. Browsers are even used as the interface to financial, accounting, or call center applications. A capable web browser is not a luxury but a necessity.

Once upon a time, the only true full-featured graphical web browser for Linux was Netscape Navigator. In a few short years, we find ourselves with an embarrassment of riches when it comes to browsers. The classic favorite is still here. The modern **Netscape Communicator** mirrors its Windows counterpart, but we no longer have to stop here. In 1998, Netscape released its source code under an open source license and its powerful cousin, **Mozilla**, was born. A great deal has changed since then. In fact, the current incarnation of Netscape (version 6.x) is based on Mozilla. I highly recommend that you consider this one.

As I write this, I tend to flip back and forth between Mozilla and KDE's own browser, **Konqueror**. Besides being a great browser, Konqueror is also a powerful file manager. If you are running KDE, you don't need to download this one. It's part of the whole KDE environment.

Not enough? GNOME has Galeon (based on Mozilla's engine) and Opera has, well, Opera, an excellent and *lightweight* browser.

> **Note**: You may have noticed that I used several browsers in screenshots throughout the book.

http://galeon.sourceforge.net	Galeon
http://www.konqueror.org	Konqueror
http://www.opera.com	Opera browser
http://www.netscape.com	Netscape Communicator
http://www.mozilla.org	Mozilla

Convincing the CIO, CFO, and CEO

When you start counting out the cost of individual licenses in a classic office environment, the advantages of a package such as StarOffice start to become apparent. Over time, using Linux in the office can become an investment in itself, one that will continue paying off as time goes on. Rest assured that yours won't be the first office to make the switch either. Have a look at M-Tech's Linux Business Application directory (see the Resources section at the end of this appendix). The list, which is far from complete, will astound you.

Linux has become very well entrenched in the role of server. Even in offices that use nothing but Windows on the desktop, it is not unusual to find a Samba server doing the job an NT server once did, or an Apache web server telling the world what those businesses have to offer. Linux is out there in their firewalls, mail servers, and internet gateways. Why not on the desktop?

The argument that there are no applications for Linux is an old one, but it has incredible staying power. So is the argument that device drivers and hardware support are weak. The best way to dispel these arguments is by actually installing and running Linux. Start with a desktop or two and work from there. Get your users excited by getting them involved. In time, the value and power of the Linux desktop will become evident.

Resources

Linux Advocacy mini-HOWTO

`http://www.linuxdoc.org/HOWTO/mini/Advocacy.html`

Linux Business Directory (businesses that use Linux day to day)

`http://www.m-tech.ab.ca/linux-biz/`

Appendix B

The GNU General Public License

This is a copy of the GNU General Public License. Those wishing to see the original can do so by visiting the Free Software Foundation website. The direct link to the license is as follows.

http://www.gnu.org/copyleft/gpl.html

Still on that website, you may also want to check out the comparative list of license types (both commercial and noncommercial) and how they compare to the GNU GPL. Most interesting here is the definition of whether a license qualifies as free and whether it is compatible with the GPL. That address is here.

http://www.gnu.org/philosophy/license-list.html

Now, without further adieu, here is the GNU GPL.

GNU General Public License

Version 2, June 1991

Preamble

The licenses for most software are designed to take away your freedom to share and change it. By contrast, the GNU General Public License is intended to guarantee your freedom to share and change free software—to make sure the software is free for all its users. This General Public License applies to most of the Free Software Foundation's software and to any other program whose authors commit to using it. (Some other Free Software Foundation software is covered by the GNU Library General Public License instead.) You can apply it to your programs, too.

When we speak of free software, we are referring to freedom, not price. Our General Public Licenses are designed to make sure that you have the freedom to distribute copies of free software (and charge for this service if you wish), that you receive source code or can get it if you want it, that you can change the software or use pieces of it in new free programs; and that you know you can do these things.

To protect your rights, we need to make restrictions that forbid anyone to deny you these rights or to ask you to surrender the rights. These restrictions translate to certain responsibilities for you if you distribute copies of the software, or if you modify it.

For example, if you distribute copies of such a program, whether gratis or for a fee, you must give the recipients all the rights that you have. You must make sure that they, too, receive or can get the source code. And you must show them these terms so they know their rights.

We protect your rights with two steps: (1) copyright the software, and (2) offer you this license which gives you legal permission to copy, distribute and/or modify the software.

Also, for each author's protection and ours, we want to make certain that everyone understands that there is no warranty for this free software. If the software is modified by someone else and passed on, we want its recipients to know that what they have is not the original, so that any problems introduced by others will not reflect on the original authors' reputations.

Finally, any free program is threatened constantly by software patents. We wish to avoid the danger that redistributors of a free program will individually obtain patent licenses, in effect making the program proprietary. To prevent this, we have made it clear that any patent must be licensed for everyone's free use or not licensed at all.

The precise terms and conditions for copying, distribution and modification follow.

GNU General Public License Terms And Conditions For Copying, Distribution and Modification

0. This License applies to any program or other work which contains a notice placed by the copyright holder saying it may be distributed under the terms of this General Public License. The "Program," below, refers to any such program or work, and a "work based on the Program" means either the Program or any

derivative work under copyright law: that is to say, a work containing the Program or a portion of it, either verbatim or with modifications and/or translated into another language. (Hereinafter, translation is included without limitation in the term "modification.") Each licensee is addressed as "you."

Activities other than copying, distribution and modification are not covered by this License; they are outside its scope. The act of running the Program is not restricted, and the output from the Program is covered only if its contents constitute a work based on the Program (independent of having been made by running the Program). Whether that is true depends on what the Program does.

1. You may copy and distribute verbatim copies of the Program's source code as you receive it, in any medium, provided that you conspicuously and appropriately publish on each copy an appropriate copyright notice and disclaimer of warranty; keep intact all the notices that refer to this License and to the absence of any warranty; and give any other recipients of the Program a copy of this License along with the Program.

You may charge a fee for the physical act of transferring a copy, and you may at your option offer warranty protection in exchange for a fee.

2. You may modify your copy or copies of the Program or any portion of it, thus forming a work based on the Program, and copy and distribute such modifications or work under the terms of Section 1 above, provided that you also meet all of these conditions:

a) You must cause the modified files to carry prominent notices stating that you changed the files and the date of any change.

b) You must cause any work that you distribute or publish, that in whole or in part contains or is derived from the Program or any part thereof, to be licensed as a whole at no charge to all third parties under the terms of this License.

c) If the modified program normally reads commands interactively when run, you must cause it, when started running for such interactive use in the most ordinary way, to print or display an announcement including an appropriate copyright notice and a notice that there is no warranty (or else, saying that you provide a warranty) and that users may redistribute the program under these conditions, and telling the user how to view a copy of this License. (Exception: if the Program itself is interactive but does not normally print such an announcement, your work based on the Program is not required to print an announcement.)

These requirements apply to the modified work as a whole. If identifiable sections of that work are not derived from the Program, and can be reasonably considered independent and separate works in themselves, then this License, and its terms, do not apply to those sections when you distribute them as separate works. But when you distribute the same sections as part of a whole which is a work based on the Program, the distribution of the whole must be on the terms of this License, whose permissions for other licensees extend to the entire whole, and thus to each and every part regardless of who wrote it.

Thus, it is not the intent of this section to claim rights or contest your rights to work written entirely by you; rather, the intent is to exercise the right to control the distribution of derivative or collective works based on the Program.

In addition, mere aggregation of another work not based on the Program with the Program (or with a work based on the Program) on a volume of a storage or distribution medium does not bring the other work under the scope of this License.

3. You may copy and distribute the Program (or a work based on it, under Section 2) in object code or executable form under the terms of Sections 1 and 2 above provided that you also do one of the following:

a) Accompany it with the complete corresponding machine-readable source code, which must be distributed under the terms of Sections 1 and 2 above on a medium customarily used for software interchange; or,

b) Accompany it with a written offer, valid for at least three years, to give any third party, for a charge no more than your cost of physically performing source distribution, a complete machine-readable copy of the corresponding source code, to be distributed under the terms of Sections 1 and 2 above on a medium customarily used for software interchange; or,

c) Accompany it with the information you received as to the offer to distribute corresponding source code. (This alternative is allowed only for noncommercial distribution and only if you received the program in object code or executable form with such an offer, in accord with Subsection b above.)

The source code for a work means the preferred form of the work for making modifications to it. For an executable work, complete source code means all the source code for all modules it contains, plus any associated interface definition files, plus the scripts used to control compilation and installation of the executable. However, as a special exception, the source code distributed need not include anything that is normally distributed (in either source or binary form) with the major components (compiler, kernel, and so on) of the operating system on which the executable runs, unless that component itself accompanies the executable.

If distribution of executable or object code is made by offering access to copy from a designated place, then offering equivalent access to copy the source code from the same place counts as distribution of the source code, even though third parties are not compelled to copy the source along with the object code.

4. You may not copy, modify, sublicense, or distribute the Program except as expressly provided under this License. Any attempt otherwise to copy, modify, sublicense or distribute the Program is void, and will automatically terminate your rights under this License. However, parties who have received copies, or rights, from you under this License will not have their licenses terminated so long as such parties remain in full compliance.

5. You are not required to accept this License, since you have not signed it. However, nothing else grants you permission to modify or distribute the Program or its derivative works. These actions are prohibited by law if you do not accept this License. Therefore, by modifying or distributing the Program (or

any work based on the Program), you indicate your acceptance of this License to do so, and all its terms and conditions for copying, distributing or modifying the Program or works based on it.

6. Each time you redistribute the Program (or any work based on the Program), the recipient automatically receives a license from the original licensor to copy, distribute or modify the Program subject to these terms and conditions. You may not impose any further restrictions on the recipients' exercise of the rights granted herein. You are not responsible for enforcing compliance by third parties to this License.

7. If, as a consequence of a court judgment or allegation of patent infringement or for any other reason (not limited to patent issues), conditions are imposed on you (whether by court order, agreement or otherwise) that contradict the conditions of this License, they do not excuse you from the conditions of this License. If you cannot distribute so as to satisfy simultaneously your obligations under this License and any other pertinent obligations, then as a consequence you may not distribute the Program at all. For example, if a patent license would not permit royalty-free redistribution of the Program by all those who receive copies directly or indirectly through you, then the only way you could satisfy both it and this License would be to refrain entirely from distribution of the Program.

If any portion of this section is held invalid or unenforceable under any particular circumstance, the balance of the section is intended to apply and the section as a whole is intended to apply in other circumstances.

It is not the purpose of this section to induce you to infringe any patents or other property right claims or to contest validity of any such claims; this section has the sole purpose of protecting the integrity of the free software distribution system, which is implemented by public license practices. Many people have made generous contributions to the wide range of software distributed through that system in reliance on consistent application of that system; it is up to the author/donor to decide if he or she is willing to distribute software through any other system and a licensee cannot impose that choice.

This section is intended to make thoroughly clear what is believed to be a consequence of the rest of this License.

8. If the distribution and/or use of the Program is restricted in certain countries either by patents or by copyrighted interfaces, the original copyright holder who places the Program under this License may add an explicit geographical distribution limitation excluding those countries, so that distribution is permitted only in or among countries not thus excluded. In such case, this License incorporates the limitation as if written in the body of this License.

9. The Free Software Foundation may publish revised and/or new versions of the General Public License from time to time. Such new versions will be similar in spirit to the present version, but may differ in detail to address new problems or concerns.

Each version is given a distinguishing version number. If the Program specifies a version number of this License which applies to it and "any later version," you have the option of following the terms and conditions either of that version or of any later version published by the Free Software Foundation. If the Program does not specify a version number of this License, you may choose any version ever published by the Free Software Foundation.

10. If you wish to incorporate parts of the Program into other free programs whose distribution conditions are different, write to the author to ask for permission. For software which is copyrighted by the Free Software Foundation, write to the Free Software Foundation; we sometimes make exceptions for this. Our decision will be guided by the two goals of preserving the free status of all derivatives of our free software and of promoting the sharing and reuse of software generally.

No Warranty

11. BECAUSE THE PROGRAM IS LICENSED FREE OF CHARGE, THERE IS NO WARRANTY FOR THE PROGRAM, TO THE EXTENT PERMITTED BY APPLICABLE LAW. EXCEPT WHEN OTHERWISE STATED IN WRITING THE COPYRIGHT HOLDERS AND/OR OTHER PARTIES PROVIDE THE PROGRAM "AS IS" WITHOUT WARRANTY OF ANY KIND, EITHER EXPRESSED OR IMPLIED, INCLUDING, BUT NOT LIMITED TO, THE IMPLIED WARRANTIES OF MERCHANTABILITY AND FITNESS FOR A PARTICULAR PURPOSE. THE ENTIRE RISK AS TO THE QUALITY AND PERFORMANCE OF THE PROGRAM IS WITH YOU. SHOULD THE PROGRAM PROVE DEFECTIVE, YOU ASSUME THE COST OF ALL NECESSARY SERVICING, REPAIR OR CORRECTION.

12. IN NO EVENT UNLESS REQUIRED BY APPLICABLE LAW OR AGREED TO IN WRITING WILL ANY COPYRIGHT HOLDER, OR ANY OTHER PARTY WHO MAY MODIFY AND/OR REDISTRIBUTE THE PROGRAM AS PERMITTED ABOVE, BE LIABLE TO YOU FOR DAMAGES, INCLUDING ANY GENERAL, SPECIAL, INCIDENTAL OR CONSEQUENTIAL DAMAGES ARISING OUT OF THE USE OR INABILITY TO USE THE PROGRAM (INCLUDING BUT NOT LIMITED TO LOSS OF DATA OR DATA BEING RENDERED INACCURATE OR LOSSES SUSTAINED BY YOU OR THIRD PARTIES OR A FAILURE OF THE PROGRAM TO OPERATE WITH ANY OTHER PROGRAMS), EVEN IF SUCH HOLDER OR OTHER PARTY HAS BEEN ADVISED OF THE POSSIBILITY OF SUCH DAMAGES.

END OF TERMS AND CONDITIONS

How to Apply These Terms to Your New Programs

If you develop a new program, and you want it to be of the greatest possible use to the public, the best way to achieve this is to make it free software which everyone can redistribute and change under these terms.

To do so, attach the following notices to the program. It is safest to attach them to the start of each source file to most effectively convey the exclusion of warranty; and each file should have at least the "copyright" line and a pointer to where the full notice is found.

```
<one line to give the program's name and a brief idea of what it
   does.>
Copyright (C) <year> <name of author>
```

This program is free software; you can redistribute it and/or modify it under the terms of the GNU General Public License as published by the Free Software Foundation; either version 2 of the License, or (at your option) any later version.

This program is distributed in the hope that it will be useful, but WITHOUT ANY WARRANTY; without even the implied warranty of MERCHANTABILITY or FITNESS FOR A PARTICULAR PURPOSE. See the GNU General Public License for more details.

You should have received a copy of the GNU General Public License along with this program; if not, write to the Free Software Foundation, Inc., 59 Temple Place, Suite 330, Boston, MA 02111-1307 USA

Also add information on how to contact you by electronic and paper mail.

If the program is interactive, make it output a short notice like this when it starts in an interactive mode:

Gnomovision version 69, Copyright (C) year name of author

Gnomovision comes with ABSOLUTELY NO WARRANTY; for details type `show w'. This is free software, and you are welcome to redistribute it under certain conditions; type `show c' for details.

The hypothetical commands `show w' and `show c' should show the appropriate parts of the General Public License. Of course, the commands you use may be called something other than `show w' and `show c' they could even be mouse-clicks or menu items—whatever suits your program.

You should also get your employer (if you work as a programmer) or your school, if any, to sign a "copyright disclaimer" for the program, if necessary. Here is a sample; alter the names:

Yoyodyne, Inc., hereby disclaims all copyright interest in the program `Gnomovision' (which makes passes at compilers) written by James Hacker.

<signature of Ty Coon>, 1 April 1989

Ty Coon, President of Vice

This General Public License does not permit incorporating your program into proprietary programs. If your program is a subroutine library, you may consider it more useful to permit linking proprietary applications with the library. If this is what you want to do, use the GNU Library General Public License instead of this License.

Index

E

G

J

K

L

Q

X

Y

Z